PLAYFAIR
FOOTBALL
ANNUAL 1994-95

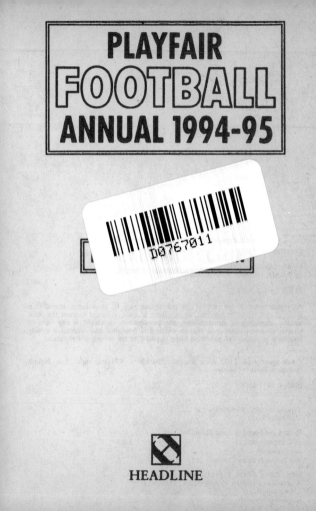

HEADLINE

First published in 1994
by HEADLINE BOOK PUBLISHING

10 9 8 7 6 5 4 3 2 1

Cover photograph Left: Alan Shearer (Blackburn Rovers); right: Luc Nijholt
(Swindon Town) (*Colorsport*)

ISBN 0 7472 4468 5

Typeset by BPC Whitefriars Ltd,
Tunbridge Wells

Printed and bound in Great Britain by
BPC Paperbacks Ltd
A member of
The British Printing Company Ltd

HEADLINE BOOK PUBLISHING
A division of Hodder Headline PLC
338 Euston Road
London NW1 3BH

CONTENTS

Other Football

Information and Records

EDITORIAL

The 'feel good' World Cup in the USA may well have ended in the unsatisfactory lottery of a penalty shoot-out to give Brazil victory over Italy, but the general, lasting impression appears to have been positive.

Perhaps the biggest bonus came from the behaviour of the crowds, which had a multi-national flavour and lacked the local involvement of spectators who were used to seeing their own country playing at the highest level.

The good-nature of those attending the finals is something which one hopes could be translated into future tournaments. But it is one thing to stage the finals in a country like the USA which has no full-time professional league set-up, watched by thousands of people each week, to a country where indiscipline by fans is more common.

The next World Cup is four years hence in France when there will be 32 finalists. But before that we have the 1996 European Championship Finals to be held in England. While it would be fervently hoped that there will be no serious trouble caused by the clash of rival supporters, one cannot really expect the virtual absence of problems off the field as appeared the situation in the recent World Cup.

However, if the same improvement can be made with spectators as was demonstrated with the conduct of the players in the USA, then we may well be on course for a new era in the development of the game both on and off the field.

FIFA itself seemed to be fairly happy that the implementation of the law preventing players being kicked by an opponent from behind when with no chance of getting the ball and the decision to allow players not interfering with play to be allowed to continue in offside situations, had worked.

The increase in goalscoring at the matches might well prevent the type of outrageous ideas which appeared likely after the 1990 finals, when bigger goals were being widely discussed for the future.

The kick-in replacing the throw-in is still being tried out, though it obviously lends itself as an adjunct to the long-ball game. Mercifully, there was little or no success achieved by teams in the USA using this method of play. Indeed the number of short, completed passes probably reached a new record in many of the matches.

FIFA celebrates its 90th birthday this year and is nearing the 200 mark in countries affiliated. It should remember that as much as changing the laws and rules affecting the game, is the need to alter the attitude of those who play it.

LEAGUE ATTENDANCES 1993–94

FA CARLING PREMIERSHIP STATISTICS

| | Average Gate | | | Season 1993/94 | |
	1992/93	1993/94	+/–%	Highest	Lowest
Arsenal	24,403	30,563	+ 25.2	36,203	21,295
Aston Villa	29,594	29,015	–2.0	45,347	16,180
Blackburn Rovers	16,246	17,721	+ 9.1	22,061	14,260
Chelsea	18,787	19,416	+ 3.3	37,064	8,923
Coventry City	14,951	13,352	–10.7	17,009	9,837
Everton	20,445	22,876	+ 11.9	38,157	13,265
Ipswich Town	18,223	16,382	–10.1	22,478	11,468
Leeds United	29,250	34,493	+ 17.9	41,127	28,717
Liverpool	37,004	38,493	+ 4.0	44,339	24,561
Manchester City	24,698	26,709	+ 8.1	35,155	20,513
Manchester United	35,152	44,244	+ 25.9	44,751	41,829
Newcastle United	29,018	33,679	+ 16.1	36,342	32,067
Norwich City	16,154	18,164	+ 12.4	21,181	14,851
Oldham Athletic	12,859	12,563	–2.3	16,708	9,633
Queens Park Rangers	15,015	14,228	–5.2	21,267	9,875
Sheffield United	18,801	19,562	+ 4.0	30,044	14,183
Sheffield Wednesday	27,263	27,191	–0.3	34,548	18,509
Southampton	15,382	14,751	–4.1	19,105	9,028
Swindon Town	10,715	15,274	+ 42.6	18,102	11,940
Tottenham Hotspur	27,740	27,160	–2.1	31,502	17,452
West Ham United	16,001	20,572	+ 28.6	28,382	15,777
Wimbledon	8,405	10,474	+ 24.6	28,553	5,536

ENDSLEIGH INSURANCE LEAGUE: DIVISION ONE STATISTICS

| | Average Gate | | | Season 1993/94 | |
	1992/93	1993/94	+/–%	Highest	Lowest
Barnsley	6,415	7,610	+ 18.6	13,270	4,380
Birmingham City	12,328	14,506	+ 17.7	28,228	9,377
Bolton Wanderers	9,062	10,498	+ 15.8	18,496	7,058
Bristol City	11,004	8,852	–19.6	20,725	5,350
Charlton Athletic	7,005	8,056	+ 15.0	12,192	6,639
Crystal Palace	15,748	15,656	–0.6	28,694	10,925
Derby County	15,020	15,937	+ 6.1	19,300	13,370
Grimsby Town	6,088	5,989	–1.6	11,930	4,014
Leicester City	15,362	16,005	+ 4.2	21,744	10,366
Luton Town	8,212	7,878	–4.1	10,053	6,201
Middlesbrough	16,724	10,400	37.8	17,056	6,286
Millwall	9,188	9,821	+ 6.9	16,731	5,887
Nottingham Forest	21,910	23,051	+ 5.2	27,010	17,584
Notts County	8,151	8,314	+ 2.0	17,911	5,302
Oxford United	6,356	6,877	+ 8.2	10,417	4,065
Peterborough United	8,064	7,412	–8.1	14,010	5,084
Portsmouth	13,706	11,692	–14.7	19,535	7,005
Southend United	5,396	6,105	+ 13.1	10,731	3,758
Stoke City	16,579	15,931	–3.9	22,565	10,138
Sunderland	17,258	16,934	–1.8	19,363	13,645
Tranmere Rovers	8,071	8,099	+ 0.3	15,603	5,526
Watford	8,275	7,907	–4.4	14,359	5,109
West Bromwich Albion	15,161	16,840	+ 11.1	25,615	13,867
Wolverhampton Wanderers	13,598	22,008	+ 61.8	28,039	15,989

ENDSLEIGH INSURANCE LEAGUE: DIVISION TWO

	Average Gate			Season 1993/94	
	1992/93	1993/94	+/-%	Highest	Lowest
AFC Bournemouth	4,454	4,355	-2.2	7,106	2,385
Barnet	3,429	2,431	29.1	3,158	1,352
Blackpool	5,501	4,757	-13.5	8,969	3,121
Bradford City	6,581	6,395	-2.8	9,501	3,472
Brentford	8,476	5,611	-33.8	6,848	4,361
Brighton & Hove Albion	6,710	7,730	+15.2	15,423	4,518
Bristol Rovers	5,745	5,338	-7.1	7,697	3,909
Burnley	10,537	11,317	+7.4	18,168	8,822
Cambridge United	5,545	3,686	-33.5	4,903	2,543
Cardiff City	8,560	6,072	-29.1	10,847	3,583
Exeter City	3,275	3,320	+1.4	6,601	1,933
Fulham	4,736	4,655	-1.7	9,797	2,998
Hartlepool United	3,139	2,076	-33.9	3,286	1,077
Huddersfield Town	5,918	6,372	+7.7	16,195	3,854
Hull City	4,672	5,943	+27.2	11,232	3,580
Leyton Orient	5,377	4,237	-21.2	6,304	2,643
Plymouth Argyle	6,377	9,003	+41.2	15,609	5,657
Port Vale	8,092	8,323	+2.9	10,710	6,484
Reading	4,782	6,932	+45.4	11,840	4,971
Rotherham United	4,769	3,736	21.7	5,543	2,643
Stockport County	5,504	5,090	-7.5	7,666	3,782
Swansea City	5,199	3,534	-32.0	5,383	2,483
Wrexham	4,987	3,961	20.6	7,253	2,090
York City	3,946	4,633	+17.4	8,481	2,409

ENDSLEIGH INSURANCE LEAGUE: DIVISION THREE

	Average Gate			Season 1993/94	
	1992/93	1993/94	+/-%	Highest	Lowest
Bury	2,670	2,597	-2.7	4,164	1,687
Carlisle United	3,611	5,524	+53.0	10,279	3,796
Chester City	2,992	3,191	+6.7	5,638	2,195
Chesterfield	3,213	3,188	-0.8	5,285	2,110
Colchester United	3,777	2,857	-24.4	3,932	2,316
Crewe Alexandra	3,455	3,991	+15.5	6,494	2,700
Darlington	1,960	2,276	+16.1	4,831	1,613
Doncaster Rovers	2,411	2,478	+2.8	4,439	1,603
Gillingham	3,301	3,148	-4.6	4,573	2,453
Hereford United	2,211	2,262	+2.3	4,280	1,429
Lincoln City	3,331	3,179	-4.6	6,030	1,631
Mansfield Town	3,730	2,718	-27.1	4,272	1,802
Northampton Town	3,139	3,454	+10.0	6,432	1,866
Preston North End	5,689	7,377	+29.7	12,790	4,941
Rochdale	2,312	2,657	+14.9	4,317	1,827
Scarborough	1,929	1,681	-12.9	2,631	1,137
Scunthorpe United	3,147	3,182	+1.1	4,587	2,122
Shrewsbury Town	3,411	4,402	+29.1	7,686	2,436
Torquay United	2,695	3,437	+27.5	4,991	2,704
Walsall	3,628	4,237	+16.8	6,473	2,519
Wigan Athletic	2,598	1,897	27.0	3,741	1,232
Wycombe Wanderers	4,602	5,448	+18.4	7,442	3,975

Adams, Tony A.	Jensen, John	Parlour, Raymond
Bould, Stephen A.	Keown, Martin R.	Read, Paul
Campbell, Kevin J.	Linighan, Andrew	Seaman, David A.
Carter, James W. C.	Marshall, Scott R.	Selley, Ian
Clarke, Adrian J.	McDonald, Christopher	Shaw, Paul
Davis, Paul	McGoldrick, Eddie J. P.	Smith, Alan M.
Dickov, Paul	Merson, Paul C.	Winterburn, Nigel
Dixon, Lee M.	Miller, Alan J.	Wright, Ian E.
Flatts, Mark	Morrow, Stephen J.	Zumrutel, Soner
Hillier, David	O'Brien, Roy	

League Appearances: Adams, T.A. 35; Bould, S.A. 23(2); Campbell, K.J. 28(9); Davis, P. 21(1); Dickov, P. (1); Dixon, L.M. 32(1); Flatts, M. 2(1); Heaney, N. 1; Hillier, D. 11(4); Jensen, J. 27; Keown, M.R. 23(10); Limpar, A. 9(1); Linighan, A. 20(1); McGoldrick, E.J. 23(3); Merson, P.C. 24(9); Miller, A.J. 3(1); Morrow, S.J. 7(4); Parlour, R. 24(3); Seaman, D.A. 39; Selley, I. 16(2); Smith, A.M. 21(4); Winterburn, N. 34; Wright, I.E. 39
League (53): Wright 23 (5 pens), Campbell 14, Merson 7, Smith 3, Parlour 2, Bould 1, own goals 3.
Coca-Cola Cup (10): Wright 6, Merson 2, Campbell 1, Smith 1.
FA Cup (4): Adams 2, Smith 1, Wright 1.
Ground: Arsenal Stadium, Highbury, London N5 1BU. Telephone 071–226 0304.
Record attendance: 73,295 v Sunderland, Div 1, 9 March 1935.
Manager: George Graham.
Secretary: K. J. Friar.
Honours – Football League: Division 1 Champions – 1930–31, 1932–33, 1933–34, 1934–35, 1937–38, 1947–48, 1952–53, 1970–71, 1988–89, 1990–91. **FA Cup winners** 1929–30, 1935–36, 1949–50, 1970–71, 1978–79, 1992–93. **Football League Cup winners** 1986–87, 1992–93. **European Competitions: European Cup-Winners Cup winners:** 1993–94. **Fairs Cup winners:** 1969–70.
Colours: Red shirts with white sleeves, white shorts, red and white stockings.

Atkinson, Dalian R.	Daley, Anthony M.	McGrath, Paul
Barrett, Earl D.	Davis, Neil	Mitchell, Andrew B.
Beinlich, Stefan	Ehiogu, Ugochuku	Murphy, John P.
Boden, Christopher D.	Evans, Darren	Murray, Scott G.
Bosnich, Mark J.	Farrell, David	Oakes, Michael C.
Breitkreutz, Mattias	Farrelly, Gareth	Parker, Garry S.
Browne, Paul	Fenton, Graham A.	Pearce, Dennis A.
Burchell, Lee A.	Froggatt, Stephen J.	Richardson, Kevin
Byfield, Darren	Hendrie, Lee A.	Saunders, Dean N.
Cowe, Steven M.	Houghton, Raymond J.	Scimeca, Riccardo
Cox, Neil J.	Kubicki, Dariusz	Small, Bryan

Spink, Nigel P.   Townsend, Andrew D.   Whittingham, Guy
Staunton, Stephen   West, Daniel   Yorke, Dwight
Teale, Shaun

League Appearances: Atkinson, D.R. 29; Barrett, E.D. 39; Beinlich, S. 6(1); Bosnich, M.J. 28; Breitkreutz, M. 1(1); Cowans, G.S. 9(2); Cox, N.J. 16(4); Daley, A.M. 19(8); Ehiogu, U. 14(3); Farrell, D. 4; Fenton, G.A. 9(3); Froggatt, S.J. 8(1); Houghton, R.J. 25(5); Kubicki, D. 1(1); McGrath, P. 30; Parker, G.S. 17(2); Richardson, K. 40; Saunders, D.N. 37(1); Small, B. 8(1); Spink, N.P. 14(1); Staunton, S. 24; Teale, S. 37(1); Townsend, A.D. 32; Whittingham, G. 13(5); Yorke, D. 2(10)
League (46): Saunders 10 (3 pens), Atkinson 8, Richardson 5, Townsend 3, Whittingham 3, Cox 2, Houghton 2, Parker 2, Staunton 2 (1 pen), Yorke 2, Beinlich 1, Daley 1, Fenton 1, Froggatt 1, McGrath 1, Teale 1, own goal 1.
Coca-Cola Cup (16): Atkinson 6, Saunders 4 (1 pen), Houghton 2, Richardson 2, Barrett 1, Teale 1.
FA Cup (3): Houghton 1, Saunders 1 (pen), Yorke 1.
Ground: Villa Park, Trinity Rd, Birmingham B6 6HE. Telephone 021–327 2299.
Record attendance: 76,588 v Derby Co, FA Cup 6th rd, 2 March 1946.
Manager: Ron Atkinson.
Secretary: Steven Stride.
Honours – Football League: Division 1 Champions – 1893–94, 1895–96, 1896–97, 1898–99, 1899–1900, 1909–10, 1980–81. Division 2 Champions – 1937–38, 1959–60. Division 3 Champions – 1971–72. **FA Cup:** Winners 1887, 1895, 1897, 1905, 1913, 1920, 1957. **Football League Cup:** Winners 1961, 1975, 1977, 1994. **European Competitions: European Cup winners:** 1981–82 , **European Super Cup winners:** 1982–83.
Colours: Claret shirts, sky blue trim, white shorts, claret and sky blue trim, white stockings, claret trim.

BARNET   DIV. 3

Affor, Louis K.   Mutchell, Robert D.   Smith, Gary N.
Alexander, Timothy M.   Newson, Mark J.   Tomlinson, Michael L.
Gibson, Terence B.   Phillips, Gary C.   Walker, Alan
Hoddle, Carl   Scott, Peter R.   Wilson, Paul R.
Macdonald, David H.

League Appearances: Affor, L.K. (3); Alexander, T. 27(5); Barnett, B.J. (2); Barnett, D. 19; Carter, M.C. 4(1); Close, S.C. 21(6); Cooper, G.V. 24(12); Dichio, D.S. 9; Dolby, T.C. 13(3); Edwards, R.J. 5; Evans, N.J. 4(8); Finnigan, A. 5(1); Gibson, T.B. 20; Haag, K.J. 31(7); Hall, M.A. 3; Haylock, P. 18(2); Hoddle, C. 43(1); Lynch, A.J. 11(11); McDonald, D.H. 10; Marwood, B. 18(5); Mutchell, R.D. 14; Newson, M.J. 29; Pape, A.M. 4; Phillips, G.C. 42; Rioch, G.J. 3; Rowe, E.B. 9(1); Scott, P.R. 30; Smith, G.N. 8(1); Tomlinson, M. 10(1); Walker, A. 38; Wilson, P.R. 34
League (41): Haag 8 (3 pens), Gibson 4, Cooper 3, Evans 3, Lynch 3, Wilson 3 (3 pens), Close 2, Dichio 2, Dolby 2, Newson 2, Rowe 2, Scott 2, Barnett D 1, Edwards 1, Finnigan 1, Hoddle 1, Walker 1.
Coca-Cola Cup (4): Lynch 2, Haag 1, Walker 1.
FA Cup (4): Close 1, Haag 1, Hoddle 1, Rowe 1.
Ground: Underhill Stadium, Barnet Lane, Barnet, Herts EN5 2BE. Telephone 081–441 6932.

Record attendance: 11,026 v Wycombe Wanderers. FA Amateur Cup 4th Round 1951–52.
Player-Manager: Gary Phillips.
Secretary: Bryan Ayres.
Honours – FA Amateur Cup winners 1945–46. GM Vauxhall Conference winners 1990–91.
Colours: Amber and black striped shirts, black shorts, amber stockings.

BARNSLEY   DIV. 1

Anderson, Vivian A.	Feeney, Mark A.	Rammell, Andrew V.
Archdeacon, Owen D.	Fleming, James G.	Redfern, Neil D.
Bennett, Tony	Hanby, Robert J.	Sheridan, Darren S.
Bishop, Darren C.	Jackson, Christopher D.	Snodin, Glynn
Brooke, David	Jones, Scott	Taggart, Gerald P.
Bullock, Martin J.	Liddell, Andrew M.	Watson, David N.
Burton, Marc A.	Moses, Adrian P.	Williams, Gareth J.
Butler, Lee S.	O'Connell, Brendan	Wilson, Daniel J.
Eaden, Nicholas J.	Payton, Andrew P.	

League Appearances: Anderson, V.A. 20; Archdeacon, O.D. 41(1); Biggins, W. 12(1); Bishop, D.C. 37(1); Boden, C. 4; Bryson, J.I. 16; Butler, L.S. 37; Currie, D.N. (3); Eaden, N.J. 36(1); Fleming, J.G. 46; Graham, D.W. 1(1); Jackson, C.D. 2(2); Liddell, A.M. 11(11); O'Connell, B. 38; Payton, A.P. 25; Rammell, A.V. 31(3); Redfearn, N.D. 46; Robinson, J. (1); Sheridan, D.S. 2(1); Snodin, G. 7(4); Taggart, G.P. 38; Watson, D.N. 9; Williams, G.J. 4(5); Wilson, D.J. 43
League (55): Payton 12, Redfearn 12 (2 pens), O'Connell 6, Rammell 6, Anderson 3, Bryson 3, Archdeacon 2 (1 pen), Biggins 2, Eaden 2, Taggart 2, Bishop 1, Currie 1, Jackson 1, Liddell 1, Williams 1.
Coca-Cola Cup (2): Archdeacon 1 (pen), Bryson 1.
FA Cup (5): Archdeacon 1, O'Connell 1, Payton 1, Rammell 1, Taggart 1.
Ground: Oakwell Ground, Grove St, Barnsley S71 1ET. Telephone Barnsley (0226) 295353.
Record attendance: 40,255 v Stoke C, FA Cup 5th rd, 15 February 1936.
Manager: Danny Wilson.
Secretary: Michael Spinks.
Honours – Football League: Division 3 (N) Champions – 1933–34, 1938–39, 1954–55.
FA Cup: Winners 1912.
Colours: Red shirts, white shorts, red stockings.

BIRMINGHAM CITY   DIV. 2

Barnett, David	Desouza, Juan M.	Dryden, Richard A.
Bennett, Ian M.	Doherty, Neil	Fenwick, Paul J.
Claridge, Stephen E.	Dominguez, Jose M. M.	Frain, John W.
Cooper, Gary	Donowa, Brian L.	Harding, Paul
Daish, Liam S.	Downing, Keith G.	Hiley, Scott P.

Hooper, Lyndon F.
Kalogeracos, Vasilios
Lowe, Kenneth
McGavin, Steven J.
Miller, Kevin
Moulden, Paul A.
Parris, George

Pschisolido, Paolo P.
Robinson, Steven E.
Saville, Andrew V.
Scott, Richard P.
Sedgemore, Benjamin R
Shearer, Peter A.
Shutt, Carl S.

Tait, Paul R.
Wallace, David L.
Whyte, Christopher A.
Willis, Roger C.
Wratten, Adam P.

League Appearances: Barnett, D. 8(1); Bennett, I.M. 22; Black, S.A. 2; Claridge, S.E. 17(1); Cooper, G. 16(2); Daish, L.S. 19; De Souza, J.M. 1(6); Doherty, N. 12(1); Dominguez, J.M. 3(2); Donowa, B.L. 14(7); Downing, K.G. 1; Dryden, R.A. 34; Fenwick, P.J. 6(3); Frain, J.W. 26; Harding, P. 14(2); Hiley, S.P. 28; Hooper, L.F. 1(4); Huxford, R.J. 5; Jenkinson, L. 2(1); Lowe, K. 10(2); McGavin, S.J. 6(2); McMinn, K.C. 19(3); Mardon/Ward, P.J./M.W 14(3); Miller, K. 24; Morgan, T.J. 1); Moulden, P.A. 5(2); Parris, G. 22(2); Peschisolido, P.P. 21(3); Potter, G.S. 7; Saville, A.V. 38(1); Scott, R.P. 5(1); Shearer, P.A. 2; Shutt, C.S. 18(8); Smith/Rogers, D./D.J. 23(3); Tait, P.R. 9(1); Wallace, D.L. 8(2); Whyte, C.A. 33; Willis, R.C. 11(5)
League (52): Saville 10 (1 pen), Peschisolido 9, Claridge 7 (2 pens), Donowa 5, Willis 5, Shutt 4, Frain 2 (1 pen), Smith 2, Cooper 1, Doherty 1, Lowe 1, McGavin 1, Wallace 1, Ward 1, own goals 2.
Coca-Cola Cup (3): Frain 1, Parris 1, Peschisolido 1.
FA Cup (1): Harding 1.
Ground: St Andrews, Birmingham B9 4NH. Telephone 021–772 0101.
Record attendance: 66,844 v Everton, FA Cup 5th rd,11 February 1939.
Manager: Barry Fry.
Secretary: Alan Jones BA, MBA
Honours – Football League: Division 2 Champions – 1892–93, 1920–21, 1947-48, 1954–55. **Football League Cup:** Winners 1963. **Leyland Data Cup:** Winners 1991.
Colours: All blue.

BLACKBURN ROVERS   FA PREMIERSHIP

Ainscough, Paul B.
Atkins, Mark N.
Batty, David
Berg, Henning
Brown, Richard A.
Dickins, Matthew J.
Flowers, Timothy D.
Gallacher, Kevin W.
Harford, Paul
Hendry, Edward C J.
Ireland, Simon P.

Le Saux, Graeme P.
Makel, Lee
Malone, Christopher J.
Marker, Nicholas R. T.
May, David
Mimms, Robert A.
Moran, Kevin B.
Morgan, Thomas P.
Morrison, Andrew C
Newell, Michael C
Pearce, Ian A.

Ripley, Stuart E.
Scott, Andrew M.
Shearer, Alan
Sherwood, Tim A.
Talia, Francesco
Tallon, Gary T
Thorne, Peter L.
Warhurst, Paul
Wilcox, Jason M
Wright, Alan

League Appearances: Andersson, P.J. 1; Atkins, M.N. 8(7); Batty, D. 26; Berg, H. 38(3); Flowers, T.D. 29; Gallacher, K W. 27(3); Hendry, E.C. 22(1); Le Saux, G.P. 40(1); Makel, L. 2(2); Marker, N.R. 16(7); May, D. 40; Mimms, R.A. 13; Moran, K.B. 19; Morrison, A.C. 1(4); Newell, M.C 27(1); Pearce, I.A. 1(4); Ripley, S.E. 40; Shearer, A. 34(6); Sherwood, T.A. 38; Warhurst, P. 4(5); Wilcox, J.M. 31(2); Wright, A. 7(5)

League (63): Shearer 31 (3 pens), Gallacher 7, Newell 6, Wilcox 6, Ripley 4, Le Saux 2, Sherwood 2, Atkins 1, Berg 1, May 1, Moran 1, Pearce 1.
Coca-Cola Cup (5): Newell 2 (1 pen), May 1, Pearce 1, Shearer 1
FA Cup (6): Shearer 2, Gallacher 1, May 1, Sherwood 1, Wilcox 1.
Ground: Ewood Park, Blackburn BB2 4JF. Telephone Blackburn (0254) 698888.
Record attendance: 61,783 v Bolton W, FA Cup 6th rd, 2 March, 1929
Manager: Kenny Dalglish MBE.
Secretary: John W. Howarth FAAI.
Honours – Football League: Division 1 Champions – 1911–12, 1913- 14. Division 2 Champions – 1938–39. Division 3 Champions – 1974–75. **FA Cup:** Winners 1884, 1885, 1886, 1890, 1891, 1928. **Full Members' Cup:** Winners 1986–87.
Colours: Blue and white halved shirts, white shorts, blue stockings.

BLACKPOOL   DIV. 2

Bamber, John D.
Beech, Christopher S.
Bonner, Mark
Briggs, Gary
Capleton, Melvin D. R.
Cook, Mitchell
Davies, Michael J.

Gore, Ian G.
Gouck, Andrew S.
Griffiths, Bryan K.
Horner, Philip M.
Martin, Lee B.
Mitchell, Neil N.

Murphy, James A.
Quinn, Stephen J.
Rodwell, Anthony
Sheedy, Kevin M.
Stoneman, Paul
Watson, Andrew A.

League Appearances: Bailey, N. 1; Bamber, J.D. 20(2); Beech, C.S. 24(11); Bonner, M. 39(1); Briggs, G. 32; Cook, M. 45; Davies, M.J. 24; Gore, I.G. 29; Gouck, A.S. 25(2); Griffiths, B.K. 42(1); Horner, P.M. 41; Leitch, G.J. 1(1); McIlhargey, S. 3(1); Martin, L.B. 43; Mitchell, N.N. 8(16); Murphy, J.A. 14(2); Quinn, S.J. 1(13); Robinson, D.J. 9(3); Rodwell, A. 28; Sheedy, K.M. 25(1); Stoneman, P. 9(1); Symons, P. (1); Thorpe, L.A. (1); Watson, A.A. 40; Whitworth, N.A. 3
League (63): Watson 20, Griffiths 16 (3 pens), Bonner 7, Bamber 4, Mitchell 3, Beech 2, Gouck 2, Horner 2, Quinn 2, Robinson 2, Briggs 1, Rodwell 1, Sheedy 1.
Coca-Cola Cup (10): Watson 5, Bamber 3, Quinn 1, own goal 1.
FA Cup (0):
Ground: Bloomfield Rd Ground, Blackpool FY1 6JJ. Telephone Blackpool (0253) 404331.
Record attendance: 38,098 v Wolverhampton W, Division 1, 17 September 1955.
Manager: —.
Secretary: D. J. Allan.
Honours – Football League: Division 2 Champions – 1929–30. **FA Cup:** Winners 1953. **Anglo-Italian Cup:** Winners 1971.
Colours: Tangerine shirts with navy and white trim, white shorts, tangerine stockings with navy blue tops.

BOLTON WANDERERS   DIV. 1

Branagan, Keith G.
Coyle, Owen C.
Davison, Aidan J.
Fisher, Neil J.

Fulton, Stephen
Green, Scott P.
Kelly, Anthony G.
Lee, David M.

Lydiate, Jason L.
Martindale, Gary
Mason, Andrew J.
McAteer, Jason W.

McGinlay, John Roscoe, Andrew R. Thomspn, Alan
McKay, Andrew S. Seagraves, Mark Walker, Andrew F.
Patterson, Mark A. Spooner, Nicholas M. Whittaker, Stuart
Phillips, James N. Stubbs, Alan Winstanley, Mark A.

League Appearances: Branagan, K.G. 10; Brown, P. 42; Burke, D.I. 11(1); Coyle, O.C. 25(5); Darby, J.T. 3(2); Davison, A.J. 30(1); Fisher, N.J. (2); Fleck, R. 6(1); Fulton, S. 4; Green, S.P. 11(11); Hoult, R. 3(1); Kelly, A.G. 35; Lee, D.M. 35(6); Lydiate, J.L. 5; McAteer, J.W. 45(1); McGinlay, J. 39; Parkinson, G. 1; Patterson, M.A. 34(1); Phillips, J.N. 41(1); Roscoe, A.R. 2(1); Seagraves, M 32(3); Spooner, N.M. 1; Stubbs, A. 41; Thompson, A. 19(8); Walker, A.F. 7(4); Walton, M.A. 3; Whittaker, S. 2; Winstanley, M.A. 19(2)
League (63): McGinlay 25 (3 pens), Coyle 7, Thompson 6, Lee 5, Green 4, McAteer 3, Walker 3, Brown 2, Fleck 1, Kelly 1, Patterson 1, Seagraves 1, Stubbs 1, own goals 3.
Coca-Cola Cup (3): Coyle 1, Kelly 1 (pen), McGinlay 1.
FA Cup (16): Coyle 5, McGinlay 3 (1 pen), McAteer 2, Stubbs 2, Brown 1, Patterson 1, Thompson 1, Walker 1.
Ground: Burnden Park, Bolton BL3 2QR. Telephone Bolton (0204) 389200.
Record attendance: 69,912 v Manchester C, FA Cup 5th rd, 18 February 1933.
Manager: Bruce Rioch.
Secretary: Des McBain.
Honours – Football League: Division 2 Champions – 1908–09, 1977–78. Division 3 Champions – 1972–73. **FA Cup winners** 1923, 1926, 1929, 1958. **Sherpa Van Trophy:** Winners 1989.
Colours: White shirts, navy blue shorts, red stockings, blue and white tops.

AFC BOURNEMOUTH DIV. 2

Aspinall, Warren McElhatton, Michael T. O'Driscoll, Sean M.
Bartram, Vincent L. Mean, Scott Pennock, Adrian B.
Beardsmore, Russell P. Morris, Mark J. Pulis, Anthony
Cotterill, Stephen Moss, Neil G. Russell, Kevin J.
Fletcher, Steven M. Murray, Robert J. Watson, Alexander F.
Leadbitter, Christopher J. O'Connor, Mark A. Williams, William J.

League Appearances: Aspinall, W. 22(2); Bartram, V.L. 41; Beardsmore, R.P. 15(9); Burns, C. 13(1); Chivers, G.P. 24(2); Cotterill, S. 36(1); Fletcher, S.M. 31(5); Kevan, D.J. (1); Leadbitter, C.J. 20(7); McElhatton, M.T. 6(4); McGorry, B.P. 16; Masters, N.B. 18; Mean, S. 1(4); Mitchell, G.L. 4; Morris, M.J. 38; Moss, N.G. 5(1); Murray, R.J. 5(15); O'Connor, M.A. 45; O'Driscoll, S.M. 7(1); Parkinson, J.S. 30; Pennock, A.B. 40; Russell, K.J. 17; Skinner, J.J. 16; Town, D.E. (1); Watson, A.F. 45; Wood, P.A. 11(5)
League (51): Cotterill 14, Fletcher 6, Aspinall 5, Wood 5, Murray 4, McGorry 3, O'Connor 3, Pennock 3, Chivers 2, Masters 2 (1 pen), Burns 1, Parkinson 1, Russell 1, Watson 1, Wood 1.
Coca-Cola Cup (4): Beardsmore 1, Fletcher 1, Masters 1, Parkinson 1.
FA Cup (7): Aspinall 1 (pen), Cotterill 1, McGorry 1, Masters 1, Pennock 1, Watson 1.
Ground: Dean Court Ground, Bournemouth BH7 7AF. Telephone Bournemouth (0202) 395381.

Record attendance: 28,799 v Manchester U, FA Cup 6th rd, 2 March 1957
Manager: Tony Pulis.
Secretary: K. R. J. MacAlister.
Honours – Football League: Division 3 Champions 1986–87 **Associate Members'
Cup:** Winners 1984.
Colours: Red shirts with white V shape & reverse V shape 3' pattern, black shorts with
white piping, black stockings with red/white turnback.

BRADFORD CITY   DIV. 2

Bowling, Ian   Richards, Dean I.   Sinnott, Lee
Duxbury, Lee E.   Robson, Gary   Stapleton, Francis A.
Jewell, Paul   Scargill, Wayne   Tolson, Neil
Oliver, Gavin R.   Showler, Paul   Tomlinson, Paul
Power, Lee M.

League Appearances: Barlow, A.J. 2; Blake, N.L. 7; Bowling, I. 23; Duxbury, L.E.
43; Duxbury , M. 12(1); Ford, T. 5; Grayston, N.J. 2; Hamilton, D.V. 2; Heseltine,
W.A. 11(1); Hoyle, C.R. 22(7); Jewell, P. 28(2); Lawford, C.B. 8(3); McCarthy, S.C. 18;
McHugh, M.B. 3(2); Oliver, G.R. 35; Partridge, S.M. (1); Power, L.M. 2(1); Reid, P.R
36(2); Richards, D.I. 46; Robson, G. 46; Showler, P. 26(6); Sinnott , L. 18; Stapleton,
F.A. 16(12); Steele, T.W. 8(3); Tolson, N. 16(6); Tomlinson, G.M. 12(5); Tomlinson, P
23; Williams, G. 31(1); Wilson, K.J. 5
League (61): McCarthy 14, Duxbury L 9, Reid 9 (2 pens), Tomlinson G 6, Jewell 5,
Showler 5, Power 2, Richards 2, Robson 2, Tolson 2, Williams 2 (2 pens), Hamilton
1, own goals 2.
Coca-Cola Cup (13): McCarthy 7, Jewell 3, Reid 1, Showler 1, Steele 1.
FA Cup (0):
Ground: Valley Parade Ground, Bradford BD8 7DY. Telephone Bradford (0274)
306062.
Record attendance: 39,146 v Burnley, FA Cup 4th rd, 11 March 1911
Manager: Lennie Lawrence.
Secretary: Shaun Harvey.
Honours – Football League: Division 2 Champions 1907–08. Division 3 Champions
1984–85. Division 3 (N) Champions 1928–29 **FA Cup:** Winners 1911
Colours: Claret and amber shirts, black shorts, black stockings.

BRENTFORD   DIV. 2

Annon, Darren C.   Harvey, Lee D.   Smith, Paul W.
Ashby, Barry J.   Hutchings, Carl E.   Statham, Brian
Bates, Jamie   Manuel, William A. J.   Stephenson, Paul
Benjamin, Ian T.   Metcalf, Matthew A.   Taylor, Robert A.
Birch, Paul   Mundee, Denny W. J.   Thompson, David
Dearden, Kevin C.   Peters, Robert A. A.   Westley, Shane L. M
Fernandes, Tamer H.   Ratcliffe, Simon   Williams, Dean P
Grainger, Martin R.   Ravenscroft, Craig

14

League Appearances: Allon, J.B. 21, Annon, D.C. 5(4); Ashby, B.J. 8; Bates, J. 45; Benjamin, I.T. 12(2); Bennett, M.R. 6(2); Benstead, G.M. 5; Cornwell, J.A. 4; Dearden, K.C. 35; Fernandes, T.H (1); Gayle, M.A. 35, Grainger, M.R. 31, Harvey, L.D. 23(3); Hutchings, C.E. 20(9); Manuel, W.A. 17(1); Metcalf, M.A. 3(4); Morgan, S. 1; Mundee, D.W. 37(2); Peters, R.A. 8(4); Ratcliffe, S. 41(2); Ravenscroft, C. 4(3); Smith, P.W. 32; Statham, B. 31; Stephenson, P. 25; Taylor, R.A. 5; Thompson, D. 9(1); Tilson, S.B. 2; Watson, K.E. 2(1); Westley, S.L. 31; Williams, D.A. 2(1); Williams, D.P 6(1)

League (57): Allon 13, Mundee 11 (4 pens) Gayle 6, Harvey 4, Ratcliffe 4, Smith 3, Bates 2, Benjamin 2, Grainger 2, Taylor 2, Annon 1, Ashby 1, Ravenscroft 1, Statham 1, Thompson 1, Williams D A 1, own goals 2.

Coca-Cola Cup (3): Westley 2, Peters 1.

FA Cup (4): Allon 2 (1 pen), Gayle 2.

Ground: Griffin Park, Braemar Rd, Brentford, Middlesex TW8 0NT Telephone 081-847 2511.

Record attendance: 39,626 v Preston NE, FA Cup 6th rd, 5 March 1938.

Manager: David Webb. **Secretary:** Polly Kates.

Honours – Football League: Division 2 Champions - 1934- 35. Division 3 Champions - 1991–92. Division 3 (S) Champions - 1932- 33. Division 4 Champions 1962–63.

Colours: Red and white vertical striped shirts, black shorts, red stockings.

BRIGHTON & HOVE ALBION   DIV. 2

Bissett, Nicholas	Funnell, Simon P.	Pates, Colin G.
Case, James R.	McCarthy, Paul J.	Rust, Nicholas C. I.
Chapman, Ian R.	McDougald, David E. J.	Ryan, John J.
Codner, Robert A. G.	Munday, Stuart C.	Simmonds, Daniel B.
Crumplin, John L.	Myall, Stuart T.	Tuck, Stuart G.
Foster, Stephen B.	Nogan, Kurt	Wilkins, Dean M

League Appearances: Andrews, P.D. 1(4); Bissett, N. 12; Case, J.R. 21, Chapman, I.R. 45; Codner, R.A. 40; Crumplin, J.L. 29(3); Dickov, P. 8; Edwards, M.D. 25(2); Farrington, M.A. 4(2); Flatts, M.M. 9(1); Foster, S.B. 34; Fox, M.S. 4(8); Fox, S.M. (1); Funnell, S.P. 14(10); Geddes, G.J. 7(5); Johnson, R.Y. 1(1); Kennedy, A.J. 8(4); McCarthy, P.J. 37; McGarrigle, K. 1; Munday, S.C. 33(1); Myall, S.T. 12(1); Nogan, K. 41; Pates, C.G. 34; Rust, N.C. 46; Simmonds, D.B. 6(8); Tuck, S.G. 5(6); Wilkins, D.M. 20(1); Wilkinson, D.B. 8(3); Wosahlo, B.E. 1

League (60): Nogan 22 (1 pen), Codner 8, Dickov 5, Edwards 4, Chapman 3 (1 pen), McCarthy 3, Crumplin 2, Foster 2, Funnell 2, Kennedy 2, Wilkins 2, Bissett 1, Farrington 1, Flatts 1, Munday 1, Geddes 1.

Coca-Cola Cup (3): Nogan 2, Kennedy 1.

FA Cup (2): Kennedy 2.

Ground: Goldstone Ground, Old Shoreham Rd, Hove, Sussex BN3 7DE. Telephone Brighton (0273) 778855.

Record attendance: 36,747 v Fulham, Division 2, 27 December 1958.

Manager: Liam Brady.

Secretary: Ron Pavey.

Honours – Football League: Division 3 (S) Champions   1957 58 Division 4 Champions - 1964–65.

Colours: Royal blue shirts with white pin stripe, royal blue sleeves, royal blue shorts with white and royal trim, royal blue stockings with red/white trim.

BRISTOL CITY   DIV. 1

Allison, Wayne
Baird, Ian J.
Bent, Junior A.
Brown, Ian O.
Bryant, Matthew
Duffin, Stuart G.
Edwards, Robert W.
Fowler, Jason K. G.
Harriott, Marvin L.

Hewlett, Paul M.
Loss, Colin P.
Martin, David
McKop, Henry G.
Milsom, Paul J.
Munro, Stuart
Osman, Russell C.
Partridge, Scott M.

Robinson, Spencer L.
Rosenior, Leroy D. G.
Rudgley, Simon P. D.
Scott, Martin
Shail, Mark E. D.
Tinnion, Brian
Welch, Keith J.
Wyatt, Michael J.

League Appearances: Aizlewood, M. 5; Allison, W. 35(4); Baird, I.J. 16(3); Barclay, D.A. 2; Bent, J.A. 17(3); Borrows, B. 6; Brown, I.O. 5(6); Brown, W.L. 1; Bryant, M. 27(1); Edwards, R.W. 31(7); Fowler, J.K. (1); Gavin, M.W. 6(2); Harriott, M.L. 17; Harrison, G.R. 1; Hewlett, P.M. 11(1); Hoyland, J.W. 6; Kamara, A.S. (1); Llewellyn, A.D. 15; McKop, H.G. 2(2); Martin, D. 33(1); Milsom, P.J. 1(2); Munro, S. 43(1); Osman, R.C. 4(1); Partridge, S.M. 7(2); Pennyfather, G. 7(5); Robinson, S.L. 31(10); Rosenior, L.D. 1(4); Scott, M. 45; Shail, M.E. 35(1); Shelton, G. 3; Tinnion, B. 40(1); Welch, K.J. 45; Wyatt, M.J. 8(2)
League (47): Allison 15, Baird 5, Scott 5 (1 pen), Tinnion 5 (3 pens), Partridge 4, Robinson 4, Bent 2, Edwards 2, Shail 2, Brown 1 1, Martin 1, Osman 1.
Coca-Cola Cup (1): Robinson 1.
FA Cup (7): Allison 4, Tinnion 2, Shail 1.
Ground: Ashton Gate, Bristol BS3 2EJ. Telephone Bristol (0272) 632812 (5 lines).
Record attendance: 43,335 v Preston NE, FA Cup 5th rd, 16 February 1935.
Manager: Russell Osman.
Secretary: Jean Harrison.
Honours – Football League: Division 2 Champions · 1905-06. Division 3 (S) Champions 1922 23, 1926-27, 1954-55. **Welsh Cup winners 1934. Anglo-Scottish Cup:** Winners 1977 78. **Freight Rover Trophy winners 1985-86.**
Colours: Red shirts, white shorts, red and white stockings.

BRISTOL ROVERS   DIV. 2

Alexander, Ian
Archer, Lee
Browning, Marcus T.
Channing, Justin A.
Clark, William R.
Davis, Michael V.
Gurney, Andrew R.
Hardyman, Paul G. T.

Maddison, Lee R.
McLean, Ian
Parkin, Brian
Paul, Martin L.
Pritchard, David M.
Skinner, Justin
Sterling, Worrel R.

Stewart, Marcus P.
Taylor, Gareth K
Taylor, John P.
Tillson, Andrew
Tovey, Paul W.
Waddock, Gary P
Wright, Ian M

League Appearances: Alexander, I. 15(3); Archer, L. 37, Browning, M T 30(1); Channing, J.A. 28(1); Clark, W.R 34(2); Davis, M.V 2(8); Evans, R.W 1(1); Gurney, A.R. 2(1); Hardyman, P.G. 17(8); Kelly, G.J. 1, McLean, I. 17(10); Maddison, L.R 36(1); Margetson, M.W. 2(1); Parkin, B. 43; Paul, M.L (4); Pounder, A.M 8(2);

Pritchard, D.M. 11; Saunders, C.S. 4(3); Skinner, J. 27(2); Sterling, W.R. 43; Stewart, M.P. 23(6); Taylor, J.P. 44(1); Tillson, A. 12(1); Tovey, P.W. (1); Waddock, G.P. 39; Wright, I.M. 29; Yates, S. 1
League (60): Taylor 23, Archer 5, Channing 5 (1 pen), Skinner 5, Sterling 5, Stewart 5 (2 pens), Browning 4, McLean 2, Pounder 2, Clark 1, Hardyman 1, Waddock 1, own goal 1.
Coca-Cola Cup (1): Sterling 1.
FA Cup (1): Archer 1.
Ground: Twerton Park, Twerton, Bath BS15 1AZ. Telephone: 0272 352508.
Record attendance: 9464 v Liverpool, FA Cup 4th rd, 8 February 1992 (Twerton Park). 38,472 v Preston NE, FA Cup 4th rd, 30 January 1960 (Eastville).
Manager: John Ward. **Secretary:** Ian Wilson.
Honours – Football League: Division 3 (S) Champions – 1952–53. Division 3 Champions – 1989–90.
Colours: Blue and white quartered shirts, white shorts, blue stockings.

BURNLEY   DIV. 1

Beresford, Marlon	Joyce, Warren G.	Pender, John P.
Brass, Christopher P.	Lancashire, Graham	Philliskirk, Anthony
Davis, Stephen M.	Livingstone, Richard	Randall, Adrian J.
Deary, John S.	McKenzie, Paul	Russell, Wayne L.
Dowell, Wayne A.	McMinn, Kevin C.	Thompson, Leslie
Eyres, David	Monington, Mark D.	Weller, Paul
Farrell, Andrew J.	Mullin, John	Williams, Paul A.
Francis, John A.	Parkinson, Gary	Wilson, Paul A.
Heath, Adrian P.	Peel, Nathan J.	

League Appearances: Beresford, M. 46; Davis, S.M. 42; Deary, J.S. 43; Eyres, D. 45; Farrell, A.J. 13(9); Francis, J.A. 31(12); Heath, A.P. 41; Joyce, W.G. 19(3); Lancashire, G. (1); McMinn, K.C. 14; Measham, I. 6; Monington, M.D. 16(4); Mullin, J. 1(5); Parkinson, G. 20; Patterson, I.D. (1); Peel, N.J. 4(9); Pender, J.P. 42; Philliskirk, A. 19; Randall, A.J. 31(6); Russell, K.J. 26(2); Smith, I.P. (1); Thompson, L. 36; Wilson, P.A. 11
League (79): Eyres 19 (6 pens), Heath 9, Davis 7, Francis 7, Philliskirk 7, Russell 6, Deary 4, Joyce 4, Randall 4, McMinn 3, Farrell 2, Peel 2, Monington 1, Mullin 1, Parkinson 1, Pender 1, own goal 1.
Coca-Cola Cup (7): Eyres 3 (1 pen), Davis 1, Deary 1, Francis 1, Russell 1.
FA Cup (7): Eyres 4, Heath 1, Joyce 1, own goal 1.
Ground: Turf Moor, Burnley BB10 4BX. Telephone Burnley (0282) 427777.
Record attendance: 54,775 v Huddersfield T, FA Cup 3rd rd, 23 February 1924.
Manager: Jimmy Mullen.
Secretary: Mark Blackbourne.
Honours – Football League: Division 1 Champions – 1920–21, 1959–60. Division 2 Champions – 1897–98, 1972–73. Division 3 Champions – 1981–82. Division 4 Champions – 1991–92. **FA Cup winners** 1913–14. **Anglo Scottish Cup:** Winners 1978–79.
Colours: Claret shirts with sky blue sleeves, white shorts and stockings.

BURY

Adekola, David
Anderson, Lee C.
Bracey, Lee M. I.
Carter, Mark C.
Cross, Ryan

Daws, Nicholas J.
Hughes, Ian
Jackson, Michael J.
Johnrose, Leonard
Kelly, Anthony O. N.

Lucketti, Christopher J.
Mauge, Ronald C.
Rigby, Antony A.
Stanislaus, Roger E. P.
Stevens, Ian D.

League Appearances: Adekola, D. 7(12); Anderson, L.C. 11; Beckford, J.N. 3; Blissett, L.L. 8(2); Bracey, L.M. 40; Carter, M.C. 36; Collings, P.W. 1; Cross, R. 16(1); Daws, N.J. 33(4); Hanson, D.P. 1; Hughes, I. 38; Jackson, M.J. 37(2); Johnrose, L. 11(3); Jones, P.A. 4; Kearney, M.J. 7(2); Kelly, A.O. 34(1); Kelly, G.A. 1; Knill, A.R. 8; Lucketti, C.J. 27; Mauge, R.C. 25(1); Mulligan, J. 2(1); Powell, G. 4(1); Reid, A. 2(2); Rigby, A.A. 33; Ryan, J.B. 8(1); Stanislaus, R.E. 35; Stevens, I.D. 28(5); Ward, D. 2(1); Woods, K. (2); Worsley, G. (1)
League (55): Carter 20 (3 pens). Kelly 7, Rigby 7, Stevens 7, Adekola 4, Mauge 3, Blissett 1, Daws 1, Kearney 1, Lucketti 1, Mulligan 1, Reid 1, own goal 1.
Coca-Cola Cup (2): Blissett 1, Powell 1.
FA Cup (0):
Ground: Gigg Lane, Bury BL9 9HR. Telephone 061 764 4881.
Record attendance: 35,000 v Bolton W, FA Cup 3rd rd, 9 January 1960.
Manager: Mike Walsh.
Assistant Secretary: J. Neville.
Honours – Football League: Division 2 Champions   1894-95. Division 3 Champions 1960-61. **FA Cup winners** 1900, 1903.
Colours: White shirts, navy blue shorts, navy stockings.

CAMBRIDGE UNITED

Barrick, Dean
Bartlett, Kevin F.
Butler, Stephen
Corazzin, Giancarlo M.
Craddock, Jody D.
Filan, John R.
Fowler, John A.

Granville, Daniel P.
Heathcote, Michael
Hunter, Alvin J.
Hyde, Micah
Jeffrey, Andrew S.
Joseph, Matthew N. A.

Livett, Simon R.
Lyne, Neil G. F.
Middleton, Craig D.
Nyamah, Kofi
O'Shea, Daniel E.
Sheffield, Jonathan

League Appearances: Barrick, D. 44; Butler, S. 33; Cheetham, M.M. 8(5); Claridge, S.E. 24; Clayton, G. 20(5); Corazzin, G.M. 28; Craddock, J.D. 19(1); Daish, L.S. 18; Danzey, M.J. 10(4); Fensome, A.B. 1(1); Filan, J.R. 46; Flatts, M.M. 5; Fowler, J.A. 16(4); Granville, D.P. 10(1); Hay, D.A. (3); Heathcote, M. 40; Hunter, A.J. 3(11); Hyde, M. 13(5); Jeffrey, A.S. 37(3); Joseph, M.N. 27; Livett, S.R. 10; Lyne, N.G.F. 5; Middleton, C.D. 17(2); Nyamah, K. 4(10); O'Shea, D.E. 36(2); Rowett, G. 24(5); Skelly, R.B. 2; Sloan, S.M. 4; Wilkins, R.J. 7
League (79): Butler 21 (5 pens). Claridge 11 (1 pen). Corrazin 10. Granville 5, Heathcote 5, Rowett 5, Clayton 4, Danzey 3, Cheetham 2, Daish 2, Hyde 2, Joseph 2, Middleton 2, Nyamah 2, Barrick 1, Flatts 1, Sloan 1.
Coca-Cola Cup (3): Claridge 3 (1 pen).

FA Cup (2): Heathcote 1, Nyamah 1.
Ground: Abbey Stadium, Newmarket Rd, Cambridge CB5 8LN. Telephone (0223) 566500.
Record attendance; 14,000 v Chelsea, Friendly, 1 May 1970.
Manager: Gary Johnson.
Secretary: Steve Greenall.
Honours – Football League: Division 3 Champions – 1990–91. Division 4 Champions – 1976–77.
Colours: Amber & black striped shirts, black shorts with amber & black trim, black & amber stockings.

CARDIFF CITY   DIV. 2

Adams, Darren S.   Fereday, Wayne   Searle, Damon P.
Aizlewood, Mark   Griffith, Cohen   Stant, Philip
Baddeley, Lee M.   Kite, Philip D.   Thompson, Garry L.
Bird, Anthony   Millar, William P.   Wigg, Nathan M.
Brazil, Derek M.   Perry, Jason   Williams, Stephen D.
Dale, Carl   Richardson, Nicholas J.

League Appearances: Adams, D.S. 9(5); Aizlewood, M. 22; Baddeley, L.M. 25(5); Bird, A. 25(10); Blake, N.A. 20; Brazil, D.M. 31; Brock, K.S. 14; Cornwell, J.A. 5; Dale, C. 7(8); Evans, D.A. (1); Evans, T. 4(1); Fereday, W. 17; Graham, B. (1); Grew, M. 11; Griffith, C. 39(3); James, R.M. 9; Jones, I.M. 2; Kite, P.D. 17(1); Knill, A.R. 4; Millar, W.P. 28(9); Perry, J. 40; Ratcliffe, K. 6; Richardson, N.J. 38(1); Searle, D.P. 41(1); Stant, P. 34(2); Thompson, G.L. 28(2); Walker, L. 1; Wigg, N.M. 8(11); Williams, S.D. 18; Young, S. 3(3)
League (66): Blake 14 (2 pens), Stant 10, Millar 7 (5 pens), Griffith 6, Bird 5, Richardson 5 (2 pens), Thompson 5, Dale 3, Aizlewood 2, Brock 2, Cornwell 2, Adams 1, Fereday 1, Perry 1, own goals 2.
Coca-Cola Cup (2): Bird 1, own goal 1.
FA Cup (10): Stant 4, Blake 3, Bird 1, Thompson 1, own goal 1.
Ground: Ninian Park, Cardiff CF1 8SX. Telephone Cardiff (0222) 398636.
Record attendance: 61,566, Wales v England, 14 October 1961.
Manager: Eddie May.
Secretary: Jim Finney.
Honours – Football League: Division 3 (S) Champions – 1946–47. **FA Cup winners** 1926–27 (only occasion the Cup has been won by a club outside England). **Welsh Cup winners** 21 times.
Colours: Blue shirts, white shorts, blue stockings.

CARLISLE UNITED   DIV. 3

Arnold, Ian   Elliott, Anthony R.   Robinson, Jamie
Burgess, David J.   Gallimore, Anthony M.   Thomas, Roderick C.
Caig, Anthony   Joyce, Joseph P.   Thorpe, Jeffrey R.
Davey, Simon   Pearson, John S.   Valentine, Peter
Day, Mervyn R.   Reddish, Shane   Walling, Dean A.
Edmondson, Darren S.   Reeves, David

League Appearances: Arnold, I. 7(7); Barnes, A.J. 2; Burgess, D.J. 36(4); Caig, A. 20; Conway, P.J. 16(2); Curran, C.P. 4(2); Davey, S. 42; Day, M.R. 16; Delap, R.J. (1); Edmondson, D.S. 21(1); Elliott, A.R. 6; Fairweather, C. 11(1); Flounders, A.J. 6(2); Gallimore, A.M. 40; Graham, D.W. 2; Holden, S.A. 1; Joyce, J.P. 28(1); McCreery, D. 6(7); McMahon, S. 2; Murray, P. 2(6); Oghani, G.W. 8(6); Peacock, L.A. (1); Pearson, J.S. 5(2); Prins, J. 2(3); Reddish, S. 33(2); Reeves, D. 34; Robinson, J. 16; Rouse, S. 1(4); Thomas, R.C. 37(1); Valentine, P. 18(2); Walling, D.A. 40
League (57): Reeves 11, Davey 9 (1 pen), Thomas 9, Arnold 5 (1 pen), Walling 5, Conway 4, Edmondson 3, Valentine 2, Burgess 1, Curran 1, Fairweather 1, Flounders 1, Gallimore 1, Graham 1, Reddish 1, Robinson 1, own goal 1.
Coca-Cola Cup (2): Davey 1, Thomas 1.
FA Cup (8): Arnold 3, Edmondson 2, Davey 1, Gallimore 1, Reeves 1.
Ground: Brunton Park, Carlisle CA1 1LL. Telephone Carlisle (0228) 26237.
Record attendance: 27,500 v Birmingham C, FA Cup 3rd rd, 5 January 1957 and v Middlesbrough, FA Cup 5th rd, 7 February 1970.
Director of Coaching: Mick Wadsworth.
Acting Secretary: Jim Thoburn.
Honours – Football League: Division 3 Champions – 1964–65.
Colours: Blue shirts, white shorts, blue stockings.

CHARLTON ATHLETIC   DIV. 1

Balmer, Stuart M.	Gritt, Stephen J.	Pardew, Alan S.
Bennett, Michael R.	Leaburn, Carl W.	Pitcher, Darren E. J.
Bowyer, Lee D.	Linger, Paul H.	Robinson, John R. C.
Brown, Steven B.	McLeary, Alan T.	Robson, Mark A.
Chandler, Dean A. R.	Mills, Daniel R.	Rufus, Richard R.
Chapple, Philip R.	Minto, Scott C.	Salmon, Michael B.
Curbishley, Llewellyn	Nelson, Garry P.	Sturgess, Paul C.
Garland, peter J.	Newton, Shaun O.	Walsh, Colin D.
Grant, Kim T.		

League Appearances: Bailey, D.L. (4); Balmer, S.M. 25(6); Bennett, M.R. 10; Brown, S.B. 18(1); Chapple, P.R. 40(4); Curbishley, L. (1); Garland, P.J. 21(6); Gorman, P.M. 7(7); Grant, K.T. 18(12); Leaburn, C.W. 39; Linger, P.H. (5); McLeary, A.T. 44; Minto, S.C. 42; Nelson, G.P. 34(9); Newton, S.O. 11(8); Pardew, A.S. 24(2); Pitcher, D.E. 42; Robinson, J.R. 27; Robson, M.A. 20(3); Salmon, M.B. 41; Small, M.A. 1(1); Sturgess, P.C. 5(3); Vaughan, J. 5(1); Walsh, C.D. 32(3)
League (61): Nelson 15, Leaburn 10, Pardew 10 (3 pens), Chapple 5, Walsh 4, McLeary 3, Minto 2 (1 pen), Newton 2, Robson 2, Balmer 1, Bennett 1, Garland 1, Gorman 1, Grant 1, Pitcher 1 (pen), Robinson 1, own goal 1.
Coca-Cola Cup (1): Leaburn 1.
FA Cup (8): Grant 2, Leaburn 2, Pitcher 2 (1 pen), Pardew 1, Robson 1.
Ground: The Valley, Floyd Road, Charlton, London SE7 8BL. Telephone 081–293 4567.
Record attendance: 75,031 v Aston Villa, FA Cup 5th rd, 12 February 1938 (at The Valley).
Managers: Steve Gritt and Alan Curbishley.
Secretary: Chris Parkes.
Honours – Football League: Division 3 (S) Champions – 1928–29, 1934–35. **FA Cup winners** 1947.
Colours: Red shirts, white shorts, red stockings.

CHELSEA   FA PREMIERSHIP

Barnard, Darren S.
Barness, Anthony
Burley, Craig W.
Clarke, Stephen
Colgan, Nicholas V.
Dow, Andrew
Duberry, Michael W.
Elliott, Paul M.
Fleck, Robert
Hall, Gareth D.

Hitchcock, Kevin
Hoddle, Glenn
Hopkin, David
Izzet, Mustafa K.
Johnsen, Erland
Kharine, Dmitri V.
Kjeldbjerg, Jakob
Lee, David J.
Myers, Andrew
Newton, Edward J. J.

Norman, Craig T.
Peacock, Gavin K.
Rowe, Ezekiel B.
Shipperley, Neil J.
Sinclair, Frank M.
Skiverton, Terence J.
Spackman, Nigel
Spencer, John
Stein, Mark E. S.
Wise, Dennis F.

League Appearances: Barnard, D.S. 9(3); Burley, C.W. 20(3); Cascarino, A.G. 16(4); Clarke, S. 39; Donaghy, M. 24(4); Dow, A. 13(1); Duberry, M.W. 1; Fleck, R. 7(2); Hall, G.D. 4(3); Hitchcock, K. 2; Hoddle, G. 16(3); Hopkin, D. 12(9); Johnsen, E. 27(1); Kharine, D.V. 40; Kjeldbjerg, J. 29; Lee, D.J. 3(4); Myers, A. 6; Newton, E.J. 33(3); Peacock, G.K. 37; Shipperley, N.J. 18(6); Sinclair, F.M. 35; Spackman, N. 5(4); Spencer, J. 13(6); Stein, E.M. 18; Wise, D.F. 35
League (49): Stein 13 (3 pens), Peacock 8, Spencer 5, Cascarino 4, Shipperley 4, Wise 4 (1 pen), Burley 3, Barnard 1, Donaghy 1, Fleck 1, Hoddle 1, Johnsen, 1, Kjeldbjerg 1, Lee 1, own goal 1.
Coca-Cola Cup (3): Wise 2, Shipperley 1.
FA Cup (13): Peacock 6, Burley 3, Spencer 2, Shipperley 1, Stein 1.
Ground: Stamford Bridge, London SW6 1HS. Telephone 071-385 5545.
Record attendance: 82,905 v Arsenal, Division 1, 12 Oct 1935.
Manager: Glenn Hoddle.
Secretary: Yvonne Todd.
Honours – Football League: Division 1 Champions – 1954–55. **FA Cup winners** 1970.
Football League Cup winners 1964–65. **Full Members' Cup winners** 1985–86. **Zenith Data Systems Cup winners** 1989–90. **European Cup-Winners' Cup winners** 1970–71.
Colours: Royal blue shirts and shorts, white stockings.

CHESTER CITY   DIV. 2

Felgate, David W.
Flitcroft, David J.
Greenall, Colin A.
Jenkins, Iain

Leonard, Mark A.
Lightfoot, Christopher I.
Preece, Roger
Pugh, David

Rimmer, Stuart A.
Thompson, David S.
Whelan, Spencer R.

League Appearances: Barrow, G. 10(3); Bishop, E.M. 9(9); Came, M.R. 30; Donnelly, D.C. 9(9); Felgate, D.W. 34; Flitcroft, D.J. 4(4); Greenall, C.A. 42; Jakub, Y. 35(1); Jenkins, I. 30(4); Lancashire, G. 10(1); Leonard, M.A. 28(4); Lightfoot, C.I. 37; McIlhargey, S. 1; Preece, R. 38(1); Pugh, D. 36(1); Rimmer, S.A. 26(9); Stewart, W.I. 7; Thompson, D.S. 40(1); Wheeler, P. 23(2); Whelan, S.R. 22
League (69): Pugh 12 (3 pens), Lightfoot 11, Leonard 8 (1 pen), Rimmer 8, Lancashire 7, Wheeler 7 (1 pen), Thompson 6, Bishop 2, Preece 2, Came 1, Flitcroft 1, Greenall 1, own goals 3.

Coca-Cola Cup (1): Rimmer 1.
FA Cup (3): Leonard 1, Lightfoot 1, Preece 1.
Ground: The Deva Stadium, Bumpers Lane, Chester CH1 4LT. Telephone Chester (0244) 371376, 371809.
Record attendance: 20,500 v Chelsea, FA Cup 3rd rd (replay), 16 January, 1952 (at Sealand Road).
Manager: Graham Barrow.
Secretary: Derek Barber JP, AMITD.
Honours – Welsh Cup winners 1908, 1933, 1947. **Debenhams Cup:** Winners 1977.
Colours: Blue and white striped shirts, black shorts, blue stockings.

CHESTERFIELD   DIV. 3

Carr, Darren	Hewitt, James R.	Morris, Andrew D.
Curtis, Thomas	Jules, Mark A.	Moss, David
Davies, Kevin C.	Law, Nicholas	Norris, Stephen M
Dennis, John A.	Leonard, Michael C.	Rogers, Lee J.
Dyche, Sean M.	Marples, Christopher	

League Appearances: Brien, A.J. 9; Carr, C.P. 20(3); Carr , D. 28; Cash, S.P. 4(2); Curtis, T. 35(1); Davies, K.C. 16(8); Dennis, J.A. 4(6); Dyche, S.M. 19(1); Gregory, N.R. 2(1); Hebberd, N.T. 14(4); Hewitt, J.R. 28(1); Jules, M.A. 28(5); Knowles, C.B. 1; Law, N. 31; Leonard, M.C. 31(1); Lyne, N.G. 5(1); McGugan, P.J. 2(3); Madden, L.D. 26; Marples, C. 11; Morris, A.D. 32(2); Moss, D. 26; Norris, S.M. 30(9); Pearson, L. (1); Rogers, L.J. 32; Spooner, S.A. 5; Stringfellow, I.R. (1); Taylor, S. 1; Trotter, M. 14(1); Turnbull, L.M. 8
League (55): Norris 19 (3 pens), Morris 11, Moss 6, Davies 4, Curtis 3, Hewitt 3, Law 2, Turnbull 2 (1 pen), Carr D 1, Gregory 1, Jules 1, Lyne 1, Trotter 1.
Coca-Cola Cup (5): Norris 2, Jules 1, Morris 1, Turnbull 1 (pen).
FA Cup (0):
Ground: Recreation Ground, Chesterfield S40 4SX. Telephone Chesterfield (0246) 209765.
Record attendance: 30,968 v Newcastle U, Division 2, 7 April 1939.
Manager: John Duncan.
Secretary: Mrs N. J. Bellamy.
Honours – Football League: Division 3 (N) Champions – 1930–31, 1935–36. Division 4 Champions – 1969–70, 1984–85. **Anglo-Scottish Cup** winners 1980–81.
Colours: Blue shirts, white shorts, blue stockings.

COLCHESTER UNITED   DIV. 3

Abrahams, Paul	Cawley, Peter	Kinsella, Mark A.
Allpress, Tim J.	Cheesewright, John	McDonough, Roy
Ball, Steven J.	English, Anthony K.	Partner, Andrew N.
Betts, Simon R.	Fry, Christopher D.	Smith, Nicholas L.
Brown, Stephen R.	Gentle, Justin D.	Walters, Scott
Butler, Neal C.	Hyslop, Christian T.	Whitton, Stephen P.

League Appearances: Abrahams, P. 1(3); Allpress, T.J. 21(2); Ball, S.J. 27(5); Barada, T. 1; Basham, M. 1; Bennett, G. 3(1); Betts, S.R. 31(2); Booty, J. (1); Brown , I.O. 4; Brown, S.R. 30(4); Campbell, S.M. 1(3); Cawley, P. 36; Cheesewright, J. 17; Cook, A.M. 1(1); Cook, J.P. (1); Desborough, M. 1; Dickens, A.W. 28(4); English, A.K. 42; Fry, C.D. 12(5); Gentle, J.D. (2); Grainger, M.R. 5(3); Hyslop, C.T 8; Keeley, J.H. 15; Kinsella, M.A. 42; Locke, A.S. 4; McDonough, R. 36(2); McGavin, S.J. 20(1); Morrow, G.R. (1); Munson, N.W. 2(1); Richardson, J. 1(7); Roberts, P. 21; Sheffield, J. 6; Smith, N.L. 29(10); Watts, G.S. 8(4); Whitton, S.P. 8
League (56): Brown S 11, Kinsella 8, McGavin 8, McDonough 7, English 4, Dickens 3, Ball 2, Grainger 2 (1 pen), Watts 2, Whitton 2, Betts 1, Brown I 1, Cawley 1, own goals 4.
Coca-Cola Cup (2): Kinsella 1, McDonough 1.
FA Cup (3): Brown S 1, English 1, McGavin 1.
Ground: Layer Rd Ground, Colchester CO2 7JJ. Telephone (0206) 574042.
Record attendance: 19,072 v Reading, FA Cup 1st rd, 27 Nov, 1948.
Manager: George Burley.
Secretary: Sue Smith.
Honours–GM Vauxhall Conference winners 1991–92. **FA Trophy winners** 1991 92.
Colours: Blue and white striped shirts, white shorts, white stockings.

COVENTRY CITY   FA PREMIERSHIP

Atherton, Peter	Gould, Jonathan A.	Rennie, David
Babb, Philip A.	Harford, Michael G.	Roberts, Brian L. F.
Boland, Willie J.	Hurst, Lee J.	Robertson, Alexander
Borrows, Brian	Jenkinson, Leigh	Robson, Stewart I.
Busst, David J.	Lovelock, Andrew J.	Sheridan, Anthony J.
Costello, Lorcan M.	Morgan, Stephen	Smith, Jason L.
Darby, Julian T.	Ndlovu, Peter	Wegerle, Roy C.
Davies, Martin L.	O'Toole, Gavin F.	Williams, John N.
Farquhar, Alistair J.	Ogrizovic, Steven	Williams, Paul R.
Flynn, Sean	Pickering, Albert G.	Wood, Simon O.
Gayle, Sean	Quinn, Michael	

League Appearances: Atherton, P. 39(1); Babb, P.A. 40; Boland, W.J. 24(3); Booty, M.J. 2; Borrows, B. 29; Busst, D.J. 2(1); Darby, J.T. 25(1); Flynn, S. 33(3); Gayle, J. 3; Gould, J.A. 9; Harford, M.G. (1); Jenkinson, L. 10(6); Kruszynski, Z. 1(1); McGrath, L.A. 10(1); Marsden, C. 5(2); Morgan, S. 39(1); Ndlovu, P. 40; Ogrizovic, S. 33; Pickering, A.G. 1(3); Quinn, M 28(4); Rennie, D. 34; Robertson, A. (3); Robson, S.I. 1; Sheridan, A.J. 4(4); Wegerle, R.C. 20(1); Williams, J.N. 27(5); Williams, P.R. 3(6)
League (43): Ndlovu 11 (2 pens), Quinn 8 (1 pen), Wegerle 6 (1 pen), Darby 5, Babb 3, Flynn 3, Williams J 3, Morgan 2, Harford 1, Rennie 1.
Coca-Cola Cup (5): Morgan 3, Babb 1, Quinn 1.
FA Cup (0):
Ground: Highfield Road Stadium, King Richard Street, Coventry CV2 4FW. Telephone (General Enquiries): (0203) 223535.
Record attendance: 51,455 v Wolverhampton W, Division 2, 29 April 1967
Manager: Phil Neal.
Secretary: Graham Hover.
Honours – Football League: Division 2 Champions 1966–67 Division 3 Champions 1963–64. Division 3 (S) Champions 1935–36. **FA Cup winners** 1986–87
Colours: All Sky blue.

Adebola, Bamberdele
Annon, Richard
Booty, Martyn J.
Ceraolo, Mark
Clarkson, Philip I.
Collins, Wayne A.
Edwards, Robert
Gardiner, Mark C.
Garvey, Stephen H.

Gayle, Mark S. R.
Hughes, Anthony B.
Lennon, Neil F.
Macauley, Steven R.
Murphy, Daniel B.
Naylor, Anthony J.
Rivers, Mark A.
Rowbotham, Darren
Smith, Gareth S.

Smith, Mark A.
Tierney, Francis
Walters, Steven P.
Ward, Ashley S.
Whalley, Gareth
Wilkinson, Ian M.
Wilson, Eugene
Woodward, Andrew S.

League Appearances: Abel, G. 18(2); Annan, R. 9(1); Booty, M.J. 30(1); Clarkson, P.I. 6(1); Collins, W.A. 27(8); Edwards, R. 8(4); Evans, S.J. 39(1); Gardiner, M.C. 31(3); Gayle, M.S. 8; Hughes, A.B. 4(2); Jones, P.L. 4(4); Lennon, N.F. 31(2); Lyons, A. 1(1); Macauley, S.R 17; Murphy, D.B. 5(7); Naylor, A.J. 30(7); Rowbotham, D. 39(1); Smith , G.S. 36(1); Smith, M.A. 32; Tierney, F. 4(4); Walters, S.P. 20; Ward, A.S. 24(1); Whalley, G. 12(3); Wilkinson, I.M. 2(1); Wilson, E. 16(2); Woodward, A.S. 9(3)

League (80): Rowbotham 15, Naylor 13, Ward 13, Evans 7, Smith S 7 (4 pens), Lennon 4, Macauley 3, Clarkson 2, Collins 2, Edwards 2, Murphy 2, Abel 1, Annan 1, Booty 1, Gardiner 1, Jones 1, Tierney 1, Walters 1, Whalley 1, own goals 2.
Coca-Cola Cup (3): Lyons 1, Rowbotham 1, Ward 1.
FA Cup (7): Edwards 1, Gardiner 1, Lennon 1, Naylor 1, Rowbotham 1, Smith S 1 (pen), Whalley 1.
Ground: Football Ground, Gresty Rd, Crewe CW2 6EB. Telephone Crewe (0270) 213014.
Record attendance: 20,000 v Tottenham H, FA Cup 4th rd, 30 January 1960.
Manager: Dario Gradi.
Secretary: Mrs Gill Palin.
Honours – Welsh Cup: Winners 1936, 1937.
Colours: Red shirts, white shorts, red stockings.

Armstrong, Christopher P.
Bowry, Robert
Coleman, Christopher
Cox, Ian G.
Dyer, Bruce A.
Glass, James R.
Gordon, Dean D.
Humphrey, John
Launders, Brian T.
Martyn, Antony N.

Matthew, Damian
Mortimer, Paul H.
Ndah, George E.
Newman, Richard A.
Osborn, Simon E.
Patterson, Darren J.
Rodger, Simon L.
Salako, John A.
Scully, Anthony D. T.

Shaw, Richard E.
Smith, Eric
Southgate, Gareth
Sparrow, Paul
Thorn, Andrew C.
Vincent, Jamie R.
Whyte, David A.
Williams, Paul A.
Young, Eric

League Appearances: Armstrong, C.P. 43; Bowry, R. 17(4); Coleman, C. 46; Dyer, B.A. 2(9); Gordon, D.D. 39(6); Humphrey, J. 32; Martyn, A.N. 46; Massey, S.A

1;Matthew, D. 11(1); Ndah, G.E. (1); Newman, R.A. 10(1); O'Connor, M.J. 2;
Osborn, S.E. 5(1); Rodger, S.L. 37(5); Salako, J.A. 34(4); Shaw, R.E. 30(4); Southgate,
G. 46; Stewart, P.A. 18; Thorn, A.C. 10; Whyte, D.A. 10(6); Williams, P.A. 21(3);
Young, E. 46
League (73): Armstrong 22, Southgate 9, Salako 8, Williams 7, Gordon 5 (2 pens),
Young 5, Coleman 3, Rodger 3, Stewart 3, Whyte 3, Shaw 2, Humphrey 1, Matthew
1, Osborn 1.
Coca-Cola Cup (7): Southgate 3, Armstrong 1, Gordon 1, Thorn 1, Whyte 1.
FA Cup (0):
Ground: Selhurst Park, London SE25 6PU. Telephone 081-653 1000.
Record attendance: 51,482 v Burnley, Division 2, 11 May 1979.
Team Manager: Alan Smith.
Club Secretary: Mike Hurst.
Honours – Football League: Division 1 – Champions 1993–94. Division 2 Champions
– 1978–79. Division 3 (S) 1920–21 **Zenith Data Systems Cup winners 1991.**
Colours: Red and blue shirts, red shorts, red stockings.

DARLINGTON   DIV. 3

Chapman, Gary A.	Himsworth, Gary P.	Reed, Adam M.
Collier, Darren	Kirkham, Peter J.	Ripley, Andrew I.
Cross, Paul	O'Shaughnessy, Stephen	Shaw, Simon R.
Gaughen, Steven E.	Painter, Peter R.	Slaven, Bernard
Gregan, Sean M.		

League Appearances: Appleby, M.W. 10; Ball, S. 15(5); Case, J.R. 1; Chapman,
G.A. 38(3); Collier, D. 42; Cooper, P. 1; Crosby, A.K. 25; Cross, P. 26; Ellison, A.L.
18(11); Fickling, A. 1; Gaughan, S.E. 32; Gregan, S.M. 21(2); Himsworth, G.P. 28;
Isaacs, A. 16(4); Joyce, J.P. 4; Juryeff, I.M. 1; Kavanagh, G.A. 5; Kirkham, P.J. 2(7);
McNab, N. 4; Madden, L.D. 5; Maddick, K.A. 1(1); O'Shaughnessy, S. 32; Painter,
P.R. 35(1); Pearson, L. 26(2); Reed, A.M. 11(2); Ripley, A.I. (2); Scott, R. (1); Shaw,
S.R. 18(12); Slaven, B. 11; Sunley, M. 17(1); Switzer, G. 12(2); White, J.G. 4
League (42): Painter 11 (1 pen), Chapman 7, Ellison 4, Pearson 4, Gaughan 3,
Himsworth 3, Cross 2, Slaven 2, Appleby 1, Ball 1, Gregan 1, Isaacs 1, Shaw 1, White
1.
Coca-Cola Cup (1): Juryeff 1.
FA Cup (2): Ellison 1, Painter 1.
Ground: Feethams Ground, Darlington DL1 5JB. Telephone Darlington (0325)
465097.
Record attendance: 21,023 v Bolton W, League Cup 3rd rd, 14 November 1960.
Manager: Alan Murray.
Secretary: T. D. Hughes.
Honours – Football League: Division 3 (N) Champions   1924–25. Division 4
Champions 1990–91.
Colours: Black and white.

DERBY COUNTY   DIV. 1

Carsley, Lee K.
Chalk, Martyn P. G.
Charles, Gary A.
Cooper, Kevin L.
Cowans, Gordon S.
Forsyth, Michael E.
Gabbiadini, Marco
Goulooze, Richard
Harkes, John A.
Hayward, Steve L.

Johnson, Thomas
Kavanagh, Jason C.
Kitson, Paul
Kuhl, Martin
Nicholson, Shane M.
Pembridge, Mark A.
Powell, Stephen R.
Round, Stephen
Short, Craig J.

Simpson, Paul D.
Stallard, Mark
Sturridge, Dean C.
Sutton, Stephen J.
Sutton, Wayne F.
Taylor, Martin J.
Tretton, Andrew D.
Wassall, Darren P.
Williams, Paul D.

League Appearances: Charles, G.A. 43; Coleman, S. 2; Cowans, G.S. 19; Forsyth, M.E. 27(1); Gabbiadini, M. 33(6); Harkes, J.A. 31(2); Hayward, S.L. 2(3); Johnson, T. 31(6); Kavanagh, J.C. 9(10); Kitson, P. 41; Kuhl, M. 27; Nicholson, S.M. 22; Pembridge, M.A. 39(2); Ramage, C.D. 3(2); Ratcliffe, K. 6; Short, C.J. 43; Simpson, P.D. 27(7); Taylor, M.J. 46; Wassall, D.P. 25; Williams, P.D. 30(4)
League (73): Gabbiadini 13, Johnson 13, Kitson 13, Pembridge 11 (4 pens), Simpson 9, Short 3, Forsyth 2, Harkes 2, Charles 1, Williams 1, Nicholson 1, own goals 4.
Coca-Cola Cup (5): Gabbiadini 2, Johnson 1, Kitson 1, Simpson 1.
FA Cup (1): Johnson 1
Ground: Baseball Ground, Shaftesbury Crescent, Derby DE3 8NB. Telephone Derby (0332) 340105.
Record attendance: 41,826 v Tottenham H, Division 1, 20 September 1969.
Manager: Roy McFarland.
General Manager/Secretary: Michael Dunford.
Honours – Football League: Division 1 Champions 1971–72, 1974–75. Division 2 Champions – 1911–12, 1914–15, 1968–69, 1986–87 Division 3 (N) 1956–57. **FA Cup** winners 1945–46.
Colours: White shirts, black sleeves, black shorts, white stockings.

DONCASTER ROVERS   DIV. 3

Beasley, Andrew
Harper, Steven J.
Hulme, Kevin
Jones, Graeme A.
Kitchen, David E.

Lawrence, James H.
Limber, Nicholas
Marquis, Paul R.
Measham, Ian
Roche, David

Swailes, Christopher W.
Thew, Lee
Wilcox, Russell
Williams, Paul L.
Yates, Mark J.

League Appearances: Atkins, I.L. 7; Beasley, A. 37; Bottomley, P.L. 10; Brentano, S.R. 1; Clarke, D.A. 15(1); Clarke, N.J. 5; Cunningham, A.E. 19(6); Dunphy, S. 1; Ford, S.T. 4(2); Fowler, L. 7(4); France, D.B. (1); Freeman, C.R. 23(2); Harper, S.J. 25(6); Hewitt, J.R. 5(1); Hulme, K. 33(1); Ingham, G. 1; Jeffrey, M.R. 8; Jones, G.A. 24(4); Kitchen, D.E. 14; Lawrence, J.H. 2(7); Limber, N. 3(1); Luscombe, L.J. 5(3); Marquis, P.R. 9; Measham, I. 21; Moss, D. 9; Page, D.R. 18(4); Prindiville, S.A. (1); Roche, D. 30; Swailes, C.W. 17; Thew, L. 6(5); Turnbull, L.M. 10(1); Whitmarsh,

26

P.2(4); Wilcox, R. 40; Williams, P.L. (1); Williamson, D.A. 10(3); Worthington, G.L. 8; Yates, M.J. 33(1)

League (44): Hulme 8, Roche 5 (1 pen), Jones 4, Page 4, Yates 4, Freeman 2, Harper 2, Moss 2, Wilcox 2, Worthington 2, Bottomley 1, Cunningham 1, Jeffrey 1, Kitchen 1, Lawrence 1, Thew 1, Turnbull 1 (pen), Whitmarsh 1, Williamson 1.

Coca-Cola Cup (3): Harper 1, Hulme 1, Wilcox 1.

FA Cup (2): Williamson 2.

Ground: Belle Vue Ground, Doncaster DN4 5HT. Telephone Doncaster (0302) 539441.

Record attendance: 37,149 v Hull C, Division 3 (N), 2 October 1948.

Manager: Sammy Chung.

Secretary: Mrs K. J. Oldale.

Honours – Football League: Division 3 (N) Champions – 1934–35, 1946–47, 1949–50. Division 4 Champions – 1965–66, 1968–69.

Colours: White shirts with red lightning stripes, red shorts, red stockings.

EVERTON   FA PREMIERSHIP

Ablett, Gary I.	Jackson, Matthew A.	Rideout, Paul D.
Angell, Brett A. M.	Kearton, Jason B.	Rowett, Gary
Barlow, Stuart	Kenny, William	Snodin, Ian
Cottee, Antony R.	Limpar, Anders	Southall, Neville
Ebbrell, John K.	Moore, Neil	Stuart, Graham C.
Grant, Anthony J.	O'Connor, Jonathan	Unsworth, David G.
Grugel, Mark A.	Parkinson, Joseph S.	Ward, Mark W.
Hinchcliffe, Andrew G.	Priest, Christopher	Warzycha, Robert
Holmes, Paul	Quigley, James D.	Watson, David
Horne, Barry		

League Appearances: Ablett, G.I. 32; Angell, B.A. 13(3); Barlow, S. 6(16); Beagrie, P.S. 29; Cottee, A.R. 36(3); Ebbrell, J.K. 39; Hinchcliffe, A.G. 25(1); Holmes, P. 15; Horne, B. 28(4); Jackson, M.A. 37(1); Limpar, A. 9; Moore, N. 4; Radosavljevic, P. 9(14); Rideout, P.D. 21(3); Rowett, G. (2); Snodin, I. 28(1); Southall, N. 42; Stuart, G.C. 26(4); Unsworth, D.G. 7(1); Ward, M.W. 26(1); Warzycha, R. 3(4); Watson, D. 27(1)

League (42): Cottee 16 (2 pens), Rideout 6, Ebbrell 4, Barlow 3, Beagrie 3, Stuart 3 (1 pen), Ablett 1, Angell 1, Horne 1, Radosavljevic 1, Ward 1, Watson 1, own goal 1.

Coca-Cola Cup (14): Rideout 4, Cottee 3, Watson 3, Beagrie 1, Snodin 1, Ward 1 (pen), own goal 1.

FA Cup (3): Barlow 2, Rideout 1.

Ground: Goodison Park, Liverpool L4 4EL. Telephone 0151–521 2020.

Record attendance: 78,299 v Liverpool, Division 1, 18 September 1948.

Manager: Mike Walker.

Secretary: Jim Greenwood.

Honours – Football League: Division 1 Champions – 1890–91, 1914–15, 1927–28, 1931–32, 1938–39, 1962–63, 1969–70, 1984–85, 1986–87. Division 2 Champions – 1930–31. **FA Cup:** Winners 1906, 1933, 1966, 1984. **European Competitions: European Cup-Winners' Cup winners:** 1984–85.

Colours: Royal blue shirts with white collar, white shorts, blue stockings.

EXETER CITY   DIV. 3

Bailey, Danny S.
Brown, Jonathan
Cecere, Michele J.
Cooper, David B. E.
Cooper, Mark N.
Coughlin, Russell

Daniels, Scott
Fox, Peter D.
Gavin, Mark W.
Minett, Jason
Robinson, Ronald

Ross, Michael P.
Storer, Stuart J.
Turner, Robert P.
Whiston, Peter
Worthington, Gary L.

League Appearances: Adekola, D. 1(2); Bailey, D.S. 29(5); Bond, K.J. 1; Brown, J. 18(5); Cecere, M.J. 2; Cooper, D.B. (1); Cooper, M.N. 21; Coughlin, R. 35; Daniels, S. 39(2); Davies, S.I. 5(1); Fox, P.D. 25(1); Gavin, M.W. 12; Gosney, A.R. 1; Harris, A. 4; Jepson, R.F. 16; Llewellyn, A.D. 15; McKnight, A.D. 9(1); Mehew, D.S. 5(2); Minett, J. 34(4); Morgan, N. 12; Pears, R.J. 6(5); Percival, J.C. (4); Phillips, M.J. 7(2); Redwood, T.R. 11(2); Richardson, J.D. 4(3); Robinson, R. 21(1); Ross, M.P. 26(1); Storer, S.J. 44; Thirlby, A.D. 7(3); Tonge, A.J. (1); Turner, R.P. 22; Veysey, K.J. 11(1); Whiston, P. 22; White, C. 7(1); Wigley, S. 22(1); Worboys, G. 4; Worthington, G.L. 8(7)
League (52): Jepson 13 (3 pens), Ross 9 (1 pen), Cooper M 8 (2 pens), Morgan 4, Turner 3, Daniels 2, Storer 2, Adekola 1, Davies 1, Minett 1, Pears 1, Robinson 1, Whiston 1, Wigley 1, Worboys 1, Worthington 1, own goals 2.
Coca-Cola Cup (3): Jepson 2 (1 pen), Storer 1.
FA Cup (6): Bailey 1, Harris 1, Jepson 1, Ross 1, Storer 1, Worthington 1.
Ground: St James Park, Exeter EX4 6PX. Telephone Exeter (0392) 54073.
Record attendance: 20,984 v Sunderland, FA Cup 6th rd (replay), 4 March 1931.
Manager: Terry Cooper.
Secretary: Margaret Bond.
Honours – Football League: Division 4 Champions - 1989–90. **Division 3 (S) Cup:** Winners 1934.
Colours: Red and white striped shirts, white shorts, red stockings.

FULHAM   DIV. 3

Angus, Terence N.
Brazil, Gary N.
Eckhardt, Jeffrey E.
Farrell, Sean P.
Ferney, Martin J.

Hails, Julian
Harrison, Lee D.
Herrera, Roberto
Jupp, Duncan A.

Marshall, John P.
Morgan, Simon C.
Stannard, James
Thomas, Glen A.

League Appearances: Angus, T.N. 28(8); Baah, P.H. 26(7); Bedrossian, A. 24(6); Brazil, G.N. 46; Cooper, M.N. 2(3); Eckhardt, J.E. 33(2); Farrell, S.P. 34; Ferney, M.J. 22(1); Hails, J. 37; Haworth, R.J. 4(7); Herrera, R. 23; Jupp, D.A. 28(2); Kelly, P.L. 1(2); Mahorn, P.G. 1(2); Marshall, J.P. 21; Mison, M. 1(3); Morgan, S.C. 36(1); Onwere, U.A. 20(2); Pike, M.R. 31(2); Stannard, J. 46; Thomas, G.A. 37; Tierling, L.A. 5(9)
League (50): Brazil 14 (1 pen), Farrell 9, Morgan 6, Eckhardt 5, Baah 4, Hails 4, Angus 2, Bedrossian 1, Haworth 1, Herrera 1, Marshall 1, Pike 1, own goal 1.
Coca-Cola Cup (5): Farrell 3, Brazil 1, own goal 1.
FA Cup (0):

28

Ground: Craven Cottage, Stevenage Rd, Fulham, London SW6 6HH. Telephone 071–736 6561.
Record attendance: 49,335 v Millwall, Division 2, 8 October 1938.
Manager: Ian Branfoot.
Secretary: Mrs Janice O'Doherty.
Honours – Football League: Division 2 Champions – 1948–49. Division 3 (S) Champions - 1931–32.
Colours: White shirts, red and black trim, black shorts, white stockings red and black trim.

GILLINGHAM   DIV. 3

Arnot, Andrew J.
Baker, David P.
Banks, Steven
Barrett, Scott
Breen, Gary
Butler, Philip A.
Carpenter, Richard

Dunne, Joseph J.
Forster, Nicholas M.
Green, Richard E.
Hague, Paul
Martin, Eliot J.
Micklewhite, Gary
Palmer, Lee J.

Ramage, Andrew W.
Reinelt, Robert S.
Smillie, Neil
Smith, Neil J.
Trott, Robin F.
Watson, Paul D.

League Appearances: Arnott, A.J. 6(4); Baker, D.P. 30(3); Banks, S. 29; Barrett, S. 13; Breen, G. 20(2); Butler, P.A. 25(2); Carpenter, R. 40; Clark, P.P. 11(2); Crane, S.J. 1(5); Dunne, J.J. 37; Forster, N.M. 35(6); Green, R.E. 38(1); Hague, P. 1; Henry, L.A. 12(2); Martin, E.J. 8(1); Micklewhite, G. 28(1); Palmer, L.J. 28; Reinelt, R.S. 16(9); Smillie, N. 38; Smith, N.J. 31(4); Trott, R.F. 1; Watson, P.D. 14
League (44): Forster 18, Baker 8, Green 4 (2 pens), Carpenter 3 (2 pens), Arnott 2, Smillie 2, Smith 2, Butler 1, Henry 1, Micklewhite 1, Reinelt 1, own goal 1.
Coca-Cola Cup (1): Reinelt 1.
FA Cup (3): Baker 1, Micklewhite 1, Smith 1.
Ground: Priestfield Stadium, Gillingham ME7 4DD. Telephone Medway (0634) 851854/576828.
Record attendance: 23,002 v QPR, FA Cup 3rd rd 10 January 1948.
Manager: Mike Flanagan.
Secretary: Bill Williams.
Honours – Football League: Division 4 Champions – 1963–64.
Colours: Blue shirts, white shorts, white stockings.

GRIMSBY TOWN   DIV. 1

Agnew, Paul
Childs, Gary P. C.
Crichton, Paul A.
Croft, Gary
Dobbin, James
Futcher, Paul
Gilbert, David J.

Gowshall, Joby
Groves, Paul
Handyside, Peter D.
Jobling, Kevin A.
Lever, Mark
Livingstone, Stephen
McDermott, John

Mendonca, Clive P.
Rees, Anthony A.
Rodger, Graham
Shakespeare, Craig R.
Watson, Thomas R.
Wilmot, Rhys J.
Woods, Neil S.

League Appearances: Agnew, P. 21(2); Childs, G.P. 30(1); Crichton, P.A. 46; Croft, G. 31(5); Crosby, G. 2(1); Daws, A. 9(1); Dobbin, J. 27(2); Ford, T. 27(2); Futcher, P. 39; Gilbert, D.J. 37; Groves, P. 46; Handyside, P.D. 11(2); Jemson, N.B. 6; Jobling, K.A. 4(7); Lever, M. 21(1); Livingstone, S. 27; McDermott, J. 26; Mendonca, C.P. 39; Okorie, C. (5); Rees, A.A. 7(9); Rodger, G. 20(4); Shakespeare, C.R. 21(12); Watson, T.R. 6(5); Woods, N.S. 3(8).
League (52): Mendonca 14 (4 pens), Groves 11, Childs 6, Dobbin 4, Gilbert 4 (1 pen), Livingstone 3, Shakespeare 3, Jemson 2 (1 pen), Croft 1, Rodger 1, Watson 1, own goals 2.
Coca-Cola Cup (6): Dobbin 2, Mendonca 2, Groves 1, Okorie 1.
FA Cup (2): Croft 1, Groves 1.
Ground: Blundell Park, Cleethorpes, South Humberside DN35 7PY. Telephone Cleethorpes (0472) 697111.
Record attendance: 31,651 v Wolverhampton W, FA Cup 5th rd, 20 February 1937.
Manager: Alan Buckley.
Secretary: Ian Fleming.
Honours – Football League: Division 2 Champions – 1900–01, 1933–34. Division 3 (N) Champions – 1925–26, 1955–56. Division 3 Champions – 1979–80. Division 4 Champions – 1971-72. **League Group Cup:** Winners 1981–82.
Colours: Black and white vertical striped shirts, black shorts with red triangular panel on side, white stockings with red band on turnover.

HARTLEPOOL UNITED   DIV. 3

Garrett, Scott	Jones, Steven	Skedd, Antony S.
Gilchrist, Philip A.	Lynch, Christopher J.	Southall, Leslie N.
Honour, Brian	McGuckin, Thomas I.	Thompson, Paul D. Z.
Houchen, Keith M.		

League Appearances: Carter, T.D. 18; Cross, P. 16; Cross, R. 17; Emerson, D. 12(1); Gallacher, J. 2; Garrett, S. 14; Gilchrist, P.A. 30(5); Halliday, S.W. 7(4); Honour, B. 17; Houchen, K.M. 34; Ingram, S.D. 13; Johnrose, L. 9(4); Jones, S. 28; Lynch, C.J. 17(2); McGuckin, T.I. 33(2); MacPhail, J. 29(3); Oliver, K. (1); Olsson, P. 29(3); Peverell, N.J. 6(10); Skedd, A.S. 21(1); Southall, L.N. 38(2); Tait, M.P. 25(1); Thompson, P.D. 20(6); West, C.W. 29(7); Wratten, P. 42
League (41): Southall 9 (2 pens), Houchen 8, West 5, Thompson 4, Honour 3 (1 pen), Johnrose 3, McGuckin 2, Olsson 2, Peverell 2, Gallacher 1, MacPhail 1, own goal 1.
Coca-Cola Cup (3): Honour 1, Tait 1, West 1.
FA Cup (0):
Ground: The Victoria Ground, Clarence Road, Hartlepool TS24 8BZ. Telephone Hartlepool (0429) 272584.
Record attendance: 17,426 v Manchester U, FA Cup 3rd rd, 5 January 1957.
Manager: John MacPhail.
Secretary: John Elliott.
Honours – Nil.
Colours: Navy/sky blue.

HEREFORD UNITED   DIV. 3

Clark, Howard W.   Eversham, Paul J.   Pike, Christopher
Davies, Gareth M.   Hall, Derek R.   Reece, Andrew J.
Downs, Gregory   Pickard, Owen A.   Steele, Timothy W.

League Appearances: Abraham, G.J. 29(1); Akinbiyi, A.P. 3(1); Anderson, C.R. 32(3); Brain, S.A. 2(1); Clark, D.B. (1); Clark, H.W. 35(2); Clements, S. 2(5); Davies, G.M. 30(1); Downs, G. 27; Eversham, P.J. 3(5); Fry, C.D. 12(4); Hall, D.R. 42; Harrison, G.R. 6; Judge, A.G. 39; Langford, C.R. 3(1); May, L.A. 5(2); Morris, D.K. 23(6); Nicholson, M. 22(5); Pickard, O.A. 30(6); Pike, C. 34; Preddy, P. 9(4); Reece, A.J. 28; Roberts, D.A. 5(1); Smith, K. 17(1); Steele, T.W. 20; Thomas, B. 3; Williams, C.J. 1(1)
League (60): Pike 18 (4 pens), Hall 9, Clark H 6, Pickard 5, Roberts 5, Nicholson 4, Fry 3, Akinbiyi 2, Steele 2, Abraham 1, Anderson 1, Eversham 1, May 1, Morris 1, Reece 1.
Coca-Cola Cup (3): Hall 2 (1 pen), May 1.
FA Cup (2): Hall 1, Pike 1.
Ground: Edgar Street, Hereford HR4 9JU. Telephone Hereford (0432) 276666.
Record attendance: 18,114 v Sheffield W, FA Cup 3rd rd, 4 January 1958.
Manager: Greg Downs.
Secretary: David Vaughan.
Honours – Football League: Division 3 Champions – 1975–76. **Welsh Cup winners:** 1990.
Colours: White shirts, black shorts, white stockings.

HUDDERSFIELD TOWN   DIV. 2

Billy, Christopher A.   Jackson, Peter A.   Robinson, Philip J.
Blackwell, Kevin P.   Jepson, Ronald F.   Rowe, Rodney C.
Booth, Andrew D.   Logan, Richard A.   Scully, Patrick J.
Bullock, Darren J.   Mitchell, Graham L.   Starbuck, Philip M.
Clayton, Gary   Mooney, Thomas   Trevitt, Simon
Collins, Simon   Onuora, Ifem   Ward, Richard
Dunn, Iain G. W.   Payne, Stephen J.   Whitehead, Scot
Dyson, Jonathan P.   Reid, Paul R.   Whitney, Jonathan D.
Francis, Stephen S.

League Appearances: Baldry, S. 10; Barnett, G.L. 1; Billy, C.A. 34; Blackwell, K.P. (1); Booth, A.D. 18(8); Bullock, D.J. 20; Clayton, G. 15(2); Collins, S. 1; Cowan, T. 10; Currie, D.N. 7; Dunn, I.G. 20(14); Dyson, J.P. 19(3); Francis, S.S. 46; Harkness, S. 5; Hicks, S.J. 20(2); Jackson, P.A. 30(3); Jepson, R.F. 19(4); Logan, R.A. 9(7); Marsden, C. 2; Mitchell, G.L. 20(2); Onuora, I. 12(10); Roberts, I.W. 14(1); Robinson, P.J. 39; Robinson , R. 2; Rowe, R.C. 7(6); Scully, P.J. 11; Starbuck, P.M. 45(1); Trevitt, S. 31; Wells, M.A. 21(1); Whitney, J.D. 14; Williams, A. 4(2)
League (58): Starbuck 12 (5 pens), Booth 10, Dunn 6, Onuora 6, Jepson 5, Roberts 4, Wells 4, Bullock 3, Baldry 2, Clayton 1, Currie 1, Hicks 1, Robinson P 1, Rowe 1, Trevitt 1.

Coca-Cola Cup (4): Dunn 3, Roberts 1.
FA Cup (2): Jackson 1, Rowe 1.
Ground: Leeds Rd, Huddersfield HD1 6PX. Telephone (0484) 420335/6.
Record attendance: 67,037 v Arsenal, FA Cup 6th rd, 27 February1932.
Manager: Neil Warnock.
Secretary: Alan D. Sykes.
Honours – Football League: Division 1 Champions – 1923–24, 1924–25, 1925–26. Division 2 Champions – 1969–70. Division 4 Champions – 1969–70. **FA Cup winners** 1922.
Colours: Blue and white striped shirts, blue shorts, blue stockings with red and white trim.

HULL CITY   DIV. 2

Abbott, Gregory S.
Allison, Neil J.
Atkinson, Graeme
Brown, Linton
Dakin, Simon M.
Dewhurst, Robert M.
Fettis, Alan

Hargreaves, Christian
Hobson, Gary
Lee, Christopher
Lowthorpe, Adam
Mail, David
Mann, Neil

Mitchell, Charles B.
Moran, Stephen J.
Norton, David W.
Peacock, Richard J.
Wilson, Stephen L.
Windass, Dean

League Appearances: Abbott, G.S. 40; Allison, N.J. 27(1); Atkinson, G. 36(4); Bound, M.T. 7; Brown, L. 38(4); Dakin, S.M. 8(1); Dewhurst, R.M. 27; Fettis, A. 37; Hargreaves, C. 21(7); Hobson, G. 36; Lee, C. 37(6); Lowthorpe, A. 3; Mail, D. 21(3); Mann, N. 2(3); Miller, R.J. 2(1); Mitchell, C.B. 9; Moran, S.J. 11(6); Norton, D.W. 44; Peacock, R.J. 4(7); Warren, L.A. 28(5); Williams, G.J. 16; Wilson, S.L. 9; Windass, D. 43
League (62): Windass 23 (6 pens), Brown 9, Atkinson 7, Abbott 6 (1 pen), Moran 5, Lee 3, Dewhurst 2, Norton 2, Williams 2, Allison 1, Bound 1, Peacock 1.
Coca-Cola Cup (3): Abbott 1, Atkinson 1, Windass 1.
FA Cup (2): Brown 1, Hargreaves 1.
Ground: Boothferry Park, Hull HU4 6EU. Telephone Hull (0482) 51119.
Record attendance: 55,019 v Manchester U, FA Cup 6th rd, 26 February 1949.
Manager: Terry Dolan.
Secretary: Tom Wilson.
Honours – Football League: Division 3 (N) Champions – 1932–33, 1948–49. Division 3 Champions – 1965–66.
Colours: Black and amber striped shirts, black shorts, amber stockings.

IPSWICH TOWN   FA PREMIERSHIP

Baker, Clive E.
Connell, Graham
Cotterell, Leo S.
Durrant, Lee R.
Forrest, Craig L.
Gregory, David S.

Gregory, Neil R.
Guentchev, Bontcho L.
Johnson, Gavin
Kiwomya, Christopher M.
Linighan, David
Marshall, Ian P.

Mason, Paul D.
Milton, Simon C.
Morgan, Philip J.
Palmer, Stephen L.
Pirie, David W.
Slater, Stuart I.

Stockwell, Michael T.   Thompson, Neil   Williams, David G.
Tanner, Adam D.   Wark, John   Yallop, Frank W.
Thompson, Gary M.   Whelan, Philip J.   Youds, Edward P.

League Appearances: Baker, C.E. 15; Durrant, L.R. 3(4); Forrest, C.L. 27; Goddard, P. 3(1); Guentchev, B.L. 9(15); Johnson, G. 16; Kiwomya, C.M. 34(3); Linighan, D. 38; Marshall, I.P. 28(1); Mason, P.D. 18(4); Milton, S.C. 11(4); Palmer, S.L. 31(5); Slater, S.I. 28; Stockwell, M.T. 42; Thompson, N. 32; Wark, J. 38; Whelan, P.J. 28(1); Whitton, S.P. 7(4); Williams, D.G. 34; Yallop, F.W. 2(5); Youds, E.P. 18(5)
League (35): Marshall 10, Kiwomya 5, Linighan 3, Mason 3, Wark 3 (2 pens), Guentchev 2 (1 pen), Johnson 1, Milton 1, Palmer 1, Slater 1, Stockwell 1, Whitton 1, Youds 1, own goals 2.
Coca-Cola Cup (6): Marshall 2, Kiwomya 1, Mason 1 (pen), Milton 1, Whitton 1.
FA Cup (8): Marshall 3, Johnson 1, Palmer 1, Stockwell 1, Thompson 1, Wark 1.
Ground: Portman Road, Ipswich, Suffolk IP1 2DA. Telephone Ipswich (0473) 219211 (4 lines).
Record attendance: 38,010 v Leeds U, FA Cup 6th rd, 8 March 1975.
Manager: John Lyall.
Secretary: David C. Rose.
Honours – Football League: Division 1 Champions – 1961–62. Division 2 Champions – 1960–61, 1967–68, 1991–92. Division 3 (S) Champions – 1953–54, 1956–57. **FA Cup:** Winners 1977 78. **European Competitions:** UEFA Cup winners: 1980–81, 1982–83.
Colours: Blue shirts, white sleeves, white shorts, blue stockings.

LEEDS UNITED   FA PREMIERSHIP

Beeney, Mark R.   Humphries, Mark   Smithard, Matthew
Bowman, Robert A.   Kelly, Garry   Speed, Gary A.
Cousin, Scott   Lukic, Jovan   Strachan, Gordon D.
Couzens, Andrew J.   McAllister, Gary   Tinkler, Mark
Deane, Brian C.   Newsome, Jon   Wallace, Raymond G.
Dorigo, Anthony R.   O'Leary, David A.   Wallace, Rodney S.
Fairclough, Courtney H.   Pemberton, John M.   Wetherall, David
Ford, Mark   Pettinger, Paul A.   Whelan, Noel
Forrester, Jamie   Sharp, Kevin   White, David
Hodge, Stephen B.

League Appearances: Batty, D. 8(1); Beeney, M.R. 22; Deane, B.C. 41; Dorigo, A.R. 37; Fairclough, C.H. 40; Ford, M. 1(1); Forrester, J. 2(1); Hodge, S.B. 7(1); Kelly, G. 42; Lukic, J. 20; McAllister, G. 42; Newsome, J. 25(4); O'Leary, D.A. 10; Pemberton, J.M. 6(3); Rocastle, D.C. 6(1); Sharp, K.R. 7(3); Speed, G.A. 35(1); Strachan, G.D. 32(1); Strandli, F. (4); Tinkler, M. (3); Wallace , Ray G. (1); Wallace, Rod S. 34(3); Wetherall, D. 31(1); Whelan, N. 6(10); White, D. 9(6)
League (65): Rod Wallace 17, Deane 11, Speed 10, McAllister 8 (1 pen), White 5, Fairclough 4, Strachan 3, Hodge 1, Newsome 1, Rocastle 1, Wetherall 1, own goals 3.
Coca-Cola Cup (2): Speed 1, Whelan 1.
FA Cup (7): Forrester 2, Deane 1, Speed 1, Strachan 1, Wetherall 1, White 1.
Ground: Elland Road, Leeds LS11 0ES. Telephone Leeds (0532) 716037 (4 lines).

Record attendance: 57,892 v Sunderland, FA Cup 5th rd (replay), 15 March 1967.
Manager: Howard Wilkinson.
Company Secretary: Nigel Pleasants.
Honours – Football League: Division 1 Champions – 1968–69, 1973–74, 1991–92. Division 2 Champions – 1923–24, 1963–64, 1989–90. **FA Cup:** Winners 1972. **Football League Cup:** Winners 1967–68. **European Competitions: European Fairs Cup winners:** 1967–68, 1970–71.
Colours: All white, yellow and blue trim.

LEICESTER CITY   FA PREMIERSHIP

Agnew, Stephen M.
Blake, Mark A.
Carey, Brian P.
Coatsworth, Gary
Eustace, Scott D.
Gee, Phillip
Grayson, Simon N.
Hill, Colin F.
Hoult, Russell

Joachim, Julian K.
Lewis, Neil A.
Lowe, David A.
Mills, Gary R.
Oldfield, David C.
Ormondroyd, Ian
Philpott, Lee
Poole, Kevin
Roberts, Iwan W.

Smith, Richard G.
Speedie, David R.
Thompson, Ian T.
Thompson, Stephen J.
Walsh, Steven
Ward, Gavin J.
Whitlow, Michael
Willis, James A.

League Appearances: Agnew, S.M. 36; Blake, M.A. 10(1); Carey, B.P. 24(3); Coatsworth, G. 15(4); Eustace, S.D. (1); Gee, P. 6(6); Gibson, C.J. 11(4); Grayson, S.N. 39(1); Hill, C.F. 30(1); James, A.C. 4(5); Joachim, J.K. 27(9); Kerr, P.A. 4(3); Lewis, N.A. 24; Lowe, D.A. 1(4); Mills, G.R. 21(2); Oldfield, D.C. 24(3); Ormondroyd, I. 30(1); Philpott, L. 10(9); Poole, K. 14; Roberts, I.W. 26; Smith, R.G. 2(6); Speedie, D.R. 37; Thompson, S.J. 30; Walsh, S. 9(1); Ward, G.J. 32; Whitlow, M. 31; Willis, J.A. 9
League (72): Roberts 13, Speedie 12, Joachim 11, Thompson 7 (6 pens), Oldfield 4, Ormondroyd 4, Walsh 4, Agnew 3, Coatsworth 2, Kerr 2 (1 pen), Whitlow 2, Blake 1, Gee 1, Grayson 1, James 1, Willis 1, own goals 3.
Coca-Cola Cup (9): Ormondroyd 2, Hill 1, Joachim 1, Oldfield 1, Speedie 1, Thompson 1, Walsh 1, Whitlow 1.
FA Cup (1): Oldfield 1.
Ground: City Stadium, Filbert St, Leicester LE2 7FL. Telephone Leicester (0533) 555000.
Record attendance: 47,298 v Tottenham H, FA Cup 5th rd, 18 February 1928.
Manager: Brian Little.
Chief Executive: Barrie Pierpoint.
Honours – Football League: Division 2 Champions – 1924–25, 1936–37, 1953–54, 1956–57, 1970–71, 1979–80. **Football League Cup:** Winners 1964.
Colours: All blue.

LEYTON ORIENT   DIV. 2

Austin, Kevin
Barnett, Gary L.
Bellamy, Gary

Bogie, Ian
Carter, Darren S.
Cockerill, Glenn

Deards, Nathan J.
Heald, Paul A.
Hendon, Ian M.

Howard, Terence
Lakin, Barry
Ludden, Dominic J. R.
Newell, Paul C.

Purse, Darren J.
Putney, Trevor A.
Ryan, Vaughan W.
Sweetman, Nicholas E.

Turner, Christopher R.
Warren, Mark W.
West, Colin

League Appearances: Austin, K. 30; Barnett, G.L. 32(4); Bellamy, G. 27(2); Benstock, D. 9(3); Bogie, I. 34; Carter, D.S. 35(1); Cockerill, G. 19; Cooper, M.D. 20(9); Gamble, B.D. 1; Hackett, W.J. 32(1); Harriott, M.L. 8; Hendon, I.M. 35(1); Howard, T. 20(5); Kitchen, D.E. 7(4); Lakin, B. 11(4); Livett, S.R. (1); Ludden, D.J. 29(5); Newell, P.C. 40; Okai, S.P. 5(6); Purse, D.J. 2(3); Putney, T.A. 20(2); Ryan, V.W. 16(1); Taylor, R.A. 12(11); Thomas, M.R. 5; Tomlinson, M L. 4; Turner, C.R. 6; Warren, M.W. 5(1); West, C. 42(1)
League (57): West 14 (1 pen), Cooper 8, Barnett 7, Carter 7, Bogie 3, Hackett 3, Cockerill 2, Hendon 2, Howard 2, Okai 2, Putney 2, Thomas 2, Bellamy 1, Taylor 1, own goal 1.
Coca-Cola Cup (0):
FA Cup (5): Hackett 2, Carter 1, Cooper 1, Lakin 1
Ground: Leyton Stadium, Brisbane Road, Leyton, London E10 5NE. Telephone 081–539 2223/4.
Record attendance: 34,345 v West Ham U, FA Cup 4th rd, 25 January 1964.
Joint Managers: Chris Turner/John Sitton.
Secretary: Miss Carol Stokes.
Honours – Football League: Division 3 Champions 1969-70. **Division 3 (S) Champions** 1955-56.
Colours: Red shirts with white pinstripe, white shorts, red stockings.

LINCOLN CITY   DIV. 3

Brown, Grant A.
Carbon, Matthew P.
Daws, Anthony
Dixon, Ben
Dumphy, Sean
Hill, David M.
Johnson, Alan K.

Johnson, David A.
Leaning, Andrew J.
Mardenborough, Stephen A.
Matthews, Neil
Parkinson, Stephen
Platnauer, Nicholas R.
Pollitt, Michael F.

Puttnam, David P.
Ridings, David
Schofield, John D.
Smith, Mark C.
Smith, Paul M.
West, Dean

League Appearances: Baraclough, I.R. 34(3); Brown, G.A. 38; Burridge, J. 4; Campbell, D.A. 2(2); Carbon, M.P. 9; Clarke, D.A. 7; Costello, P. 6(5); Daws, A. 14; Dixon, B. 5(3); Dunphy, S. 14(3); Flitcroft, D.J. 2; Hill, D.M. 27(5); Hirst, L.W. 7; Huckerby, D.C. (6); Johnson, A.K. 16; Johnson, D.A. 38(3); Jones, G. (4); Leaning, A.J. 8; Lormor, A. 5(5); Loughlan, A.J. 4(8); Mardenborough, S.A. 14(7); Matthews, N. 31(5); Parkinson, S. 1(2); Platnauer, N.R. 13; Pollitt, M.F. 30; Puttnam, D.P. 13; Ridings, D. 10; Schofield, J.D. 40; Smith, M.C. 20; Smith, P.M. 33(3); West, D. 13(5); Williams, S.R. 4(4)
League (52): Johnson D 8, Matthews 7, West 6, Baraclough 5 (4 pens), Brown 3, Daws 3, Hill 3, Jones 2, Loughlan 2, Mardenborough 2, Schofield 2, Campbell 1, Clarke 1, Huckerby 1, Lormor 1, Puttnam 1, Smith M 1, Williams 1, own goals 2.
Coca-Cola Cup (7): Johnson D 2, Lormor 2, Baraclough 1 (pen), Brown 1, Matthews 1

FA Cup (3): Johnson D 1, Lormor 1, West 1.
Ground: Sincil Bank, Lincoln LN5 8LD. Telephone Lincoln (0522) 522224.
Record attendance: 23,196 v Derby Co, League Cup 4th rd, 15 November 1967.
Manager: Sam Ellis.
Secretary: Phil Hough.
Honours – Football League: Division 3 (N) Champions – 1931–32, 1947–48, 1951–52.
Division 4 Champions – 1975–76.
Colours: Red and white striped shirts, black shorts, red stockings with white trim.

LIVERPOOL   FA PREMIERSHIP

Barnes, John C. B.	Hutchison, Donald	Piechnik, Torben
Brunskill, Iain R.	James, David B.	Redknapp, Jamie F.
Brydon, Lee	Jones, Phillip L.	Ruddock, Neil
Charnock, Philip A.	Jones, Robert M.	Rush, Ian J.
Clough, Nigel H.	Matteo, Dominic	Stewart, Paul A.
Dicks, Julian A.	McManaman, Steven	Tanner, Nicholas
Fowler, Robert B.	Molby, Ian	Thomas, Michael L.
Frodsham, Ian T.	Neal, Ashley J.	Walters, Mark E.
Harkness, Steven	Nicol, Stephen	Warner, Anthony R.
Harris, Andrew D. D.	O'Donnell, Paul G.	Wright, Mark

League Appearances: Barnes, J.C. 24(2); Bjornebye, S.I. 6(3); Burrows, D. 3(1); Clough, N.H. 25(2); Dicks, J.A. 24; Fowler, R.B. 27(1); Grobbelaar, B.D. 29; Harkness, S. 10(1); Hutchison, D. 6(5); James, D.B. 13(1); Jones, R.M. 38; McManaman, S. 29(1); Marsh, M.A. (2); Matteo, D. 11; Molby, J. 11; Nicol, S. 27(4); Piechnik, T. 1; Redknapp, J.F. 29(6); Rosenthal, R. (3); Ruddock, N. 39; Rush, I.J. 41(1); Stewart, P.A. 7(1); Thomas, M.L. 1(6); Walters, M.E. 7(10); Whelan, R.A. 23; Wright, M. 31
League (59): Rush 14, Fowler 12 (1 pen), Clough 7, Redknapp 4, Barnes 3, Dicks 3 (2 pens), Ruddock 3, McManaman 2, Molby 2 (2 pens), Marsh 1, Nicol 1, Whelan 1, Wright 1, own goals 5.
Coca-Cola Cup (14): Fowler 6, Rush 4, Clough 1, Molby 1 (pen), Ruddock 1, own goal 1.
FA Cup (1): Rush 1.
Ground: Anfield Road, Liverpool L4 0TH. Telephone 0151–263 2361.
Record attendance: 61,905 v Wolverhampton W, FA Cup 4th rd, 2 February 1952.
Manager: Roy Evans.
Chief Executive/General Secretary: Peter Robinson.
Honours – Football League: Division 1 – Champions 1900–01, 1905–06, 1921–22, 1922–23, 1946–47, 1963–64, 1965–66, 1976–77, 1978–79, 1979–80, 1981–82, 1982–83, 1983–84, 1985–86, 1987–88, 1989–90 (Liverpool have a record number of 18 League Championship wins). Division 2 Champions – 1893–94, 1895–96, 1904–05, 1961–62. **FA Cup:** Winners 1965, 1974, 1986, 1989, 1992. **League Super Cup:** Winners 1985–86. **European Competitions: European Cup winners:** 1976–77, 1977–78, 1980–81, 1983–84. **UEFA Cup winners:** 1972–73, 1975–76. **Super Cup winners:** 1977.
Colours: All red with white markings.

Aunger, Geoffrey E.
Campbell, Jamie
Dixon, Kerry M.
Greene, David M.
Harper, Alan
Hartson, John
Harvey, Richard G.
Houghton, Scott A.

Hughes, Ceri M.
James, Julian C.
Johnson, Marvin A.
Linton, Desmond M.
McLaren, Paul A.
Oakes, Scott J.
Petterson, Andrew K.
Preece, David W.

Rioch, Gregor J.
Skelton, Aaron M.
Sommer, Juergen P.
Telfer, Paul N.
Thomas, Mitchell A.
Thorpe, Anthony
Williams, Martin K.

League Appearances: Aunger, G.E. 5; Benjamin, I.T. 2(1); Burke, M.S. 2(1); Campbell, J. 4(12); Davis, K.G. 1; Dickov, P. 8(7); Dixon, K.M. 27(2); Dreyer, J.B. 40; Greene, D.M. 10; Harper, A. 40(1); Hartson, J. 21(13); Houghton, S.A. 6(9); Hughes, C.M. 42; James, J.C. 29(4); Johnson, M.A. 17; Linton, D.M. 32(1); McLaren, P.A. (1); Oakes, S.J. 33(3); Peake, T. 36; Petterson, A.K. 2(3); Preece, D.W. 28(1); Rees, J.M. 8(2); Sommer, J.P. 43; Telfer, P.N. 44(1); Thomas, M.A. 17(3); Thorpe, A. 4(10); Williams, M.K. 5(10)
League (56): Dixon 9, Oakes 8, Hughes 7, Telfer 7 (1 pen), Hartson 6, Preece 5, Dreyer 3 (2 pens), James 3, Aunger 1, Benjamin 1, Dickov 1, Harper 1, Houghton 1, Thomas 1, Thorpe 1, Williams 1.
Coca-Cola Cup (0):
FA Cup (9): Oakes 5, Hartson 1, Preece 1, Telfer 1, Thorpe 1.
Ground: Kenilworth Road Stadium, 1 Maple Rd, Luton, Beds. LU4 8AW. Telephone, Offices: Luton (0582) 411622; Ticket Office: (0582) 416976.
Record attendance: 30,069 v Blackpool, FA Cup 6th rd replay, 4 March 1959.
Manager: David Pleat.
Secretary: J. K. Smylie.
Honours – Football League: Division 2 Champions – 1981–82. Division 4 Champions – 1967–68. Division 3 (S) Champions – 1936–37. **Football League Cup winners** 1987–88.
Colours: White shirts with navy and orange trim, navy shorts with orange and white trim, white stockings with navy and orange trim.

Beagrie, Peter S.
Beech, Christopher
Bentley, James G.
Brightwell, David J.
Brightwell, Ian R.
Coton, Anthony P.
Curle, Keith
Dibble, Andrew
Edghill, Richard A.
Finney, Stephen K.
Flitcroft, Gary W.

Foster, John C.
Griffiths, Carl B.
Groenendijk, Alfons
Harkin, Joseph
Hill, Andrew R.
Ingram, Rae
Karl, Steffen
Kernaghan, Alan N.
Kerr, David W.
Lake, Paul A.

Lomas, Stephen M.
Margetson, Martyn W.
McMahon, Stephen
Phelan, Terry
Quigley, Michael A.
Quinn, Niall J.
Rocastle, David C.
Rosler, Uwe
Sharpe, John J.
Sheron, Michael N.

Simpson, Fitzroy   Thomas, Scott L.   Walsh, Paul A.
Smith, Ian R.   Vonk, Michel C.   Whitley, James

League Appearances: Beagrie, P.S. 9; Brightwell, D.J. 19(3); Brightwell , I.R. 6(1); Coton, A.P. 31; Curle, K. 29; Dibble, A. 11; Edghill, R.A. 22; Flitcroft, G.W. 19(2); Foster, J.C. 1; Griffiths, C.B. 11(5); Groenendijk, A. 9; Hill, A.R. 15(2); Holden, R.W. 9; Ingebrigtsen, K. 2(6); Karl, S. 4(2); Kernaghan, A.N. 23(1); Kerr, D.W. 2; Lomas, S.M. 17(6); McMahon, S. 35; Mike, A.R. 1(8); Phelan, T. 30; Quigley, M.A. 2; Quinn, N.J. 14(1); Reid, P. 1(3); Rocastle, D.C. 21; Rosler, U. 12; Sheron, M.N. 29(4); Shutt, C.S. 5(1); Simpson, F. 12(3); Vonk, M.C. 34(1); Walsh, P.A. 11; White, D. 16
League (38): Sheron 6, Quinn 5, Rosler 5, Griffiths 4, Walsh 4, Flitcroft 3, Rocastle 2, Beagrie 1, Brightwell D 1, Curle 1 (pen), Karl 1, Mike 1, Phelan 1, Vonk 1, White 1, own goal 1.
Coca-Cola Cup (5): White 2, Lomas 1, Quinn 1, Vonk 1.
FA Cup (4): Ingebrigtsen 3, Kernaghan 1.
Ground: Maine Road, Moss Side, Manchester M14 7WN. Telephone 061 226 1191/2.
Record attendance: 84,569 v Stoke C, FA Cup 6th rd, 3 March 1934 (British record for any game outside London or Glasgow).
Manager: Brian Horton.
General Secretary: J. B. Halford.
Honours – Football League: Division 1 Champions   1936–37, 1967–68. Division 2 Champions   1898–99, 1902–03, 1909–10, 1927–28, 1946–47, 1965–66. **FA Cup** winners 1904, 1934, 1956, 1969. **Football League Cup** winners 1970, 1976. **European Competitions: European Cup-Winners' Cup** winners: 1969–70.
Colours: Sky blue shirts, white shorts, sky blue stockings.

MANCHESTER UNITED   FA PREMIERSHIP

Beckham, David R. J.   Ince, Paul E. C.   Pallister, Garry A.
Bruce, Stephen R.   Irving, Richard J.   Parker, Paul A.
Butt, Nicholas   Irwin, Joseph D.   Pilkington, Kevin W.
Cantona, Eric   Kanchelskis, Andrei   Rawlinson, Mark D.
Casper, Christopher M.   Keane, Roy M.   Schmeichel, Peter B.
Davies, Simon I.   McClair, Brian J.   Scholes, Paul
Dean, Craig   McGibbon, Patrick, C. G.   Sharpe, Lee S.
Dublin, Dion   McKee, Colin   Thornley, Benjamin L.
Giggs, Ryan J.   Murdoch, Colin J.   Walsh, Gary
Gillespie, Keith R.   Neville, Gary A.   Whitworth, Neil A.
Hughes, Leslie M.   O'Kane, John A.

League Appearances: Bruce, S.R. 41; Butt, N. (1); Cantona, E. 34; Dublin, D. 1(4); Ferguson, D. 1(2); Giggs, R.J. 32(6); Hughes, L.M. 36; Ince, P.E. 39; Irwin, J.D. 42; Kanchelskis, A. 28(3); Keane, R.M. 34(3); McClair, B.J. 12(14); McKee, C. 1; Martin, L.A. 1; Neville, G.A. 1; Pallister, G.A. 41; Parker, P.A. 39(1); Phelan, M.C. 1(1); Robson, B. 10(5); Schmeichel, P.B. 40; Sharpe, L.S. 26(4); Thornley, B. (1); Walsh, G. 2(1)
League (80): Cantona 18 (2 pens), Giggs 13, Hughes 11, Sharpe 9, Ince 8, Kanchelskis 6, Keane 5, Bruce 3, Irwin 2, Dublin 1, McClair 1, Pallister 1, Robson 1, own goal 1.

Coca-Cola Cup (19): Hughes 5, McClair 4, Giggs 3, Bruce 2, Sharpe 2, Cantona 1, Dublin 1, Kanchelskis 1.
FA Cup (18): Cantona 4 (2 pens), Hughes 4, Kanchelskis 3, Irwin 2, Giggs 1, Ince 1, Keane 1, McClair 1, Robson 1.
Ground: Old Trafford, Manchester M16 0RA. Telephone 0161–872 1661.
Record attendance: 76,962 Wolverhampton W v Grimsby T, FA Cup semi-final. 25 March 1939.
Manager: Alex Ferguson.
Secretary: Kenneth Merrett.
Honours – FA Premier League: Champions – 1992–93, 1993–94. **Football League: Division 1 Champions** – 1907–8, 1910–11, 1951–52, 1955–56, 1956–57, 1964–65, 1966–67. Division 2 Champions – 1935–36, 1974–75. **FA Cup winners** 1909, 1948, 1963, 1977, 1983, 1985, 1990, 1994. **Football League Cup winners** 1991–92. **European Competitions:** European Cup winners: 1967–68. European Cup-Winners' Cup winners: 1990–91. **European Fairs Cup winners:** 1964–65. **Super Cup winners:** 1991.
Colours: Red shirts, white shorts, black stockings.

MANSFIELD TOWN   DIV. 3

Boothroyd, Adrian N.	Holland, Paul	Timons, Christopher
Castledine, Gary J.	Noteman, Kevin S.	Ward, Darren
Gray, Kevin J.	Parkin, Stephen J.	Wilkinson, Stephen J.
Hadley, Stewart	Pearcey, Jason K.	

League Appearances: Blissett, L.L. 4(1); Boothroyd, A.N. 22(1); Castledine, G.J. 14(7); Clarke, N.J. 14(1); Fairclough, W.R. 27(2); Fleming, P. 25(3); Foster, S. 2(3); Gray, K.J. 42; Hadley, S. 14; Holland, P. 38; Ireland, S.P. 8(1); Kerry, C.B. 1(1); Lampkin, K. 11(2); McLoughlin, P.B. 19(4); Noteman, K.S. 29(4); Parkin, S.J. 21(2); Pearcey, J.K. 9; Perkins, C.P. 2(1); Platnauer, N.R. 25; Reed, J.P. 12(1); Rees, J.M. 15; Stant, P. 4; Stark, W.R. (1); Stringfellow, I.R. 10(4); Sykes, A.B. 1(1); Timons, C. 15(1); Ward, D. 33; Wilkinson, S.J. 36(6); Wilson, L. 9(5)
League (53): Wilkinson 10, Holland 7, Hadley 5, Noteman 5 (1 pen), Clarke 3, Stringfellow 3, Fairclough 2, Gray 2, McLoughlin 2, Reed 2, Blissett 1, Boothroyd 1, Ireland 1, Lampkin 1, Parkin 1, Rees 1, Stant 1, Sykes 1, Timons 1, Wilson 1, own goals 2.
Coca-Cola Cup (3): McLoughlin 1, Noteman 1, Stant 1.
FA Cup (1): Wilkinson 1.
Ground: Field Mill Ground, Quarry Lane, Mansfield.
Record attendance: 24,467 v Nottingham F, FA Cup 3rd rd, 10 January 1953.
Manager: Andy King.
Secretary: Mick Horton.
Honours – Football League: Division 3 Champions – 1976–77. Division 4 Champions – 1974–75. **Freight Rover Trophy winners** 1986–87.
Colours: All yellow with navy blue trim.

MIDDLESBROUGH   DIV. 1

Agiadis, Nicholas	Byrne, Wesley J.	Fleming, Curtis
Barron, Michael J.	Collett, Andrew A.	Hendrie, John G.

Hignett, Craig
Johnson, Ian
Kavanagh, Graham A.
Liburd, Richard J.
McGargle, Stephen
McKinlay, David H.
Mohan, Nicholas
Moore, Alan

Morris, Christopher B.
Mustoe, Robbie
Norton, Paul
Oliver, Michael
Peake, Andrew M.
Pears, Stephen
Pollock, Jamie
Roberts, Ben J.

Stamp, Philip L.
Taylor, Mark S.
Todd, Andrew J. J.
Vickers, Stephen
Ward, Richard T.
Whyte, Derek
Wilkinson, Paul
Wright, Thomas E.

League Appearances: Barron, M.J. 1(1); Fleming, C. 35(5); Forrester, P. (1); Gannon, J.S. 6(1); Hendrie, J.G. 28(1); Hignett, C. 25(4); Illman, N.D. (1); Johnson, I. 1(1); Kavanagh, G.A. 5(6); Kernaghan, A.N. 6; Liburd, R.J. 41; Mohan, N. 22(4); Moore, A. 42; Morris, C.B. 14(1); Mustoe, R. 38; Peake, A.M. 30; Pears, S. 46; Pollock, J. 34; Stamp, P.L. 8(2); Todd, A.J. 2(1); Vickers, S. 25(1); Whyte, D. 42; Wilkinson, P. 45; Winnie, D. 1; Wright, T.E. 9(7)
League (66): Wilkinson 15 (1 pen), Hendrie 13, Moore 10, Pollock 9, Hignett 5, Vickers 3, Kavanagh 2, Mustoe 2, Kernaghan 1, Liburd 1, Peake 1, Whyte 1, own goals 3.
Coca-Cola Cup (10): Hignett 5, Hendrie 3, Mustoe 1, Wilkinson 1.
FA Cup (3): Kavanagh 1, Moore 1, Wilkinson 1
Ground: Ayresome Park, Middlesbrough, Cleveland TS1 4PB. Telephone Middlesbrough (0642) 819659.
Record attendance: 53,596 v Newcastle U, Division 1, 27 December 1949.
Manager: Bryan Robson.
Chief Executive/Secretary: Keith Lamb.
Honours – Football League: Division 2 Champions 1926-27, 1928-29, 1973-74.
Amateur Cup winners 1895, 1898, **Anglo-Scottish Cup:** Winners 1975-76.
Colours: Red shirts, white shorts, red stockings.

MILLWALL   DIV. 1

Allen, Clive D.
Barber, Phillip A.
Beard, Mark
Berry, Greg J.
Carter, Timothy D.
Chapman, Daniel G.
Connor, James R.
Cunningham, Kenneth E.
Dawes, Ian R.
Dolby, Tony C.
Emberson, Carl W.
Emblen, Neil R.

Goodman, Jonathan
Harle, Michael J.
Huxford, Richard J.
Keller, Kasey
Kennedy, Mark
Kerr, John
Maguire, Gavin T.
May, Andrew M.
McCarthy, Anthony P.
McCarthy, Michael
Middleton, Matthew J.
Mitchell, David S.

Moralee, Jamie D.
Murray, Bruce
Pitcher, Geoffrey
Rae, Alex
Roberts, Andrew J.
Saddington, James
Stevens, Keith H.
Thatcher, Ben D.
Van Denhauwe, Patrick W.
Verveer, Etienne
Wietecha, David
Wright, Jermaine M.

League Appearances: Allen, C.D. 11(1); Barber, P.A. 32(3); Beard, M. 8(6); Berry, G.J. 5(5); Bogie, I. 4; Byrne, J.F 1(3); Carter, T.D. 2; Cunningham, K.E. 39; Dawes, I.R. 20(1); Dolby, T.C. 13(4); Emblen, N.R. 12; Goodman, J. 18(1); Hurlock, T.A. 13; Huxford, R.J. 25(6); Keller, K. 44; Kennedy, M 9(3); Kerr, J. 13(10); Luscombe, L.J

(2); McCarthy, A.P. 2; Maguire, G.T. 3; May, A.M. 1(2); Mitchell, D.S. 26(1);Moralee, J.D. 25(5); Murray, B. 7(6); Patmore, W.J. (1); Rae, A. 34(2); Roberts, A.J. 42; Stevens, K.H. 44; Thatcher, B.D. 8; Van Den Hauwe, P.W. 23; Verveer, E. 22(8)
League (58): Rae 13 (4 pens), Mitchell 9, Goodman 7, Verveer 5, Kennedy 4, Kerr 4, Moralee 4, Murray 2, Roberts 2, Beard 1, Berry 1, Bogie 1, Cunningham 1, Stevens 1, own goals 3.
Coca-Cola Cup (4): Huxford 1, Moralee 1, Murray 1, Verveer 1.
FA Cup (0):
Ground: The Den, Zampa Road, Bermondsey SE16 3LN. Telephone 071–232 1222.
Manager: Mick McCarthy.
Chief Executive Secretary: Graham Hortop.
Honours – Football League: Division 2 Champions – 1987–88. Division 3 (S) Champions – 1927–28, 1937–38. Division 4 Champions – 1961–62. **Football League Trophy winners 1982–83.**
Colours: Blue shirts, white shorts, blue stockings.

NEWCASTLE UNITED · FA PREMIERSHIP

Allen, Malcolm
Appleby, Matthew W.
Appleby, Richard D.
Armstrong, Alun
Beardsley, Peter A.
Beresford, John
Bracewell, Paul W.
Clark, Lee
Cole, Andrew
Elliott, Robert J.
Fox, Ruel A.
Harper, Stephen
Holland, Christopher J.
Hooper, Michael D.
Howey, Stephen N.
Jeffrey, Michael R.
Lee, Robert M.
Mathie, Alexander
Murray, Nathan
Neilson, Alan B.
Papavassiliou, Nicodemos
Peacock, Darren
Robinson, Mark
Sellars, Scott
Srnicek, Pavel
Venison, Barry
Watson, Stephen C.

League Appearances: Allen, M. 9; Appleby, M.W. 1; Beardsley, P.A. 35; Beresford, J. 34; Bracewell, P.W. 32; Clark, L. 29; Cole, A. 40; Elliott, R.J. 13(2); Fox, R.A. 14; Holland, C.J. 2(1); Hooper, M.D. 19; Howey, S.N. 13(1); Jeffrey, M.R. 2; Kilcline, B. 1; Lee, R.M. 41; Mathie, A. (16); Neilson, A.B. 10(4); O'Brien, L.F. 4(2); Papavassiliou, N. 7; Peacock, D. 9; Robinson, M. 12(4); Scott, K.W. 18; Sellars, S. 29(1); Srnicek, P. 21; Venison, B. 36(1); Watson, S.C. 29(3); Wright, T.J. 2(1)
League (82): Cole 34, Beardsley 21 (7 pens), Lee 7, Allen 5 (2 pens), Mathie 3, Sellars 3, Clark 2, Fox 2, Watson 2, Bracewell 1, own goals 2.
Coca-Cola Cup (12): Cole 6, Allen 2 (1 pen), Beardsley 1, Bracewell 1, Lee 1, Sellars 1.
FA Cup (3): Beardsley 2 (1 pen), Cole 1.
Ground: St James' Park, Newcastle-upon-Tyne NE1 4ST. Telephone 091–232 8361.
Record attendance: 68,386 v Chelsea, Division 1, 3 Sept 1930.
Manager: Kevin Keegan.
General Manager/Secretary: R. Cushing.
Honours – Football League: Division I – Champions 1904–05, 1906–07, 1908–09, 1926–27, 1992–93. Division 2 Champions – 1964–65. **FA Cup winners** 1910, 1924, 1932, 1951, 1952, 1955. **Texaco Cup winners** 1973–74, 1974–75. **European Competitions: European Fairs Cup winners:** 1968–69. **Anglo-Italian Cup winners:** Winners 1973.
Colours: Black and white striped shirts, black shorts, black stockings.

NORTHAMPTON TOWN   DIV. 3

Aldridge, Martin J.   Harmon, Darren J.   Phillips, Leslie M.
Bell, Michael   Harrison, Garry M.   Richardson, Barry
Colkin, Lee   Patmore, Warren J.   Wilkin, Kevin
Fleming, Terry M.

League Appearances: Aldridge, M.J. 23(6); Bell, M. 37(1); Brown, S. 24; Burnham, J.J. 15(2); Chard, P.J. 25(3); Colkin, L. 17(3); Cornwell, J.A. 13; Elad, D.E. 8(2); Fitzpatrick, P.J. 1(1); Fleming, T.M. 26(5); Francis, S.R. (1); Gallacher, B. 5; Gillard, K.J. 13(1); Gilzean, I.R. 29(4); Harmon, D.J. 28(3); Harrison, G.M. 2; Hyslop, C.T. 8; Parsons, M.C. 19; Patmore, W.J. 11(6); Phillips, L.M. 26; Preston, R.J. 1; Richardson, B. 27; Sampson, I. 8; Sherwood, S. 15(1); Stackman, H.S. (1); Terry, S.G. 39; Warburton, R. 17; Wilkin, K. 24; Wood, D. 1
League (44): Gilzean 10, Aldridge 8, Harmon 7, Wilkin 5, Brown 4 (1 pen), Patmore 2, Chard 1, Colkin 1, Cornwell 1, Fitzpatrick 1, Fleming 1 (pen), Terry 1, Warburton 1, own goal 1.
Coca-Cola Cup (0):
FA Cup (1): Aldridge 1.
Ground: Sixfields, Upton Way, Northampton NN5 4EG. Telephone Northampton (0604) 234100.
Record attendance: 24,523 v Fulham, Division 1, 23 April 1966.
Manager: John Barnwell.
Secretary: Barry Collins.
Honours – Football League: Division 3 Champions 1962–63. Division 4 Champions 1986–87.
Colours: Claret and white.

NORWICH CITY   FA PREMIERSHIP

Adams, Neil J.   Ekoku, Efangwu   Polston, John D.
Akinbiyi, Adeola P.   Goss, Jeremy   Prior, Spencer
Bowen, Mark R.   Gunn, Bryan   Robins, Mark G.
Butterworth, Ian S.   Howie, Scott   Smith, David
Crook, Ian S.   Johnson, Andrew J.   Sutch, Daryl
Culverhouse, Ian B.   Marshall, Andrew J.   Sutton, Christopher R.
Cureton, Jamie   Megson, Gary J.   Ullathorne, Robert
Eadie, Darren M.   Newman, Robert N.   Woodthorpe, Colin J.

League Appearances: Adams, N.J. 11(3); Akinbiyi, A.P. (2); Bowen, M.R. 41; Butterworth, I.S. 23(2); Crook, I.S. 38; Culverhouse, I.B. 42; Eadie, D.M. 9(6); Ekoku, E. 20(7); Fox, R.A. 25; Goss, J. 34; Gunn, B. 41; Howie, S. 1(1); Johnson, A.J. (2); Megson, G.J. 21(1); Newman, R.N. 32; Polston, J.D. 24; Power, L.M. 2(3); Prior, S. 13; Robins, M.G. 9(4); Smith, D. 5(2); Sutch, D. 1(2); Sutton, C.R. 41; Ullathorne, R. 11(5); Woodthorpe, C.J. 18(2)
League (65): Sutton 25 (1 pen), Ekoku 12, Fox 7 (1 pen), Goss 6, Bowen 5, Eadie 3, Newman 2, Ullathorne 2, Culverhouse 1, Robins 1, own goal 1.
Coca-Cola Cup (5): Fox 2, Crook 1, Ekoku 1, Sutton 1.

FA Cup (2): Sutton 2.
Ground: Carrow Road, Norwich NR1 1JE. Telephone Norwich (0603) 760760.
Record attendance: 43,984 v Leicester C, FA Cup 6th rd, 30 March 1963.
Manager: John Deehan.
Secretary: A. R. W. Neville.
Honours – Football League: Division 2 Champions – 1971–72, 1985–86. Division 3 (S) Champions – 1933–34. **Football League Cup:** Winners 1962, 1985.
Colours: Yellow shirts, green trim, green shorts, yellow trim, yellow stockings.

NOTTINGHAM FOREST   FA PREMIERSHIP

Armstrong, Craig
Black, Kingsley
Blatherwick, Steven S.
Bohinen, Lars
Bowyer, Gary D.
Bull, Gary W.
Carbone, Anthony
Chettle, Stephen
Clark, Richard P.
Collymore, Stanley V.
Cooper, Colin T.
Crosby, Gary
Crossley, Mark G.
Drury, Nathan
Finnigan, John
Gemmill, Scot
Gilmore, Craig

Glover, Edward L.
Guinan, Stephen
Haaland, Alf-Inge R.
Haywood, Paul
Hinshelwood, Danny
Howe, Stephen
Hughes, Luke
Kilford, Ian A.
Laws, Brian
Lee, Jason B.
Lyttle, Desmond
Marshall, Lee
McGregor, Paul A.
Mendum, Craig
Pearce, Stuart
Phillips, David O.
Rookyard, Carl

Rosario, Robert M.
Smith, Richard
Stone, Stephen B.
Stratford, Lee
Thom, Stuart P.
Tiler, Carl
Walker, Justin
Walley, Mark
Warner, Vance
Watkins, Darren
Webb, Neil J.
Wilson, Ross E.
Woan, Ian S.
Woolford, Stephen
Wright, Dale C.
Wright, Thomas J.

League Appearances: Black, K. 30(7); Blatherwick, S.S. 3; Bohinen, L. 22(1); Bull, G.W. 3(8); Chettle, S. 46; Collymore, S.V. 27(1); Cooper, C.T. 36(1); Crosby, G. 4(2); Crossley, M.G. 36(1); Gemmill, S. 30(1); Glover, E.L. 15(3); Haaland, A-I.R. 3; Harvey, L.D. (2); Howe, S. 2(2); Kilford, I.A. (1); Laws, B. 6(1); Lee, J.B. 10(3); Lyttle, D. 37; Pearce, S. 42; Phillips, D.O. 40(3); Rosario, R.M. 15(1); Stone, S.B. 45; Tiler, C. 3; Warner, V. 1; Webb, N.J. 17(4); Woan, I.S. 23(1); Wright, T.J. 10
League (74): Collymore 19, Gemmill 8, Cooper 7, Pearce 6 (3 pens), Glover 5, Stone 5, Woan 5, Phillips 4, Black 3, Webb 3, Lee 2, Rosario 2, Bohinen 1, Chettle 1, Lyttle 1, own goals 2.
Coca-Cola Cup(11): Collymore 5, Black 2,Cooper 1, Crosby 1,Gemmill 1, Webb 1.
FA Cup (1): Cooper 1.
Ground: City Ground, Nottingham NG2 5FJ. Telephone Nottingham (0602) 526000.
Record attendance: 49,945 v Manchester U, Division 1, 28 October 1967.
Manager: Frank Clark.
Secretary: P. White.
Honours – Football League: Division 1 – Champions 1977–78. Division 2 Champions – 1906–07, 1921–22. Division 3 (S) Champions – 1950–51. **FA Cup:** Winners 1898, 1959. **Football League Cup:** Winners 1977–78, 1978–79, 1988–89, 1989–90. **Anglo-Scottish Cup:** Winners 1976–77. **Simod Cup:** Winners 1989. **Zenith Data Systems Cup:** Winners 1991–92. **European Competitions: European Cup winners:** 1978–79, 1979–80, 1980–81. **Super Cup winners:** 1979–80.
Colours: Red shirts, white shorts, red stockings.

NOTTS COUNTY

Agana, Patrick A. O.
Cherry, Steven R.
Cox, Paul R.
Devlin, Paul J.
Dijkstra, Meindert
Dolan, Kenneth P.
Draper, Mark A.
Gallagher, Thomas D.
Galloway, Michael A.

Johnson, Michael O.
Legg, Andrew
Lund, Gary J.
Matthews, Robert
McSwegan, Gary J.
Murphy, Shaun P.
Palmer, Charles A.
Sherlock, Paul G.
Short, Christian M.

Simpson, Michael
Slawson, Stephen M.
Snook, Edward K.
Thomas, Dean R.
Turner, Philip
Walker, Richard N.
Wilson, Kevin J.
Worboys, Gavin
Yates, Dean R.

League Appearances: Agana, P.A. 18(2); Catlin, R. 1; Cherry, S.R. 45; Cox, P.R. 15(4); Devlin, P.J. 40(1); Dijkstra, M. 16(2); Draper, M.A. 44; Foster, C.J. 9; Gallagher, T.D. 13; Gannon, J.P. 2; Goater, L.S. 1; Johnson, M.O. 33(1); King, P.G. 6; Legg, A. 29(1); Lund, G.J. 45(1); McSwegan, G.J. 28(9); Matthews, R. 6(6); Murphy, S.P. 11; Palmer, C.A. 22; Reeves, D. 1(3); Reid, P. 5; Robinson, D.A. 2; Sherlock, P.G. 6(1); Short, C.M. 5(1); Simpson, M. 5(1); Slawson, S.M. 4; Thomas, D.R. 5(2); Turner, P. 40; Walker, R.N. 21; Williams, A. 1(1); Wilson, K.J. 27(2); Yates, D.R. (1)

League (65): McSwegan 15 (2 pens), Draper 13 (3 pens), Lund 11, Devlin 7, Agana 4, Matthews 3, Turner P 3, Legg 2, Dijkstra 1, Murphy 1, Palmer 1, Robinson 1, Simpson 1, Walker 1, Wilson 1.

Coca-Cola Cup (5): Cox 1, Draper 1, Lund 1, McSwegan 1, own goal 1.

FA Cup (4): Agana 1, Devlin 1, Draper 1, Lund 1.

Ground: County Ground, Meadow Lane, Nottingham NG2 3HJ. Telephone Nottingham (0602) 861155/529000.

Record attendance: 47,310 v York C, FA Cup 6th rd, 12 March 1955.

Manager: Mick Walker.

Secretary: N. E. Hook MCIM, AMLD.

Honours – Football League: Division 2 Champions – 1896–97, 1913–14, 1922–23. Division 3 (S) Champions – 1930–31, 1949–50. Division 4 Champions – 1970–71. **FA Cup:** Winners 1893–94.

Colours: Black and white striped shirts, white shorts, black stockings.

OLDHAM ATHLETIC

Barlow, Andrew J.
Beckford, Darren R.
Bernard, Paul R. J.
Brennan, Mark R.
Eyre, John R.
Fleming, Craig
Gerrard, Paul W.
Graham, Richard E.

Hallworth, Jonathan G.
Henry, Nicholas I.
Holden, Andrew I.
Holden, Richard W.
Jobson, Richard I.
Makin, Christopher
McCarthy, Sean C.

Milligan, Michael J.
Olney, Ian D.
Pointon, Neil G.
Redmond, Stephen
Rickers, Paul S.
Ritchie, Andrew T.
Sharp, Graeme M.

League Appearances: Adams, N.J. 7(6); Barlow, A.J. 3(3); Beckford, D.R. 13(9); Beresford, D. (1); Bernard, P.R. 32; Brennan, M.R. 11; Eyre, J.R. 1(1); Fleming, C. 37; Gerrard, P.W. 15(1); Graham, R.E. 4(1); Halle, G. 22(1); Hallworth, J.G. 19; Henry, N.I. 22; Holden, R.W. 28(1); Jobson, R.I. 37; Key, L.W. 2; McCarthy, S.C. 19(1); McDonald, N.R. 3; Makin, C. 26(1); Milligan, M.J. 39; Olney, I.D. 10; Palmer, R.N. 1(7); Pedersen, T. 7(3); Pointon, N.G. 23(1); Redmond, S. 31(2); Ritchie, A.T. 13(9); Sharp, G.M. 31(3); Walsh, G. 6
League (42): Sharp 9, Beckford 6, Holden 6 (1 pen). Bernard 5, Jobson 5, McCarthy 4, Halle 1, Makin 1, Olney 1, Redmond 1, Ritchie 1 (pen), own goals 2.
Coca-Cola Cup (5): Sharp 2, Beckford 1, Bernard 1, Halle 1.
FA Cup (7): Beckford 3, Pointon 2, Holden 1, Ritchie 1.
Ground: Boundary Park, Oldham. Telephone 0161–624 4972.
Record attendance: 47,671 v Sheffield W, FA Cup 4th rd. 25 January 1930.
Manager: Joe Royle.
Secretary: Terry Cale.
Honours – Football League: Division 2 Champions – 1990–91, Division 3 (N) Champions – 1952-53. Division 3 Champions – 1973-74.
Colours: All blue with red piping.

OXFORD UNITED   DIV. 2

Allen, Christopher A.	Elliott, Matthew S.	Penney, David M.
Beauchamp, Joseph D.	Ford, Michael P.	Reece, Paul J.
Byrne, John F.	Ford, Robert J.	Robinson, Leslie
Collins, David D.	Lewis, Michael	Rogan, Anthony G. P.
Cusack, Nicholas J.	Moody, Paul	Wanless, Paul S.
Druce, Mark A.	Murphy, Matthew S.	Whitehead, Philip M.
Dyer, Alexander C.		

League Appearances: Allen, C.A. 34(11); Beauchamp, J.D. 43(2); Byrne, J.F. 27(3); Carter, J.W. 5; Collins, D.D. 18(8); Cusack, N.J. 18(2); Druce, M.A. 5(14); Dyer, A.C. 30(8); Elliott, M.S. 32; Ford, M.P. 41; Ford, R.J. 12(2); Jackson, D.W. 1(1); Kee, P.V. 3; Keeble, M.E. (1); Lewis, M. 46; Magilton, J. 29; Moody, P. 15; Narbett, J.V. 1; Penney, D.M. 13(3); Reece, P.J. 4; Robinson, L. 36; Rogan, A.G. 29; Saunders, C.S. 2(3); Smart, G.J. 22(1); Wanless, P.S. 1(8); Whitehead, P.M. 39
League (54): Moody 8 (3 pens), Byrne 7, Beauchamp 6, Cusack 6, Dyer 5, Elliott 5, Magilton 5 (4 pens), Allen 3, Penney 2, Robinson 2, Rogan 2, Ford M 1, own goals 2.
Coca-Cola Cup (2): Beauchamp 1, Wanless 1.
FA Cup (8): Byrne 2, Elliott 2, Allen 1, Beauchamp 1, Dyer 1, Magilton 1.
Ground: Manor Ground, Headington, Oxford OX3 7RS. Telephone Oxford (0865) 61503.
Record attendance: 22,750 v Preston NE, FA Cup 6th rd, 29 February 1964.
Manager: Denis Smith.
Secretary: Mick Brown.
Honours – Football League: Division 2 Champions – 1984-85. Division 3 Champions – 1967-68, 1983-84. **Football League Cup:** Winners 1985-86.
Colours: Gold shirts with blue sleeves, blue shorts, gold stockings.

PETERBOROUGH UNITED DIV. 2

Adcock, Anthony C.
Barber, Frederick
Bradshaw, Darren S.
Brissett, Jason C.
Carter, Ian N.
Charlery, Kenneth
Cooksey, Scott A.

Ebdon, Marcus
Greenman, Christopher
Hackett, Gary S.
Halsall, Michael
Howarth, Lee
Iorfa, Dominic
McGlashan, John

McGorry, Brian P.
Morrison, David E.
Peters, Mark
Spearing, Anthony
Walsh, Stephen
Williams, Lee

League Appearances: Adcock, A.C. 40(2); Anthrobus, S. 2; Barber, F. 24; Barnes, D.O. 5(3); Bennett, I.M. 19; Bradshaw, D.S. 38(1); Brissett, J.C. 23(7); Carter, I.N. 9(2); Charlery, K. 26; Clark, S. 1; Cooksey, S.A. 3; Cooper, G. 13(1); Ebdon, M. 10; Fulton, S. 3; Furnell, A.P. 5(5); Gibson, T.B. 1; Greenman, C. 24(1); Hackett, G.S. 18(4); Halsall, M. (1); Howarth, L. 24(1); Iorfa, D. 24(10); Kruszynski, Z. 2(1); McDonald, D.H. 28(1); McGee, P. 5(1); McGlashan, J. 26(2); McGorry, B.P. 14(4); Peters, M. 17(2); Philliskirk, A. 6(5); Rush, D. 2(2); Spearing, A. 33(1); Welsh, S. 45; Williams, L. 16(2)
League (48): Adcock 12 (3 pens), Charlery 8, Iorfa 8, Philliskirk 4 (1 pen), McGorry 3, McGlashan 3, Cooper 2 (1 pen), Barnes 1, Bradshaw 1, Furnell 1, Hackett 1, Rush 1, Spearing 1, Welsh 1, own goal 1.
Coca-Cola Cup (8): Adcock 1, Bradshaw 1, Brissett 1, Hackett 1, McGlashan 1, Oliver 1, Philliskirk 1, Rush 1.
FA Cup (2): Brissett 1, Charlery 1.
Ground: London Road Ground, Peterborough PE2 8AL. Telephone Peterborough (0733) 63947.
Record attendance: 30,096 v Swansea T, FA Cup 5th rd, 20 February 1965.
Manager: John Still.
Company Secretary: Miss Caroline Hand.
Honours – Football League: Division 4 Champions – 1960–61, 1973–74.
Colours: Royal blue shirts, white shorts, white stockings.

PLYMOUTH ARGYLE DIV. 2

Barlow, Martin D.
Burnett, Wayne
Castle, Stephen C.
Comyn, Andrew J.
Crocker, Marcus A.
Dalton, Paul

Edworthy, Marc
Evans, Michael J.
Hill, Keith J.
Landon, Richard J.
Marshall, Dwight W.
McCall, Stephen H.

Naylor, Dominic J.
Nicholls, Alan
Nugent, Kevin P.
Williams, Martin K.

League Appearances: Barlow, M.D. 22(4); Boardman, P. (1); Burnett, W. 30(2); Burrows, A.M. 20(2); Castle, S.C. 44; Comyn, A.J. 46; Crocker, M.A. (1); Dalton, P. 40; Edworthy, M. 7(5); Evans, M.J. 16(6); Hill, K.J. 28(1); Landon, R.J. 3(3); McCall, S.H. 44(1); McCarthy, A.J. 1(1); Marshall, D.W. 28(3); Naylor, D.J. 42(1); Newland, R.J. 4(1); Nicholls, A. 38; Nugent, K.P. 39; Patterson, M. 41; Shilton, P.L. 4; Skinner, C.R. 9(7)

46

League (88): Castle 21 (1 pen), Nugent 14, Dalton 12, Marshall 12, Evans 9, Comyn 5, Landon 5, Barlow 2, Burnett 2, McCall 2, Hill 1, own goals 3.
Coca-Cola Cup (2): Barlow 1, Marshall 1.
FA Cup (7): Dalton 3, Nugent 3, Marshall 1.
Ground: Home Park, Plymouth, Devon PL2 3DQ. Telephone Plymouth (0752) 562561.
Record attendance: 43,596 v Aston Villa, Division 2, 10 October 1936.
Manager: Peter Shilton.
Secretary: Michael Holladay.
Honours – Football League: Division 3 (S) Champions 1929-30, 1951 52. Division 3 Champions – 1958–59.
Colours: Green and black striped shirts, black shorts, black stockings.

PORTSMOUTH   DIV. 1

Awford, Andrew T.	Doling, Stuart J.	McLoughlin, Alan F.
Burns, Christopher	Durnin, John	Neill, Warren A.
Burton, Deon J.	Flahavan, Aaron A.	Pethick, Robert J.
Butters, Guy	Gittens, John	Powell, Darryl A.
Creaney, Gerard	Hall, Paul A.	Russell, Lee
Cunningham, Aaron M.	Igoe, Samuel G.	Stimson, Mark
Daniel, Raymond C.	Knight, Alan E.	Symons, Christopher J.
Dobson, Anthony J.	Kristensen, Bjorn	Wood, Paul A.

League Appearances: Aspinall, W. (5); Awford, A.T. 35; Blake, M.A. 15; Boere, J.W. 4(1); Burns, C. 8(4); Burton, D.J. 1(1); Butters, G. 12(3); Chamberlain, M.V. 12(7); Chapman, L.R. 5; Creaney, G. 18; Daniel, R.C. 14(2); Dobson, A.J. 23(1); Doling, S.J. 9(4); Durnin, J. 23(5); Gittens, J. 30; Hall, P.A. 16(12); Horne, B. 3; Knight, A.E. 43; Kristensen, B. 31(5); McLoughlin, A.F. 37(1); Neill, W.A. 35; Pethick, R.J. 14(4); Powell, D.A. 17(11); Power, L.M. 1(1); Price, C.J. 1(4); Russell, L. 5(5); Stimson, M. 28(1); Symons, C.J. 29; Walsh, P.A. 30; Wood, P.A. 7(5)
League (52): Creaney 11 (2 pens), Durnin 6, McLoughlin 6, Powell 5, Walsh 5, Hall 4, Symons 3 (2 pens), Chapman 2, Dobson 2, Neill 2, Butters 1, Chamberlain 1, Doling 1, Gittens 1, Stimson 1, Wood 1.
Coca-Cola Cup (10): Walsh 4, Durnin 2, Burns 1, Kristensen 1, McLoughlin 1, Stimson 1.
FA Cup (4): McLoughlin 4.
Ground: Fratton Park, Frogmore Rd, Portsmouth PO4 8RA Telephone Portsmouth (0705) 731204.
Record attendance: 51,385 v Derby Co, FA Cup 6th rd, 26 February 1949.
Manager: Jim Smith.
Secretary: Paul Weld.
Honours – Football League: Division 1 Champions 1948–49, 1949 50. Division 3 (S) Champions 1923-24. Division 3 Champions 1961 -62, 1982 -83 **FA Cup:** Winners 1939.
Colours: Blue shirts, white shorts, red stockings.

PORT VALE   DIV. 1

Allon, Joseph B.   Jeffers, John J.   Stokes, Dean A.
Aspin, Neil   Kent, Kevin J.   Swan, Peter H.
Billing, Peter G.   Kerr, Paul A.   Tankard, Allen J.
Foyle, Martin J.   Musselwhite, Paul S.   Taylor, Ian K.
Glover, Dean V.   Porter, Andrew M.   Van Der Laan, Robertus P.
Griffiths, Gareth J.   Sandeman, Bradley R.   Walker, Raymond
Heald, Oliver R.

League Appearances: Allon, J.B. 3(1); Aspin, N. 40; Billing, P.G. 7(1); Cross, N.J. 29(8); Foyle, M.J. 36(1); Glover, D.V. 46; Griffiths, G.J. 3(1); Jeffers, J.J. 21(4); Kent, K.J. 23(7); Kerr, P.A. 24(1); Livingstone, S. 4(1); Lowe, D.A. 18(1); Musselwhite, P.S. 46; Newhouse, A.R. (2); Porter, A.M. 28(9); Sandeman, B.R. 4(5); Slaven, B. 20(3); Stokes, D.A. 21; Swan, P.H. 40; Tankard, A.J. 22(4); Taylor, I.K. 42; Van der Laan, R.P. 29(4)
League (79): Foyle 18, Taylor 13, Cross 12, Slaven 7, Lowe 5, Kent 4, Kerr 4, Van der Laan 4, Glover 3, Allon 2, Griffiths 2, Aspin 1, Jeffers 1, own goals 3.
Coca-Cola Cup (2): Slaven 1, Taylor 1.
FA Cup (5): Foyle 1, Kerr 1, Porter 1, Slaven 1, Tankard 1.
Ground: Vale Park, Burslem, Stoke-on-Trent ST4 4EG. Telephone Stoke-on-Trent (0782) 814134.
Record attendance: 50,000 v Aston Villa, FA Cup 5th rd, 20 February 1960.
Manager: John Rudge.
Secretary: R. A. Allan.
Honours – Football League: Division 3 (N) Champions – 1929–30, 1953–54. Division 4 Champions – 1958–59.
Colours: White shirts, black shorts, black and white stockings.

PRESTON NORTH END   DIV. 3

Ainsworth, Gareth   Holmes, Steven P.   Norbury, Michael S.
Bryson, James I. C.   Kidd, Ryan A.   O'Hanlon, Kelham G.
Cartwright, Lee   Kilbane, Farrell N.   Raynor, Paul J.
Challender, Gregory L.   Lucas, Richard   Squires, James A.
Conroy, Michael K.   Magee, Kevin   Sulley, Christopher S.
Ellis, Anthony J.   Matthewson, Trevor   Watson, Liam
Fensome, Andrew B.   Moyes, David W.   Whalley, David N.
Hicks, Stuart J.   Nebbeling, Gavin M.   Woods, Stephen G.

League Appearances: Ainsworth, G. 34(4); Bamber, L.E. (1); Bryson, J.I. 24(1); Burton, S.P. 2(1); Callaghan, A.J. 1; Cartwright, L. 36(3); Challender, G.L. 5(5); Conroy, M.K. 28(4); Ellis, A.J. 36(1); Fensome, A.B. 31; Hicks, S.J. 3(1); Holland, C. (1); Kidd, R.A. 35(1); Kilbane, F.N. (1); Lucas, R. 21(3); Magee, K. 5(2); Masefield, P.D. 6; Matthewson, T. 12; Moyes, D.W. 29; Nebbeling, G.M. 22; Norbury, M.S. 11(10); O'Hanlon, K.G. 23; Raynor, P.J. 36(3); Squires, J.A. 4; Sulley, C.S. 21; Watson, L. 1; Whalley, D.N. 17(4); Woods, S.G. 19(1)

League (79): Ellis 26 (3 pens), Conroy 12, Ainsworth 11, Raynor 6, Norbury 5, Moyes 4, Nebbeling 4, Bryson 2, Challender 2, Cartwright 1, Fensome 1, Kidd 1, Matthewson 1, Sulley 1, own goals 2.
Coca-Cola Cup (2): Cartwright 1, Ellis 1.
FA Cup (5): Ellis 2 (1 pen), Conroy 1, Moyes 1, Raynor 1.
Ground: Deepdale, Preston PR1 6RU. Telephone Preston (0772) 795919.
Record attendance: 42,684 v Arsenal, Division 1, 23 April 1938.
Manager: John Beck.
Secretary: Audrey Shaw.
Honours – Football League: Division 1 Champions – 1888–89 (first champions), 1889–90. Division 2 Champions – 1903–04, 1912–13, 1950–51. Division 3 Champions – 1970–71. **FA Cup winners** 1889, 1938.
Colours: White and navy shirts, navy shorts, navy stockings.

QUEENS PARK RANGERS   FA PREMIERSHIP

Allen, Bradley J.
Bailey, Dennis L.
Bardsley, David J.
Barker, Simon
Brevett, Rufus E.
Bryan, Marvin L.
Caldwell, Peter J.
Croft, Brian G.
Dichio, Daniele S. E.
Doyle, Maurice

Ferdinand, Leslie
Freedman, Douglas A.
Gallen, Kevin A.
Graham, Mark R.
Holloway, Ian S.
Impey, Andrew R.
Maddix, Daniel S.
McCarthy, Alan J.
McDonald, Alan
Meaker, Michael J.

Penrice, Gary K.
Ready, Karl
Roberts, Anthony M.
Sinclair, Trevor
Stejskal, Jan
White, Devon W.
Wilson, Clive
Witter, Anthony J.
Yates, Stephen

League Appearances: Allen, B.J. 14(7); Bardsley, D.J. 32; Barker, S. 35(2); Brevett, R.E. 3(4); Doyle, M. 1; Ferdinand, L. 35(1); Holloway, I.S. 19(6); Impey, A.R. 31(2); McCarthy, A.J. 4; McDonald, A. 12; Meaker, M.J. 11(3); Peacock, D. 30; Penrice, G.K. 23(3); Ready, K. 19(3); Roberts, A.M. 16; Sinclair, T. 30(2); Stejskal, J. 26; White, D.W. 12(6); Wilkins, R.C. 39; Wilson, C. 42; Witter, A.J. 1; Yates, S. 27(2)
League (62): Ferdinand 16, Penrice 6, Allen 7, White 7, Barker 5, Sinclair 4, Impey 3, Peacock 3, Wilson 3 (3 pens), McDonald 1, Meaker 1, Ready 1, Wilkins 1, own goals 2.
Coca-Cola Cup (10): Allen 3, Barker 2, Ferdinand 2, Impey 1, Meaker 1, Sinclair 1.
FA Cup (1): Barker 1.
Ground: South Africa Road, W12 7PA. Telephone 081-743 0262.
Record attendance: 35,353 v Leeds U, Division 1, 27 April 1974.
Manager: Gerry Francis.
Secretary: Miss S. F. Marson.
Honours – Football League: Division 2 Champions – 1982–83. Division 3 (S) Champions – 1947–48. Division 3 Champions – 1966–67. **Football League Cup winners** 1966–67.
Colours: Blue and white hooped shirts, white shorts, white stockings.

READING

Barkus, Lea P.
Bass, David
Gilkes, Earl G. M.
Gooding, Michael C.
Gray, Andrew
Hartenberger, Uwe

Hislop, Neil S.
Hopkins, Jeffrey
Jones, Tom
Kerr, Dylan
Lambert, Christopher J. P.
Lovell, Stuart A.

McPherson, Keith A.
Parkinson, Philip J.
Quinn, James M.
Ranson, Raymond
Taylor, Scott D.
Williams, Adrian

League Appearances: Bass, D. (1); Carey, A.W. (1); Dillon, K.P. 31(1); Gilkes, E.G.M. 29(10); Gooding, M.C. 41; Gray, A. (5); Hartenberger, U. (9); Hislop, N.S. 46; Hopkins, J. 40(2); Humphrey, J. 8; Jones, T. 11(6); Kerr, D. 45; Lambert, C.J. 1(5); Lovell, S.A. 43(2); McPherson, K.A. 19(1); Parkinson, P.J. 42; Quinn, J.M. 46; Ranson, R. 22(2); Taylor, S.D. 34(4); Wallace, R.G. 3; Williams, A. 41; Witter, A.J. 4
League (81): Quinn 35 (6 pens), Lovell 20, Gooding 7, Taylor 6, Parkinson 3, Gilkes 2, Hartenberger 2, Hopkins 2, Kerr 2, McPherson 1, own goal 1.
Coca-Cola Cup (7): Lovell 2, Quinn 2, Dillon 1, Gray 1, Parkinson 1.
FA Cup (1): Gooding 1.
Ground: Elm Park, Norfolk Road, Reading RG3 2EF. Telephone Reading (0734) 507878.
Record attendance: 33,042 v Brentford, FA Cup 5th rd, 19 February 1927.
Manager: Mark McGhee.
Secretary: Jayne E. Hill.
Honours – Football League: Division 2 Champions – 1993–94. Division 3 Champions – 1985–86. Division 3 (S) Champions – 1925–26. Division 4 Champions – 1978–79 Simod Cup winners 1987–88.
Colours: Navy and white hooped shirts, white shorts, white stockings.

ROCHDALE

Bowden, Jon L.
Butler, Paul J.
Doyle, Stephen C.
Formby, Kevin
Hodge, Martin J.
Lancaster, David

Matthews, Neil P.
Milner, Andrew J.
Oliver, Darren
Peake, Jason W.
Reeves, Alan
Reid, Shaun

Stuart, Mark R.
Taylor, Jamie L.
Thackeray, Andrew J.
Whitehall, Steven C
Williams, Paul A.

League Appearances: Bowden, J.L. 11(18); Butler, P.J. 38; Doyle, S.C. 32(2); Finley, A.J. 1; Flounders, A.J. 9(2); Formby, K. 2(3); Graham, J. 28(1); Hodge, M.J. 42; Howard, A.P. (5); Jones, A. 3(1); Lancaster, D. 37(3); Matthews, N.P. 5(1); Milner, A.J. 14(11); Mulrain, S.F. (2); Oliver, D. 14(5); Peake, J.W. 10; Reeves, A. 41; Reid, S. 39; Ryan, J.B. 10(2); Shelton, G. 3; Snowden, T. (1); Stuart, M.R. 41(1); Taylor, J.L. 1(9); Thackeray, A.J. 35(2); Whitehall, S.C. 37(2); Williams, P.A. 9(2)
League (63): Lancaster 14, Whitehall 14, Stuart 13 (1 pen), Thackeray 4, Bowden 3, Reeves 3, Reid 3, Butler 2, Milner 2, Williams 2, Doyle 1, Howard 1, Taylor 1
Coca-Cola Cup (4): Flounders 1 (pen), Lancaster 1, Stuart 1, own goal 1
FA Cup (2): Stuart 1 (pen), Whitehall 1 (pen).

Ground: Spotland, Sandy Lane, Rochdale OL11 5DS. Telephone Rochdale (0706) 44648.
Record attendance: 24,231 v Notts Co, FA Cup 2nd rd, 10 December 1949.
Manager: Dave Sutton.
Secretary: Keith Clegg.
Honours – Nil.
Colours: Blue with red and white chevrons.

ROTHERHAM UNITED   DIV. 2

Banks, Ian F.	Hazel, Desmond L.	Richardson, Neil T.
Breckin, Ian	Helliwell, Ian	Roberts, Glyn S.
Brien, Anthony J.	Howard, Jonathan	Smith, Scott D.
Clarke, Matthew J.	Hurst, Paul M.	Todd, Mark K.
Dolby, Christopher J.	Jacobs, Wayne G.	Varadi, Imre
Goater, Leonardo S.	Marginson, Karl K.	Wilder, Christopher J.
Goodwin, Shaun L.	Mercer, William	Williams, Andrew

League Appearances: Banks, I.F. 31; Barras, A. 5; Breckin, I. 10; Brien, A.J. 25(1); Clarke, M.J. 29(1); Dolby, C.J. (1); Goater, L.S. 25(14); Goodwin, S.L. 38; Hazel, D.L. 26(3); Helliwell, I. 37(3); Howard, J. 4(4); Hurst, P.M. 3(1); Hutchings, C. 5(2); Jacobs, W.G. 40(2); Kiwomya, A.D. 4(3); Law, N. 10; Marginson, K.K. 6; Marshall, S.R. 10; Mercer, W. 17; Pickering, A.G. 12; Richardson, N.T. 27; Roberts, G.S. 11(3); Smith, S.D. 7; Todd, M.K. 9(2); Varadi, I. 38(1); Whitworth, N.A. 8; Wilder, C.J. 35(2); Williams, A. 34
League (63): Varadi 19, Goater 13, Goodwin 8, Banks 3 (1 pen), Hazel 3, Helliwell 3, Brien 2, Jacobs 2, Wilder 2 (1 pen), Williams 2, Barras 1, Marshall 1, Pickering 1, Roberts 1, Todd 1, Whitworth 1.
Coca-Cola Cup (5): Banks 1, Hazel 1, Law 1, Varadi 1, own goal 1.
FA Cup (1): Wilder 1 (pen).
Ground: Millmoor Ground, Rotherham S60 1HR. Telephone Rotherham (0709) 562434.
Record attendance: 25,000 v Sheffield U, Division 2, 13 December 1952 and v Sheffield W, Division 2, 26 January 1952.
Manager: Phil Henson.
Secretary: N. Darnill.
Honours – Football League: Division 3 Champions – 1980–81. Division 3 (N) Champions – 1950–51. Division 4 Champions – 1988–89.
Colours: Red shirts, white shorts, red stockings.

SCARBOROUGH   DIV. 3

Calvert, Mark R.	Harper, Lee J.	Swales, Stephen C.
Charles, Stephen	Knowles, Darren T.	Thompson, Simon L.
Davis, Darren J.	McHugh, Michael B.	Toman, James A.
Dineen, Jack	Meyer, Adrian M.	White, Jason G.
Evans, Mark	Murray, Shaun	Whittington, Craig
Foreman, Darren	Rockett, Jason	Young, Stuart R.

League Appearances: Ashdjian, J.A. 2(5); Burridge, J. 3; Calvert, M.R. 42; Cawthorn, P.J. 6(2); Charles, S. 37; Davis, D.J. 24(1); Dineen, J. 1(1); Evans, M. 2; Foreman, D. (3); Harper, L.J. (2); Hawke, W.R. (1); Henderson, D.M. 17; Horsfield, G. 6; Knowles, D.T. 42; McHugh, M.B. 1(2); Maguire, G.T. 2; Meyer, A.M. 36; Mockler, A.J. 6; Murray, S. 29; Oakes, M.C. 1; Robinson, P. 3(1); Rockett, J. 33(1); Sheppard, S. 9; Swales, S.C. 24(2); Thompson, S.L. 29(3); Toman, J.A. 12(1); White, J.G. 24; Whitington, C. 26(1); Young, S.R. 21(7)
League (55): Whitington 10, White 9, Young 9, Charles 7 (3 pens), Henderson 5, Murray 5, Calvert 3, Thompson 2, Cawthorn 1, Davis 1, Knowles 1, Meyer 1, Toman 1.
Coca-Cola Cup (0):
FA Cup (1): Young 1.
Ground: The McCain Stadium, Seamer Road, Scarborough YO12 4HF. Telephone (0723) 375094.
Manager: Steve Wicks.
Administrator: Eric Hall.
Honours – FA Trophy: Winners 1973, 1976, 1977. **GM Vauxhall Conference:** Winners 1987.
Colours: Red shirts, white shorts, red stockings.

SCUNTHORPE UNITED   DIV. 3

Alexander, Graham	Hope, Christopher J.	Ryan, Tim J.
Bradley, Russell	Housham, Steven J.	Samways, Mark
Bullimore, Wayne A.	Juryeff, Ian M.	Sansam, Christian
Carmichael, Matthew	Knill, Alan R.	Smith, Mark C.
Goodacre, Samuel D.	Martin, Dean S.	Thompstone, Ian P.
Henderson, Damian M.	Mudd, Paul A.	Thornber, Stephen J.

League Appearances: Alexander, G. 40(1); Bradley, R. 34; Bullimore, W.A. 17(1); Carmichael, M. 42; Danzey, M.J. 3; Elliott, M.S. 14; Goodacre, S.D. 10(8); Heath, M. 1(1); Henderson, D.M. 15(5); Hope, C.J. 37(4); Juryeff, I.M. 20(3); Knill, A.R. 25; Martin, D.S. 26; Mudd, P.A. 31(2); Ryan, T.J. (1); Samways, M. 41; Sansam, C. 4(6); Smith, M.C. 26(4); Thompstone, I.P. 29(1); Thornber, S.J. 21(3); Toman, J.A. 15; Trebble, N.D. 8(6); Watson, J.I. 1(4); White, J.G. 2(7)
League (64): Carmichael 18 (2 pens), Smith 6, Juryeff 5, Thompstone 5, Toman 5, Alexander 4, Bullimore 3 (1 pen), Goodacre 3, Mudd 3, Martin 2, Thornber 2, Trebble 2, Bradley 1, Danzey 1, Elliott 1, Henderson 1, Knill 1, own goal 1.
Coca-Cola Cup (1): Martin 1.
FA Cup (4): Goodacre 2, Carmichael 1, Toman 1.
Ground: Glanford Park, Scunthorpe, South Humberside DN15 8TD. Telephone Scunthorpe (0724) 848077.
Record attendance: Old Showground: 23,935 v Portsmouth, FA Cup 4th rd, 30 January 1954. Glanford Park: 8775 v Rotherham U, Division 4, 1 May 1989.
Team Manager: David Moore.
Secretary: A. D. Rowing.
Honours – Division 3 (N) Champions – 1957–58.
Colours: White shirts, claret and blue trim, sky blue shorts, claret and white trim, sky blue stockings, claret and white trim.

Anthony, Graham J.
Battersby, Tony
Beesley, Paul
Bibbo, Salvatore
Blake, Nathan A.
Blount, Mark
Bradshaw, Carl
Brocklehurst, David
Carr, Franz A.
Cowan, Thomas
Davidson, Ross
Fickling, Ashley
Flo, Jostein
Foran, Mark J.
Foreman, Matthew
Gage, Kevin W.
Gannon, John S.
Gayle, Brian W.
Hartfield, Charles J.
Hodges, Glyn P.
Hoyland, Jamie W.
Kelly, Alan T.
Littlejohn, Adrian S.
Nilsen, Roger
Reed, John P.
Rogers, Paul A.
Scott, Andrew
Scott, Robert
Thomson, Martin
Tracey, Simon P.
Tuttle, David P.
Ward, Mitchum D.
Whitehouse, Dane L.

League Appearances: Barnes, D. 2; Beesley, P. 22(3); Blake, N.A. 7(5); Bradshaw, C. 39(1); Carr, F.A. 10; Cork, A.G. 7(12); Cowan, T. 4; Davison, R. 8(1); Falconer, W.H. 21(2); Flo, J. 32(1); Gage, K.W. 16(5); Gannon, J.S. 14; Gayle, B.W. 13; Hartfield, C.J. 3(2); Hodges, G.P. 19(12); Hoyland, J.W. 17(1); Kamara, C. 15(1); Kelly, A.T. 29(1); Littlejohn, A.S. 12(7); Nilsen, R. 21(1); Pemberton, J.M. 8; Rogers, P.A. 24(1); Scott, A. 12(3); Tracey, S.P. 13(2); Tuttle, D.P. 31; Ward, M.D. 20(2); Whitehouse, D.L. 35(3); Wirmola, J.F. 8
League (42): Flo 9, Blake 5, Whitehouse 5 (3 pens), Cork 3, Falconer 3, Gayle 3, Littlejohn 3, Rogers 3, Hodges 2, Bradshaw 1, Carr 1, Ward 1, own goals 3.
Coca-Cola Cup (2): Davison 1, Ward 1.
FA Cup (0):
Ground: Bramall Lane Ground, Sheffield S2 4SU. Telephone Sheffield (0742) 738955.
Record attendance: 68,287 v Leeds U, FA Cup 5th rd, 15 February 1936.
Team Manager: Dave Bassett.
Secretary: D. Capper AFA.
Honours – Football League: Division 1 Champions – 1897–98. Division 2 Champions – 1952–53. Division 4 Champions – 1981–82. **FA Cup:** Winners 1899, 1902, 1915, 1925.
Colours: Red and white striped shirts, black shorts, black stockings.

Barker, Richard I.
Bart-Williams, Christopher G.
Bright, Mark A.
Brown, Steven M.
Coleman, Simon
Faulkner, David P.
Hardwick, Matthew J.
Hirst, David E.
Holmes, Darren P.
Hyde, Graham
Jemson, Nigel B.
Jones, Ryan A.
Kearn, Stewart
Key, Lance W.
King, Philip G.
Linighan, Brian
Palmer, Carlton L.
Pearce, Andrew J.
Pearson, Nigel G.
Poric, Aden
Pressman, Kevin P.
Sheridan, John J.
Sinton, Andrew
Stewart, Simon A.
Waddle, Christopher R.
Walker, Desmond S.

Watson, Gordon W. G. Williams, Michael A. Worthington, Nigel
Watts, Julian Woods, Christopher C.

League Appearances: Bart-Williams, C.G. 30(7); Bright, M.A. 36(4); Briscoe, L.S. (1); Coleman, S. 10(5); Francis, T.J. (1); Hirst, D.E. 6(1); Hyde, G. 27(9); Jemson, N.B. 10(8); Jones, R.A. 24(3); King, P.G. 7(3); Linighan , B. 1; Nilsson, R.N. 38; Palmer, C.L. 37; Pearce, A.J. 29(3); Pearson, N.G. 4(1); Poric, A. 2(4); Pressman, K.P. 32; Sheridan, J.J. 19(1); Sinton, A. 25; Waddle, CR. 19; Walker, D.S. 42; Warhurst, P. 4; Watson, G.W. 15(8); Watts, J. 1; Williams, M.A. 4; Woods, C.C. 10; Worthington, N. 30(1)

League (76): Bright 19, Watson 12, Bart-Williams 8, Jones 6, Jemson 5, Palmer 5, Pearce 3, Sheridan 3 (3 pens), Sinton 3, Waddle 3, Coleman 1, Hirst 1, Hyde 1, Worthington 1, own goals 5.

Coca-Cola Cup (10): Bright 2, Palmer 2, Watson 2, Bart-Williams 1, Hirst 1, Jemson 1, Jones 1.

FA Cup (5): Bright 2, Bart-Williams 1, Hyde 1, Pearce 1.

Ground: Hillsborough, Sheffield, S6 1SW. Telephone Sheffield (0742) 343122.

Record attendance: 72,841 v Manchester C, FA Cup 5th rd, 17 February 1934.

Manager: Trevor Francis.

Secretary: G. H. Mackrell FCCA.

Honours – Football League: Division 1 Champions – 1902–03, 1903–04, 1928–29, 1929–30. Division 2 Champions – 1899–1900, 1925–26, 1951–52, 1955–56, 1958–59. FA Cup winners 1896, 1907, 1935. Football League Cup winners 1990–91.

Colours: Blue and white striped shirts, blue shorts, blue stockings.

SHREWSBURY TOWN   DIV. 2

Brown, Michael A. Hockaday, David Summerfield, Kevin
Clarke, Timothy J. Lynch, Thomas M. Taylor, Robert M.
Clarke, Wayne Patterson, Gary Walton, David L.
Edwards, Paul Seabury, Kevin Williams, Mark S.
Evans, Paul S. Smith, Mark A. Withe, Christopher
Gallen, Joseph M. Spink, Dean P.

League Appearances: Blake, M.C. 15; Brough, J.R. 1(1); Brown, M.A. 40(1); Clarke, W. 27(1); Croft, B.G. 4; Donaldson, O.M. 6(3); Donowa, B.L. 4; Edwards, P. 42; Evans, P.S. 11(2); Gallen, J.M. 4(2); Griffiths, C.B. 8(1); Hockaday, D. 30(2); Lynch, T.M. 32(3); MacKenzie, S. 3; Patterson, G. 35(4); Rutherford, M.R. 7(7); Smith, M.A. 4(4); Spink, D.P. 38(2); Summerfield, K. 18(15); Taylor, R.M. 41; Walton, D.L. 27; Williams, M.S. 35(1); Withe, C. 23(3); Woods, R.G. 7(2)

League (63): Spink 18, Clarke 11 (3 pens), Brown 7, Griffiths 5, Walton 5, Lynch 4, Summerfield 3, Donaldson 2, Taylor 2, Gallen 1, Patterson 1, Williams 1, Woods 1, own goals 2.

Coca-Cola Cup (7): Summerfield 3, Brown 1, Evans 1, Griffiths 1, MacKenzie 1 (pen).

FA Cup (3): Gallen 1, Spink 1, Walton 1.

Ground: Gay Meadow, Shrewsbury SY2 6AB. Telephone Shrewsbury (0743) 360111.

Record attendance: 18,917 v Walsall, Division 3, 26 April 1961.

Manager: Fred Davies.

Secretary: M. J. Starkey.
Honours – Football League: Division 3 Champions – 1978–79, 1993–94. **Welsh Cup** winners 1891, 1938, 1977, 1979, 1984, 1985.
Colours: Amber/blue trim shirts, blue shorts, amber stockings, blue trim.

SOUTHAMPTON   FA PREMIERSHIP

Allan, Derek T.
Allen, Paul K.
Andrews, Ian E.
Banger, Nicholas L.
Barlett, Neal
Beasant, David
Benali, Francis V.
Bennett, Frank
Bound, Mathew T.
Charlton, Simon T.

Cramb, Colin
Dodd, Jason R.
Doherty, Kevin T.
Dowie, Iain
Groves, Perry
Hall, Richard A.
Heaney, Neil
Hughes, David R.
Kenna, Jeffrey J.
Le Tissier, Matthew P.

Maddison, Neil S.
Magilton, James
Maskell, Craig D.
McDonald, Paul
Monkou, Kenneth J.
Robinson, Matthew R.
Sheerin, Paul
Tisdale, Paul R.
Widdrington, Thomas

League Appearances: Adams, M.R. 17(2); Allen, P.K. 29(3); Andrews, I.E. 5; Banger, N.L. 4(10); Bartlett, N. 4(3); Beasant, D. 25; Benali, F.V. 34(3); Bennett, F. (8); Bound, M.T. 1; Charlton, S.T. 29(4); Cockerill, G. 12(2); Cramb, C. (1); Dodd, J.R. 5(5); Dowie, I. 39; Flowers, T.D. 12; Hall, R.A. 4; Heaney, N. 2; Hughes, D.R. (2); Hurlock, T.A. 2; Kenna, J.J. 40(1); Le Tissier, M.P. 38; Maddison, N.S. 41; Magilton, J. 15; Maskell, C.D. 6(4); Monkou, K.J. 35; Moody, P. 3(2); Moore, K.T. 14; Powell, L. 1; Reid, P. 7; Widdrington, T. 11; Wood, S.A. 27
League (49): Le Tissier 25 (6 pens), Maddison 7, Dowie 5, Monkou 4, Kenna 2, Allen 1, Bennett 1, Charlton 1, Maskell 1, Widdrington 1, own goal 1.
Coca-Cola Cup (1): Moore 1.
FA Cup (1): Dowie 1.
Ground: The Dell, Milton Road, Southampton SO9 4XX. Telephone Southampton (0703) 220505.
Record attendance: 31,044 v Manchester U, Division 1, 8 October 1969.
Manager: Alan Ball.
Secretary: Brian Truscott.
Honours – Football League: Division 3 (S) Champions – 1921–22. Division 3 Champions – 1959–60. **FA Cup:** Winners 1975–76.
Colours: Red and white striped shirts, black shorts, black stockings.

SOUTHEND UNITED   DIV. 1

Ansah, Andrew
Bodley, Michael J.
Bressington, Graham
Cornwell, John A.
Davidson, Craig L.
Edwards, Andrew D.
Gridelet, Philip R.
Hall, Mark A.

Howell, David C.
Hunt, Jonathan R.
Jones, Gary
Jones, Keith A.
Locke, Adam S.
Martin, Jae A.
Mooney, Thomas J.
Otto, Ricky

Payne, Derek R.
Poole, Gary J.
Powell, Christopher G. R.
Royce, Simon
Sansome, Paul E.
Southon, Jamie P.
Sussex, Andrew R.
Tilson, Stephen B.

League Appearances: Allon, J.B. 2(1); Angell, B. 17; Ansah, A. 23(4); Beadle, P.C. 8; Bodley, M.J. 16; Bressington, G. 27(1); Edwards, A.D. 41(1); Gridelet, P.R. 21(8); Harding, P. 2(3); Howell, D.C. 6; Hunt, J.R. 36(6); Jones , G. 14(8); Jones, K.A. 19(1); Lee, J.B. 18(6); Locke, A.S. 7(1); Martin, J.A. 1(3); Mooney, T.J. 9(5); Nogan, L.M. 4(1); Otto, R. 44(1); Payne, D.R. 32(3); Poole, G.J. 38; Powell, C.G. 46; Royce, S. 4(2); Sansome, P.E. 42; Scully, P.J. 8; Sussex, A.R. 18(3); Tilson, S.B. 3(7)
League (63): Otto 13, Ansah 7, Angell 6, Hunt 6, Sussex 6 (1 pen), Jones K 5, Mooney 5, Bressington 3 (3 pens), Jones G 3, Lee 3, Poole 2 (1 pen), Beadle 1, Bodley 1, Edwards 1, own goal 1.
Coca-Cola Cup (1): Angell 1.
FA Cup (0):
Ground: Roots Hall Football Ground, Victoria Avenue, Southend-on-Sea SS2 6NQ. Telephone Southend (0702) 340707.
Record attendance: 31,090 v Liverpool FA Cup 3rd rd, 10 January 1979.
Manager: Peter Taylor.
Secretary: J. W. Adams.
Honours – Football League: Division 4 Champions – 1980–81.
Colours: Blue shirts, yellow trim, blue shorts, blue trim, blue stockings.

STOCKPORT COUNTY   DIV. 2

Barras, Anthony	Frain, David	Owen, Phillip J. G.
Beaumont, Christopher P.	Francis, Kevin D. M.	Preece, Andrew P.
Cantona, Joel	Gannon, James P.	Todd, Lee
Connelly, Sean P.	Ironside, Ian	Wallace, Michael
Edwards, Neil R.	James, Martin J.	Ward, Peter
Emerson, Dean	Keeley, John H.	Williams, William R.
Flynn, Michael A.	Miller, David B.	

League Appearances: Barras, A. 3; Beaumont, C.P. 26(6); Cantona, J. (3); Connelly, S.P. 30(2); Edwards, N.R. 26; Emerson, D. 7(1); Finley, A.J. 7; Flynn, M.A. 46; Frain, D. 32(1); Francis, K.D. 45; Gannon, J.P. 31(4); Ironside, I. 10(1); James, M.J. 9(15); Keeley, J.H. 10; Miller, D.B. 36(2); Murray, B. 2(1); Preece, A.P. 43; Quinn, S.J. (1); Ryan, D.T. 26(6); Todd, L. 31(2); Wallace, M. 36(1); Ward, P. 34(1); Williams, W.R. 16
League (74): Francis 28 (2 pens), Preece 21, Ryan 6, Gannon 4, Frain 3, Wallace 3, Ward 3, Beaumont 1, Flynn 1, Williams B 1, own goals 3.
Coca-Cola Cup (2): Francis 1, Ryan 1.
FA Cup (9): Francis 3, Preece 2, Beaumont 1, Frain 1, Todd 1, Wallace 1.
Ground: Edgeley Park, Hardcastle Road, Stockport, Cheshire SK3 9DD. Telephone 0161–480 8888.
Record attendance: 27,833 v Liverpool, FA Cup 5th rd, 11 February 1950.
Manager: Danny Bergara.
Secretary: Gary Glendenning BA ACCA.
Honours – Football League: Division 3 (N) Champions – 1921–22, 1936–37. Division 4 Champions – 1966–67.
Colours: Royal and pale blue shirts with red trim, white shorts, white stockings, blue trim.

STOKE CITY
DIV. 1

Adams, Michael R.
Beeston, Carl F.
Biggins, Wayne
Butler, John E.
Carruthers, Martin G.
Clark, John B.
Clarkson, Ian S.
Cranson, Ian
Devlin, Mark A.

Gleghorn, Nigel W.
Gynn, Michael
Leslie, Steven
Macari, Paul
Mulligan, James
Orlygsson, Thorvaldur
Overson, Vincent D.
Potter, Graham S.

Prudhoe, Mark
Regis, David
Sandford, Lee R.
Shaw, Graham P.
Sinclair, Ronald M.
Straney, Paul B.
Sturridge, Simon A.
Ware, Paul D.

League Appearances: Adams, M.R. 10; Bannister, G. 10(5); Biggins, W. 10; Butler, J.E. 34(1); Carruthers, M.G. 24(10); Clark, J.B. 12; Clarkson, I.S. 14; Cowan, T. 14; Cranson, I. 44; Foley, S. 42(1); Gleghorn, N.W. 38(2); Gynn, M. 14(7); Harbey, G.K. 2; Kevan, D.J. 1; Lowe, K. 3(6); Marshall, G.B. 10; Muggleton, C.D. 6; Orlygsson, T. 42(3); Overson, V.D. 39; Potter, G.S. 2(1); Prudhoe, M. 30; Regis, D. 33(5); Sandford, L.R. 41(1); Shaw, G.P. 2(2); Stein, E.M. 12; Sturridge, S.A. 5(8); Walters, M. 9; Ware, P.D. 1; Williams, B. 2
League (57): Regis 10, Orlygsson 9 (1 pen) Stein 8 (1 pen), Carruthers 5, Biggins 4 (2 pens), Adams 3, Gleghorn 3, Bannister 2, Foley 2, Overson 2, Walters 2, Sandford 1, own goals 6.
Coca-Cola Cup (7): Stein 4, Carruthers 1, Gleghorn 1, Regis 1.
FA Cup (4): Regis 2, Cranson 1, Orlygsson 1.
Ground: Victoria Ground, Stoke-on-Trent ST4 4EG. Telephone Stoke-on-Trent (0782) 413511.
Record attendance: 51,380 v Arsenal, Division 1, 29 March 1937.
Manager: Joe Jordan.
Secretary: M. J. Potts.
Honours – Football League: Division 2 Champions – 1932–33, 1962-63, 1992-93. Division 3 (N) Champions – 1926–27. **Football League Cup:** Winners 1971-72. Autoglass Trophy winners 1992.
Colours: Red and white striped shirts, white shorts, red stockings.

SUNDERLAND
DIV. 1

Angel, Mark
Armstrong, Gordon I.
Atkinson, Brian
Ball, Kevin A.
Bennett, Gary E.
Brodie, Stephen E.
Chamberlain, Alec F. R.
Cunnington, Shaun G.
Ferguson, Derek
Goodman, Donald R.

Gray, Martin D.
Gray, Michael
Gray, Philip
Helgason, Gudni R.
Howey, Lee M.
Kay, John
Lawless, Christopher J.
Melville, Andrew R.
Musgrave, Sean

Norman, Anthony J.
Ord, Richard J.
Owers, Gary
Rodgerson, Ian
Rush, David
Russell, Craig S.
Sampson, Ian
Smith, Anthony
Smith, Martin

League Appearances: Armstrong, G.I. 22(4); Atkinson, B. 21(8); Ball, K.A.

36;Bennett, G.E. 37(1); Brodie, S.E. (4); Chamberlain, A.F. 43; Cunnington, S.G. 11; Ferguson, D. 41; Goodman, D.R. 34(1); Gray, P. 39(2); Howey, L.M. 7(7); Kay, J. X; Kubicki, D. 15; Lawrence, J.H. 2(2); Martin D Gray 16(6); Martin Gray 16(6); Melville, A.R. 44; Norman, A.J. 3; Ord, R.J. 24(4); Owers, G. 30; Power, L.M. 1(2); Rodgerson, I. 2(2); Rush, D. (5); Russell, C.S. 29(6); Sampson, I. 2(2); Smith, A. 1; Smith, M. 27(2)

League (54): Gray P 14 (3 pens), Goodman 10, Russell 9, Smith 8, Howey 3, Armstrong 2, Melville 2, Ord 2, Owers 2, Cunnington 1, Michael Gray 1.
Coca-Cola Cup (8): Goodman 4, Gray P 3, Power 1.
FA Cup (3): Ferguson 1, Howey 1, Smith 1.
Ground: Roker Park Ground, Sunderland SR6 9SW. Telephone Sunderland 091-514 0332.
Record attendance: 75,118 v Derby Co, FA Cup 6th rd replay, 8 March 1933.
Manager: Mick Buxton.
Secretary: G. Davidson FCA.
Honours – Football League: Division 1 Champions – 1891–92, 1892–93, 1894–95, 1901–02, 1912–13, 1935–36. Division 2 Champions – 1975–76. Division 3 Champions – 1987–88. **FA Cup:** Winners 1937, 1973.
Colours: Red and white striped shirts, black shorts, red stockings, white turnover.

SWANSEA CITY   DIV. 2

Ampadu, Patrick K.	Cook, Andrew C.	Jenkins, Stephen R.
Barnhouse, David J.	Cornforth, John M.	Jones, Lee
Basham, Michael	Ford, Jonathan S.	McFarlane, Andrew A.
Bowen, Jason P.	Freestone, Roger	Pascoe, Colin J.
Chappell, Shaun R.	Harris, Mark A.	Perrett, Darren J.
Clode, Mark J.	Hayes, Martin	Torpey, Stephen D. J.
Coates, Jonathan S.	Hodge, John	Walker, Keith C.

League Appearances: Ampadu, P.K. 11(2); Aspinall, W. 5; Barnhouse, D.J. 2(1); Basham, M. 5; Bowen, J.P. 39(2); Burns, C. 4; Chapple, S.R. 19(10); Clode, M.J. 26(2); Coates, J.S. (4); Cook, A.C. 23(5); Cornforth, J.M. 37(1); Ford, J.S. 21(6); Freestone, R. 46; Harris, M.A. 46; Hayes, M. 22; Hodge, J. 15(12); Jenkins, S.R. 38(2); Jones, R.J. 6(1); McFarlane, A.A. 15(13); Moore, M.T. (1); Pascoe, C.J. 31(2); Penney, D.M. 11; Perrett, D.J. 8(3); Rush, M.J. 13; Torpey, S.D. 36(4); Walker, K.C. 27
League (56): Bowen 11, Torpey 9, Cornforth 6 (1 pen), Pascoe 5, Hayes 4, Chapple 3, Harris 3, McFarlane 3, Hodge 2, Penney 2 (1 pen), Walker 2, Clode 1, Coates 1, Ford 1, Jenkins 1, Perrett 1, own goal 1.
Coca-Cola Cup (4): Bowen 2, Pascoe 1, Torpey 1.
FA Cup (2): Torpey 2.
Ground: Vetch Field, Swansea SA1 3SU. Telephone Swansea (0792) 474114.
Record attendance: 32,796 v Arsenal, FA Cup 4th rd, 17 February 1968.
Team Manager: Frank Burrows.
Secretary: George Taylor.
Honours – Football League: Division 3 (S) Champions – 1924–25, 1948–49. **Autoglass Trophy:** Winners 1994. **Welsh Cup:** Winners 9 times.
Colours: White shirts, white shorts, black stockings.

SWINDON TOWN

Berkley, Austin J.
Bodin, Paul
Digby, Fraser C.
Fenwick, Terence W.
Fjortoft, Jan A.
Gooden, Ty M.
Hammond, Nicholas D.
Hamon, Christopher
Horlock, Kevin

Kilcline, Brian
Ling, Martin
Maclaren, Ross
Middleton, Lee J.
Moncur, John F.
Murray, Edwin J.
Mutch, Andrew
Nijholt, Luc
O'Sullivan, Wayne S.

Phillips, Marcus S.
Scott, Keith
Summerbee, Nicholas J.
Taylor, Shaun
Thomson, Andrew
Viveash, Adrian L.
Whitbread, Adrian R.
White, Stephen J.

League Appearances: Bodin, P. 28(4); Digby, F.C. 28; Fenwick, T.W. 23(3); Fjortoft, J-A. 26(10); Gooden, T.M. 2(2); Hammond, N.D. 11(2); Hamon, C. (1); Hazard, M. 7(2); Heald, P.A. 1(1); Horlock, K. 32(6); Kilcline, B. 10; Ling, M. 29(4); McAvennie, F. 3(4); MacLaren, R. 10(2); Maskell, C.D. 8(6); Moncur, J.F. 41; Mutch, A. 27(3); Nijholt, L. 31(1); Sanchez, L.P. 6(2); Scott, K. 22(5); Sheffield, J. 2; Summerbee, N.J. 36(2); Taylor, S. 42; Thomson, A. 1; Whitbread, A.R. 34(1); White, S.J. 2(4)
League (47): Fjortoft 12 (2 pens), Bodin 7 (5 pens), Mutch 6, Moncur 4, Scott 4, Taylor 4, Maskell 3 (1 pen), Summerbee 3, Ling 1, Nijholt 1, Whitbread 1, own goal 1.
Coca-Cola Cup (3): Summerbee 2, Mutch 1.
FA Cup (2): Fjortoft 1, Mutch 1.
Ground: County Ground, Swindon, Wiltshire SN1 2ED. Telephone Swindon (0793) 430430.
Record attendance: 32,000 v Arsenal, FA Cup 3rd rd, 15 January 1972.
Manager: John Gorman.
Secretary: Jon Pollard.
Honours – Football League: Division 4 Champions – 1985–86. **Football League Cup:** Winners 1968–69. **Anglo-Italian Cup:** Winners 1970.
Colours: All red.

TORQUAY UNITED

Barrow, Lee A.
Bayes, Ashley J.
Buckle, Paul J.
Burton, Nicholas J.
Colcombe, Scott
Curran, Christopher
Darby, Duane A.

Foster, Adrian M.
Goodridge, Gregory R. S.
Hancox, Richard
Hardy, Paul A.
Hathaway, Ian A.
Hodges, Kevin
Kelly, Thomas J.

Moore, Darren M.
O'Riordan, Donald J.
Okorie, Chima
Sale, Mark D.
Stamps, Scott
Trollope, Paul J.

League Appearances: Barrow, L.A. 19(1); Bayes, A.J. 32; Buckle, P.J. 16; Burton, N.J. 7(1); Byng, D.G. 2(1); Colcombe, S. 27; Curran, C. 41; Darby, D.A. 21(15); Foster, A.M. 32(7); Goodridge, G.R 5(3); Hancox, R 1(2); Hardy, P.A. (1); Hathaway, I.A. 38(3); Hodges, K. 26(3); Kelly, T.J. 33(2); Laight, E.S. (1); Loram, M.J. (1); Lowe, M.I. 10; Moore, D.M. 37; Myers, C. 6; Okorie, C. 6(3);

O'Riordan,D.J. 31; O'Toole, C. 3; Sale, M.D. 20(13); Stacey, S.J. 1; Stamps, S. 6; Trollope, P.J. 42
League (64): Foster 15, Trollope 10, Darby 8, Hathaway 7, Sale 6, Buckle 2 (2 pens), Burton 2, Byng 2, Hodges 2, Kelly 2, Moore 2, O'Riordan 2, Curran 1, Goodridge 1, Okorie 1, own goal 1.
Coca-Cola Cup (2): Foster 1, Trollope 1.
FA Cup (2): Moore 1, Sale 1.
Ground: Plainmoor Ground, Torquay, Devon TQ1 3PS. Telephone Torquay (0803) 328666.
Record attendance: 21,908 v Huddersfield T, FA Cup 4th rd, 29 January 1955.
Player-Manager: Don O'Riordan.
Secretary/General Manager: D. F. Turner.
Honours – Nil
Colours: Yellow and navy hooped shirts, navy shorts, yellow stockings.

TOTTENHAM HOTSPUR   FA PREMIERSHIP

Anderton, Darren R.
Austin, Dean B.
Barmby, Nicholas J.
Beadle, Peter C.
Brady, Gary
Calderwood, Colin
Campbell, Soloman
Carr, Stephen
Caskey, Darren M.
Cundy, Jason V.
Day, Christopher N.
Dozzell, Jason A. W.

Edinburgh, Justin C.
Gray, Andrew A.
Grogan, Darren M.
Hazard, Michael
Hendry, John
Hill, Daniel, R. L.
Howells, David
Kerslake, David
Mabbutt, Gary V.
Mahorn, Paul G.
McMahon, Gerard J.
Nethercott, Stuart

Robinson, Stephen
Rosenthal, Ronny
Samways, Vincent
Scott, Kevin W.
Sedgley, Stephen P.
Sheringham, Edward P.
Simpson, Robert A.
Thorstvedt, Erik
Turner, Andrew P.
Walker, Ian M.
Watson, Kevin E.

League Appearances: Allen, P.K. (1); Anderton, D.R. 35(2); Austin, D.B. 20(3); Barmby, N.J. 27; Calderwood, C. 26; Campbell, S. 27(7); Carr, S. 1; Caskey, D.M. 16(9); Dozzell, J.A. 28(4); Durie, G.S. 10; Edinburgh, J.C. 24(1); Gray, A.A. (2); Hazard, M. 13(4); Hendry, J. (3); Hill, D.R. 1(2); Howells, D. 15(3); Kerslake, D. 16(1); Mabbutt, G.V. 29; Mahorn, P.G. 1; Moran, P. (5); Nethercott, S. 9(1); Robinson, S. 1(1); Rosenthal, R. 11(4); Samways, V. 39; Scott, K.W. 12; Sedgley, S.P. 42; Sheringham, E.P. 17(2); Thorstvedt, E. 32; Turner, A.P. (1); Walker, I.M. 10(1)
League (54): Sheringham 14 (4 pens), Dozzell 8, Anderton 6, Barmby 5 (1 pen), Sedgley 5, Caskey 4, Samways 3, Hazard 2 (1 pen), Rosenthal 2, Durie 1, Gray 1 (pen), Howells 1, Scott 1, own goal 1.
Coca-Cola Cup (6): Sheringham 2, Barmby 1, Campbell 1, Caskey 1, Howells 1.
FA Cup (2): Barmby 1, Dozzell 1.
Ground: 748 High Rd, Tottenham, London N17 0AP. Telephone 081–365 5000.
Record attendance: 75,038 v Sunderland, FA Cup 6th rd, 5 March 1938.
Manager: Ossie Ardiles
Secretary: Peter Barnes.
Honours – Football League: Division 1 Champions – 1950–51, 1960–61. Division 2 Champions – 1919–20, 1949–50. **FA Cup:** Winners 1901 (as non-League club), 1921, 1961, 1962, 1967, 1981, 1982, 1991 (8 wins stands as the record). **Football League Cup:** Winners 1970–71, 1972–73. **European Competitions: European Cup-Winners' Cup winners:** 1962–63. **UEFA Cup winners:** 1971–72, 1983–84.
Colours: White shirts, navy blue shorts, white stockings.

60

TRANMERE ROVERS

DIV. 1

Aldridge, John W.
Branch, Graham
Brannon, Gerald D.
Coyne, Daniel
Edwards, Michael
Evans, John D.
Garnett, Shaun M.
Higgins, David A.
Irons, Kenneth

Johnson, Philip
Jones, Gary S.
Jones, Martin W.
Kenworthy, Jonathan R.
Malkin, Christopher G.
McGreal, John
Morgan, Alan M.
Morrissey, John J.

Muir, Ian J.
Mungall, Steven H.
Nevin, Patrick K. F.
Nixon, Eric W.
Nolan, Iain R.
O'Brien, Liam F.
Proctor, Mark G.
Thomas, Tony

League Appearances: Aldridge, J.W. 34; Branch, G. 6(7); Brannan, G.D. 45; Coyne, D. 4(1); Garnett, S.M. 26; Higgins, D.A. 37; Hughes, M. 7(1); Irons, K. 29(5); Jones, G.S. 2(4); Kenworthy, J.R. 11(5); McGreal, J. 14(1); Malkin, C.G. 27(1); Martindale, D. 12(1); Morrissey, J.J. 22(3); Muir, I.J. 10(6); Mungall, S.H. 8(4); Nevin, P.K. 45; Nixon, E.W. 42; Nolan, I.R. 39(1); O'Brien, L.F. 17; Proctor, M.G. 18; Thomas, T. 40; Vickers, S. 11
League (69): Aldridge 21 (3 pens), Brannan 9, Muir 9, Malkin 8, Nevin 8, Irons 3, Garnett 2, Jones 2, Kenworthy 2, Thomas 2, McGreal 1, Morrissey 1, O'Brien 1.
Coca-Cola Cup (20): Aldridge 7 (1 pen), Nevin 4, Brannan 2, Irons 2 (1 pen), Hughes 1, Malkin 1, Nolan 1, Thomas 1, Vickers 1.
FA Cup (0):
Ground: Prenton Park, Prenton Road West, Birkenhead. Telephone 0151–608 3677.
Record attendance: 24,424 v Stoke C, FA Cup 4th rd, 5 February 1972.
Manager: John King.
Secretary: Norman Wilson FAAI.
Honours – Football League Division 3 (N) Champions – 1937–38. **Welsh Cup:** Winners 1935. **Leyland Daf Cup:** Winners 1990.
Colours: All white.

WALSALL

DIV. 3

Butler, Martin N.
Edwards, David J.
Evans, Duncan W.
Keister, John E. S.
Knight, Richard
Lightbourne, Kyle L.

Marsh, Christopher J.
McDonald, Rodney
McManus, Steven
Ntamark, Charles B.
O'Connor, Martin J.

Peer, Dean
Ryder, Stuart H.
Smith, Dean
Walker, James B.
Watkiss, Stuart P.

League Appearances: Butler, M.N. 9(6); Byrne, D.S. 5; Cecere, M.J. 4(2); Evans, D.W. 41; Gayle, J. 4; Gayle, M.S. 9(1); Keister, J.E. 17(5); Knight, R. 1(1); Lightbourne, K.L. 34(1); Lillis, J.W. 14(10); Livingstone, G. 2(1); McDonald, R. 34(1); Marsh, C.J. 39; Ntamark, C.B. 34(3); O'Connor, M.J. 14; O'Hara, S. 15(6); Peer, D. 33; Reece, A.J. 6; Ryder, S.H. 20(6); Saunders, C.S. 1(1); Smith, D. 35(1); Tinkler, J. 6; Walker, J.B. 31; Watkiss, S.P. 38(1); Wright, E. 16(13)
League (48): Peer 8, Lightbourne 7, Lillis 6, McDonald 6, Wright 5, Marsh 4, Butler 3, Cecere 2, O'Connor 2 (2 pens), Watkiss 2, Gayle J 1, Keister 1, Smith 1.

Coca-Cola Cup (1): McDonald 1.
FA Cup (4): Lightbourne 2, McDonald 1, Wright 1.
Ground: Bescot Stadium, Bescot Cresent, Walsall WS1 4SA. Telephone Walsall (0922) 22791.
Record attendance: 10,628 B International, England v Switzerland, 20 May 1991.
Manager: Kenny Hibbitt.
Secretary/Commercial Manager: Roy Whalley.
Honours – Football League: Division 4 Champions – 1959–60.
Colours: Red and white striped shirts, black shorts, red stockings.

WATFORD   DIV. 1

Alsford, Julian	Gibbs, Nigel J.	Page, Robert J.
Barnes, David	Hessenthaler, Andrew	Porter, Gary
Bazeley, Darren S.	Holdsworth, David G.	Ramage, Craig D.
Digweed, Perry M.	Inglethorpe, Alex M.	Sheppard, Simon
Drysdale, Jason	Johnson, Richard M.	Soloman, Jason R.
Dublin, Keith B. L.	Lavin, Gerard	Watson, Mark S.
Foster, Colin J.	Millen, Keith D.	White, John S.
Furlong, Paul A.	Nogan, Lee M.	Wilkerson, Paul S.

League Appearances: Alsford, J. 7(1); Ashby, B.J. 16(1); Bailey, D.L. 2(6); Barnes, D. 5; Bazeley, D.S. 6(4); Charlery, K. 15(1); Digweed, P.M. 26; Drysdale, J. 19; Dublin, K.B. 30(3); Dyer, B.A. 29; Foster, C.J. 6; Furlong, P.A. 38; Harding, P. 1(1); Hessenthaler, A. 42; Holdsworth, D.G. 28; Inglethorpe, A M. 1(8); Johnson, R.M. 22(5); Lavin, G. 46; McCarthy, A.J. 8(1); Millen, K.D. 10; Mooney, T.J. 10; Nogan, L.M. 21(5); Page, R.J. 4; Porter, G. 43; Ramage, C.D. 11(2); Sheppard, S. 18; Soloman, J.R. 21(4); Suckling, P.J. 2; Watson, M.S. 17; Willis, R.C. 2(2).
League (66): Furlong 18 (1 pen), Porter 9 (1 pen), Dyer 6, Hessenthaler 5, Bailey 4, Lavin 3, Nogan 3, Soloman 3, Ashby 2, Charlery 2, Inglethorpe 2, Mooney 2, Alsford 1, Bazeley 1, Dublin 1, Foster 1, own goals 3.
Coca-Cola Cup (8): Dyer 2, Furlong 1, Hessenthaler 1, Holdsworth 1, Nogan 1, Porter 1, Soloman 1.
FA Cup (1): Porter 1 (pen).
Ground: Vicarage Road Stadium, Watford WD1 8ER. Telephone Watford (0923) 230933.
Record attendance: 34,099 v Manchester U, FA Cup 4th rd (replay), 3 February 1969.
Team Manager: Glenn Roeder.
Chief Executive: Eddie Plumley FAAI.
Honours – Football League: Division 3 Division 1 1968–69 Division 4 Champions – 1977–78.
Colours: Yellow shirts, black shorts, black stockings.

WEST BROMWICH ALBION   DIV. 1

Ashcroft, Lee	Coldicott, Stacy	Donovan, Kevin
Bradley, Darren M.	Cutler, Neil A.	Dudley, Derek A.
Burgess, Daryl	Darton, Scott R.	Edwards, Paul R

Hamilton, Ian R.
Heggs, Carl S.
Herbert, Craig J.
Hunt, Andrew
Hunter, Roy I.
Lange, Anthony S.
Lilwall, Stephen

Macdonald, William
Mardon, Paul J.
McCue, James G.
McNally, Bernard A.
Mellon, Michael J.
Naylor, Stuart W.

O'Regan, Kieran
Parsley, Neil
Raven, Paul D.
Smith, David
Strodder, Gary J.
Taylor, Robert

League Appearances: Ampadu, P.K. 8(3); Ashcroft, L. 17(4); Bradley, D.M. 24; Burgess, D. 43; Coldicott, S. 4(1); Darton, S.R. 6; Donovan, K. 33(4); Edwards, P.R. 15; Fenton, G.A. 7; Fereday, W. 7(3); Garner, S. 4(4); Hamilton, I.R. 41(1); Heggs, C.S. 3(3); Hunt, A. 35; Hunter, R.I. (2); Lange, A.S. 27(2); Lilwall, S. 13; McNally, B.A. 4(4); Mardon, P.J. 22; Mellon, M.J. 18(3); Naylor, S.W. 19(1); O'Regan, K. 24(1); Parsley, N. 19(1); Raven, P.D. 34; Reid, N.S. 3(2); Smith, D. 18; Strodder, G.J. 11(10); Taylor, R. 42; Williams, P.R. 5
League (60): Taylor 18 (1 pen), Hunt 12, Donovan 8, Ashcroft 3, Fenton 3, Hamilton 3, Bradley 2, Burgess 2, Mellon 2, O'Regan 2, Strodder 2, Mardon 1, Raven 1, own goal 1.
Coca-Cola Cup (6): Donovan 3, Burgess 1, Hunt 1, Taylor 1.
FA Cup (1): Hunt 1.
Ground: The Hawthorns, West Bromwich B71 4LF. Telephone 021–525 8888 (all Depts).
Record attendance: 64,815 v Arsenal, FA Cup 6th rd, 6 March 1937.
Manager: Keith Burkinshaw.
Secretary: Dr. John J. Evans BA, PHD. (Wales).
Honours – Football League: Division 1 Champions – 1919–20. Division 2 Champions – 1901–02, 1910–11. **FA Cup:** Winners 1888, 1892, 1931, 1954, 1968. **Football League Cup:** Winners 1965–66.
Colours: Navy blue and white striped shirts, white shorts, blue and white stockings.

WEST HAM UNITED

FA PREMIERSHIP

Allen, Martin J.
Bishop, Ian W.
Boere, Jeroen W. J.
Breacker, Timothy S.
Brown, Kenneth J.
Burrows, David
Butler, Peter J. F.
Canham, Scott W.
Chapman, Lee R.
Currie, Darren

Feuer, Anthony I.
Gordon, Dale A.
Holland, Matthew R.
Holmes, Matthew J. E.
Jones, Stephen G.
Marsh, Michael A.
Martin, Alvin E.
McPherson, Malcolm
Miklosko, Ludek

Mitchell, Paul R.
Morley, Trevor W.
Peyton, Gerald J.
Potts, Steven J.
Pratt, David J.
Rowland, Keith
Rush, Matthew J.
Webster, Simon P.
Williamson, Daniel A.

League Appearances: Allen, C.D. 7; Allen, M.J. 20(6); Bishop, I.W. 36; Boere, J.W. (4); Breacker, T.S. 40; Brown, K.J. 6(3); Burrows, D. 25; Butler, P.J. 26; Chapman, L.R. 26(4); Dicks, J.A. 7; Foster, C.J. 5; Gale, A.P. 31(1); Gordon, D.A. 8; Holmes, M.J. 33(1); Jones, S.G. 3(5); Marquis, P.R. (1); Marsh, M.A. 33; Martin, A.E. 6(1); Miklosko, L. 42; Mitchell, P.R. (1); Morley, T.W. 39(3); Potts, S.J. 41; Robson, M.A. 1(2); Rowland, K. 16(7); Rush, M.J. 9(1); Williamson, D.A. 2(1)

63

League (47): Morley 13 (2 pens), Chapman 7, Allen M 6, Breacker 3, Holmes 3, Allen C 2, Jones 2, Martin 2, Bishop 1, Burrows 1, Butler 1, Gordon 1, Marsh 1, Rush 1, Williamson 1, own goals 2.
Coca-Cola Cup (8): Morley 3 (1 pen), Chapman 2, Allen M 1, Boere 1, Burrows 1.
FA Cup (7): Allen M 2, Chapman 2, Bishop 1, Jones 1, Marsh 1.
Ground: Boleyn Ground, Green Street, Upton Park, London E13 9AZ. Telephone 081 548-2748.
Record attendance: 42,322 v Tottenham H, Division 1, 17 October 1970.
Manager: Billy Bonds MBE.
Secretary: Tom Finn.
Honours – Football League: Division 2 Champions – 1957–58, 1980–81. **FA Cup: Winners** 1964, 1975, 1980. **European Competitions: European Cup-Winners' Cup winners:** 1964–65.
Colours: Claret shirts, white shorts, white stockings.

WIGAN ATHLETIC   DIV. 3

Carragher, Mathew	Lyons, Andrew	Rimmer, Neill
Daley, Phillip	McKearney, David J.	Robertson, John N.
Doolan, John	Morton, Neil	Strong, Greg
Duffy, Christopher J.	Ogden, Neil	West, Paul D.
Farnworth, Simon	Patterson, Ian D.	Wright, Mark A.
Gavin, Patrick J.	Rennie, Paul A.	

League Appearances: Carragher, M. 27(5); Connelly, D. 8(5); Daley, P. 11(7); Duffy, C.J. 15(12); Farnworth, S. 42; Furlong, C.D. 1(1); Gavin, P.J. 28(2); Gillespie, K.R. 8; Hollis, S.J. (1); Johnson, A.K. 16; Kennedy, M.F. 15(2); Kilford, I.A. 7(1); Langley, K.J. 28(5); Lyons, A. 33; McKearney, D.J. 28; Morton, N. 32(7); Ogden, N. (2); Patterson, I.D. 2(2); Rennie, P.A. 25(1); Rimmer, N. 19(1); Robertson, J.N. 34; Skipper, P.D. 41; Strong, G. 16(2); Thorne, P.L. 10(1); Vaughan, J.D. 2(2); West, P.D. 1(1); Wright, M.A. 13(1)
League (51): Lyons 11 (1 pen), Gavin 6, Gillespie 4, McKearney 4, Morton 4, Daley 3, Kilford 3, Skipper 3, Langley 2, Rennie 2, Connelly 1, Duffy 1, Furlong 1, Johnson 1, Kennedy 1, Robertson 1, Strong 1, Wright 1, own goal 1.
Coca-Cola Cup (2): Gavin 1, Morton 1.
FA Cup (6): Duffy 1, Gavin 1, McKearney 1 (pen), Morton 1, Skipper 1, own goal 1.
Ground: Springfield Park, Wigan WN6 7BA. Telephone Wigan (0942) 44433.
Record attendance: 27,500 v Hereford U, 12 December 1953.
Manager: Kenny Swain.
Secretary: Mrs Brenda Spencer.
Honours – Freight Rover Trophy: Winners 1984–85.
Colours: Black and blue striped shirts, black shorts, blue stockings.

WIMBLEDON   FA PREMIERSHIP

Anthrobus, Stephen A.	Blackwell, Dean R.	Clarke, Andrew W.
Ardley, Neal C.	Blissett, Gary P.	Dobbs, Gerald F.
Barton, Warren D.	Castledine, Stewart M.	Earle, Robert G.

Elkins, Gary	Joseph, Roger A.	Perry, Christopher J.
Fashanu, John	Kimble, Alan F.	Scales, John R.
Fear, Peter	McAllister, Brian	Segers, Hans
Fitzgerald, Scott B.	McCarthy, Jamie	Skinner, Justin J.
Gayle, Marcus A.	McGee, Paul	Sullivan, Neil
Holdsworth, Dean C.	Miller, Paul A.	Talboys, Steven
Jones, Vincent P.	Payne, Grant	Thomas, Mark L.

League Appearances: Ardley, N.C. 14(2); Barton, W.D. 37(2); Berry, G.J. 4; Blackwell, D.R. 16(2); Blissett, G.P. 6(12); Castledine, S.M. 3; Clarke, A.W. 9(14); Dobbs, G.F. 3(7); Earle, R.G. 42; Elkins, G. 18; Fashanu, J. 35(1); Fear, P. 23; Fitzgerald, S.B. 27(1); Gayle, M.A. 10; Holdsworth, D.C. 42; Jones, V.P. 33; Joseph, R.A. 13; Kimble, A.F. 14; McAllister, B. 13; Perry, C.J. (2); Sanchez, L.P. 15; Scales, J.R. 37; Segers, H. 41; Sullivan, N. 1(1); Talboys, S. 6(1)
League (56): Holdsworth 17 (1 pen), Fashanu 11, Earle 9, Blissett 3, Barton 2, Clarke 2, Jones 2, Sanchez 2, Ardley 1, Berry 1, Castledine 1, Elkins 1, Fear 1, own goals 3.
Coca-Cola Cup (11): Holdsworth 4, Earle 3, Ardley 1, Barton 1, Clarke 1, Jones 1.
FA Cup (5): Holdsworth 3, Fashanu 1, Scales 1.
Ground: Selhurst Park, South Norwood, London SE25 6PY. Telephone 081 771–2233.
Record attendance: 30,115 v Manchester U, FA Premier League, 9 May 1993.
Manager: Joe Kinnear.
Secretary: Steve Rooke.
Honours – Football League: Division 4 Champions – 1982–83. **FA Cup:** Winners 1987–88.
Colours: All navy blue with gold trim.

WOLVERHAMPTON WANDERERS DIV. 1

Bennett, Thomas M.	Kelly, David T.	Simkin, Darren S.
Birch, Paul	Kelly, James	Smith, James J. A.
Blades, Paul A.	Marsden, Christopher	Smith, Jason J.
Bull, Stephen G.	Masters, Neil B.	Stowell, Michael
Cook, Paul A.	Mills, Rowan L.	Thomas, Geoffrey R.
De Bont, Andrew C.	Piearce, Stephen	Thompson, Andrew R.
Denison, Robert	Rankine, Simon M.	Venus, Mark
Ferguson, Darren	Shaw, Darren R.	Voice, Scott H.
Jones, Paul S.	Shirtliff, Peter A.	
Keen, Kevin I.		

League Appearances: Bennett, T.M. 8(2); Birch, P. 25(7); Blades, P.A. 35; Bull, S.G. 27; Burke, M.S. 10(2); Cook, P.A. 34(2); Dennison, R. 10(4); Edwards, P.R. 10(1); Ferguson, D. 12(2); Keen, K.I. 36(5); Kelly, D.T. 35(1); Kelly, J. 4; Marsden, C. 8; Masters, N.B. 4; Mills, R.L. 6(8); Mountfield, D.N. 17(2); Rankine, S.M. 28(3); Regis, C. 8(11); Shirtliff, P.A. 39; Simkin, D.S. 7(1); Small, M.A. 2(1); Stowell, M. 46; Thomas, G.R. 8; Thompson, A.R. 36(1); Venus, M. 38(1); Whittingham, G. 13

League (60): Bull 14, Kelly D 11, Whittingham 8, Keen 7, Thomas 4, Thompson 3 (2 pens), Cook 2 (2 pens), Dennison 2, Regis 2, Birch 1, Blades 1, Burke 1, Mills 1, Mountfield 1, Small 1, Venus 1.
Coca-Cola Cup (2): Burke 1, Mountfield 1.
FA Cup (6): Kelly D 2, Blades 1, Keen 1, Mills 1, Thompson 1.
Ground: Molineux Grounds, Wolverhampton WV1 4QR. Telephone (0902) 712181.
Record attendance: 61,315 v Liverpool, FA Cup 5th rd, 11 February 1939.
Team Manager: Graham Taylor.
Secretary: Keith Pearson ACIS.
Honours – Football League: Division 1 Champions – 1953–54, 1957–58, 1958–59. Division 2 Champions – 1931–32, 1976–77. Division 3 (N) Champions – 1923–24. Division 3 Champions – 1988–89. Division 4 Champions – 1987–88. **FA Cup:** Winners 1893, 1908, 1949, 1960. **Football League Cup:** Winners 1973–74, 1979–80. **Sherpa Van Trophy winners** 1988.
Colours: Gold shirts, black shorts, gold stockings.

WREXHAM   DIV. 2

Bennett, Gary M.	Hunter, Barry V.	Phillips, Wayne
Brammer, David	Jones, Barry	Pugh, Stephen
Connolly, Karl	Lake, Michael C.	Roden, Damian J.
Cross, Jonathan N.	Marriott, Andrew	Taylor, Peter M. R.
Durkan, Kieron J.	Owen, Gareth	Watkin, Stephen
Hardy, Philip	Pejic, Melvyn	Williams, Scott J.
Humes, Anthony		

League Appearances: Bennett, G.M. 41; Brace, D.P. 1; Brammer, D. 16(6); Connolly, K. 38(1); Cross, J.N. 20(5); Durkan, K.J. 9(1); Hardy, P. 25; Hughes, B. 3(8); Humes, A. 25(2); Hunter, B.V. 23; Jones, B. 33; Jones, K.R. 5; Kelly, J. 9; Lake, M.C. 29(1); Marriott, A. 36; Morris, M. 4; Owen, G. 24(3); Paskin, W.J. 4(11); Pejic, M. 40; Phillips, W. 20(1); Pugh, S. 2(5); Sertori, M.A. 15; Taylor, P.M. 28(2); Walton, M.A. 6; Watkin, S. 39(1); Williams, S.J. 11(3).
League (66): Bennett 32 (8 pens), Watkin 9 (1 pen), Taylor 7, Owen 3, Brammer 2, Connolly 2, Cross 2, Jones B 2, Durkan 1, Humes 1, Hunter 1, Lake 1, Phillips 1, Sertori 1, own goal 1.
Coca-Cola Cup (8): Bennett 3 (2 pens), Paskin 2, Connolly 1, Pejic 1, own goal 1.
FA Cup (1): Watkin 1.
Ground: Racecourse Ground, Mold Road, Wrexham. Telephone Wrexham (0978) 262129.
Record attendance: 34,445 v Manchester U, FA Cup 4th rd, 26 January 1957.
Manager: Brian Flynn.
Secretary: D. L. Rhodes.
Honours – Football League: Division 3 Champions – 1977–78. **Welsh Cup:** Winners 22 times.
Colours: Red shirts, white shorts, red stockings.

Brown, Stephen
Carroll, David F.
Cousins, Jason M.
Creaser, Glyn R.
Crossley, Matthew J. W.
Evans, Terence W.

Garner, Simon
Guppy, Stephen A.
Hemmings, Anthony G.
Horton, Duncan
Hutchinson, Simon
Hyde, Paul D.

Langford, Timothy
Ryan, Keith J.
Stapleton, Simon J.
Titterton, David S. J.
Turnbull, Lee M.

League Appearances: Blatherwick, S.S. 2; Brown, S. 8(1); Carroll, D.F. 41; Cooper, M.N. (2); Cousins, J.M. 37; Creaser, G.R. 15; Crossley, M.J. 39; Cunningham, A.E. 4(1); Cusack, N.J. 2(2); Evans, T.W. 20(2); Garner, S. 10(2); Guppy, S.A. 41; Hayrettin, H. 15(4); Hemmings, A.G. 18(8); Hodges, L.L. 2(2); Horton, D. 15; Hutchinson, S. 2(6); Hyde, P.D. 42; Kerr, A.A. 12(2); Langford, T. 18(11); Potter, G.S. 2(1); Reid, N.S. 3(2); Rogers, D.J. (1); Ryan, K.J. 42; Scott, K. 15; Stapleton, S.J. 21(1); Thompson, S. 16(11); Titterton, D.S. 14(4); Turnbull, L.M. 6

League (67): Scott 10 (3 pens), Guppy 8, Langford 8, Hemmings 7, Carroll 6, Evans 6, Garner 4, Kerr 3, Creaser 2, Crossley 2, Brown 1, Cooper 1, Cousins 1, Cusack 1, Hayrettin 1, Ryan 1, Stapleton 1, Thompson 1, Titterton 1, own goals 2.

Coca-Cola Cup (7): Scott 2, Cousins 1, Evans 1, Langford 1, Ryan 1, Thompson 1.

FA Cup (3): Carroll 1, Hemmings 1, Langford 1.

Ground: Adams Park, Hillbottom Road, Sands, High Wycombe HP12 4HJ. Telephone 0494 472100.

Manager: Martin O'Neill MBE.

Secretary: John Goldsworthy.

Honours – GM Vauxhall Conference winners: 1993. **FA Trophy winners:** 1991, 1993.

Colours: Light & dark blue quartered shirts, navy blue shorts, sky blue stockings.

Atkin, Paul A.	Hall, Wayne	Pepper, Colin N.
Barnes, Paul L.	Jordan, Scott D.	Stancliffe, Paul I.
Barrett, Anthony	Kiely, Dean L.	Swann, Gary
Blackstone, Ian K.	McCarthy, Jonathan D.	Tutill, Stephen A.
Bushell, Stephen	McMillan, Lyndon A.	Warburton, Raymond
Canham, Anthony	Murty, Graeme S.	
Cooper, Stephen B.	Naylor, Glenn	

League Appearances: Atkin, P.A. 13(1); Barnes, P.L. 42; Barratt, A. 5(14); Blackstone, I.K. 24(8); Bushell, S. 30(1); Canham, A. 36; Cooper, S.B. 28(1); Hall, W. 45; Kiely, D.L. 46; McCarthy, J.D. 44; McMillan, L.A. 46; Murty, G.S. 1; Naylor, G. 5(5); Pepper, C.N. 18(5); Stancliffe, P.I. 28; Swann, G. 44; Tutill, S.A. 46; Warburton, R. 5(1)
League (64): Barnes 24 (3 pens), Blackstone 7, McCarthy 7, Cooper 5, Bushell 4, Swann 4, Tutill 4, Canham 3, Barratt 2, Naylor 1, Stancliffe 1, own goals 2.
Coca-Cola Cup (0):
FA Cup (2): Canham 1, McCarthy 1.
Ground: Bootham Crescent, York YO3 7AQ. Telephone York 0904 624447.
Record attendance: 28,123 v Huddersfield T, FA Cup 6th rd, 5 March 1938.
Manager: Alan Little.
Secretary: Keith Usher.
Honours – Football League: Division 4 Champions – 1983–84.
Colours: Red shirts, blue shorts, red stockings.

LEAGUE REVIEW

Manchester United duly retained their FA Premier League title, though under its new heading of FA Carling Premiership. Only when the first League table was compiled did they not appear in first place. United were simply the best team in the top echelon when on their best form.

Oddly enough, Chelsea managed to beat them twice 1-0, though these were just two defeats out of four sustained in the competition. United's nearest challengers Blackburn Rovers came close to achieving the double over them, however, leading 1-0 at Old Trafford on Boxing Day until Paul Ince's equaliser in the 88th minute and winning the second match 2-0 at Ewood Park on 2 April.

But Rovers, who took their free-spending to a massive £27 million in the recent summer when they paid a record fee of £5 million for Norwich City's Chris Sutton, relied heavily on the goalscoring of Alan Shearer. He contributed 31 of Blackburn's 63 League goals.

In contrast, Manchester United had three players with double figure goal tallies: Eric Cantona (18), Ryan Giggs (13) and Mark Hughes (11). But United were deprived of a unique treble of honours when Aston Villa beat them in the Coca Cup Final and in the FA Cup there was a measure of consolation for them when they defeated Chelsea 4-0 at Wembley.

It was also a satisfactory season in Europe for Arsenal, who notched their 100th goal in the major continental competitions in winning the Cup-Winners Cup at the expense of Italy's Parma.

Domestically, attendances again showed up well despite the problems caused by the lingering recession. Crowds in the Premiership reached the highest in the top division since 1981–82 with an aggregate of ten and a quarter million. With Endsleigh Insurance League figures from the Football League itself, the overall increase was more than one million.

There was less convincing information concerning goalscoring. For the four national divisions the average number of goals per game was short by just 0.02 on 1992–93 and registered 2.67 from the 5418 goals scored. The record number of goals was set up in 1960–61 when the average number of goals per game was 3.44.

Teams in the Premiership wore squad numbers as did some in the Football League, but there was criticism about the system. Arsenal even reverted to normal numbering but found it too expensive having to produce a variety of shirt name combinations.

There was a warning note from the number of sendings-off during the first-class matches when the total touched a new high of 288, even before the play-offs.

HOME TEAM	Arsenal	Aston Villa	Blackburn R	Chelsea	Coventry C	Everton	Ipswich T	Leeds U	Liverpool
Arsenal	—	1-2	1-0	1-0	0-3	2-0	4-0	2-1	1-0
Aston Villa	1-2	—	0-1	1-0	0-0	0-0	0-1	1-0	2-1
Blackburn R	1-1	1-0	—	2-0	2-1	2-0	0-0	2-1	2-0
Chelsea	0-2	1-1	1-2	—	1-2	4-2	1-1	1-1	1-0
Coventry C	1-0	0-1	2-1	1-1	—	2-1	1-0	0-2	1-0
Everton	1-1	0-1	0-3	4-2	0-0	—	0-0	1-1	2-0
Ipswich T	1-5	1-2	1-0	1-0	0-2	0-2	—	0-0	1-2
Leeds U	2-1	2-0	3-3	4-1	1-0	3-0	0-0	—	2-0
Liverpool	0-0	2-1	0-1	2-1	1-0	2-1	1-0	2-0	—
Manchester C	0-0	3-0	0-2	2-2	1-1	1-0	2-1	1-1	1-1
Manchester U	1-0	3-1	1-1	0-1	0-0	1-0	0-0	0-0	1-0
Newcastle U	2-0	5-1	1-1	0-0	4-0	1-0	2-0	1-1	3-0
Norwich C	1-1	1-2	2-2	1-1	1-0	3-0	1-0	2-1	2-2
Oldham Ath	0-0	1-1	1-2	2-1	3-3	0-1	0-3	1-1	0-3
QPR	1-1	2-2	1-0	1-1	5-1	2-1	3-0	0-4	1-3
Sheffield U	1-1	1-2	1-2	1-0	0-0	0-0	1-1	2-2	0-0
Sheffield W	0-1	0-0	1-2	3-1	0-0	5-1	5-0	3-3	3-1
Southampton	0-4	4-1	3-1	3-1	1-0	0-2	0-1	0-2	4-2
Swindon T	0-4	1-2	1-3	1-3	3-1	1-1	2-2	0-5	0-5
Tottenham H	0-1	1-1	0-2	1-1	1-2	3-2	1-1	1 1	3-3
West Ham U	0-0	0-0	1-2	1-0	3-2	0-1	2-1	0-1	1-2
Wimbledon	0-3	2-2	4-1	1-1	1-2	1 1	0-2	1-0	1 1

1993–94 RESULTS

Manchester C	Manchester U	Newcastle U	Norwich C	Oldham Ath	QPR	Sheffield U	Sheffield W	Southampton	Swindon T	Tottenham H	West Ham U	Wimbledon
0-0	2-2	2-1	0-0	1-1	0-0	3-0	1-0	1-0	1-1	1-1	0-2	1-1
0-0	1-2	0-2	0-0	1-2	4-1	1-0	2-2	0-2	5-0	1-0	3-1	0-1
2-0	2-0	1-0	2-3	1-0	1-1	0-0	1-1	2-0	3-1	1-0	0-2	3-0
0-0	1-0	1-0	1-2	0-1	2-0	3-2	1-1	2-0	2-0	4-3	2-0	2-0
4-0	0-1	2-1	2-1	1-1	0-0	1-1	1-1	1-1	1-1	1-0	1-1	1-2
1-0	0-1	0-2	1-5	2-1	0-3	4-2	0-2	1-0	6-2	0-1	0-1	3-2
2-2	1-2	1-1	2-1	0-0	1-3	3-2	1-4	1-0	1-1	2-2	1-1	0-0
3-2	0-2	1-1	0-4	1-0	1-1	2-1	2-2	0-0	3-0	2-0	1-0	4-0
2-1	3-3	0-2	0-1	2-1	3-2	1-2	2-0	4-2	2-2	1-2	2-0	1-1
	2-3	2-1	1-1	1-1	3-0	0-0	1-3	1-1	2-1	0-2	0-0	0-1
2-0		1-1	2-2	3-2	2-1	3-0	5-0	2-0	4-2	2-1	3-0	3-1
2-0	1-1		3-0	3-2	1-2	4-0	4-2	1-2	7-1	0-1	2-0	4-0
1-1	0-2	1-2		1-1	3-4	0-1	1-1	4-5	0-0	1-2	0-0	0-1
0-0	2-5	1-3	2-1		4-1	1-1	0-0	2-1	2-1	0-2	1-2	1-1
1-1	2-3	1-2	2-2	2-0		2-1	1-2	2-1	1-3	1-1	0-0	1-0
0-1	0-3	2-0	1-2	2-1	1-1		1-1	0-0	3-1	2-2	3-2	2-1
1-1	2-3	0-1	3-3	3-0	3-1	3-1		2-0	3-3	1-0	5-0	2-2
0-1	1-3	2-1	0-1	1-3	0-1	3-3	1-1		5-1	1-0	0-2	1-0
1-3	2-2	2-2	3-3	0-1	1-0	0-0	0-1	2-1		2-1	1-1	2-4
1-0	0-1	1-2	1-3	5-0	1-2	2-2	1-3	3-0	1-1		1-4	1-1
3-1	2-2	2-4	3-3	2-0	0-4	0-0	2-0	3-3	0-0	1-3		0-2
1-0	1-0	4-2	3-1	3-0	1-1	2-0	2-1	1-0	3-0	2-1	1-2	

ENDSLEIGH INSURANCE LEAGUE

HOME TEAM	Barnsley	Birmingham C	Bolton W	Bristol C	Charlton Ath	Crystal Palace	Derby Co	Grimsby T	Leicester C
Barnsley		2-3	1-1	1-1	0-1	1-3	0-1	1-2	0-1
Birmingham C	0-2	–	2-1	2-2	1-0	2-4	3-0	1-1	0-3
Bolton W	2-3	1-1	–	2-2	3-2	1-0	0-2	1-1	1-2
Bristol C	0-2	3-0	2-0	–	0-0	2-0	0-0	1-0	1-3
Charlton Ath	2-1	1-0	3-0	3-1	—	0-0	1-2	0-1	2-1
Crystal Palace	1-0	2-1	1-1	4-1	2-0	—	1-1	1-0	2-1
Derby Co	2-0	1-1	2-0	1-0	0-2	3-1	–	2-1	3-2
Grimsby T	2-2	1-0	0-0	1-0	0-1	1-1	1-1	–	0-0
Leicester C	0-1	1-1	1-1	3-0	2-1	1-1	3-3	1-1	
Luton T	5-0	1-1	0-2	0-2	1-0	0-1	2-1	2-1	0-2
Middlesbrough	5-0	2-2	0-1	0-1	2-0	2-3	3-0	1-0	2-0
Millwall	2-0	2-1	1-0	0-0	2-1	3-0	0-0	1-0	0-0
Nottingham F	2-1	1-0	3-2	0-0	1-1	1-1	1-1	5-3	4-0
Notts Co	3-1	2-1	2-1	2-0	3-3	3-2	4-1	2-1	4-1
Oxford U	1-1	2-0	0-2	4-2	0-4	1-3	2-0	2-2	2-2
Peterborough U	4-1	1-0	2-3	0-2	0-1	1-1	2-2	1-2	1-1
Portsmouth	2-1	0-2	0-0	0-0	1-2	0-1	3-2	3-1	0-1
Southend U	0-3	3-1	2-0	0-1	4-2	1-2	4-3	1-2	0-0
Stoke C	5-4	2-1	2-0	3-0	1-0	0-2	2-1	1-0	1-0
Sunderland	1-0	1-0	2-0	0-0	4-0	1-0	1-0	2-2	2-3
Tranmere R	0-3	1-2	2-1	2-2	2-0	0-1	4-0	1-2	1-0
Watford	0-2	5-2	4-3	1-1	2-2	1-3	3-4	0-3	1-1
WBA	1-1	2-4	2-2	0-1	2-0	1-4	1-2	1-0	1-2
Wolverhampton W	1-1	3-0	1-0	3-1	1-1	2-0	2-2	0-0	1-1

– DIVISION 1 1993–94 RESULTS

Luton T	Middlesbrough	Millwall	Nottingham F	Notts Co	Oxford U	Peterborough U	Portsmouth	Southend U	Stoke C	Sunderland	Tranmere R	Watford	WBA	Wolverhampton W
1-0	1-4	0-1	1-0	0-3	1-0	1-0	2-0	1-3	3-0	4-0	1-0	0-1	1-1	2-0
1-1	1-0	1-0	0-3	2-3	1-1	0-0	0-1	3-1	3-1	0-0	0-3	1-0	2-0	2-2
2-1	4-1	4-0	4-3	4-2	1-0	1-1	1-1	0-2	1-1	0-0	2-1	3-1	1-1	1-3
1-0	0-0	2-2	1-4	0-2	0-1	4-1	1-0	2-1	0-0	2-0	2-0	1-1	0-0	2-1
1-0	2-5	0-0	0-1	5-1	1-0	5-1	0-1	4-3	2-0	0-0	3-1	2-1	2-1	0-1
3-2	0-1	1-0	2-0	1-2	2-1	3-2	5-1	1-0	4-1	1-0	0-0	0-2	1-0	1-1
2-1	0-1	0-0	0-2	1-1	2-1	2-0	1-0	1-3	4-2	5-0	4-0	1-2	5-3	0-4
2-0	1-1	0-0	0-0	2-2	1-0	2-1	1-1	4-0	0-0	0-1	0-0	2-2	2-2	2-0
2-1	2-0	4-0	1-0	3-2	2-3	2-1	0-3	3-0	1-1	2-1	1-1	4-4	4-2	2-2
—	1-1	1-1	1-2	1-0	3-0	2-0	4-1	1-1	6-2	2-1	0-1	2-1	3-2	0-2
0-0	—	4-2	2-2	3-0	2-1	1-1	0-2	1-0	1-2	4-1	0-0	1-1	3-0	1-0
2-2	1-1	—	2-2	2-0	2-2	0-0	1-4	2-0	2-1	3-1	4-1	2-1	1-0	1-0
2-0	1-1	1-3	—	1-0	0-0	2-0	1-1	2-0	2-3	2-2	2-1	2-1	1-0	1-0
1-2	2-3	1-3	2-1	—	2-1	2-1	1-1	2-1	2-0	1-0	0-0	1-0	1-0	0-2
0-1	1-1	0-2	1-0	2-1	—	1-2	3-2	2-1	1-0	0-3	1-0	2-3	1-1	4-0
0-0	1-0	0-0	2-3	1-1	3-1	—	2-2	3-1	1-1	1-3	0-0	3-4	2-0	0-1
1-0	2-0	2-2	2-1	0-0	1-1	0-2	—	2-1	3-3	0-1	2-0	2-0	0-1	3-0
2-1	1-0	1-1	1-1	3-0	6-1	3-0	2-1	—	0-0	0-1	1-2	2-0	0-3	1-1
2-2	3-1	1-2	0-1	0-1	1-3	0-0	0-1	2-1	—	1-0	1-2	2-0	1-0	1-1
2-0	2-1	2-1	2-3	2-0	2-3	0-0	1-2	0-2	0-1	—	3-2	2-0	1-0	0-2
4-1	4-0	3-2	1-2	3-1	2-0	2-1	3-1	1-1	2-0	4-1	—	2-1	3-0	1-1
2-2	2-0	2-0	1-2	3-1	2-1	2-1	1-0	3-0	1-3	1-1	1-2	—	0-1	1-0
1-1	1-1	0-0	0-2	3-0	3-1	3-0	4-1	2-2	0-0	2-1	1-3	4-1	—	3-2
1-0	2-3	2-0	1-1	3-0	2-1	1-1	1-1	0-1	1-1	1-1	2-1	2-0	1-2	—

ENDSLEIGH INSURANCE LEAGUE

HOME TEAM	Barnet	Blackpool	Bournemouth	Bradford C	Brentford	Brighton & HA	Bristol R	Burnley	Cambridge U
Barnet		0-1	1 2	1 2	0-0	1 1	1 2	1 1	2 3
Blackpool	3-1		2 1	1 3	1 1	2-0	0-1	1 2	2 3
Bournemouth	1-1	1-0		1 1	0-3	2-1	3-0	1-0	1 2
Bradford C	2 1	2 1	0-0		1-0	2-0	0-1	0-1	2-0
Brentford	1-0	3-0	1 1	2-0		1 1	3-4	0-0	3 3
Brighton & HA	1-0	3-2	3-3	0-1	2 1		0-2	1-1	4 1
Bristol R	5-2	0-0	0-1	4-3	1-4	1-0		3 1	2-1
Burnley	5-0	3-1	4-0	0-1	4-1	3-0	3-1	–	3-0
Cambridge U	1 1	3-2	3-2	2 1	1 1	2 1	1 3	0-1	–
Cardiff C	0-0	0-2	2 1	1 1	1 1	2 2	1 2	2 1	2 7
Exeter C	0-0	1-0	0-2	0-0	2 2	1 1	1-0	4-1	0-5
Fulham	3-0	1-0	0-2	1 1	0-0	0-1	0-1	3-2	0-2
Hartlepool U	2 1	2-0	1 1	1 2	0-1	2 2	2 1	4 1	0-2
Huddersfield T	1 2	2 1	1 1	1 1	1 1	1 3	1 3	1-0	1 1
Hull C	4-4	0-0	1 1	3-1	1-0	0-0	3-0	1 2	2-0
Leyton Orient	4-2	2-0	0-0	2 1	1 1	1 3	1-0	3-1	2 1
Plymouth Arg	1-0	2 1	2-0	3-1	1 1	1 1	3-3	3-2	0-3
Port Vale	6-0	2-0	2 1	0-0	1-0	4-0	2-0	1 1	2 2
Reading	4-1	1 1	3-0	1 1	2 1	2-0	2-0	2 1	3-1
Rotherham U	1 1	0-2	1 2	1 2	2-0	0-1	1 1	3-2	3-0
Stockport Co	2 1	1-0	0-2	4-1	3-1	3-0	0-2	2 1	3-1
Swansea C	2-0	4-4	1 1	2-0	1 1	3-0	2-0	3-1	4 2
Wrexham	4-0	2 3	2 1	0-3	1 2	1 3	3-2	1-0	1 1
York C	1 1	2 1	2-0	1 1	0-2	3-1	0-1	0-0	2-0

– DIVISION 2 1993–94 RESULTS

Cardiff C	Exeter C	Fulham	Hartlepool U	Huddersfield T	Hull C	Leyton Orient	Plymouth Arg	Port Vale	Reading	Rotherham U	Stockport Co	Swansea C	Wrexham	York C
0-0	2-1	0-2	3-2	0-1	1-2	3-1	0-0	2-3	0-1	2-1	0-0	0-1	1-2	1-3
1-0	1-0	2-3	2-1	2-1	6-2	4-1	2-1	1-3	0-4	1-2	2-0	1-1	4-1	0-5
3-2	1-1	1-3	0-0	1-2	0-2	1-1	0-1	2-1	2-1	0-0	1-1	0-1	1-2	3-1
2-0	6-0	0-0	2-1	3-0	1-1	0-0	1-5	2-1	2-4	2-1	1-2	2-1	1-0	0-0
1-1	2-1	1-2	1-0	1-2	0-3	0-1	1-1	1-2	1-0	2-2	1-1	1-1	2-1	1-1
3-5	0-0	2-0	1-1	2-2	3-0	2-0	2-1	1-3	0-1	0-2	1-1	4-1	1-1	2-0
2-1	1-1	2-1	1-1	0-0	1-1	1-1	0-0	2-0	1-1	0-1	1-1	1-2	3-1	0-1
2-0	3-2	3-1	2-0	1-1	3-1	4-1	4-2	2-1	0-1	0-0	1-1	1-1	2-1	2-1
1-1	3-0	3-0	1-0	4-5	3-4	3-1	2-0	1-0	0-1	0-1	0-0	2-0	2-2	0-2
—	2-0	1-0	2-2	2-2	3-4	2-0	2-3	1-3	3-0	1-0	3-1	1-0	5-1	0-0
2-2	—	6-4	2-1	2-3	0-1	1-0	2-3	1-1	4-6	1-1	1-2	1-0	5-0	1-2
1-3	0-2	—	2-0	1-1	0-1	2-3	1-1	0-0	1-0	1-0	0-1	3-1	0-0	0-1
3-0	1-2	0-1	—	1-4	0-1	1-1	1-8	1-4	1-4	2-0	1-0	1-0	1-2	0-2
2-0	0-1	1-0	1-1	—	0-2	1-0	1-0	1-1	0-3	2-1	1-1	1-1	3-0	3-2
1-0	5-1	1-1	1-0	2-1	—	0-1	2-2	0-0	1-2	4-1	0-1	0-1	0-0	1-1
2-2	1-1	2-2	1-2	1-0	3-1	—	2-1	2-3	1-1	1-1	0-0	2-1	2-2	2-0
1-2	1-0	3-1	2-0	2-0	2-1	3-1	—	2-0	3-1	4-2	2-3	2-1	1-1	2-1
2-2	3-0	2-2	1-0	1-1	2-1	2-1	2-1	—	0-4	2-1	1-1	3-0	3-0	2-1
1-1	1-0	1-0	4-0	0-0	1-1	2-1	3-2	1-2	—	0-0	2-0	2-1	0-1	2-1
5-2	1-2	7-0	2-3	1-0	0-3	0-2	2-2			—	1-2	1-1	2-1	2-1
2-2	4-0	2-4	5-0	3-0	0-0	3-0	2-3	2-1	1-1	2-0	—	4-0	1-0	1-3
1-0	2-0	2-1	1-1	1-0	1-0	1-1	0-1	0-1	1-1	0-0	1-2	—	3-1	1-2
3-1	1-1	2-0	2-0	3-1	3-0	4-2	0-3	2-1	3-2	3-3	0-1	3-2	—	1-1
5-0	3-0	2-0	3-0	0-2	0-0	3-0	0-0	1-0	1-0	0-0	1-2	2-1	1-1	—

ENDSLEIGH INSURANCE LEAGUE

HOME TEAM	Bury	Carlisle U	Chester C	Chesterfield	Colchester U	Crewe Alex	Darlington	Doncaster R
Bury	—	2-1	1-1	2-1	0-1	1-0	5-1	4-0
Carlisle U	1-2	—	1-0	3-0	2-0	1-2	2-0	4-2
Chester C	3-0	0-0	—	3-1	2-1	1-2	0-0	0-1
Chesterfield	1-1	3-0	1-2	—	0-0	2-0	1-1	1-1
Colchester U	4-1	2-1	0-0	0-2	—	2-4	1-2	3-1
Crewe Alex	2-4	2-3	2-1	0-1	2-1	—	2-1	2-0
Darlington	1-0	1-3	1-2	0-0	7-3	1-0	—	1-3
Doncaster R	1-3	0-0	3-4	0-0	2-1	0-0	1-3	—
Gillingham	1-0	2-0	2-2	0-2	3-0	1-3	2-1	0-0
Hereford U	3-0	0-0	0-5	0-3	5-0	1 2	1-1	2-1
Lincoln C	2-2	0-0	0-3	1-2	2-0	1 2	1 1	2-1
Mansfield T	2-2	0-1	0-4	1-2	1-1	1 2	0-3	2-1
Northampton T	0-1	1-1	1-0	2-2	1 1	2-2	1-0	0-0
Preston NE	3-1	0-3	1-1	4-1	1-0	0-2	3-2	3-1
Rochdale	2-1	0-1	2-0	5-1	1-1	2-1	0-0	1-1
Scarborough	1-0	0-3	0-1	1-1	0-2	1-2	3-0	2-0
Scunthorpe U	1-1	2-1	1-1	2-2	1 1	2-1	3-0	1-3
Shrewsbury T	1-0	1-0	3-0	0-0	2-1	2-2	1-1	0-1
Torquay U	0-0	1-1	1-3	1-0	3-3	3-3	2-1	2-1
Walsall	0-1	0-1	1-1	0-1	1-2	2-2	3-0	1-2
Wigan Ath	3-1	0-2	6-3	1-0	0-1	2-2	2-0	0-0
Wycombe W	2-1	2-0	1-0	0-1	2-5	3-1	2-0	1-0

	Gillingham	Hereford U	Lincoln C	Mansfield T	Northampton T	Preston NE	Rochdale	Scarborough	Scunthorpe U	Shrewsbury T	Torquay U	Walsall	Wigan Ath	Wycombe W
	0-0	5-3	1-0	2-2	0-0	1-1	0-1	0-2	1-0	2-3	1-1	1-2	3-0	1-2
	1-2	1-2	3-3	1-1	0-1	0-1	0-1	2-0	3-1	2-1	1-1	2-1	3-0	2-2
	1-0	3-1	1-1	1-1	1-0	3-2	3-1	4-1	0-2	1-0	1-1	2-1	2-1	3-1
	3-2	3-1	2-2	0-2	4-0	1-1	1-1	1-0	1-1	1-2	3-1	0-1	1-0	2-3
	1-2	1-0	1-0	0-0	3-2	1-1	2-5	1-2	2-1	3-3	1-2	0-1	3-1	0-2
	1-0	6-0	2-2	2-1	3-1	4-3	2-1	1-1	3-3	0-0	2-3	1-2	4-1	2-1
	2-1	1-3	3-2	2-0	0-1	0-2	1-1	0-2	2-1	0-2	1-2	0-0	0-0	0-0
	0-0	1-0	1-0	0-1	2-1	1-1	2-1	0-4	3-1	0-0	0-2	4-0	3-1	0-3
	–	2-0	1-1	1-0	1-0	2-2	1-2	2-2	1-0	0-2	2-2	1-1	2-2	0-1
	2-0	–	1-2	2-3	1-1	2-3	5-1	0-1	1-2	0-1	2-2	0-1	3-0	3-4
	3-1	3-1	–	1-2	4-3	0-2	1-1	0-1	2-0	0-1	1-0	1-2	0-1	1-3
	2-1	2-1	1-0	–	1-0	2-2	0-1	4-2	0-1	1-0	2-1	1-2	2-3	3-0
	1-2	0-1	0-0	5-1	–	2-0	1-2	3-2	4-0	0-3	0-1	0-1	0-2	1-1
	0-0	3-0	2-0	3-1	1-1	–	2-1	2-2	2-2	6-1	3-1	2-0	3-0	2-3
	3-0	2-0	0-1	1-1	6-2	2-1	–	2-1	2-3	1-2	4-1	0-0	1-2	2-2
	1-1	0-1	2-2	1-1	2-1	3-4	2-1	–	0-1	1-3	1-2	1-0	4-1	3-1
	1-1	1-2	2-0	2-3	7-0	3-1	2-1	1-1	–	1-4	1-3	5-0	1-0	0-0
	2-2	2-0	1-2	2-2	2-1	1-0	1-1	2-0	0-0	–	3-2	1-2	0-0	1-0
	0-1	1-1	3-2	1-0	2-0	4-3	1-1	2-0	1-1	0-0	–	0-1	1-1	1-1
	1-0	3-3	5-2	0-2	1-3	2-0	1-0	1-0	0-0	0-1	1-2	–	1-1	4-2
	2-0	3-4	0-1	4-1	1-1	2-2	0-0	1-2	0-2	2-5	1-3	2-2	–	1-1
	1-1	3-2	2-3	1-0	1-0	1-1	1-1	4-0	2-2	1 1	1-1	3-0	0-1	–

F.A. Carling Premiership

	P	Home			Goals		Away			Goals		Pts	GD
		W	D	L	F	A	W	D	L	F	A		
1 Manchester U	42	14	6	1	39	13	13	5	3	41	25	92	+42
2 Blackburn R	42	14	5	2	31	11	11	4	6	32	25	84	+27
3 Newcastle U	42	14	4	3	51	14	9	4	8	31	27	77	+41
4 Arsenal	42	10	8	3	25	15	8	9	4	28	13	71	+25
5 Leeds U	42	13	6	2	37	18	5	10	6	28	21	70	+26
6 Wimbledon	42	12	5	4	35	21	6	6	9	21	32	65	+3
7 Sheffield W	42	10	7	4	48	24	6	9	6	28	30	64	+22
8 Liverpool	42	12	4	5	33	23	5	5	11	26	32	60	+4
9 QPR	42	8	7	6	32	29	8	5	8	30	32	60	+1
10 Aston Villa	42	8	5	8	23	18	7	7	7	23	32	57	−4
11 Coventry C	42	9	7	5	23	17	5	7	9	20	28	56	−2
12 Norwich C	42	4	9	8	26	29	8	8	5	39	32	53	+4
13 West Ham U	42	6	7	8	26	31	7	6	8	21	27	52	−11
14 Chelsea	42	11	5	5	31	20	2	7	12	18	33	51	−4
15 Tottenham H	42	4	8	9	29	33	7	4	10	25	26	45	−5
16 Manchester C	42	6	10	5	24	22	3	8	10	14	27	45	−11
17 Everton	42	8	4	9	26	30	4	4	13	16	33	44	−21
18 Southampton	42	9	2	10	30	31	3	5	13	19	35	43	−17
19 Ipswich T	42	5	8	8	21	32	4	8	9	14	26	43	−23
20 Sheffield U	42	6	10	5	24	23	2	8	11	18	37	42	−18
21 Oldham Ath	42	5	8	8	24	33	4	5	12	18	35	40	−26
22 Swindon T	42	4	7	10	25	45	1	8	12	22	55	30	−53

LEADING GOALSCORERS 1993–94

FA PREMIER LEAGUE	League	FA Cup	Coca Cola Cup	Other Cups	Total
Andy Cole (*Newcastle U*)	34	1	6	0	41
Alan Shearer (*Blackburn R*)	31	2	1	0	34
Chris Sutton (*Norwich C*)	25	2	1	0	28
Matthew Le Tissier (*Southampton*)	25	0	0	0	25
Ian Wright (*Arsenal*)	23	1	6	3	33
Peter Beardsley (*Newcastle U*)	21	2	1	0	24
Mark Bright (*Sheffield W*)	19	2	2	0	23
Eric Cantona (*Manchester U*)	18	4	1	2	25
Dean Holdsworth (*Wimbledon*)	17	3	4	0	24
Rodney Wallace (*Leeds U*)	17	0	0	0	17
Tony Cottee (*Everton*)	16	0	3	0	19
Les Ferninand (*QPR*)	16	0	2	0	18
Ian Rush (*Liverpool*)	14	1	4	0	19
Kevin Campbell (*Arsenal*)	14	0	1	4	19

Endsleigh Insurance League Division 1

		Home			Goals		Away			Goals			
	P	W	D	L	F	A	W	D	L	F	A	Pts	GD
1 Crystal Palace	46	16	4	3	39	18	11	5	7	34	28	90	+27
2 Nottingham F	46	12	9	2	38	22	11	5	7	36	27	83	+25
3 Millwall	46	14	8	1	36	17	5	9	9	22	32	74	+9
4 Leicester C	46	11	9	3	45	30	8	7	8	27	29	73	+13
5 Tranmere R	46	15	3	5	48	23	6	6	11	21	30	72	+16
6 Derby C	46	15	3	5	44	25	5	8	10	29	43	71	+5
7 Notts C	46	16	3	4	43	26	4	5	14	22	43	68	-4
8 Wolverhampton W	46	10	10	3	34	19	7	9	7	26	28	68	+13
9 Middlesbrough	46	12	6	5	40	19	6	7	10	26	35	67	+12
10 Stoke C	46	14	4	5	35	19	4	9	10	22	40	67	-2
11 Charlton Ath	46	14	3	6	39	22	5	5	13	22	36	65	+3
12 Sunderland	46	14	2	7	35	22	5	6	12	19	35	65	-3
13 Bristol C	46	11	7	5	27	18	5	9	9	20	32	64	-3
14 Bolton W	46	10	8	5	40	31	5	6	12	23	33	59	-1
15 Southend U	46	10	5	8	34	28	7	3	12	29	39	59	-4
16 Grimsby T	46	7	14	2	26	16	6	6	11	26	31	59	+5
17 Portsmouth	46	10	6	7	29	22	5	7	11	23	36	58	-6
18 Barnsley	46	9	3	11	25	26	7	4	12	30	41	55	-12
19 Watford	46	10	5	8	39	35	5	4	14	27	45	54	-14
20 Luton T	46	12	4	7	38	25	2	7	14	18	35	53	-4
21 WBA	46	9	7	7	38	31	4	5	14	24	40	51	-9
22 Birmingham C	46	9	7	7	28	29	4	5	14	24	40	51	-17
23 Oxford U	46	10	5	8	33	33	3	5	15	21	42	49	-21
24 Peterborough	46	6	9	8	31	30	2	4	17	17	46	37	-28

ENDSLEIGH INSURANCE DIVISION 1

John McGinlay (*Bolton W*)	25	3	1	4	33
Chris Armstrong (*C Palace*)	22	0	1	1	24
John Aldridge (*Tranmere R*)	21	0	7	0	28
Stan Collymore (*Notingham F*)	19	0	5	1	25
Bob Taylor (*WBA*)	18	0	1	2	21
Paul Furlong (*Watford*)	18	0	1	0	19
Wayne Allison (*Bristol C*)	15	4	0	1	20
Paul Wilkinson (*Middlesbrough*)	15	1	1	2	19
Gary McSwegan (*Notts Co*)	15	0	1	1	17
Phil Gray (*Sunderland*)	14	0	3	0	17
Clive Mendonca (*Grimsby Town*)	14	0	2	1	17
Steve Bull (*Wolverhampton W*)	14	0	0	1	15
John Hendrie (*Middlesbrough*)	13	0	3	3	19
Tommy Johnson (*Derby Co*)	13	1	1	1	16
Paul Kitson (*Derby Co*)	13	1	0	1	15
Marco Gabbiadini (*Derby Co*)	13	0	2	0	15

Endsleigh Insurance League Division 2

		Home			Goals		Away			Goals		
	P	W	D	L	F	A	W	D	L	F	A	Pts	GD
1 Reading	46	15	6	2	40	16	11	5	7	41	28	89	+37
2 Port Vale	46	16	6	1	46	18	10	4	9	33	28	88	+33
3 Plymouth Arg	46	16	4	3	46	26	9	6	8	42	30	85	+32
4 Stockport Co	46	15	3	5	50	22	9	10	4	24	22	85	+30
5 York C	46	12	7	4	33	13	9	5	9	31	27	75	+24
6 Burnley	46	17	4	2	55	18	4	6	13	24	40	73	+21
7 Bradford C	46	13	5	5	34	20	6	8	9	27	33	70	+8
8 Bristol R	46	10	8	5	33	26	10	2	11	27	33	70	+1
9 Hull C	46	9	9	5	33	20	9	5	9	29	34	68	+8
10 Cambridge U	46	11	5	7	38	29	8	4	11	41	44	66	+6
11 Huddersfield T	46	9	8	6	27	26	8	6	9	31	35	65	−3
12 Wrexham	46	13	4	6	45	33	4	7	12	21	44	62	−11
13 Swansea C	46	12	7	4	37	20	4	5	14	19	38	60	−2
14 Brighton & H A	46	10	7	6	38	29	5	7	11	22	38	59	−7
15 Rotherham U	46	11	4	8	42	30	4	9	10	21	30	58	+3
16 Brentford	46	7	10	6	30	28	6	9	8	27	27	58	+2
17 Bournemouth	46	8	7	8	26	27	6	8	9	25	32	57	−8
18 Leyton Orient	46	11	9	3	38	26	3	5	15	19	45	56	−14
19 Cardiff C	46	10	7	6	39	33	3	8	12	27	46	54	−13
20 Blackpool	46	12	2	9	41	37	4	3	16	22	38	53	−12
21 Fulham	46	7	6	10	20	23	7	4	12	30	40	52	−13
22 Exeter C	46	8	7	8	38	37	3	5	15	14	46	45	−31
23 Hartlepool U	46	8	3	12	28	40	1	6	16	13	47	36	−46
24 Barnet	46	4	6	13	22	32	1	7	15	19	54	28	−45

DIVISION 2

Jimmy Quinn (*Reading*)	35	2	0	3	40
Gary Bennett (*Wrexham*)	32	3	0	1	36
Kevin Francis (*Stockport Co*)	28	3	1	2	34
Paul Barnes (*York C*)	24	0	0	1	25
Dean Windass (*Hull C*)	23	1	0	0	24
John Taylor (*Bristol R*)	23	0	0	0	23
Kurt Nogan (*Brighton & HA*)	22	0	2	2	26
Andy Preece (*Stockport Co*)	21	2	0	5	28
Steve Castle (*Plymouth Arg*)	21	0	0	1	22
Steve Butler (*Cambridge U*)	21	0	0	0	21
Stuart Lovell (*Reading*)	20	0	0	1	21
David Eyres (*Burnley*)	19	4	3	1	27
Imre Varadi (*Rotherham U*)	19	1	0	1	21
Martin Foyle (*Port Vale*)	18	0	1	2	21

Endsleigh Insurance League Division 3

		Home			Goals		Away			Goals			
	P	W	D	L	F	A	W	D	L	F	A	Pts	GD
1 Shrewsbury T	42	10	8	3	28	17	12	5	4	35	22	79	+24
2 Chester C	42	13	5	3	35	18	8	6	7	34	28	74	+23
3 Crewe Alex	42	12	4	5	45	30	9	6	6	35	31	73	+19
4 Wycombe W	42	11	6	4	34	21	8	7	6	33	32	70	+14
5 Preston NE	42	13	5	3	46	23	5	8	8	33	37	67	+19
6 Torquay U	42	8	10	3	30	24	9	6	6	34	32	67	+8
7 Carlisle U	42	10	4	7	35	23	8	6	7	22	19	64	+15
8 Chesterfield	42	8	8	5	32	22	8	6	7	23	26	62	+7
9 Rochdale	42	10	5	6	38	22	6	8	25	29	60	+12
10 Walsall	42	7	5	9	28	26	10	4	7	20	27	60	−5
11 Scunthorpe U	42	9	7	5	40	26	6	7	8	24	30	59	+8
12 Mansfield T	42	9	3	9	28	30	6	7	8	25	32	55	−9
13 Bury	42	9	6	6	33	22	5	5	11	22	34	53	−1
14 Scarborough	42	8	4	9	29	28	7	4	10	26	33	53	−6
15 Doncaster R	42	8	6	7	24	26	6	4	11	20	31	52	−13
16 Gillingham	42	8	8	5	27	23	4	7	10	17	28	51	−7
17 Colchester U	42	8	4	9	31	33	6	6	10	25	38	49	−15
18 Lincoln C	42	7	4	10	26	29	5	7	9	26	34	47	−11
19 Wigan Ath	42	6	7	8	33	33	5	5	11	18	37	45	−19
20 Hereford U	42	6	4	11	34	33	6	2	13	26	46	42	−19
21 Darlington	42	7	5	9	24	28	3	6	12	18	36	41	−22
22 Northampton T	42	6	7	8	25	23	3	4	14	19	43	38	−22

DIVISION 3

Tony Ellis (*Preston NE*)	26	2	1	1	30
Mark Carter (*Bury*)	20	0	0	0	20
Steve Norris (*Chesterfield*)	19	2	0	1	22
Matt Carmichael (*Scunthorpe U*)	18	1	0	5	24
Dean Spink (*Shrewsbury*)	18	1	0	1	20
Chris Pike (*Hereford U*)	18	1	0	0	19
Nick Forster (*Gillingham*)	18	0	0	0	18
Darren Rowbotham (*Crewe Alex*)	15	1	1	0	17
Adrian Foster (*Torquay U*)	15	0	1	0	16
Steve Whitehall (*Rochdale*)	14	1	0	0	15
Tony Naylor (*Crewe Alex*)	13	1	0	2	16
David Reeves (*Carlisle U*)	11	1	0	3	15

N.B. Players are listed in order of the League goals scored. Only those who scored in one division are included in the list. Other cup goals refer to those in European matches, Autoglass Trophy and Anglo-Italian Cup, but not in the play-offs.

LEAGUE POSITIONS: FA PREMIER 1992–93 AND DIVISION 1 1968–69 TO 1991–92

	1992–93	1991–92	1990–91	1989–90	1988–89	1987–88	1986–87	1985–86	1984–85	1983–84	1982–83	1981–82	1980–81
Arsenal	10	4	1	4	1	6	4	7	7	6	10	5	3
Aston Villa	2	7	17	2	17	–	22	16	10	10	6	11	1
Birmingham C	–	–	–	–	–	–	–	21	–	20	17	16	13
Blackburn R	4	–	–	–	–	–	–	–	–	–	–	–	–
Blackpool	–	–	–	–	–	–	–	–	–	–	–	–	–
Bolton W	–	–	–	–	–	–	–	–	–	–	–	–	22
Brighton & HA	–	–	–	–	–	–	–	–	–	–	22	13	19
Bristol C	–	–	–	–	–	–	–	–	–	–	–	–	–
Burnley	–	–	–	–	–	–	–	–	–	–	–	–	–
Carlisle U	–	–	–	–	–	–	–	–	–	–	–	–	–
Charlton Ath	–	–	–	19	14	17	19	–	–	–	–	–	–
Chelsea	11	14	11	5	–	18	14	6	6	–	–	–	–
Coventry C	15	19	16	12	7	10	10	17	18	19	19	14	16
Crystal Palace	20	10	3	15	–	–	–	–	–	–	–	–	22
Derby Co	–	–	20	16	5	15	–	–	–	–	–	–	–
Everton	13	12	9	6	8	4	1	2	1	7	7	8	15
Huddersfield T	–	–	–	–	–	–	–	–	–	–	–	–	–
Ipswich T	16	–	–	–	–	–	–	20	17	12	9	2	2
Leeds U	17	1	4	–	–	–	–	–	–	–	–	20	9
Leicester C	–	–	–	–	–	–	20	19	15	15	–	–	21
Liverpool	6	6	2	1	2	1	2	1	2	1	1	1	5
Luton T	–	20	18	17	16	9	7	9	13	16	18	–	–
Manchester C	9	5	5	14	–	–	21	15	–	–	20	10	12
Manchester U	1	2	6	13	11	2	11	4	4	4	3	3	8
Middlesbrough	21	–	–	–	18	–	–	–	–	–	–	22	14
Millwall	–	–	–	20	10	–	–	–	–	–	–	–	–
Newcastle U	–	–	–	–	20	8	17	11	14	–	–	–	–
Norwich C	3	18	15	10	4	14	5	–	20	14	14	–	20
Nottingham F	22	8	8	9	3	3	8	8	9	3	5	12	7
Notts Co	–	21	–	–	–	–	–	–	–	21	15	15	–
Oldham Ath	19	17	–	–	–	–	–	–	–	–	–	–	–
Oxford U	–	–	–	–	–	21	18	18	–	–	–	–	–
Portsmouth	–	–	–	–	–	19	–	–	–	–	–	–	–
QPR	5	11	12	11	9	5	16	13	19	5	–	–	–
Sheffield U	14	9	13	–	–	–	–	–	–	–	–	–	–
Sheffield W	7	3	–	18	15	11	13	5	8	–	–	–	–
Southampton	18	16	14	7	13	12	12	14	5	2	12	7	6
Stoke C	–	–	–	–	–	–	–	–	22	18	13	18	11
Sunderland	–	–	19	–	–	–	–	–	21	13	16	19	17
Swansea C	–	–	–	–	–	–	–	–	–	–	21	6	–
Tottenham H	8	15	10	3	6	13	3	10	3	8	4	4	10
Watford	–	–	–	–	–	20	9	12	11	11	2	–	–
WBA	–	–	–	–	–	–	–	22	12	17	11	17	4
West Ham U	–	22	–	–	19	16	15	3	16	9	8	9	–
Wimbledon	12	13	7	8	12	7	6	–	–	–	–	–	–
Wolv'hampton W	–	–	–	–	–	–	–	–	–	22	–	21	18

1979-80	1978-79	1977-78	1976-77	1975-76	1974-75	1973-74	1972-73	1971-72	1970-71	1969-70	1968-69	
4	7	5	8	17	16	10	2	5	1	12	4	Arsenal
7	8	8	4	16	–	–	–	–	–	–	–	Aston Villa
–	21	11	13	19	17	19	10	–	–	–	–	Birmingham C
–	–	–	–	–	–	–	–	–	–	–	–	Blackburn R
–	–	–	–	–	–	–	–	–	22	–	–	Blackpool
22	17	–	–	–	–	–	–	–	–	–	–	Bolton W
16	–	–	–	–	–	–	–	–	–	–	–	Brighton & HA
20	13	17	18	–	–	–	–	–	–	–	–	Bristol C
–	–	–	–	21	10	6	–	–	21	14	14	Burnley
–	–	–	–	–	22	–	–	–	–	–	–	Carlisle U
–	–	–	–	–	–	–	–	–	–	–	–	Charlton Ath
–	22	16	–	–	21	17	12	7	6	3	5	Chelsea
15	10	7	19	14	14	16	19	18	10	6	20	Coventry C
13	–	–	–	–	–	–	21	20	18	20	–	Crystal Palace
21	19	12	15	4	1	3	7	1	9	4	–	Derby Co
19	4	3	9	11	4	7	17	15	14	1	3	Everton
–	–	–	–	–	–	–	–	22	15	–	–	Huddersfield T
3	6	18	3	6	3	4	4	13	19	18	12	Ipswich T
11	5	9	10	5	9	1	3	2	2	2	1	Leeds U
–	–	22	11	7	18	9	16	12	–	–	21	Leicester C
1	1	2	1	1	2	2	1	3	5	5	2	Liverpool
–	–	–	–	–	20	–	–	–	–	–	–	Luton T
17	15	4	2	8	8	14	11	4	11	10	13	Manchester C
2	9	10	6	3	–	21	18	8	8	8	11	Manchester U
9	12	14	12	13	7	–	–	–	–	–	–	Middlesbrough
–	–	–	–	–	–	–	–	–	–	–	–	Millwall
–	–	21	5	15	15	15	9	11	12	7	9	Newcastle U
12	16	13	16	10	–	22	20	–	–	–	–	Norwich C
5	2	1	–	–	–	–	–	21	16	15	18	Nottingham F
–	–	–	–	–	–	–	–	–	–	–	–	Notts Co
–	–	–	–	–	–	–	–	–	–	–	–	Oldham Ath
–	–	–	–	–	–	–	–	–	–	–	–	Oxford U
–	–	–	–	–	–	–	–	–	–	–	–	Portsmouth
–	20	19	14	2	11	8	–	–	–	–	22	QPR
–	–	–	–	22	6	13	14	10	–	–	–	Sheffield U
–	–	–	–	–	–	–	–	–	–	22	15	Sheffield W
8	14	–	–	–	–	20	13	19	7	19	7	Southampton
18	–	–	21	12	5	5	15	17	13	9	19	Stoke C
–	–	–	20	–	–	–	–	–	–	21	17	Sunderland
–	–	–	–	–	–	–	–	–	–	–	–	Swansea C
14	11	–	22	9	19	11	8	6	3	11	6	Tottenham H
–	–	–	–	–	–	–	–	–	–	–	–	Watford
10	3	6	7	–	–	–	22	16	17	16	10	WBA
–	–	20	17	18	13	18	6	14	20	17	8	West Ham U
–	–	–	–	–	–	–	–	–	–	–	–	Wimbledon
6	18	15	–	20	12	12	5	9	4	13	16	Wolv'hampton W

LEAGUE POSITIONS: DIVISION 1
1992–93 AND DIVISION 2 1968–69 TO 1991–92

	1992-93	1991-92	1990-91	1989-90	1988-89	1987-88	1986-87	1985-86	1984-85	1983-84	1982-83	1981-82	1980-81
Aston Villa	–	–	–	–	–	2	–	–	–	–	–	–	–
Barnsley	13	16	8	19	7	14	11	12	11	14	10	6	–
Birmingham C	19	–	–	–	23	19	19	–	2	–	–	–	–
Blackburn R	–	6	19	5	5	5	12	19	5	6	11	10	4
Blackpool	–	–	–	–	–	–	–	–	–	–	–	–	–
Bolton W	–	–	–	–	–	–	–	–	–	22	19	18	–
Bournemouth	–	–	–	22	12	17	–	–	–	–	–	–	–
Bradford C	–	–	–	23	14	4	10	13	–	–	–	–	–
Brentford	22	–	–	–	–	–	–	–	–	–	–	–	–
Brighton & HA	–	23	–	6	18	19	–	22	11	6	9	–	–
Bristol C	15	17	9	–	–	–	–	–	–	–	–	–	21
Bristol R	24	13	13	–	–	–	–	–	–	–	–	–	22
Burnley	–	–	–	–	–	–	–	–	–	–	21	–	–
Bury	–	–	–	–	–	–	–	–	–	–	–	–	–
Cambridge U	23	5	–	–	–	–	–	–	–	22	12	14	13
Cardiff C	–	–	–	–	–	–	–	21	15	–	20	19	
Carlisle U	–	–	–	–	–	–	20	16	7	14	–	–	–
Charlton Ath	12	7	16	–	–	–	2	17	13	17	13	–	–
Chelsea	–	–	–	–	1	–	–	–	1	18	12	12	
Crystal Palace	–	–	–	3	6	6	5	15	18	15	15	–	–
Derby Co	8	3	–	–	–	–	1	–	–	20	13	16	6
Fulham	–	–	–	–	–	–	–	22	9	11	4	–	–
Grimsby T	9	19	–	–	–	–	21	15	10	5	19	17	7
Hereford U	–	–	–	–	–	–	–	–	–	–	–	–	–
Huddersfield T	–	–	–	–	–	23	17	16	13	12	–	–	–
Hull C	–	–	24	14	21	15	14	6	–	–	–	–	–
Ipswich T	–	1	14	9	8	8	5	–	–	–	–	–	–
Leeds U	–	–	–	1	10	7	4	14	7	10	8	–	–
Leicester C	6	4	22	13	15	13	–	–	–	–	3	8	–
Leyton Orient	–	–	–	–	–	–	–	–	–	–	–	22	17
Luton T	20	–	–	–	–	–	–	–	–	–	–	1	5
Manchester C	–	–	–	–	2	9	–	–	3	4	–	–	–
Manchester U	–	–	–	–	–	–	–	–	–	–	–	–	–
Mansfield T	–	–	–	–	–	–	–	–	–	–	–	–	–
Middlesbrough	–	2	7	21	–	3	–	21	19	17	16	–	–
Millwall	7	15	5	–	–	1	16	9	–	–	–	–	–
Newcastle U	1	20	11	3	–	–	–	–	–	3	5	9	11
Norwich C	–	–	–	–	–	–	–	1	–	–	3	–	–
Nottingham F	–	–	–	–	–	–	–	–	–	–	–	–	–
Notts Co	17	–	4	–	–	–	–	–	20	–	–	–	2
Oldham Ath	–	–	1	8	16	10	3	8	14	19	7	11	15
Oxford U	14	21	10	17	17	–	–	–	1	–	–	–	–
Peterborough U	10	–	–	–	–	–	–	–	–	–	–	–	–
Plymouth Arg	–	22	18	16	18	16	7	–	–	–	–	–	–
Port Vale	–	24	15	11	–	–	–	–	–	–	–	–	–
Portsmouth	3	9	17	12	20	–	2	4	4	16	–	–	–
Preston NE	–	–	–	–	–	–	–	–	–	–	–	–	20
QPR	–	–	–	–	–	–	–	–	–	–	1	5	8

1979-80	1978-79	1977-78	1976-77	1975-76	1974-75	1973-74	1972-73	1971-72	1970-71	1969-70	1968-69	
–	–	–	–	–	2	14	3	–	–	21	18	Aston Villa
–	–	–	–	–	–	–	–	–	–	–	–	Barnsley
3	–	–	–	–	–	–	2	9	18	7	–	Birmingham C
–	22	5	12	15	–	–	–	21	8	19	–	Blackburn R
–	20	5	10	7	5	7	6	–	2	8	–	Blackpool
–	–	1	4	4	10	11	–	–	22	16	17	Bolton W
–	–	–	–	–	–	–	–	–	–	–	–	Bournemouth
–	–	–	–	–	–	–	–	–	–	–	–	Bradford C
–	–	–	–	–	–	–	–	–	–	–	–	Brentford
–	2	4	–	–	–	22	–	–	–	–	–	Brighton & HA
–	–	–	2	5	16	5	8	19	14	16	–	Bristol C
19	16	18	15	18	19	–	–	–	–	–	–	Bristol R
21	13	11	16	–	–	1	7	–	–	–	–	Burnley
–	–	–	–	–	–	–	–	–	–	–	21	Bury
8	12	–	–	–	–	–	–	–	–	–	–	Cambridge U
15	9	19	18	–	21	17	20	19	3	7	5	Cardiff C
–	–	20	19	–	3	18	10	4	12	12	–	Carlisle U
22	19	17	7	9	–	–	21	20	20	3	–	Charlton Ath
4	–	–	2	11	–	–	–	–	–	–	–	Chelsea
–	1	9	–	–	20	–	–	–	–	–	2	Crystal Palace
–	–	–	–	–	–	–	–	–	–	–	1	Derby Co
20	10	10	17	12	9	13	9	20	–	22	–	Fulham
–	–	–	–	–	–	–	–	–	–	–	–	Grimsby T
–	–	–	22	–	–	–	–	–	–	–	–	Hereford U
–	–	–	–	–	–	21	–	–	1	6	–	Huddersfield T
–	22	14	14	8	9	13	12	5	13	11	–	Hull C
–	–	–	–	–	–	–	–	–	–	–	–	Ipswich T
–	–	–	–	–	–	–	–	–	–	–	–	Leeds U
1	17	–	–	–	–	–	–	1	3	–	–	Leicester C
14	11	14	19	13	12	4	15	17	17	–	–	Leyton Orient
6	18	13	6	7	–	2	12	13	6	–	–	Luton T
–	–	–	–	–	–	–	–	–	–	–	–	Manchester C
–	–	–	–	–	–	–	–	–	–	–	–	Manchester U
–	–	21	–	–	–	–	–	–	–	–	–	Mansfield T
–	–	–	–	–	1	4	9	7	4	4	–	Middlesbrough
–	21	16	10	–	20	12	11	3	8	10	10	Millwall
9	8	–	–	–	–	–	–	–	–	–	–	Newcastle U
–	–	–	–	3	–	–	1	10	11	13	–	Norwich C
–	–	3	8	16	7	14	–	–	–	–	–	Nottingham F
17	6	15	8	5	14	10	–	–	–	–	–	Notts Co
11	14	8	13	17	18	–	–	–	–	–	–	Oldham Ath
–	–	–	20	11	18	8	15	14	15	20	–	Oxford U
–	–	–	–	–	–	–	–	–	–	–	–	Peterborough U
–	–	–	21	16	–	–	–	–	–	–	–	Plymouth Arg
–	–	–	–	–	–	–	–	–	–	–	–	Port Vale
–	–	–	22	17	15	17	16	16	17	15	–	Portsmouth
10	7	–	–	–	21	19	18	–	22	14	–	Preston NE
5	–	–	–	–	–	2	4	11	9	–	–	QPR

	1992-93	1991-92	1990-91	1989-90	1988-89	1987-88	1986-87	1985-86	1984-85	1983-84	1982-83	1981-82	1980-81
Reading	–	–	–	–	–	22	13	–	–	–	–	–	–
Rotherham U	–	–	–	–	–	–	–	–	–	–	20	7	–
Sheffield U	–	–	–	2	–	21	9	7	18	–	–	–	–
Sheffield W	–	–	3	–	–	–	–	–	–	2	6	4	10
Shrewsbury T	–	–	–	–	22	18	18	17	8	8	9	18	14
Southampton	–	–	–	–	–	–	–	–	–	–	–	–	–
Southend U	18	12	–	–	–	–	–	–	–	–	–	–	–
Stoke C	–	–	–	24	13	11	8	10	–	–	–	–	–
Sunderland	21	18	–	6	11	–	20	18	–	–	–	–	–
Swansea C	–	–	–	–	–	–	–	–	–	21	–	–	3
Swindon T	5	8	21	4	6	12	–	–	–	–	–	–	–
Tottenham H	–	–	–	–	–	–	–	–	–	–	–	–	–
Tranmere R	4	14	–	–	–	–	–	–	–	–	–	–	–
Walsall	–	–	–	–	24	–	–	–	–	–	–	–	–
Watford	16	10	20	15	4	–	–	–	–	–	–	2	9
WBA	–	–	23	20	9	20	15	–	–	–	–	–	–
West Ham U	2	–	2	7	–	–	–	–	–	–	–	–	1
Wimbledon	–	–	–	–	–	–	–	3	12	–	–	–	–
Wolv'hampton W	11	11	12	10	–	–	–	–	22	–	2	–	–
Wrexham	–	–	–	–	–	–	–	–	–	–	–	21	16
York C	–	–	–	–	–	–	–	–	–	–	–	–	–

LEAGUE POSITIONS: DIVISION 2
1992–93 AND DIVISION 3 1968–69 TO 1991–92

	1992-93	1991-92	1990-91	1989-90	1988-89	1987-88	1986-87	1985-86	1984-85	1983-84	1982-83	1981-82	1980-81
Aldershot	–	–	–	–	24	20	–	–	–	–	–	–	–
Aston Villa	–	–	–	–	–	–	–	–	–	–	–	–	–
Barnsley	–	–	–	–	–	–	–	–	–	–	–	–	2
Barrow	–	–	–	–	–	–	–	–	–	–	–	–	–
Birmingham C	–	2	12	7	–	–	–	–	–	–	–	–	–
Blackburn R	–	–	–	–	–	–	–	–	–	–	–	–	–
Blackpool	18	–	–	23	19	10	9	12	–	–	–	–	23
Bolton W	2	13	4	6	10	–	21	18	17	10	–	–	–
Bournemouth	17	8	9	–	–	–	1	15	10	17	14	–	–
Bradford C	10	16	8	–	–	–	–	–	1	7	12	–	–
Brentford	–	1	6	13	7	12	11	10	13	20	9	8	9
Brighton & HA	9	–	–	–	–	2	–	–	–	–	–	–	–
Bristol C	–	–	–	2	11	5	6	9	5	–	–	23	–
Bristol R	–	–	–	1	5	8	19	16	6	5	7	15	–

	1979-80	1978-79	1977-78	1976-77	1975-76	1974-75	1973-74	1972-73	1971-72	1970-71	1969-70	1968-69
Reading	-	-	-	-	-	-	-	-	-	-	-	-
Rotherham U	-	-	-	-	-	-	-	-	-	-	-	-
Sheffield U	-	20	12	11	-	-	-	-	-	2	6	9
Sheffield W	-	-	-	-	22	19	10	14	15	-	-	-
Shrewsbury T	13	-	-	-	-	-	-	-	-	-	-	-
Southampton	-	-	2	9	6	13	-	-	-	-	-	-
Southend U	-	-	-	-	-	-	-	-	-	-	-	-
Stoke C	-	3	7	-	-	-	-	-	-	-	-	-
Sunderland	2	4	6	-	1	4	6	6	5	13	-	-
Swansea C	12	-	-	-	-	-	-	-	-	-	-	-
Swindon T	-	-	-	-	-	22	16	11	12	5	-	-
Tottenham H	-	-	3	-	-	-	-	-	-	-	-	-
Tranmere R	-	-	-	-	-	-	-	-	-	-	-	-
Walsall	-	-	-	-	-	-	-	-	-	-	-	-
Watford	18	-	-	-	-	-	-	-	22	18	19	-
WBA	-	-	-	-	3	6	8	-	-	-	-	-
West Ham U	7	5	-	-	-	-	-	-	-	-	-	-
Wimbledon	-	-	-	-	-	-	-	-	-	-	-	-
Wolv'hampton W	-	-	1	-	-	-	-	-	-	-	-	-
Wrexham	16	15	-	-	-	-	-	-	-	-	-	-
York C	-	-	-	21	15	-	-	-	-	-	-	-

	1979-80	1978-79	1977-78	1976-77	1975-76	1974-75	1973-74	1972-73	1971-72	1970-71	1969-70	1968-69
Aldershot	-	-	-	21	20	8	-	-	-	-	-	-
Aston Villa	-	-	-	-	-	-	-	-	1	4	-	-
Barnsley	11	-	-	-	-	-	-	-	22	12	7	10
Barrow	-	-	-	-	-	-	-	-	-	-	23	19
Birmingham C	-	-	-	-	-	-	-	-	-	-	-	-
Blackburn R	2	-	-	-	-	1	13	3	10	-	-	-
Blackpool	18	12	-	-	-	-	-	-	-	-	-	-
Bolton W	-	-	-	-	-	-	-	1	7	-	-	-
Bournemouth	-	-	-	-	21	11	7	3	-	21	4	-
Bradford C	-	-	22	-	-	-	-	-	24	19	10	-
Brentford	19	10	-	-	-	-	-	22	-	-	-	-
Brighton & HA	-	-	-	2	4	19	19	-	2	14	5	12
Bristol C	-	-	-	-	-	-	-	-	-	-	-	-
Bristol R	-	-	-	-	-	-	2	5	6	6	3	16

	1992–93	1991–92	1990–91	1989–90	1988–89	1987–88	1986–87	1985–86	1984–85	1983–84	1982–83	1981–82	1980–81
Burnley	13	–	–	–	–	–	–	–	21	12	–	1	8
Bury	–	21	7	5	13	14	16	20	–	–	–	–	–
Cambridge U	.	–	1	–	–	–	–	–	24	–	–	–	–
Cardiff C	–	–	–	21	16	–	–	22	–	–	2	–	–
Carlisle U	–	–	–	–	–	–	22	–	–	–	–	2	19
Charlton Ath	–	–	–	–	–	–	–	–	–	–	–	–	3
Chester C	24	18	19	16	8	15	15	–	–	–	–	24	18
Chesterfield	–	–	–	–	22	18	17	17	–	–	24	11	5
Colchester U	–	–	–	–	–	–	–	–	–	–	–	–	22
Crewe Alex	–	–	22	12	–	–	–	–	–	–	–	–	–
Crystal Palace	–	–	–	–	–	–	–	–	–	–	–	–	–
Darlington	–	24	–	–	–	–	22	13	–	–	–	–	–
Derby Co	–	–	–	–	–	–	–	3	7	–	–	–	–
Doncaster R	–	–	–	–	24	13	11	14	–	23	19	–	–
Exeter C	19	20	16	–	–	–	–	–	–	24	19	18	11
Fulham	12	9	21	20	4	9	18	–	–	–	–	3	13
Gillingham	–	–	–	–	23	13	5	5	4	8	13	6	15
Grimsby T	–	–	3	–	–	22	–	–	–	–	–	–	–
Halifax T	–	–	–	–	–	–	–	–	–	–	–	–	–
Hartlepool U	16	11	–	–	–	–	–	–	–	–	–	–	–
Hereford U	–	–	–	–	–	–	–	–	–	–	–	–	–
Huddersfield T	15	3	11	8	14	–	–	–	–	–	3	17	4
Hull C	20	14	–	–	–	–	–	–	3	4	–	–	24
Leyton Orient	7	10	13	14	–	–	–	22	11	20	–	–	–
Lincoln C	–	–	–	–	–	–	21	19	14	6	4	–	–
Luton T	–	–	–	–	–	–	–	–	–	–	–	–	–
Mansfield T	22	–	24	15	15	19	10	–	–	–	–	–	–
Middlesbrough	–	–	–	–	–	–	2	–	–	–	–	–	–
Millwall	–	–	–	–	–	–	–	–	2	9	17	9	16
Newport Co	–	–	–	–	–	–	23	19	18	13	4	16	12
Northampton T	–	–	–	22	20	6	–	–	–	–	–	–	–
Notts Co	–	–	–	3	9	4	7	8	–	–	–	–	–
Oldham Ath	–	–	–	–	–	–	–	–	–	–	–	–	–
Oxford U	–	–	–	–	–	–	–	–	–	1	5	5	14
Peterborough U	–	6	–	–	–	–	–	–	–	–	–	–	–
Plymouth Arg	14	–	–	–	–	–	2	15	19	8	10	7	–
Portsmouth	–	–	–	–	–	–	–	–	–	–	1	13	6
Port Vale	3	–	–	–	3	11	12	–	23	–	–	–	–
Preston NE	21	17	17	19	6	16	–	23	16	16	14	–	–
Reading	8	12	15	10	18	–	–	1	9	–	21	12	10
Rochdale	–	–	–	–	–	–	–	–	–	–	–	–	–
Rotherham U	11	–	23	9	–	21	14	14	12	18	–	–	1
Scunthorpe U	–	–	–	–	–	–	–	–	–	21	–	–	–
Sheffield U	–	–	–	–	2	–	–	–	3	11	–	–	21
Sheffield W	–	–	–	–	–	–	–	–	–	–	–	–	–
Shrewsbury T	–	22	18	11	–	–	–	–	–	–	–	–	–
Southend U	–	–	2	–	21	17	–	–	–	22	15	7	–
Southport	–	–	–	–	–	–	–	–	–	–	–	–	–

1979-80	1978-79	1977-78	1976-77	1975-76	1974-75	1973-74	1972-73	1971-72	1970-71	1969-70	1968-69	
-	-	-	-	-	-	-	-	-	-	-	-	Burnley
21	19	15	7	13	14	-	-	-	22	19	-	Bury
-	-	2	-	-	-	21	-	-	-	-	-	Cambridge U
-	-	-	-	2	-	-	-	-	-	-	-	Cardiff C
6	6	13	-	-	-	-	-	-	-	-	-	Carlisle U
-	-	-	-	3	14	11	-	-	-	-	-	Charlton Ath
9	16	5	13	17	-	-	-	-	-	-	-	Chester C
4	20	9	18	15	15	5	16	13	5	-	-	Chesterfield
5	7	8	-	22	11	-	-	-	-	-	-	Colchester U
-	-	-	-	-	-	-	-	-	-	-	23	Crewe Alex
-	-	-	3	5	5	-	-	-	-	-	-	Crystal Palace
-	-	-	-	-	-	-	-	-	-	-	-	Darlington
-	-	-	-	-	-	-	-	-	-	-	-	Derby C
-	-	-	-	-	-	-	-	-	23	11	-	Doncaster R
8	9	17	-	-	-	-	-	-	-	-	-	Exeter C
-	-	-	-	-	-	-	-	-	2	4	-	Fulham
16	4	7	12	14	10	-	-	-	24	20	20	Gillingham
1	-	-	23	18	16	6	9	-	-	-	-	Grimsby T
-	-	-	24	17	9	20	17	3	18	-	-	Halifax T
-	-	-	-	-	-	-	-	-	-	-	22	Hartlepool U
-	23	-	1	12	18	-	-	-	-	-	-	Hereford U
-	-	-	-	24	10	-	-	-	-	-	-	Huddersfield T
20	8	-	-	-	-	-	-	-	-	-	-	Hull C
-	-	-	-	-	-	-	-	-	-	1	18	Leyton Orient
-	24	16	9	-	-	-	-	-	-	-	-	Lincoln C
-	-	-	-	-	-	-	-	-	2	3	-	Luton T
23	18	-	1	11	-	-	-	21	7	6	15	Mansfield T
-	-	-	-	-	-	-	-	-	-	-	-	Middlesbrough
14	-	-	-	3	-	-	-	-	-	-	-	Millwall
-	-	-	-	-	-	-	-	-	-	-	-	Newport Co
-	-	22	-	-	-	-	-	-	-	-	21	Northampton T
-	-	-	-	-	-	2	4	-	-	-	-	Notts Co
-	-	-	-	1	4	11	-	-	-	-	24	Oldham Ath
17	11	18	17	-	-	-	-	-	-	-	-	Oxford U
-	21	4	16	10	7	-	-	-	-	-	-	Peterborough U
15	15	19	-	2	17	8	8	15	17	5	-	Plymouth Arg
-	-	-	24	20	-	-	-	-	-	-	-	Portsmouth
-	-	21	19	12	6	20	6	15	17	-	-	Port Vale
-	-	3	6	8	9	-	-	-	1	-	-	Preston NE
7	-	-	21	-	-	-	-	21	8	14	-	Reading
-	-	-	-	-	24	13	18	16	9	-	-	Rochdale
13	17	20	4	16	-	-	21	5	8	14	11	Rotherham U
-	-	-	-	-	-	-	24	-	-	-	-	Scunthorpe U
12	-	-	-	-	-	-	-	-	-	-	-	Sheffield U
3	14	14	8	20	-	-	-	-	-	-	-	Sheffield W
-	1	11	10	9	-	22	15	12	13	15	17	Shrewsbury T
22	13	-	-	23	18	12	14	-	-	-	-	Southend U
-	-	-	-	-	-	23	-	-	-	22	8	Southport

LEAGUE POSITIONS: DIVISION 2
1992–93 AND DIVISION 3 1968–69 TO 1991–92 (cont.)

	1992-93	1991-92	1990-91	1989-90	1988-89	1987-88	1986-87	1985-86	1984-85	1983-84	1982-83	1981-82	1980-81
Stockport Co	6	5	–	–	–	–	–	–	–	–	–	–	–
Stoke C	1	4	14	–	–	–	–	–	–	–	–	–	–
Sunderland	–	–	–	–	–	1	–	–	–	–	–	–	–
Swansea C	5	19	20	17	12	–	–	24	20	–	–	–	–
Swindon T	–	–	–	–	–	3	–	–	–	–	–	22	17
Torquay U	–	23	–	–	–	–	–	–	–	–	–	–	–
Tranmere R	–	–	5	4	–	–	–	–	–	–	–	–	–
Walsall	5	–	–	24	–	3	8	6	11	6	10	20	20
Watford	–	–	–	–	–	–	–	–	–	–	–	–	–
WBA	4	7	–	–	–	–	–	–	–	–	–	–	–
Wigan Ath	23	15	10	18	17	7	4	4	16	15	18	–	–
Wimbledon	–	–	–	–	–	–	–	–	–	2	–	21	–
Wolv'hampton W	–	–	–	–	1	–	–	23	–	–	–	–	–
Wrexham	–	–	–	–	–	–	–	–	–	–	–	22	–
York City	–	–	–	–	–	–	23	20	7	8	–	–	–

LEAGUE POSITIONS: DIVISION 3
1992–93 AND DIVISION 4 1968–69 TO 1991–92

	1992-93	1991-92	1990-91	1989-90	1988-89	1987-88	1986-87	1985-86	1984-85	1983-84	1982-83	1981-82	1980-81
Aldershot	–	*	23	22	–	–	6	16	13	5	18	16	6
Barnet	3	7	–	–	–	–	–	–	–	–	–	–	–
Barnsley	–	–	–	–	–	–	–	–	–	–	–	–	–
Barrow	–	–	–	–	–	–	–	–	–	–	–	–	–
Blackpool	–	4	5	–	–	–	–	2	6	21	12	–	–
Bolton W	–	–	–	–	–	3	–	–	–	–	–	–	–
Bournemouth	–	–	–	–	–	–	–	–	–	–	–	4	13
Bradford C	–	–	–	–	–	–	–	–	–	–	–	2	14
Bradford PA	–	–	–	–	–	–	–	–	–	–	–	–	–
Brentford	–	–	–	–	–	–	–	–	–	–	–	–	–
Bristol C	–	–	–	–	–	–	–	–	–	4	14	–	–
Burnley	–	1	6	16	16	10	22	14	–	–	–	–	–
Bury	7	–	–	–	–	–	–	–	4	15	5	9	12
Cambridge U	–	–	–	6	8	15	11	22	–	–	–	–	–
Cardiff C	1	9	13	–	–	2	13	–	–	–	–	–	–
Carlisle U	18	22	20	8	12	23	–	–	–	–	–	–	–
Chester C	–	–	–	–	–	–	–	2	16	24	13	–	–
Chesterfield	12	13	18	7	–	–	–	–	–	1	13	–	–

*Record expunged

Team	1979-80	1978-79	1977-78	1976-77	1975-76	1974-75	1973-74	1972-73	1971-72	1970-71	1969-70	1968-69
Stockport Co	-	-	-	-	-	-	-	-	-	-	24	9
Stoke C	-	-	-	-	-	-	-	-	-	-	-	-
Sunderland	-	-	-	-	-	-	-	-	-	-	-	-
Swansea C	-	3	-	-	-	-	-	23	14	11	-	-
Swindon T	10	5	10	11	19	4	-	-	-	-	-	2
Torquay U	-	-	-	-	-	-	-	-	23	10	13	6
Tranmere R	-	23	12	14	-	22	16	10	20	18	16	7
Walsall	-	22	6	15	7	8	15	17	9	20	12	13
Watford	-	2	-	-	23	7	19	-	-	-	-	1
WBA	-	-	-	-	-	-	-	-	-	-	-	-
Wigan Ath	-	-	-	-	-	-	-	-	-	-	-	-
Wimbledon	24	-	-	-	-	-	-	-	-	-	-	-
Wolv'hampton W	-	-	-	-	-	-	-	-	-	-	-	-
Wrexham	-	-	1	5	6	13	4	12	16	9	-	-
York City	-	-	24	-	-	3	18	19	-	-	-	-

Team	1979-80	1978-79	1977-78	1976-77	1975-76	1974-75	1973-74	1972-73	1971-72	1970-71	1969-70	1968-69
Aldershot	10	5	5	17	-	-	-	4	17	13	6	15
Barnet	-	-	-	-	-	-	-	-	-	-	-	-
Barnsley	-	4	7	6	12	15	13	14	-	-	-	-
Barrow	-	-	-	-	-	-	22	24	-	-	-	-
Blackpool	-	-	-	-	-	-	-	-	-	-	-	-
Bolton W	11	18	17	13	6	-	-	-	2	-	-	-
Bournemouth	5	15	-	4	17	10	8	16	-	-	-	4
Bradford C	-	-	-	-	-	-	-	-	-	24	24	-
Bradford PA	-	-	-	-	-	-	-	-	-	-	-	-
Brentford	-	-	4	15	18	8	19	-	3	14	5	11
Bristol C	-	-	-	-	-	-	-	-	-	-	-	-
Burnley	-	-	-	-	-	-	-	-	-	-	-	-
Bury	-	-	-	-	-	4	12	9	-	-	-	-
Cambridge U	-	-	1	13	6	-	3	10	20	-	-	-
Cardiff C	-	-	-	-	-	-	-	-	-	-	-	-
Carlisle U	-	-	-	-	-	-	-	-	-	-	-	-
Chester C	-	-	-	-	-	4	7	15	20	5	11	14
Chesterfield	-	-	-	-	-	-	-	-	-	-	1	20

LEAGUE POSITIONS: DIVISION 3 1992–93 AND DIVISION 4 1968–69 TO 1991–92 (cont.)

	1992-93	1991-92	1990-91	1989-90	1988-89	1987-88	1986-87	1985-86	1984-85	1983-84	1982-83	1981-82	1980-81
Colchester U	10	–	–	24	22	9	5	6	7	8	6	6	–
Crewe Alex	6	6	–	–	3	17	17	12	10	16	23	24	18
Darlington	15	–	1	–	24	13	–	–	3	14	17	13	8
Doncaster R	16	21	11	20	23	–	–	–	–	2	–	–	3
Exeter C	–	–	–	1	13	22	14	21	18	–	–	–	–
Gillingham	21	11	15	14	–	–	–	–	–	–	–	–	–
Grimsby T	–	–	–	2	9	–	–	–	–	–	–	–	–
Halifax T	22	20	22	23	21	18	15	20	21	21	11	19	23
Hartlepool U	–	–	3	19	19	16	18	7	19	23	22	14	9
Hereford U	17	17	17	17	15	19	16	10	5	11	24	10	22
Huddersfield T	–	–	–	–	–	–	–	–	–	–	–	–	–
Hull C	–	–	–	–	–	–	–	–	–	–	2	8	–
Leyton Orient	–	–	–	–	6	8	7	5	–	–	–	–	–
Lincoln C	8	10	14	10	10	–	24	–	–	–	–	–	2
Maidstone U	–	18	19	5	–	–	–	–	–	–	–	–	–
Mansfield T	–	3	–	–	–	–	–	3	14	19	10	20	7
Newport Co	–	–	–	–	–	24	–	–	–	–	–	–	–
Northampton T	20	16	10	–	–	–	1	8	23	18	15	22	10
Notts Co	–	–	–	–	–	–	–	–	–	–	–	–	–
Oldham Ath	–	–	–	–	–	–	–	–	–	–	–	–	–
Peterborough U	–	–	4	9	17	7	10	17	11	7	9	5	5
Portsmouth	–	–	–	–	–	–	–	–	–	–	–	–	–
Port Vale	–	–	–	–	–	–	–	4	12	–	3	7	19
Preston NE	–	–	–	–	–	–	2	23	–	–	–	–	–
Reading	–	–	–	–	–	–	–	–	–	3	–	–	–
Rochdale	11	8	12	12	18	21	21	18	17	22	20	21	15
Rotherham U	–	2	–	–	1	–	–	–	–	–	–	–	–
Scarborough	13	12	9	18	5	12	–	–	–	–	–	–	–
Scunthorpe U	14	5	8	11	4	4	8	15	9	–	4	23	16
Sheffield U	–	–	–	–	–	–	–	–	–	–	–	1	–
Shrewsbury T	9	–	–	–	–	–	–	–	–	–	–	–	–
Southend U	–	–	–	3	–	–	3	9	20	–	–	–	1
Southport	–	–	–	–	–	–	–	–	–	–	–	–	–
Stockport Co	–	–	2	4	20	20	19	11	22	12	16	18	20
Swansea C	–	–	–	–	–	6	12	–	–	–	–	–	–
Swindon T	–	–	–	–	–	–	–	1	8	17	8	–	–
Torquay U	19	–	7	15	14	5	23	24	24	9	12	15	17
Tranmere R	–	–	–	–	2	14	20	19	6	10	19	11	21
Walsall	5	15	16	–	–	–	–	–	–	–	–	–	–
Watford	–	–	–	–	–	–	–	–	–	–	–	–	–
Wigan Ath	–	–	–	–	–	–	–	–	–	–	–	3	11
Wimbledon	–	–	–	–	–	–	–	–	–	–	1	–	4
Wolv'hampton W	–	–	–	–	–	1	4	–	–	–	–	–	–
Workington	–	–	–	–	–	–	–	–	–	–	–	–	–
Wrexham	2	14	24	21	7	11	9	13	15	20	–	–	–
York C	4	19	21	13	11	–	–	–	–	1	7	17	24

1979-80	1978-79	1977-78	1976-77	1975-76	1974-75	1973-74	1972-73	1971-72	1970-71	1969-70	1968-69	
–	–	–	3	–	–	3	22	11	6	10	6	Colchester U
23	24	15	12	16	18	21	21	24	15	15	–	Crewe Alex
22	21	19	11	20	21	20	24	19	12	22	5	Darlington
12	22	12	8	10	17	22	17	12	–	–	1	Doncaster R
–	–	–	2	7	9	10	8	15	9	18	17	Exeter C
–	–	–	–	–	–	2	9	13	–	–	–	Gillingham
–	2	6	–	–	–	–	–	1	19	16	23	Grimsby T
18	23	20	21	–	–	–	–	–	–	–	2	Halifax T
19	13	21	22	14	13	11	20	18	23	23	–	Hartlepool U
21	14	–	–	–	–	–	2	–	–	–	–	Hereford U
1	9	11	9	5	–	–	–	–	–	–	–	Huddersfield T
–	–	–	–	–	–	–	–	–	–	–	–	Hull C
–	–	–	–	–	–	–	–	–	–	–	–	Leyton Orient
7	–	–	1	5	12	10	5	21	8	8	–	Lincoln C
–	–	–	–	–	–	–	–	–	–	–	–	Maidstone U
–	–	–	–	1	17	6	–	–	–	–	–	Mansfield T
3	8	16	19	22	12	9	5	14	22	21	22	Newport C
13	19	10	–	2	16	5	23	21	7	14	–	Northampton T
–	–	–	–	–	–	–	–	1	7	19	–	Notts Co
–	–	–	–	–	–	–	–	3	19	–	–	Oldham Ath
8	–	–	–	–	1	19	8	16	9	18	–	Peterborough U
4	7	–	–	–	–	–	–	–	–	–	–	Portsmouth
20	16	–	–	–	–	–	–	–	4	13	–	Port Vale
–	–	–	–	–	–	–	–	–	–	–	–	Preston NE
–	1	8	–	3	7	6	7	16	–	–	–	Reading
24	20	24	18	15	19	–	–	–	–	–	3	Rochdale
–	–	–	–	3	15	–	–	–	–	–	–	Rotherham U
–	–	–	–	–	–	–	–	–	–	–	–	Scarborough
14	12	14	20	19	24	18	–	4	17	12	16	Scunthorpe U
–	–	–	–	–	2	–	–	–	–	–	–	Sheffield U
–	–	2	10	–	–	–	1	2	18	17	7	Shrewsbury T
–	–	23	23	23	11	–	1	7	8	–	–	Southend U
–	–	–	–	–	–	–	–	–	–	–	–	Southport
16	17	18	14	21	20	24	11	23	11	–	–	Stockport Co
–	–	3	5	11	22	14	–	–	–	3	10	Swansea C
–	–	–	–	–	–	–	–	–	–	–	–	Swindon T
9	11	9	16	9	14	16	18	–	–	–	–	Torquay U
15	–	–	–	4	–	–	–	–	–	–	–	Tranmere R
2	–	–	–	–	–	–	–	–	–	–	–	Walsall
–	–	1	7	8	–	–	–	–	–	–	–	Watford
6	6	–	–	–	–	–	–	–	–	–	–	Wigan Ath
–	3	13	–	–	–	–	–	–	–	–	–	Wimbledon
–	–	–	–	–	–	–	–	–	–	–	–	Wolv'hampton W
–	–	24	24	24	23	23	13	6	10	20	12	Workington
–	–	–	–	–	–	–	–	–	–	2	9	Wrexham
17	10	22	–	–	–	–	–	–	4	13	21	York C

LEAGUE CHAMPIONSHIP HONOURS

FA PREMIER LEAGUE
Maximum points: 126

	First	Pts	Second	Pts	Third	Pts
1992–93	Manchester U	84	Aston Villa	74	Norwich C	72
1993–94	Manchester U	92	Blackburn R	84	Newcastle U	77

DIVISION 1
Maximum points: 138

1992–93	Newcastle U	96	West Ham U	88	Portsmouth††	88
1993–94	Crystal Palace	90	Nottingham F	83	Millwall††	74

DIVISION 2
Maximum points: 138

1992–93	Stoke C	93	Bolton W	90	Port Vale††	89
1993–94	Reading	89	Port Vale	88	Plymouth Arg††	85

DIVISION 3
Maximum points: 126

1992–93	Cardiff C	83	Wrexham	80	Barnet	79
1993–94	Shrewsbury T	79	Chester C	74	Crewe Alex	73

†† *Not promoted after play-offs.*

FOOTBALL LEAGUE

	First	Pts	Second	Pts	Third	Pts
1888–89*a*	Preston NE	40	Aston Villa	29	Wolverhampton W	28
1889–90*a*	Preston NE	33	Everton	31	Blackburn R	27
1890–91*a*	Everton	29	Preston NE	27	Notts Co	26
1891–92*b*	Sunderland	42	Preston NE	37	Bolton W	36

DIVISION 1 to 1991–92
Maximum points: a 44; b 52; c 60; d 68; e 76; f 84; g 126; h 120; k 114.

1892–93*c*	Sunderland	48	Preston NE	37	Everton	36
1893–94*c*	Aston Villa	44	Sunderland	38	Derby Co	36
1894–95*c*	Sunderland	47	Everton	42	Aston Villa	39
1895–96*c*	Aston Villa	45	Derby Co	41	Everton	39
1896–97*c*	Aston Villa	47	Sheffield U*	36	Derby Co	36
1897–98*c*	Sheffield U	42	Sunderland	37	Wolverhampton W*	35
1898–99*d*	Aston Villa	45	Liverpool	43	Burnley	39
1899–1900*d*	Aston Villa	50	Sheffield U	48	Sunderland	41
1900–01*d*	Liverpool	45	Sunderland	43	Notts Co	40
1901–02*d*	Sunderland	44	Everton	41	Newcastle U	37
1902–03*d*	The Wednesday	42	Aston Villa*	41	Sunderland	41
1903–04*d*	The Wednesday	47	Manchester C	44	Everton	43
1904–05*d*	Newcastle U	48	Everton	47	Manchester C	46
1905–06*e*	Liverpool	51	Preston NE	47	The Wednesday	44
1906–07*e*	Newcastle U	51	Bristol C	48	Everton*	45
1907–08*e*	Manchester U	52	Aston Villa*	43	Manchester C	43
1908–09*e*	Newcastle U	53	Everton	46	Sunderland	44

	First	Pts	Second	Pts	Third	Pts
1909–10e	Aston Villa	53	Liverpool	48	Blackburn R*	45
1910–11e	Manchester U	52	Aston Villa	51	Sunderland*	45
1911–12e	Blackburn R	49	Everton	46	Newcastle U	44
1912–13e	Sunderland	54	Aston Villa	50	Sheffield W	49
1913–14e	Blackburn R	51	Aston Villa	44	Middlesbrough*	43
1914–15e	Everton	46	Oldham Ath	45	Blackburn R*	43
1919–20f	WBA	60	Burnley	51	Chelsea	49
1920–21f	Burnley	59	Manchester C	54	Bolton W	52
1921–22f	Liverpool	57	Tottenham H	51	Burnley	49
1922–23f	Liverpool	60	Sunderland	54	Huddersfield T	53
1923–24f	Huddersfield T*	57	Cardiff C	57	Sunderland	53
1924–25f	Huddersfield T	58	WBA	56	Bolton W	55
1925–26f	Huddersfield T	57	Arsenal	52	Sunderland	48
1926–27f	Newcastle U	56	Huddersfield T	51	Sunderland	49
1927–28f	Everton	53	Huddersfield T	51	Leicester C	48
1928–29f	Sheffield W	52	Leicester C	51	Aston Villa	50
1929–30f	Sheffield W	60	Derby Co	50	Manchester C*	47
1930–31f	Arsenal	66	Aston Villa	59	Sheffield W	52
1931–32f	Everton	56	Arsenal	54	Sheffield W	50
1932–33f	Arsenal	58	Aston Villa	54	Sheffield W	51
1933–34f	Arsenal	59	Huddersfield T	56	Tottenham H	49
1934–35f	Arsenal	58	Sunderland	54	Sheffield W	49
1935–36f	Sunderland	56	Derby Co*	48	Huddersfield T	48
1936–37f	Manchester C	57	Charlton Ath	54	Arsenal	52
1937–38f	Arsenal	52	Wolverhampton W	51	Preston NE	49
1938–39f	Everton	59	Wolverhampton W	55	Charlton Ath	50
1946–47f	Liverpool	57	Manchester U*	56	Wolverhampton W	56
1947–48f	Arsenal	59	Manchester U*	52	Burnley	52
1948–49f	Portsmouth	58	Manchester U*	53	Derby Co	53
1949–50f	Portsmouth*	53	Wolverhampton W	53	Sunderland	52
1950–51f	Tottenham H	60	Manchester U	56	Blackpool	50
1951–52f	Manchester U	57	Tottenham H*	53	Arsenal	53
1952–53f	Arsenal*	54	Preston NE	54	Wolverhampton W	51
1953–54f	Wolverhampton W	57	WBA	53	Huddersfield T	51
1954–55f	Chelsea	52	Wolverhampton W*	48	Portsmouth*	48
1955–56f	Manchester U	60	Blackpool*	49	Wolverhampton W	49
1956–57f	Manchester U	64	Tottenham H*	56	Preston NE	56
1957–58f	Wolverhampton W	64	Preston NE	59	Tottenham H	51
1958–59f	Wolverhampton W	61	Manchester U	55	Arsenal*	50
1959–60f	Burnley	55	Wolverhampton W	54	Tottenham H	53
1960–61f	Tottenham H	66	Sheffield W	58	Wolverhampton W	57
1961–62f	Ipswich T	56	Burnley	53	Tottenham H	52
1962–63f	Everton	61	Tottenham H	55	Burnley	54
1963–64f	Liverpool	57	Manchester U	53	Everton	52
1964–65f	Manchester U*	61	Leeds U	61	Chelsea	56
1965–66f	Liverpool	61	Leeds U*	55	Burnley	55
1966–67f	Manchester U	60	Nottingham F*	56	Tottenham H	56
1967–68f	Manchester C	58	Manchester U	56	Liverpool	55
1968–69f	Leeds U	67	Liverpool	61	Everton	57
1969–70f	Everton	66	Leeds U	57	Chelsea	55
1970–71f	Arsenal	65	Leeds U	64	Tottenham H*	52
1971–72f	Derby Co	58	Leeds U*	57	Liverpool*	57
1972–73f	Liverpool	60	Arsenal	57	Leeds U	53
1973–74f	Leeds U	62	Liverpool	57	Derby Co	48
1974–75f	Derby Co	53	Liverpool*	51	Ipswich T	57

* Won or placed on goal average.

	First	Pts	Second	Pts	Third	Pts
1975–76f	Liverpool	60	QPR	59	Manchester U	56
1976–77f	Liverpool	57	Manchester C	56	Ipswich T	52
1977–78f	Nottingham F	64	Liverpool	57	Everton	55
1978–79f	Liverpool	68	Nottingham F	60	WBA	59
1979–80f	Liverpool	60	Manchester U	58	Ipswich T	53
1980–81f	Aston Villa	60	Ipswich T	56	Arsenal	53
1981–82g	Liverpool	87	Ipswich T	83	Manchester U	78
1982–83g	Liverpool	82	Watford	71	Manchester U	70
1983–84g	Liverpool	80	Southampton	77	Nottingham F*	74
1984–85g	Everton	90	Liverpool*	77	Tottenham H	77
1985–86g	Liverpool	88	Everton	86	West Ham U	84
1986–87g	Everton	86	Liverpool	77	Tottenham H	71
1987–88h	Liverpool	90	Manchester U	81	Nottingham F	73
1988–89k	Arsenal*	76	Liverpool	76	Nottingham F	64
1989–90k	Liverpool	79	Aston Villa	70	Tottenham H	63
1990–91k	Arsenal†	83	Liverpool	76	Crystal Palace	69
1991–92g	Leeds U	82	Manchester U	78	Sheffield W	75

No official competition during 1915–19 and 1939–46.

† 2 pts deducted

DIVISION 2 to 1991–92

Maximum points: a 44; b 56; c 60; d 68; e 76; f 84; g 126; h 132; k 138.

	First	Pts	Second	Pts	Third	Pts
1892–93a	Small Heath	36	Sheffield U	35	Darwen	30
1893–94b	Liverpool	50	Small Heath	42	Notts Co	39
1894–95c	Bury	48	Notts Co	39	Newton Heath*	38
1895–96c	Liverpool*	46	Manchester C	46	Grimsby T*	42
1896–97c	Notts Co	42	Newton Heath	39	Grimsby T	38
1897–98c	Burnley	48	Newcastle U	45	Manchester C	39
1898–99d	Manchester C	52	Glossop NE	46	Leicester Fosse	45
1899–1900d	The Wednesday	54	Bolton W	52	Small Heath	46
1900–01d	Grimsby T	49	Small Heath	48	Burnley	44
1901–02d	WBA	55	Middlesbrough	51	Preston NE*	42
1902–03d	Manchester C	54	Small Heath	51	Woolwich A	48
1903–04d	Preston NE	50	Woolwich A	49	Manchester U	48
1904–05d	Liverpool	58	Bolton W	56	Manchester U	53
1905–06e	Bristol C	66	Manchester U	62	Chelsea	53
1906–07e	Nottingham F	60	Chelsea	57	Leicester Fosse	48
1907–08e	Bradford C	54	Leicester Fosse	52	Oldham Ath	50
1908–09e	Bolton W	52	Tottenham H*	51	WBA	51
1909–10e	Manchester C	54	Oldham Ath*	53	Hull C*	53
1910–11e	WBA	53	Bolton W	51	Chelsea	49
1911–12e	Derby Co*	54	Chelsea	54	Burnley	52
1912–13e	Preston NE	53	Burnley	50	Birmingham	46
1913–14e	Notts Co	53	Bradford PA*	49	Woolwich A	49
1914–15e	Derby Co	53	Preston NE	50	Barnsley	47
1919–20f	Tottenham H	70	Huddersfield T	64	Birmingham	56
1920–21f	Birmingham*	58	Cardiff C	58	Bristol C	51
1921–22f	Nottingham F	56	Stoke C*	52	Barnsley	52
1922–23f	Notts Co	53	West Ham U*	51	Leicester C	51
1923–24f	Leeds U	54	Bury*	51	Derby Co	51
1924–25f	Leicester C	59	Manchester U	57	Derby Co	55
1925–26f	Sheffield W	60	Derby Co	57	Chelsea	52
1926–27f	Middlesbrough	62	Portsmouth*	54	Manchester C	54
1927–28f	Manchester C	59	Leeds U	57	Chelsea	54

	First	Pts	Second	Pts	Third	Pts
1928–29f	Middlesbrough	55	Grimsby T	53	Bradford*	48
1929–30f	Blackpool	58	Chelsea	55	Oldham Ath	53
1930–31f	Everton	61	WBA	54	Tottenham H	51
1931–32f	Wolverhampton W	56	Leeds U	54	Stoke C	52
1932–33f	Stoke C	56	Tottenham H	55	Fulham	50
1933–34f	Grimsby T	59	Preston NE	52	Bolton W*	51
1934–35f	Brentford	61	Bolton W*	56	West Ham U	56
1935–36f	Manchester U	56	Charlton Ath	55	Sheffield U*	52
1936–37f	Leicester C	56	Blackpool	55	Bury	52
1937–38f	Aston Villa	57	Manchester U*	53	Sheffield U	53
1938–39f	Blackburn R	55	Sheffield U	54	Sheffield W	53
1946–47f	Manchester C	62	Burnley	58	Birmingham C	55
1947–48f	Birmingham C	59	Newcastle U	56	Southampton	52
1948–49f	Fulham	57	WBA	56	Southampton	55
1949–50f	Tottenham H	61	Sheffield W*	52	Sheffield U*	52
1950–51f	Preston NE	57	Manchester C	52	Cardiff C	50
1951–52f	Sheffield W	53	Cardiff C*	51	Birmingham C	51
1952–53f	Sheffield U	60	Huddersfield T	58	Luton T	52
1953–54f	Leicester C*	56	Everton	56	Blackburn R	55
1954–55f	Birmingham C*	54	Luton T*	54	Rotherham U	54
1955–56f	Sheffield W	55	Leeds U	52	Liverpool*	48
1956–57f	Leicester C	61	Nottingham F	54	Liverpool	53
1957–58f	West Ham U	57	Blackburn R	56	Charlton Ath	55
1958–59f	Sheffield W	62	Fulham	60	Sheffield U*	53
1959–60f	Aston Villa	59	Cardiff C	58	Liverpool*	50
1960–61f	Ipswich T	59	Sheffield U	58	Liverpool	52
1961–62f	Liverpool	62	Leyton O	54	Sunderland	53
1962–63f	Stoke C	53	Chelsea*	52	Sunderland	52
1963–64f	Leeds U	63	Sunderland	61	Preston NE	56
1964–65f	Newcastle U	57	Northampton T	56	Bolton W	50
1965–66f	Manchester C	59	Southampton	54	Coventry C	53
1966–67f	Coventry C	59	Wolverhampton W	58	Carlisle U	52
1967–68f	Ipswich T	59	QPR*	58	Blackpool	58
1968–69f	Derby Co	63	Crystal Palace	56	Charlton Ath	50
1969–70f	Huddersfield T	60	Blackpool	53	Leicester C	51
1970–71f	Leicester C	59	Sheffield U	56	Cardiff C*	53
1971–72f	Norwich C	57	Birmingham C	56	Millwall	55
1972–73f	Burnley	62	QPR	61	Aston Villa	50
1973–74f	Middlesbrough	65	Luton T	50	Carlisle U	49
1974–75f	Manchester U	61	Aston Villa	58	Norwich C	53
1975–76f	Sunderland	56	Bristol C*	53	WBA	53
1976–77f	Wolverhampton W	57	Chelsea	55	Nottingham F	52
1977–78f	Bolton W	58	Southampton	57	Tottenham H*	56
1978–79f	Crystal Palace	57	Brighton*	56	Stoke C	56
1979–80f	Leicester C	55	Sunderland	54	Birmingham C*	53
1980–81f	West Ham U	66	Notts Co	53	Swansea C*	50
1981–82g	Luton T	88	Watford	80	Norwich C	71
1982–83g	QPR	85	Wolverhampton W	75	Leicester C	70
1983–84g	Chelsea*	88	Sheffield W	88	Newcastle U	80
1984–85g	Oxford U	84	Birmingham C	82	Manchester C	74
1985–86g	Norwich C	84	Charlton Ath	77	Wimbledon	76
1986–87g	Derby Co	84	Portsmouth	78	Oldham Ath††	75
1987–88h	Millwall	82	Aston Villa*	78	Middlesbrough	78
1988–89k	Chelsea	99	Manchester C	82	Crystal Palace	81

* Won or placed on goal average/goal difference.

†† Not promoted after play-offs.

97

	First	*Pts*	*Second*	*Pts*	*Third*	*Pts*
1989–90k	Leeds U*	85	Sheffield U	85	Newcastle U††	80
1990–91l	Oldham Ath	88	West Ham U	87	Sheffield W	82
1991–92k	Ipswich T	84	Middlesbrough	80	Derby Co	78

No competition during 1915–19 and 1939–46.

DIVISION 3 to 1991–92

Maximum points: 92; 138 from 1981–82.

	First	*Pts*	*Second*	*Pts*	*Third*	*Pts*
1958–59	Plymouth Arg	62	Hull C	61	Brentford*	57
1959–60	Southampton	61	Norwich C	59	Shrewsbury T*	52
1960–61	Bury	68	Walsall	62	QPR	60
1961–62	Portsmouth	65	Grimsby T	62	Bournemouth*	59
1962–63	Northampton T	62	Swindon T	58	Port Vale	54
1963–64	Coventry C*	60	Crystal Palace	60	Watford	58
1964–65	Carlisle U	60	Bristol C*	59	Mansfield T	57
1965–66	Hull C	69	Millwall	65	QPR	57
1966–67	QPR	67	Middlesbrough	55	Watford	54
1967–68	Oxford U	57	Bury	56	Shrewsbury T	55
1968–69	Watford*	64	Swindon T	64	Luton T	61
1969–70	Orient	62	Luton T	60	Bristol R	56
1970–71	Preston NE	61	Fulham	60	Halifax T	56
1971–72	Aston Villa	70	Brighton	65	Bournemouth*	62
1972–73	Bolton W	61	Notts Co	57	Blackburn R	55
1973–74	Oldham Ath	62	Bristol R*	61	York C	61
1974–75	Blackburn R	60	Plymouth Arg	59	Charlton Ath	55
1975–76	Hereford U	63	Cardiff C	57	Millwall	56
1976–77	Mansfield T	64	Brighton & HA	61	Crystal Palace*	59
1977–78	Wrexham	61	Cambridge U	58	Preston NE*	56
1978–79	Shrewsbury T	61	Watford*	60	Swansea C	60
1979–80	Grimsby T	62	Blackburn R	59	Sheffield W	58
1980–81	Rotherham U	61	Barnsley*	59	Charlton Ath	59
1981–82	Burnley*	80	Carlisle U	80	Fulham	78
1982–83	Portsmouth	91	Cardiff C	86	Huddersfield T	82
1983–84	Oxford U	95	Wimbledon	87	Sheffield U*	83
1984–85	Bradford C	94	Millwall	90	Hull C	87
1985–86	Reading	94	Plymouth Arg	87	Derby Co	84
1986–87	Bournemouth	97	Middlesbrough	94	Swindon T	87
1987–88	Sunderland	93	Brighton & HA	84	Walsall	82
1988–89	Wolverhampton W	92	Sheffield U	84	Port Vale	84
1989–90	Bristol R	93	Bristol C	91	Notts Co	87
1990–91	Cambridge U	86	Southend U	85	Grimsby T*	83
1991–92	Brentford	82	Birmingham C	81	Huddersfield T	78

* Won or placed on goal average/goal difference.

DIVISION 4 (1958–1992)

Maximum points: 92; 138 from 1981-82.

	First	*Pts*	*Second*	*Pts*	*Third*	*Pts*
1958–59	Port Vale	64	Coventry C*	60	York C	60
1959–60	Walsall	65	Notts Co*	60	Torquay U	60
1960–61	Peterborough U	66	Crystal Palace	64	Northampton T*	60
1961–62†	Millwalh	56	Colchester U	55	Wrexham	53
1962–63	Brentford	62	Oldham Ath*	59	Crewe Alex	59
1963–64	Gillingham*	60	Carlisle U	60	Workington T	59
1964–65	Brighton	63	Millwall*	62	York C	62

98

	First	Pts	Second	Pts	Third	Pts
1965–66	Doncaster R*	59	Darlington	59	Torquay U	58
1966–67	Stockport Co	64	Southport*	59	Barrow	59
1967–68	Luton T	66	Barnsley	61	Hartlepools U	60
1968–69	Doncaster R	59	Halifax T	57	Rochdale*	56
1969–70	Chesterfield	64	Wrexham	61	Swansea C	60
1970–71	Notts Co	69	Bournemouth	60	Oldham Ath	59
1971–72	Grimsby T	63	Southend U	60	Brentford	59
1972–73	Southport	62	Hereford U	58	Cambridge U	57
1973–74	Peterborough U	65	Gillingham	62	Colchester U	60
1974–75	Mansfield T	68	Shrewsbury T	62	Rotherham U	59
1975–76	Lincoln C	74	Northampton T	68	Reading	60
1976–77	Cambridge U	65	Exeter C	62	Colchester U*	59
1977–78	Watford	71	Southend U	60	Swansea C*	56
1978–79	Reading	65	Grimsby T*	61	Wimbledon*	61
1979–80	Huddersfield T	66	Walsall	64	Newport Co	61
1980–81	Southend U	67	Lincoln C	65	Doncaster R	56
1981–82	Sheffield U	96	Bradford C*	91	Wigan Ath	91
1982–83	Wimbledon	98	Hull C	90	Port Vale	88
1983–84	York C	101	Doncaster R	85	Reading*	82
1984–85	Chesterfield	91	Blackpool	86	Darlington	85
1985–86	Swindon T	102	Chester C	84	Mansfield T	81
1986–87	Northampton T	99	Preston NE	90	Southend U	80
1987–88	Wolverhampton W	90	Cardiff C	85	Bolton W	78
1988–89	Rotherham U	82	Tranmere R	80	Crewe Alex	78
1989–90	Exeter C	89	Grimsby T	79	Southend U	75
1990–91	Darlington	83	Stockport Co†	82	Hartlepool U	82
1991–92†*	Burnley	80	Rotherham U*	77	Mansfield T	77

†*Maximum points:* 88 owing to Accrington Stanley's resignation.   ††*Not promoted after play-offs.*
†* *Maximum points:* 126 owing to Aldershot being expelled.

DIVISION 3—SOUTH (1920–1958)

Maximum points: a 84; b 92.

	First	Pts	Second	Pts	Third	Pts
1920–21a	Crystal Palace	59	Southampton	54	QPR	53
1921–22a	Southampton*	61	Plymouth Arg	61	Portsmouth	53
1922–23a	Bristol C	59	Plymouth Arg*	53	Swansea C	53
1923–24a	Portsmouth	59	Plymouth Arg	55	Millwall	54
1924–25a	Swansea T	57	Plymouth Arg	56	Bristol C	53
1925–26a	Reading	57	Plymouth Arg	56	Millwall	53
1926–27a	Bristol C	62	Plymouth Arg	60	Millwall	56
1927–28a	Millwall	65	Northampton T	55	Plymouth Arg	53
1928–29a	Charlton Ath*	54	Crystal Palace	54	Northampton T*	52
1929–30a	Plymouth Arg	68	Brentford	61	QPR	51
1930–31a	Notts Co	59	Crystal Palace	51	Brentford	50
1931–32a	Fulham	57	Reading	55	Southend U	53
1932–33a	Brentford	62	Exeter C	58	Norwich C	57
1933–34a	Norwich C	61	Coventry C*	54	Reading*	54
1934–35a	Charlton Ath	61	Reading	53	Coventry C	51
1935–36a	Coventry C	57	Luton T	56	Reading	54
1936–37a	Luton T	58	Notts Co	56	Brighton	53
1937–38a	Millwall	56	Bristol C	55	QPR*	53
1938–39a	Newport Co	55	Crystal Palace	52	Brighton	49
1939–46	Competition cancelled owing to war.					
1946–47a	Cardiff C	66	QPR	57	Bristol C	51
1947–48a	QPR	61	Bournemouth	57	Walsall	51

	First	Pts	Second	Pts	Third	Pts
1948–49a	Swansea T	62	Reading	55	Bournemouth	52
1949–50a	Notts Co	58	Northampton T*	51	Southend U	51
1950–51b	Nottingham F	70	Norwich C	64	Reading*	57
1951–52b	Plymouth Arg	66	Reading*	61	Norwich C	61
1952–53b	Bristol R	64	Millwall*	62	Northampton T	62
1953–54b	Ipswich T	64	Brighton	61	Bristol C	56
1954–55b	Bristol C	70	Leyton O	61	Southampton	59
1955–56b	Leyton O	66	Brighton	65	Ipswich T	64
1956–57b	Ipswich T*	59	Torquay U	59	Colchester U	58
1957–58b	Brighton	60	Brentford*	58	Plymouth Arg	58

* Won or placed on goal average.

DIVISION 3—NORTH (1921–1958)

Maximum points: a 76; b 84; c 80; d 92.

	First	Pts	Second	Pts	Third	Pts
1921–22a	Stockport Co	56	Darlington*	50	Grimsby T	50
1922–23a	Nelson	51	Bradford PA	47	Walsall	46
1923–24b	Wolverhampton W	63	Rochdale	62	Chesterfield	54
1924–25b	Darlington	58	Nelson*	53	New Brighton	53
1925–26b	Grimsby T	61	Bradford PA	60	Rochdale	59
1926–27b	Stoke C	63	Rochdale	58	Bradford PA	55
1927–28b	Bradford PA	63	Lincoln C	55	Stockport Co	54
1928–29g	Bradford C	63	Stockport Co	62	Wrexham	52
1929–30b	Port Vale	67	Stockport Co	63	Darlington*	50
1930–31b	Chesterfield	58	Lincoln C	57	Wrexham*	54
1931–32c	Lincoln C*	57	Gateshead	57	Chester	50
1932–33b	Hull C	59	Wrexham	57	Stockport Co	54
1933–34b	Barnsley	62	Chesterfield	61	Stockport Co	59
1934–35b	Doncaster R	57	Halifax T	55	Chester	54
1935–36b	Chesterfield	60	Chester*	55	Tranmere R	55
1936–37b	Stockport Co	60	Lincoln C	57	Chester	53
1937–38b	Tranmere R	56	Doncaster R	54	Hull C	53
1938–39b	Barnsley	67	Doncaster R	56	Bradford C	52
1939–46	Competition cancelled owing to war.					
1946–47b	Doncaster R	72	Rotherham U	60	Chester	56
1947–48b	Lincoln C	60	Rotherham U	59	Wrexham	50
1948–49b	Hull C	65	Rotherham U	62	Doncaster R	50
1949–50b	Doncaster R	55	Gateshead	53	Rochdale*	51
1950–51d	Rotherham U	71	Mansfield T	64	Carlisle U	62
1951–52d	Lincoln C	69	Grimsby T	66	Stockport Co	59
1952–53d	Oldham Ath	59	Port Vale	58	Wrexham	56
1953–54d	Port Vale	69	Barnsley	58	Scunthorpe U	57
1954–55d	Barnsley	65	Accrington S	61	Scunthorpe U*	58
1955–56d	Grimsby T	68	Derby Co	63	Accrington S	58
1956–57d	Derby Co	63	Hartlepool U	59	Accrington S*	58
1957–58d	Scunthorpe U	66	Accrington S	59	Bradford C	57

* Won or placed on goal average

PROMOTED AFTER PLAY-OFFS
(Not accounted for in previous section)

1986–87	Aldershot to Division 3.
1987–88	Swansea C to Division 3.
1988–89	Leyton O to Division 3.
1989–90	Cambridge U to Division 3; Notts Co to Division 2; Sunderland to Division 1.

1990–91 Notts Co to Division 1; Tranmere R to Division 2; Torquay U to Division 3.
1991–92 Blackburn R to Premier League; Peterborough U to Division 1.
1992–93 Swindon T to Premier League; WBA to Division 1; York C to Division 2.
1993–94 Leicester C to Premier League; Burnley to Division 1; Wycombe W to Division 2

RELEGATED CLUBS

FA PREMIER LEAGUE TO DIVISION 1

1992–93 Crystal Palace, Middlesbrough, Nottingham Forest
1993–94 Sheffield U, Oldham Ath, Swindon T

DIVISION 1 TO DIVISION 2

1898–99 Bolton W and Sheffield W
1899–1900 Burnley and Glossop
1900–01 Preston NE and WBA
1901–02 Small Heath and Manchester C
1902–03 Grimsby T and Bolton W
1903–04 Liverpool and WBA
1904–05 League extended. Bury and Notts Co, two bottom clubs in First Division, re-elected.
1905–06 Nottingham F and Wolverhampton W
1906–07 Derby Co and Stoke C
1907–08 Bolton W and Birmingham C
1908–09 Manchester C and Leicester Fosse
1909–10 Bolton W and Chelsea
1910–11 Bristol C and Nottingham F
1911–12 Preston NE and Bury
1912–13 Notts Co and Woolwich Arsenal
1913–14 Preston NE and Derby Co
1914–15 Tottenham H and Chelsea*
1919–20 Notts Co and Sheffield W
1920–21 Derby Co and Bradford PA
1921–22 Bradford C and Manchester U
1922–23 Stoke C and Oldham Ath
1923–24 Chelsea and Middlesbrough
1924–25 Preston NE and Nottingham F
1925–26 Manchester C and Notts Co
1926–27 Leeds U and WBA
1927–28 Tottenham H and Middlesbrough
1928–29 Bury and Cardiff C
1929–30 Burnley and Everton
1930–31 Leeds U and Manchester U
1931–32 Grimsby T and West Ham U
1932–33 Bolton W and Blackpool
1933–34 Newcastle U and Sheffield U

1934–35 Leicester C and Tottenham H
1935–36 Aston Villa and Blackburn R
1936–37 Manchester U and Sheffield W
1937–38 Manchester C and WBA
1938–39 Birmingham C and Leicester C
1946–47 Brentford and Leeds U
1947–48 Blackburn R and Grimsby T
1948–49 Preston NE and Sheffield U
1949–50 Manchester C and Birmingham C
1950–51 Sheffield W and Everton
1951–52 Huddersfield and Fulham
1952–53 Stoke C and Derby Co
1953–54 Middlesbrough and Liverpool
1954–55 Leicester C and Sheffield W
1955–56 Huddersfield and Sheffield U
1956–57 Charlton Ath and Cardiff C
1957–58 Sheffield W and Sunderland
1958–59 Portsmouth and Aston Villa
1959–60 Luton T and Leeds U
1960–61 Preston NE and Newcastle U
1961–62 Chelsea and Cardiff C
1962–63 Majchester C and Leyton O
1963–64 Bolton W and Ipswich T
1964–65 Wolverhampton W and Birmingham C
1965–66 Northampton T and Blackburn R
1966–67 Aston Villa and Blackpool
1967–68 Fulham and Sheffield U
1968–69 Leicester C and QPR
1969–70 Sunderland and Sheffield W
1970–71 Burnley and Blackpool
1971–72 Huddersfield T and Nottingham F
1972–73 Crystal Palace and WBA
1973–74 Southampton, Manchester U, Norwich C

1974–75 Luton T, Chelsea, Carlisle U
1975–76 Wolverhampton W, Burnley, Sheffield U
1976–77 Sunderland, Stoke C, Tottenham H
1977–78 West Ham U, Newcastle U, Leicester C
1978–79 QPR, Birmingham C, Chelsea
1979–80 Bristol C, Derby Co, Bolton W
1980–81 Norwich C, Leicester C, Crystal Palace
1981–82 Leeds U, Wolverhampton W, Middlesbrough
1982–83 Manchester C, Swansea C, Brighton & HA
1983–84 Birmingham C, Notts Co, Wolverhampton W

1984–85 Norwich C, Sunderland, Stoke C
1985–86 Ipswich T, Birmingham C, WBA
1986–87 Leicester C, Manchester C, Aston Villa
1987–88 Chelsea**, Portsmouth, Watford, Oxford U
1988–89 Middlesbrough, West Ham U, Newcastle U
1989–90 Sheffield W, Charlton Ath, Millwall
1990–91 Sunderland and Derby Co
1991–92 Luton T, Notts Co, West Ham U
1992–93 Brentford, Cambridge U, Bristol R
1993–94 Birmingham C, Oxford U, Peterborough U

**Relegated after play-offs.*
Subsequently re-elected to Division 1 when League was extended after the War.

DIVISION 2 TO DIVISION 3

1920–21 Stockport Co
1921–22 Bradford and Bristol C
1922–23 Rotherham C and Wolverhampton W
1923–24 Nelson and Bristol C
1924–25 Crystal Palace and Coventry C
1925–26 Stoke C and Stockport Co
1926–27 Darlington and Bradford C
1927–28 Fulham and South Shields
1928–29 Port Vale and Clapton O
1929–30 Hull C and Notts Co
1930–31 Reading and Cardiff C
1931–32 Barnsley and Bristol C
1932–33 Chesterfield and Charlton Ath
1933–34 Millwall and Lincoln C
1934–35 Oldham Ath and Notts Co
1935–36 Port Vale and Hull C
1936–37 Doncaster R and Bradford C
1937–38 Barnsley and Stockport Co
1938–39 Norwich C and Tranmere R
1946–47 Swansea T and Newport Co
1947–48 Doncaster R and Millwall
1948–49 Nottingham F and Lincoln C
1949–50 Plymouth Arg and Bradford
1950–51 Grimsby T and Chesterfield
1951–52 Coventry C and QPR
1952–53 Southampton and Barnsley
1953–54 Brentford and Oldham Ath
1954–55 Ipswich T and Derby Co
1955–56 Plymouth Arg and Hull C
1956–57 Port Vale and Bury

1957–58 Doncaster R and Notts Co
1958–59 Barnsley and Grimsby T
1959–60 Bristol C and Hull C
1960–61 Lincoln C and Portsmouth
1961–62 Brighton & HA and Bristol R
1962–63 Walsall and Luton T
1963–64 Grimsby T and Scunthorpe U
1964–65 Swindon T and Swansea T
1965–66 Middlesbrough and Leyton O
1966–67 Northampton T and Bury
1967–68 Plymouth Arg and Rotherham U
1968–69 Fulham and Bury
1969–70 Preston NE and Aston Villa
1970–71 Blackburn R and Bolton W
1971–72 Charlton Ath and Watford
1972–73 Huddersfield T and Brighton & HA
1973–74 Crystal Palace, Preston NE, Swindon T
1974–75 Millwall, Cardiff C, Sheffield W
1975–76 Oxford U, York C, Portsmouth
1976–77 Carlisle U, Plymouth Arg, Hereford U
1977–78 Blackpool, Mansfield T, Hull C
1978–79 Sheffield U, Millwall, Blackburn R
1979–80 Fulham, Burnley, Charlton Ath
1980–81 Preston NE, Bristol C, Bristol R
1981–82 Cardiff C, Wrexham, Orient

1982–83 Rotherham U, Burnley, Bolton W

1983–84 Derby Co, Swansea C, Cambridge U

1984–85 Notts Co, Cardiff C, Wolverhampton W

1985–86 Carlisle U, Middlesbrough, Fulham

1986–87 Sunderland**, Grimsby T, Brighton & HA

1987–88 Huddersfield T, Reading, Sheffield U**

1988–89 Shrewsbury T, Birmingham C, Walsall

1989–90 Bournemouth, Bradford, Stoke C

1990–91 WBA and Hull C

1991–92 Plymouth Arg, Brighton & HA, Port Vale

1992–93 Preston NE, Mansfield T, Wigan Ath, Chester C

1993–94 Fulham, Exeter C, Hartlepool U, Barnet

DIVISION 3 TO DIVISION 4

1958–59 Rochdale, Notts Co, Doncaster R and Stockport

1959–60 Accrington S, Wrexham, Mansfield T and York C

1960–61 Chesterfield, Colchester U, Bradford C and Tranmere R

1961–62 Newport Co, Brentford, Lincoln C and Torquay U

1962–63 Bradford PA, Brighton, Carlisle U and Halifax T

1963–64 Millwall, Crewe Alex, Wrexham and Notts Co

1964–65 Luton T, Port Vale, Colchester U and Barnsley

1965–66 Southend U, Exeter C, Brentford and York C

1966–67 Doncaster R, Workington, Darlington and Swansea T

1967–68 Scunthorpe U, Colchester U, Grimsby T and Peterborough U (demoted)

1968–69 Oldham Ath, Crewe Alex, Hartlepool and Northampton

1969–70 Bournemouth, Southport, Barrow, Stockport Co

1970–71 Reading, Bury, Doncaster R, Gillingham

1971–72 Mansfield T, Barnsley, Torquay U, Bradford C

1972–73 Rotherham U, Brentford, Swansea C, Scunthorpe U

1973–74 Cambridge U, Shrewsbury T, Southport, Rochdale

1974–75 AFC Bournemouth, Tranmere R, Watford, Huddersfield T

1975–76 Aldershot, Colchester U, Southend U, Halifax T

1976–77 Reading, Northampton T, Grimsby T, York C

1977–78 Port Vale, Bradford C, Hereford U, Portsmouth

1978–79 Peterborough U, Walsall, Tranmere R, Lincoln C

1979–80 Bury, Southend U, Mansfield T, Wimbledon

1980–81 Sheffield U, Colchester U, Blackpool, Hull C

1981–82 Wimbledon, Swindon T, Bristol C, Chester

1982–83 Reading, Wrexham, Doncaster R, Chesterfield

1983–84 Scunthorpe U, Southend U, Port Vale, Exeter C

1984–85 Burnley, Orient, Preston NE, Cambridge U

1985–86 Lincoln C, Cardiff C, Wolverhampton W, Swansea C

11986–87 Bolton W**, Carlisle U, Darlington, Newport Co

1987–88 Doncaster R, York C, Grimsby T, Rotherham U**

1988–89 Southend U, Chesterfield, Gillingham, Aldershot

1989–90 Cardiff C, Northampton T, Blackpool, Walsall

1990–91 Crewe Alex, Rotherham U, Mansfield T

1991–92 Bury, Shrewsbury T, Torquay U, Darlington

** *Relegated after play-offs.*

103

LEAGUE TITLE WINS

FA PREMIER LEAGUE – Manchester U 2.

LEAGUE DIVISION 1 – Liverpool 18, Arsenal 10, Everton 9, Manchester U 7, Aston Villa 7, Sunderland 6, Newcastle U 5, Sheffield W 4, Huddersfield T 3, Leeds U 3, Wolverhampton W 3, Blackburn R 2, Portsmouth 2, Preston NE 2, Burnley 2, Manchester C 2, Tottenham H 2, Derby Co 2, Chelsea 1, Sheffield U 1, WBA 1, Ipswich T 1, Nottingham F 1, Crystal Palace 1.

LEAGUE DIVISION 2 – Leicester C 6, Manchester C 6, Sheffield W 5, Birmingham C (one as Small Heath) 4, Derby Co 4, Liverpool 4, Ipswich T 3, Leeds U 3, Notts Co 3, Preston NE 3, Middlesbrough 3, Stoke C 3, Grimsby T 2, Norwich C 2, Nottingham F 2, Tottenham H 2, WBA 2, Aston Villa 2, Burnley 2, Chelsea 2, Manchester U 2, West Ham U 2, Wolverhampton W 2, Bolton W 2, Huddersfield T, Bristol C, Brentford, Bury, Bradford C, Everton, Fulham, Sheffield U, Newcastle U, Coventry C, Blackpool, Blackburn R, Sunderland, Crystal Palace, Luton T, QPR, Oxford U, Millwall, Oldham Ath, Reading 1 each.

LEAGUE DIVISION 3 – Portsmouth 2, Oxford U 2, Shrewsbury T 2, Plymouth Arg, Southampton, Bury, Northampton T, Coventry C, Carlisle U, Hull C, QPR, Watford, Leyton O, Preston NE, Bolton W, Oldham Ath, Blackburn R, Hereford U, Mansfield T, Wrexham, Grimsby T, Rotherham U, Burnley, Bradford C, Bournemouth, Reading, Sunderland, Wolverhampton W, Bristol R, Cambridge U, Brentford, Cardiff C 1 each.

LEAGUE DIVISION 4 – Chesterfield 2, Doncaster R 2, Peterborough U 2, Port Vale, Walsall, Millwall, Brentford, Gillingham, Brighton, Stockport Co, Luton T, Notts Co, Grimsby T, Southport, Mansfield T, Lincoln C, Cambridge U, Watford, Reading, Huddersfield T, Southend U, Sheffield U, Wimbledon, York C, Swindon T, Northampton T, Wolverhampton W, Rotherham U, Exeter C, Darlington, Burnley 1 each.

To 1957-58

DIVISION 3 (South) – Bristol C 3; Charlton Ath, Ipswich T, Millwall, Notts Co, Plymouth Arg, Swansea T 2 each; Brentford, Bristol R, Cardiff C, Crystal Palace, Coventry C, Fulham, Leyton O, Luton T, Newport Co, Nottingham F, Norwich C, Portsmouth, QPR, Reading, Southampton, Brighton 1 each.

DIVISION 3 (North) – Barnsley, Doncaster R, Lincoln C 3 each; Chesterfield, Grimsby T, Hull C, Port Vale, Stockport Co 2 each; Bradford PA, Bradford C, Darlington, Derby Co, Nelson, Oldham Ath, Rotherham U, Stoke C, Tranmere R, Wolverhampton W, Scunthorpe U 1 each.

TRANSFERS 1993–94

June 1993

24 Banks, Steven	West Ham United	Gillingham
1 Bradley, Russell	Halifax Town	Scunthorpe United
9 Burgess, David J.	Blackpool	Carlisle United
8 Charlton, Simon T.	Huddersfield Town	Southampton
7 Clough, Nigel H.	Nottingham Forest	Liverpool
21 Cooper, Colin T.	Millwall	Nottingham Forest
15 Dennis, John A.	Cambridge United	Chesterfield
24 Hannigan, Al James	Marlow	Enfield
18 Hunt, Andrew	Newcastle United	West Bromwich Albion
3 Jones, Gary	Boston United	Southend United
15 Keen, Mark A.	Enfield	Chelmsford City
24 Kelly, David T.	Newcastle United	Wolverhampton Wanderers
17 Luscombe, Lee	Brentford	Millwall
18 McGoldrick, Eddie J.P.	Crystal Palace	Arsenal
24 Pearce, Andrew J.	Coventry City	Sheffield Wednesday
24 Prior, Spencer	Southend United	Norwich City
4 Prudhoe, Mark	Darlington	Stoke City
2 Richardson, Stephen J.	Wimborne Town	Poole Town
28 Russell, Kevin J.	Stoke City	Burnley
24 Thomas, Geoffrey R.	Crystal Palace	Wolverhampton Wanderers
30 Webster, Simon	Charlton Athletic	West Ham United

July 1993

29 Baird, Ian	Heart of Midlothian	Bristol City
16 Beardsley, Peter A.	Everton	Newcastle United
30 Blackwood, Bevon A.	Winsford United	Witton Albion
23 Blissett, Gary	Brentford	Wimbledon
28 Bowling, Ian	Lincoln City	Bradford City
9 Bressington, Graham	Lincoln City	Southend United
19 Bye, Andrew G.	Farnborough Town	Yeovil Town
16 Carey, Brian P.	Manchester United	Leicester City
16 Carmichael, Matthew	Lincoln City	Scunthorpe United
21 Carr, Darren	Crewe Alexandra	Chesterfield
9 Carruthers, Martin G.	Aston Villa	Stoke City
29 Charles, Gary A.	Nottingham Forest	Derby County
8 Clarke, Michael D.	Sutton Coldfield Town	Solihull Borough
8 Colgate, Mark S.	Woodford Town	Harlow Town
28 Collier, Darren	Blackburn Rovers	Darlington
5 Collymore, Stanley V.	Southend United	Nottingham Forest
2 Cormack, Lee D.	Waterlooville	Newport (IOW)
1 Coyle, Owen C.	Airdrieonians	Bolton Wanderers
16 Crawshaw, Gary	Staines Town	Hendon
20 Curran, Christopher P.	Scarborough	Carlisle United
26 Davison, Aidan J.	Millwall	Bolton Wanderers
14 Deane, Brian C.	Sheffield United	Leeds United
1 Durrin, John	Oxford United	Portsmouth
27 Eyres, David	Blackpool	Burnley
29 Ferguson, Derek	Heart of Midlothian	Sunderland
22 Fletcher, Gary I.	Salisbury City	Wimborne Town
30 Francis, Stephen S.	Reading	Huddersfield Town
13 Gallimore, Anthony	Stoke City	Carlisle United
8 Gentle, Justin	Boreham Wood	Luton Town
19 Gray, Philip	Luton Town	Sunderland
23 Griffiths, Bryan K.	Wigan Athletic	Blackpool
19 Harford, Michael G.	Sunderland	Coventry City
16 Hava, Vassos	Woodford Town	Harlow Town
16 Hill, David M.	Scunthorpe United	Lincoln City
14 Hodge, John	Exeter City	Swansea City
15 Hoddle, Glenn	Swindon Town	Chelsea
4 Hulme, Kevin	Bury	Doncaster Rovers
9 Jeffrey, Andrew S.	Cambridge City	Cambridge United
7 Joyce, Warren G.	Plymouth Argyle	Burnley
21 Keane, Roy M.	Nottingham Forest	Manchester United
29 Keeley, John H.	Oldham Athletic	Colchester United

7	Keen, Kevin I.	West Ham United	Wolverhampton Wanderers
15	Kerr, Dylan	Leeds United	Reading
27	Kimble, Alan F.	Cambridge United	Wimbledon
23	Legg, Andrew	Swansea City	Notts County
27	Lyttle, Desmond	Swansea City	Nottingham Forest
12	Mardenborough, Stephen A.	Darlington	Lincoln City
28	McMinn, Kevin C.	Derby County	Birmingham City
14	McSwegan, Gary	Glasgow Rangers	Notts County
5	Mooney, Thomas J.	Scarborough	Southend United
19	Morgan, Stephen A.	Plymouth Argyle	Coventry City
2	Myers, Christopher	Torquay United	Dundee United
20	O'Hanlon, Kelham G.	Carlisle United	Preston North End
26	Onuorah, Chike	Bournemouth	Wimborne Town
8	O'Regan, Kieran	Huddersfield Town	West Bromwich Albion
9	Otto, Ricky	Leyton Orient	Southend United
21	Patterson, Mark	Derby County	Plymouth Argyle
21	Phillips, James N.	Middlesbrough	Bolton Wanderers
9	Poole, Gary J.	Plymouth Argyle	Southend United
2	Raynor, Paul J.	Cambridge United	Preston North End
22	Redman, Ian F.	Curzon Ashton	Ashton United
14	Robinson, Spencer L.	Bury	Bristol City
23	Rodgerson, Ian	Birmingham City	Sunderland
6	Rowbotham, Darren	Birmingham City	Crewe Alexandra
22	Ruddock, Neil	Tottenham Hotspur	Liverpool
14	Shakespeare, Craig R.	West Bromwich Albion	Grimsby Town
5	Speedie, David R.	Southampton	Leicester City
30	Sterling, Worrel R.	Peterborough United	Bristol Rovers
23	Stimson, Mark	Newcastle United	Portsmouth
26	Tankard, Allen J.	Wigan Athletic	Port Vale
19	Taverner, Neil. J.	Woodford Town	Harlow Town
19	Thomas, Karl	Witton Albion	Runcorn
26	Townsend, Andrew D.	Chelsea	Aston Villa
16	Ward, Gavin J.	Cardiff City	Leicester City
1	Webster, Simon	Charlton Athletic	West Ham United
30	Whitbread, Adrian R.	Leyton Orient	Swindon Town
28	Williams, Dean A.	St Albans City	Brentford
1	Williams, John M.	Newport (IOW)	Waterlooville
16	Wright, Evran	Stourbridge	Halesowen Harriers

Temporary transfers

23	Allardyce, Craig. S	Preston North End	Macclesfield Town
26	Hargreaves, Christian	Grimsby Town	Hull City
22	Hoult, Russell	Leicester City	Kettering Town
14	Smith, Mark C.	Grimsby Town	Scunthorpe United

August 1993

20	Alford, Carl P.	Witton Albion	Macclesfield Town
13	Allen, Malcolm	Millwall	Newcastle United
20	Ashby, Nicholas. R.	Aylesbury United	Kettering Town
11	Ashcroft, Lee	Preston North End	West Bromwich Albion
20	Barnett, Gary L.	Huddersfield Town	Leyton Orient
11	Barrick, Dean	Rotherham United	Cambridge United
19	Benton, David	Kidderminster Harriers	Worcester City
5	Blake, Mark A.	Aston Villa	Portsmouth
16	Bloomfield, Paul	Cheltenham Town	Gloucester City
23	Bracey, Lee	Halifax Town	Bury
27	Brown, Steven R.	Scunthorpe United	Colchester United
12	Bryson, James I.C.	Sheffield United	Barnsley
9	Burnett, Wayne	Blackburn Rovers	Plymouth Argyle
13	Carter, Timothy D.	Sunderland	Hartlepool United
13	Casey, Kim T.	Wycombe Wanderers	Solihull Borough
11	Chapman, Lee R.	Leeds United	Portsmouth
13	Chapple, Philip R.	Cambridge United	Charlton Athletic
19	Clarke, Matthew L.	Cradley Town	Halesowen Harriers
13	Clarke, Wayne	Walsall	Shrewsbury Town
11	Comyn, Andrew J.	Derby County	Plymouth Argyle
20	Conroy, Michael K.	Burnley	Preston North End
2	Cook, Andrew C.	Exeter City	Swansea City
3	Cooper, Stephen B.	Tranmere Rovers	York City

14 Cotterill, Stephen	Wimbledon	AFC Bournemouth
4 Coughlin, Russell	Swansea City	Exeter City
27 Dennis, Leonard C.	Welling United	Woking
1 Dozzell, Jason	Ipswich Town	Tottenham Hotspur
4 Falconer, William H.	Middlesbrough	Sheffield United
5 Farnworth, Simon	Preston North End	Wigan Athletic
31 Foran, Mark J.	Millwall	Sheffield United
9 Fulton, Stephen	Celtic	Bolton Wanderers
25 Gormley, Edward J.	Doncaster Rovers	Drogheda United
3 Hall, Neil	Winsford United	Witton Albion
17 Harkes, John A.	Sheffield Wednesday	Derby County
20 Harrop, Mark	Dover Athletic	Gravesend & Northfleet
6 Helliwell, Ian	Scunthorpe United	Rotherham United
9 Hendon, Ian M.	Tottenham Hotspur	Leyton Orient
27 Hicks, Stuart J.	Doncaster Rovers	Huddersfield Town
13 Houghton, Scott A.	Tottenham Hotspur	Luton Town
6 Hunter, Barry V.	Crusaders	Wrexham
13 Jackson, Michael J.	Crewe Alexandra	Bury
20 Johnson, David A.	Sheffield Wednesday	Lincoln City
20 Juryeff, Ian M.	Darlington	Scunthorpe United
1 Kurila, Alan	Burton Albion	Rushden & Diamonds
16 Leadbitter, Christopher J.	Cambridge United	AFC Bournemouth
2 Lee, Andrew G.	Telford United	Runcorn
13 Leonard, Mark A.	Preston North End	Chester City
20 Leworthy, David J.	Farnborough Town	Dover Athletic
9 Loveridge, Peter J.	Salisbury City	Wimborne Town
12 Marshall, Ian P.	Oldham Athletic	Ipswich Town
20 Matthewson, Trevor	Birmingham City	Preston North End
5 McKearney, David J.	Crewe Alexandra	Wigan Athletic
4 Melville, Andrew R.	Oxford United	Sunderland
12 Mitchell, Paul R.	AFC Bournemouth	West Ham United
9 Mooney, Simon G.	Radcliffe Borough	Mossley
9 Morrison, Andrew C.	Plymouth Argyle	Blackburn Rovers
4 Mutch, Andrew T.	Wolverhampton Wanderers	Swindon Town
9 Nuttell, Michael J.	Dagenham & Redbridge	Rushden & Diamonds
2 Pascoe, Colin J.	Sunderland	Swansea City
12 Peacock, Gavin K.	Newcastle United	Chelsea
20 Phillips, David O.	Norwich City	Nottingham Forest
2 Putney, Trevor A.	Watford	Leyton Orient
23 Pye, Mark	Harrow Borough	Enfield
7 Ramsey, Paul	Cardiff City	St Johnstone
1 Rennie, Paul A.	Stoke City	Wigan Athletic
2 Rhodes, Jason P.	Armitage 90	Burton Albion
7 Richardson, Paul A.	Dagenham & Redbridge	Rushden & Diamonds
6 Robinson, Ronald	Peterborough United	Exeter City
9 Rogan, Anthony G.P.	Sunderland	Oxford United
13 Ross, Michael P.	Portsmouth	Exeter City
10 Rowland, Keith	AFC Bournemouth	West Ham United
19 Scott, Robert	Sutton United	Sheffield United
5 Selby, Neil	Havant Town	Waterlooville
12 Sheridan, Darren S.	Winsford United	Barnsley
20 Shirtliff, Peter A.	Sheffield Wednesday	Wolverhampton Wanderers
13 Sinclair, Trevor L.	Blackpool	Queens Park Rangers
9 Sinton, Andrew	Queens Park Rangers	Sheffield Wednesday
13 Smith, Mark C.	Notts County	Lincoln City
5 Smith, Mark C.	Grimsby Town	Scunthorpe United
16 Stanborough Nicholas D.	Hinckley Athletic	Gresley Rovers
5 Thompson, Alan	Newcastle United	Bolton Wanderers
20 Toman, James A.	Darlington	Scunthorpe United
6 Torpey, Stephen D.J.	Bradford City	Swansea City
2 Tuttle, David P.	Tottenham Hotspur	Sheffield United
20 Valentine, Peter	Bury	Carlisle United
20 Warner, Steven P.	Dover Athletic	Billericay Town
3 Whittingham, Guy	Portsmouth	Aston Villa
4 Whyte, Christopher A.	Leeds United	Birmingham City
4 Wilcox, Russell	Hull City	Doncaster Rovers
8 Williams, Dean P.	Tamworth	Brentford
17 Williams, Paul R.C.	Stockport County	Coventry City
12 Wilson, Daniel J.	Sheffield Wednesday	Barnsley

2 Woods, Gordon W.	Ashton United	Curzon Ashton
24 Wright, Evran	Ashton United	Walsall
17 Yates, Steven	Bristol Rovers	Queens Park Rangers

Temporary transfers

20 Allardyce, Craig S.	Preston North End	Macclesfield Town
27 Aspinall, Warren	Portsmouth	AFC Bournemouth
19 Austin, Kevin	Saffron Walden Town	Leyton Orient
12 Barness, Anthony	Chelsea	Middlesbrough
2 Bottomley, Paul L.	Bridlington Town	Doncaster Rovers
27 Bound, Matthew T.	Southampton	Hull City
17 Clarke, Christopher	Bolton Wanderers	Morecambe
13 Cornwell, John A.	Southend United	Cardiff City
23 Crosby, Gary	Nottingham Forest	Grimsby Town
1 Dixon, Kerry M.	Southampton	Luton Town
26 Evans, Terence W.	Brentford	Wycombe Wanderers
3 Fickling, Ashley	Sheffield United	Darlington
20 Gayle, John	Birmingham City	Walsall
1 Gormley, Edward J.	Doncaster Rovers	Drogheda United
27 Greene, Dennis B.	Wycombe Wanderers	Woking
13 Hague, Paul	Gillingham	Cork City
26 Harding, Paul J.	Notts County	Southend United
7 Harper, Steeen J.	Burnley	Doncaster Rovers
9 Heavey, Paul A.	Preston North End	Netherfield
11 Heritage, Peter M.	Doncaster Rovers	Hastings Town
20 Hicks, Stuart J.	Doncaster Rovers	Huddersfield Town
2 Jones, Gary	Southend United	Dagenham & Redbridge
2 Jones, Graeme A.	Bridlington Town	Doncaster Rovers
13 Kaminsky, Jason M.G.	Nottingham Forest	Cobh Ramblers
24 Lambert, Christopher J.P.	Reading	Blackburn Rovers
6 Lee, Jason	Lincoln City	Southend United
13 Muggleton, Carl D.	Leicester City	Stoke City
28 Mulligan, James	Stoke City	Northwich Victoria
16 Murray, Shaun	Portsmouth	Millwall
31 Payne, Christopher A.	Billericay	Brighton & Hove Albion
23 Power, Lee M.	Norwich City	Sunderland
12 Reece, Andrew J.	Bristol Rovers	Walsall
23 Shutt, Carl S.	Leeds United	Birmingham City
12 Stant, Philip	Cardiff City	Mansfield Town
4 Walton, Mark A.	Norwich City	Wrexham
27 West, Dean	Lincoln City	Boston United
30 White, Jason G.	Scunthorpe United	Darlington
27 Whitehead, Philip M.	Barnsley	Stockport County
26 Wietecha, David	Millwall	Crewe Alexandra
20 Williams, Brett	Nottingham Forest	Stoke City

September 1993

16 Allen, Paul K.	Tottenham Hotspur	Southampton
24 Benjamin, Ian T.	Luton Town	Brentford
6 Bullock, Martin J.	Eastwood Town	Barnsley
17 Burrows, David	Liverpool	West Ham United
10 Carter, Mark C.	Barnet	Bury
17 Chapman, Lee R.	Portsmouth	West Ham United
13 Clarkson, Ian S.	Birmingham City	Stoke City
17 Dicks, Julian A.	West Ham United	Liverpool
16 Gayle, John	Birmingham City	Coventry City
3 Hackett, Gary S.	West Bromwich Albion	Peterborough United
29 Hargreaves, Christian	Grimsby Town	Hull City
24 Harper, Steven J.	Burnley	Doncaster Rovers
8 Hemmings, Anthony G.	Northwich Victoria	Wycombe Wanderers
3 Higginbotham, Paul A.	Stalybridge Celtic	Barrow
23 Hooper, Michael D.	Liverpool	Newcastle United
21 Ironside, Ian	Middlesbrough	Stockport County
20 Kernaghan, Alan N.	Middlesbrough	Manchester City
24 Kerslake, David	Leeds United	Tottenham Hotspur
6 Lee, Jason B	Lincoln City	Southend United
17 Marsh, Michael A.	Liverpool	West Ham United
9 Martin, Dean E.	West Ham United	Kettering Town
16 Measham, Ian	Burnley	Doncaster Rovers

20 Moyes, David W.	Hamilton Academical	Preston North End
9 Parsley, Neil R.	Huddersfield Town	West Bromwich Albion
24 Sturridge, Simon A.	Birmingham City	Stoke City
9 Van Den Hauwe, Patrick W.	Tottenham Hotspur	Millwall
3 Warhurst, Paul	Sheffield Wednesday	Blackburn Rovers
20 Westley, Graham N.	Aylesbury United	Harrow Borough
24 Wright, Thomas J.	Newcastle United	Nottingham Forest

Temporary transfers

27 Allardyce, Craig S.	Preston North End	Netherfield
16 Allon, Joseph B.	Brentford	Southend United
10 Angell, Brett	Southend United	Everton
12 Barness, Anthony	Chelsea	Middlesbrough
27 Bennett, Craig	Doncaster Rovers	Bridlington Town
24 Benstead, Graham	Brentford	Kettering Town
8 Benton, Stephen	Bristol City	Clevedon Town
7 Borrows, Brian	Coventry City	Bristol City
3 Clark, Paul D.	Cambridge United	Walton & Hersham
29 Colgan, Nicholas V.	Chelsea	Crewe Alexandra
16 Cornwell, John A.	Southend United	Brentford
28 Davison, Robert	Leicester City	Sheffield United
17 Dixon, Kerry M.	Southampton	Luton Town
12 Dobson, Anthony J.	Blackburn Rovers	Portsmouth
25 Dowell, Wayne A.	Burnley	Witton Albion
17 Flitcroft, David J.	Preston North End	Lincoln City
16 Ford, Tony	Grimsby Town	Bradford City
13 Gillespie, Keith R.	Manchester United	Wigan Athletic
13 Hall, Mark A.	Southend United	Barnet
24 Harkness, Steven	Liverpool	Huddersfield Town
8 Harper, Steven J.	Preston North End	Doncaster Rovers
9 Heavey, Paul A.	Preston North End	Netherfield
3 Hine, Mark	Doncaster Rovers	Gateshead
8 Howarth, Neil	Burnley	Macclesfield Town
10 Jemson, Nigel B.	Sheffield Wednesday	Grimsby Town
17 Jones, Gary	Southend United	Lincoln City
3 Jones, Philip L.	Liverpool	Crewe Alexandra
23 Joyce, Joseph P.	Carlisle United	Darlington
24 Kelly, Anthony O.N.	Stoke City	Bury
24 Knill, Alan R.	Bury	Cardiff City
3 Livingstone, Stephen	Chelsea	Port Vale
24 Lyne, Neil G.F.	Cambridge United	Chesterfield
22 Mahorn, Paul G.	Tottenham Hotspur	Fulham
13 Makin, Christopher	Oldham Athletic	Preston North End
24 McIlhargey, Stephen	Blackpool	Chester City
7 Milsom, Paul J.	Bristol City	Clevedon Town
13 Muggleton, Carl D.	Leicester City	Stoke City
7 Muir, John G.	Preston North End	Telford United
27 Murphy, Shaun P.	Notts County	Lincoln City
16 Painter, Peter R.	Burnley	Darlington
27 Parkinson, Stephen	Lincoln City	Kings Lynn
28 Peel, Nathan J.	Sheffield United	Burnley
21 Potter, Graham S.	Birmingham City	Wycombe Wanderers
23 Reed, John P.	Sheffield United	Mansfield Town
7 Rioch, Gregor J.	Luton Town	Barnet
24 Small, Michael A.	West Ham United	Wolverhampton Wanderers
16 Tilson, Stephen B.	Southend United	Brentford
2 Whitehead, Philip M.	Halifax Town	Stockport County
29 Whitehead, Philip M.	Barnsley	Oxford United
13 Williams, Andrew	Notts County	Huddersfield Town
23 Wright, Ian M.	Stoke City	Bristol Rovers

October 1993

14 Austin, Kevin L.	Saffron Walden Town	Leyton Orient
26 Batty, David	Leeds United	Blackburn Rovers
8 Brien, Anthony J.	Chesterfield	Rotherham United
1 Carter, Richard.	Solihull Borough	Bromsgrove Rovers
29 Darby, Julian T.	Bolton Wanderers	Coventry City
15 Evans, Terence W.	Brentford	Wycombe Wanderers
21 Grainger, Martin R.	Colchester United	Brentford

29 Griffiths, Carl B.	Shrewsbury Town	Manchester City
13 Hawkes, Leigh R.	Enfield	Billericay Town
27 Hewitt, James R.	Doncaster Rovers	Chesterfield
11 Holden, Richard W.	Manchester City	Oldham Athletic
4 Jeffrey, Michael R.	Doncaster Rovers	Newcastle United
26 Judd, Robin A.	Atherstone United	Solihull Borough
18 Kelly, Anthony O. N.	Stoke City	Bury
12 Lambert, Colin A.	Macclesfield Town	Halifax Town
8 Law, Nicholas	Rotherham United	Chesterfield
16 Leicester, Stuart	Macclesfield Town	Stalybridge Celtic
8 Livett, Simon R.	Leyton Orient	Cambridge United
1 Lucketti, Christopher J.	Halifax Town	Bury
8 Moss, David A.	Doncaster Rovers	Chesterfield
8 Oliver, Darren	Bolton Wanderers	Rochdale
4 Pearce, Ian A.	Chelsea	Blackburn Rovers
25 Peel, Nathan J.	Sheffield United	Burnley
1 Pethick, Robert J.	Weymouth	Portsmouth
29 Pickering, Albert G.	Rotherham United	Coventry City
8 Power, Philip D.	Stalybridge Celtic	Macclesfield Town
7 Pritchard, Dean B.	Emley	Witton Albion
1 Roche, David	Newcastle United	Doncaster Rovers
2 Slater, Stuart	Celtic	Ipswich Town
2 Stein, Earl M. S.	Stoke City	Chelsea
8 Turnbull, Lee M.	Chesterfield	Doncaster Rovers
15 Wallace, David L.	Manchester United	Birmingham City
21 Whitney, John D.	Winsford United	Huddersfield Town
21 Williams, Andrew	Notts County	Rotherham United
7 Woods, Stephen G.	Clydebank	Preston North End
29 Wright, Ian M.	Stoke City	Bristol Rovers

Temporary transfers

14 Aspinall, Warren	Portsmouth	Swansea City
29 Bailey, Dennis L.	Queens Park Rangers	Charlton Athletic
28 Benstead, Graham M.	Brentford	Kettering Town
22 Benton, Stephen	Bristol City	Cobh Ramblers
15 Blissett, Luther	Bury	Derry City
15 Boden, Christopher D.	Aston Villa	Barnsley
14 Bogie, Ian	Millwall	Leyton Orient
22 Costello, Peter	Lincoln City	Halifax Town
1 Cowan, Thomas	Sheffield United	Stoke City
4 Craddock, Jodie D.	Cambridge United	Woking
12 Crosby, Andrew K.	Doncaster Rovers	Halifax Town
28 Davison, Robert	Leicester City	Sheffield United
8 Dickov, Paul	Arsenal	Luton Town
28 Dickson, Benjamin M.	Lincoln City	Witton Albion
26 Dobson, Anthony J.	Blackburn Rovers	Portsmouth
23 Dowell, Wayne A.	Burnley	Witton Albion
15 Dumphy, Sean	Lincoln City	Doncaster Rovers
1 Esdaille, David	Bury	Witton Albion
15 Fairbairn, Neil	Wimbledon	Stevenage Borough
8 Fensome, Andrew B.	Cambridge United	Preston North End
12 Fernandes, Tamer	Brentford	Wealdstone
14 Flatts, Mark M.	Arsenal	Cambridge United
28 Flounders, Andrew J.	Rochdale	Carlisle United
12 France, Darren B.	Doncaster Rovers	Halifax Town
3 Gillespie, Keith R.	Manchester United	Wigan Athletic
8 Gray, Andrew	Reading	Woking
1 Greene, Dennis B.	Wycombe Wanderers	Enfield
1 Harriott, Marvin L.	Barnsley	Leyton Orient
13 Heavey, Paul A.	Preston North End	Netherfield
29 Herrera, Roberto	Queens Park Rangers	Fulham
8 Hewitt, James R.	Doncaster Rovers	Chesterfield
3 Hine, Mark	Doncaster Rovers	Gateshead
4 Jones, Philip L.	Liverpool	Crewe Alexandra
12 Key, Lance W.	Sheffield Wednesday	Oldham Athletic
22 King, Philip G.	Sheffield Wednesday	Notts County
1 Livett, Simon R.	Leyton Orient	Cambridge United
29 Livingstone, Stephen	Chelsea	Grimsby Town
8 Locke, Adam S.	Southend United	Colchester United

1 Lyons, Andrew	Crewe Alexandra	Wigan Athletic
8 Marriott, Andrew	Nottingham Forest	Wrexham
20 Muggleton, Carl D.	Leicester City	Stoke City
4 Oliver, Darren	Bolton Wanderers	Peterborough United
18 Painter, Peter R.	Burnley	Darlington
1 Parkinson, Stephen	Lincoln City	Kings Lynn
28 Parkinson, Stephen	Lincoln City	Witton Albion
5 Payne, Christopher	Billericay Town	Brighton & Hove Albion
15 Power, Lee M.	Norwich City	Portsmouth
23 Reed, John P.	Sheffield United	Mansfield Town
1 Reeves, David	Notts County	Carlisle United
27 Rush, David	Sunderland	Peterborough United
8 Whitworth, Neil A.	Manchester United	Rotherham United
8 Williamson, Daniel A.	West Ham United	Doncaster Rovers

November 1993

9 Bale, Kevin	Salisbury City	Newport (IOW)
11 Bashir, Naseem	Chesham United	Aylesbury United
4 Beasant, David	Chelsea	Southampton
25 Biggins, Wayne	Barnsley	Celtic
1 Boyce, David J.	Waterlooville	Gravesend & Northfleet
29 Bryson, James I. C.	Barnsley	Preston North End
22 Bullock, Darren J.	Nuneaton Borough	Huddersfield Town
1 Byrne, John F.	Millwall	Oxford United
1 Cook, Timothy J.	Burnham	Maidenhead United
30 Coyne, Thomas	Tranmere Rovers	Motherwell
18 Cross, Paul	Hartlepool United	Darlington
5 Davison, Robert	Leicester City	Sheffield United
5 Elliott, Matthew S.	Scunthorpe United	Oxford United
6 Emblen, Neil R.	Sittingbourne	Millwall
18 Emerson, Dean	Hartlepool United	Stockport County
19 Fensome, Andrew B.	Cambridge United	Preston North End
4 Flowers, Timothy D.	Southampton	Blackburn Rovers
16 Gardiner, Aaron R.	Halstead Town	Cornard United
6 Harle, Michael J.	Sittingbourne	Millwall
3 Hazard, Michael	Swindon Town	Tottenham Hotspur
6 King, Arthur	Hednesford Town	Dudley Town
5 Knill, Alan R.	Bury	Scunthorpe United
2 Lyons, Andrew	Crewe Alexandra	Wigan Athletic
19 McRobert, Lee P.	Ashford Town	Sittingbourne
18 Mardon, Paul J.	Birmingham City	West Bromwich Albion
1 Murray, Shaun	Portsmouth	Scarborough
17 Page, Donald R.	Rotherham United	Doncaster Rovers
25 Payton, Andrew P.	Celtic	Barnsley
12 Pemberton, John M.	Sheffield United	Leeds United
8 Power, John J.	Sutton United	Dulwich Hamlet
25 Roberts, Iwan W.	Huddersfield Town	Leicester City
17 Robson, Mark A.	West Ham United	Charlton Athletic
18 Scott, Keith	Wycombe Wanderers	Swindon Town
1 Shutt, Carl S.	Leeds United	Birmingham City
26 Sinfield, Mark R.	Enfield	Billericay Town
26 Southgate, Darren	Billericay Town	Ford United
5 Tate, Steven K.	Havant Town	Waterlooville
30 Vickers, Stephen	Tranmere Rovers	Middlesbrough
1 Whitehead, Philip M.	Barnsley	Oxford United
19 Whitington, Craig	Crawley Town	Scarborough
15 Wilson, Craig	Poole Town	Waterlooville
12 Zelem, Alan W.	Curzon Ashton	Mossley

Temporary transfers

12 Anders, Jason S.	Rochdale	Northwich Victoria
26 Adebola, Bamberdele	Crewe Alexandra	Bangor City
25 Appleby, Matthew W.	Newcastle United	Darlington
1 Barlow, Andrew J.	Oldham Athletic	Bradford City
18 Basham, Michael	West Ham United	Colchester United
4 Bogie, Ian	Millwall	Leyton Orient
30 Coleman, Simon	Derby County	Sheffield Wednesday
1 Cowan, Thomas	Sheffield United	Stoke City
23 Davies, Martin L.	Coventry City	Stafford Rangers

111

19 Dickins, Matthew J.	Blackburn Rovers	Lincoln City
9 Dickov, Paul	Arsenal	Luton City
27 Dobson, Anthony J.	Blackburn Rovers	Portsmouth
2 Edwards, Russell J.	Crystal Palace	Slough Town
2 Eeles, Anthony G.	Gillingham	Cork City
22 Fairbairn, Neil	Wimbledon	Kingstonian
8 Fensome, Andrew B.	Cambridge United	Preston North End
15 Fernandes, Tamer	Brentford	Wealdstone
5 Gannon, John S.	Sheffield United	Middlesbrough
12 Goater, Leonardo S.	Rotherham United	Middlesbrough
29 Graham, Deiniol W. T.	Barnsley	Notts County
11 Gray, Andrew	Reading	Carlisle United
2 Harding, Paul	Notts County	Woking
1 Harriott, Marvin L.	Barnsley	Watford
11 Harrison, Gerald R.	Bristol Rovers	Leyton Orient
28 Herrera, Roberto	Queens Park Rangers	Hereford United
11 Hine, Mark	Doncaster Rovers	Fulham
18 Holden, Stephen A.	Carlisle United	Gateshead
1 Hoult, Russell	Leicester City	Kettering Town
1 Jenkinson, Leigh	Coventry City	Bolton Wanderers
22 Kabia, Jason	Lincoln City	Birmingham City
29 Livingstone, Stephen	Chelsea	Stafford Rangers
2 Luscombe, Lee	Millwall	Grimsby Town
26 McCarthy, Alan J.	Queens Park Rangers	Sittingbourne
2 Manning, Paul J.	Millwall	Watford
2 Marsden, Christopher	Huddersfield Town	Slough Town
26 Muggleton Carl D.	Leicester City	Coventry City
2 Mulligan, James	Stoke City	Sheffield United
1 Murray, Shaun	Portsmouth	Bury
26 Oakes, Michael C.	Aston Villa	Scarborough
18 Painter, Peter R.	Burnley	Scarborough
22 Philips, Justin	Derby County	Darlington
5 Reece, Andrew J.	Bristol Rovers	Cork City
23 Reed, John P.	Sheffield United	Hereford United
5 Rogers, Darren J.	Birmingham City	Mansfield Town
2 Rowe, Ezekiel B.	Chelsea	Wycombe Wanderers
8 Saddington, James	Millwall	Barnet
12 Thomas, Mitchell A.	West Ham United	Sittingbourne
19 Trotter, Michael	Leicester City	Luton Town
2 Wallbridge, Andrew J.	Oxford United	Chesterfield
19 Walsh, Gary	Manchester United	Worcester City
2 Walton, David L.	Sheffield United	Oldham Athletic
7 Whitworth, Neil A.	Manchester United	Shrewsbury Town
5 Williams, Paul A.	Stockport County	Rotherham United
19 Williams, Paul R. C.	Coventry City	Rochdale
8 Williamson, Daniel A.	West Ham United	West Bromwich Albion
		Doncaster Rovers

December 1993

17 Bennett, Ian M.	Peterborough United	Birmingham City
10 Blake, Noel L.	Bradford City	Dundee
10 Bogie, Ian	Millwall	Leyton Orient
2 Boothroyd, Adrian N.	Heart of Midlothian	Mansfield Town
16 Charley, Kenneth L.	Watford	Peterborough United
10 Charles, Lee	Yeading	Chertsey Town
17 Cooper, Gary	Peterborough United	Birmingham City
21 Dobson, Anthony J.	Blackburn Rovers	Portsmouth
10 Finney, Kevin	Leek Town	Stafford Rangers
2 Flitcroft, David J.	Preston North End	Chester City
15 Fowler, Lee E.	Preston North End	Doncaster Rovers
24 Fry, Christopher D.	Hereford United	Colchester United
21 Gayle, Mark S. R.	Walsall	Crewe Alexandra
24 Harriott, Marvin L.	Barnsley	Bristol City
10 Henderson, Damian M	Scarborough	Scunthorpe United
1 Jepson, Ronald F.	Exeter City	Huddersfield Town
7 Johnrose, Leonard	Hartlepool United	Bury
20 Lowe, Kenneth	Stoke City	Birmingham City
3 McCarthy, Sean C.	Bradford City	Oldham Athletic
1 Marriott, Andrew	Nottingham Forest	Wrexham
22 Masters, Neil B.	AFC Bournemouth	Wolverhampton Wanderers

112

18 Mutchell, Robert D.	Oxford United	Barnet
24 Painter, Peter R.	Burnley	Darlington
9 Patmore, Warren J.	Millwall	Northampton Town
20 Potter, Graham S.	Birmingham City	Stoke City
7 Reece, Andrew J.	Bristol Rovers	Hereford United
23 Reeves, David	Notts County	Carlisle United
22 Rocastle, David C.	Leeds United	Manchester City
8 Rodwell, James	Hednesford Town	Nuneaton Borough
24 Ryan, John B.	Rochdale	Bury
18 Simpkins, John P.	Bashley	Newport (IOW)
11 Taylor, Stephen C.	Rushall Olympic	Bromsgrove Rovers
3 Tolson, Neil	Oldham Athletic	Bradford City
3 Toman, James A.	Scunthorpe United	Scarborough
17 Wallace, Matthew	Atherstone United	Hednesford Town
23 Walton, David L.	Sheffield United	Shrewsbury Town
22 White, David	Manchester City	Leeds United
8 White, Jason G.	Scunthorpe United	Scarborough
31 Willis, Roger C.	Watford	Birmingham City
30 Wilmot, Richard	Scunthorpe United	Halifax Town

Temporary transfers

31 Aspinall, Warren	Portsmouth	AFC Bournemouth
31 Barnes, Andrew J.	Crystal Palace	Carlisle United
20 Barnett, David	Barnet	Birmingham City
23 Blissett, Luther	Bury	Mansfield Town
17 Burns, Christopher	Portsmouht	Swansea
16 Clarke, Nicholas J.	Mansfield Town	Doncaster Rovers
31 Coleman, Simon	Derby County	Sheffield Wednesday
1 Cowan, Thomas	Sheffield United	Stoke City
10 Croft, Brian G. A.	Queens Park Rangers	Shrewsbury Town
7 Cross, Ryan	Hartlepool United	Bury
17 Davies, Simon I.	Manchester United	Exeter City
8 Dickov, Paul	Arsenal	Luton Town
23 Fairbairn, Neil	Wimbledon	Kingstonian
31 Finley, Alan J.	Stockport County	Rochdale
31 Flatts, Mark M.	Arsenal	Brighton & Hove Albion
7 Fleck, Robert	Chelsea	Bolton Wanderers
24 Fulton, Stephen	Bolton Wanderers	Peterborough United
7 Gannon, John S.	Sheffield United	Middlesbrough
3 Harding, Paul J.	Notts County	Birmingham City
9 Harriott, Marvin L.	Barnsley	Bristol City
20 Harrison, Gerald R.	Bristol City	Hereford United
23 Harrison, Michael	Port Vale	Stafford Rangers
30 Herrera, Roberto	Queens Park Rangers	Fulham
3 Hirst, Lee W.	Coventry City	Lincoln City
31 Hodges, Lee L.	Tottenham Hotspur	Wycombe Wanderers
18 Holden, Steven A.	Carlisle United	Kettering Town
7 Holmes, Keith N.	Oxford United	Worcester City
3 Hoult, Russell	Leicester City	Bolton Wanderers
9 Humphrey, John	Crystal Palace	Reading
10 Hyslop, Christian T.	Southend United	Northampton Town
23 Kee, Paul	Oxford United	Ards
30 Kilford, Ian A.	Nottingham Forest	Wigan Athletic
31 Lowe, Kenneth	Stoke City	Birmingham City
24 McCarthy, Alan J.	Queens Park Rangers	Watford
8 Margetson, Martyn W.	Manchester City	Bristol Rovers
5 Marsden, Christopher	Huddersfield Town	Coventry City
3 Marshall, Scott R.	Arsenal	Rotherham United
8 Myers, Christopher	Dundee United	Torquay United
5 Newhouse, Aidan R.	Wimbledon	Tranmere Rovers
17 Pape, Andrew M.	Barnet	Enfield
8 Rees, Jason M.	Luton Town	Mansfield Town
10 Roberts, Darren A.	Wolverhampton Wanderers	Telford United
6 Rogers, Darren J.	Birmingham City	Wycome Wanderers
5 Rowe, Ezekiel B.	Chelsea	Barnet
7 Saddington, James	Millwall	Sittingbourne
8 Sampson, Ian	Sunderland	Northampton Town
23 Sheffield, Jonathan	Cambridge United	Colchester United
31 Shutt, Carl S.	Birmingham City	Manchester City

9 Sinnott, Lee	Crystal Palace	Bradford City
23 Stringfellow, Ian R.	Mansfield Town	Chesterfield
17 Thomas, Mark L.	Wimbledon	Bromley
15 Thomas, Mitchell A.	West Ham United	Luton Town
20 Trotter, Michael	Leicester City	Chesterfield
4 Walton, David L.	Sheffield United	Shrewsbury Town
10 Whitworth, Neil A.	Manchester United	Blackpool
15 Wietecha, David	Millwall	Rotherham
8 Williamson, Daniel A.	West Ham United	Doncaster Rovers
10 Woods, Kenneth S.	Bury	Stalybridge Celtic
6 Worboys, Gavin	Notts County	Exeter City

January 1994

21 Angell, Brett A. M.	Southend United	Everton
14 Barnes, David	Sheffield United	Watford
21 Brown, John C.	Stalybridge Celtic	Leek Town
13 Cecere, Michele J.	Walsall	Exeter City
7 Claridge, Stephen E.	Cambridge United	Birmingham City
3 Clarke, David A.	Lincoln City	Doncaster Rovers
21 Coleman, Simon	Derby County	Sheffield Wednesday
14 Connor, Terence F.	Yeovil Town	Calne Town
11 Cross, Ryan	Hartlepool United	Bury
8 Edwards, Paul R.	Wolverhampton Wanderers	West Bromwich Albion
13 Ferguson, Darren	Manchester United	Wolverhampton Wanderers
20 Grange, Damian	Leek Town	Kidsgrove Athletic
28 Green, Gary	Dorchester Town	Havant Town
5 Harding, Paul	Notts County	Birmingham City
20 Kilcline, Brian	Newcastle United	Swindon Town
20 Livingstone, Stephen	Chelsea	Grimsby Town
7 McGavin, Steven J.	Colchester United	Birmingham City
4 McPherson, Malcolm	Yeovil Town	West Ham United
1 Marsden, Christopher	Huddersfield Town	Wolverhampton Wanderers
13 Mottashead, Nigel J.	Havant Town	Weymouth
11 Muggleton, Carl D.	Leicester City	Celtic
11 Nicholls, Danny	Witney Town	Buckingham Town
21 O'Brien, Liam F.	Newcastle United	Tranmere Rovers
27 Parkinson, Gary	Bolton Wanderers	Burnley
21 Philliskirk, Anthony	Peterborough United	Burnley
4 Robertson, Alexander	Rangers	Coventry City
28 Robinson, Jamie	Barnsley	Carlisle United
26 Rosenthal, Ronnie	Liverpool	Tottenham Hotspur
5 Shearer, Peter A.	AFC Bournemouth	Birmingham City
10 Sinnott, Lee	Crystal Palace	Bradford City
21 Smith, David	Birmingham City	West Bromwich Albion
21 Turnbull, Lee M.	Doncaster Rovers	Wycombe Wanderers

Temporary transfers

31 Adebola, Bamberdele	Crewe Alexandra	Northwich Victoria
21 Akinbiyi, Adeola P.	Norwich City	Hereford United
14 Angell, Brett	Southend United	Everton
21 Anthrobus, Stephen A.	Wimbledon	Peterborough United
8 Appleby, Matthew W.	Newcastle United	Darlington
6 Carter, Timothy D.	Hartlepool United	Millwall
14 Collins, Simon	Huddersfield Town	Halifax Town
25 Creaney, Gerard	Celtic	Portsmouth
7 Crocker, Marcus	Plymouth Argyle	Weymouth Town
10 Currie, David N.	Barnsley	Huddersfield Town
10 Daish, Liam S.	Cambridge United	Birmingham City
16 Davies, Simon I.	Manchester United	Exeter City
27 Donowa, Brian L.	Birmingham City	Shrewsbury Town
21 Edey, Darren	Peterborough United	Cambridge City
31 Fairbairn, Neil	Wimbledon	Kingstonian
7 Feeney, Mark A.	Barnsley	Coleraine
10 Fenton, Graham A.	Aston Villa	West Bromwich Albion
10 Foster, Colin J.	West Ham United	Notts County
14 Gannon, James P.	Stockport County	Notts County
12 Granville, Daniel P.	Cambridge United	Saffron Walden Town
13 Hague, Paul	Gillingham	Sittingbourne
26 Hirst, Lee	Coventry City	Lincoln City

18 Holden, Steven A.	Carlisle United	Kettering Town
5 Hoult, Russell	Leicester City	Bolton Wanderers
10 Humphrey, John	Crystal Palace	Reading
9 Hyslop, Christian T.	Southend United	Northampton Town
10 Jobling, Kevin A.	Grimsby Town	Scunthorpe United
11 Kerr, Stewart	Celtic	Swindon Town
7 Knight, Craig	Wrexham	Crusaders
27 Lancashire, Graham	Burnley	Chester
28 Murphy, Matthew S.	Oxford United	Kettering Town
21 Newhouse, Aiden R.	Wimbledon	Port Vale
26 Peters, Robert A. A.	Brentford	Slough Town
24 Rees, Jason	Luton Town	Mansfield Town
9 Roberts, Darren A.	Wolverhampton Wanderers	Telford United
13 Robinson, Ronald	Exeter City	Huddersfield Town
5 Rowe, Ezekiel B.	Chelsea	Barnet
10 Rush, Matthew J.	West Ham United	Swansea City
8 Sampson, Ian	Sunderland	Northampton Town
28 Sheffield, Johnathan	Cambridge United	Swindon Town
7 Snowden, Trevor	Rochdale	Northwich Victoria
14 Steele, Timothy W.	Bradford City	Hereford United
2 Stewart, Paul A.	Liverpool	Crystal Palace
14 Thomas, Mitchell A.	West Ham United	Luton Town
28 Tomlinson, Michael L.	Leyton Orient	St Albans City
31 Warren, Mark W.	Leyton Orient	West Ham United
7 Watts, Grant S.	Crystal Palace	Colchester United
28 West, Mark	Wycombe Wanderers	Aylesbury United
17 Wietecha, David	Millwall	Rotherham United
6 Williams, Gareth J.	Barnsley	Hull City
13 Wilson, Kevin J.	Notts County	Bradford City

February 1994

17 Adams, Neil J.	Oldham Athletic	Norwich City
16 Ampadu, Patrick K.	West Bromwich Albion	Swansea City
2 Aspinall, Warren	Portsmouth	AFC Bournemouth
21 Barnett, David	Barnet	Birmingham City
8 Beale, Dean J.	Newport (IOW)	Poole Town
5 Blackwood, Bevon A.	Witton Albion	Buxton
21 Blake, Nathan A.	Cardiff City	Sheffield United
11 Blount, Mark	Gresley Rovers	Sheffield United
9 Brown, Stephen	Northampton Town	Wycombe Wanderers
3 Buckle, Paul J.	Brentford	Torquay United
10 Clark, John B.	Dundee United	Stoke City
18 Clayton, Gary	Cambridge United	Huddersfield Town
3 Cowans, Gordon S.	Aston Villa	Derby County
3 Creaney, Gerard	Celtic	Portsmouth
2 Daish, Liam S.	Cambridge United	Birmingham City
15 Daws, Anthony	Grimsby Town	Lincoln City
23 Endersby, Lee A.	Wembley	Harrow Borough
2 Fox, Ruel A.	Norwich City	Newcastle United
4 Garner, Simon	West Bromwich Albion	Wycome Wanderers
11 Gavin, Mark W.	Bristol City	Exeter City
4 Hanks, Christopher	Bromsgrove Rovers	Gresley Rovers
17 Hyslop, Christian T.	Southend United	Colchester United
11 Johnson, Alan K.	Wigan Athletic	Lincoln City
10 McGorry, Brian P.	AFC Bournemouth	Peterborough United
7 McKinnon, Raymond	Nottingham Forest	Aberdeen
11 Magilton, James	Oxford United	Southampton
7 Maskell, Craig D.	Swindon Town	Southampton
21 Matthew, Damian	Chelsea	Crystal Palace
4 Moody, Paul	Southampton	Oxford United
25 Pritchard, David M.	Telford United	Bristol Rovers
21 Ramage, Craig D.	Derby County	Watford
22 Ridings, David	Halifax Town	Lincoln City
1 Scott, Kevin W.	Newcastle United	Tottenham Hotspur
11 Smith, Eric G.	Halesowen Town	Bilston Town
3 Steele, Timothy W.	Bradford City	Hereford United
1 Thompson, David	Bristol City	Brentford
4 Turner, Robert P.	Notts County	Exeter City
18 Washington, Darren T.	Congleton Town	Leek Town

| 7 Williams, Paul A. | Stockport County | Rochdale |
| 28 Wood, Paul A. | AFC Bournemouth | Portsmouth |

Temporary transfers

2 Adebola, Bamberdele	Crewe Alexandra	Northwich Victoria
18 Adekola, David	Bury	Exeter City
21 Anthrobus, Stephen A.	Wimbledon	Peterborough United
3 Arnold, Ian	Carlisle United	Stalybridge Celtic
25 Barras, Anthony	Stockport County	Rotherham United
8 Blatherwick, Steven S.	Nottingham Forest	Wycombe Wanderers
25 Brock, Kevin	Newcastle United	Cardiff City
11 Byrne, David S.	Partick Thistle	Walsall
7 Campbell, David A.	Burnley	Lincoln City
18 Cornwell, John A.	Southend United	Northampton Town
2 Creaser, Glyn	Wycombe Wanderers	Yeovil Town
15 Currie, David N.	Barnsley	Huddersfield Town
4 Danzey, Michael J.	Cambridge United	Scunthorpe United
18 Dichio, Daniele S.	Queens Park Rangers	Welling United
16 Dolby, Tony C.	Millwall	Barnet
4 Edwards, Michael	Tranmere Rovers	Stalybridge Celtic
1 Flatts, Mark M.	Arsenal	Brighton & Hove Albion
7 Flounders, Andrew J.	Rochdale	Carlisle United
14 Foster, Colin J.	West Ham United	Notts County
25 Gayle, Mark S. R.	Crewe Alexandra	Liverpool
12 Granville, Daniel P.	Cambridge United	Saffron Walden Town
3 Gregory, Neil R.	Ipswich Town	Chesterfield
8 Hague, Paul	Gillingham	Sittingbourne
25 Harrison, Garry M.	Northampton Town	Bashley
21 Harrison, Gerald R.	Bristol City	Bath City
4 Hoult, Russell	Leicester City	Bolton Wanderers
4 Howarth, Neil	Burnley	Macclesfield Town
21 Huxford, Richard J.	Millwall	Birmingham City
25 Kavanagh, Graham A.	Middlesbrough	Darlington
10 Kelly, Gary A.	Bury	West Ham United
2 Kerr, Stuart P.	AFC Bournemouth	Bashley
10 Kitchen, David E.	Leyton Orient	Doncaster Rovers
4 Lakin, Barry	Leyton Orient	Woking
18 Leitch, Grant	Blackpool	Fleetwood Town
18 Lormor, Anthony	Lincoln City	Halifax Town
18 Lowe, David A.	Leicester City	Port Vale
11 McCarthy, Alan J.	Queens Park Rangers	Plymouth Argyle
25 McPherson, Malcolm	West Ham United	Dorchester Town
11 Margetson, Martyn W.	Manchester City	Bolton Wanderers
14 O'Connor, Martyn J.	Crystal Palace	Walsall
27 Peters, Robert A.	Brentford	Slough Town
7 Ramage, Andrew	Gillingham	Hastings Town
23 Rees, Jason	Luton Town	Mansfield Town
24 Rutherford, Mark R.	Shelbourne	Shrewsbury Town
11 Shelton, Gary	Bristol City	Rochdale
25 Sloan, Scott M.	Falkirk	Cambridge United
28 Small, Michael A.	West Ham United	Charlton Athletic
18 Snowden, Trevor	Rochdale	Northwich Victoria
18 Stewart, Paul A.	Liverpool	Crystal Palace
26 Sweetman, Nicholas	Leyton Orient	Baldock Town
21 Tait, Paul R.	Birmingham City	Millwall
2 Tomlinson, Michael	Leyton Orient	St Albans City
4 Warburton, Raymond	York City	Northampton Town
8 Watts, Grant	Crystal Palace	Colchester United
28 Whittingham, Guy	Aston Villa	Wolverhampton Wanderers
17 Wietecha, David	Millwall	Rotherham United
4 Wilkerson, Paul S.	Millwall	Stevenage Borough
7 Williams, Gareth J.	Barnsley	Hull City
11 Williams, Lee	Aston Villa	Peterborough United
11 Witter, Anthony J.	Queens Park Rangers	Reading
9 Wood, Paul A.	AFC Bournemouth	Portsmouth
25 Wright, Dale C.	Nottingham Forest	Slough Town

March 1994

| 24 Allen, Clive D. | West Ham United | Millwall |

116

24	Allon, Joseph B.	Brentford	Port Vale
25	Arter, David J.	Sittingbourne	Ashford Town
22	Ashby, Barry J.	Watford	Brentford
24	Basham, Michael	West Ham United	Swansea City
24	Beagrie, Peter S.	Everton	Manchester City
21	Berks, Peter R.	Hednesford Town	Bilston Town
24	Berry, Greg J.	Wimbledon	Millwall
24	Biggins, Wayne	Celtic	Stoke City
24	Blake, Mark A.	Portsmouth	Leicester City
25	Blondrage, Andrew J.	Hastings Town	Sittingbourne
12	Bye, Andrew G.	Yeovil Town	Bashley
23	Carter, Timothy D.	Hartlepool United	Millwall
8	Cox, Ian	Carlshalton Athletic	Crystal Palace
24	Cunningham, Anthony E.	Doncaster Rovers	Wycombe Wanderers
1	Diaz, Jorge	Dorchester Town	Weymouth
10	Dyer, Bruce A.	Watford	Crystal Palace
14	Fereday, Wayne	West Bromwich Albion	Cardiff City
24	Formby, Kevin	Burscough	Rochdale
23	Foster, Colin J.	West Ham United	Watford
24	Gayle, Marcus A.	Brentford	Wimbledon
24	Harrison, Gerald R.	Bristol City	Huddersfield Town
31	Harrison, Michael	Port Vale	Hednesford Town
22	Heaney, Neil	Arsenal	Southampton
24	Herrera, Roberto	Queens Park Rangers	Fulham
24	Hicks, Stuart J.	Huddersfield Town	Preston North End
24	Jones, Alexander	Rochdale	Halifax Town
25	Keast, Douglas W	Corby Town	Rushden & Diamonds
8	Kitchen, David E.	Leyton Orient	Doncaster Rovers
17	Lawrence, James H.	Sunderland	Doncaster Rovers
24	Lee, Jason B.	Southend United	Nottingham Forest
3	Limber, Nicholas	Manchester City	Doncaster Rovers
24	Limpar, Anders	Arsenal	Everton
24	McHugh, Michael B.	Bradford City	Scarborough
24	Marchant, Giles R.	Walton & Hersham	Sutton United
24	Martindale, Gary	Burscough	Bolton Wanderers
22	Millen, Keith D.	Brentford	Watford
24	Parkinson, Joseph S.	AFC Bournemouth	Everton
24	Patterson, Ian D.	Burnley	Wigan Athletic
24	Peacock, Darren	Queens Park Rangers	Newcastle United
26	Peake, Jason W.	Halifax Town	Rochdale
8	Power, Lee M.	Norwich City	Bradford City
1	Rowett, Gary	Cambridge United	Everton
3	Russell, Kevin J.	Burnley	AFC Bournemouth
24	Scully, Patrick J.	Southend United	Huddersfield Town
24	Taylor, Robert A.	Leyton Orient	Brentford
24	Thomas, Mitchell A.	West Ham United	Luton Town
21	Tomlinson, Michael L.	Leyton Orient	Barnet
11	Walsh, Paul A.	Portsmouth	Manchester City
24	Whitton, Stephen P.	Ipswich Town	Colchester United
24	Williams, Lee	Aston Villa	Peterborough United

Temporary transfers

3	Adebola, Bamberdele	Crewe Alexandra	Northwich Victoria
28	Alsford, Julian	Watford	Slough Town
24	Bailey, Dennis L.	Queens Park Rangers	Watford
4	Beadle, Peter C.	Tottenham Hotspur	Southend United
24	Beckford, Jason N.	Birmingham City	Bury
26	Benton, Stephen	Bristol City	Weston Super Mare
24	Blissett, Luther	Bury	Southport
24	Boere, Jerome W.	West Ham United	Portsmouth
4	Bradbury, Shaun D.	Wolverhampton Wanderers	Telford United
22	Brown, Ian O.	Bristol City	Colchester United
4	Burke, Mark S.	Wolverhampton Wanderers	Luton Town
11	Burns, Christopher	Portsmouth	AFC Bournemouth
18	Burton, Simon P.	Preston North End	Altrincham
17	Campbell, David	Burnley	Portadown
24	Carmichael, David	Coventry City	Nuneaton Borough
23	Carter, James W. C.	Arsenal	Oxford United
7	Carter, Timothy D.	Hartlepool United	Millwall

30 Clarke, Christopher	Bolton Wanderers	Chorley
21 Clarke, Nicholas J.	Bromsgrove Rovers	Preston North End
18 Cornwell, John A.	Southend United	Northampton Town
3 Costello, Peter	Lincoln City	Kettering Town
24 Cowan, Thomas	Sheffield United	Huddersfield Town
24 Cronin, Gareth	Sunderland	Bradford City
24 Cusack, Nicholas J.	Oxford United	Wycombe Wanderers
4 Dempsey, Mark A.	Gillingham	Kettering Town
24 Dichio, Daniele S. E.	Queens Park Rangers	Barnet
23 Dickov, Paul	Arsenal	Brighton & Hove Albion
17 Dolby, Tony C.	Millwall	Barnet
18 Duffin, Stuart	Bristol City	Weymouth
28 Durbin, Gary	Bristol City	Weymouth
31 Gonzague, Michael	Southend United	Enfield
3 Gregory, Neil R.	Ipswich Town	Chesterfield
24 Heald, Paul A.	Leyton Orient	Swindon Town
18 Heavey, Paul A.	Preston North End	Fleetwood Town
31 Holmes, Steven P.	Preston North End	Bromsgrove Rovers
6 Howarth, Neil	Burnley	Macclesfield Town
4 Hoyland, Jamie W.	Sheffield United	Bristol City
18 Ireland, Simon P.	Blackburn Rovers	Mansfield Town
23 Jones, Terence P.	Everton	Northwich Victoria
23 Kee, Paul V.	Oxford United	Reading
24 Kelly, Gary A.	Bury	West Ham United
11 Kelly, James	Wolverhampton Wanderers	Wrexham
31 Kelly, Paul	Fulham	Hendon
24 Kerr, Paul A.	Port Vale	Leicester City
24 Kerr, Stuart P.	AFC Bournemouth	Bashley
24 Kilford, Ian A.	Nottingham Forest	Wigan Athletic
4 Kubicki, Dariusz	Aston Villa	Sunderland
8 Lakin, Barry	Leyton Orient	Woking
24 Lancashire, Graham	Burnley	Chester City
30 Livett, Simon R.	Cambridge United	Dagenham & Redbridge
10 Llewellyn, Andrew D.	Bristol City	Exeter City
3 Lormor, Anthony	Lincoln City	Halifax Town
24 Lowe, David A.	Leicester City	Port Vale
31 Lynch, Anthony J.	Barnet	Stevenage Borough
24 Lyne, Neil G. F.	Cambridge United	Chesterfield
24 McGee, Paul	Wimbledon	Peterborough United
4 McMinn, Kevin C.	Birmingham City	Burnley
24 Maguire, Gavin T.	Millwall	Scarborough
21 Marshall, Scott R.	Arsenal	Oxford United
24 Mehew, David S.	Bristol Rovers	Exeter City
24 Mooney, Thomas J.	Southend United	Watford
31 Morgan, Scott	Brentford	Wokingham Town
24 Murray, Bruce E.	Millwall	Stockport County
17 Nogan, Lee M.	Watford	Southend United
24 Oakes, Michael C.	Aston Villa	Tranmere Rovers
4 Parkinson, Stephen	Lincoln City	Kings Lynn
24 Penney, David M.	Oxford United	Swansea City
28 Peters, Robert A.	Brentford	Slough Town
2 Quinn, Stephen J.	Blackpool	Stockport County
24 Reid, Brian	Rangers	Newcastle United
18 Roberts, Darren A.	Wolverhampton Wanderers	Hereford United
9 Sertori, Mark A.	Wrexham	Preston North End
31 Sheppard, Simon	Watford	Scarborough
31 Skidmore, Robert J.	Bristol City	Clevedon Town
7 Skinner, Justin J.	Wimbledon	AFC Bournemouth
24 Small, Michael A.	West Ham United	Charlton Athletic
24 Southon, Jamie P.	Southend United	Stevenage Borough
30 Stewart, Paul A.	Liverpool	Crystal Palace
24 Swales, Stephen C.	Scarborough	Millwall
25 Sweetman, Nicholas E.	Leyton Orient	Baldock Town
11 Thorne, Peter L.	Blackburn Rovers	Wigan Athletic
1 Wallace, Raymond G.	Leeds United	Reading
24 Walters, Mark	Liverpool	Stoke City
4 Warburton, Raymond	York City	Northampton Town
24 Ward, Mark W.	Everton	Birmingham City
31 Ward, Richard	Huddersfield Town	Stalybridge Celtic

24	Watson, Kevin E.	Tottenham Hotspur	Brentford
9	Watts, Grant	Crystal Palace	Colchester United
24	West, Mark	Wycombe Wanderers	Yeovil Town
24	White, Christopher J.	Exeter City	Yeovil Town
31	Whitmarsh, Paul	Doncaster Rovers	Gateshead
27	Whittingham, Guy	Aston Villa	Wolverhampton Wanderers
10	Williams, Gareth J.	Barnsley	Hull City
11	Williams, Lee	Aston Villa	Peterborough United
22	Wilson, Lee	Mansfield Town	Telford United
24	Winnie, David	Aberdeen	Middlesbrough
24	Woods, Raymond G.	Coventry City	Shrewsbury Town
24	Worthington, Gary L.	Exeter City	Doncaster Rovers

April 1994

5	McMinn, Kevin C.	Birmingham City	Burnley

Temporary transfers

5	Gonzague, Michael A.	Southend United	Enfield
2	Harrison, Garry M.	Northampton Town	Racing Club Warwick

May 1994

26	Bushay, Ansil	St Albans City	Slough Town
26	Furlong, Paul A.	Watford	Chelsea
31	Hodges, Lee L.	Tottenham Hotspur	Barnet
12	McDougald, David E. J.	Tottenham Hotspur	Brighton & Hove Albion
28	Minto, Scott C.	Charlton Athletic	Chelsea
12	Morrison, David E.	Chelmsford City	Peterborough United
11	Munday, Mark	Herne Bay	Gravesend & Northfleet
17	O'Connor, Martyn J.	Crystal Palace	Walsall
17	Reid, Paul R.	Bradford City	Huddersfield Town

Temporary transfers

1	Skidmore, Robert	Bristol City	Clevedon Town

FA CUP REVIEW

Once Gavin Peacock's far-out drop shot had nudged the crossbar and bounced to safety, you had the feeling Chelsea would pay for this measure of misfortune. Manchester United went on to score four times without reply to become the fourth team this century to complete the League and Cup double and the sixth overall.

But for an hour Chelsea were the more cohesive of two struggling sides on a wet surface. Neither team was able to deliver a final pass of any threat, before Eddie Newton upended Dennis Irwin inside the penalty area and Harrow schoolmaster David Elleray unhesitantly pointed to the spot. From that moment Chelsea were heading for a caning.

Eric Cantona, who had a quiet game along with several other Manchester United players up to that time and might have been substituted because of a sciatica problem, scored from the penalty. Five minutes later Frank Sinclair jostled for possession with an Andrei Kanchelskis in full flight and Elleray awarded a second penalty for United, though the infringement was just outside the area. Cantona completed the formality again, the first time two penalties had been awarded in an FA Cup Final for one team.

The Frenchman should have made to a hat-trick shortly afterwards, but pulled his shot wide of the upright when clean through. However goal number three came after Sinclair missed his footing and Hughes swept through at an angle. Inside eight minutes Chelsea were out of the reckoning, but there was still time for them to concede a fourth goal, when substitute Brian McClair was left with a simple tap-in.

To their credit Chelsea did not give up. In fact over the 90 minutes they had more goal attempts than United, but never really looked capable of scoring. Mark Stein leading the attack did not appear match fit after returning not long ago from injury and departed from the scene before the end. Moreover their passing game did not allow for players to take opponents on individually and on this tricky surface it might have paid better dividends.

For United Giggs was only seen in flashes. Paul Ince and Mark Hughes were probably their best players. Referee Elleray booked Erland Johnsen for a body check on Giggs and Steve Bruce for an indiscretion of his own.

Manchester United thus became the joint most successful team in FA Cup history with eight wins shared with Tottenham and equalled their previous biggest win, achieved when they defeated Brighton and Hove Albion 4-0 in the replay of the 1983 final.

United avoided a hat-trick of defeats against chelsea in the season, which had seen Peacock twice score the only goal of the FA Carling Premiership matches with them. But who knows what might have happened had his attempt gone in.

FINAL at Wembley
14 MAY
Manchester U (0) 4 *(Cantona 2 (2 pens), Hughes, McClair)*
Chelsea (0) 0 79,634
Manchester U: Schmeichel; Parker, Irwin (Sharpe), Bruce, Kanchelskis (McClair), Pallister, Cantona, Ince, Keane, Hughes, Giggs.
Chelsea: Kharine; Clarke, Sinclair, Kjeldbjerg, Johnsen, Burley (Hoddle), Spencer, Newton, Stein (Cascarino), Peacock, Wise.
Referee: D. Elleray (Harrow).

FA CUP 1993–94

FIRST ROUND

Leek	(0) 2	Wigan Ath	(1) 2
Barnet	(0) 2	Carshalton	(1) 1
Bournemouth	(3) 4	Brighton & HA	(1) 2
Bradford C	(0) 0	Chester C	(0) 0
Burnley	(0) 0	York C	(0) 0
Cambridge U	(0) 0	Reading	(0) 0
Chesterfield	(0) 0	Rochdale	(0) 1
Colchester U	(1) 3	Sutton U	(2) 4
Crewe Alex	(2) 4	Darlington	(2) 2
Enfield	(0) 0	Cardiff C	(0) 0
Farnborough	(1) 1	Exeter C	(0) 3
Gretna	(2) 2	Bolton W	(1) 3
Kidderminster	(0) 3	Kettering	(0) 0
Knowsley	(1) 1	Carlisle U	(3) 4
Leyton Orient	(1) 2	Gravesend & N	(1) 1
Macclesfield	(2) 2	Hartlepool U	(0) 0
Mansfield T	(0) 1	Preston NE	(0) 2
Marlow	(0) 0	Plymouth Arg	(0) 2
Met Police	(0) 0	Crawley	(0) 2
Molesey	(0) 0	Bath	(4) 4
Northampton T	(0) 1	Bromsgrove	(1) 2
Port Vale	(2) 2	Blackpool	(0) 0
Rotherham U	(0) 1	Stockport Co	(0) 2
Runcorn	0	Hull City	1
Scarborough	(0) 1	Bury	(0) 0
Shrewsbury T	(0) 1	Doncaster R	(0) 1
Slough	(0) 1	Torquay U	(2) 2
Stalybridge	(1) 1	Marine	(1) 1
Swansea C	(0) 1	Nuneaton	(0) 1
Telford	(1) 1	Huddersfield T	(1) 1
VS Rugby	(0) 0	Brentford	(1) 3
Witton	(0) 0	Lincoln C	(0) 2
Woking	(1) 2	Weston Super Mare	(2) 2
Wrexham	(1) 1	Walsall	(1) 1
Yeading	(0) 0	Gillingham	(0) 0
Accrington S	(0) 2	Scunthorpe U	(1) 3
Bristol R	(1) 1	Wycombe W	(1) 2
Cambridge C	(0) 0	Hereford U	(0) 1
Halifax T	(2) 2	WBA	(0) 1
Yeovil	(0) 1	Fulham	(0) 0
Runcorn	(0) 0	Hull C	(0) 2

FIRST ROUND REPLAYS

Huddersfield T	(0) 1	Telford	(0) 0
Nuneaton	(0) 2	Swansea C	(1) 1
Walsall	(0) 2	Wrexham	(0) 0
Weston Super Mare	(0) 0	Woking	(0) 1
Reading	(1) 1	Cambridge U	(1) 2
Marine	(2) 4	Stalybridge	(2) 4

Cardiff C	(0) 1	Enfield	(0) 0
Chester C	(1) 1	Bradford C	(0) 0
Gillingham	(3) 3	Yeading	(0) 1
Wigan Ath	(1) 3	Leek	(0) 0
York C	(1) 2	Burnley	(2) 3
Doncaster R	(0) 1	Shrewsbury T	(0) 2

SECOND ROUND

Port Vale	(0) 1	Huddersfield T	(0) 0
Bournemouth	(0) 1	Nuneaton	(0) 1
Brentford	(0) 1	Cardiff C	(1) 3
Burnley	(2) 4	Rochdale	(0) 1
Carlisle U	(2) 3	Stalybridge	(0) 1
Chester C	(2) 2	Hull C	(0) 0
Crawley	(0) 1	Barnet	(0) 2
Crewe Alex	(2) 2	Macclesfield	(0) 1
Kidderminster	(0) 1	Woking	(0) 0
Leyton Orient	(1) 1	Exeter C	(1) 1
Lincoln C	(1) 1	Bolton W	(1) 3
Plymouth Arg	(1) 2	Gillingham	(0) 0
Shrewsbury T	(0) 0	Preston NE	(1) 1
Stockport Co	(1) 5	Halifax T	(0) 1
Torquay U	(0) 0	Sutton U	(0) 1
Walsall	(1) 1	Scunthorpe U	(1) 1
Wigan Ath	(0) 1	Scarborough	(0) 0
Wycombe W	(0) 1	Cambridge U	(0) 0
Yeovil	(0) 0	Bromsgrove	(2) 2
Bath	(1) 2	Hereford U	(0) 1

SECOND ROUND REPLAYS

Exeter C	(0) 2	Leyton Orient	(0) 2
Scunthorpe U	(0) 0	Walsall	(0) 0
Nuneaton	(0) 0	Bournemouth	(1) 1

THIRD ROUND

Barnet	(0) 0	Chelsea	(0) 0
Birmingham C	(1) 1	Kidderminster	(1) 2
Blackburn R	(1) 3	Portsmouth	(0) 3
Bolton W	(0) 1	Everton	(0) 0
Bristol C	(1) 1	Liverpool	(1) 1
Bromsgrove	(1) 1	Barnsley	(0) 2
Cardiff C	(0) 2	Middlesbrough	(1) 2
Charlton Ath	(1) 3	Burnley	(0) 0
Exeter C	(0) 0	Aston Villa	(0) 1
Grimsby T	(0) 1	Wigan Ath	(0) 0
Leeds U	(1) 3	Crewe Alex	(1) 1
Manchester C	(0) 4	Leicester C	(0) 1
Newcastle U	(1) 2	Coventry C	(0) 0
Notts Co	(2) 3	Sutton U	(0) 2
Oldham Ath	(0) 2	Derby Co	(1) 1
Oxford U	(1) 2	Tranmere R	(0) 0
Peterborough U	(0) 1	Tottenham H	(0) 1

Plymouth Arg	(0) 1	Chester C	(0) 0
Preston NE	(0) 2	Bournemouth	(0) 1
Sheffield W	(1) 1	Nottingham F	(0) 1
Southampton	(1) 1	Port Vale	(1) 1
Stockport Co	(1) 2	QPR	(1) 1
Stoke C	(0) 0	Bath	(0) 0
Sunderland	(1) 1	Carlisle U	(0) 0
Swindon T	(1) 1	Ipswich T	(0) 1
West Ham U	(0) 2	Watford	(1) 1
Wimbledon	(2) 3	Scunthorpe U	(0) 0
Wolverhampton W	(0) 1	Crystal Palace	(0) 0
Wycombe W	(0) 0	Norwich C	(1) 2
Sheffield U	(0) 0	Manchester U	(0) 1
Millwall	(0) 0	Arsenal	(0) 1
Luton T	(0) 1	Southend U	(0) 0

THIRD ROUND REPLAYS

Bath	(0) 1	Stoke C	(2) 4
Carlisle U	(0) 0	Sunderland	(0) 1
Ipswich T	(1) 2	Swindon T	(0) 1
Port Vale	(1) 1	Southampton	(0) 0

THIRD ROUND

| Bristol C | (0) 1 | Liverpool | (0) 1 |

THIRD ROUND REPLAYS

Chelsea	(2) 4	Barnet	(0) 0
Everton	(1) 2	Bolton W	(0) 3
Middlesbrough	(0) 1	Cardiff C	(1) 2
Nottingham F	(0) 0	Sheffield W	(0) 2
Portsmouth	(0) 1	Blackburn R	(1) 3
Tottenham H	(1) 1	Peterborough U	(1) 1
Liverpool	(0) 0	Bristol C	(0) 1

FOURTH ROUND

Cardiff C	(0) 1	Manchester C	(0) 0
Charlton Ath	(0) 0	Blackburn R	(0) 0
Chelsea	(1) 1	Sheffield W	(0) 1
Grimsby T	(0) 1	Aston Villa	(1) 2
Ipswich T	(0) 3	Tottenham H	(0) 0
Kidderminster	(0) 1	Preston NE	(0) 0
Newcastle U	(0) 1	Luton T	(0) 1
Notts Co	(1) 1	West Ham U	(1) 1
Oldham Ath	(0) 0	Stoke C	(0) 0
Oxford U	(2) 2	Leeds U	(1) 2
Plymouth Arg	(0) 2	Barnsley	(1) 2
Port Vale	(0) 0	Wolverhampton W	(1) 2
Wimbledon	(1) 2	Sunderland	(1) 1
Norwich C	(0) 0	Manchester U	(1) 2
Bolton W	(1) 2	Arsenal	(0) 2

FOURTH ROUND REPLAY

| Blackburn R | (0) 0 | Charlton Ath | (1) 1 |

FOURTH ROUND

| Stockport Co | (0) 0 | Bristol C | (1) 4 |

FOURTH ROUND REPLAYS

Arsenal	(1) 1	Bolton W	(1) 3
Barnsley	(0) 1	Plymouth Arg	(0) 0
Leeds U	(0) 2	Oxford U	(0) 3
Luton T	(1) 2	Newcastle U	(0) 0
Sheffield W	(1) 1	Chelsea	(1) 3
Stoke C	(0) 0	Oldham Ath	(1) 1
West Ham U	(0) 1	Notts Co	(0) 0
			aet

FIFTH ROUND

Bristol C	(1) 1	Charlton Ath	(0) 1
Kidderminster	(0) 0	West Ham U	(0) 1
Oldham Ath	(0) 1	Barnsley	(0) 0
Oxford U	(1) 1	Chelsea	(2) 2
Wolverhampton W	(0) 1	Ipswich T	(1) 1
Bolton W	(0) 1	Aston Villa	(0) 0
Cardiff C	(0) 1	Luton T	(1) 2
Wimbledon	(0) 0	Manchester U	(1) 3

FIFTH ROUND REPLAYS

| Charlton Ath | (1) 2 | Bristol C | (0) 0 |
| Ipswich T | (0) 1 | Wolverhampton W | (2) 2 |

SIXTH ROUND

Bolton W	(0) 0	Oldham Ath	(0) 1
Manchester U	(0) 3	Charlton Ath	(0) 1
Chelsea	(0) 1	Wolverhampton W	(0) 0
West Ham U	(0) 0	Luton T	(0) 0

SIXTH ROUND REPLAY

| Luton T | (1) 3 | West Ham U | (1) 2 |

SEMI-FINALS at Wembley

| Chelsea | (1) 2 | Luton T | (0) 0 |
| Manchester U | (0) 1 | Oldham Ath | (0) 1 |

SEMI-FINAL REPLAY at Maine Road

| Manchester U | (2) 4 | Oldham Ath | (1) 1 |

FINAL at Wembley

| Manchester U | (0) 4 | Chelsea | (0) 0 |

PAST FA CUP FINALS

Details of one goalscorer is not available in 1878.

1872	The Wanderers .... 1 *Betts*	Royal Engineers........................0	
1873	The Wanderers .... 2 *Kinnaird, Wollaston*	Oxford University 0	
1874	Oxford University .... 2 *Mackarness, Patton*	Royal Engineers........................0	
1875	Royal Engineers........... 1 *Renny-Tailyour*	Old Etonians ....1* *Bonsor*	
Replay	Royal Engineers........... 2 *Renny-Tailyour, Stafford*	Old Etonians 0	
1876	The Wanderers .... 1 *Edwards*	Old Etonians ....1* *Bonsor*	
Replay	The Wanderers .... 3 *Wollaston, Hughes 2*	Old Etonians 0	
1877	The Wanderers .... 2 *Kenrick, Heron*	Oxford University ....1* *Kinnaird (og)*	
1878	The Wanderers .... 3 *Kenrick 2, Kinnaird*	Royal Engineers........................1 *Unknown*	
1879	Old Etonians .... 1 *Clerke*	Clapham Rovers 0	
1880	Clapham Rovers .... 1 *Lloyd-Jones*	Oxford University 0	
1881	Old Carthusians .... 3 *Wyngard, Parry, Todd*	Old Etonians 0	
1882	Old Etonians .... 1 *Anderson*	Blackburn Rovers....................0	
1883	Blackburn Olympic .... 2 *Costley, Matthews*	Old Etonians ....1* *Goodhart*	
1884	Blackburn Rovers.......... 2 *Brown, Forrest*	Queen's Park, Glasgow ....1 *Christie*	
1885	Blackburn Rovers.......... 2 *Forrest, Brown*	Queen's Park, Glasgow 0	
1886	Blackburn Rovers.......... 0	West Bromwich Albion 0	
Replay	Blackburn Rovers.......... 2 *Brown, Sowerbutts*	West Bromwich Albion 0	
1887	Aston Villa .... 2 *Hunter, Hodgetts*	West Bromwich Albion 0	
1888	West Bromwich Albion . 2 *Woodhall, Bayliss*	Preston NE ....1 *Goodall*	
1889	Preston NE .... 3 *Dewhurst, Ross, Thompson*	Wolverhampton W 0	
1890	Blackburn Rovers.......... 6 *Dewar, John Southworth, Lofthouse, Townley 3*	Sheffield W ....1 *Bennett*	

125

Year	Winner		Runner-up	
1891	Blackburn Rovers	3	Notts Co	1
	Dewar, John Southworth, Townley		Oswald	
1892	West Bromwich Albion	3	Aston Villa	0
	Geddes, Nicholls, Reynolds			
1893	Wolverhampton W	1	Everton	0
	Allen			
1894	Notts Co	4	Bolton W	1
	Watson, Logan 3		Cassidy	
1895	Aston Villa	1	West Bromwich Albion	0
	Devey			
1896	Sheffield W	2	Wolverhampton W	1
	Spiksley 2		Black	
1897	Aston Villa	3	Everton	2
	Campbell, Wheldon, Crabtree		Boyle, Bell	
1898	Nottingham F	3	Derby Co	1
	Capes 2, McPherson		Bloomer	
1899	Sheffield U	4	Derby Co	1
	Bennett, Beers, Almond, Priest		Boag	
1900	Bury	4	Southampton	0
	McLuckie 2, Wood, Plant			
1901	Tottenham H	2	Sheffield U	2
	Brown 2		Bennett, Priest	
Replay	Tottenham H	3	Sheffield U	1
	Cameron, Smith, Brown		Priest	
1902	Sheffield U	1	Southampton	1
	Common		Wood	
Replay	Sheffield U	2	Southampton	1
	Hedley, Barnes		Brown	
1903	Bury	6	Derby Co	0
	Ross, Sagar, Leeming 2, Wood, Plant			
1904	Manchester C	1	Bolton W	0
	Meredith			
1905	Aston Villa	2	Newcastle U	0
	Hampton 2			
1906	Everton	1	Newcastle U	0
	Young			
1907	Sheffield W	2	Everton	1
	Stewart, Simpson		Sharp	
1908	Wolverhampton W	3	Newcastle U	1
	Hunt, Hedley, Harrison		Howie	
1909	Manchester U	1	Bristol C	0
	A. Turnbull			
1910	Newcastle U	1	Barnsley	1
	Rutherford		Tuffnell	
Replay	Newcastle U	2	Barnsley	0
	Shepherd 2 (1 pen)			

1911	Bradford C 0	Newcastle U 0
Replay	Bradford C 1	Newcastle U 0
	Spiers	
1912	Barnsley 0	West Bromwich Albion 0
Replay	Barnsley 1	West Bromwich Albion 0*
	Tuffnell	
1913	Aston Villa 1	Sunderland 0
	Barber	
1914	Burnley 1	Liverpool 0
	Freeman	
1915	Sheffield U 3	Chelsea 0
	Simmons, Fazackerley, Kitchen	
1920	Aston Villa 1	Huddersfield T 0*
	Kirton	
1921	Tottenham H 1	Wolverhampton W 0
	Dimmock	
1922	Huddersfield T ....,..... 1	Preston NE 0
	Smith (pen)	
1923	Bolton W 2	West Ham U 0
	Jack, J.R. Smith	
1924	Newcastle U 2	Aston Villa 0
	Harris, Seymour	
1925	Sheffield U 1	Cardiff C 0
	Tunstall	
1926	Bolton W 1	Manchester C 0
	Jack	
1927	Cardiff C 1	Arsenal 0
	Ferguson	
1928	Blackburn Rovers 3	Huddersfield T 1
	Roscamp 2, McLean	*A. Jackson*
1929	Bolton W 2	Portsmouth 0
	Butler, Blackmore	
1930	Arsenal 2	Huddersfield T 0
	James, Lambert	
1931	West Bromwich Albion . 2	Birmingham 1
	W.G. Richardson 2	*Bradford*
1932	Newcastle U 2	Arsenal 1
	Allen 2	*John*
1933	Everton 3	Manchester C 0
	Stein, Dean, Dunn	
1934	Manchester C 2	Portsmouth 1
	Tilson 2	*Rutherford*
1935	Sheffield W 4	West Bromwich Albion 2
	Rimmer 2, Palethorpe, Hooper	*Boyes, Sandford*
1936	Arsenal 1	Sheffield U 0
	Drake	
1937	Sunderland 3	Preston NE 1
	Gurney, Carter, Burbanks	*F. O'Donnell*

1938	Preston NE 1	Huddersfield T.........................0*
	Mutch (pen)	
1939	Portsmouth 4	Wolverhampton W 1
	Parker 2, Barlow, Anderson	*Dorsett*
1946	Derby Co 4	Charlton Ath...........................1*
	H. Turner (og), Doherty, Stamps 2	*H. Turner*
1947	Charlton Ath 1	Burnley 0*
	Duffy	
1948	Manchester U 4	Blackpool 2
	Rowley 2, Pearson, Anderson	*Shimwell (pen), Mortensen*
1949	Wolverhampton W 3	Leicester C 1
	Pye 2, Smyth, Lewis 2	*Griffiths*
1950	Arsenal 2	Liverpool................................0
	Lewis 2	
1951	Newcastle U 2	Blackpool 0
	Milburn 2	
1952	Newcastle U 1	Arsenal 0
	G. Robledo	
1953	Blackpool 4	Bolton W..............................3
	Mortensen 3, Perry	*Lofthouse, Moir, Bell*
1954	West Bromwich Albion .3	Preston NE............................2
	Allen 2 (1 pen), Griffin	*Morrison, Wayman*
1955	Newcastle U 3	Manchester C.........................1
	Milburn, Mitchell, Hannah	*Johnstone*
1956	Manchester C 3	Birmingham C.........................1
	Hayes, Dyson, Johnstone	*Kinsey*
1957	Aston Villa 2	Manchester U.........................1
	McParland 2	*T. Taylor*
1958	Bolton W 2	Manchester U.........................0
	Lofthouse 2	
1959	Nottingham F 2	Luton T.................................1
	Dwight, Wilson	*Pacey*
1960	Wolverhampton W 3	Blackburn Rovers....................0
	McGrath (og), Deeley 2	
1961	Tottenham H.............. 2	Leicester C 0
	Smith, Dyson	
1962	Tottenham H................ 3	Burnley 1
	Greaves, Smith, Blanchflower (pen)	*Robson*
1963	Manchester U 3	Leicester C 1
	Herd 2, Law	*Keyworth*
1964	West Ham U 3	Preston NE.............................2
	Sissons, Hurst, Boyce	*Holden, Dawson*
1965	Liverpool.................... 2	Leeds U 1*
	Hunt, St John	*Bremner*

1966	Everton	3	Sheffield W	2
	Trebilcock 2, Temple		McCalliog, Ford	
1967	Tottenham H	2	Chelsea	1
	Robertson, Saul		Tambling	
1968	West Bromwich Albion	1	Everton	0*
	Astle			
1969	Manchester C	1	Leicester C	0
	Young			
1970	Chelsea	2	Leeds U	2*
	Houseman, Hutchinson		Charlton, Jones	
Replay	Chelsea	2	Leeds U	1*
	Osgood, Webb		Jones	
1971	Arsenal	2	Liverpool	1*
	Kelly, George		Heighway	
1972	Leeds U	1	Arsenal	0
	Clarke			
1973	Sunderland	1	Leeds U	0
	Porterfield			
1974	Liverpool	3	Newcastle	0
	Keegan 2, Heighway			
1975	West Ham U	2	Fulham	0
	A. Taylor 2			
1976	Southampton	1	Manchester U	0
	Stokes			
1977	Manchester U	2	Liverpool	1
	Pearson, J. Greenhoff		Case	
1978	Ipswich T	1	Arsenal	0
	Osborne			
1979	Arsenal	3	Manchester U	2
	Talbot, Stapleton,		McQueen, McIlroy	
	Sunderland			
1980	West Ham U	1	Arsenal	0
	Brooking			
1981	Tottenham H	1	Manchester C	1*
	Hutchison (og)		Hutchison	
Replay	Tottenham H	3	Manchester C	2
	Villa 2, Crooks		Mackenzie, Reeves (pen)	
1982	Tottenham H	1	QPR	1*
	Hoddle		Fenwick	
Replay	Tottenham H	1	QPR	0
	Hoddle (pen)			
1983	Manchester U	2	Brighton & HA	2*
	Stapleton, Wilkins		Smith, Stevens	
Replay	Manchester U	4	Brighton & HA	0
	Robson 2, Whiteside, Muhren		(pen)	
1984	Everton	2	Watford	0
	Sharp, Gray			
1985	Manchester U	1	Everton	0*
	Whiteside			

1986	Liverpool ....3 *Rush 2, Johnston*	Everton ....1 *Lineker*	
1987	Coventry C ....3 *Bennett, Houchen, Mabbutt (og)*	Tottenham H....................2* *C. Allen, Kilcline (og)*	
1988	Wimbledon ....1 *Sanchez*	Liverpool 0	
1989	Liverpool ....3 *Aldridge, Rush 2*	Everton ....2* *McCall 2*	
1990	Manchester U ....3 *Robson, Hughes 2*	Crystal Palace ....3* *O'Reilly, Wright 2*	
Replay	Manchester U ....1 *Martin*	Crystal Palace 0	
1991	Tottenham H.................2 *Stewart, Walker (og)*	Nottingham F ....1* *Pearce*	
1992	Liverpool ....2 *Thomas, Rush*	Sunderland.......................0	
1993	Arsenal...........................1 *Wright*	Sheffield W ....1 *Hirst*	
Replay	Arsenal...........................2 *Wright, Linighan*	Sheffield W ....1 *Waddle*	
1994	Manchester U ....4 *Cantona 2 (2 pens), Kanchelskis, McClair*	Chelsea 0	

*After extra-time

SUMMARY OF FA CUP WINNERS SINCE 1871

Manchester United.................8	Barnsley 1
Tottenham Hotspur 8	Blackburn Olympic...............1
Aston Villa.............................7	Blackpool 1
Blackburn Rovers...................6	Bradford City.......................1
Newcastle United 6	Burnley 1
Arsenal...................................6	Cardiff City.........................1
Liverpool 5	Charlton Athletic.................1
The Wanderers 5	Chelsea 1
West Bromwich Albion 5	Clapham Rovers...................1
Bolton Wanderers 4	Coventry City......................1
Everton 4	Derby County......................1
Manchester City 4	Huddersfield Town 1
Sheffield United.....................4	Ipswich Town......................1
Wolverhampton Wanderers 4	Leeds United........................1
Sheffield Wednesday 3	Notts County.......................1
West Ham United 3	Old Carthusians...................1
Bury 2	Oxford University................1
Nottingham Forest..................2	Portsmouth..........................1
Old Etonians 2	Royal Engineers...................1
Preston North End 2	Southampton 1
Sunderland..............................2	Wimbledon 1

APPEARANCES IN FA CUP FINAL

Arsenal	12	Blackpool	3
Manchester United	12	Burnley	3
Everton	11	Nottingham Forest	3
Newcastle United	11	Portsmouth	3
Liverpool	10	Southampton	3
West Bromwich Albion	10	Barnsley	2
Aston Villa	9	Birmingham City	2
Tottenham Hotspur	9	Bury	2
Blackburn Rovers	8	Cardiff City	2
Manchester City	8	Charlton Athletic	2
Wolverhampton Wanderers	8	Clapham Rovers	2
Bolton Wanderers	7	Notts County	2
Preston North End	7	Queen's Park (Glasgow)	2
Old Etonians	6	Blackburn Olympic	1
Sheffield United	6	Bradford City	1
Sheffield Wednesday	6	Brighton & Hove Albion	1
Huddersfield Town	5	Bristol City	1
The Wanderers	5	Coventry City	1
Chelsea	4	Crystal Palace	1
Derby County	4	Fulham	1
Leeds United	4	Ipswich Town	1
Leicester City	4	Luton Town	1
Oxford University	4	Old Carthusians	1
Royal Engineers	4	Queen's Park Rangers	1
Sunderland	4	Watford	1
West Ham United	4	Wimbledon	1

COCA-COLA CUP REVIEW

Aston Villa, the initial winners of the League Cup competition in 1961, equalled the four wins achieved by Liverpool and Nottingham Forest with a convincing 3-1 success over Manchester United, who at the time were chasing an historic treble of domestic titles.

Back at the beginning of the first round, Bradford City had led the goalscoring with an aggregate 11-1 win over Darlington. Bradford then took a 2-1 lead in the first leg of the second round against Norwich City before losing at Carrow Road by three clear goals.

Holders Arsenal also began the defence of their crown in scoring form with a 5-0 win at Huddersfield Town, before being held 1-1 at Highbury in the second leg. Other goal rushes in the first leg saw Leicester take a 6-1 lead at Rochdale, Middlesbrough beat Brighton 5-0 and Tranmere and West Ham establish 5-1 leads respectively over Oxford and Chesterfield.

Newcastle United outscored everyone in the second legs, winning 7-1 at Notts County for an 11-1 aggregate success. Andy Cole achieved a hat-trick in both games. But the best individual effort came from Liverpool's Robbie Fowler with all five goals against Fulham.

Premiership casualties were Sheffield United against Blackpool, Leeds against Sunderland, and Southampton at the hands of Shrewsbury, while Coventry needed extra time to dispose of Endsleigh Insurance League newcomers Wycombe Wanderers.

Aston Villa and Manchester United emerged safely beating Birmingham and Stoke respectively. Both had easy wins in the third round, Villa 4-1 at Sunderland, United 5-1 at home to Leicester. Arsenal needed a replay before eliminating Norwich away 3-0.

A Dalian Atkinson goal after just four minutes at Highbury gave Villa a 1-0 triumph over the holders, while United were winning 2-0 at Everton. Villa then completed a North London double by winning 2-1 at Tottenham in the fifth round.

However, Manchester United found Portsmouth more durable opponents and they were forced into a replay at Fratton Park before emerging. Meanwhile last year's beaten finalists Sheffield Wednesday were progressing along with Endsleigh First Division Tranmere.

Wednesday restricted United to a 1-0 lead in their semi-final at Old Trafford, but the Reds eased through at Hillsborough 4-1. Not so the other semi where Tranmere took a deserved 3-1 lead in the first leg.

At Villa Park, Tranmere looked to be through still leading 4-3 on aggregate with two minutes remaining. Then Atkinson levelled the scores and Villa won 5-4 on penalties after extra time with Mark Bosnich the hero in the Villa goal. However he had been fortunate to escape a red card for a first half foul on John Aldridge which gave Tranmere their goal from the spot.

Handball by Andrei Kanchelskis gave Villa a last minute penalty in the final and a red card for United. But the game really had been won and lost at 2-0 with goals in 25 and 75 minutes from Atkinson and Dean Saunders respectively.

COCA COLA CUP 1993–94

FIRST ROUND FIRST LEG

Doncaster R	(0) 0	Blackpool	(0) 1
Birmingham C	(2) 3	Plymouth Arg	(0) 0
Bolton W	(0) 0	Bury	(2) 2
Bournemouth	(2) 3	Cardiff C	(1) 1
Brentford	(0) 2	Watford	(1) 2
Cambridge U	(1) 1	Luton T	(0) 0
Chesterfield	(1) 3	Carlisle U	(1) 1
Crewe Alex	(0) 0	Wrexham	(0) 1
Darlington	(1) 1	Bradford C	(2) 5
Fulham	(0) 2	Colchester U	(0) 0
Gillingham	(0) 1	Brighton & HA	(0) 0
Hereford U	(0) 0	Torquay U	(2) 2
Huddersfield T	(0) 0	Scarborough	(0) 0
Leyton Orient	(0) 0	Wycombe W	(1) 2
Notts Co	(2) 2	Hull C	(0) 0
Port Vale	(0) 2	Lincoln C	(0) 2
Preston NE	(1) 1	Burnley	(1) 2
Rochdale	(0) 2	York C	(0) 0
Shrewsbury T	(1) 1	Scunthorpe U	(0) 0
Stockport Co	(1) 1	Hartlepool U	(1) 1
Sunderland	(0) 3	Chester C	(1) 1
Swansea C	(0) 0	Bristol C	(0) 1
Walsall	(0) 0	Exeter C	(0) 0
Wigan Ath	(0) 0	Rotherham U	(0) 1
Bristol R	(1) 1	WBA	(2) 4
Reading	(0) 3	Northampton T	(0) 0
Southend U	(0) 0	Barnet	(0) 2
Stoke C	(1) 2	Mansfield T	(2) 2

FIRST ROUND SECOND LEG

Barnet	(0) 1	Southend U	(0) 1
Blackpool	(1) 3	Doncaster R	(3) 3
Bristol C	(0) 0	Swansea C	(1) 2
Bury	(0) 0	Bolton W	(1) 2
Cardiff C	(1) 1	Bournemouth	(1) 1
Carlisle U	(1) 1	Chesterfield	(1) 1
Chester C	(0) 0	Sunderland	(0) 0
Colchester U	(0) 0	Fulham	(0) 2
Hartlepool U	(0) 2	Stockport Co	(1) 1
Hull C	(3) 3	Notts Co	(0) 1
Lincoln C	(0) 0	Port Vale	(0) 0
Luton T	(0) 0	Cambridge U	(0) 1
Mansfield T	(1) 1	Stoke C	(1) 3
Plymouth Arg	(0) 2	Birmingham C	(0) 0
Rotherham U	(3) 4	Wigan Ath	(1) 2
Scarborough	(0) 0	Huddersfield T	(1) 3
Scunthorpe U	(0) 1	Shrewsbury T	(0) 0
Torquay U	(0) 0	Hereford U	(0) 2
Watford	(1) 3	Brentford	(1) 1

Wrexham	(2) 3	Crewe Alex	(1) 3
Wycombe W	(1) 1	Leyton Orient	(0) 0
York C	(0) 0	Rochdale	(0) 0
Bradford C	(3) 6	Darlington	(0) 0
Brighton & HA	(1) 2	Gillingham	(0) 0
Burnley	(1) 4	Preston NE	(0) 1
Exeter C	(1) 2	Walsall	(1) 1
WBA	(0) 0	Bristol R	(0) 0
Northampton T	(0) 0	Reading	(1) 2

SECOND ROUND FIRST LEG

Barnet	(0) 1	QPR	(2) 2
Barnsley	(0) 1	Peterborough U	(0) 1
Birmingham C	(0) 0	Aston Villa	(0) 1
Blackburn R	(1) 1	Bournemouth	(0) 0
Blackpool	(2) 3	Sheffield U	(0) 0
Bolton W	(0) 1	Sheffield W	(0) 1
Crystal Palace	(1) 3	Charlton Ath	(0) 1
Grimsby T	(1) 3	Hartlepool U	(0) 0
Huddersfield T	(0) 0	Arsenal	(2) 5
Ipswich T	(1) 2	Cambridge U	(0) 0
Lincoln C	(1) 3	Everton	(1) 4
Middlesbrough	(4) 5	Brighton & HA	(0) 0
Rochdale	(1) 1	Leicester C	(1) 6
Rotherham U	(0) 0	Portsmouth	(0) 0
Sunderland	(1) 2	Leeds U	(1) 1
Swansea C	(2) 2	Oldham Ath	(1) 1
Tranmere R	(1) 5	Oxford U	(0) 1
Watford	(0) 0	Millwall	(0) 0
Wrexham	(0) 3	Nottingham F	(2) 3
Bradford C	(1) 2	Norwich C	(0) 1
Burnley	(0) 0	Tottenham H	(0) 0
Coventry C	(2) 3	Wycombe W	(0) 0
Exeter C	(1) 1	Derby Co	(1) 3
Fulham	(0) 1	Liverpool	(2) 3
Hereford U	(0) 0	Wimbledon	(1) 1
Manchester C	(1) 1	Reading	(0) 0
Newcastle U	(1) 4	Notts Co	(1) 1
Southampton	(1) 1	Shrewsbury T	(0) 0
Stoke C	(1) 2	Manchester U	(0) 1
Swindon T	(1) 2	Wolverhampton W	(0) 0
WBA	(1) 1	Chelsea	(0) 1
West Ham U	(3) 5	Chesterfield	(0) 1

SECOND ROUND SECOND LEG

Arsenal	(0) 1	Huddersfield T	(1) 1
Bournemouth	(0) 0	Blackburn R	(0) 0
Cambridge U	(0) 0	Ipswich T	(0) 2
Charlton Ath	(0) 0	Crystal Palace	(0) 1
Chesterfield	(0) 0	West Ham U	(0) 2
Hartlepool U	(0) 0	Grimsby T	(1) 2
Liverpool	(2) 5	Fulham	(0) 0
Notts Co	(0) 1	Newcastle U	(3) 7

134

Oxford U	(0) 1	Tranmere R	(1) 1
Peterborough U	(1) 3	Barnsley	(0) 1
Portsmouth	(3) 5	Rotherham U	(0) 1
Sheffield U	(0) 2	Blackpool	(0) 0
Wimbledon	(3) 4	Hereford U	(0) 1
Wolverhampton W	(0) 2	Swindon T	(0) 1
Wycombe W	(1) 4	Coventry C	(0) 2
Aston Villa	(0) 1	Birmingham C	(0) 0
Brighton & HA	(0) 1	Middlesbrough	(2) 3
Chelsea	(1) 2	WBA	(1) 1
Derby Co	(1) 2	Exeter C	(0) 0
Everton	(1) 4	Lincoln C	(0) 2
Leeds U	(0) 1	Sunderland	(2) 2
Leicester C	(1) 2	Rochdale	(1) 1
Manchester U	(0) 2	Stoke C	(0) 0
Millwall	(2) 4	Watford	(2) 3
Norwich C	(0) 3	Bradford C	(0) 0
Nottingham F	(1) 3	Wrexham	(0) 1
Oldham Ath	(2) 2	Swansea C	(0) 0
QPR	(2) 4	Barnet	(0) 0
Reading	(0) 1	Manchester C	(1) 2
Sheffield W	(0) 1	Bolton W	(0) 0
Shrewsbury T	(1) 2	Southampton	(0) 0
Tottenham H	(1) 3	Burnley	(1) 1

THIRD ROUND

Arsenal	(0) 1	Norwich C	(1) 1
Blackburn R	(0) 0	Shrewsbury T	(0) 0
Blackpool	(1) 2	Peterborough U	(1) 2
Everton	(0) 2	Crystal Palace	(0) 2
Manchester C	(0) 1	Chelsea	(0) 0
Oldham Ath	(1) 2	Coventry C	(0) 0
Portsmouth	(0) 2	Swindon T	(0) 0
Sunderland	(0) 1	Aston Villa	(2) 4
Tranmere R	(2) 4	Grimsby T	(0) 1
Derby Co	(0) 0	Tottenham H	(0) 1
Liverpool	(2) 3	Ipswich T	(1) 2
Manchester U	(2) 5	Leicester C	(0) 0
Middlesbrough	(0) 1	Sheffield W	(0) 1
Nottingham F	(1) 2	West Ham U	(0) 1
QPR	(2) 3	Millwall	(0) 0
Wimbledon	(1) 2	Newcastle U	(1) 1

THIRD ROUND REPLAYS

Peterborough U	(2) 2	Blackpool	(1) 1
Shrewsbury T	(1) 3	Blackburn R	(1) 4
Crystal Palace	(1) 1	Everton	(0) 4
Norwich C	(0) 0	Arsenal	(2) 3
Sheffield W	(1) 2	Middlesbrough	(1) 1

FOURTH ROUND

Arsenal	(0) 0	Aston Villa	(1) 1

135

Everton	(0) 0	Manchester U	(1) 2
Peterborough U	(0) 0	Portsmouth	(0) 0
Tranmere R	(0) 3	Oldham Ath	(0) 0
Liverpool	(1) 1	Wimbledon	(0) 1
Nottingham F	(0) 0	Manchester C	(0) 0
QPR	(1) 1	Sheffield W	(1) 2
Tottenham H	(0) 1	Blackburn R	(0) 0

FOURTH ROUND REPLAYS

Wimbledon	(1) 2	Liverpool	(1) 2
Manchester C	(1) 1	Nottingham F	(2) 2
Portsmouth	(0) 1	Peterborough U	(0) 0

FIFTH ROUND

Wimbledon	(0) 1	Sheffield W	(0) 2
Manchester U	(1) 2	Portsmouth	(1) 2
Tottenham H	(0) 1	Aston Villa	(0) 2
Nottingham F	(0) 1	Tranmere R	(0) 1

FIFTH ROUND REPLAYS

| Portsmouth | (0) 0 | Manchester U | (1) 1 |
| Tranmere R | (1) 2 | Nottingham F | (0) 0 |

SEMI-FINAL FIRST LEG

| Manchester U | (1) 1 | Sheffield W | (0) 0 |
| Tranmere R | (2) 3 | Aston Villa | (0) 1 |

SEMI-FINAL SECOND LEG

| Aston Villa | (2) 3 | Tranmere R | (1) 1 |
| Sheffield W | (1) 1 | Manchester U | (3) 4 |

FINAL at Wembley

| Aston Villa | (1) 3 | Manchester U | (0) 1 |

*after extra time   †won on penalties   ††won on away goals

FINAL at Wembley
27 MAR
Aston Villa (1) 3 *(Atkinson, Saunders 2 (1 pen))*

Manchester U (0) 1 *(Hughes)*   77,231

Aston Villa: Bosnich; Barrett, Staunton (Cox), Teale, McGrath, Richardson, Daley, Townsend, Saunders, Atkinson, Fenton.
Manchester U: Sealey; Parker, Irwin, Bruce (McClair), Kanchelskis, Pallister, Cantona, Ince, Keane, Hughes, Giggs (Sharpe).
Referee: K. Cooper (Pontypridd).

PAST LEAGUE CUP FINALS

Played as two legs up to 1966

1961	Rotherham U.............2	Aston Villa.............0
	Webster, Kirkman	
	Aston Villa.............3	Rotherham U.............0*
	O'Neill, Burrows, McParland	
1962	Rochdale.............0	Norwich C.............3
		Lythgoe 2, Punton
	Norwich C.............1	Rochdale.............0
	Hill	
1963	Birmingham C.............3	Aston Villa.............1
	Leek 2, Bloomfield	*Thomson*
	Aston Villa.............0	Birmingham C.............0
1964	Stoke C.............1	Leicester C.............1
	Bebbington	*Gibson*
	Leicester C.............3	Stoke C.............2
	Stringfellow, Gibson, Riley	*Viollet, Kinnell*
1965	Chelsea.............3	Leicester C.............2
	Tambling, Venables (pen), McCreadie	*Appleton, Goodfellow*
	Leicester C.............0	Chelsea.............0
1966	West Ham U.............2	WBA.............1
	Moore, Byrne	*Astle*
	WBA.............4	West Ham U.............1
	Kaye, Brown, Clark, Williams	*Peters*
1967	QPR.............3	WBA.............2
	Morgan R, Marsh, Lazarus	*Clark C 2*
1968	Leeds U.............1	Arsenal.............0
	Cooper	
1969	Swindon T.............3	Arsenal.............1*
	Smart, Rogers 2	*Gould*
1970	Manchester C.............2	WBA.............1*
	Doyle, Pardoe	*Astle*
1971	Tottenham H.............2	Aston Villa.............0
	Chivers 2	
1972	Chelsea.............1	Stoke C.............2
	Osgood	*Conroy, Eastham*
1973	Tottenham H.............1	Norwich C.............0
	Coates	
1974	Wolverhampton W.............2	Manchester C.............1
	Hibbitt, Richards	*Bell*
1975	Aston Villa.............1	Norwich C.............0
	Graydon	
1976	Manchester C.............2	Newcastle U.............1
	Barnes, Tueart	*Gowling*
1977	Aston Villa.............0	Everton.............0
Replay	Aston Villa.............1	Everton.............1*
	Kenyon (og)	*Latchford*

Replay	Aston Villa.............................3	Everton 2*	
	Little 2, Nicholl	*Latchford, Lyons*	
1978	Nottingham F.......................0	Liverpool............................0*	
Replay	Nottingham F.......................1	Liverpool............................0	
	Robertson (pen)		
1979	Nottingham F.......................3	Southampton 2	
	Birtles 2, Woodcock	*Peach, Holmes*	
1980	Wolverhampton W 1	Nottingham F.....................0	
	Gray		
1981	Liverpool.............................1	West Ham U.......................1*	
	Kennedy, A	*Stewart (pen)*	
Replay	Liverpool.............................2	West Ham U.......................1	
	Dalglish, Hansen	*Goddard*	
1982	Liverpool.............................3	Tottenham H 1*	
	Whelan 2, Rush	*Archibald*	
1983	Liverpool.............................2	Manchester U 1*	
	Kennedy, Whelan	*Whiteside*	
1984	Liverpool.............................0	Everton 0*	
Replay	Liverpool.............................1	Everton 0	
	Souness		
1985	Norwich C 1	Sunderland 0	
	Chisholm (og)		
1986	Oxford U 3	QPR 0	
	Hebberd, Houghton, Charles		
1987	Arsenal................................2	Liverpool............................1	
	Nicholas 2	*Rush*	
1988	Luton T 3	Arsenal...............................2	
	Stein B 2, Wilson	*Hayes, Smith*	
1989	Nottingham F.......................3	Luton T 1	
	Clough 2, Webb	*Harford*	
1990	Nottingham F.......................1	Oldham Ath........................0	
	Jemson		
1991	Sheffield W 1	Manchester U 0	
	Sheridan		
1992	Manchester U 1	Nottingham F.....................0	
	McClair		
1993	Arsenal................................2	Sheffield W 1	
	Merson, Morrow	*Harkes*	

*After extra time

ANGLO-ITALIAN CUP 1993–94

PRELIMINARY ROUND

Grimsby T	(1) 2	Middlesbrough	(0) 1
Notts Co	(1) 3	Derby Co	(0) 2
Peterborough U	(2) 4	Leicester C	(1) 3
Portsmouth	(2) 3	Bristol C	(1) 1
Sunderland	(0) 2	Tranmere R	(0) 0
Watford	(1) 2	Luton T	(1) 1
Wolverhampton W	(1) 3	Stoke Co	(2) 3
Millwall	(2) 2	Charlton Ath	(1) 2
Bristol C	(1) 2	Oxford U	(0) 1
Charlton Ath	(2) 4	Crystal Palace	(1) 1
Luton T	(0) 1	Southend U	(0) 1
Middlesbrough	(1) 3	Barnsley	(0) 0
Stoke C	(1) 2	Birmingham C	(0) 0
Tranmere R	(0) 1	Bolton W	(2) 2
Derby Co	(0) 3	Nottingham F	(0) 2
Leicester C	(0) 0	WBA	(0) 0
Barnsley	(0) 2	Grimsby T	(1) 1
Birmingham C	(0) 2	Wolverhampton W	(0) 2
Bolton W	(0) 2	Sunderland	(0) 0
Crystal Palace	(2) 3	Millwall	(0) 0
Oxford U	(0) 0	Portsmouth	(2) 2
Nottingham F	(0) 1	Notts Co	(1) 1
Southend U	(3) 3	Watford	(0) 0
WBA	(1) 3	Peterborough U	(0) 1

International Stage
Group A

Bolton W	(1) 5	Ancona	(0) 0
Brescia	(1) 2	Charlton Ath	(0) 0
Notts Co	(2) 4	Ascoli	(0) 2
Pisa	(0) 3	Middlesbrough	(0) 1

Group B

Fiorentina	(1) 3	Southend U	(0) 0
Padova	(0) 0	Portsmouth	(0) 0
Stoke C	(1) 2	Cosenza	(0) 1
WBA	(1) 1	Pescara	(2) 2

Group A

Ancona	(0) 1	Charlton Ath	(0) 1
Bolton W	(1) 3	Brescia	(1) 3
Notts Co	(2) 3	Pisa	(1) 2

Group B

Cosenza	(0) 1	Southend U	(1) 2
Pescara	(1) 2	Portsmouth	(1) 1
WBA	(2) 3	Padova	(2) 4
Stoke C	(0) 0	Fiorentina	(0) 0

Group A

Brescia	(2) 3	Notts Co	(1) 1
Charlton Ath	(0) 0	Ascoli	(2) 3
Middlesbrough	(0) 0	Ancona	(0) 0
Pisa	(1) 1	Bolton W	(1) 1

Group B

Fiorentina	(1) 2	WBA	(0) 0
Padova	(1) 3	Stoke C	(0) 0
Portsmouth	(0) 3	Cosenza	(0) 0
Southend U	(0) 1	Pescara	(2) 3

Group A

Ascoli	(1) 3	Middlesbrough	(0) 0
Ancona	(0) 0	Notts Co	(0) 1
Ascoli	(0) 1	Bolton W	(0) 1
Charlton Ath	(0) 0	Pisa	(2) 3
Middlesbrough	(0) 0	Brescia	(0) 1

Group B

Cosenza	(1) 2	WBA	(1) 1
Pescara	(1) 2	Stoke C	(1) 1
Portsmouth	(1) 2	Fiorentina	(0) 3
Southend U	(0) 5	Padova	(1) 2

SEMI-FINAL FIRST LEG

Brescia	(0) 1	Pescara	(0) 0
Southend U	(1) 1	Notts Co	(0) 0

SEMI-FINAL SECOND LEG

Notts Co	(0) 1	Southend U	(0) 0
Pescara	(1) 3	Brescia	(1) 2

FINAL at Wembley

Notts Co	(0) 0	Brescia	(0) 1

FINAL at Wembley
20 MAR
Notts Co (0) 0
Brescia (0) 1 *(Ambrosetti)*   *17,185*

Notts Co: Cherry; Wilson, Dijkstra, Turner, Johnson, Palmer, Devlin, Draper, Lund, McSwegan (Agana), Legg.
Brescia: Landucci; Marangon, Giunta, Domini, Baronchelli, Bonometti, Schenardi, Sabau, Ambrosetti (Piovanelli), Hagi, Gallo.

AUTOGLASS TROPHY 1993–94

First Round

Scarborough	(2) 2	Scunthorpe U	(0) 2

Blackpool	(1) 1	Chester C	(1) 2
Carlisle U	(1) 2	Preston NE	(0) 0
Fulham	(2) 4	Brighton & HA	(1) 1
Gillingham	(0) 0	Colchester U	(0) 0
Hartlepool U	(0) 1	Darlington	(0) 1
Hereford U	(1) 1	Walsall	(0) 1
Huddersfield T	(1) 3	Doncaster R	(0) 1
Lincoln C	(1) 1	Mansfield T	(0) 1
Plymouth Arg	(0) 1	Swansea C	(1) 3
Stockport Co	(1) 2	Wigan Ath	(0) 0
Torquay U	(0) 0	Bristol R	(0) 1
Wrexham	(2) 3	Shrewsbury T	(1) 1
Wycombe W	(1) 1	Barnet	(0) 0
Doncaster R	(0) 1	Rotherham U	(1) 2
Barnet	(1) 2	Brentford	(1) 2
Chester C	(1) 2	Crewe Alex	(1) 2
Colchester U	(1) 2	Cambridge U	(0) 2
Darlington	(0) 0	York C	(1) 1
Mansfield T	(1) 3	Chesterfield	(1) 1
Preston NE	(0) 2	Burnley	(0) 1
Scunthorpe U	(0) 1	Hull C	(1) 1
Shrewsbury T	(1) 2	Port Vale	(1) 2
Swansea C	(2) 2	Exeter C	(0) 0
Walsall	(0) 0	Northampton T	(0) 0
Wigan Ath	(0) 1	Bury	(0) 3
Brighton & HA	(2) 2	Reading	(0) 2
Bristol R	(1) 3	Cardiff C	(0) 0
Brentford	(0) 2	Wycombe W	(2) 3
Burnley	(0) 1	Carlisle U	(1) 2
Bury	(1) 1	Stockport Co	(2) 3
Cambridge U	(1) 2	Gillingham	(0) 0
Cardiff C	(0) 2	Torquay U	(0) 0
Chesterfield	(0) 1	Lincoln C	(0) 2
Exeter C	(0) 1	Plymouth Arg	(0) 0
Hull C	(0) 0	Scarborough	(2) 2
Northampton T	(1) 1	Hereford U	(1) 1
Port Vale	(0) 0	Wrexham	(0) 0
Rotherham U	(0) 1	Huddersfield T	(1) 1
York C	(1) 2	Hartlepool U	(0) 0
Reading	(0) 1	Fulham	(0) 0
Crewe Alex	(1) 2	Blackpool	(2) 2

Second Round

Cambridge U	(1) 2	Port Vale	(1) 4
Carlisle U	(1) 2	Bury	(1) 1
Hereford U	(0) 1	Brentford	(2) 2
Huddersfield T	(0) 0	Preston NE	(0) 0
Lincoln C	(0) 3	Darlington	(2) 2
Stockport Co	(1) 4	Rochdale	(0) 0
Bristol R	(1) 2	Fulham	(0) 0
Reading	(2) 4	Northampton T	(0) 1
Scarborough	(0) 0	Scunthorpe U	(0) 2
Wrexham	(0) 0	Colchester U	(0) 1

York C	(0) 1	Mansfield T	(0) 1
Chester C	(1) 1	Rotherham U	(0) 0
Bradford C	(1) 2	Crewe Alex	(1) 3
Swansea C	(0) 2	Exeter C	(0) 1
Wycombe W	(0) 3	Cardiff C	(0) 2
Bournemouth	(0) 1	Leyton Orient	(1) 1

Northern quarter-finals

Carlisle U	(1) 2	Mansfield T	(0) 1
Huddersfield T	(2) 3	Crewe Alex	(1) 2
Lincoln C	(1) 1	Chester C	(0) 0
Stockport Co	(0) 2	Scunthorpe U	(0) 0

Southern quarter-finals

Colchester U	(0) 0	Wycombe W	(0) 1
Fulham	(0) 1	Reading	(0) 0
Leyton Orient	(0) 1	Brentford	(0) 0
Swansea C	(0) 1	Port Vale	(0) 0

Northern semi-final

Carlisle U	(1) 2	Lincoln C	(0) 1

Southern semi-finals

Fulham	(1) 2	Wycombe W	(0) 2
Leyton Orient	(0) 0	Swansea C	(2) 2

Northern semi-final

Stockport Co	(0) 0	Huddersfield T	(0) 1

Southern final first leg

Swansea C	(2) 3	Wycombe W	(1) 1

Northern final first leg

Huddersfield T	(1) 4	Carlisle U	(1) 1

Northern final second leg

Carlisle U	(2) 2	Huddersfield T	(0) 0

Southern final second leg

Wycombe W	(1) 1	Swansea C	(0) 0

Final at Wembley

Huddersfield T	(0) 1	Swansea C	(1) 1

Final at Wembley
24 APR

Huddersfield T (0) 1 *(Logan)*
Swansea C (1) 1 *(McFarlane)*   *47,733*

Huddersfield T: Francis; Billy, Cowan, Starbuck, Scully, Mitchell, Logan, Robinson P, Booth, Bullock (Dunn), Baldry.
Swansea C: Freestone; Jenkins, Clode (Torpey), Basham, Harris, Pascoe, Bowen, Ampadu, McFarlane, Cornforth, Hodge (Ford).
aet; Swansea C won 3-1 on penalties

FA CHARITY SHIELD WINNERS 1908–93

1908	Manchester U v QPR	
	4-0 after 1-1 draw	
1909	Newcastle U v Northampton T	2-0
1910	Brighton v Aston Villa	1-0
1911	Manchester U v Swindon T	8-4
1912	Blackburn R v QPR	2-1
1913	Professionals v Amateurs	7-2
1920	WBA v Tottenham H	2-0
1921	Tottenham H v Burnley	2-0
1922	Huddersfield T v Liverpool	1-0
1923	Professionals v Amateurs	2-0
1924	Professionals v Amateurs	3-1
1925	Amateurs v Professionals	6-1
1926	Amateurs v Professionals	6-3
1927	Cardiff C v Corinthians	2-1
1928	Everton v Blackburn R	2-1
1929	Professionals v Amateurs	3-0
1930	Arsenal v Sheffield W	2-1
1931	Arsenal v WBA	1-0
1932	Everton v Newcastle U	5-3
1933	Arsenal v Everton	3-0
1934	Arsenal v Manchester C	4-0
1935	Sheffield W v Arsenal	1-0
1936	Sunderland v Arsenal	2-1
1937	Manchester C v Sunderland	2-0
1938	Arsenal v Preston NE	2-1
1948	Arsenal v Manchester U	4-3
1949	Portsmouth v Wolverhampton W	1-1*
1950	World Cup Team v Canadian	
	Touring Team	4-2
1951	Tottenham H v Newcastle U	2-1
1952	Manchester U v Newcastle U	4-2
1953	Arsenal v Blackpool	3-1
1954	Wolverhampton W v WBA	4-4*
1955	Chelsea v Newcastle U	3-0
1956	Manchester U v Manchester C	1-0
1957	Manchester U v Aston Villa	4-0

1958	Bolton W v Wolverhampton W	4-1
1959	Wolverhampton W v	
	Nottingham F	3-1
1960	Burnley v Wolverhampton W	2-2*
1961	Tottenham H v FA XI	3-2
1962	Tottenham H v Ipswich T	5-1
1963	Everton v Manchester U	4-0
1964	Liverpool v West Ham U	2-2*
1965	Manchester U v Liverpool	2-2*
1966	Liverpool v Everton	1-0
1967	Manchester U v Tottenham H	3-3*
1968	Manchester C v WBA	6-1
1969	Leeds U v Manchester C	2-1
1970	Everton v Chelsea	2-1
1971	Leicester C v Liverpool	1-0
1972	Manchester C v Aston Villa	1-0
1973	Burnley v Manchester C	1-0
1974	Liverpool† v Leeds U	1-1
1975	Derby Co v West Ham U	2-0
1976	Liverpool v Southampton	1-0
1977	Liverpool v Manchester U	0-0*
1978	Nottingham F v Ipswich T	5-0
1979	Liverpool v Arsenal	3-1
1980	Liverpool v West Ham U	1-0
1981	Aston Villa v Tottenham H	2-2*
1982	Liverpool v Tottenham H	1-0
1983	Manchester U v Liverpool	2-0
1984	Everton v Liverpool	1-0
1985	Everton v Manchester U	2-0
1986	Everton v Liverpool	1-1*
1987	Everton v Coventry C	1-0
1988	Liverpool v Wimbledon	2-1
1989	Liverpool v Arsenal	1-0
1990	Liverpool v Manchester U	1-1*
1991	Arsenal v Tottenham H	0-0*
1992	Leeds U v Liverpool	4-3

*Each club retained shield for six months. †Won on penalties.

FA CHARITY SHIELD 1993

Arsenal (1) 1, Manchester U (1) 1
(Manchester U won 5-4 on penalties)

At Wembley, 7 August 1993, attendance 66,519

Arsenal: Seaman; Dixon (Keown), Winterburn, Davis, Linighan, Adams, Jensen, Wright, Campbell, Merson, Limpar (McGoldrick).
Scorer: Wright.

Manchester U: Schmeichel; Parker, Irwin, Bruce, Kanchelskis, Pallister, Cantona, Ince, Keane, Hughes, Giggs (Robson).
Scorer: Hughes.

ABERDEEN PREM. DIV.

Ground: Pittodrie Stadium, Aberdeen AB2 1QH (0224 632328)
Colours: All red with white trim.
Manager: William Miller.
League Appearances: Aitken, R (1); Bett, J 6; Booth, S 14(11); Burridge, J 3; Connor, R 21(4); Gibson, A 1(1); Grant, B 26(4); Irvine, B 42; Jess, E 38(3); Kane, P 39; McKimmie, S 40; McKinnon, R 5; McLeish, A 35; Miller, J 24(3); Paatelainen, M 14(22); Richardson, L 31(4); Robertson, H 6(2); Roddie, A 3(3); Shearer, D 39(4); Smith, G 19(2); Snelders, T 33; Stillie, D 4(1); Ten Caat, T 1(2); Thomson, S (3); Watt, M 4; Winnie, D 2(4); Wright, S 34(2)
Goals-League (58): Shearer 17, Irvine 7, Jess 6, Paatelainen 5, Booth 4, Miller 4, Richardson 4, Kane 3, Grant 2, Connor 1, Roddie 1, own goals 3.
Scottish Cup (8): Shearer 4, Booth 1, Miller 1, Richardson 1, own goal 1.
League Cup (11): Shearer 4 (1 pen), Booth 2, Miller 2, Jess 1, McLeish 1, Richardson 1.

AIRDRIEONIANS DIV. 1

Ground: Broomfield Park, Gartlea Road, Airdrie ML6 9JL (0236 62067)
Colours: White shirts with red diamond, white shorts.
Manager: Alex MacDonald.
League Appearances: Abercromby, M 1(6); Balfour, E 18(7); Black, K 40; Boyle, J 17(10); Caesar, G 16; Conn, S (2); Connelly, G 3(2); Davenport, P 35(3); Ferguson, I 26(2); Harvey, P 9(4); Hay, G 11; Honor, C 32(2); Jack, P 32(3); Kirkwood, D 28(1); Lawrence, A 20(7); McCulloch, W (1); McIntyre, J 8(5); McVicar, D 20(1); Martin, J 44; Reid, W 14(4); Sandison, J 33; Smith, Andr 25(13); Smith, Anth 4(2); Stewart, A 36; Tomnay, D 1; Wilson, M 11
Goals-League (58): Kirkwood 10 (5 pens), Davenport 9, Ferguson 9, Andrew Smith 7, Lawrence 5, Honor 2 (1 pen), Reid 2, Stewart 2, Black 1, Boyle 1, Caesar 1, Harvey 1, Hay 1, Jack 1, Anthony Smith 1, Wilson 1, own goals 4.
Scottish Cup (5): Kirkwood 4 (4 pens), Ferguson 1.
League Cup (4): Balfour 1, Davenport 1, Kirkwood 1, Lawrence 1.
B&Q Cup (3): Abercromby 1, Black 1, McIntyre 1.

ALBION ROVERS DIV. 3

Ground: Cliftonhill Stadium, Main Street, Coatbridge ML5 3RB (0236 432350)
Colours: Yellow shirts with red trim, red shorts with yellow stripes.
Managers: Tom Spence/Sam Conn.
League Appearances: Beattie, J 14(1); Burns, R 16; Cadden, S 20(1); Collins, L 19(1); Conn, S 31; Fraser, A 15(13); Friar, P (1); Gallagher, J 20(8); Horne, J 7; Kelly, J 19; Kerrigan, S 22(2); Lynch, M 1(2); McBride, J 8; McBride, M 24(8); McCafferty, T 1; McCaffrey, J 22; McConnachie , R 22(1); McDonald, D 6; McKeown, D 35(1); McQuade, A (5); Mirner, E 7(2); Murray, D 1; Riley, D 26; Ryan, M 1; Scott, M 36(1); Seggie, D 21(8); Spence, T 12; Taylor, G 8(2); Thompson, D 3(2); Walker, D 11; Watson, E 1(2)
Goals-League (37): Scott 17 (3 pens), Kerrigan 6, Seggie 3, McBride M 2, Walker 2, Cadden 1, Conn 1, Fraser 1, Gallagher 1, Kelly 1, own goals 2.
Scottish Cup (3): Fraser 1, McCaffrey 1, Scott 1 (pen).
League Cup (3): Fraser 1, Kerrigan 1, Scott 1.
B&Q Cup (2): McBride M 1, Scott 1.

ALLOA   DIV. 3

Ground: Recreation Park, Alloa FK10 1RR (0259 722695)
Colours: Gold shirts with black trim, black shorts.
Manager: Billy Lamont.
League Appearances: Bennett, N 14(1); Butter, J 39; Cadden, S 10; Campbell, C 34(1); Crombie, L (2); Dempsey, J 3; Diver, D 7; Gibson, J 8(6); Hendry, M 5; Herd, W 4(3); Kemp, B 12; Lamont, P 17(6); Lawrie, D 10; Lee, R 13; McAnenay, M 19(5); McAvoy, N 23(6); McCormack, J 7; McCormick, S 13(10); McCulloch, K 36; Mackay, J 3(3); McNiven, J 34(1); Moffat, B 20(7); Neil, C 1; Nelson, M 2; Newbigging, W 33; Ramsay, S 30; Russell, G 3(4); Tait, G 9(15); Willock, A 20(6)
Goals–League (41): Newbigging 7 (7 pens), McCormick S 6 (1 pen), Moffat 4, Ramsay 4, Willock 4, Lamont 3, Diver 2, Gibson 2, McAnenay 2, McAvoy 2, Cadden 1, Hendry 1, Kemp 1, McCulloch 1, Russell 1.
Scottish Cup (6): Lamont 1, McAnenay 1, McAvoy 1, McCormick S 1, McCulloch 1, own goal 1.
League Cup (1): Hendry 1.
B&Q Cup (1): Newbigging 1.

ARBROATH   DIV. 3

Ground: Gayfield Park, Arbroath DD11 1QB (0241 872157)
Colours: Maroon shirts with sky blue trim, white shorts.
Managers: George Mackie/Donald Park.
League Appearances: Adam, C 31; Buckley, G 18(7); Clouston, B 25(2); Diver, D 21; Duncan, R 1; Elliot, D 7(7); Farnan, C 29(5); Feeney, P 6(2); Florence, S 36; Glennie, R 11; Hamilton, J 14(1); Harkness, M 1; Hindson, P (1); Jackson, D 36; King, T 25(1); McClelland, J 2; McGregor, S 3(4); McKeown, J 1; McKillop, A 11(1); McKinnon, C 29; Martin, C 22(3); Martin, M 7; Mitchell, B 22; Russell, R 1; Scott, D 6(14); Sorbie, S 33(3); Strachan, J 8(1); Tindal, K 7(6); Tosh, S 6(1); Will, B 10
Goals–League (42): Diver 10, Sorbie 8, McKinnon 7, Martin 4, Adam 3, Tindal 3, Feeney 2, King 2 (1 pen), Clouston 1, Farnan 1, Tosh 1.
Scottish Cup (5): McKinnon 2, Adam 1, Buckley 1, Sorbie 1.
League Cup (4): Elliot 1, Martin 1, Strachan 1, Tindal 1.
B&Q Cup (1): Diver 1.

AYR UNITED   DIV. 1

Ground: Somerset Park, Ayr KA8 9NB (0292 263435)
Colours: White shirts with black trim, black shorts.
Manager: Simon Stainrod.
League Appearances: Albiston, A 1; Beattie, J 3; Biggart, K 16(2); Bilsland, B 5(8); Bryce, S 12(5); Burley, G 12(1); Burns, H 35; Connie, C 2(4); Donaldson, D 1; Duncan, C 31; George, D 18; Grierson, G (1); Hood, G 26(1); Howard, N 5; Jack, R 14(4); Kennedy, D 6(3); Lennox, G 23; McGivern, S 38(2); McGlashan, C 34(2); McKilligan, N 8; McNab, N 4; McQuilter, R 7(1); McVicar, D 10; Mair, G 25(1); Moore, V 19; Robertson, G 20(1); Scott, B 12(2); Shotton, M 38; Spence, W 13; Stainrod, S 7(3); Traynor, J 34(8); Walker, T 2(2); Williams, R (1); Woods, T 3(8)
Goals–League (42): McGivern 12, Hood 3, McGlashan 3, Traynor 3, Biggart 2, Bilsland 2, Bryce 2, Burns 2 (1 pen), Moore 2, McGlashan 2, Shotton 2, Stainrod 2, Howard 1, Lennox 1, McKilligan 1, Scott 1, Woods 1, own goals 2.
Scottish Cup (1): Bryce 1.
League Cup (0):
B&Q Cup (8): McGivern 3, Burns 2 (1 pen), Bryce 1, McGlashan 1, own goal 1.

BERWICK RANGERS   DIV. 2

Ground: Shielfield Park, Berwick-on-Tweed TD15 2EF (0289 307424)
Colours: Black and gold striped shirts, black shorts.
Manager: Jim Crease.
League Appearances: Banks, A 36(1); Boyle, L 6(1); Ceccarelli, P 1; Coughlin, J 11; Cowan, M 37; Cunningham, C 7(6); Donaldson, G 1(1); Forrester, P 2(3); Gallacher, S 2(2); Gibson, K 22(1); Graham, T 14(11); Hall, A 28(3); Hawke, W 20; Healer, A 1; Irvine, W 37(1); Kane, K 34(2); King, T 1(4); Kirkwood, G 1; Lawson, O 1; Neil, M 28; O'Connor, G 26; Osborne, M 6; Richardson, S 17(5); Romaines, S 4; Scott, D 11(7); Sokoluk, J (1); Tait, A 1; Valentine, C 39; Wilson, M 23(3); Young, K 9(7); Young, N 3(1)
Goals–League (75): Irvine 15, Hawke 12, Kane 10 (2 pens), Neil 7, Banks 6 (1 pen), Cowan 4, Cunningham 4, Forrester 3, Scott 3, Young K 3, Graham 2, Hall 2, Wilson 2, Coughlin 1, own goal 1.
Scottish Cup (1): Kane 1.
League Cup (0): **B&Q Cup** (1): Banks 1.

BRECHIN CITY   DIV. 2

Ground: Glebe Park, Brechin DD9 6BJ (0356 622856)
Colours: Red with white trim.
Manager: Ian Redford.
League Appearances: Alexander, B 13(1); Allan, R 19; Baillie, R 1; Balfour, D 12; Bell, S 7(3); Brand, R 25(1); Brown, R 38(1); Cairney, H 28; Christie, G 26(2); Conway, F 35; Fisher, D 3; Gray, B 1(3); Greig, L 3(1); Hutt, G 10; Kemlo, S 4(1); Kopel, S 4; Lees, G 7(2); Lorimer, R 4(1); McLaren, P 24(2); McNeill, W 19(11); Miller, M 39; Nicolson, K 24; O'Brien, P 10(4); Redford, I 40(3); Ross, A 31(4); Scott, D 33; Vannett, R 24(1)
Goals–League (30): Miller 10 (1 pen), Brand 4, Brown 3, Redford 3, Christie 2, McNeill 2, Ross 2, Conway 1, Nicolson 1, Scott 1, Vannett 1.
Scottish Cup (0):
League Cup (0): **B&Q Cup** (4): Brown 2, Miller 2.

CALEDONIAN THISTLE   DIV. 3

Ground: Telford Street Park, Inverness. (0463 230274)
Colours: Royal blue shirts with white trim, white shorts.
Manager: Sergei Baltacha.

CELTIC   PREM. DIV.

Ground: Celtic Park, Glasgow G40 3RE (041-556 2611)
Colours: Green and white hooped shirts, white shorts.
Manager: —
League Appearances: Biggins, W 4(5); Bonner, P 31; Boyd, T 38; Byrne, P 18(4); Collins, J 38; Creaney, G 17(1); Donnelly, S 10(2); Falconer, W 14; Galloway, M 16(6); Gillespie, G 25(2); Grant, P 27(1); Hay, C 2; McAvennie, F 8(3); McGinlay, P 39(2); McLaughlin, B (8); McNally, M 30(2); McStay, P 35; Marshall, G 1; Martin, L 15; Mowbray, A 20(2); Muggleton, C 12; Nicholas, C 30(5); O'Neil, B 14(14); Payton, A 1(6); Slater, S 3(1); Smith, B 6(1); Vata, R 6(4); Wdowczyk, D 24(1)
Goals–League (51): McGinlay 10, Collins 8 (1 pen), Nicholas 8, Creaney 5, Donnelly 5, Byrne 2, McNally 2, McStay 2, O'Neil 2, Payton 2, Falconer 1, McAvennie 1, Mowbray 1, Slater 1, Vata 1. **Scottish Cup (0):**
League Cup (12): McAvennie 5, Payton 3, McGinlay 2, McNally 1, Nicholas 1.

CLYDE   DIV. 2

Ground: Broadwood Stadium, Cumbernauld G68 9NE (0236 451511)
Colours: White shirts with red and black trim, black shorts.
Manager: Alex Smith.
League Appearances: Bell, D 13(5); Brown, J 1(3); Clark, M 12; Clarke, S 16; Dickson, J 8(4); Fridge, L 42; Hillcoat, J 1(1); Howie, S 1; Knox, K 44; McAulay, J 21(6); McCarron, J 26(5); McCheyne, G 23(1); McConnell, I 23(3); McFarlane, R 34; McGill, D 4(12); Mackenzie, A 18; Morrison, S 13(7); Neill, A 36(3); O'Neill, M 8(1); Parks, G 19(9); Quinn, K 3(10); Ronald, P 9(5); Sludden, J 16(1); Strain, B 19(6); Tennant, S 30(1); Thomson, J 35; Tierney, P 1(1); Wright, A 2(1); Wylde, G 6
Goals–League (35): McConnell 5, Parks 5, Sludden 4, Strain 3, Thomson 3, Clarke S 2, McAulay 2, McGill 2, Tennant 2 (1 pen), Dickson 1, Knox 1, Mackenzie 1, Morrison 1 (pen), O'Neill 1, Quinn 1, own goal 1.
Scottish Cup (1): McCheyne 1. **League Cup (1):** McAulay 1.
B&Q Cup (0):

CLYDEBANK   DIV. 1

Ground: Kilbowie Park, Clydebank G81 2PB (041-952 2887)
Colours: White, black and red trim, white shorts.
Manager: John Steedman.
League Appearances: Bowman, G (1); Cooper, D 14(4); Crawford, D 22(1); Crawford, J 15(3); Currie, T 26(4); Eadie, K 19(2); Elliot, D (1); Ferguson, G 14(2); Flannigan, C 34(2); Harris, C 16(4); Harvey, P 26; Hay, G 22; Henry, J 42(2); Jack, S 33(1); Kerrigan, S 9(6); Lansdowne, A 11(9); Lee, K 3(2); McIntosh, M 2(2); McQueen, J 12; Maher, J 1; Matthews, G 7; Monaghan, A 15; Murdoch, S 34; Nelson, M 3(3); Quigg, S 1; Smith, S 16(10); Sutherland, C 12(2); Sweeney, S 31; Thomson, I 19(4); Treanor, M 14; Walker, J 4(2); Woods, S 10
Goals–League (56): Eadie 11, Flannigan 11, Henry 7, Jack 6, Harvey 3, Smith 3, Ferguson 2, Thomson 2 (1 pen), Treanor 2, Walker 2, Crawford J 1, Currie 1, Harris 1, Lansdowne 1, McIntosh 1, Sutherland 1, own goal 1.
Scottish Cup (2): Henry 1, Sweeney 1.
League Cup (0):
B&Q Cup (6): Flannigan 2, Lansdowne 1, Lee 1, Nelson 1, own goal 1.

COWDENBEATH DIV. 3

Ground: Central Park, Cowdenbeath KY4 9EY (0383 610166)
Colours: Royal blue shadow vertical stripes with white trim, white shorts.
Manager: Patrick Dolan.
League Appearances: Barclay, S 7(9); Bowmaker, K 4(2); Burke, P 1; Callaghan, W 33; Carr, R 17(3); Davidson, I 21(8); Douglas, H 1; Filshill, S 18; Hamill, A 9; Harris, C 9(1); Henderson, N 22; Herd, W 33; Hunter, P 23(2); Law, G 1(1); Lee, I 24(1); Macdonald, K 10; McMahon, B 32(2); McMahon, S 2; Maloney, J 4; Maratea, D 17(3); Moffat, J 17; Petrie, E 26(3); Reilly, H 1; Russell, R 2(4); Scott, C 17; Sim, A 5; Stout, D 5(5); Thomson, J 17(2); Watt, D 35; Young, A 7(2)
Goals–League (40): Callaghan 11, Henderson 9, Hunter 6, Herd 4 (1 pen), McMahon B 2, Carr 1, Davidson 1, Harris 1, Law 1, Lee 1, Macdonald 1, Young 1, own goal 1.
Scottish Cup (8): Callaghan 3, Henderson 3, Hunter 1, Reilly 1.
League Cup (1): Henderson 1.
B&Q Cup (2): Callaghan 1, Lee 1.

DUMBARTON DIV. 2

Ground: Boghead Park, Dumbarton G82 2JA (0389 62569 and 67864)
Colours: All Gold.
Manager: Murdo MacLeod.
League Appearances: Boyd, J 11(3); Campbell, C 12(2); Cunnington, E 13; Docherty, R (1); Fabiani, R 36(3); Farrell, G (1); Foster, A 22(5); Gibson, C 44; Gilmour, J 1(5); Gow, S 12(2); McAnenay, M (1); McConville, R 19(2); McDonald, J 3(3); MacFarlane, I 43; McGarvey, M 27(8); MacLeod, M 42; McQuade, J 3; Marsland, J 32(4); Martin, P 17(2); Meechan, J 31(5); Meechan, K 1; Melvin, M 42; Mooney, M 41(2); Nelson, M (3); Walker, T 6(2); Ward, H 7(3); Wilson, T 19
Goals–League (48): Gibson 13, Mooney 9 (2 pens), Meechan 4, Melvin 4, Cunnington 3, McGarvey 3, Boyd 2, Foster 2, McDonald 2, Gow 1, McConville 1, MacLeod 1, Marsland 1, Walker 1, Ward 1. **Scottish Cup (1):** Mooney (pen).
League Cup (0): B&Q Cup (1): Foster 1.

DUNDEE DIV. 1

Ground: Dens Park, Dundee DD3 7JY (0382 826104)
Colours: Dark blue shirts with red and white trim, white shorts.
Manager: Jim Duffy.
League Appearances: Adamczuk, D 7(4); Anderson, I (1); Armstrong, L (1); Bain, K 4(3); Blake, N 23; Britton, G 15(2); Christie, M 1; Czachowski, P 18; David, I 1; Dinnie, A 7; Dodds, W 23(1); Duffy, C 9; Duffy, J 35; Farningham, R 20(4); Frail, S 28(4); Hamilton, J (1); McCann, N 20(2); McGowan, J 11(3); McKeown, G 18(1); McMartin, G 1(2); McQuillan, J 27(7); Mathers, P 33; Mobilio, D (2); Pageaud, M 11; Paterson, G 17(3); Pittman, S 35(1); Ristic, D 16(2); Ritchie, P 10(7); Shaw, G 17; Stainrod, S 1; Teasdale, M 2(3); Tosh, P 14(12); Tully, C 1; Vrto, D 38; Wieghorst, M 21(3)
Goals–League (42): Ristic 6, Shaw 6, Dodds 5 (1 pen), Pittman 3, Blake 2, Duffy N 2, Farningham 2, McKeown 2, Paterson 2, Ritchie 2, Wieghorst 2, Adamczuk 1, Anderson 1 (pen), Britton 1, Czachowski 1, McCann 1, Tosh 1, own goals 2.
Scottish Cup (6): Britton 3, Shaw 2, Tosh 1.
League Cup (2): Nielsen 1, own goal 1.

148

DUNDEE UNITED   PREM. DIV.

Ground: Tannadice Park, Dundee DD3 7JW (0382 833166)
Colours: Tangerine shirts with black trim, black shorts.
Manager: Ivan Golac.
League Appearances: Bollan, G 10(2); Bowman, D 35; Brewster, C 30(3); Clark, J 13(1); Cleland, A 32(1); Connolly, P 21(7); Crabbe, S 10(11); Dailly, C 29(9); Flies, B 1; Hannah, D 6(4); Johnson, G 8(2); McBain, R (1); McInally, J 29(2); McKinlay, W 39; McLaren, A 18(9); Main, A 18; Malpas, M 35; Myers, C 4(1); Narey, D 6; Nixon, J 7(8); O'Neil, J 8(4); Perry, M 8(1); Petric, G 27; Van De Kamp, G 25; Van Der Hoorn, F 28; Welsh, B 37
Goals–League (47): Brewster 16, McKinlay 9, Connolly 5, Dailly 4, Bowman 2, Crabbe 2, Hannah 2, Cleland 1, McLaren 1, Nixon 1, O'Neil 1, Petric 1, Welsh 1, own goal 1.
Scottish Cup (11): Brewster 4, McKinlay 2 (1 pen), Welsh 2, Crabbe 1, McInally 1, McLaren 1.
League Cup (5): Clark 2, Connolly 1, McKinlay 1, McLaren 1.

DUNFERMLINE ATHLETIC   DIV. 1

Ground: East End Park, Dunfermline KY12 7RB (0383 724295)
Colours: Black and white striped shirts, black shorts.
Manager: Bert Paton.
League Appearances: Baillie, A 14(1); Bowes, M 4(2); Cooper, N 30; Cunnington, E 7(2); Davies, W 3(1); Den Bieman, I 33(8); French, H 31(5); Hamilton, L 28; Hillcoat, J 8; Laing, D 11(16); McCathie, N 43; McNamara, J 38(1); McWilliams, D 12(8); Moore, A 2(6); Moyes, D 1; O'Boyle, G 28(4); Petrie, S 30(7); Preston, A 20(6); Robertson, C 40; Sharp, R 30; Sinclair, C 1(5); Smith, P 43(1); Tod, A 19(3); Westwater, I 8
Goals–League (93): O'Boyle 17 (1 pen), French 15, Tod 11, Smith 9, Laing 8, McCathie 8, Petrie 6, Preston 5 (3 pens), Den Bieman 3, McWilliams 3, Robertson 3, Cooper 2, Sharp 1, Sinclair 1, own goal 1.
Scottish Cup (2): Tod 2.
League Cup (2): French 1, Robertson 1.
B&Q Cup (7): Laing 2, O'Boyle 2, Den Bieman 1, Sharp 1, Smith 1.

EAST FIFE   DIV. 2

Ground: Bayview Park, Methil, Fife KY8 3AG (0333 426323)
Colours: Amber shirts with black trim, amber shorts.
Manager: Alex Totten.
League Appearances: Allan, G 31(2); Andrew, B 17(7); Barron, D 20(2); Beaton, D 38; Beedie, S 25; Bell, G 16(2); Burns, W 29; Charles, R 20; Cusick, J 5(1); Dow, C 8(1); Elliott, D 1; Gibb, R 19(6); Gowrie, R (2); Hildersley, R 21(4); Hope, D 15(1); Irvine, AJ 22(8); Jackson, S (3); Logan, P (2); Long, D (2); McBride, J 8(7); Reilly, J 7(2); Scott, R 27(3); Sneddon, A 33(1); Taylor, PH 13(6); Williamson, A 34; Wilson, E 19(1); Yardley, M 1
Goals–League (58): Scott 10, Irvine 9, Beaton 5, Reilly 5, Allan 4 (1 pen), Andrew 4, Williamson 4, Burns 3 (2 pens), Hildersley 2, Hope 2, McBride 2, Sneddon 2, Bell 1, Cusick 1, Dow 1, Taylor 1, own goals 2.
Scottish Cup (5): Scott 3, Hildersley 1, Hope 1.
League Cup (1): Scott 1.
B&Q Cup (1): Allan 1.

EAST STIRLING   DIV. 3

Ground: Firs Park, Falkirk FK2 7AY (0324 623583)
Colours: Black and white hoops, black shorts.
Manager: Billy Little.
League Appearances: Conroy, J 15(1); Conway, M 17(1); Craig, D 38; Crews, B 24(5); Docherty, A 1(4); Geraghty, M 32(1); Horne, J (1); Imrie, P 1; Kemp, B 19; Lee, D 4(3); Lee, I 10; Lee, R 18; Loney, J 21(10); McAulay, I 16(5); McCallum, M 16; Macdonald, K 11(3); McDougall, G 38; McInally, M (3); McKinnon, C 3; Millar, G 35(1); Roberts, P 8(4); Robertson, S 11(7); Ross, B 34; Russell, G 36; Speirs, A 3(4); Teasdale, J 3; Tierney, S 1(3); Yates, D 14(2)
Goals–League (54): McCallum 12, Geraghty 7, Macdonald 5 (2 pens), Craig 4 (1 pen), Millar 4, Kemp 3 (2 pens) Lee I 3 (1 pen), Russell 3, Conroy 2, Crews 2, McAulay 2, Robertson 1, Speirs 1, Tierney 1, Yates 1, own goals 3.
Scottish Cup (5): Geraghty 3, McAulay 1, Robertson 1.
League Cup (1): Conroy 1.
B&Q Cup (0).

FALKIRK   PREM. DIV.

Ground: Brockville Park, Falkirk FK1 5AX (0324 624121 and 632487)
Colours: Dark blue shirts with white trim, white shorts.
Manager: Jim Jefferies.
League Appearances: Burley, G 1; Cadette, R 39; Drinkell, K 18(2); Duffy, C 23; Gallacher, J 2(4); Hamilton, G 7; Henderson, N 8(2); Hughes, J 28(1); Johnston, F 14(1); McCall, I 32(3); McDonald, C 5(11); McGowan, J 6(3); MacKenzie, S 14(5); McLaren, C (1); McLaughlin, J 38; McQueen, T 26; May, E 34(4); Oliver, N 30(2); Parks, A 41; Rice, B 36(1); Ristic, D 12; Shaw, G 18(10); Sloan, S 8(4); Taggart, C 4(9); Weir, D 37; Westwater, I 3; Young, K (1)
Goals–League (81): Cadette 18, Shaw 10, Duffy 9, May 9 (1 pen), Drinkell 6, Ristic 4, Hughes 3, Rice 3, Weir 3, Henderson 2, McCall 2, McGowan 2, McLaughlin 2, Oliver 2, Johnston 1, McDonald 1, Sloan 1, Taggart 1, own goals 2.
Scottish Cup (1): Hughes 1.
League Cup (6): Cadette 4, Duffy 1, May 1. **B&Q Cup (15):** Cadette 6, McDonald 2, May 2 (1 pen), Sloan 2, Drinkell 1, Duffy 1, Hughes 1.

FORFAR ATHLETIC   DIV. 3

Ground: Station Park, Forfar, Angus (0307 463576)
Colours: Royal/sky/white patterned shirts, white shorts.
Manager: Tommy Campbell.
League Appearances: Archibald, E 24; Arthur, G 24; Bingham, D 38; Buchan, S 5; Donaldson, G 11; Downie, I 22(11); Gray, B (1); Hamill, A 25(2); Heddle, I 39; Kopel, S 22(5); Leddie, P 18(3); Lees, G 16(3); McCafferty, A 1(3); McIntyre, S 6; McPhee, I 35; Mann, R 37; Mearns, G 17(1); Morris, R 7(6); Petrie, S 3; Philliben, R 34(1); Russell, N 10; Sheridan, J 2; Smith, R 9(13); Thomson, S 5; Winter, G 21(2)
Goals–League (58): Bingham 13, Heddle 8, Downie 6, Kopel 6, Smith 6, Donaldson 3, Petrie 3, Winter 3 (3 pens), Lees 2, McPhee 2, Mann 2, Archibald 1, Hamill 1, Leddie 1, own goal 1. **Scottish Cup (8):** Bingham 3 (1 pen), Downie 2, Heddle 2, Kopel 1.
League Cup (1): Hamill 1.
B&Q Cup (2): Bingham 1, Smith 1.

HAMILTON ACADEMICAL
DIV. 1

Ground: Douglas Park, Hamilton ML3 0DF (0698 286103)
Colours: Red and white hooped shirts, white shorts.
Manager: Iain Munro.
League Appearances: Baptie, C 33(3); Campbell, D 21(1); Chalmers, P 14(6); Clark, G 29(3); Clark, P 6(4); Cormack, D 4; Duffield, P 33(3); Ferguson, A 40; Fitzpatrick, P 17(1); Hillcoat, C 1; Lorimer, K 1; McEntegart, S 27(2); McGill, D 13(3); McIntosh, M 13; McInulty, S 31(3); McKenzie, P 33(3); McLean, C 9(9); McQuade, J 21(10); Miller, C 31; Moyes, D 5; Napier, C 27; Nicholls, D 4; Powell, L 2(3); Reid, W 30; Sherry, J 5; Walsh, D (1); Ward, K 24(6); Weir, J 2
Goals–League (66): Duffield 19 (2 pens), Clark G 9 (3 pens), Ward 8, McLean 7, Campbell 6, Chalmers 5, McGill 3, Baptie 2, McIntosh 2, Napier 2, Fitzpatrick 1, Sherry 1, own goal 1. **Scottish Cup** (0):
League Cup (0):
B&Q Cup (1) Baptie 1.

HEART OF MIDLOTHIAN
PREM. DIV.

Ground: Tynecastle Park, Gorgie Road, Edinburgh EH11 2NL (031-337 6132)
Colours: Maroon shirts, white shorts.
Manager: Tommy McLean.
League Appearances: Berry, N 30; Colquhoun, J 38(3); Fashanu, J 10(1); Ferguson, I 3(3); Foster, W 8(9); Frail, S 9; Harrison, T 1; Hogg, G 16(1); Johnston, A 5(23); Johnston, M 31; Leitch, S 24(4); Levein, C 30; Locke, G 29(4); Mackay, G 34(2); McKinlay, T 43; McLaren, A 37; Millar, J 16(4); Robertson, J 32(4); Smith, H 27; Thomas, K 7(5); Van De Ven, P 2; Walker, N 17; Weir, J 25(1); Wright, G 10(2)
Goals–League (37): Robertson 10 (1 pen), Colquhoun 4, Johnston M 4 (1 pen), Millar 4, Levein 3, Frail 2, Leitch 2, Fashanu 1, Ferguson 1, Foster 1, Johnston A 1, Mackay 1, McLaren 1, own goals 2.
Scottish Cup (3): Foster 1, Johnston M 1, Robertson 1.
League Cup (2): Robertson 2.

HIBERNIAN
PREM. DIV.

Ground: Easter Road Stadium, Edinburgh EH7 5QG (031-661 2159)
Colours: Green shirts with white sleeves and collar, white shorts.
Manager: Alex Miller.
League Appearances: Bannon, E 1; Beaumont, D 24(2); Donald, G 2(4); Evans, G 23(17); Farrell, D 26(9); Findlay, W 15(5); Hamilton, B 40(2); Harper, K 1(1); Hunter, G 29; Jackson, C 8(3); Jackson, D 29(11); Leighton, J 44; Lennon, D 3(2); Love, G 3(1); McAllister, K 36; McGraw, M (2); McIntyre, T 11; Miller, G (1); Miller, W 37; Mitchell, G 36; O'Neill, M 36; Tortolano, J 12(6); Tweed, S 27(2); Wright, K 41(1)
Goals–League (53): Wright 16, Jackson D 7, McAllister 6, Evans 4, Findlay 3, O'Neill 3 (1 pen), Tweed 3, Beaumont 2, Farrell 2, Hamilton 2, Hunter 2, Lennon 2, Mitchell 1, Tortolano 1, own goal 1.
Scottish Cup (3): McAllister 1, O'Neill 1, Wright 1.
League Cup (8): McAllister 2, Wright 2, Donald 1, Hunter 1, Jackson D 1, own goal 1.

KILMARNOCK

Ground: Rugby Park, Kilmarnock KA1 2DP (0563 25184)
Colours: Blue and white striped shirts, blue shorts.
Manager: Tommy Burns.
League Appearances: Black, T 44; Brown, T 26(5); Burns, T 12; Campbell, C (1); Crainie, D 6(8); Geddes, R 44; Lauchlan, J (1); McCloy, S 1(5); McCluskey, G 16(7); McInally, A 2(6); MacPherson, A 43; McSkimming, S 40; Millen, A 44; Mitchell, A 34; Montgomerie, R 42; Napier, C 10(5); Paterson, C 4(2); Porteous, I 7(6); Reilly, M 37(1); Roberts, M 7(6); Skilling, M 23; Stark, W 6(2); Williamson, R 36(2)
Goals–League (36): Williamson 7, Brown 5, Mitchell 5, Black 4 (2 pens), McSkimming 3, Skilling 3, McCluskey 2, MacPherson 2, Roberts 2, Crainie 1, McCloy 1, Porteous 1.
Scottish Cup (5): Black 2 (1 pen), Brown 1, McSkimming 1, Williamson 1. **League Cup** (1): Mitchell 1.

MEADOWBANK THISTLE

Ground: Meadowbank Stadium, Edinburgh EH7 6AE (031-661 5351)
Colours: Amber with black trim, black shorts.
Manager: Michael Lawson.
League Appearances: Bailey, L 29(8); Brock, J 3(6); Coulston, D (2); Coyle, M 4(4); Davidson, G 9; Douglas, R 4; Duthie, M 10(7); Elder, S 3(3); Ellison, S 24(1); Fleming, D 38; Gardner, L 10(6); Graham, T 19(2); Hutchison, M 15(6); Ingram, N (3); Little, I 38(1); McCartney, C (3); McLeod, G 35; MacLeod, I 19(2); McQueen, J 11; Murray, M 39; Price, G 5(7); Rutherford, P 32; Scott, S 7; Thorburn, S 7(4); Williamson, R 2; Williamson, S 32; Wilson, S 34(1)
Goals–League (62): Little 12, Bailey 11, McLeod G 9 (2 pens), Rutherford 8, Murray 4, Wilson 4, Duthie 3, Fleming 2, Graham 2, Hutchison 2, Brock 1, Coyle 1, Price 1, Scott 1, own goal 1. **Scottish Cup** (1): Rutherford 1.
League Cup (1): Little 1. **B&Q Cup** (8): Brock 2, Little 2, Rutherford 2, Bailey 1, McLeod G 1 (pen).

MONTROSE

Ground: Links Park, Montrose DD10 8QD (0674 673200)
Colours: Blue with white trim, white shorts.
Manager: John Holt.
League Appearances: Beedie, S 12; Cooper, C 22(6); Craib, M 23; Craib, S 15(2); Garden, M 3(4); Grant, D 35(1); Haro, M 8; Holt, J (1); Houghton, G 5(3); Irvine, N 22; Jack, R (3); Kennedy, A 35(2); Larter, D 37; Lavelle, M 27; McKenna, I 9(11); Massie, R 2; Masson, P 1; Milne, C 16; Robertson, I 35; Smith, J 31; Stephen, L 28(5); Taylor, D 6(10); Tindal, K 9(2); Tosh, J 26(1); Wilkins, G (1); Wolecki, E 6(9); Yeats, C 16(2)
Goals–League (56): Grant 12, Kennedy 11 (2 pens), Taylor 6, Milne 5, Stephen 4, Cooper 3, Craib M 3, McKenna 3, Wolecki 3 (1 pen), Yeats 3, Garden 1, Lavelle 1, Tindal 1.
Scottish Cup (2): Kennedy 1, own goal 1.
League Cup (0):
B&Q Cup (6): Kennedy 2, Yeats 2, Craib M 1, Wolecki 1.

GREENOCK MORTON   DIV. 2

Ground: Cappielow Park, Greenock (0475 23511)
Colours: Royal blue tartan shirts, royal blue shorts.
Manager: Allan McGraw
League Appearances: Aitken, S 3(1); Alexander, R 35(1); Anderson, J 19; Beaton, S 2; Blair, P (1); Brown, C 4; Collins, D 35(2); Doak, M 15; Donaghy, M 15(6); Fowler, J 34(4); Gahagan, J 7(6); Grace, A 2(1); Hunter, J 21; Johnstone, D 22; Lilley, D 34(4); Lothian, D 1; McArthur, S 35(5); McCahill, S 8; McCann, M (1); McDonald, I 3(2); McEwan, A 12(6); McInnes, D 16; Mahood, A 11(1); Pickering, M 25; Rafferty, S 19(7); Sexton, B 4; Shearer, N 16; Thomson, R 7(15); Tolmie, J 35(1); Wylie, D 44
Goals–League (44): Alexander 11, McEwan 6, Lilley 5, Doak 4 (1 pen), Mahood 3, Anderson 2, McArthur 2, Thomson 2, Tolmie 2, Collins 1, Donaghy 1, Hunter 1, McCahill 1, McInnes 1, own goals 2.
Scottish Cup (40): McEwan 2, Anderson 1, Lilley 1. **League Cup (2):** Lilley 1, Tolmie 1.
B&Q Cup (2): Alexander 1, Tolmie 1.

MOTHERWELL   PREM. DIV.

Ground: Fir Park, Motherwell ML1 2QN (0698 261437/8/9)
Colours: Amber shirts with claret trim, claret shorts.
Manager: —
League Appearances: Angus, I 8(3); Arnott, D 25(4); Burley, G 3(2); Burns, A 2(2); Cooper, D 2(8); Coyne, T 26; Davies, W 6(4); Dolan, J 32(4); Dykstra, S 44; Ferguson, I 1; Graham, A 2(3); Griffin, J 1(2); Kirk, S 25(11); Krivokapic, M 42; Lambert, P 30(2); McCart, C 36; McGrillen, P 20(20); McKinnon, R 42; McMillan, S 1; Martin, B 43; O'Donnell, P 35; Philliben, J 18(10); Shannon, R 41(2)
Goals–League (58): Coyne 12 (3 pens), Arnott 8, Kirk 7, O'Donnell 7, McGrillen 5, McKinnon 4 (1 pen), Lambert 3, Martin 2, Philliben 2, Burns 1, Krivokapic 1, own goals 6.
Scottish Cup (3): Coyne 1, Kirk 1, Philliben 1.
League Cup (8): Arnott 3, McGrillen 2, Ferguson 1, Graham 1, Shannon 1.

PARTICK THISTLE   PREM. DIV.

Ground: Firhill Park, Glasgow G20 7BA (041-945 4811)
Colours: Red and yellow striped shirts, black shorts.
Manager: John Lambie.
League Appearances: Barnes, D 3(4); Britton, G 20(2); Byrne, D 21(2); Cameron, I 37(4); Charnley, J 25(1); Clark, M 10(1); Craig, A 37(1); English, I 25(11); Farningham, R 2; Gibson, A 6(5); Grant, R 35(2); Jamieson, W 42(1); Kinnaird, P 2(1); Law, R 25; McGlashan, C (1); McKee, K 22(1); McKilligan, N 1(2); Milne, C 29(2); Murdoch, A 5(1); Nelson, C 39; Shaw, G 13(4); Smith, T 3(5); Taylor, A 27(5); Tierney, G 18(4); Watson, G 37
Goals–League (46): Craig 14 (1 pen), Grant 13, English 4, Taylor 4, Britton 3, Shaw 2, Cameron 1, Charnley 1 (pen), Jamieson 1, Milne 1, Smith 1, Tierney 1.
Scottish Cup (0): League Cup (14): Cameron 4, Craig 4, Grant 2, Britton 1, English 1, Jamieson 1, Law 1.

QUEEN OF THE SOUTH   DIV. 2

Ground: Palmerston Park, Dumfries DG2 9BA (0387 54853)
Colours: Royal blue shirts, white shorts.
Manager: William McLaren.
League Appearances: Bell, A 23; Bryce, T 34(3); Davidson, A 14; Jackson, D 7(13); Kelly, P 22(7); Kennedy, D 17; Leslie, S 5(1); McColm, R 6; McFarlane, A 22; McGhie, W 30(1); McGuire, D 19(9); McKeown, B 35; McLaren, J 12(7); Mallan, S 37; Mills, D 30; Proudfoot, K 7; Purdie, D 19; Rowe, G 30; Sermanni, P 15(12); Shanks, D 13(1); Thomson, A 32(3)
Goals–League (69): Thomson 29 (2 pens), Mallan 11, Bryce 7, McGuire 6 (1 pen), Kelly 3, Bell 2, Kennedy 2, McGhie 2, McLaren 2, Sermanni 2 (1 pen), McFarlane 1, Mills 1, own goal 1. **Scottish Cup (3):** Thomson 2, Mills 1.
League Cup (1): Shanks 1.
B&Q Cup (2): Kelly 1, Thomson 1.

QUEEN'S PARK   DIV. 3

Ground: Hampden Park, Glasgow G42 9BA (041-632 1275)
Colours: Black and white hooped shirts, white shorts.
Coach: Eddie Hunter.
League Appearances: Black, S 6(2); Brodie, D 12(13); Campbell, S 5(2); Cassidy, M (1); Caven, R 33; Chalmers, J 38; Elder, G 30; Ferguson, P 7(1); Fitzpatrick, S 37; Graham, D 31(4); Henrici, G 4(1); Kavanagh, J 7(3); Kerr, G 19(2); Lynch, M (1); McCormick, S 29(7); Mackenzie, K 2; McPhee, B 14(5); Maxwell, I 26; Moir, A 2; Moonie, D 1; O'Brien, J 2(1); O'Neill, J 39; Orr, G 39; Orr, J 19; Rodden, J 10(6); Sneddon, S 2; Stevenson, C 15(6)
Goals–League (52): O'Neill 18 (3 pens), McCormick 7, McPhee 7, Caven 6, Graham 6, Orr G 3, Brodie 2, Maxwell 1, O'Brien 1, Rodden 1.
Scottish Cup (3): McPhee 1, O'Neill 1, Rodden 1. **League Cup (0):**
B&Q Cup (0).

RAITH ROVERS   DIV. 1

Ground: Stark's Park, Pratt Street, Kirkcaldy KY1 1SA (0592 263514)
Colours: Navy blue shirts, white shorts.
Manager: Jimmy Nicholl.
League Appearances: Arthur, G 1; Broddle, J 16(2); Cameron, C 30(11); Carson, T 8; Coyle, R 41; Crawford, S 24(12); Dair, J 35(3); Dalziel, G 20(7); Dennis, S 43; Graham, A 35(1); Hawke, W 1(1); Hetherston, P 34; Kelly, N 1(3); Lennon, D 7; McAnespie, S 2(1); McGeachie, G 18(2); MacLeod, I 3; McStay, J 35(2); Nicholl, J 33(1); Potter, B 1; Rowbotham, J 33(3); Sinclair, D 29(7); Thomson, S 34
Goals–League (46): Dalziel 8 (2 pens): Cameron 6, Dair 6, Crawford 5, Graham 5, Hetherston 5 (2 pens), Dennis 3, McStay 2, Sinclair 2, Coyle 1, Nicholl 1, Rowbotham 1, own goal 1. **Scottish Cup (2):** Dair 1, McStay 1.
League Cup (1): Cameron 1.

RANGERS   PREM. DIV.

Ground: Ibrox Stadium, Glasgow G51 2XD (041-427 8500)
Colours: Royal blue shirts, red and white trim, white shorts.
Manager: Walter Smith.
League Appearances: Brown, J 24; Durie, G 23(1); Durrant , I 14(9); Ferguson, D 7(3); Ferguson, I 35; Goram, A 8; Gough, R 37; Hagen, D 4(2); Hateley, M 40(2); Huistra, P 10(11); Kouznetsov, O 4(2); McCall, S 34; McCoist, A 16(5); McPherson, D 27(1); Maxwell, A 31(1); Mikhailichenko, A 24(10); Miller, C 2(1); Moore, C 1; Morrow, J 2; Murray, N 20(2); Pressley, S 17(6); Robertson, D 32; Scott, C 5(1); Steven, T 32; Stevens, G 28(1); Vinnicombe, C 2(2); Wishart, F 5
Goals–League (74): Hateley 22 (2 pens), Durie 12, McCoist 7 (1 pen), Huistra 6, Ferguson I 5, Mikhailichenko 5, Steven 4, Gough 3, McCall 3, Ferguson D 1, Hagen 1, Kuznetsov 1, MacPherson 1, Pressley 1, Robertson 1, own goal 1.
Scottish Cup (14): Hateley 4 (1 pen), McCoist 3 (1 pen), Brown 1, Durie 1, Ferguson I 1, McPherson 1, Robertson 1, Steven 1, own goal 1. **League Cup** (8): Ferguson I 3, Hateley 2 (1 pen), Durrant 1, McCoist 1, Steven 1.

ROSS COUNTY   DIV. 3

Ground: Victoria Park, Dingwall IV15 9QW (0349 862253)
Colours: Dark blue shirts, white shorts.
Manager: Bobby Wilson.

ST JOHNSTONE   DIV. 1

Ground: McDiarmid Park, Crieff Road, Perth PH1 2SJ (0738 26961)
Colours: Royal blue shirts with white trim, white shorts.
Manager: Paul Sturrock.
League Appearances: Arkins, V (1); Budden, J 1(1); Buglione, M 3(7); Cherry, P 31(2); Cole, A 1; Curran, H 39; Davies, J 30(2); Deas, P 35(1); Dodds, W 20; Ferguson, I 22; Inglis, J 25; Irons, D 1; McAuley, S 28; McClelland, J 1; McGinnis, G 28; McGowne, K 37(3); McMartin, G (6); Maskrey, S 1(3); Miller, C 12; Moore, A 7(6); Morgan, A (3); Preston, A 3(6); Ramsey, P 22; Rhodes, A 44; Scott, P 19(5); Torfason, G 21(8); Turner, T 37(2); Wright, P 16(1)
Goals–League (35): Wright 7 (2 pens), Dodds 6 (1 pen), Davies 5, Torfason 5 (1 pen), Curran 3, Ferguson 3, Scott 3, Inglis 1, McGinnis 1, Moore 1.
Scottish Cup (8): Dodds 4, Ferguson 2, McMartin 1, Scott 1.
League Cup (2): Moore 1, Wright 1.

ST MIRREN   DIV. 1

Ground: St Mirren Park, Paisley PA3 2EJ (041-889 2558 and 041-840 1337)
Colours: Black and white halved shirts, white shorts.
Manager: Jimmy Bone.
League Appearances: Archdeacon, P (2); Baker, M 37(1); Bone, A 21(12); Combe, A 16; Dawson, R 38; Dick, J 31(4); Elliot, D 34(2); Farrell, S 4(4); Fullarton, J 37; Gallagher, E 11(5); Gardner, J 14(7); Gillies, K 3(6); Gillies, R 10(12); Harvie, S 4(2); Hetherston, B (3); Hewitt, J 27(4); Lambert, P 3; Lavety, B 35(7); McGrotty, G 1; McIntyre, P 39(3); McLaughlin, B 18(5); McWhirter, N 27; Money, C 28; Orr, N 24; Paterson, A 2; Peacock, J 5(1); Smith, Benj 2; Smith, Bria (2); Taylor, S 13(1)

Goals–League (61): Lavety 10, Elliot 8, McIntyre 8, McWhirter 7, Bone 5, Gallagher 5, Dick 4, Hewitt 4, Dawson 3 (3 pens), Gillies R 2, Baker 1, Gardner 1, Harvie 1, McLaughlin 1, Orr 1. **Scottish Cup** (3): Bone 1, Elliot 1, Lavety 1.
League Cup (1): Dick 1.
B&Q Cup (8): Gallagher 4, Lavety 2, Harvie 1, McIntyre 1.

STENHOUSEMUIR   DIV. 2

Ground: Ochilview Park, Stenhousemuir FK5 5QL (0324 562992)
Colours: Maroon shirts with silver trim, white shorts.
Manager: Terry Christie.
League Appearances: Aitken, N 36(1); Armstrong, G 39; Christie, M 13(5); Clarke, J 21(4); Clouston, B 3; Dickov, S 4(11); Donaldson, E 1(3); Fisher, J 30; Gallacher, I 1; Godfrey, P 29; Haddow, L 21(1); Hallford, E 10(1); Harkness, M 36; Irvine, J 18(2); Logan, S 22(4); McConnell, I 1; Mathieson, M 36; O'Neill, P 2; Robertson, S 3; Roseburgh, D 28; Sludden, J 18; Sprott, A 32(3); Steel, T 26(7); Swanson, D 2(5)
Goals–League (62): Mathieson 14, Sludden 13, Steel 8, Roseburgh 7 (1 pen), Irvine 6, Sprott 6, Fisher 3, Aitken 1, Godfrey 1, Haddow 1, Swanson 1, own goal 1.
Scottish Cup (0):
League Cup (4): Clouston 1, Fisher 1, Irvine 1, Mathieson 1.
B&Q Cup (0):

STIRLING ALBION   DIV. 2

Ground: Forthbank Stadium, Springkerse Industrial Estate, Stirling FK7 7UJ (0786 450399)
Colours: Red shirts with white sleeves, white shorts.
Manager/chief coach: Kevin Drinkell.
League Appearances: Armstrong, P 39; Callaghan, T 27(5); Docherty, A 1(6); Drinkell, K 10(1); Flynn, D 16(4); Gibson, J 16(5); Hamilton, J 21(1); Kerr, J 4; Kinross, S (1); Lawrie, D 21; McAnenay, P 1; McCallum, M 8(3); McCormack, JT 10; Macdonald, K (1); McGeown, M 43; McInnes, I 12(13); McKenna, A 6(1); McLeod, J 17(1); McQuilter, R 18; Mitchell, C 43; Monaghan, M 1(1); Moore, V 5; Pew, D 21(10); Reid, W 11; Reilly, R 17(5); Roberts, P 16(4); Tait, T 42; Watson, P 29(1); Watters, W 29(11)
Goals–League (41): Watters 13, Armstrong 6, Flynn 3, McInnes 3, Callaghan 2, Lawrie 2, McKenna 2, Mitchell 2, Drinkell 1, Gibson 1, Kerr 1, McCallum 1, Pew 1, Reilly 1, Tait 1, own goal 1.
Scottish Cup (4): Roberts 2, Armstrong 1, Pew 1. **League Cup** (0):
B&Q Cup (0).

STRANRAER   DIV. 1

Ground: Stair Park, Stranraer DG9 8BS (0776 3271)
Colours: Royal blue shirts with geometrical design, white shorts.
Manager: Alex McAnespie.
League Appearances: Brannigan, K 36; Brown, J 5(1); Cody, S 29; Diver, D 1(4); Duffy, B 30(2); Duncan, G 35; Ferguson, W 8(21); Gallagher, A 26(3); Grant, A 32; Henderson, D 35; Hughes, J 24(1); Johnston, S 2; McCaffrey, J 10; McCann, J (1); McIntyre, S 16(8); McLean, P 20(5); Millar, G 36; Ross, S 9; Sloan, T 38; Spittal, I 25(4); Walker, D (2); Walker, T 12
Goals–League (63): Sloan 16, Duncan 8 (4 pens), Ferguson 6, Grant 6, Henderson 6, Gallagher 5, Walker T 5, Diver 4, Cody 3, McIntyre 2, Brannigan 1, McLean.
Scottish Cup (11): Sloan 8, Duncan 1 (pen), Ferguson 1, Henderson 1.
League Cup (2): Henderson 2. **B&Q Cup** (2): Henderson 1, Sloan 1.

SCOTTISH REVIEW

Rangers were again the team to beat, though they were by no means as convincing as they had been previously. The lack of a consistent rival probably accounted for a situation which is not healthy for the overall benefit of football in Scotland.

Celtic looked capable of a serious challenge in the first half of the season but fell away and it was again left to Aberdeen to finish runners-up, their fifth second place in six years.

However, Motherwell could be pleased with third place just a point behind the Dons. With drastic reorganisation in sight, there was considerable pressure on teams at the bottom of the table.

The three relegation places were filled by St Johnstone, Raith Rovers and Dundee, but Kilmarnock and Partick Thistle only escaped by goal difference at the expense of the Saints.

The one precious promotion place from the First Division went to Falkirk in a two-horse race with Dunfermline Athletic. Free-scoring Dunfermline were hoping for a Falkirk defeat at Clydebank on the last day of the season, but the Bairns drew 1-1 and the Fifers' 5-0 win over Clyde still left them a point adrift.

Dunfermline thus joined in with the teams finishing down to seventh place and the three relegated from the Premier Division to form a new-look Division One of ten.

Those in the last five positions were coupled with the teams finishing from second place to sixth in the Second Division to form a Division Two, while those in seventh to 14th place in the Second Division were supplemented by the arrival of two new clubs, Caledonian Thistle and Ross County from the Highland League in a ten-club Division Three.

Escaping from these mathematical deliberations were Stranraer, champions of the Second Division, who enjoyed the best season in their history and deservedly so, after going so close in 1993. They were clear winners and will take their place in the new Division One.

The newcomers have interesting pedigrees. Caledonian Thistle are an amalgamation of two Inverness clubs Caley and Thistle, while Ross County have had a string of successes in the early rounds of the Scottish FA Cup to back them.

Next season the Scottish League will also revert to the English style of three points for a win. This it is hoped will give a fresh impetus to the attitude on the field. In the Premier Division last season a fifth of the matches were drawn.

SCOTTISH LEAGUE – PREMIER DIVISION RESULTS 1993–94

	Aberdeen	Celtic	Dundee	Dundee United	Hearts	Hibernian	Kilmarnock	Motherwell	Partick Thistle	Raith Rovers	Rangers	St Johnstone
Aberdeen	—	1-1	1-1	2-0	2-0	4-0	1-0	1-0	2-0	4-0	2-0	0-1
Celtic	0-2	—	2-1	1-1	0-0	2-3	0-3	2-2	2-1	1-0	0-0	1-1
Dundee	2-2	1-2	—	0-2	2-2	2-2	0-0	0-1	3-1	2-1	0-0	0-1
Dundee United	0-1	1-3	1-1	—	0-3	2-1	3-0	1-1	1-2	2-2	2-4	1-1
Hearts	0-1	0-2	1-1	1-0	—	2-1	0-0	2-0	2-1	2-2	1-1	1-0
Hibernian	1-1	0-1	0-0	1-1	3-1	—	1-1	1-0	5-1	1-0	1-1	0-2
Kilmarnock	1-1	0-0	1-0	2-0	0-2	1-1	—	0-1	1-2	4-1	0-2	0-1
Motherwell	3-1	2-2	2-0	1-2	0-1	1-0	2-0	—	1-2	1-1	2-2	1-2
Partick Thistle	3-1	1-1	3-0	1-2	0-0	0-0	2-2	3-2	—	2-2	1-2	0-0
Raith Rovers	0-2	1-4	2-1	0-3	2-2	0-2	2-2	0-3	1-1	—	1-1	0-0
Rangers	2-0	1-1	1-3	0-3	2-2	2-1	2-1	3-0	5-1	4-0	—	4-0
St Johnstone	0-0	2-1	2-1	2-1	2-0	2-2	0-1	2-1	1-0	2-0	0-4	—

SCOTTISH LEAGUE – DIVISION I RESULTS 1993–94

	Airdrieonians	Ayr United	Brechin City	Clyde	Clydebank	Dumbarton	Dunfermline Athletic	Falkirk	Hamilton Academical	Greenock Morton	St Mirren	Stirling Albion
Airdrieonians	—	1-2	0-2	0-2	0-1	1-2	3-2	2-0	4-0	2-0	1-2	3-2
Ayr United	2-3	—	2-1	3-1	2-0	1-1	0-2	1-0	1-1	2-2	0-2	2-1
Brechin City	0-2	2-4	—	4-1	0-1	1-1	0-1	3-0	1-0	2-1	1-1	1-2
Clyde	0-2	1-1	1-1	—	1-1	1-3	2-1	0-2	2-0	0-3	1-1	2-0
Clydebank	1-2	3-2	2-0	2-0	—	2-2	0-2	0-2	0-2	2-0	0-3	3-0
Dumbarton	0-0	1-1	1-0	2-0	2-4	—	3-2	1-1	2-2	3-0	1-3	2-1
Dunfermline Athletic	3-2	6-1	4-0	5-0	0-2	1-1	—	3-2	0-1	2-0	0-3	1-2
Falkirk	2-0	2-1	2-0	4-2	0-4	4-0	0-2	—	4-0	4-0	3-3	3-0
Hamilton Academical	3-2	2-1	2-1	9-0	0-0	2-1	2-1	2-0	—	5-1	4-2	2-0
Greenock Morton	0-0	1-1	2-0	2-0	3-0	0-0	0-2	2-2	2-0	—	4-0	3-1
St Mirren	3-0	3-1	2-1	0-1	2-0	0-3	2-2	0-3	0-2	5-1	—	0-1
Stirling Albion	1-1	1-3	0-3	0-1	1-2	2-0	2-0	0-1	1-1	1-3	1-0	—

SCOTTISH LEAGUE – DIVISION II RESULTS 1993–94

	Albion Rovers	Alloa	Arbroath	Berwick Rangers	Cowdenbeath	East Fife	East Stirlingshire	Forfar Athletic	Meadowbank Thistle	Montrose	Queen of the South	Queen's Park	Stenhousemuir	Stranraer
Albion Rovers	—	0-2	1-7	0-2	0-1	1	1-3	1-3	0-2	3-4	1	2-1	1-2	1-2
Alloa	1-1	—	2-3		0-1	2-1	1-5	1-3	3-2	1-0	1-9	0-0	1-0	0-1
Arbroath	1-0	0-1	—	0-4	0-2	2-2	0-0	1-3	3-2	2-0	2-5	2-0	2-0	0-0
Berwick Rangers	1-0	1-1	2-0	—	3-2	0-1	2-2	1-2	1-1	0-3	0-3	6-0	2-0	0-2
Cowdenbeath	0-1	4-1	5-0	1-2	—	1-2	1-3	3-1	1-2	0-1	1-2	3-4	3-0	1-2
East Fife	3-1	0-1	1-0	1-2	3-2	—	1-2	3-1	0-2	5-2	3-2	5-5	1-1	1-1
East Stirlingshire	3-0	0-3	1-2	2-1	3-2	2-1	—	1-2	0-1	2-3	0-1	2-0	3-1	0-1
Forfar Athletic	4-2	3-2	2-1	1-1	0-3	1-0	4-2	—	0-1	1-2	1-2	4-0	3-1	1-3
Meadowbank Thistle	1-0	2-2	3-0	2-1	2-1	0-2	2-2	1	—	1-0	2-0	1-2	0-2	2-2
Montrose	1-2	0-1	0-0	2-5	1-1	3-0	5-0	1-0	0-3	—	4-0	4-0	2-3	1-3
Queen of the South	2-0	2-1	6-0	0-0	1-3	4-2	1-1	1-0	5-1	1-0	—	5-2	3-1	0-2
Queen's Park	5-1	1-0	4-0	2-1	1-1	0-1	2-0	0-3	2-1	2-1	1-1	—	0-0	0-0
Stenhousemuir	2-0	1-0	2-0	3-0	4-0	3-2	1-0	2-0	1-2	3-1	3-0	2-0	—	2-2
Stranraer	2-1	1-1	1-0	2-1	2-0	1-2	1-0	2-1	3-1	2-4	3-3	2-0	1-0	—

SCOTTISH LEAGUE FINAL TABLES 1993—94

Premier Divsion	P	Home W	D	L	Goals F	A	Away W	D	L	Goals F	A	Pt	GD
Rangers	44	12	6	4	43	22	10	8	4	31	19	58	+33
Aberdeen	44	11	9	2	33	12	6	12	4	25	24	55	+22
Motherwell	44	11	7	4	31	20	9	7	6	27	23	54	+15
Celtic	44	8	11	3	25	17	7	9	6	26	21	50	+13
Hibernian	44	11	7	4	29	15	5	8	9	24	33	47	+5
Dundee U	44	5	11	6	26	25	6	9	7	21	23	42	−1
Hearts	44	6	9	7	22	24	5	11	6	15	19	42	−6
Kilmarnock	44	6	10	6	18	19	6	6	10	18	26	40	−9
Partick T	44	9	8	5	23	17	3	8	11	23	40	40	−11
St Johnstone	44	7	7	8	24	26	3	13	6	11	21	40	−12
Raith R	44	3	12	7	25	35	3	7	12	21	45	31	−34
Dundee	44	6	7	9	26	26	2	6	14	16	31	29	−15

First Division	P	Home W	D	L	Goals F	A	Away W	D	L	Goals F	A	Pt	GD
Falkirk	44	16	4	2	47	16	10	10	2	34	16	66	+49
Dunfermline Ath	44	18	2	2	61	18	11	5	6	32	17	65	+58
Airdrieonians	44	9	9	4	28	18	11	5	6	30	20	54	+20
Hamilton A	44	13	5	4	43	20	6	7	9	23	34	50	+12
Clydebank	44	11	5	6	30	28	7	9	6	26	20	50	+8
St Mirren	44	10	3	9	30	25	11	5	6	31	30	50	+6
Ayr U	44	6	8	8	20	28	8	6	8	22	24	42	−10
Dumbarton	44	5	8	9	25	29	6	6	10	23	30	36	−11
Stirling Albion	44	7	6	9	23	30	6	3	13	18	38	35	−27
Clyde	44	6	7	9	18	20	4	5	13	17	38	32	−23
Morton	44	3	11	8	22	29	3	6	13	22	46	29	−31
Brechin C	44	4	3	15	13	34	2	4	16	17	47	19	−51

Second Division	P	Home W	D	L	Goals F	A	Away W	D	L	Goals F	A	Pt	GD
Stranraer	39	15	2	3	38	18	8	8	3	25	17	56	+28
Berwick R	39	9	7	4	40	23	9	5	5	35	23	48	+29
Stenhousemuir	39	10	6	3	35	15	9	3	8	27	29	47	+18
Meadowbank T	39	9	8	2	36	24	8	5	7	26	24	47	+14
Queen of the S	39	9	3	7	36	20	8	6	6	33	28	43	+21
East Fife	39	9	5	5	33	23	6	6	8	25	29	41	+6
Alloa	39	6	8	6	16	17	6	9	4	25	22	41	+2
Forfar Ath	39	6	6	8	27	32	8	5	6	31	26	39	—
East Stirling	39	7	3	9	29	31	6	8	6	25	26	37	−3
Montrose	39	6	5	8	24	25	8	3	9	32	36	36	−5
Queen's Park	39	10	4	6	34	32	2	6	11	18	44	34	−24
Arbroath	39	6	8	5	24	28	6	1	13	18	39	33	−25
Albion R	39	3	5	12	18	33	4	5	10	19	33	24	−29
Cowdenbeath	39	1	4	15	19	39	5	4	10	21	33	20	−32

SCOTTISH LEAGUE HONOURS

PREMIER DIVISION
Maximum points: 72

	First	*Pts*	*Second*	*Pts*	*Third*	*Pts*
1975–76	Rangers	54	Celtic	48	Hibernian	43
1976–77	Celtic	55	Rangers	46	Aberdeen	43
1977–78	Rangers	55	Aberdeen	53	Dundee U	40
1978–79	Celtic	48	Rangers	45	Dundee U	44
1979–80	Aberdeen	48	Celtic	47	St Mirren	42
1980–81	Celtic	56	Aberdeen	49	Rangers*	44
1981–82	Celtic	55	Aberdeen	53	Rangers	43
1982–83	Dundee U	56	Celtic*	55	Aberdeen	55
1983–84	Aberdeen	57	Celtic	50	Dundee U	47
1984–85	Aberdeen	59	Celtic	52	Dundee U	47
1985–86	Celtic*	50	Hearts	50	Dundee U	47

Maximum points: 88

1986–87	Rangers	69	Celtic	63	Dundee U	60
1987–88	Celtic	72	Hearts	62	Rangers	60

Maximum points: 72

1988–89	Rangers	56	Aberdeen	50	Celtic	46
1989–90	Rangers	51	Aberdeen*	44	Hearts	44
1990–91	Rangers	55	Aberdeen	53	Celtic*	41

Maximum points: 88

1991–92	Rangers	72	Hearts	63	Celtic	62
1992–93	Rangers	73	Aberdeen	64	Celtic	60
1993–94	Rangers	58	Aberdeen	55	Motherwell	54

DIVISION 1
Maximum points: 52

1975–76	Partick T	41	Kilmarnock	35	Montrose	30

Maximum points: 78

1976–77	St Mirren	62	Clydebank	58	Dundee	51
1977–78	Morton*	58	Hearts	58	Dundee	57
1978–79	Dundee	55	Kilmarnock*	54	Clydebank	54
1979–80	Hearts	53	Airdrieonians	51	Ayr U	44
1980–81	Hibernian	57	Dundee	52	St Johnstone	51
1981–82	Motherwell	61	Kilmarnock	51	Hearts	50
1982–83	St Johnstone	55	Hearts	54	Clydebank	50
1983–84	Morton	54	Dumbarton	51	Partick T	46
1984–85	Motherwell	50	Clydebank	48	Falkirk	45
1985–86	Hamilton A	56	Falkirk	45	Kilmarnock	44

Maximum points: 88

1986–87	Morton	57	Dunfermline Ath	56	Dumbarton	53
1987–88	Hamilton A	56	Meadowbank T	52	Clydebank	49

			Maximum points: 78			
1988–89	Dunfermline Ath	54	Falkirk	52	Clydebank	48
1989–90	St Johnstone	58	Airdrieonians	54	Clydebank	44
1990–91	Falkirk	54	Airdrieonians	53	Dundee	52
			Maximum points: 88			
1991–92	Dundee	58	Partick T*	57	Hamilton A	57
1992–93	Raith R	65	Kilmarnock	54	Dunfermline Ath	52
1993–94	Falkirk	66	Dunfermline Ath	65	Airdrieonians	54

DIVISION 2

Maximum points: 52

1975–77	Clydebank*	40	Raith R	40	Alloa	35
			Maximum points: 78			
1976–77	Stirling A	55	Alloa	51	Dunfermline Ath	50
1977–78	Clyde*	53	Raith R	53	Dunfermline Ath	48
1978–79	Berwick R	54	Dunfermline Ath	52	Falkirk	50
1979–80	Falkirk	50	East Stirling	49	Forfar Ath	46
1980–81	Queen's Park	50	Queen of the S	46	Cowdenbeath	45
1981–82	Clyde	59	Alloa*	50	Arbroath	50
1982–83	Brechin C	55	Meadowbank T	54	Arbroath	49
1983–84	Forfar Ath	63	East Fife	47	Berwick R	43
1984–85	Montrose	53	Alloa	50	Dunfermline Ath	49
1985–86	Dunfermline Ath	57	Queen of the S	55	Meadowbank T	49
1986–87	Meadowbank T	55	Raith R*	52	Stirling A	52
1987–88	Ayr U	61	St Johnstone	59	Queen's Park	51
1988–89	Albion R	50	Alloa	45	Brechin C	43
1989–90	Brechin C	49	Kilmarnock	48	Stirling A	47
1990–91	Stirling A	54	Montrose	46	Cowdenbeath	45
			Maximum points: 78			
1991–92	Dumbarton	52	Cowdenbeath	51	Alloa	50
1992–93	Clyde	54	Brechin C*	53	Stranraer	53
1993–94	Stranraer	56	Berwick R	48	Stenhousemuir*	47

DIVISION 1 to 1974–75

Maximum points: a 36; b 44; c 40; d 52; e 60; f 68; g 76; h 84.

	First	Pts	Second	Pts	Third	Pts
1890–91*a*††	Dumbarton	29	Rangers	29	Celtic	24
1891–92*b*	Dumbarton	37	Celtic	35	Hearts	30
1892–93*a*	Celtic	29	Rangers	28	St Mirren	23

1893–94a	Celtic	29	Hearts	26	St Bernard's	22
1894–95a	Hearts	31	Celtic	26	Rangers	21
1895–96a	Celtic	30	Rangers	26	Hibernian	24
1896–97a	Hearts	28	Hibernian	26	Rangers	25
1897–98a	Celtic	33	Rangers	29	Hibernian	22
1898–99a	Rangers	36	Hearts	26	Celtic	24
1899–						
1900a	Rangers	32	Celtic	25	Hibernian	24
1900–01c	Rangers	35	Celtic	29	Hibernian	25
1901–02a	Rangers	28	Celtic	26	Hearts	22
1902–03b	Hibernian	37	Dundee	31	Rangers	29
1903–04d	Third Lanark	43	Hearts	39	Rangers*	38
1904–05d	Celtic‡	41	Rangers	41	Third Lanark	35
1905–06e	Celtic	49	Hearts	43	Airdrieonians	38
1906–07f	Celtic	55	Dundee	48	Rangers	45
1907–08f	Celtic	55	Falkirk	51	Rangers	50
1908–09f	Celtic	51	Dundee	50	Clyde	48
1909–10f	Celtic	54	Falkirk	52	Rangers	46
1910–11f	Rangers	52	Aberdeen	48	Falkirk	44
1911–12f	Rangers	51	Celtic	45	Clyde	42
1912–13f	Rangers	53	Celtic	49	Hearts*	41
1913–14g	Celtic	65	Rangers	59	Hearts*	54
1914–15g	Celtic	65	Hearts	61	Rangers	50
1915–16g	Celtic	67	Rangers	56	Morton	51
1916–17g	Celtic	64	Morton	54	Rangers	53
1917–18f	Rangers	56	Celtic	55	Kilmarnock	43
1918–19f	Celtic	58	Rangers	57	Morton	47
1919–20h	Rangers	71	Celtic	68	Motherwell	57
1920–21h	Rangers	76	Celtic	66	Hearts	56
1921–22h	Celtic	67	Rangers	66	Raith R	56
1922–23g	Rangers	55	Airdrieonians	50	Celtic	46
1923–24g	Rangers	59	Airdrieonians	50	Celtic	41
1924–25g	Rangers	60	Airdrieonians	57	Hibernian	52
1925–26g	Celtic	58	Airdrieonians*	50	Hearts	50
1926–27g	Rangers	56	Motherwell	51	Celtic	49
1927–28g	Rangers	60	Celtic*	55	Motherwell	55
1928–29g	Rangers	67	Celtic	51	Motherwell	50
1929–30g	Rangers	60	Motherwell	55	Aberdeen	53
1930–31g	Rangers	60	Celtic	58	Motherwell	56
1931–32g	Motherwell	66	Rangers	61	Celtic	48
1932–33g	Rangers	62	Motherwell	59	Hearts	50
1933–34g	Rangers	66	Motherwell	62	Celtic	47
1934–35g	Rangers	55	Celtic	52	Hearts	50
1935–36g	Celtic	66	Rangers*	61	Aberdeen	61
1936–37g	Rangers	61	Aberdeen	54	Celtic	52
1937–38g	Celtic	61	Hearts	58	Rangers	49
1938–39g	Rangers	59	Celtic	48	Aberdeen	46
1946–47e	Rangers	46	Hibernian	44	Aberdeen	39
1947–48e	Hibernian	48	Rangers	46	Partick T	36

1948–49e	Rangers	46	Dundee	45	Hibernian	39
1949–50e	Rangers	50	Hibernian	48	Hearts	43
1950–51e	Hibernian	48	Rangers*	38	Dundee	38
1951–52e	Hibernian	45	Rangers	41	East Fife	37
1952–53e	Rangers*	43	Hibernian	43	East Fife	39
1953–54e	Celtic	43	Hearts	38	Partick T	35
1954–55e	Aberdeen	49	Celtic	46	Rangers	41
1955–56f	Rangers	52	Aberdeen	46	Hearts*	45
1956–57f	Rangers	55	Hearts	53	Kilmarnock	42
1957–58f	Hearts	62	Rangers	49	Celtic	46
1958–59f	Rangers	50	Hearts	48	Motherwell	46
1959–60f	Hearts	54	Kilmarnock	50	Rangers*	42
1960–61f	Rangers	51	Kilmarnock	50	Third Lanark	42
1961–62f	Dundee	54	Rangers	51	Celtic	46
1962–63f	Rangers	57	Kilmarnock	48	Partick T	46
1963–64f	Rangers	55	Kilmarnock	49	Celtic*	47
1964–65f	Kilmarnock*	50	Hearts	50	Dunfermline Ath	49
1965–66f	Celtic	57	Rangers	55	Kilmarnock	45
1966–67f	Celtic	58	Rangers	55	Clyde	46
1967–68f	Celtic	63	Rangers	61	Hibernian	45
1968–69f	Celtic	54	Rangers	49	Dunfermline Ath	45
1969–70f	Celtic	57	Rangers	45	Hibernian	44
1970–71f	Celtic	56	Aberdeen	54	St Johnstone	44
1971–72f	Celtic	60	Aberdeen	50	Rangers	44
1972–73f	Celtic	57	Rangers	56	Hibernian	45
1973–74f	Celtic	53	Hibernian	49	Rangers	48
1974–75f	Rangers	56	Hibernian	49	Celtic	45

DIVISION 2 to 1974–75

Maximum points. a 76; *b* 72; *c* 68; *d* 52; *e* 60; *f* 36; *g* 44; *h* 52.

1893–94f	Hibernian	29	Cowlairs	27	Clyde	24
1894–95f	Hibernian	30	Motherwell	22	Port Glasgow	20
1895–96f	Abercorn	27	Leith Ath	23	Renton	21
1896–97f	Partick T	31	Leith Ath	27	Kilmarnock	21
1897–98f	Kilmarnock	29	Port Glasgow	25	Morton	22
1898–99f	Kilmarnock	32	Leith Ath	27	Port Glasgow	25
1899–1900f	Partick T	29	Morton	26	Port Glasgow	20
1900–01f	St Bernard's	26	Airdrieonians	23	Abercorn	21
1901–02g	Port Glasgow	32	Partick T	31	Motherwell	26
1902–03g	Airdrieonians	35	Motherwell	28	Ayr U	27
1903–04g	Hamilton A	37	Clyde	29	Ayr U	28
1904–05g	Clyde	32	Falkirk	28	Hamilton A	27
1905–06g	Leith Ath	34	Clyde	31	Albion R	27
1906–07g	St Bernard's	32	Vale of Leven*	27	Arthurlie	27
1907–08g	Raith R	30	Dumbarton	‡‡27	Ayr U	27

Year	Winner	Pts	Second	Pts	Third	Pts
1908–09g	Abercorn	31	Raith R*	28	Vale of Leven	28
1909–10g‡	Leith Ath	33	Raith R	33	St Bernard's	27
1910–11g	Dumbarton	31	Ayr U	27	Albion R	25
1911–12g	Ayr U	35	Abercorn	30	Dumbarton	27
1912–13h	Ayr U	34	Dunfarmline Ath	33	East Stirling	32
1913–14g	Cowdenbeath	31	Albion R	27	Dunfermline Ath	26
1914–15h	Cowdenbeath*	37	St Bernard's*	37	Leith Ath	37
1921–22a	Alloa	60	Cowdenbeath	47	Armadale	45
1922–23a	Queen's Park	57	Clydebank	¶50	St Johnstone	¶45
1923–24a	St Johnstone	56	Cowdenbeath	55	Bathgate	44
1924–25a	Dundee U	50	Clydebank	48	Clyde	47
1925–26a	Dunfermline Ath	59	Clyde	53	Ayr U	52
1926–27a	Bo'ness	56	Raith R	49	Clydebank	45
1927–28a	Ayr U	54	Third Lanark	45	King's Park	44
1928–29b	Dundee U	51	Morton	50	Arbroath	47
1929–30a	Leith Ath*	57	East Fife	57	Albion R	54
1930–31a	Third Lanark	61	Dundee U	50	Dunfermline Ath	47
1931–32a	East Stirling*	55	St Johnstone	55	Raith Rovers*	46
1932–33c	Hibernian	54	Queen of the S	49	Dunfermline Ath	47
1933–34c	Albion R	45	Dunfermline Ath*	44	Arbroath	44
1934–35c	Third Lanark	52	Arbroath	50	St Bernard's	47
1935–36c	Falkirk	59	St Mirren	59	Morton	48
1936–37c	Ayr U	54	Morton	51	St Bernard's	48
1937–38c	Raith R	59	Albion R	48	Airdrieonians	47
1938–39c	Cowdenbeath	60	Alloa*	48	East Fife	48
1946–47d	Dundee	45	Airdrieonians	42	East Fife	31
1947–48e	East Fife	53	Albion R	42	Hamilton A	40
1948–49e	Raith R*	42	Stirling Albion	42	Airdrieonians*	41
1949–50e	Morton	47	Airdrieonians	44	St Johnstone*	36
1950–51e	Queen of the S*	45	Stirling Albion	45	Ayr U	36
1951–52e	Clyde	44	Falkirk	43	Ayr U	39
1952–53e	Stirling Albion	44	Hamilton A	43	Queen's Park	37
1953–54e	Motherwell	45	Kilmarnock	42	Third Lanark*	36
1954–55e	Airdrieonians	46	Dunfermline Ath	42	Hamilton A	39
1955–56b	Queen's Park	54	Ayr U	51	St Johnstone	49
1956–57b	Clyde	64	Third Lanark	51	Cowdenbeath	45
1957–58b	Stirling Albion	55	Dunfermline Ath	53	Arbroath	47
1958–59b	Ayr U	60	Arbroath	51	Stenhousemuir	40
1959–60b	St Johnstone	53	Dundee U	50	Queen of the S	49
1960–61b	Stirling Albion	55	Falkirk	54	Stenhousemuir	50
1961–62b	Clyde	54	Queen of the S	53	Morton	441
1962–63b	St Johnstone	55	East Stirling	49	Morton	48

1963–64b	Morton	67	Clyde	53	Arbroath	46
1964–65b	Stirling Albion	59	Hamilton A	50	Queen of the S	45
1965–66b	Ayr U	53	Airdrieonians	50	Queen of the S	49
1966–67b	Morton	69	Raith R	58	Arbroath	57
1967–68b	St Mirren	62	Arbroath	53	East Fife	40
1968–69b	Motherwell	64	Ayr U	53	East Fife*	47
1969–70b	Falkirk	56	Cowdenbeath	55	Queen of the S	50
1970–71b	Partick T	56	East Fife	51	Arbroath	46
1971–72b	Dumbarton*	52	Arbroath	52	Stirling Albion	50
1972–73b	Clyde	56	Dumfermline Ath	52	Raith R*	47
1973–74b	Airdrieonians	60	Kilmarnock	59	Hamilton A	55
1974–75a	Falkirk	54	Queen of the S	53	Montrose	53

Elected to Division 1: 1894 Clyde; 1897 Partick T; 1899 Kilmarnock; 1900 Partick T; 1902 Partick T; 1903 Airdrieonians; 1905 Falkirk, Aberdeen and Hamilton A; 1906 Clyde; 1910 Raith R; 1913 Ayr U.

RELEGATED CLUBS

From Premier Division

1975–76 Dundee, St Johnstone
1976–77 Hearts, Kilmarnock
1977–78 Ayr U, Clydebank
1978–79 Hearts, Motherwell
1979–80 Dundee, Hibernian
1980–81 Kilmarnock, Hearts
1981–82 Partick T, Airdrieonians
1982–83 Morton, Kilmarnock
1983–84 St Johnstone, Motherwell
1984–85 Dumbarton, Morton
1985–86 *No relegation due to League reorganization*
1986–87 Clydebank, Hamilton A
1987–88 Falkirk, Dunfermline Ath, Morton
1988–89 Hamilton A
1989–90 Dundee
1990–91 None
1991–92 St Mirren, Dunfermline Ath
1992–93 Falkirk, Airdrieonians
1993–94 Reorganisation into four divisions

From Division 1

1975–76 Dunfermline Ath, Clyde
1976–77 Raith R, Falkirk
1977–78 Alloa Ath, East Fife
1978–79 Montrose, Queen of the S
1979–80 Arbroath, Clyde
1980–81 Stirling A, Berwick R
1981–82 East Stirling, Queen of the S
1982–83 Dunfermline Ath, Queen's Park
1983–84 Raith R, Alloa
1984–85 Meadowbank T, St Johnstone
1985–86 Ayr U, Alloa
1986–87 Brechin C, Montrose
1987–88 East Fife, Dumbarton
1988–89 Kilmarnock, Queen of the S
1989–90 Albion R, Alloa
1990–91 Clyde, Brechin C
1991–92 Montrose, Forfar Ath
1992–93 Meadowbank T, Cowdenbeath

Relegated from Division 1 1973–74

1921–22 *Queen's Park, Dumbarton, Clydebank
1922–23 Albion R, Alloa Ath

1951 52 Morton, Stirling Albion
1952–53 Motherwell, Third Lanark
1953–54 Airdrieonians, Hamilton A

1923–24 Clyde, Clydebank	1954–55 No clubs relegated
1924–25 Third Lanark, Ayr U	1955–56 Stirling Albion, Clyde
1925–26 Raith R, Clydebank	1956–57 Dunfermline Ath, Ayr U
1926–27 Morton, Dundee U	1957–58 East Fife, Queen's Park
1927–28 Dunfermline Ath, Bo'ness	1958–59 Queen of the S, Falkirk
1928–29 Third Lanark, Raith R	1959–60 Arbroath, Stirling Albion
1929–30 St Johnstone, Dundee U	1960–61 Ayr U, Clyde
1930–31 Hibernian, East Fife	1961–62 St Johnstone, Stirling Albion
1931–32 Dundee U, Leith Ath	1962–63 Clyde, Raith R
1932–33 Morton, East Stirling	1963–64 Queen of the S, East Stirling
1933–34 Third Lanark, Cowdenbeath	1964–65 Airdrieonians, Third Lanark
1934–35 St Mirren, Falkirk	1965–66 Morton, Hamilton A
1935–36 Airdrieonians, Ayr U	1966–67 St Mirren, Ayr U
1936–37 Dunfermline Ath, Albion R	1967–68 Motherwell, Stirling Albion
1937–38 Dundee, Morton	1968–69 Falkirk, Arbroath
1938–39 Queen's Park, Raith R	1969–70 Raith R, Partick T
1946–47 Kilmarnock, Hamilton A	1970–71 St Mirren, Cowdenbeath
1947–48 Airdrieonians, Queen's Park	1971–72 Clyde, Dunfermline Ath
1948–49 Morton, Albion R	1972–73 Kilmarnock, Airdrieonians
1949–50 Queen of the S, Stirling Albion	1973–74 East Fife, Falkirk
1950–51 Clyde, Falkirk	

*Season 1921–22 – only 1 club promoted, 3 clubs relegated.

Scottish League championship wins: Rangers 44, Celtic 35, Aberdeen 4, Hearts 4, Hibernian 4, Dumbarton 2, Dundee 1, Dundee United 1, Kilmarnock 1, Motherwell 1, Third Lanark 1.

The Scottish Football League was reconstructed into three divisions at the end of the 1974–75 season, so the usual relegation statistics do not apply. Further reorganization took place at the end of the 1985–86 season. From 1986–87, the Premier and First Division had 12 teams each. The Second Division remains at 14. From 1988–89, the Premier Division reverted to 10 teams, and the First Division to 14 teams but in 1991–92 the Premier and First Division reverted to 12.

SCOTTISH LEAGUE CUP 1993–94

FIRST ROUND

Alloa	(0) 1	Berwick R	(0) 0
East Fife	(1) 1	Albion R	(1) 2
Queen's Park	(0) 0	Arbroath	(0) 1
Stenhousemuir	(1) 3	Forfar Ath	(1) 1
Montrose	(0) 0	East Stirling	(1) 1
Queen of the S	(1) 1	Stranraer	(1) 2

SECOND ROUND

Aberdeen	(1) 5	Clydebank	(0) 0
Airdrieonians	(2) 2	Cowdenbeath	(0) 1
Ayr U	(0) 0	Motherwell	(2) 6
Brechin C	(0) 0	St Mirren	(0) 1
Hamilton A	(0) 0	Dundee U	(0) 1
Hibernian	(0) 2	Alloa	(0) 0
Kilmarnock	(1) 1	Morton	(1) 2
Meadowbank T	(1) 1	Dundee	(1) 1
Stenhousemuir	(1) 1	Falkirk	(1) 2
Stirling Albion	(0) 0	Celtic	(0) 2
Albion R	(0) 1	Partick T	(2) 11
Clyde	(0) 1	St Johnstone	(1) 2
Dunfermline Ath	(0) 2	East Stirling	(0) 0
Hearts	(1) 2	Stranraer	(0) 0
Raith R	(1) 1	Arbroath	(1) 2
Rangers	(0) 1	Dumbarton	(0) 0

THIRD ROUND

Aberdeen	(1) 5	Motherwell	(0) 2
Dunfermline Ath	(0) 0	Rangers	(2) 2
Hibernian	(2) 2	Dundee	(0) 1
Morton	(0) 0	Partick T	(0) 1
St Mirren	(0) 0	Dundee U	(0) 1
Arbroath	(0) 1	Celtic	(4) 9
Hearts	(0) 0	Falkirk	(0) 1
St Johnstone	(0) 0	Airdrieonians	(2) 2

QUARTER-FINALS

Celtic	(0) 1	Airdrieonians	(0) 0
Dundee U	(1) 3	Falkirk	(0) 3
Partick T	(1) 2	Hibernian	(0) 2
Rangers	(1) 2	Aberdeen	(0) 1

SEMI-FINALS

Dundee U	(0) 0	Hibernian	(1) 1
Celtic	(0) 0	Rangers	(1) 1

FINAL at Celtic Park

Rangers	(0) 2	Hibernian	(0) 1

PAST SCOTTISH LEAGUE CUP FINALS

Season	Winner			Runner-up		
1946–47	Rangers		4	Aberdeen		0
1947–48	East Fife	0	4	Falkirk	0*	1
1948–49	Rangers		2	Raith Rovers		0
1949–50	East Fife		3	Dunfermline		0
1950–51	Motherwell		3	Hibernian		0
1951–52	Dundee		3	Rangers		2
1952–53	Dundee		2	Kilmarnock		0
1953–54	East Fife		3	Partick Thistle		2
1954–55	Hearts		4	Motherwell		2
1955–56	Aberdeen		2	St Mirren		1
1956–57	Celtic	0	3	Partick Thistle	0	0
1957–58	Celtic		7	Rangers		1
1958–59	Hearts		5	Partick Thistle		1
1959–60	Hearts		2	Third Lanark		1
1960–61	Rangers		2	Kilmarnock		0
1961–62	Rangers	1	3	Hearts	1	1
1962–63	Hearts		1	Kilmarnock		0
1963–64	Rangers		5	Morton		0
1964–65	Rangers		2	Celtic		1
1965–66	Celtic		2	Rangers		1
1966–67	Celtic		1	Rangers		0
1967–68	Celtic		5	Dundee		3
1968–69	Celtic		6	Hibernian		2
1969–70	Celtic		1	St Johnstone		0
1970–71	Rangers		1	Celtic		0
1971–72	Partick Thistle		4	Celtic		1
1972–73	Hibernian		2	Celtic		1
1973–74	Dundee		1	Celtic		0
1974–75	Celtic		6	Hibernian		3
1975–76	Rangers		1	Celtic		0
1976–77	Aberdeen		2	Celtic		1*
1977–78	Rangers		2	Celtic		1*
1978–79	Rangers		2	Aberdeen		1
1979–80	Aberdeen	0	0	Dundee U	0*	3
1980–81	Dundee		0	Dundee U		3
1981–82	Rangers		2	Dundee U		1
1982–83	Celtic		2	Rangers		1
1983–84	Rangers		3	Celtic		2
1984–85	Rangers		1	Dundee U		0
1985–86	Aberdeen		3	Hibernian		0
1986–87	Rangers		2	Celtic		1
1987–88	Rangers†		3	Aberdeen		3*
1988–89	Aberdeen		2	Rangers		3*
1989–90	Aberdeen		2	Rangers		1
1990–91	Rangers		2	Celtic		1
1991–92	Rangers		2	Aberdeen		1
1992–93	Rangers		2	Aberdeen		1*

†Won on penalties   *After extra time

B & Q CUP 1993–94

FIRST ROUND

Albion R	(0) 2	Cowdenbeath	(2) 2*
(Cowdenbeath won 3-2 on penalties)			
Ayr U	(1) 3	East Fife	(0) 1
Dumbarton	(1) 1	Stranraer	(2) 2
Stenhousemuir	(0) 0	Clydebank	(3) 5
Brechin C	(0) 3	Arbroath	(0) 1
Clyde	(0) 0	St Mirren	(1) 1
Falkirk	(1) 2	Alloa	(0) 1
Forfar Ath	(1) 2	Meadowbank T	(1) 3*
Montrose	(4) 5	East Stirling	(0) 0
Queen of the S	(0) 2	Berwick R	(1) 1

SECOND ROUND

Airdrieonians	(2) 3	Hamilton A	(0) 1
Ayr U	(1) 2	Brechin C	(0) 1*
Falkirk	(2) 3	Cowdenbeath	(0) 0
Morton	(0) 2	St Mirren	(1) 4
Queen's Park	(0) 0	Clydebank	(0) 1
Meadowbank T	(1) 2	Stirling Albion	(0) 0
Montrose	(0) 0	Stranraer	(0) 0*
Queen of the S	(0) 0	Dunfermline Ath	(4) 6
(Montrose won 6-5 on penalties)			

QUARTER-FINALS

Airdrieonians	(0) 0	St Mirren	(0) 2
Ayr U	(1) 2	Clydebank	(0) 0
Falkirk	(1) 4	Dunfermline Ath	(0) 1
Meadowbank T	(1) 1	Montrose	(1) 1*
(Meadowbank T won 3-1 on penalties)			

SEMI-FINALS

Ayr U	(0) 1	St Mirren	(0) 2
Falkirk	(0) 3	Meadowbank T	(0) 2

FINAL at Fir Park, Motherwell, 13,763

Falkirk	(0) 3	St Mirren	(0) 0

* after extra time

SCOTTISH CUP 1994

FIRST ROUND

Albion R	(0) 0	Huntly	(0) 0
Cowdenbeath	(1) 1	Queen's Park	(1) 1
East Fife	(3) 5	Rothes	(0) 0
Forfar Ath	(4) 8	Queen of the S	(1) 3
Ross County	(9)11	St Cuthbert Wanderers	(0) 0
Stranraer	(1) 3	Whitehill Welfare	(2) 3

FIRST ROUND REPLAYS

Queen's Park	(0) 2	Cowdenbeath	(3) 3
Whitehill Welfare	(0) 0	Stranraer	(3) 4
Huntly	(0) 5	Albion R	(1) 3

SECOND ROUND

Berwick R	(1) 1	East Fife	(0) 0
East Stirling	(0) 4	Cove R	(0) 1
Forfar Ath	(0) 0	Ross County	(2) 4
Meadowbank T	(1) 1	Montrose	(1) 2
Alloa	(2) 4	Gala Fairydean	(0) 0
Cowdenbeath	(1) 1	Stenhousemuir	(0) 0
Selkirk	(0) 0	Arbroath	(2) 3
Huntly	(1) 1	Stranraer	(0) 2

THIRD ROUND

Airdrieonians	(0) 1	Dunfermline Ath	(0) 1
Arbroath	(0) 2	Dundee U	(2) 3
Clydebank	(1) 1	Dundee	(0) 1
Hibernian	(0) 2	Clyde	(0) 0
Kilmarnock	(1) 2	Ayr U	(1) 1
Morton	(0) 2	Cowdenbeath	(2) 2
Motherwell	(0) 1	Celtic	(0) 0
Partick T	(0) 0	Hearts	(1) 1
Raith R	(2) 2	Brechin C	(0) 0
Rangers	(3) 4	Dumbarton	(0) 1
St Johnstone	(0) 2	Hamilton A	(0) 0
St Mirren	(1) 2	Montrose	(0) 0
Stirling Albion	(0) 1	Berwick R	(0) 0
Stranraer	(1) 2	Falkirk	(0) 0
Alloa	(2) 2	Ross County	(0) 0
East Stirling	(0) 1	Aberdeen	(0) 3

THIRD ROUND REPLAYS

Cowdenbeath	(0) 1	Morton	(1) 2
Dunfermline Ath	(0) 1	Airdrieonians	(2) 3
Dundee	(2) 2	Clydebank	(0) 0

FOURTH ROUND

Aberdeen	(0) 1	Raith R	(0) 0
Airdrieonians	(0) 1	Stranraer	(0) 0

Dundee U	(1) 2	Motherwell	(1) 2
Morton	(0) 0	Kilmarnock	(1) 1
Rangers	(2) 6	Alloa	(0) 0
Dundee	(1) 3	St Mirren	(1) 1
Hibernian	(1) 1	Hearts	(1) 2
St Johnstone	(1) 3	Stirling Albion	(2) 3

FOURTH ROUND REPLAYS

Motherwell	(0) 0	Dundee U	(0) 1
Stirling Albion	(0) 0	St Johnstone	(2) 2

QUARTER-FINALS

Airdrieonians	(0) 0	Dundee U	(0) 0
Kilmarnock	(1) 1	Dundee	(0) 0
Rangers	(0) 2	Hearts	(0) 0
St Johnstone	(0) 1	Aberdeen	(1) 1

QUARTER-FINAL REPLAYS

Aberdeen	(2) 2	St Johnstone	(0) 0
Dundee U	(2) 2	Airdrieonians	(0) 0

SEMI-FINALS at Hampden Park

Dundee U	(0) 1	Aberdeen	(1) 1
Kilmarnock	(0) 0	Rangers	(0) 0

SEMI-FINAL REPLAYS at Hampden Park

Dundee U	(0) 1	Aberdeen	(0) 0
Kilmarnock	(1) 1	Rangers	(0) 2

FINAL at Hampden Park, 37,450

Dundee U	(0) 1	Rangers	(0) 0

Brewster

PAST SCOTTISH CUP FINALS

Year	Team 1	Score	Team 2	Score
1874	Queens Park	2	Clydesdale	0
1875	Queen's Park	3	Renton	0
1876	Queen's Park	1 2	Third Lanark	1 0
1877	Vale of Leven	0 1 3	Rangers	0 1 2
1878	Vale of Leven	1	Third Lanark	0
1879	Vale of Leven	1	Rangers	1
	Vale of Leven awarded, Rangers did not appear for replay			
1880	Queen's Park	3	Thornlibank	0
1881	Queen's Park	2 3	Dumbarton	1 1
	Replayed because of protest			
1882	Queen's Park	2 4	Dumbarton	2 1
1883	Dumbarton	2 2	Vale of Leven	2 1
1884	*Queen's Park awarded cup when Vale of Leven did not appear for the final*			
1885	Renton	0 3	Vale of Leven	0 1
1886	Queen's Park	3	Renton	1
1887	Hibernian	2	Dumbarton	1
1888	Renton	6	Cambuslang	1
1889	Third Lanark	3 2	Celtic	0 1
	Replayed because of protest			
1890	Queen's Park	1 2	Vale of Leven	1 1
1891	Hearts	1	Dumbarton	0
1892	Celtic	15	Queen's Park	0 1
	Replayed because of protest			
1893	Queen's Park	2	Celtic	1
1894	Rangers	3	Celtic	1
1895	St Bernards	3	Renton	1
1896	Hearts	3	Hibernian	1
1897	Rangers	5	Dumbarton	1
1898	Rangers	2	Kilmarnock	0
1899	Celtic	2	Rangers	0
1900	Celtic	4	Queen's Park	3
1901	Hearts	4	Celtic	3
1902	Hibernian	1	Celtic	0
1903	Rangers	1 0 2	Hearts	1 0 0
1904	Celtic	3	Rangers	2
1905	Third Lanark	0 3	Rangers	0 1
1906	Hearts	1	Third Lanark	0
1907	Celtic	3	Hearts	0
1908	Celtic	5	St Mirren	1
1909	*After two drawn games between Celtic and Rangers, 2.2, 1.1, there was a riot and the cup was withheld*			
1910	Dundee	2 0 2	Clyde	2 0 1
1911	Celtic	0 2	Hamilton Acad	0 0
1912	Celtic	2	Clyde	0
1913	Falkirk	2	Raith Albion R	2
1921	Partick Th	1	Rangers	0
1922	Morton	1	Rangers	0
1923	Celtic	1	Hibernian	0
1924	Airdrieonians	2	Hibernian	0
1925	Celtic	2	Dundee	1
1926	St Mirren	2	Celtic	0
1927	Celtic	3	East Fife	1
1928	Rangers	4	Celtic	0
1929	Kilmarnock	2	Rangers	0
1930	Rangers	0 2	Partick Th	0 1

1931	Celtic	2 4	Motherwell	2 2
1932	Rangers	1 3	Kilmarnock	1 0
1933	Celtic	1	Motherwell	0
1934	Rangers	5	St Mirren	0
1935	Rangers	2	Hamilton Acad	1
1936	Rangers	1	Third Lanark	0
1937	Celtic	2	Aberdeen	1
1938	East Fife	1 4	Kilmarnock	1 2
1939	Clyde	4	Motherwell	0
1947	Aberdeen	2	Hibernian	1
1948	Rangers	1 1	Morton	1 0
1949	Rangers	4	Clyde	1
1950	Rangers	3	East Fife	0
1951	Celtic	1	Motherwell	0
1952	Motherwell	4	Dundee	0
1953	Rangers	1 1	Aberdeen	1 0
1954	Celtic	2	Aberdeen	1
1955	Clyde	1 1	Celtic	1 0
1956	Hearts	3	Celtic	1
1957	Falkirk	1 2	Kilmarnock	1 1
1958	Clyde	1	Hibernian	0
1959	St Mirren	3	Aberdeen	1
1960	Rangers	2	Kilmarnock	0
1961	Dunfermline Ath	0 2	Celtic	0 0
1962	Rangers	2	St Mirren	0
1963	Rangers	1 3	Celtic	1 0
1964	Rangers	3	Dundee	1
1965	Celtic	3	Dunfermline Ath	2
1966	Rangers	0 1	Celtic	0 0
1967	Celtic	2	Aberdeen	0
1968	Dunfermline Ath	3	Hearts	1
1969	Celtic	4	Rangers	0
1970	Aberdeen	3	Celtic	1
1971	Celtic	1 2	Rangers	1 1
1972	Celtic	6	Hibernian	1
1973	Rangers	3	Celtic	2
1974	Celtic	3	Dundee U	0
1975	Celtic	3	Airdrieonians	1
1976	Rangers	3	Hearts	1
1977	Celtic	1	Rangers	0
1978	Rangers	2	Aberdeen	1
1979	Rangers	0 0 3	Hibernian	0 0 2
1980	Celtic	1	Rangers	0
1981	Rangers	0 4	Dundee U	0 1
1982	Aberdeen	4	Rangers	1 (aet)
1983	Aberdeen	1	Rangers	0 (aet)
1984	Aberdeen	2	Celtic	1 (aet)
1985	Celtic	2	Dundee U	1
1986	Aberdeen	3	Hearts	0
1987	St Mirren	1	Dundee U	0 (aet)
1988	Celtic	2	Dundee U	1
1989	Celtic	1	Rangers	0
1990	Aberdeen†	0	Celtic	0
1991	Motherwell	4	Dundee U	3 (aet)
1992	Rangers	2	Airdrieonians	1
1993	Rangers	2	Aberdeen	1

†won on penalties

WELSH FOOTBALL 1993–94

KONICA LEAGUE OF WALES

		Home			Goals		Away			Goals		
	P	W	D	L	F	A	W	D	L	F	A	Pts
Bangor City	38	15	4	0	51	10	11	1	7	31	16	83
Inter Cardiff	38	15	1	3	46	19	11	2	6	51	25	81
Ton Pentre	38	12	5	2	35	12	9	3	7	27	25	71
Flint Town United	38	13	3	3	42	19	7	3	9	28	28	66
Holywell Town	38	13	5	1	48	19	5	5	9	26	38	64
Newtown	38	10	5	4	27	21	8	4	7	25	27	63
Connah's Quay Nomads	38	10	4	5	37	24	6	7	6	22	23	59
Cwmbran Town	38	11	5	3	31	19	5	4	10	20	27	57
Ebbw Vale	38	9	4	6	37	34	7	5	7	31	32	57
Aberystwyth Town	38	8	6	5	26	22	7	4	8	31	34	55
Porthmadog	38	7	4	8	38	28	7	3	9	52	43	49
Llanelli	38	8	1	10	44	46	6	3	10	32	54	46
Conwy United	38	7	3	9	29	29	6	3	10	26	41	45
Mold Alexandra	38	5	5	9	29	36	7	2	10	30	39	43
Haverfordwest County	38	3	5	11	17	43	7	5	7	23	38	40
Afan Lido	38	4	8	7	29	32	4	7	8	23	34	39
Caersws	38	6	4	9	23	28	3	8	8	16	28	39
Llansantffraid	38	7	3	9	26	32	2	4	13	20	45	34
Maesteg Park Athletic	38	3	4	12	17	36	5	5	9	26	35	33
Briton Ferry Athletic	38	4	4	11	32	52	4	5	10	21	32	33

THE WELSH FOOTBALL LEAGUE

		Home			Goals		Away			Goals		
Division One	P	W	D	L	F	A	W	D	L	F	A	Pts
Barry Town	34	15	0	2	50	9	12	4	1	44	19	85
Aberaman	34	9	1	7	32	24	11	3	3	39	25	64
AFC Porth	34	7	3	7	31	24	12	3	2	37	14	63
Caldicot	34	6	8	3	38	31	10	3	4	45	28	59
Pontypridd	34	8	5	4	31	19	7	3	7	22	24	52
Pembroke Boro	34	9	4	4	37	23	6	2	9	22	26	51
Cardiff Civil Service	34	10	2	5	37	20	5	4	8	22	30	51
Llanwern	34	9	2	6	30	21	4	5	8	20	32	46
Ammanford	34	7	4	6	27	24	6	2	9	25	31	45
Caerleon	34	9	4	4	33	27	3	5	9	17	32	45
Morriston	34	5	5	7	22	21	6	5	6	23	28	43
Brecon	34	6	2	9	33	37	5	6	6	24	31	41
Caerau	34	7	5	5	30	20	3	5	9	16	30	40
Abergavenny	34	7	6	4	24	21	3	3	11	16	47	39
Ferndale	34	5	6	6	22	24	2	7	8	14	38	34
Port Talbot	34	4	5	8	25	34	5	2	10	18	37	34
Blaenrhondda	34	6	3	8	28	26	2	5	10	19	38	32
Bridgend Town	34	4	4	9	26	34	2	2	13	17	47	24

Division Two	P	W	D	L	F	A	W	D	L	F	A	Pts
		Home			*Goals*		*Away*			*Goals*		
Taffs Wells	26	10	1	2	39	13	7	4	2	27	12	56
Treowen	26	11	2	0	31	6	6	3	4	21	19	56
Carmarthen	26	8	1	4	28	19	7	2	4	30	28	48
Risca	26	8	1	4	35	19	6	2	5	15	15	45
B.P.	27	7	2	4	26	15	5	4	4	24	22	42
Fields Park/Pont.	26	5	6	2	26	19	5	3	5	16	17	39
Garw	26	7	2	4	25	19	4	4	5	16	16	39
Skewen	26	5	6	2	20	16	5	2	6	24	27	38
Cardiff Corries	26	6	2	5	20	21	4	2	7	14	30	34
Pontyclun	26	4	4	5	21	14	3	3	7	12	23	28
Newport YMCA	26	5	3	5	21	18	2	3	8	15	32	27
Seven Sisters	26	5	0	8	17	22	2	1	10	13	32	22
Tonyrefail	26	2	2	9	19	29	4	1	8	17	25	21
Milford	26	2	4	7	15	27	1	2	10	13	45	15

SMIRNOFF IRISH LEAGUE CHAMPIONSHIP
FINAL TABLE

	P	W	D	L	F	A	Pts
Linfield	30	21	7	2	63	22	70
Portadown	30	20	8	2	76	21	68
Glenavon	30	21	5	4	69	29	68
Crusaders	30	17	7	6	53	30	58
Bangor	30	14	3	13	45	49	45
Ards	30	13	2	15	59	55	41
Distillery	30	11	8	11	41	40	41
Cliftonville	30	11	10	9	40	32	40
Glentoran	30	10	7	13	46	43	37
Coleraine	30	10	7	13	41	50	37
Ballymena	30	9	6	15	38	56	33
Ballyclare	30	9	6	15	36	58	33
Carrick	30	6	7	17	42	81	25
Newry	30	5	9	16	26	52	24
Omagh T.	30	6	5	19	32	58	23
Larne	30	5	7	18	30	62	22

EUROPEAN REVIEW

One of the finest exhibitions of football seen in a European Cup Final for many years ended with AC Milan deservedly beating Barcelona 4-0. Deprived of several key players through injury and suspension, the Italian champions gave a masterly performance of skill, application and resolve and completely dominated their opponents.

The Spanish might well have lost the match before the kick-off as they were too confident of victory against such depleted opponents. Having just snatched the Spanish title on the last weekend of the season, Johan Cruyff's team appeared overwhelming favourites for the crown.

Even with the presence of two World Cup strikers in Romario (Brazil) and Hristo Stoichkov (Bulgaria), the Barcelona attack was never allowed to get into gear as Milan held all the aces in midfield.

Arsenal brought the Cup-Winners Cup to England after beating the Italian club Parma 1-0 in a low-key final. Alan Smith was the marksman in the 19th minute. In the first round, Arsenal's initial goal against the Danish club Odense had been their 100th in European competition.

This victory prevented a possible treble for Italian clubs as Internazionale provided a Milan double by beating Salzburg of Austria 1-0 in both legs of their UEFA Cup Final.

The growth of member nations in UEFA, has increased the number of clubs playing in European competitions and the challenge for domestic honours has increased as a result. There were again notable successes for teams in both League and Cup tournaments.

Anderlecht achieved the double in Belgium as did Levski Sofia in Bulgaria. But in Italy, AC Milan won the title scoring only 36 goals in 34 matches, the lowest total achieved by a championship-winning team in the country. This was, of course, in sharp contrast to their excellent showing in Europe.

But the decision to allow only 24 teams in the European Cup for 1994-95 has meant that the remaining full members of the 47-strong European body are now taking part in the UEFA Cup.

There are seeded teams in the Champions Cup: Manchester United, Barcelona, Bayern Munich, Spartak Moscow, Benfica, Anderlecht, AC Milan and Ajax.

These are exempt from the preliminary round which will consist of the remaining 16 teams. There will also be four mini-leagues in the European Cup, this part of the tournament being known again as the Champions League.

EUROPEAN CUP 1993–94

Preliminary Round, First Leg

B68 Toftir	(0) 0	Croatia Zagreb	(3) 5
Cwmbran Town	(3) 3	Cork City	(0) 2
Ekranas	(0) 0	Floriana	(0) 1
HJK Helsinki	(1) 1	Norma Tallinn	(1) 1
Omonia	(1) 2	Aarau	(0) 1
Rosenborg	(1) 2	Avenir Beggen	(0) 0
Skonto Riga	(0) 0	Olimpija Ljubljana	(1) 1
Tbilisi Dynamo	(1) 2	Linfield	(0) 1
Zimbrul	(0) 1	Beitar Jerusalem	(1) 1
Partizani Tirana	(0) 0	IA Akranes	(0) 0

Preliminary Round, Second Leg

Aarau	(2) 2	Omonia	(0) 0
IA Akranes	(0) 3	Partizani Tirana	(0) 0
Beitar Jerusalem	(1) 2	Zimbrul	(0) 0
Cork City	(0) 2	Cwmbran Town	(1) 1
Croatia Zagreb	(1) 6	B68 Toftir	(0) 0
Floriana	(0) 1	Ekranas	(0) 0
Linfield	(0) 1	Tbilisi Dynamo	(0) 1
Norma Tallinn	(0) 0	HJK Helsinki	(0) 1
Olimpija Ljubljana	(0) 0	Skonto Riga	(0) 1
Skonto Riga won 12-10 on penalties			
Rosenborg	(0) 1	Avenir Beggen	(0) 0

First Round, First Leg

Aarau	(0) 0	AC Milan	(0) 1
AIK Stockholm	(1) 1	Sparta Prague	(0) 0
IA Akranes	(0) 1	Feyenoord	(0) 0
Galatasaray	(1) 2	Cork City	(0) 1
HJK Helsinki	(0) 0	Anderlecht	(0) 3
Dynamo Kiev	(2) 3	Barcelona	(1) 1
Kispest Honved	(1) 2	Manchester United	(3) 3
Lech Poznan	(2) 3	Beitar Jerusalem	(0) 0
Linfield	(2) 3	FC Copenhagen	(0) 0
Monaco	(0) 1	AEK Athens	(0) 0
Porto	(1) 2	Floriana	(0) 0
Rangers	(1) 3	Levski Sofia	(0) 2
Rosenborg	(3) 3	FK Austria	(0) 2
Skonto Riga	(0) 0	Moscow Spartak	(4) 5
Steaua	(1) 1	Croatia Zagreb	(1) 2
Werder Bremen	(2) 5	Dynamo Minsk	(0) 2

First Round, Second Leg

AEK Athens	(1) 1	Monaco	(1) 1
Anderlecht	(3) 3	HJK Helsinki	(0) 0
Barcelona	(2) 4	Dynamo Kiev	(1) 1
Beitar Jerusalem	(1) 2	Lech Poznan	(3) 4

179

FC Copenhagen	(2) 4	Linfield	(0) 0
Cork City	(0) 0	Galatasaray	(0) 1
Croatia Zagreb	(1) 2	Steaua	(1) 3
Feyenoord	(1) 3	IA Akranes	(0) 0
FK Austria	(1) 4	Rosenborg	(1) 1
Floriana	(0) 0	Porto	(0) 0
Levski Sofia	(1) 2	Rangers	(1) 1
Manchester United	(0) 2	Kispest Honved	(0) 1
AC Milan	(0) 0	Aarau	(0) 0
Dynamo Minsk	(1) 1	Werder Bremen	(0) 1
Moscow Spartak	(3) 4	Skonto Riga	(0) 0
Sparta Prague	(1) 2	AIK Stockholm	(0) 0

Second Round, First Leg

Barcelona	(1) 3	FK Austria	(0) 0
FC Copenhagen	(0) 0	AC Milan	(3) 6
Lech Poznan	(1) 1	Moscow Spartak	(3) 5
Levski Sofia	(0) 2	Werder Bremen	(0) 2
Manchester United	(2) 3	Galatasaray	(2) 3
Monaco	(0) 4	Steaua	(1) 1
Porto	(0) 1	Feyenoord	(0) 0
Sparta Prague	(0) 0	Anderlecht	(0) 1

Second Round, Second Leg

Anderlecht	(1) 4	Sparta Prague	(1) 2
Feyenoord	(0) 0	Porto	(0) 0
FK Austria	(1) 1	Barcelona	(1) 2
AC Milan	(1) 1	FC Copenhagen	(0) 0
Moscow Spartak	(1) 2	Lech Poznan	(1) 1
Steaua	(0) 1	Monaco	(0) 0
Werder Bremen	(0) 1	Levski Sofia	(0) 0
Galatasaray	(0) 0	Manchester United	(0) 0

Champions League
Group A

Monaco	(2) 4	Spartak Moscow	(0) 1
Galatasaray	(0) 0	Barcelona	(0) 0
Barcelona	(2) 2	Monaco	(0) 0
Spartak Moscow	(0) 0	Galatasaray	(0) 0
Monaco	(2) 2	Galatasaray	(0) 0
Spartak Moscow	(0) 2	Barcelona	(1) 2
Barcelona	(1) 5	Spartak Moscow	(1) 1
Galatasaray	(0) 0	Monaco	(0) 2
Barcelona	(1) 3	Galatasaray	(0) 0
Spartak Moscow	(0) 0	Monaco	(0) 0
Galatasaray	(0) 1	Spartak Moscow	(0) 2
Monaco	(0) 0	Barcelona	(1) 1

Final table

	P	W	D	L	F	A	Pts
Barcelona	6	4	2	0	13	3	10
Monaco	6	3	1	2	9	4	7
Spartak Moscow	6	1	3	2	6	12	5
Galatasaray	6	0	2	4	1	10	2

Group B

Anderlecht	(0) 0	AC Milan	(0) 0
Porto	(2) 3	Werder Bremen	(0) 2
Werder Bremen	(0) 5	Anderlecht	(3) 3
AC Milan	(2) 3	Porto	(0) 0
AC Milan	(0) 2	Werder Bremen	(0) 1
Anderlecht	(0) 1	Porto	(0) 0
Werder Bremen	(0) 1	AC Milan	(0) 1
Porto	(1) 2	Anderlecht	(0) 0
AC Milan	(0) 0	Anderlecht	(0) 0
Werder Bremen	(0) 0	Porto	(2) 5
Anderlecht	(1) 1	Werder Bremen	(1) 2
Porto	(0) 0	AC Milan	(0) 0

Final table

	P	W	D	L	F	A	Pts
AC Milan	6	2	4	0	6	2	8
Porto	6	3	1	2	10	6	7
Werder Bremen	6	2	1	3	11	15	5
Anderlecht	6	1	2	3	5	9	4

Semi-finals

Barcelona	(2) 3	Porto	(0) 0
AC Milan	(1) 3	Monaco	(0) 0

Final: AC Milan (2) 4, Barcelona (0) 0
(in Athens, 18 May 1994, 70,000)

AC Milan: Rossi; Tassotti, Galli, Maldini (Nava 85), Panucci, Boban, Albertini, Desailly, Donadoni, Savicevic, Massaro.
Scorers: Massaro 22, 45, Savicevic 47, Desailly 58.
Barcelona: Zubizarreta; Ferrer, Koeman, Nadal, Beguiristain (Eusebio 51), Bakero, Guardiola, Amor, Sergi (Quique), Stoichkov, Romero.
Referee: Don (England).

EUROPEAN CUP-WINNERS'CUP 1993–94

Preliminary Round, First Leg

Balzers	3	Albpetrol	1
RAF Jelgava	0	Havnar Boltfelag	1
Dudelange	(0) 0	Maccabi Haifa	(1) 1
Lugano	(1) 5	Neman Grodno	(0) 0
Valur	(0) 3	MyPa	(1) 1
Sliema Wanderers	(0) 1	Degerfors	(2) 3
Bangor	(1) 1	Apoel	(1) 1
Nikol Tallinn	(0) 0	Lillestrom	(4) 4
Kosice	(2) 2	Zalgiris	(0) 0
Karpaty Lvov	(0) 1	Shelbourne	(0) 0
Publikum Celje	(0) 0	Odense	(0) 1

Preliminary Round, Second Leg

Albpetrol	0	Balzers	0
Degerfors	(2) 3	Sliema Wanderers	(0) 0
Havnar Boltfelag w.o. RAF Jelgava failed to fulfill fixture.			
Apoel	(1) 2	Bangor	(1) 1
Lillestrom	(3) 4	Nikol Tallinn	(0) 1
Maccabi Haifa	(2) 6	Dudelange	(0) 1
MyPa	(0) 0	Valur	(0) 1
Neman Grodno	(0) 2	Lugano	(1) 1
Odense	(0) 0	Publikum Celje	(0) 0
Shelbourne	(1) 3	Karpaty Lvov	(0) 1
Zalgiris	(0) 0	Kosice	(1) 1

First Round, First Leg

Apoel	(0) 0	Paris St Germain	(0) 1
Bayer Leverkusen	(1) 2	Boby Brno	(0) 0
Degerfors	(0) 1	Parma	(0) 2
Valur	(0) 0	Aberdeen	(2) 3
Benfica	(0) 1	Katowice	(0) 0
CSKA Sofia	(3) 8	Balzers	(0) 0
Hajduk Split	(1) 1	Ajax	(0) 0
Innsbruck	(0) 3	Ferencvaros	(0) 0
Kosice	(0) 2	Besiktas	(1) 1
Lillestrom	(0) 0	Torino	(1) 2
Moscow Torpedo	(0) 1	Maccabi Haifa	(0) 0
Odense	(1) 1	Arsenal	(1) 2
Panathinaikos	(2) 3	Shelbourne	(0) 0
Real Madrid	(1) 3	Lugano	(0) 0
Standard Liege	(1) 5	Cardiff City	(1) 2
Uni Craiova	(0) 4	Havnar Boltfelag	(0) 0

First Round, Second Leg

Cardiff City	(0) 1	Standard Liege	(2) 3
Maccabi Haifa	(1) 3	Moscow Torpedo	(1) 1
Paris St Germain	(2) 2	Apoel	(0) 0
Parma	(1) 2	Degerfors	(0) 0

Aberdeen	(0) 4	Valur	(0) 0
Ajax	(2) 6	Hajduk Split	(0) 0
Arsenal	(0) 1	Odense	(0) 1
Balzers	(0) 1	CSKA Sofia	(1) 3
Besiktas	(1) 2	Kosice	(0) 0
Boby Brno	(0) 0	Bayer Leverkusen	(1) 3
Ferencvaros	(0) 1	Innsbruck	(1) 2
Katowice	(0) 1	Benfica	(0) 1
Havnar Boltfelag	(0) 0	Uni Craiova	(2) 3
Lugano	(0) 1	Real Madrid	(1) 3
Shelbourne	(0) 1	Panathinaikos	(1) 2
Torino	(1) 1	Lillestrom	(0) 2

Second Round, First Leg

Ajax	(0) 2	Besiktas	(1) 1
Arsenal	(1) 3	Standard Liege	(0) 0
Benfica	(2) 3	CSKA Sofia	(0) 1
Innsbruck	(0) 1	Real Madrid	(1) 1
Maccabi Haifa	(0) 0	Parma	(0) 1
Panathinaikos	(1) 1	Bayer Leverkusen	(1) 4
Paris St Germain	(2) 4	Uni Craiova	(0) 0
Torino	(1) 3	Aberdeen	(2) 2

Second Round, Second Leg

Aberdeen	(1) 1	Torino	(1) 2
CSKA Sofia	(0) 1	Benfica	(1) 3
Parma	(0) 0	Maccabi Haifa	(0) 1
Parma won 3-1 on penalties			
Real Madrid	(1) 3	Innsbruck	(0) 0
Uni Craiova	(0) 0	Paris St Germain	(1) 2
Standard Liege	(0) 0	Arsenal	(4) 7
Bayer Leverkusen	(0) 1	Panathinaikos	(1) 2
Besiktas	(0) 0	Ajax	(1) 4

Quarter-finals, First Leg

Benfica	(0) 1	Bayer Leverkusen	(0) 1
Torino	(0) 0	Arsenal	(0) 0
Ajax	(0) 0	Parma	(0) 0
Real Madrid	(0) 0	Paris St Germain	(1) 1

Quarter-finals, Second Leg

Arsenal	(0) 1	Torino	(0) 0
Bayer Leverkusen	(1) 4	Benfica	(0) 4
Paris St Germain	(0) 1	Real Madrid	(1) 1
Parma	(1) 2	Ajax	(0) 0

Semi-finals, First Leg

Paris St Germain	(0) 1	Arsenal	(1) 1
Benfica	(1) 2	Parma	(1) 1

Semi-finals, Second Leg

Arsenal	(1) 1	Paris St Germanin	(0) 0
Parma	(0) 1	Benfica	(0) 0

Final: Arsenal (0) 1, Parma (0) 0
(in Copenhagen, 4 May 1994, 33,765)

Arsenal: Seaman; Dixon, Winterburn, Davis, Bould, Adams, Campbell, Morrow, Smith, Merson (McGoldrick 86), Selley.
Scorer: Smith.
Parma: Bucci; Benarrivo, Di Chiara, Minotti, Apolloni, Sensini, Brolin, Pin (Melli 70), Crippa, Zola, Asprilla.
Referee: Krondl (Czech Republic).

UEFA CUP 1993–94

First Round, First Leg

Aalborg	(0) 1	La Coruna	(0) 0
Antwerp	(0) 2	Maritimo	(0) 0
Salzburg	(1) 2	Dunajska Streda	(0) 0
Bohemians	(0) 0	Bordeaux	(1) 1
Crusaders	(0) 0	Servette	(0) 0
Dnepr	(0) 1	Admira Wacker	(0) 0
Hearts	(0) 2	Atletico Madrid	(0) 1
Karlsruhe	(2) 2	PSV Eindhoven	(1) 1
Kuusysi	(3) 4	Waregem	(0) 0
			2000
Dynamo Moscow	(0) 0	Eintracht Frankfurt	(3) 6
Union Luxembourg	(0) 0	Boavista	(1) 1
Vac	(1) 2	Apollon	(0) 0
Young Boys	(0) 0	Celtic	(0) 0
Borussia Dortmund	(0) 0	Vladikavkaz	(0) 0
Botev Plovdiv	(1) 2	Olympiakos	(1) 3
Brondby	(1) 2	Dundee United	(0) 0
Gloria Bistrita	(0) 0	Branik Maribor	(0) 0
Internazionale	(1) 3	Rapid Bucharest	(0) 1
Juventus	(0) 3	Lokomotiv Moscow	(0) 0
Kocaelispor	(0) 0	Sporting Lisbon	(0) 0
Lazio	(1) 2	Lokomotiv Plovdiv	(0) 0
Norrkoping	(0) 0	Mechelen	(1) 1
Norwich City	(0) 3	Vitesse	(0) 0
Osters	(1) 1	Kongsvinger	(1) 3
Slavia Prague	(0) 1	Ofi Crete	(0) 1
Slovan Bratislava	(0) 0	Aston Villa	(0) 0
Tenerife	(1) 2	Auxerre	(2) 2
Trabzonspor	(3) 3	Valletta	(1) 1
Twente	(0) 2	Bayern Munich	(2) 2
Dinamo Bucharest	(2) 3	Cagliari	(2) 2
FC Reykjavik	(0) 1	MTK Budapest	(1) 2
Nantes	(1) 1	Valencia	(1) 1

First Round, Second Leg

Admira Wacker	(1) 2	Dnepr	(1) 3
Atletico Madrid	(1) 3	Hearts	(0) 0
Boavista	(3) 4	Union Luxembourg	(0) 0
Bordeaux	(2) 5	Bohemians	(0) 0
Dunajska Streda	(0) 0	Salzburg	(1) 2
Dundee United	(0) 3	Brondby	(0) 1
Eintracht Frankfurt	(0) 1	Moscow Dynamo	(1) 2
La Coruna	(1) 5	Aalborg	(0) 0
Lokomotiv Moscow	(0) 0	Juventus	(0) 1
Maritimo	(0) 2	Antwerp	(2) 2
Mechelen	(0) 1	Norrkoping	(1) 1
PSV Eindhoven	(0) 0	Karlsruhe	(0) 0
Servette	(0) 4	Crusaders	(0) 0
Vladikavkaz	(0) 0	Borussia Dortmund	(0) 1

Apollon	(1) 4	Vac	(0) 0
Aston Villa	(2) 2	Slovan Bratislava	(0) 1
Auxerre	(0) 0	Tenerife	(0) 1
Bayern Munich	(2) 3	Twente	(0) 0
Branik Maribor	(1) 2	Gloria Bistrita	(0) 0
Cagliari	(1) 2	Dinamo Bucharest	(0) 0
Celtic	(0) 1	Young Boys	(0) 0
Kongsvinger	(2) 4	Osters	(1) 1
Lokomotiv Plovdiv	(0) 0	Lazio	(1) 2
MTK Budapest	(0) 0	FC Reykjavik	(0) 1
Ofi Crete	(1) 1	Slavia Prague	(0) 0
Olympiakos	(1) 5	Botev Plovdiv	(0) 1
Rapid Bucharest	(0) 0	Internazionale	(0) 2
Sporting Lisbon	(1) 2	Kocaelispor	(0) 0
Valletta	(1) 1	Trabzonspor	(2) 3
Vitesse	(0) 0	Norwich City	(0) 0
Waregem	(0) 1	Kuusysi	(0) 2
Valencia	(0) 3	Nantes	(0) 1

Second Round, First Leg

Branik Maribor	0	Borussia Dortmund	0
Celtic	(1) 1	Sporting Lisbon	(0) 0
Internazionale	(1) 1	Apollon	(0) 0
Kongsvinger	(0) 1	Juventus	(0) 1
Lazio	(0) 1	Boavista	(0) 0
Mechelen	(1) 5	MTK Budapest	(0) 0
Trabzonspor	(1) 1	Cagliari	(0) 1
Valencia	(1) 3	Karlsruhe	(0) 1
Atletico Madrid	(0) 1	Ofi Crete	(0) 0
Salzburg	(0) 1	Antwerp	(0) 0
Bayern Munich	(1) 1	Norwich City	(2) 2
Bordeaux	(1) 2	Servette	(0) 1
Eintracht Frankfurt	(0) 2	Dnepr	(0) 0
Kuusysi	(1) 1	Brondby	(1) 4
La Coruna	(0) 1	Aston Villa	(0) 0
Tenerife	(1) 2	Olympiakos	(1) 1

Second Round, Second Leg

Antwerp	(0) 0	Salzburg	(0) 1
Juventus	(1) 2	Kongsvinger	(0) 0
Karlsruhe	(3) 7	Valencia	(0) 0
MTK Budapest	(0) 1	Mechelen	(1) 1
Ofi Crete	(0) 2	Atletico Madrid	(0) 0
Apollon	(2) 3	Internazionale	(3) 3
Aston Villa	(0) 0	La Coruna	(1) 1
Borussia Dortmund	(0) 2	Branik Maribor	(1) 1
Brondby	(1) 3	Kuusysi	(1) 1
Caligari	0	Trabzonspor	0
Dnepr	(1) 1	Eintracht Frankfurt	(0) 0
Norwich City	(0) 1	Bayern Munich	(1) 1
Servette	(0) 0	Bordeaux	(0) 1
Sporting Lisbon	(1) 2	Celtic	(0) 0
Boavista	(1) 2	Lazio	(0) 0

Olympiakos	(2) 4	Tenerife	(1) 3

Third Round, First Leg

Bordeaux	(0) 1	Karlsruhe	(0) 0
Eintracht Frankfurt	(0) 1	La Coruna	(0) 0
Ofi Crete	(0) 1	Boavista	(3) 4
Brondby	(1) 1	Borussia Dortmund	(0) 1
Juventus	(1) 3	Tenerife	(0) 0
Norwich City	(0) 0	Internazionale	(0) 1
Sporting Lisbon	(1) 2	Salzburg	(0) 0
Mechelen	(1) 1	Cagliari	(1) 3

Third Round, Second Leg

Salzburg	(0) 3	Sporting Lisbon	(0) 0
Boavista	(1) 2	Ofi Crete	(0) 0
Karlsruhe	(1) 3	Bordeaux	(0) 0
La Coruna	(0) 0	Eintracht Frankfurt	(1) 1
Borussia Dortmund	(1) 1	Brondby	(0) 0
Cagliari	(1) 2	Mechelen	(0) 0
Internazionale	(0) 1	Norwich City	(0) 0
Tenerife	(1) 2	Juventus	(0) 1

Quarter-finals, First Leg

Boavista	(1) 1	Karlsruhe	(0) 1
Borussia Dortmund	(0) 1	Internazionale	(2) 3
Cagliari	(0) 1	Juventus	(0) 0
Salzburg	(1) 1	Eintracht Frankfurt	(0) 0

Quarter-finals, Second Leg

Eintracht Frankfurt	(1) 1	Salzburg	(0) 0
Juventus	(1) 1	Cagliari	(1) 2
Karlsruhe	(1) 1	Boavista	(0) 0
Internazionale	(0) 1	Borussia Dortmund	(1) 2

Semi-finals, First Leg

Salzburg	0	Karlsruhe	0
Cagliari	(1) 3	Internazionale	(1) 2

Semi-finals, Second Leg

Internazionale	(1) 3	Cagliari	(0) 0
Karlsruhe	(0) 1	Salzburg	(1) 1

Final, First Leg: Salzburg (0) 0, Internazionale (1) 1
(in Vienna, 26 April 1994, 47,500)

Salzburg: Konrad; Lainer, Weber, Winklhofer (Steiner 61), Furstaller, Aigner, Amerhauser (Muzek 46), Artner, Marquinho, Pfeifenberger, Stadler.
Internazionale: Zenga; Paganin A, Orlando, Jonk, Bergomi, Battistini, Bianchi, Manicone, Berti, Bergkamp (Dell'Anno 89), Sosa (Ferri 74).
Scorer: Berti 35.
Referee: Nielsen (Denmark).

Final, Second Leg: Internazionale (0) 1, Salzburg (0) 0
(in Milan, 11 May 1994, 80,326)

Internazionale: Zenga; Paganin A, Fontolan (Ferri 67), Jonk, Bergomi, Battistini, Orlando, Manicone, Berti, Bergkamp (Paganin M 89), Sosa.

Scorer: Jonk 62.

Salzburg: Konrad; Lainer, Weber, Winklhofer (Amerhauser 67), Furstaller, Aigner, Jurcevic, Artner (Steiner 75), Marquinho, Feiersinger, Hutter.

Referee: McCluskey (Scotland).

EUROPEAN CUP DRAWS 1994–95

Champions Cup Preliminary Round

Paris St Germain v VAC Samsung (Hungary), Legia Warsaw v Hajduk Split, Steaua Bucharest v Servette (Switzerland), Sparta Prague v IFK Gothenburg, AEK Athens v Rangers, Maccabi Haifa (Israel) v Casino Salzburg, Silkeborg (Denmark) v Dynamo Kiev (Ukraine), Avenir Beggen (Luxembourg) v Galatasaray.

Champions League Draw

Group 1: Avenir Beggen or Galatasaray, Manchester United, Sparta Prague or IFK Gothenburg, Barcelona.
Group 2: Bayern Munich, Silkeborg or Dynamo Kiev, Spartak Moscow, Paris St Germain or VAC FC Samsung.
Group 3: Steaua Bucharest or Servette, Legia Warsaw or Hajduk Split, Benfica, Anderlecht.
Group 4: AC Milan, Maccabi Haifa or Salzburg, AEK Athens or Rangers, Ajax Amsterdam.

Cup-Winners' Cup Preliminary Round

FC Pirin (Bulgaria) v Schaan (Liechtenstein), Norma Tallinn (Estonia) v Maribor Branik (Slovenia), Fandok Bobruisk (Belarus) v Tirana (Albania), Tiligul Tiraspol (Moldova) v Omonia Nicosia (Cyprus), Ferencvaros (Hungary) v F91 Dudelange (Luxembourg), Floriana (Malta) v Sligo Rovers, Barry Town v Zalgiris Vilnius (Lithuania), Bodo Glimt (Norway) v Olimpija Riga (Latvia), Viktoria Zizkov (Czech Republic) v IFK Noorkoping (Sweden), Sandoyar Itrottarfelag (Faeroes) v HJK Helsinki, IBK Keflavik (Iceland) v Maccabi Tel-Aviv (Israel), Bangor (Northern Ireland) v Tatran Presov (Slovakia).

UEFA Cup Preliminary Round

Slavia Prague v Cork City, Motherwell v Havnar Boltfelag (Faeroes), FC Copenhagen v FC Jazz (Finland), Portadown v Slovan Bratislava, Bangor (Wales) v Akranes (Iceland), Anjalankoski (Finland) v Inter Bratislava, Odense BK v Flora Tallinn (Estonia), Lillestrom v Shakhter Donetsk (Ukraine), Gotu Itrottarfelag (Faeroes) v Trelleboras (Sweden), Gornik Zabrze (Poland) v Shamrock Rovers.
FC Romar (Lithuania) v AIK Solna (Sweden), Hafnarfjordur (Iceland) v Linfield, Skonto Riga (Latvia) v Aberdeen, Inter Cardiff v GKS Katowice, Rosenborg BK (Norway) v CS Grevenmacher (Luxembourg), Aarau (Switzerland) v FC Mura (Slovenia), Anorthosis Famagusta (Cyprus) v FC Chumen (Blugaria), Dynamo Tbilisi (Georgia) v Universitatae Craiova (Romania), FC Badar (Macedonia) v Bekescsabai (Hungary), SCT Olimpija (Slovenia) v Levski Sofia (Bulgaria), Fenerbahce (Turkey) v Touran (Azerbaijan).
Valletta (Malta) v Rapid Bucuresti (Romania), Kispest Honved (Hungary) v Zimbru Chisinau (Moldova), Ararat Erevan (Armenia) v CSKA Sofia, Dynamo Minsk (Belarus) v Hibernians (Malta), Teuta (Albania) v Apollon (Cyprus), Aris Thessaloniki (Greece) v Hapoel Beer Sheva (Israel).

PAST EUROPEAN CUP FINALS

1956	Real Madrid	4	Stade de Rheims	3
1957	Real Madrid	2	Fiorentina	0
1958	Real Madrid	3	AC Milan	2*
1959	Real Madrid	2	Stade de Rheims	0
1960	Real Madrid	7	Eintracht Frankfurt	3
1961	Benfica	3	Barcelona	2
1962	Benfica	5	Real Madrid	3
1963	AC Milan	2	Benfica	1
1964	Internazionale	3	Real Madrid	1
1965	Internazionale	1	SL Benfica	0
1966	Real Madrid	2	Partizan Belgrade	1
1967	Celtic	2	Internazionale	1
1968	Manchester U	4	Benfica	1*
1969	AC Milan	4	Ajax	1
1970	Feyenoord	2	Celtic	1*
1971	Ajax	2	Panathinaikos	0
1972	Ajax	2	Internazionale	0
1973	Ajax	1	Juventus	0
1974	Bayern Munich	1 4	Atletico Madrid	1 0
1975	Bayern Munich	2	Leeds U	0
1976	Bayern Munich	1	St Etienne	0
1977	Liverpool	3	Borussia Moenchengladbach	1
1978	Liverpool	1	FC Brugge	0
1979	Nottingham F	1	Malmö	0
1980	Nottingham F	1	Hamburg	0
1981	Liverpool	1	Real Madrid	0
1982	Aston Villa	1	Bayern Munich	0
1983	Hamburg	1	Juventus	0
1984	Liverpool†	1	Roma	1
1985	Juventus	1	Liverpool	0
1986	Steaua Bucharest†	0	Barcelona	0
1987	Porto	2	Bayern Munich	1
1988	PSV Eindhoven†	0	Benfica	0
1989	AC Milan	4	Steaua Bucharest	0
1990	AC Milan	1	Benfica	0
1991	Red Star Belgrade†	0	Marseille	0
1992	Barcelona	1	Sampdoria	0
1993	Marseille	1	AC Milan	0

(Marseille subsequently stripped of title)

PAST EUROPEAN CUP-WINNERS' CUP FINALS

1961	Fiorentina	4	Rangers	1‡
1962	Atletico Madrid	1 3	Fiorentina	1 0
1963	Tottenham H	5	Atletico Madrid	1
1964	Sporting Lisbon	3 1	MTK Budapest	3* 0
1965	West Ham U	2	Munich 1860	0
1966	Borussia Dortmund	2	Liverpool	1*
1967	Bayern Munich	1	Rangers	0*
1968	AC Milan	2	Hamburg	0

190

Year	Winner		Runner-up	
1969	Slovan Bratislava	3	Barcelona	2
1970	Manchester C	2	Gornik Zabrze	1
1971	Chelsea	1 2	Real Madrid	1* 1*
1972	Rangers	3	Dynamo Moscow	2
1973	AC Milan	1	Leeds U	0
1974	Magdeburg	2	AC Milan	0
1975	Dynamo Kiev	3	Ferencvaros	0
1976	Anderlecht	4	West Ham U	2
1977	Hamburg	2	Anderlecht	0
1978	Anderlecht	4	Austria Vienna	0
1979	Barcelona	4	Fortuna Dusseldorf	3*
1980	Valencia†	0	Arsenal	0
1981	Dynamo Tbilisi	2	Carl Zeiss Jena	1
1982	Barcelona	2	Standard Liege	1
1983	Aberdeen	2	Real Madrid	1*
1984	Juventus	2	Porto	1
1985	Everton	3	Rapid Vienna	1
1986	Dynamo Kiev	3	Atletico Madrid	0
1987	Ajax	1	Lokomotiv Leipzig	0
1988	Mechelen	1	Ajax	0
1989	Barcelona	2	Sampdoria	0
1990	Sampdoria	2	Anderlecht	0
1991	Manchester U	2	Barcelona	1
1992	Werder Bremen	2	Monaco	0
1993	Parma	3	Antwerp	1

FAIRS CUP FINALS

Year	Winner		Runner-up	
1958	Barcelona	8	London	2‡
1960	Barcelona	4	Birmingham C	1‡
1961	Roma	4	Birmingham C	2‡
1962	Valencia	7	Barcelona	3‡
1963	Valencia	4	Dynamo Zagreb	1‡
1964	Real Zaragoza	2	Valencia	1
1965	Ferencvaros	1	Juventus	0
1966	Barcelona	4	Real Zaragoza	3‡
1967	Dynamo Zagreb	2	Leeds U	0‡
1968	Leeds U	1	Ferencvaros	0‡
1969	Newcastle U	6	Ujpest Dozsa	2‡
1970	Arsenal	4	Anderlecht	3‡
1971	Leeds U	3**	Juventus	3‡

PAST UEFA CUP FINALS

Year	Winner			Runner-up		
1972	Tottenham H	2	1	Wolverhampton W	1	1
1973	Liverpool	3	0	Borussia Moenchengladbach	0	2
1974	Feyenoord	2	2	Tottenham H	2	0
1975	Borussia Moenchengladbach	0	5	Twente Enschede	0	1
1976	Liverpool	3	1	FC Bruges	2	1
1977	Juventus**	1	1	Athletic Bilbao	0	2
1978	PSV Eindhoven	0	3	SEC Bastia	0	0

1979	Borussia Moenchengladbach	1 1	Red Star Belgrade	1 0
1980	Borussia Moenchengladbach	3 0	Eintracht Frankfurt**	2 1
1981	Ipswich T	3 2	AZ 67 Alkmaar	0 4
1982	IFK Gothenburg	1 3	SV Hamburg	0 0
1983	Anderlecht	1 1	Benfica	0 1
1984	Tottenham H†	1 1	RSC Anderlecht	1 1
1985	Real Madrid	3 0	Videoton	0 1
1986	Real Madrid	5'0	Cologne	1 2
1987	IFK Gothenburg	1 1	Dundee U	0 1
1988	Bayer Leverkusen†	0 3	Espanol	3 0
1989	Napoli	2 3	Stuttgart	1 3
1990	Juventus	3 0	Fiorentina	1 0
1991	Internazionale	2 0	AS Roma	0 1
1992	Ajax**	0 2	Torino	0 2
1993	Juventus	3 3	Borussia Dortmund	1 0

After extra time ** *Won on away goals* † *Won on penalties* ‡ *Aggregate score*

PAST EUROPEAN CHAMPIONSHIP FINALS

Paris, 10 July 1960 USSR 2, YUGOSLAVIA 1*
USSR: Yachin; Tchekeli, Kroutikov, Voinov, Maslenkin, Netto, Metreveli, Ivanov, Ponedelnik, Bubukin, Meshki. **Scorers:** Metreveli, Ponedelnik.
Yugoslavia: Vidinic; Durkovic, Jusufi, Zanetic, Miladinovic, Perusic, Sekularac, Jerkovic, Galic, Matus, Kostic. **Scorer:** Netto (og).

Madrid, 21 June 1964 SPAIN 2, USSR 1
Spain: Iribar; Rivilla, Calleja, Fuste, Olivella, Zoco, Amancio, Pereda, Marcellino, Suarez, Lapetra. **Scorers:** Perede, Marcellino.
USSR: Yachin; Chustikov, Mudrik, Voronin, Shesternjev, Anitchkin, Chislenko, Ivanov, Ponedelnik, Kornaev, Khusainov. **Scorer:** Khusainov.

Rome, 8 June 1968 ITALY 1, YUGOSLAVIA 1
Italy: Zoff; Burgnich, Facchetti, Ferrini, Guarneri, Castano, Domenghini, Juliano, Anastasi, Lodetti, Prati. **Scorer:** Domenghini.
Yugoslavia: Pandelic; Fazlagic, Damjanovic, Pavlovic, Paunovic, Holcer, Petkovic, Acimovic, Musemic, Trivic, Dzajic. **Scorer:** Dzajic.

Replay: Rome, 10 June 1968 ITALY 2, YUGLOSLAVIA 0
Italy: Zoff; Burgnich, Facchetti, Rosato, Guarneri, Salvadore, Domenghini, Mazzola, Anastasi, De Sista, Riva. **Scorers:** Riva, Anastasi.
Yugoslavia: Pantelic; Fazlagic, Damjanovic, Pavlovic, Paunovic, Holcer, Hosic, Acimovic, Musemic, Trivic, Dzajic.

Brussels, 18 June 1972 WEST GERMANY 3, USSR 0
West Germany: Maier; Hottges, Schwarzenbeck, Beckenbauer, Breitner, Hoeness, Wimmer, Netzer, Heynckes, Müller, Kremers. **Scorers:** Müller 2, Wimmer.
USSR: Rudakov; Dzodzuashvili, Khurtsilava, Kaplichny, Istomin, Troshkin, Kolotov, Baidachni, Konkov (Dolmatov), Banishevski (Konzinkievits), Onishenko.

Belgrade, 20 June 1976 CZECHOSLOVAKIA 2, WEST GERMANY 2*
Czechoslovakia: Viktor; Dobias (Vesely F), Pivarnik, Ondrus, Capkovic, Gogh, Moder, Panenka, Svehlik (Jurkemik), Masny, Nehoda. **Scorers:** Svehlik, Dobias.
West Germany: Maier; Vogts, Beckenbauer, Schwarzenbeck, Dietz, Bonhof, Wimmer (Flohe), Müller D, Beer (Bongartz), Hoeness, Holzenbein. **Scorers:** Müller, Holzenbein.
Czechoslovakia won 5-3 on penalties.

Rome, 22 June 1980 WEST GERMANY 2, BELGIUM 1
West Germany: Schumacher; Briegel, Forster K, Dietz, Schuster, Rummenigge, Hrubesch, Müller, Allofs, Stielike, Kalz. **Scorers:** Hrubesch 2.
Belgium: Pfaff; Gerets, Millecamps, Meeuws, Renquin, Cools, Van der Eycken, Van Moer, Mommens, Van der Elst, Ceulemans. **Scorer:** Van der Eycken.

Paris, 27 June 1984 FRANCE 2, SPAIN 0
France: Bats; Battiston (Amoros), Le Roux, Bossis, Domergue, Giresse, Platini, Tigana, Fernandez, Lacombe (Genghini), Bellone. **Scorers:** Platini, Bellone.
Spain: Arconada; Urquiaga, Salva (Roberto), Gallego, Camacho, Francisco, Julio Alberto (Sarabia), Senor, Victor, Carrasco, Santilana.

Munich, 25 June 1988 HOLLAND 2, USSR 0
Holland: Van Breukelen; Van Aerle, Van Tiggelen, Wouters, Koeman R, Rijkaard, Vanenburg, Gullit, Van Basten, Muhren, Koeman E. **Scorers:** Gullit, Van Basten.
USSR: Dassayev; Khidiatulin, Aleinikov, Mikhailichenko, Litovchenko, Demianenko, Belanov, Gotsmanov (Baltacha), Protasov (Pasulko), Zavarov, Rats.

Gothenburg, 26 June 1992 DENMARK 2, GERMANY 0
Denmark: Schmeichel; Sivebaek (Christiansen), Nielsen, K, Olsen, L, Christofte, Jensen, Povlsen, Laudrup, Piechnik, Larsen, Vilfort. **Scorers:** Jensen, Vilfort.
Germany: Illgner; Reuter, Brehme, Kohler, Buchwald, Hässler, Riedle, Helmer, Sammer (Doll), Effenberg (Thon), Klinsmann.

* *After extra time*

OLYMPIC FOOTBALL

Previous winners

1896	Athens*	1.	Denmark	1956	Melbourne	1. USSR
		2.	Greece			2. Yugoslavia
1900	Paris*	1.	England			3. Bulgaria
		2.	France	1960	Rome	1. Yugoslavia
1904	St Louis**	1.	Canada			2. Denmark
		2.	USA			3. Hungary
1908	London	1.	England	1964	Tokyo	1. Hungary
		2.	Denmark			2. Czechoslovakia
		3.	Holland			3. East Germany
1912	Stockholm	1.	England	1968	Mexico City	1. Hungary
		2.	Denmark			2. Bulgaria
		3.	Holland			3. Japan
1920	Antwerp	1.	Belgium	1972	Munich	1. Poland
		2.	Spain			2. Hungary
		3.	Holland			3. East Germany/
1924	Paris	1.	Uruguay			USSR joint bronze
		2.	Switzerland	1976	Montreal	1. East Germany
		3.	Sweden			2. Poland
1928	Amsterdam	1.	Uruguay			3. USSR
		2.	Argentina	1980	Moscow	1. Czechoslovakia
		3.	Italy			2. East Germany
1932	Los Angeles no competition					3. USSR
1936	Berlin	1.	Italy	1984	Los Angeles	1. France
		2.	Austria			2. Brazil
		3.	Norway			3. Yugoslavia
1948	London	1.	Sweden	1988	Seoul	1. USSR
		2.	Yugoslavia			2. Brazil
		3.	Denmark			3. West Germany
1952	Helsinki	1.	Hungary	1992	Barcelona	1. Spain
		2.	Yugoslavia			2. Poland
		3.	Sweden			3. Ghana

*No official tournament
**No official tournament but gold medal later awarded by IOC

WORLD CLUB CHAMPIONSHIP

Played annually up to 1974 and intermittently since then between the winners of the European Cup and the winners of the South American Champions Cup— known as the Copa Libertadores. In 1980 the winners were decided by one match arranged in Tokyo in February 1981 and the venue has been the same since. AC Milan replaced Marseille who had been stripped of their European Cup title in 1993.

1960	Real Madrid beat Penarol 0-0, 5-1
1961	Penarol beat Benfica 0-1, 5-0, 2-1
1962	Santos beat Benfica 3-2, 5-2
1963	Santos beat AC Milan 2-4, 4-2, 1-0
1964	Inter-Milan beat Independiente 0-1, 2-0, 1-0
1965	Inter-Milan beat Independiente 3-0, 0-0
1966	Penarol beat Real Madrid 2-0, 2-0
1967	Racing Club beat Celtic 0-1, 2-1, 1-0
1968	Estudiantes beat Manchester United 1-0, 1-1
1969	AC Milan beat Estudiantes 3-0, 1-2
1970	Feyenoord beat Estudiantes 2-2, 1-0
1971	Nacional beat Panathinaikos* 1-1, 2-1
1972	Ajax beat Independiente 1-1, 3-0
1973	Independiente beat Juventus* 1-0
1974	Atletico Madrid* beat Independiente 0-1, 2-0
1975	Independiente and Bayern Munich could not agree dates; no matches.
1976	Bayern Munich beat Cruzeiro 2-0, 0-0
1977	Boca Juniors beat Borussia Moenchengladbach* 2-2, 3-0
1978	Not contested
1979	Olimpia beat Malmö* 1-0, 2-1
1980	Nacional beat Nottingham Forest 1-0
1981	Flamengo beat Liverpool 3-0
1982	Penarol beat Aston Villa 2-0
1983	Gremio Porto Alegre beat SV Hamburg 2-1
1984	Independiente beat Liverpool 1-0
1985	Juventus beat Argentinos Juniors 4-2 on penalties after a 2-2 draw
1986	River Plate beat Steaua Bucharest 1-0
1987	FC Porto beat Penarol 2-1 after extra time
1988	Nacional (Uru) beat PSV Eindhoven 7-6 on penalties after 1-1 draw
1989	AC Milan beat Atletico Nacional (Col) 1-0 after extra time
1990	AC Milan beat Olimpia 3-0
1991	Red Star Belgrade beat Colo Colo 3-0
1992	Sao Paulo beat Barcelona 2-1

*European Cup runners-up; winners declined to take part.

1993

12 December in Tokyo

AC Milan (0) 2 (*Massaro 48, Papin 81*)

Sao Paulo (1) 3 (*Palinha 19, Cerezo 60, Muller 87*) 80,000

AC Milan: Rossi; Panucci, Maldini, Albertini (Orlando 80), Costacurta, Baresi, Donadoni, Desailly, Papin, Massaro, Raducioiu (Tassotti 80).
Sao Paulo: Zetti; Cafu, Valber, Ronaldo, Doriva, Andre, Muller, Dinho, Palhinha (Juninho 75), Leonardo, Cerezo.
Referee: Quiniou (France).

WORLD CUP REVIEW

Brazil became the first country to win the World Cup four times, and although a penalty shoot-out final against Italy was not the ideal manner of deciding the outcome, there was little to deny that they were the most accomplished team in the USA tournament.

Those misgivings which had been widely expressed as to the sense of holding the competition in North America, where soccer takes a back seat to Basketball, American Football and Baseball, were swept away by the largely friendly atmosphere which pervaded the matches in question.

Crowds were bigger than ever before in a final tournament. The aggregate was 3,567,415 for an average 68,604. FIFA's decision to insist that their referees clamp down on the so-called tackle from behind and not penalise a player standing in an offside position when not interfering with play, helped to promote better conduct and increase scoring. But inevitably there were instances of sendings-off and bookings which were harsh in the extreme, not to mention goals scored which should have been correctly ruled offside.

The total number of yellow cards flashed was 227, while 15 players received their red version. This gave a distorted picture of the generally sensible discipline shown by the players.

The highest attendance was 94,194 for the final itself. The match ended goalless after extra time and needed the lottery of a penalty shoot-out to divide the teams. This was a World Cup first and there were others.

Lothar Matthaus (Germany) equalled Uwe Seeler (Germany), Wladyslaw Zmuda (Yugoslavia) and Diego Maradona (Argentina) with his 21st appearance in a match in the final tournament. He would have beaten it had Germany progressed as would Maradona, had he not been found guilty of taking a banned substance and suspended from the competition.

Of the 141 goals scored, the fastest was in the second minute by Batistuta for Argentina v Greece; the latest came in the third minute of injury time on two occasions by Bulgarians: Borimirov v Greece and Sirakov against Argentina.

For the first time in the cup there was an indoor match, held in the Pontiac Silverdome, Detroit. Salenko (Russia) scored a record five goals in one match and on two occasions three substitutes were used, the first when Italy's goalkeeper was sent off against Norway and when another was withdrawn from a game.

There was only one own goal, by Escobar of Colombia. In a tragic aftermath the player was shot and killed on his return to South America.

Three points for a win in the group games was inconclusive. Had two points been awarded, the placings would have remained the same.

PAST WORLD CUP FINALS

Uruguay 1930
URUGUAY 4, ARGENTINA 2 (1–2) *Montevideo*
Uruguay: Ballesteros; Nasazzi (capt), Mascheroni, Andrade, Fernandez, Gestido, Dorado, Scarone, Castro, Cea, Iriarte. **Scorers:** Dorado, Cea, Iriarte, Castro.
Argentina: Botasso; Della, Torre, Paternoster, Evaristo, J., Monti, Suarez, Peucelle, Varallo, Stabile, Ferreira (capt), Evaristo, M. **Scorers:** Peucelle, Stabile.
Leading scorer: Stabile (Argentina) 8.

Italy 1934
ITALY 2, CZECHOSLOVAKIA 1 (0–0) (1–1)* *Rome*
Italy: Combi (capt); Monseglio, Allemandi, Ferraris IV, Monti, Bertolini, Guaita, Meazza, Schiavio, Ferrari, Orsi. **Scorers:** Orsi, Schiavio.
Czechoslovakia: Planicka (capt); Zenisek, Ctyroky, Kostalek, Cambal, Krcil, Junek, Svoboda, Sobotka, Nejedly, Puc. **Scorer:** Puc.
Leading scorers: Schiavio (Italy), Nejedly (Czechoslovakia), Conen (Germany) each 4.

France 1938
ITALY 4, HUNGARY 2 (3–1) *Paris*
Italy: Olivieri; Foni, Rava, Serantoni, Andreolo, Locatelli, Biavati, Meassa (capt), Piola, Ferrari, Colaussi. **Scorers:** Colaussi 2, Piola 2.
Hungary: Szabo; Polgar, Biro, Szalay, Szucs, Lazar, Vincze, Sarosi (capt), Szengeller, Titkos. **Scorers:** Titkos, Sarosi.
Leading scorer: Leonidas (Brazil) 8.

Brazil 1950
Final pool (replaced knock-out system)
Uruguay 2, Spain 2   Brazil 6, Spain 1
Brazil 7, Sweden 1   Sweden 3, Spain 1
Uruguay 3, Sweden 2   Uruguay 2, Brazil 1

Final positions	P	W	D	L	F	A	Pts
Uruguay	3	2	1	0	7	5	5
Brazil	3	2	0	1	14	4	4
Sweden	3	1	0	2	6	11	2
Spain	3	0	1	2	4	11	1

Leading scorers: Ademir (Brazil) 7, Schiaffino (Uruguay), Basora (Spain) 5.

Switzerland 1954
WEST GERMANY 3, HUNGARY 2 (2–2) *Berne*
West Germany: Turek; Posipal, Kohlmeyer, Eckel, Liebrich, Rahn, Morlock, Walter, O., Walter, F. (capt), Schaefer. **Scorers:** Morlock, Rahn 2.
Hungary: Grosics; Buzansky, Lantos, Bozsik, Lorant, Zakarias, Czibor, Kocsis, Hidegkuti, Puskas (capt), Toth, J. **Scorers:** Puskas, Czibor.
Leading scorer: Kocsis (Hungary) 11.

Sweden 1958
BRAZIL 5, SWEDEN 2 (2–1) *Stockholm*
Brazil: Gilmar; Santos, D., Santos, N., Zito, Bellini, Orlando, Garrincha, Didi, Vavà, Pelé, Zagalo **Scorers:** Vavà 2, Pelé 2, Zagalo.
Sweden: Svensson; Bergmark, Axbom, Boerjesson, Gustavsson, Parling, Hamrin, Gren, Simonsson, Liedholm, Skoglund. **Scorers:** Liedholm, Simonsson.
Leading scorer: Fontaine (France) 13 (present record total).

Chile 1962
BRAZIL 3, CZECHOSLOVAKIA 1 (1–1) *Santiago*
Brazil: Gilmar; Santos, D., Mauro, Zozimo, Santos, N., Zito, Didi, Garrincha, Vavà, Amarildo, Zagalo. **Scorers:** Amarildo, Zito, Vavà.
Czechoslovakia: Schroiff; Tichy, Novak, Pluskal, Popluhar, Masopust, Pospichal, Scherer, Kvasniak, Kadraba, Jelinek. **Scorer:** Masopust.
Leading scorer: Jerkovic (Yugoslavia) 5.

England 1966
ENGLAND 4, WEST GERMANY 2 (1–1) (2–2)* *Wembley*
England: Banks; Cohen, Wilson, Stiles, Charlton, J., Moore, Ball, Hurst, Hunt, Charlton, R., Peters. **Scorers:** Hurst 3, Peters.
West Germany: Tilkowski; Hottges, Schulz, Weber, Schnellinger, Haller, Beckenbauer, Overath, Seeler, Held, Emmerich. **Scorers:** Haller, Weber.
Leading scorer: Eusebio (Portugal) 9.

Mexico 1970
BRAZIL 4, ITALY 1 (1–1) *Mexico City*
Brazil: Felix; Carlos Alberto, Piazza, Everaldo, Gerson, Clodoaldo, Jairzinho, Pelé, Tostão, Rivelino. **Scorers:** Pelé, Gerson, Jairzinho, Carlos Alberto.
Italy: Albertosi; Burgnich, Cera, Rosato, Fachetti, Bertini (Juliano), Riva, Domenghini, Mazzola, De Sista, Boninsegna (Rivera). **Scorer:** Boninsegna.
Leading scorer: Müller (West Germany) 10.

West Germany 1974
WEST GERMANY 2, HOLLAND 1 (2–1) *Munich*
West Germany: Maier; Vogts, Schwarzenbeck, Beckenbauer, Breitner, Bonhof, Hoeness, Overath, Grabowski, Müller, Holzenbein. **Scorers:** Breitner (pen), Müller.
Holland: Jongbloed: Suurbier, Rijsbergen (De Jong), Haan, Krol, Jansen, Van Hanegem, Neeskens, Rep (Nanninga), Cruyff, Rensenbrink (Van der Kerkhof, R.) **Scorer:** Neeskens (pen).
Leading scorer: Lato (Poland) 7.

Argentina 1978
ARGENTINA 3, HOLLAND 1 (1–1)* *Buenos Aires*
Argentina: Fillol; Olguin, Passarella, Galvan, Tarantini, Ardiles (Larrosa), Gallego,Ortiz (Houseman), Bertoni, Luque, Kempes. **Scorers:** Kempes 2, Bertoni.
Holland: Jongbloed; Poortvliet, Brandts, Krol, Jansen (Suurbier), Neeskens, Van der Kerkhof, W., Van der Kerkhof, R., Haan, Rep (Nanninga), Rensenbrink. **Scorer:** Nanninga.
Leading scorer: Kempes (Argentina) 6.

Spain 1982
ITALY 3 WEST GERMANY 1 (0–0) *Madrid*
Italy: Zoff; Bergomi, Cabrini, Collovati, Scirea, Gentile, Oriali, Tardelli, Conti, Graziani (Altobelli), Rossi (Causio). **Scorers:** Rossi, Tardelli, Altobelli.
West Germany: Schumacher; Kaltz, Forster, K-H., Stielike, Forster, B. Breitner, Dremmler (Hrubesch), Littbarski, Briegel, Fischer, Rummenigge (Müller). **Scorer:** Breitner.
Leading scorer: Rossi (Italy) 6.

Mexico 1986
ARGENTINA 3, WEST GERMANY 2 (1–0) *Mexico City*
Argentina: Pumpido; Cuciuffo, Olarticoechea, Ruggeri, Brown, Giusti, Burruchaga (Trobbiani), Batista, Valdano, Maradona, Enrique. **Scorers:** Brown, Valdano, Burruchaga.

West Germany: Schumacher; Berthold, Briegel, Jakobs, Forster, Eder, Brehme, Matthaus, Állofs (Voller), Magath (Hoeness), Rummenigge. **Scorers:** Rummenigge, Voller.
Leading scorer: Lineker (England) 6.

Italy 1990
WEST GERMANY 1, ARGENTINA 0 (0–0) *Rome*
West Germany: Illgner; Berthold (Reuter 73), Kohler, Augenthaler, Buchwald, Brehme, Littbarski, Hässler, Matthäus, Völler, Klinsmann. **Scorer:** Brehme (pen).
Argentina: Goycochea; Lorenzo, Serrizuela, Sensini, Ruggeri (Monzon 46), Simon, Basualdo, Burruchaga (Calderon 53), Maradona, Troglio, Dezotti.
Referee: Codesal (Mexico). Monzon and Dezotti sent off.
Leading scorer: Schillaci (Italy) 6.

*After extra time

199

WORLD CUP 1994 Qualifying Tournament

Europe
Germany qualified as holders
Group 1
Tallinn, 16 August 1992, 3000
Estonia (0) 0

Switzerland (2) 6 *(Chapuisat 23, 68, Bregy 29, Knup 46, Ohrel 66, Sforza 84)*

Estonia: Poom; Hepner, Kaljen, Kallaste T, Lindmaa (Veensalu 78), Kristal, Olumets, Linnumae, Kallaste R, Reim, Pushtov (Kirs 64).
Switzerland: Pascolo; Egli, Geiger, Hottiger, Rothenbuhler, Bregy, Sutter B (Bonvin 79), Ohrel, Sforza, Chapuisat, Knup.

Berne, 9 September 1992, 10,000
Switzerland (1) 3 *(Knup 2, 71, Bregy 81)*

Scotland (1) 1 *(McCoist)*

Switzerland: Pascolo; Hottiger, Quentin, Egli, Geiger, Bregy (Piffaretti 89), Sutter A, Ohrel, Knup (Sutter B 86), Sforza, Chapuisat.
Scotland: Goram; Gough, Malpas, McCall, Boyd (Gallacher 75), McPherson, Durie, McAllister, McCoist, McStay, McClair (Durrant 57).

Cagliari, 14 October 1992, 34,000
Italy (0) 2 *(Roberto Baggio 83, Eranio 89)*

Switzerland (2) 2 *(Ohrel 17, Chapuisat 21)*

Italy: Marchegiani; Tassotti, Di Chiara, Eranio, Costacurta, Lanna, Lentini, Donadoni (Albertini 71), Vialli, Roberto Baggio, Evani (Bianchi 48).
Switzerland: Pascolo; Hottiger, Quentin, Egli, Geiger, Bregy, Sutter A, Ohrel (Piffaretti 56), Knup, Sforza, Chapuisat (Sutter B 89).

Ibrox, 14 October 1992, 22,583
Scotland (0) 0

Portugal (0) 0

Scotland: Goram; Malpas, Boyd, McCall, Whyte, Levein, Gallacher (McClair 33), McStay, McCoist, McAllister, Collins (Durrant 71).
Portugal: Vitor Baia; Joao Pinto I, Helder, Veloso, Fernando Couto, Oceano, Vitor Paneira, Semedo (Figo 53), Domingos, Futre, Andre.

Valletta, 25 October 1992, 8000
Malta (0) 0

Estonia (0) 0

Malta: Cluett; Gregory (Suda 78), Vella S, Galea, Brincat, Buttigieg, Busuttil, Vella R, Zerafa (Saliba 78), Laferla, Sultana.
Estonia: Poom; Kaljend, Hepner, Prins, Kallaste T, Ratnikov, Olumets, Pushtov (Rajala 75), Kirs (Kristal 81), Reim, Kallaste R.

Ibrox, 18 November 1992, 33,029
Scotland (0) 0

Italy (0) 0

Scotland: Goram; McPherson, Malpas, McStay, McLaren, Whyte, Durie (Jess 71), McAllister, McCoist, Durrant (Robertson 88), Boyd.
Italy: Pagliuca; Mannini, Di Chiara (Costacurta 7), Maldini, Baresi, Lentini, Albertini, Eranio, Bianchi, Signori (Donadoni 65), Roberto Baggio.

Berne, 18 November 1992, 14,200
Switzerland (2) 3 *(Bickel 2, Sforza 42, Chapuisat 89)*

Malta (0) 0

Switzerland: Pascolo; Hottiger, Geiger, Egli, Rothenbuhler, Bickel (Bonvin 82), Bregy, Sforza, Sutter A, Knup (Turkyilmaz 75), Chapuisat.
Malta: Cluett; Buttigieg, Buhagiar, Galea (Camilleri E 17), Vella S, Brincat, Gregory, Camilleri J, Saliba, Vella R (Scerri 75), Busuttil.

Valletta, 19 December 1992, 15,000
Malta (0) 1 *(Gregory 85)*

Italy (0) 2 *(Vialli 59, Signori 62)*

Malta: Cluett; Vella S, Buhagiar (Camilleri J 46), Galea, Brincat, Buttigieg, Busuttil, Saliba (Vella R 73), Gregory, Laferla, Scerri.
Italy: Pagliuca; Maldini, Di Chiara (Bianchi 46), Baresi, Costacurta, Eranio, Albertini, Donadoni (Simone 58), Evani, Vialli, Signori.

Valletta, 24 January 1993, 10,000
Malta (0) 0

Portugal (0) 1 *(Rui Aguas 56)*

Malta: Cluett; Vella S, Galea, Brincat, Buhagiar, Buttigieg, Vella R (Suda 75), Busuttil, Gregory, Laferla, Scerri (Degiorgio 65).
Portugal: Vitor Baia; Joao Pinto I, Veloso, Fernando Couto, Helder, Oceano, Vitor Paneira (Joao Pinto II 56), Samedo (Jaime Magalhaes 75), Domingos, Rui Aguas, Figo.

Ibrox, 17 February 1993, 35,490
Scotland (1) 3 *(McCoist 15, 68, Nevin 84)*

Malta (0) 0

Scotland: Goram; McPherson (Robertson 64), Boyd, McStay, McLeich, McLaren, Nevin, McAllister (Ferguson 73), McCoist, Collins, Jess.
Malta: Cluett; Vella S, Buhagiar (Camilleri E 83), Galea, Brincat, Buttigieg, Busuttil, Saliba, Camilleri J, Laferla, Sultana (Vella R 74).

Oporto, 24 February 1993, 70,000
Portugal (0) 1 *(Couto 57)*

Italy (2) 3 *(Roberto Baggio 2, Casiraghi 24, Dino Baggio 75)*

Portugal: Vitor Baia; Joao Pinto I, Helder (Rui Barros 35), Fernando Mendes, Fernando Couto, Oceano, Semedo, Figo, Domingos, Futre, Carlos Xavier (Rui Aguas 46).
Italy: Pagliuca; Tassotti, Maldini, Dino Baggio, Costacurta, Vierchowod, Fuser, Albertini, Casiraghi (Lentini 26), Roberto Baggio (Mancini 85), Signori.

Palermo, 24 March 1993, 35,000
Italy (2) 6 *(Dino Baggio 19, Signori 38, Vierchowod 48, Mancini 59, 89, Maldini 73)*

Malta (0) 1 *(Busuttil 68 (pen))*

Italy: Pagliuca (Marchegiani 80); Porrini, Maldini, Dino Baggio, Vierchowod, Baresi, Fuser, Albertini, Melli, Mancini, Signori.
Malta: Cluett; Vella S, Zerafa, Galea, Saliba, Laferla, Busuttil, Vella R, Gregory (Delia 57), Degiorgio (Suda 73), Scerri.

Berne, 31 March 1993, 31,200
Switzerland (1) 1 *(Chapuisat 39)*

Portugal (1) 1 *(Semedo 44)*

Switzerland: Pascolo; Hottiger, Herr, Geiger, Rothenbuhler, Ohrel, Bregy, Sforza, Sutter A, Knup (Bonvin 46), Chapuisat.
Portugal: Vitor Baia; Peixe, Oceano, Jorge Costa, Semedo (Fernando Mendes 50), Abel Xavier, Rui Costa, Paulo Sousa, Figo (Rui Barros 68), Futre, Rui Aguas.

Trieste, 14 April 1993, 33,000
Italy (1) 2 *(Roberto Baggio 21, Signori 86)*

Estonia (0) 0

Italy: Pagliuca; Porrini (Mannini 46), Di Chiara, Dino Baggio (Di Mauro 68), Vierchowod, Baresi, Fuser, Albertini, Melli, Roberto Baggio, Signori.
Estonia: Poom; Kallaste R, Lemsalu, Prins, Kaljend, Kallaste T, Borisov, Kristal, Reim (Olumets 89), Ratnikov, Pushtov (Rajala 83).

Valletta, 17 April 1993, 8000
Malta (0) 0

Switzerland (1) 2 *(Ohrel 31, Turkyilmaz 89)*

Malta: Cluett; Vella S, Brincat, Galea, Buhagiar, Busuttil, Buttigieg, Camilleri J (Delia 74), Saliba (Carabott 55), Laferla, Scerri.
Switzerland: Pascolo; Hottiger, Herr, Geiger, Rothenbuhler (Sylvestre 50), Henchoz, Sforza, Sutter A, Ohrel, Grassi, Bonvin (Turkyilmaz 60).

Lisbon, 28 April 1993, 28,000
Portugal (2) 5 *(Rui Barros 5, 70, Cadete 45, 72, Futre 67)*

Scotland (0) 0

Portugal: Vitor Baia; Abel Xavier, Jorge Costa, Rui Costa (Veloso 53), Fernando Couto, Oceano, Rui Barros, Paulo Sousa, Semedo, Futre, Cadete (Domingos 81).
Scotland: Goram; Gough, McInally, McPherson, McKimmie, Levein (Nevin 60), McStay, McCall, McCoist, Collins (Durrant 75), Gallacher.

Berne, 1 May 1993, 31,000
Switzerland (0) 1 *(Hottiger 55)*

Italy (0) 0

Switzerland: Pascolo; Hottiger, Geiger, Herr, Quentin, Bregy, Ohrel, Sforza, Sutter A, Knup (Grassi 76), Chapuisat.
Italy: Pagliuca; Mannini, Baresi, Vierchowod, Maldini, Fuser, Zoratto (Lentini 64), Dino Baggio, Signori, Mancini (Di Mauro 46), Roberto Baggio.

Tallinn, 12 May 1993, 14,000
Estonia (0) 0

Malta (1) 1 *(Laferla 16)*

Estonia: Poom; Kallaste R (Bragin 75), Lemsalu, Prins, Kaljend, Kallaste T, Borisov, Kristal, Reim, Ratnikov (Olumets 20), Pushtov.
Malta: Cluett; Vella S, Buhagiar, Saliba, Brincat, Buttigieg, Gregory (Delia 77), Vella R, Carabott (Sultana 46), Laferla, Camilleri J.

202

Tallinn, 19 May 1993, 5100
Estonia (0) 0

Scotland (1) 3 *(Gallacher 43, Collins 59, Booth 73)*

Estonia: Poom; Kallaste R, Lemsalu, Prins, Kaljend, Kallaste T, Borisov, Kristal (Hepner 46), Reim, Veensalu (Pushtov 76), Bragin.
Scotland: Gunn; Wright (McLaren 80), Boyd, McStay, Hendry, Irvine, Gallacher, Bowman, Robertson (Booth 61), McClair, Collins.

Aberdeen, 2 June 1993, 14,309
Scotland (2) 3 *(McClair 16, Nevin 27, 72 (pen))*

Estonia (0) 1 *(Bragin 57)*

Scotland: Gunn; McLaren (McKimmie 72), Boyd, McStay, Hendry, Irvine, Gallacher, Ferguson (Booth 55), McClair, Collins, Nevin.
Estonia: Poom; Kallaste R, Lemsalu (Bragin 46), Prins, Kaljend, Kallaste T, Borisov, Kristal, Reim, Olumets (Veensalu 73), Rajala.

Oporto, 19 June 1993, 7000
Portugal (3) 4 *(Nogueira 2, Rui Costa 9, Joao Pinto II 23, Cadete 87)*

Malta (0) 0

Portugal: Vitor Baia; Nogueira (Figo 70), Fernando Couto, Oceano, Abel Xavier, Semedo, Paulo Sousa, Rui Costa, Joao Pinto II, Cadete, Domingos (Rui Aguas 46).
Malta: Cluett; Vella S, Buhagiar, Delia, Cauchi, Buttigieg, Saliba, Gregory, Camilleri J (Scerri 66), Laferla, Zerafa (Vella R 41).

Tallinn, 5 September 1993, 2750
Estonia (0) 0

Portugal (0) 2 *(Rui Costa 61, Folha 76)*

Estonia: Poom; Alonen, Prins, Hepner, Kallaste T, Kallaste R, Kristal (Vilderson 72), Bregin, Klavan (Olumets 88), Borisov, Reim.
Portugal: Vitor Baia; Abel Xavier, Fernando Couto, Oceano, Nogueira, Rui Costa (Joao Pinto I 74), Paulo Sousa, Folha, Joao Pinto II, Futre, Cadete (Cesar Brito 72).

Aberdeen, 8 September 1993, 24,000
Scotland (0) 1 *(Collins 50)*

Switzerland (0) 1 *(Bregy 69 (pen))*

Scotland: Gunn; McKimmie, Robertson D, Bowman (O'Donnell 75), Irvine, McAllister, Levein, Collins, Booth (Jess 69), Durie, Nevin.
Switzerland: Pascolo; Quentin, Geiger, Herr, Rothenbuhler (Grassi 61), Bregy (Rueda 87), Sutter A, Ohrel, Sforza, Knup, Chapuisat.

Tallinn, 22 September 1993, 6000
Estonia (0) 0

Italy (1) 3 *(Roberto Baggio 18 (pen), 73, Mancini 59)*

Estonia: Poom; Hepner, Kallaste R, Bragin (Olumets 56), Prins, Alonen, Kallaste T, Borisov, Kristal, Reim, Klavan (Ratnikov 88).
Italy: Pagliuca; Baresi, Benarrivo, Costacurta, Fortunato, Lombardo (Mancini 46), Albertini, Manicone, Eranio, Casiraghi, Roberto Baggio.

203

Rome, 13 October 1993, 61,178
Italy (2) 3 *(Donadoni 3, Casiraghi 16, Eranio 81)*
Scotland (1) 1 *(Gallacher 16)*

Italy: Pagliuca; Mussi (Lanna 69), Baresi, Costacurta, Benarrivo, Eranio, Dino Baggio, Donadoni, Roberto Baggio, Stroppa (Zola 89), Casiraghi.
Scotland: Gunn; McKimmie, McLaren, Irvine, Boyd, Bowman (McStay 71), Jess (Durrant 46), McAllister, Gallacher, Durie, McCall.

Oporto, 13 October 1993, 48,000
Portugal (1) 1 *(Joao Pinto II 9)*
Switzerland (0) 0

Portugal: Vitor Baia; Joao Pinto I, Jorge Costa, Oceano, Paulo Sousa, Peixe, Semedo (Vitor Paneira 82), Rui Costa, Joao Pinto II, Futre, Cadete (Nogueira 57).
Switzerland: Pascolo; Hottiger, Geiger, Quentin, Herr, Bregy, Sutter A, Ohrel, Sforza, Knup (Grassi 82), Chapuisat.

Lisbon, 10 November 1993, 100,000
Portugal (2) 3 *(Futre 4, Oceano 40 (pen), Rui Aguas 85)*
Estonia (0) 0

Portugal: Vitor Baia; Joao Pinto I, Oceano, Fernando Couto, Nogueira (Folha 75), Paulo Sousa, Rui Barros, Rui Costa (Vitor Paneira 60), Joao Pinto II, Futre, Rui Aguas.
Estonia: Poom; Kallaste R, Prins, Kaljend, Hepner, Ratnikov, Bragin, Borisov, Klavan (Linnumae 70), Rajala (Pushtov 46), Reim.

Milan, 17 November 1993, 71,531
Italy (0) 1 *(Dino Baggio 83)*
Portugal (0) 0

Italy: Pagliuca; Benarrivo, Costacurta, Baresi, Maldini, Stroppa (Albertini 61), Dino Baggio, Signori (Mancini 76), Casiraghi, Donadoni, Roberto Baggio.
Portugal: Vitor Baia; Fernando Couto, Peixe, Jorge Costa, Joao Pinto I (Rui Aguas 76), Rui Costa (Domingos 68), Paulo Sousa, Rui Barros, Veloso, Joao Pinto II, Futre.

Ta Quali, 17 November 1993, 8000
Malta (0) 0
Scotland (1) 2 *(McKinlay 16, Hendry 73)*

Malta: Cluett; Brincat, Galea, Buttigieg, Buhagiar (Saliba 46), Vella S, Busuttil, Spiteri, Laferla, Gregory, Suda (Scerri 68).
Scotland: Leighton; McLaren, Hendry, McKinnon, Irvine, Durrant (Boyd 68), McAllister, McKinlay (Booth 46), Nevin, Ferguson, Gallacher.

Zurich, 17 November 1993, 20,000
Switzerland (3) 4 *(Knup 31, Herr 34, Ohrel 45, Chapuisat 61)*
Estonia (0) 0

Switzerland: Pascolo; Hottiger, Herr, Geiger, Quentin (Turkyilmaz 63), Ohrel (Rueda 46), Bregy, Bickel, Sutter A, Knup, Chapuisat.
Estonia: Poom; Hepner, Kaljend, Prins, Kallaste R, Borisov, Olumets, Bragin, Klavan (Pushtov 78), Reim, Rajala.

Group 1

	P	W	D	L	F	A	Pts
Italy	10	7	2	1	22	7	16
Switzerland	10	6	3	1	23	6	15
Portugal	10	6	2	2	18	5	14
Scotland	10	4	3	3	14	13	11
Malta	10	1	1	8	3	23	3
Estonia	10	0	1	9	1	27	1

Italy and Switzerland qualified

Group 2
Oslo, 9 September 1992, 6511
Norway (4) 10 *(Rekdal 5, 79, Halle 6, 51, 69, Sorloth 15, 21, Nilsen 46, 67, Mykland 74)*

San Marino (0) 0

Norway: Thorstvedt; Pedersen T, Bratseth, Nilsen R, Halle, Mykland, Rekdal, Leonhardsen (Ingebrigtsen 57), Jakobsen JI, Sorloth (Fjortoft 75), Flo.
San Marino: Benedettini; Guerra, Gobbi, Canti, Gennari, Mazza M, Bonini, Francini (Matteoni 70), Manzaroli P, Mazza P, Pasolini O (Muccioli B 46).

Oslo, 23 September 1992, 19,998
Norway (1) 2 *(Rekdal 9 (pen), Sorloth 78)*

Holland (1) 1 *(Bergkamp 10)*

Norway: Thorstvedt; Nilsen R, Pedersen T, Bratseth, Bjornebye, Halle (Strandli 60), Mykland, Ingebrigtsen, Rekdal, Sorloth (Flo 81), Jakobsen JI.
Holland: Menzo; Koeman R, Blind, Silooy, De Boer F, Van't Schip (Taument 81), Wouters (Kieft 85), Rijkaard, Rob Witschge, Bergkamp, Van Basten.

Poznan, 23 September 1992, 11,000
Poland (1) 1 *(Waldoch 33)*

Turkey (0) 0

Poland: Bako; Rzepka, Szewczyk, Lesiak, Waldoch, Czachowski, Brzeczek, Warzycha R, Araszkiewicz (Kowalczyk 61), Kosecki (Fedoruk 64), Juskowiak.
Turkey: Hayrettin; Recep (Aykut 74), Bulent, Gokhan, Ogun, Tugay, Hami, Riza, Hakan, Oguz (Mehmet 64), Orhan.

Serravalle, 7 October 1992, 1187
San Marino (0) 0

Norway (2) 2 *(Jakobsen JI 7, Flo 19)*

San Marino: Benedettini; Guerra, Gobbi, Gennari, Bonini, Francini (Muccioli B 84), Manzaroli, Mazza M, Matteoni, Zanotti, Mazza P (Bacciocchi 25).
Norway: Thorstvedt; Bratseth, Nilsen R, Pedersen T, Halle (Bjornebye 46), Jakobsen JI, Leonhardsen (Ingebrigtsen 68), Mykland, Rekdal, Flo, Sorloth.

Wembley, 14 October 1992, 51,441
England (0) 1 *(Platt 55)*

Norway (0) 1 *(Rekdal 76)*

England: Woods; Dixon (Palmer 89), Walker, Adams, Pearce, Batty, Ince, Platt, Gascoigne, Wright (Merson 69), Shearer.
Norway: Thorstvedt; Nilsen R, Bratseth, Pedersen T (Berg 19), Bjornebye, Halle, Jakobsen JI, Ingebrigtsen, Mykland (Flo 78), Rekdal, Sorloth.

Rotterdam, 14 October 1992, 13,000
Holland (1) 2 *(Van Vossen 43, 46)*

Poland (2) 2 *(Kosecki 18, Kowalczyk 20)*

Holland: Menzo; Van Aerle, Koeman R, Rijkaard (Fraser 80), Jonk, Wouters, Numan (Vanenburg 39), Rob Witschge, Bergkamp, Van Basten, Van Vossen.
Poland: Bako; Lesiak, Szewczyk, Kozminski, Adamczuk, Czachowski (Rzepka 39), Brzeczek, Kowalczyk (Smolarek 67), Warzycha R, Kosecki, Ziober.

Ankara, 28 October 1992, 35,000
Turkey (1) 4 *(Hakan 37, 89, Orhan 87, Hami 90)*

San Marino (0) 1 *(Bacciocchi 53)*

Turkey: Hayrettin; Riza (Mehmet 73), Bulent, Gokhan, Ogun, Orhan, Okan, Ridvan, Hakan, Oguz, Aykut (Hami 46).
San Marino: Benedettini; Gobbi, Gennari, Della Valle (Bizzocchi 84), Matteoni, Guerra, Manzaroli, Mazza P, Bacciocchi, Bonini, Francini (Zanotti 65).

Wembley, 18 November 1992, 42,984
England (2) 4 *(Gascoigne 16, 61, Shearer 28, Pearce 60)*

Turkey (0) 0

England: Woods; Dixon, Pearce, Palmer, Walker, Adams, Platt, Gascoigne, Shearer, Wright I, Ince.
Turkey: Hayrettin; Recep, Bulent, Gokhan, Ogun, Orhan, Hami (Riza 69), Unal, Mehmet (Ugur 46), Oguz, Hakan.

Istanbul, 16 December 1992, 15,000
Turkey (0) 1 *(Feyyaz 60)*

Holland (0) 3 *(Van Vossen 57, 87, Gullit 59)*

Turkey: Hayrettin; Recep, Bulent, Gokhan, Ogun, Unal (Hami 77), Oguz, Tugay, Orhan, Saffet (Feyyaz 46), Hakan.
Holland: De Goey; Silooy, Koeman R, Jonk (De Boer F 65), Rijkaard, Wouters, Rob Witschge, Gullit, Viscaal, Winter (Numan 76), Van Vossen.

Wembley, 17 February 1993, 51,154
England (2) 6 *(Platt 13, 24, 67, 83, Palmer 76, Ferdinand 86)*

San Marino (0) 0

England: Woods; Dixon, Walker, Adams, Dorigo, Gascoigne, Batty, Platt, Palmer, Ferdinand, Barnes.
San Marino: Benedettini; Muccioli B, Zanotti, Mazza M, Gennari, Canti, Guerra, Manzaroli, Bacciocchi (Mazza P 63), Bonini, Francini (Matteoni 80).

Utrecht, 24 February 1993, 14,000
Holland (2) 3 *(Overmars 4, Rob Witschge 37, 57)*

Turkey (1) 1 *(Feyyaz 36 (pen))*

Holland: De Goey; Silooy, De Kock, Koeman R, Rob Witschge, Wouters (Winter 74), Jonk, Bergkamp, Van Vossen (De Boer F 46), Gullit, Overmars.
Turkey: Engin; Recep, Bulent, Gokhan, Ali Nail, Tugay (Serhat 78), Feyyaz (Saffet 61), Unal, Hakan, Oguz, Orhan.

Serravalle, 10 March 1993, 957
San Marino (0) 0
Turkey (0) 0

San Marino: Benedettini (Muccioli S 9); Canti, Gennari, Zanotti, Valentini, Guerra, Manzaroli, Mazza M (Matteoni 61), Mazza P, Bacciocchi, Francini.
Turkey: Engin; Serhat (Hami 62), Bulent, Ali Nail, Ogun, Tugay, Aykut, Unal, Mehmet, Saffet, Orhan.

Utrecht, 24 March 1993, 17,000
Holland (2) 6 *(Van Den Brom 2, Canti (og) 29, De Wolf 52, 85, De Boer R 68 (pen), Van Vossen 78)*

San Marino (0) 0

Holland: De Goey; De Wolf, De Boer F, Winter, Rob Witschge, Wouters, Overmars, Meyer, Eykelkamp (De Boer R 46), Van Den Brom, Blinker (Van Vossen 67).
San Marino: Muccioli S; Canti, Gennari, Matteoni (Zanotti 22), Valentini, Guerra, Manzaroli, Mazza M, Bacciocchi, Bonini, Francini.

Izmir, 31 March 1993, 60,000
Turkey (0) 0
England (2) 2 *(Platt 6, Gascoigne 44)*

Turkey: Engin (Hayrettin 42); Recep (Hami 69), Ogun, Ali Nail, Tugay, Bulent, Feyyaz, Unal, Mehmet, Oguz, Orhan.
England: Woods; Dixon (Clough 46), Sinton, Palmer, Walker, Adams, Platt, Gascoigne, Barnes, Wright I (Sharpe 84), Ince.

Wembley, 28 April 1993, 73,163
England (2) 2 *(Barnes 2, Platt 23)*
Holland (1) 2 *(Bergkamp 34, Van Vossen 85 (pen))*

England: Woods; Dixon, Walker, Adams, Keown, Ince, Gascoigne (Merson 46), Palmer, Barnes, Platt, Ferdinand.
Holland: De Goey; Blind, De Boer F, Rijkaard, Winter, Wouters, Rob Witschge, Gullit (Van Vossen 69), Bergkamp, Bosman (De Wolf 46), Overmars.

Oslo, 28 April 1993, 21,530
Norway (2) 3 *(Rekdal 14, Fjortoft 17, Jakobsen JI 55)*
Turkey (0) 1 *(Feyyaz 57)*

Norway: Rossbach; Halle, Pedersen T, Bratseth, Bjornebye, Flo, Mykland (Nilsen R 82), Rekdal, Leonhardsen (Ingebrigtsen 30), Jakobsen JI, Fjortoft.
Turkey: Hayrettin; Recep, Ogun, Sedat, Serhat, Bulent, Feyyaz, Unal, Mehmet (Hamza 81), Hakan (Hami 66), Orhan.

Lodz, 28 April 1993, 10,000
Poland (0) 1 *(Furtok 68)*
San Marino (0) 0

Poland: Klak; Czachowski, Szewczyk, Kozminski, Waldoch, Brzeczek, Pisz, Juskowiak (Staniek 66), Furtok, Kosecki, Ziober.
San Marino: Benedettini; Canti, Gennari, Zanotti (Francini 79), Gobbi, Valentini, Manzaroli, Della Valle, Mazza M, Bonini (Mazza P 70), Bacciocchi.

Serravalle, 19 May 1993, 1500
San Marino (0) 0

Poland (0) 3 *(Lesniak 52, 80, Warzycha K 56)*

San Marino: Benedettini; Canti, Gennari, Zanotti, Gobbi, Valentini, Manzaroli, Francini (Muccioli B 60), Mazza M, Bonini, Bacciocchi (Mazza P 72).
Poland: Matysek; Czachowski, Brzeczek, Szewczyk, Rudy, Lesniak, Swierczewski, Warzycha K, Furtok (Staniek 82), Kosecki, Ziober.

Chorzow, 29 May 1993, 60,000
Poland (1) 1 *(Adamczuk 34)*

England (0) 1 *(Wright I 84)*

Poland: Bako; Czachowski, Szewczyk, Kozminski, Lesiak, Brzeczek (Jalocha 84), Swierczewski, Adamczuk, Furtok, Kosecki, Lesniak (Wegrzyn 75).
England: Woods; Bardsley, Dorigo, Palmer (Wright I 72), Walker, Adams, Platt, Gascoigne (Clough 79), Sheringham, Barnes, Ince.

Oslo, 2 June 1993, 22,250
Norway (1) 2 *(Leonhardsen 42, Bohinen 48)*

England (0) 0

Norway: Thorstvedt; Halle, Pedersen T, Bratseth (Nilsen R 82), Bjornebye, Flo, Mykland, Leonhardsen, Fjortoft (Sorloth 57), Rekdal, Bohinen.
England: Woods; Dixon, Pallister, Palmer, Walker (Clough 63), Adams, Platt, Gascoigne, Ferdinand, Sheringham (Wright I 46), Sharpe.

Rotterdam, 9 June 1993, 40,000
Holland (0) 0

Norway (0) 0

Holland: De Goey; Van Gobbel (Winter 81), Rijkaard, Koeman R, De Boer F, Wouters, Overmars, Jonk, Bosman (Van Vossen 46), Bergkamp, Blinker.
Norway: Thorstvedt; Johnsen (Brandsaether 85), Pedersen T, Bratseth, Bjornebye (Nilsen R 46), Flo, Mykland, Leonhardsen, Fjortoft, Rekdal, Bohinen.

Wembley, 8 September 1993, 71,220
England (1) 3 *(Ferdinand 5, Gascoigne 49, Pearce 53)*

Poland (0) 0

England: Seaman; Jones, Pearce, Ince, Pallister, Adams, Platt, Gascoigne, Ferdinand, Wright, Sharpe.
Poland: Bako; Czachowski, Brzeczek, Kozminski, Lesiak, Warzycha R, Swierczewski, Adamczuk (Bak 77), Kosecki, Furtok (Ziober 46), Lesniak.

Oslo, 22 September 1993, 23,000
Norway (0) 1 *(Flo 55)*

Poland (0) 0

Norway: Thorstvedt; Bratseth, Halle, Pedersen T, Bjornebye (Nilsen 46), Flo, Berg, Ingebrigtsen (Grodas 56), Rekdal, Bohinen, Fjortoft.
Poland: Bako; Bak, Szewczyk, Wegrzyn, Swierczewski, Rudy, Kosecki, Warzycha (Brzeczek 85), Kozminski, Lesniak, Ziober.

Bologna, 22 September 1993, 1000
San Marino (0) 0

Holland (3) 7 *(Bosman l, 66, 77, Jonk 21, 44, Koeman R 52,79 (pen))*

San Marino: Benedettini; Gobbi, Conti, Gennari, Valentini, Della Valle, Toccaceli, Mazza M, Mazza P (Matteoni 76), Bonini, Bacciocchi (Gualtieri 58).
Holland: De Goey; De Boer F, Koeman R, Wouters, Jonk, Overmars, Rijkaard, Kieft (De Boer R 56), Bergkamp, Bosman, Roy.

Rotterdam, 13 October 1993, 48,000
Holland (0) 2 *(Koeman R 62, Bergkamp 68)*

England (0) 0

Holland: De Goey; De Wolf, Koeman R, De Boer F, Rijkaard, Wouters, Bergkamp, Koeman E, Overmars (Winter 75), De Boer R (Van Gobbel 90), Roy.
England: Seaman; Parker, Dorigo, Palmer (Sinton 46), Adams, Pallister, Platt, Ince, Shearer, Merson (Wright 69), Sharpe.

Poznan, 13 October 1993, 50,000
Poland (0) 0

Norway (0) 3 *(Flo 68, Fjortoft 70, Johnsen 89)*

Poland: Bako; Bak, Wegrzyn, Kozminski, Swierczewski, Rudy, Waldoch, Ziober, Kosecki (Brzeczek 25), Lesniak, Warzycha.
Norway: Grodas; Bratseth, Halle, Pedersen T, Bjornebye, Flo, Berg, Mykland, Rekdal, Bohinen, Fjortoft.

Istanbul, 27 October 1993, 15,000
Turkey (0) 2 *(Hakan 53, Bulent K 67)*

Poland (1) 1 *(Kowalczyk 18)*

Turkey: Engin; Bulent, Gokhan, Emre, Recep, Tugay, Bulent K, Oguz, Abdullah (Mehmet 80), Hakan, Orhan (Ertugrul 73).
Poland: Matysek; Lewandovski, Michalski, Kruszankin, Waldoch, Jalocha, Pisz, Adamczuk, Staniek, Kowalczyk, Juskowiak (Ziober 50).

Istanbul, 10 November 1993, 10,500
Turkey (2) 2 *(Ertugrul 5, 26)*

Norway (0) 1 *(Bohinen 47)*

Turkey: Hayrettin; Ogun (Emre 55), Gokhan, Bulent, Yusuf, Suat (Mehmet 80), Oguz, Tugay, Abdullah, Ertugrul, Orhan.
Norway: Thorstvedt; Berg, Bratseth, Pedersen T, Bjornebye, Halle, Mykland (Hardelsen 55), Rekdal, Bohinen, Johnsen (Aage 71), Jakobsen Jl.

Bologna, 17 November 1993, 2500
San Marino (1) 1 *(Gualteri 1)*

England (3) 7 *(Ince 21, 73, Wright 32, 46, 78, 88, Ferdinand 37)*

San Marino: Benedettini; Valentini (Gobby 47), Zanotti, Canti, Gennari, Guerra, Manzaroli, Dalla Valle, Bacciocchi (Mazza P 61), Bonini, Gualtieri.
England: Seaman; Dixon, Pearce, Ince, Walker, Pallister, Ripley, Wright, Ferdinand, Platt, Sinton.

Poznan, 17 November 1993, 20,000
Poland (1) 1 *(Lesniak 13)*

Holland (1) 3 *(Bergkamp 10, 56, De Boer R 88)*

Poland: Matysek; Waldoch, Michalski, Kozminski, Jalocha (Czerwiec 79), Kruszankin, Warzycha R (Celuba 70), Lewandowski, Adamczuk, Kowalczyk, Lesniak.
Holland: De Goey; Van Gobbel, Koeman R, De Boer F, Winter, Wouters, Bergkamp, Koeman E, Overmars, De Boer R, Roy.

Group 2

	P	W	D	L	F	A	Pts
Norway	10	7	2	1	25	5	16
Holland	10	6	3	1	29	9	15
England	10	5	3	2	26	9	13
Poland	10	3	2	5	10	15	8
Turkey	10	3	1	6	11	19	7
San Marino	10	0	1	9	2	46	1

Norway and Holland qualified

Group 3
Seville, 22 April 1992, 10,000
Spain (1) 3 *(Michel 2, 66 (pen), Hierro 87)*

Albania (0) 0

Spain: Zubizarreta; Abelardo, Nando, Giner, Michel (Eusebio 85), Amor, Hierro, Vizcaino, Manolo (Bakero 53), Butragueno, Goicoechea.
Albania: Strakosha (Dani 69); Josa (Peqini 55), Kola B, Lekbello, Aya, Abazi, Kushta, Barballushi, Millo, Kola A, Demollari.

Windsor Park, 28 April 1992, 4500
Northern Ireland (2) 2 *(Wilson 13, Taggart 16)*

Lithuania (1) 2 *(Narberkovas 41, Fridrikas 48)*

Northern Ireland: Fettis; Donaghy (Fleming 46), Taggart, McDonald, Worthington, Black, Magilton, Wilson, Hughes, Quinn, Dowie (Rogan 80).
Lithuania: Martinkenas; Buzmakovas, Mika, Janonis, Mazeikis, Tautkas, Urbanas, Fridrikas (Zuta 90), Narbekovas, Baranauskas, Ivanauskas (Danisevicius 89).

Dublin, 26 May 1992, 29,727
Republic of Ireland (0) 2 *(Aldridge 60, McGrath 80)*

Albania (0) 0

Republic of Ireland: Bonner; Irwin, Staunton, O'Leary, McGrath, Townsend, Keane, Houghton, Quinn, Aldridge (Coyne 83), Sheedy (McCarthy 52).
Albania: Dani; Zmijani, Qendro (Pali 71), Peqini, Vata, Abazi, Kushta, Vasi, Rraklli, Zola A (Sokoll 80), Demollari.

Tirana, 3 June 1992, 15,000
Albania (0) 1 *(Abazi 77)*

Lithuania (0) 0

Albania: Dani; Zmijani, Peqini, Lekbello, Vata, Abazi, Kushta, Milori (Rrafi 46), Millo (Fortuzi 89), Vasi, Demollari.
Lithuania: Martinkenas; Buzmakovas, Sukristovas, Mazeikis, Ziukas, Danisevicius, Baranauskas, Tautkas (Zuta 82), Urbanas, Ramelis (Zdancius 52), Kvitkauskas.

Riga, 12 August 1992, 2000
Latvia (1) 1 *(Linards 15)*
Lithuania (0) 2 *(Poderis 65, Tereskinas 86)*

Latvia: Karavayev; Ivanovs, Sprogis (Zemniskis 65), Gnedois, Glazovs (Sitik 46), Popkovs, Shevljakovs, Alexeyenko, Semionovs, Linards, Stradins.
Lithuania: Martinkenas; Buzmakovas, Janonis, Sukristovas (Poderis 56), Vainoras, Mazeikis, Baltusnikas, Baranauskas, Narbekovas (Tereskinas 2), Fridrikas, Ivanauskas.

Riga, 26 August 1992, 10,000
Latvia (0) 0
Denmark (0) 0

Latvia: Karavayev; Shevljakovs, Alexeyenko, Ivanovs, Gnedois, Popkovs (Astafjevs 65), Sprogis, Stradins, Yeliseyevs, Linards (Bulders 86), Glazovs.
Denmark: Schmeichel; Sivebaek (Elstrup 46), Olsen, Piechnik, Christofte, Heintze, Vilfort, Jensen, Laudrup B, Povlsen, Christensen.

Dublin, 9 September 1992, 32,000
Republic of Ireland (1) 4 *(Sheedy 30, Aldridge 59, 82 (pen), 86)*
Latvia (0) 0

Republic of Ireland: Bonner; Irwin, Staunton, Kernaghan, McGrath, Townsend, Keane, Whelan, Quinn (Coyne 61), Aldridge, Sheedy (Phelan 76).
Latvia: Igoshin; Astafjevs, Alexeyenko, Bulders, Gnedois, Popkovs (Semionovs 63), Sprogis, Abzinovs (Sidorovs 36), Yeliseyevs, Linards, Glazovs.

Windsor Park, 9 September 1992, 8000
Northern Ireland (3) 3 *(Clarke, Wilson, Magilton)*
Albania (0) 0

Northern Ireland: Wright; Fleming, Worthington, Taggart, McDonald, Donaghy, Wilson, Magilton, Clarke (O'Neill M 77), Dowie, Hughes.
Albania: Strakosha; Zmijani, Peqini, Lekbello, Vata, Abazi, Kushta, Milori (Bilali 69), Millo, Kepa, Rraklli.

Riga, 23 September 1992, 60,000
Latvia (0) 0
Spain (0) 0

Latvia: Karavayev; Shevljakovs, Alexeyenko, Ivanovs, Gnedois, Popkovs (Astafjevs 70), Sprogis, Stradins, Bulders (Gilis 81), Linards, Glazovs.
Spain: Zubizarreta; Ferrer, Toni, Solazabal, Lopez, Vizcaino, Goicoechea, Fonseca (Alfonso 72), Bakero, Martin Vazquez, Alvaro (Amor 59).

Vilnius, 23 September 1992, 9500
Lithuania (0) 0
Denmark (0) 0

Lithuania: Martinkenas; Mazeikis, Sukristovas, Baltusnikas, Buzmakovas, Pankratjevas, Zuta (Poderis 87), Zdancius, Tereskinas, Baranauskas, Olsanskis.
Denmark: Schmeichel; Olsen, Piechnik, Sivebaek, Christofte, Larsen, Jensen, Vilfort, Laudrup B, Elstrup, Christensen (Moller 80).

211

Copenhagen, 14 October 1992, 40,100
Denmark (0) 0

Republic of Ireland (0) 0

Denmark: Schmeichel; Olsen, Piechnik, Sivebaek, Heintze, Rieper, Jensen, Vilfort, Larsen, Laudrup B, Povlsen (Christensen 77).
Republic of Ireland: Bonner; Irwin, Phelan, Moran, Kernaghan, Keane, Townsend, Houghton (Kelly 73), Quinn, Aldridge, McGoldrick.

Windsor Park, 14 October 1992, 9500
Northern Ireland (0) 0

Spain (0) 0

Northern Ireland: Wright; Fleming, Worthington, Taggart, McDonald, Donaghy, Black (Morrow 61), Wilson, Clarke, Quinn, Hughes.
Spain: Zubizarreta; Ferrer, Toni, Solazabal, Lopez, Hierro, Amor, Michel, Claudio (Guardiola 63), Martin Vazquez, Manolo (Alfonso 60).

Vilnius, 28 October 1992, 5000
Lithuania (0) 1 *(Fridrikas 85)*

Latvia (1) 1 *(Linards 44)*

Lithuania: Martinkenas; Buzmakovas, Baltusnikas, Tumasonis (Zuta 61), Tereskinas, Sukristovas, Baranauskas, Ivanauskas, Pankratjevas, Fridrikas, Zdancius (Vainoras 68).
Latvia: Karavayev; Astafjevs, Alexeyenko, Ivanovs, Gnedois, Popkovs (Jemeljanovs 74), Sprogis, Stradins, Bulders, Linards, Glazovs.

Tirana, 11 November 1992, 3500
Albania (0) 1 *(Kepa 67)*

Latvia (1) 1 *(Alexeyenko 3)*

Albania: Strakosha; Zmijani, Lekbello, Vata, Peqini, Demollari, Fortuzi, Kacaj, Rraklli, Kushta (Prenja 67) (Bisha 74), Kepa.
Latvia: Karavayev; Gnedois, Sprogis, Bulders, Ivanovs, Glazovs (Popkovs 46), Shevljakovs, Alexeyenko, Stradins, Linards, Astafjevs.

Windsor Park, 18 November 1992, 11,000
Northern Ireland (0) 0

Denmark (0) 1 *(Larsen 51)*

Northern Ireland: Fettis; Fleming, Taggart, McDonald, Worthington, Donaghy, Magilton, Wilson (Black), Hughes, Clarke (Gray), Quinn.
Denmark: Schmeichel; Sivebaek (Kjeldbjerg 46), Rieper, Olsen, Heintze, Vilfort, Jensen, Larsen (Goldbaek 73), Povlsen, Laudrup B, Elstrup.

Seville, 18 November 1992, 33,000
Spain (0) 0

Republic of Ireland (0) 0

Spain: Zubizarreta; Ferrer, Goicoechea, Solazabal, Lopez, Hierro, Salinas (Bakero 52), Michel, Butragueno (Beguiristain 60), Martin Vazquez, Amor.
Republic of Ireland: Bonner; Irwin, Phelan, Moran, Keane, Townsend, McGrath, Houghton, Staunton, Aldridge, Quinn.

Seville, 16 December 1992, 24,500
Spain (0) 5 *(Bakero 49, Guardiola 51, Alfonso 79, Beguiristain 81, 82)*
Latvia (0) 0

Spain: Zubizarreta; Ferrer, Toni, Solazabal, Vizcaino, Amor, Claudio (Alfonso 55), Guardiola, Bakero (Martin Vazquez 62), Quico, Beguiristain.
Latvia: Karavayev; Erglis, Alexeyendo, Ivanovs, Astafjevs, Popkovs, Gilis, Stradins, Bulders, Linards, Glazovs.

Tirana, 17 February 1993, 12,000
Albania (0) 1 *(Rrakli 89)*
Northern Ireland (0) 2 *(Magilton 14, McDonald 38)*

Albania: Kapliani; Zmijani (Peqini 46), Kacaj, Bano, Vata, Bazgo, Lekbello (Shulku 46), Fortuzi, Abazi, Rraklli, Demollari.
Northern Ireland: Wright; Fleming, Morrow, Taggart, Magilton, McDonald, Donaghy, Gray, Dowie (Quinn 73), O'Neill, Black.

Seville, 24 February 1993, 21,000
Spain (3) 5 *(Cristobal 5, Bakero 13, Beguiristain 18, Christiansen 86, Aldana 89)*
Lithuania (0) 0

Spain: Zubizarreta; Ferrer, Lasa, Alcorta, Giner, Cristobal, Guardiola, Guerrero (Aldana 59), Salinas (Christiansen 69), Bakero, Beguiristain.
Lithuania: Martinkenas; Buzmakovas, Vainoras, Mazeikis, Janonis, Sukristovas, Baranauskas, Ivanauskas, Tereskinas (Zuta 69), Fridrikas, Zdancius.

Copenhagen, 31 March 1993, 40,272
Denmark (1) 1 *(Povlsen 20)*
Spain (0) 0

Denmark: Schmeichel; Olsen, Rieper, Kjeldbjerg, Vilfort, Jensen, Larsen (Hansen 76), Nielsen B, Laudrup B (Tofting 86), Elstrup, Povlsen.
Spain: Zubizarreta; Cristobal, Ferrer, Giner, Alcorta, Toni (Goicoechea 55), Amor, Guardiola (Nadal 46), Beguiristain, Aldana, Salinas.

Dublin, 31 March 1993, 33,000
Republic of Ireland (3) 3 *(Townsend 20, Quinn 22, Staunton 28)*
Northern Ireland (0) 0

Republic of Ireland: Bonner; Irwin, Phelan, McGrath, Moran, Keane, Townsend, Houghton, Quinn (McGoldrick 84), Coyne (Cascarino 78), Staunton.
Northern Ireland: Wright; Donaghy, Worthington, Taggart, McDonald, Morrow, Magilton (Quinn 51), O'Neill M (Black 74), Dowie, Gray, Hughes.

Copenhagen, 14 April 1993, 29,088
Denmark (1) 2 *(Vilfort 23, Strudal 76)*
Latvia (0) 0

Denmark: Schmeichel; Nielsen S, Rieper, Olsen, Kjeldbjerg, Goldbaek, Jensen (Larsen 61), Vilfort, Pingel (Strudal 70), Elstrup, Laudrup B.
Latvia: Karavayev; Gnedois, Shevljakovs, Ivanovs, Zeminskis, Erglis, Glazovs, Astafjevs, Zelberlins (Gilis 46), Linards, Stradins (Bulders 64).

Vilnius, 14 April 1993, 12,000
Lithuania (2) 3 *(Baltusnikas 20, Sukristovas 25, Baranauskas 63)*

Albania (0) 1 *(Demollari 86)*

Lithuania: Martinkenas (Stauce 60); Ziukas, Baltusnikas, Mazeikis, Kalvaitis, Apanavicius (Slekys 63), Baranauskas, Sukristovas, Poderis, Kirilovas, Zdancius.
Albania: Kapilani; Dema, Shulku, Bano, Taho, Ocelli, Kushta, Peqini, Dalipi (Dosti 46), Fortuzi, Demollari.

Dublin, 28 April 1993, 33,000
Republic of Ireland (0) 1 *(Quinn 75)*

Denmark (1) 1 *(Vilfort 27)*

Republic of Ireland: Bonner; Irwin, McGoldrick, McGrath, Kernaghan, Keane, Townsend, Houghton, Quinn, Aldridge (Cascarino 62), Staunton.
Denmark: Schmeichel; Nielsen S, Rieper, Olsen, Kjeldbjerg, Hansen F, Jensen, Vilfort, Pingel (Kristensen 60), Elstrup, Laudrup B.

Seville, 28 April 1993, 20,000
Spain (3) 3 *(Salinas 21, 26, Hierro 41)*

Northern Ireland (1) 1 *(Wilson 11)*

Spain: Zubizarreta; Ferrer, Giner, Toni, Alcorta, Hierro, Guerrero, Aldana, Beguiristain (Bakero 76), Salinas, Claudio (Quico 59).
Northern Ireland: Wright, Fleming, Worthington, Donaghy, Taggart, McDonald, Black (Dennison 73), Wilson, O'Neill M (Dowie 73), Gray, Hughes.

Riga, 15 May 1993, 1810
Latvia (0) 0

Albania (0) 0

Latvia: Lajzans; Ergils, Shevljakovs, Ivanovs, Gnedois, Popkovs, Troickis, Astafjevs (Semionovs 46), Zelberlins (Sarando 62), Linards, Gorjacilovs.
Albania: Nailbani; Ocelli, Bano, Shala, Vata, Skulku, Kushta, Zalla (Kapidani 88), Pequini, Milori, Fortuzi (Dalipi 77).

Vilnius, 25 May 1993, 4000
Lithuania (0) 0

Northern Ireland (1) 1 *(Dowie 8)*

Lithuania. Martinkenas; Baltusnikas, Buzmakovas (Bicka 68), Mazeikis, Ziukas, Olsanskis (Sleyks 46), Baranauskas, Sukristovas, Kirilovas, Fridrikas, Zdancius.
Northern Ireland: Wright; Fleming, Taggart, McDonald, Worthington, Donaghy, Magilton, O'Neill, Wilson, Hughes, Dowie.

Tirana, 26 May 1993, 10,000
Albania (1) 1 *(Kushta 7)*

Republic of Ireland (1) 2 *(Staunton 13, Cascarino 77)*

Albania: Musta; Zmijani (Fortuzi 58), Shulku, Shala, Vata, Lekbello, Kushta, Pequini, Rraklli (Bozgo 76), Milori, Demollari.
Republic of Ireland: Bonner, Irwin, Phelan, Kernaghan, Moran, Keane, Townsend, Houghton, Quinn, Aldridge (Cascarino 76), Staunton.

214

Vilnius, 2 June 1993, 7000
Lithuania (0) 0

Spain (0) 2 *(Guerrero 73, 77)*

Lithuania: Martinkenas; Ziukas, Baltusnikas, Mazeikis, Buzmakovas, Olsanskis, Baranauskas, Sukristovas, Kirilovas, Fridrikas (Zdancius 54), Skarbalius.
Spain: Zubizarreta; Ferrer, Lasa (Beguiristain 62), Alcorta, Giner, Hierro, Salinas (Quique 54), Nadal, Claudio, Guerrero, Amor.

Copenhagen, 2 June 1993, 39,504
Denmark (4) 4 *(Jensen 11, Pingel 20, 40, Moller 28)*

Albania (0) 0

Denmark: Schmeichel; Nielsen S, Rieper, Olsen, Kjeldbjerg, Larsen M, Jensen (Goldbaek 83), Vilfort, Pingel, Moller (Johansen 64), Laudrup B.
Albania: Musta; Fortuzi (Zala 83), Zmijani, Shulku, Ocelli, Pequini, Bano, Demollari (Bozgo 17), Kushta, Vata, Rraklli.

Riga, 2 June 1993, 2000
Latvia (0) 1 *(Linards 55)*

Northern Ireland (2) 2 *(Magilton 4, Taggart 15)*

Latvia: Karavayev; Erglis, Shevljakovs, Ivanovs, Gnedois, Popkovs, Sarando (Yeliseyevs 46), Astafjevs, Zelberlins (Babicevs 63), Linards, Gorjacilovs.
Northern Ireland: Wright; Fleming, McDonald, Taggart, Worthington, O'Neill (Quinn 85), Magilton, Donaghy, Wilson, Hughes, Dowie.

Riga, 9 June 1993, 7000
Latvia (0) 0

Republic of Ireland (2) 2 *(Aldridge 14, McGrath 42)*

Latvia: Karavayev; Erglis, Shevljakovs, Astafjevs, Ivanovs, Gnedois, Popkovs, Bulders, Babicevs (Yeliseyevs 46), Sarando (Gorjacilovs 54), Linards.
Republic of Ireland: Bonner; Irwin, Kernaghan, McGrath, Phelan, Houghton, Townsend, Keane, Staunton, Aldridge (Sheridan 80), Quinn (Cascarino 74).

Vilnius, 16 June 1993, 6000
Lithuania (0) 0

Republic of Ireland (1) 1 *(Staunton 38)*

Lithuania: Martinkenas; Ziukas, Baltusnikas, Mazeikis, Buzmakovas, Skarbalius (Zdancius 46), Baranauskas, Urbanas (Ramelis 67), Stumbrys, Kirilovas, Slekys.
Republic of Ireland: Bonner; Irwin, Phelan, McGrath, Kernaghan, Keane, Townsend, Houghton, Quinn, Aldridge (Whelan 76), Staunton.

Copenhagen, 25 August 1993, 40,300
Denmark (2) 4 *(Olsen 13, Pingel 43, Laudrup B 63, Baltusnikas (og) 70)*

Lithuania (0) 0

Denmark: Schmeichel; Olsen, Kjeldbjerg, Rieper, Hansen, Jensen (Hogh 80), Vilfort, Laudrup M, Nielsen, Laudrup B, Pingel.
Lithuania: Stauce; Ziukas, Baltusnikas, Mazeikis, Teresnikas, Olsanskis, Baranauskas, Skarbalius, Stumbrys (Apalonikas 56), Kirilovas, Slekys (Chadancus 70).

Windsor Park, 8 September 1993, 6400
Northern Ireland (1) 2 *(Quinn 35, Gray 80)*

Latvia (0) 0

Northern Ireland: Wright; Fleming, Worthington, Taggart, Donaghy, Magilton, Wilson, Gray, Quinn, Dowie, Hughes.
Latvia: Karavayev; Troickis, Alexeyenko, Ivanovs, Gnedois, Popkovs, Sarando, Shevljakovs, Babicevs, Linards, Elisevs.

Dublin, 8 September 1993, 33,000
Republic of Ireland (2) 2 *(Aldridge 4, Kernaghan 25)*

Lithuania (0) 0

Republic of Ireland: Bonner; Irwin, Phelan, Moran, Kernaghan, Keane, Houghton, Townsend (Whelan 68), Quinn (Cascarino 74), Aldridge, Staunton.
Lithuania: Stauce; Ziukas, Baltusnikas, Kalvaitis, Tereskinas, Skarbalius (Sakalinas 84), Stumbrys, Kirilovas (Maciuvicis 69), Apanavicius, Baranauskas, Slekys.

Tirana, 8 September 1993, 8000
Albania (0) 0

Denmark (0) 1 *(Pingel 64)*

Albania: Strakosha; Lekbello, Zmijani, Abazo, Millo, Shulku, Bano, Vata, Kushta, Fortuzi, Demollari.
Denmark: Schmeichel; Rieper, Olsen, Kjeldbjerg, Nielsen (Larsen 70), Hansen (Hogh 60), Vilfort, Jensen, Laudrup M, Pingel, Laudrup B.

Tirana, 22 September 1993, 8000
Albania (1) 1 *(Kushta 41)*

Spain (3) 5 *(Salinas 4, 30, 61, Toni 19, Caminero 67)*

Albania: Strakosha; Abazi, Dashi, Vata, Shulku, Kacaj, Kepa (Dalipi 79), Kushta, Shehu, Millo, Fortuzi.
Spain: Zubizarreta; Alcorta, Nadal, Camarasa, Toni, Goicoechea, Hierro, Caminero, Guerrero, Alfonso (Quique 67), Salinas.

Copenhagen, 13 October 1993, 40,200
Denmark (0) 1 *(Laudrup B 81)*

Northern Ireland (0) 0

Denmark: Schmeichel; Rieper, Olsen, Kjeldbjerg, Vilfort, Jensen, Nielsen, Laudrup M, Laudrup B, Povlsen, Pingel (Larsen H 62).
Northern Ireland: Wright; Fleming, Worthington, Taggart, McDonald, Donaghy, Magilton, Wilson (Black 61), Dowie (Quinn 83), Gray, Hughes.

Dublin, 13 October 1993, 33,000
Republic of Ireland (0) 1 *(Sheridan 74)*

Spain (3) 3 *(Caminero 12, Salinas 15, 26)*

Republic of Ireland: Bonner; Irwin, Phelan, Moran (Sheridan 22), Kernaghan, Keane, McGrath, Houghton, Quinn, Whelan, Staunton (Cascarino 46).
Spain: Zubizarreta; Ferrer, Voro, Nadal, Giner, Hierro, Goicoechea, Camarasa, Luis Enrique, Salinas (Guardiola 72), Caminero (Bakero 30).

Windsor Park, 17 November 1993, 10,500
Northern Ireland (0) 1 *(Quinn 73)*

Republic of Ireland (0) 1 *(McLoughlin 76)*

Northern Ireland: Wright; Fleming, Worthington, Taggart, McDonald, Donaghy, Magilton, Wilson (Black 83), Quinn, Gray (Dowie 73), Hughes.
Republic of Ireland: Bonner; Irwin, Phelan, Kernaghan, McGrath, Keane, Houghton (McLoughlin 66), Townsend, Quinn, Aldridge (Cascarino 81), McGoldrick.

Seville, 17 November 1993, 50,000
Spain (0) 1 *(Hierro 62)*

Denmark (0) 0

Spain: Zubizarreta; Ferrer, Giner, Alcorta, Nadal, Hierro, Goicoechea, Camarasa (Canizares 11), Bakero, Salinas (Quique 53), Luis Enrique.
Denmark: Schmeichel; Hansen, Olsen, Rieper, Nielsen (Hogh 46), Jensen, Larsen, Vilfort, Laudrup M, Povlsen (Christensen 71), Laudrup B.

Group 3

	P	W	D	L	F	A	Pts
Spain	12	8	3	1	27	4	19
Republic of Ireland	12	7	4	1	19	6	18
Denmark	12	7	4	1	15	2	18
Northern Ireland	12	5	3	4	14	13	13
Lithuania	12	2	3	7	8	21	7
Latvia	12	0	5	7	4	21	5
Albania	12	1	2	9	6	26	4

Spain and Republic of Ireland qualified

Group 4
Brussels, 22 April 1992, 18,000
Belgium (1) 1 *(Wilmots 24)*

Cyprus (0) 0

Belgium: Preud'homme; Albert, Grun, Van der Elst, Emmers, Scifo, Walem, Boffin (Borkelmans 82), Wilmots (Hofmans 75), Degryse, Oliveira.
Cyprus: Christofi M; Costa, Pittas, Constantinou C, Nicolau, Yiangudakis, Ioannou D, Larku (Constantinou G 88), Sotiriou, Papavasiliou, Hadjilukas (Panayi 70).

Bucharest, 6 May 1992, 10,000
Romania (5) 7 *(Balint 4, 40, 78, Hagi 14, Lacatus 28 (pen), Lupescu 44, Pana 55)*

Faeroes (0) 0

Romania: Stelea; Petrescu, Mihali, Popescu, Munteanu, Pana, Balint, Lupescu (Cheregi 78), Hagi, Lacatus (Gane 63), Rotariu.
Faeroes: Knudsen; Jakobsen, Hansen T, Danielsen, Justinussen, Morkore A, Jarnskor (Nielsen T 50), Dam (Jonsson 60), Hansen A, Reynheim, Muller.

Bucharest, 20 May 1992, 23,000
Romania (5) 5 *(Hagi 5, 35, Lupescu 7, 24, Balint 31)*

Wales (0) 1 *(Rush 50)*

Romania: Stelea; Petrescu, Mihali, Belodedici, Munteanu, Sabau (Timofte I 80), Popescu, Lupescu, Hagi (Gerstenmaier 71), Lacatus, Balint.
Wales: Southall; Phillips, Bowen (Blackmore 71), Aizlewood, Melville, Horne, Speed, Pembridge (Giggs 59), Hughes, Rush, Saunders.

Toftir, 3 June 1992, 5156
Faeroes (0) 0
Belgium (1) 3 *(Albert 30, Wilmots 65,71)*

Faeroes: Johannesen; Jakobsen, Hansen T, Danielsen, Jonsson T (Jensen 71), Morkore A (Justinussen 83), Nielsen T, Dam, Hansen A, Reynheim, Muller.
Belgium: Preud'homme: Staelens, Grun, Albert, Emmers, Boffin (Versavel 75), Van der Elst, Denil, Degryse, Scifo, Oliveira (Wilmots 65).

Toftir, 16 June 1992, 4500
Faeroes (0) 0
Cyprus (1) 2 *(Sotiriou 30, Papavasiliou 58)*

Faeroes: Johannesen; Jakobsen, Hansen T, Danielsen, Jonsson, Morkore A, Hansen A, Nielsen (Jarnskor 62), Rasmussen, Reynheim, Muller (Jensen 66).
Cyprus: Christofi M; Costa (Larku 46), Pittas, Constantinou C, Nicolau, Yiangudakis, Ioannou D, Charalambous, Savidis, Sotiriou (Panayi 84), Papavasiliou.

Prague, 2 September 1992, 9000
Czechoslovakia (0) 1 *(Kadlec 77)*
Belgium (1) 2 *(Chovanec (og) 44, Czerniatynski 83)*

Czechoslovakia: Stejskal; Chovanec, Glonek, Kadlec, Mistr, Nemecek, Kubik (Hapal 65), Nemec, Kula K (Dubovsky 77), Skuhravy, Moravcik.
Belgium: Preud'homme; Emmers, Medved, Albert, Smidts, Grun, Scifo, Van der Elst, Staelens (Dauwen 87), Czerniatynski, Degryse (Wilmots 66).

Cardiff, 9 September 1992, 7000
Wales (3) 6 *(Rush 5, 64, 89, Saunders 28, Bowen 37, Blackmore 71)*
Faeroes (0) 0

Wales: Southall; Phillips, Bowen (Giggs 66), Symons, Young, Blackmore, Horne, Saunders, Rush, Hughes, Speed.
Faeroes: Knudsen; Jakobsen, Hansen T, Danielsen, Hansen O, Morkore A, Simonsen, Dam (Justinussen 56), Jonsson, Reynheim, Muller.

Kosice, 23 September 1992, 17,000
Czechoslovakia (1) 4 *(Nemecek 24, Kuka 85, 87, Dubovsky 89 (pen))*
Faeroes (0) 0

Czechoslovakia: Stejskal; Glonek, Suchoparek, Novotny, Mistr (Latal 82), Moravcik, Nemecek, Dubovsky, Nemec, Hapal (Timko 68), Kuka.
Faeroes: Knudsen; Jakobsen, Johannesen, Hansen T, Justinussen, Simonsen, Dam, Hansen O (Morkore A 58), Jonsson, Reynheim, Muller (Arge 81).

Brussels, 14 October 1992, 21,000
Belgium (1) 1 *(Smidts 27)*
Romania (0) 0

Belgium: Preud'homme; Medved, Albert, Grun, Smidts, Boffin, Staelens, Van der Elst, Scifo, Degryse, Czerniatynski (Wilmots 69).
Romania: Stelea; Petrescu, Selymes, Mihali, Lupescu, Belodedici, Munteanu, Sabau, Dumitrescu (Badea 78), Lacatus, Hagi.

Nicosia, 14 October 1992, 15,000
Cyprus (0) 0

Wales (0) 1 *(Hughes 51)*

Cyprus: Christofi M; Costa, Pittas (Hadjilukas 71), Constantinou C, Nicolau, Yiangudakis, Ioannou D, Charalambous, Sotiriou (Yiannos Ioannou 59), Papavasiliou, Savidis.
Wales: Southall; Phillips, Bowen, Blackmore, Young, Symons, Horne, Saunders, Rush, Hughes, Speed.

Bucharest, 14 November 1992, 30,000
Romania (0) 1 *(Dumitrescu 48)*

Czechoslovakia (0) 1 *(Nemecek 79 (pen))*

Romania: Stelea; Petrescu, Belodedici, Mihali, Munteanu, Sabau, Lupescu (Timofte D 78), Hagi, Dumitrescu, Lacatus, Hanganu (Vladoiu 66).
Czechoslovakia: Kouba; Novotny, Glonek, Suchoparek, Hapal, Latal, Nemecek, Moravcik, Nemec (Frydek 15), Siegl, Skuhravy (Kuka P 37).

Brussels, 18 November 1992, 21,000
Belgium (0) 2 *(Staelens 53, Degryse 58)*

Wales (0) 0

Belgium: Preud'homme; Medved, Grun, Albert, Smidts, Staelens (Wilmots 82), Van der Elst, Boffin, Degryse, Scifo, Czerniatynski (Nilis 46).
Wales: Southall; Phillips, Bowen (Giggs 60), Blackmore, Young, Symons, Horne, Saunders, Rush, Hughes, Speed (Pembridge 80).

Larnaca, 29 November 1992, 3000
Cyprus (1) 1 *(Pittas 39 (pen))*

Romania (2) 4 *(Popescu 4, Raducioiu 36, Hagi 73, Hanganu 86)*

Cyprus: Christofi M; Kalotheu, Pittas, Constantinou C, Ioannou D, Yiangudakis, Andreou (Hadjilukas 25), Christofi P, Yiannos Ioannou (Sotiriou 62), Papavasiliou, Savidis.
Romania: Stelea; Petrescu, Belodedici, Mihali, Lupescu, Popescu, Lacatus, Dumitrescu, Raducioiu (Hanganu 58), Hagi, Munteanu.

Nicosia, 13 February 1993, 3000
Cyprus (0) 0

Belgium (2) 3 *(Scifo 2, 4, Albert 87)*

Cyprus: Onisferou; Costa, Yiannos Ioannou, Constantinou C, Kalotheu (Sotiriou 70), Pittas, Savidis, Yiangudakis (Charalambous 60), Papavasiliou, Christofi P, Ioannou D.
Belgium: Preud'homme; Medved, Grun, Albert, Smidts, Staelens, Scifo (Goossens 87), Van der Elst, Boffin, Degryse, Nilis (Czerniatynski 75).

Limassol, 24 March 1993, 3000
Cyprus (0) 1 *(Sotiriou 47)*

Czechoslovakia (1) 1 *(Moravcik 33)*

Cyprus: Yiannakis Ioannou; Costa, Pittas, Ioannou D, Christofi E, Yiangudakis, Xiuruppas (Panayi 86), Charalambous, Papavasiliou (Larku 71), Savidis.
Czechoslovakia: Kouba; Novotny, Suchoparek (Berger 74), Vrabec, Glonek, Nemecek, Nemec, Hapal (Latal 46), Kuka P, Skuhravy, Moravcik.

Cardiff, 31 March 1993, 27,002
Wales (2) 2 *(Giggs 18, Rush 39)*
Belgium (0) 0

Wales: Southall; Horne, Bodin, Aizlewood, Young, Ratcliffe, Saunders, Speed (Phillips 88), Rush, Hughes, Giggs (Bowen 89).
Belgium: Preud'homme; Medved (Oliveira 46), Grun, Albert, Smidts, Staelens, Van der Elst, Boffin, Degryse, Scifo, Czerniatynski (Severeyns 67).

Bucharest, 14 April 1993, 30,000
Romania (1) 2 *(Dumitrescu 33, 55)*
Cyprus (1) 1 *(Sotiriou 23)*

Romania: Stelea; Petrescu, Selymes, Sandoi, Belodedici, Munteanu, Lacatus (Stinga 78), Sabau, Ceausila (Predatu 64), Hagi, Dumitrescu.
Cyprus: Petridis; Kalotheu, Pittas, Constantinou C, Christofi E, Yiangudakis, Charalambous (Xiuruppas 78), Larku, Sotiriou, Papavasiliou, Savidis (Panayi 89).

Limassol, 25 April 1993, 4000
Cyprus (2) 3 *(Xiuruppas 7, Sotiriou 43, Ioannou Y 75)*
Faeroes (0) 1 *(Arge 82)*

Cyprus: Petridis; Charalambous, Christofi E, Pittas, Constantinou C, Yiangudakis, Larku, Xiuruppas (Yiannos Ioannou 65), Papavasiliou, Sotiriou (Hadjilukas 76), Savidis.
Faeroes: Knudsen; Jakobsen, Johannesen, Morkore K, Justinussen, Morkore A, Faero (Nielsen 46), Olsen, Reynheim (Arge 54), Hansen A, Jonsson.

Ostrava, 28 April 1993, 16,000
Czechoslovakia (1) 1 *(Latal 41)*
Wales (1) 1 *(Hughes 31)*

Czechoslovakia: Kouba; Glonek (Bejbl 66), Kadlec, Novotny, Vrabec, Latal, Nemec (Dubovsky 79), Kubik, Nemecek, Kuka P, Luhovy.
Wales: Southall; Phillips, Bodin (Bowen 52), Melville, Symons, Blackmore, Horne, Saunders, Rush, Hughes, Giggs.

Brussels, 22 May 1993, 20,641
Belgium (1) 3 *(Wilmots 32, 75, Scifo 50 (pen))*
Faeroes (0) 0

Belgium: Preud'homme; Smidts (Oliveira 76), Emmers, Grun, Staelens, Boffin, Van der Elst, Degryse, Wilmots, Scifo, Nilis.
Faeroes: Knudsen; Jakobsen, Olsen, Morkore K (Reynatugvu 89), Justinussen, Morkore A, Dam, Hansen A, Nielsen T, Arge (Rasmussen 87), Reynheim.

Kosice, 2 June 1993, 15,000
Czechoslovakia (2) 5 *(Vrabec 13, Latal 37, Dubovsky 58, 83, 89)*
Romania (1) 2 *(Raducioiu 26, 55)*

Czechoslovakia: Kouba; Suchoparek, Novotny, Vrabec, Latal, Moravcik, Nemecek, Kubik (Nemec 46), Dubovsky, Kuka P (Glonek 81), Skuhravy.
Romania: Lung; Belodedici, Prodan (Hanganu 77), Popescu, Munteanu, Sabau, Hagi, Lupescu, Dumitrescu, Lacatus (Panduru 65), Raducioiu.

Toftir, 6 June 1993, 4209
Faeroes (0) 0

Wales (2) 3 *(Saunders 22, Young 31, Rush 69)*

Faeroes: Knudsen; Jakobsen, Hansen T, Johannesen, Justinussen, Reynatugvu (Ramussen 49), Nielsen T, Dam, Hansen A, Reynheim (Mohr 59), Arge.
Wales: Southall; Phillips, Bodin, Aizlewood, Young (Melville 49), Symons, Horne, Saunders, Rush, Hughes (Speed 75), Giggs.

Toftir, 16 June 1993, 1000
Faeroes (0) 0

Czechoslovakia (3) 3 *(Hasek 3, Postulka 38,44)*

Faeroes: Knudsen; Justinussen R (Rasmussen 68), Johannesen, Jakobsen (Hansen T 70), Morkore K, Justinussen A, Morkore A, Reynatugvu, Hansen A, Dam, Nielsen.
Czechoslovakia: Kouba; Suchoparek, Hasek, Repka, Latal, Nemecek, Dubovsky, Postulka, Berger, Kuka P (Kinder 54), Moravcik (Kubik 81).

Toftir, 8 September 1993, 2500
Faeroes (0) 0

Romania (1) 4 *(Raducioiu 24,58,60,77)*

Faeroes: Johannesen, Jakobsen, Morkore K, Justinussen, Hansen A, Dam, Jarnskor, Morkore A (Nolsee 78), Reynheim, Hansen O (Reynatugvu 78).
Romania: Prunea; Petrescu (Panduru 77), Prodan, Popescu, Selymes, Sabau, Lupescu, Hagi, Munteanu, Vladoiu (Craioveanu 68), Raducioiu.

Cardiff, 8 September 1993, 37,558
Wales (2) 2 *(Giggs 21, Rush 35)*

Czechoslovakia (1) 2 *(Kuka 16, Dubovsky 67)*

Wales: Southall; Phillips, Symons, Aizlewood (Melville 78), Young, Bowen (Speed 75), Horne, Saunders, Rush, Hughes, Giggs.
Czechoslovakia: Kouba; Latal (Skuhravy 59), Kadlec, Nemecek, Novotny, Suchoparek, Hapal, Hasek, Moravcik, Kuka, Dubovsky.

Bucharest, 13 October 1993, 25,000
Romania (0) 2 *(Radicioiu 67 (pen), Dumitrescu 84)*

Belgium (0) 1 *(Scifo 87 (pen))*

Romania: Prunea; Belodedici, Petrescu, Prodan, Munteanu, Sabau (Selymes 27), Popescu, Lupescu, Hagi (Vladoiu 86), Dumitrescu, Raducioiu.
Belgium: Preud'homme; Medved, Grun, Albert, Smidts, Borkelmans (Oliveira 70), Scifo, Staelens, Van der Elst, Boffin, Wilmots (Czerniatynski 78).

Cardiff, 13 October 1993, 10,000
Wales (0) 2 *(Saunders 70, Rush 82)*

Cyprus (0) 0

Wales: Southall; Phillips, Horne, Aizlewood, Young, Symons (Goss 70), Giggs, Rush, Saunders, Hughes, Speed.
Cyprus: Petridis; Constantinou G, Pittas, Ioannou D (Panayi 71), Evagoras, Yargoudakis (Xiuruppas 75), Charalambous, Kosta, Sotiriou, Larku, Papavasiliou.

Kosice, 27 October 1993, 15,600
Czechoslovakia (2) 3 *(Dubovsky 12, Hapal 23, Skuhravy 77)*

Cyprus (0) 0

Czechoslovakia: Molnar; Suchoparek, Kadlec, Novotny, Moravcik, Nemecek, Dubovsky, Hapal, Smicer (Timko 72), Skuhravy, Kuka (Postulka 80).
Cyprus: Petridis; Constantinou G, Andreou (Kalotheu 69), Constantinou C, Panayi, Kleanthous, Larku, Papavasiliou, Chatsiloukas, Sotiriou, Xiuruppas (Stephani 62).

Brussels, 17 November 1993, 30,000
Belgium (0) 0

Czechoslovakia (0) 0

Belgium: De Wilde; Medved, De Wolf, Albert, Smidts, Staelens, Van der Elst, Scifo, Versavel, Nilis (Czerniatynski 78), Oliveira (Boffin 52).
Czechoslovakia: Kouba; Novotny, Kadlec, Suchoparek (Timio 80), Moravcik, Hazek, Hapal (Latal 70), Dubovsky, Nemecek, Skuhravy, Kuka.

Cardiff, 17 November 1993, 40,000
Wales (0) 1 *(Saunders 60)*

Romania (1) 2 *(Hagi 33, Radicioiu 83)*

Wales: Southall; Phillips, Young, Melville, Bodin (Allen 69), Symons (Goss 53), Giggs, Horne, Rush, Saunders, Speed.
Romania: Prunea; Belodedici, Petrescu, Prodan, Selymes (Monteanu 53), Sabau, Popescu, Lupescu, Hagi, Raducioiu, Dumitrescu (Michali 89).

Group 4

	P	W	D	L	F	A	Pts
Romania	10	7	1	2	29	12	15
Belgium	10	7	1	2	16	5	15
Czechoslovakia	10	4	5	1	21	9	13
Wales	10	5	2	3	19	12	12
Cyprus	10	2	1	7	8	18	5
Faeroes	10	0	0	10	1	38	0

Romania and Belgium qualified

Group 5
Yugoslavia excluded due to UN sanctions.
Athens, 13 May 1992, 10,000
Greece (1) 1 *(Sofanidis 28)*

Iceland (0) 0

Greece: Papadopoulos; Apostolakis, Kalitzakis, Manolas, Mitsibonas, Tsaluhidis Y, Tsaluhidis P, Sofiandis, Tursunidis (Noblias 77), Alexandria, Tsiantakis (Borbokis 60).
Iceland: Kristinsson B; Jonsson Kr, Marteinsson (Magnusson 74), Vaisson, Bergsson, Jonsson K, Gudjohnsen, Bjarnasson, Gretarsson, Sverrisson, Kristinsson R.

Budapest, 3 June 1992, 10,000
Hungary (1) 1 *(Kiprich 3)*

Iceland (0) 2 *(Orlygsson 51, Magnusson 73)*

Hungary: Petry; Telek, Kovacs E, Lorincz, Simon, Limperger, Pisont (Balog 78), Vincze (Eszenyi 54), Keller, Kiprich, Kovacs K.
Iceland: Kristinsson B; Gretarsson S (Magnusson 64), Bergsson, Orlygsson, Kristinsson R, Gretarsson A, Valsson, Jonsson Kr, Jonsson K (Bragason 80), Bjarnasson, Marteinsson.

Luxembourg, 9 September 1992, 3000
Luxembourg (0) 0

Hungary (1) 3 *(Detari 16, Kovacs K 52, 79)*

Luxembourg: Van Rijswijck; Bossi, Wolf, Petry, Birsens, Girres, Hellers, Weis, Salbene (Holtz 58), Langers, Malget (Thill 80).
Hungary: Petry; Nagy T, Disztl L, Keller, Lorincz, Limperger (Telek 65), Kiprich, Balog, Pisont (Bognar G 81), Detari, Kovacs K.

Reykjavik, 7 October 1992, 6350
Iceland (0) 0

Greece (0) 1 *(Tsaluhidis P 61)*

Iceland: Kristinsson B; Bergsson, Jonsson Kr, Gudjohnsen, Marteinsson (Margeirsson 29), Kristinsson R, Bjarnasson (Hakonarsson 71), Gretarsson A, Orlygsson, Gretarsson S, Sverrisson.
Greece: Mirtsos; Apostolakis, Kalitsodakis, Manolas, Kalitzakis, Papaioannou (Mitropoulos 55), Tsiantakis, Tsaluhidis P, Dimitriadis (Franceskos 69), Noblias, Donis.

Moscow, 14 October 1992, 13,000
Russia (0) 1 *(Yuran 64)*

Iceland (0) 0

Russia: Cherchesov; Khlestov, Onopko, Kulkov, Kolotovkin, Shalimov, Dobrovolski, Karpin, Lediakhov (Tatarchuk 46), Yuran (Kolivanov 76), Kiriakov.
Iceland: Kristinsson B; Marteinsson, Jonsson Kr, Valsson, Gretarsson A, Kristinsson R (Hakonarsson 88), Bergsson, Orlygsson, Margeirsson, Gudjohnsen (Bjarnasson 76), Gretarsson S.

Moscow, 28 October 1992, 1750
Russia (2) 2 *(Yuran 4, Radchenko 23)*

Luxembourg (0) 0

Russia: Cherchesov; Khlestov, Onopko, Kulkov, Karpin, Shalimov, Dobrovolski, Mostovoi, Radchenko (Tatarchuk 80), Kiriakov (Borodyuk 63), Yuran.
Luxembourg: Van Rijswijck; Birsens, Bossi, Wolf, Hellers, Girres, Salbene (Thill 77), Weis, Holtz (Groff 53), Langers, Malget.

Salonika, 11 November 1992, 40,000
Greece (0) 0

Hungary (0) 0

Greece: Mirtsos; Apostolakis, Pahaturidis, Manolas, Kolitsidakis, Tsaluhidis P, Mitropoulos, Nioblias, Dimitriadis (Valtsis 46), Tursunidis, Tsiantakis (Franceskos 63).
Hungary: Petry; Disztl L, Limperger, Lorincz, Nagy, Urban, Lipcsei, Kiprich (Salloi 32), Meszaros (Paling 78), Balog, Kovacs K.

Athens, 17 February 1993, 40,000
Greece (1) 2 *(Dimitriadis 30 (pen), Mitropoulos 65)*

Luxembourg (0) 0

Greece: Minou; Manolas, Apostolakis, Kalitzakis, Tsaluhidis P, Nioblias, Tsiantakis, Dimitriadis, Donis (Mitropoulos 58), Franceskos (Karapialis 56), Karataidis.
Luxembourg: Koch; Petry, Wolf, Bossi, Birsens, Salbene, Hellers, Weis, Groff (Scuto 67), Malget, Langers.

Budapest, 31 March 1993, 30,000
Hungary (0) 0

Greece (0) 1 *(Apostolakis 70)*

Hungary: Petry; Telek, Csabo, Disztl L (Nagy T 36), Pisont (Balog 71), Urban, Detari, Eszenyi, Duro, Kiprich, Kovacs K.
Greece: Minou; Manolas, Kalitzakis, Kolitsidakis, Tsiantakis, Apostolakis, Mitropoulos, Nioblias, Tsaluhidis P, Maragos (Antoniou 63), Mahias (Franceskos 82).

Luxembourg, 14 April 1993, 3000
Luxembourg (0) 0

Russia (1) 4 *(Kiriakov 12, 46, Shalimov 57, Kulkov 90)*

Luxembourg: Koch; Petry, Bossi, Birsens, Wolf, Salbene (Scuto 80), Hellers, Weis, Groff, Malget, Morocutti (Thill 60).
Russia: Cherchesov; Onopko, Gorlukovich, Ivanov, Shalimov, Kolivanov, Dobrovolski, Korneyev (Kulkov 60), Kanchelskis, Yuran, Kiriakov (Popov 75).

Moscow, 28 April 1993, 30,000
Russia (0) 3 *(Kanchelskis 55, Kolivanov 60, Yuran 86)*

Hungary (0) 0

Russia: Kharine; Gorlukovich, Ivanov A, Onopko, Kanchelskis, Shalimov, Dobrovolski, Korneyev (Kulkov 57), Kolivanov, Yuran, Kiriakov (Mostovoi 72).
Hungary: Petry; Telek, Nagy T, Lorincz, Pisont, Marton, Detari, Balog (Vincze 64), Duro (Banfi 64), Kovacs K, Csabi.

Luxembourg, 20 May 1993, 2000
Luxembourg (0) 1 *(Birgison (og) 70)*

Iceland (1) 1 *(Gudjohnsen 40)*

Luxembourg: Van Rijswijck; Ferron (Carboni 64), Petry, Birsens, Wolf, Holtz, Salbene, Hellers, Groff (Scuto 50), Langers, Malget.
Iceland: Kristinsson B; Birgison, Bergsson, Jonsson Kr, Orlygsson, Kristinsson R, Gretarsson A, Ingolfsson (Martinsson 82), Gudjohnsen, Gunnlaugsson (Thordarsson 56), Sverrisson.

Moscow, 23 May 1993, 40,000
Russia (0) 1 *(Dobrovolski 75 (pen))*

Greece (1) 1 *(Mitropoulos 45)*

Russia: Kharine; Gorlukovich, Onopko, Ivanov A, Kanchelskis, Shalimov, Dobrovolski, Kulkov (Tatarchuk 62), Kolivanov, Yuran, Kiriakov.
Greece: Minou; Apostolakis, Kolitsidakis, Manolas, Kalitzakis, Tsaluhidis P, Marangos, Nioblias, Mahias (Antoniou 82), Mitropoulos (Karapialis 64), Tsiantakis.

Reykjavik, 2 June 1993, 3096
Iceland (1) 1 *(Sverrisson 26)*

Russia (1) 1 *(Kiriakov 38)*

Iceland: Kristinsson B; Bergsson, Birgison, Jonsson Kr, Dervic, Stefansson, Thordarsson, Kristinsson R (Gretarsson A 78), Gudjohnsen, Sverrisson (Ingolfsson 83), Gunnlaugsson.
Russia: Kharine; Gorlukovich, Onopko, Kulkov, Ivanov, Kanchelskis, Dobrovolski, Tatarchuk (Korneyev 63), Kolivanov, Yuran (Lediakhov 75), Kiriakov.

Reykjavik, 16 June 1993, 5000
Iceland (1) 2 *(Sverrisson 13, Gudjohnsen 77)*

Hungary (0) 0

Iceland: Kristinsson B; Bjarnsson, Bergsson, Jonsson Kr, Dervic, Thordarsson, Kristinsson R, Stefansson (Gretarsson A 64), Gunnlaugsson, Gudjohnsen, Sverrisson.
Hungary: Petry; Simon, Telek, Lorincz, Urban, Pisont, Marton, Balog, Kerezturi, Orosz (Hamori 64), Hamar (Salloi 80).

Budapest, 8 September 1993, 5000
Hungary (1) 1 *(Nikiforov 21 (og))*

Russia (1) 3 *(Piatnicki 15, Kiriakov 53, Borodyuk 90)*

Hungary: Vegh; Banfi, Bordas, Puglits, Kuttor, Lipczei (Halmai 69), Vincze, Detari, Albert (Kovacs 64), Klausz, Csertoi.
Russia: Kharine; Gorlukovich, Onopko, Ivanov, Nikiforov, Kanchelskis, Shalimov, Piatnicki (Dobrovolski 71), Kolivanov, Yuran (Borodyuk 56), Kiriakov.

Reykjavik, 8 September 1993, 3969
Iceland (0) 1 *(Ingolfsson 54 (pen))*

Luxembourg (0) 0

Iceland: Kristinsson B; Birgison, Bergsson, Jonsson Kr, Thordarsson, Jonsson S, Ingolfsson, Kristinsson R, Gudjohnsen, Gudjonsson, Gunnlaugsson.
Luxembourg: Koch; Bossi, Petry, Birsens, Wolf, Holtz, Hellers, Salbene, Groff, Langers (Morocutti 65), Malget (Cardoni 82).

Luxembourg, 12 October 1993, 2558
Luxembourg (0) 1 *(Fanelli 83)*

Greece (1) 3 *(Mahlas 31, Apostolakis 65, Saravakos 73)*

Luxembourg: Koch; Ferron, Petry, Strasser, Wolf, Holtz, Birsens, Cardoni (Malget 46), Groff, Morocutti (Fanelli 69), Langers.
Greece: Minou; Apostolakis, Mahlas, Manolas, Kalitzakis, Tsaluhidis P, Saravakos, Nioblias, Mitropoulos (Alexandris 78), Dimitriadis (Maragos 46), Tsiantakis.

Budapest, 27 October 1993, 1500
Hungary (1) 1 *(Detari 20)*

Luxembourg (0) 0

Hungary: Vegh; Banfi, Mracko, Kuttor, Bordas, Csertai, Detari, Lipcsei, Fule (Orosz 46), Klausz, Vincze (Puglits 23).
Luxembourg: Koch; Bossi, Petry, Wolf, Strasser, Hellers, Saibane, Birsens, Groff (Malget 75), Langers, Fanello (Morocutti 76).

Athens, 17 November 1993, 60,000
Greece (0) 1 *(Mahlas 68)*

Russia (0) 6

Greece: Minou; Apostolakis, Ioannidis, Manolas, Karataidis, Tsaluhidis P, Saravakos (Alexandris 77), Nioblias, Mahlas, Mitropoulos (Marangos 33), Tsiantakis.
Russia: Cherchesov; Khlestov, Onopko, Popov (Mostovoi 80), Kulkov, Nikiforov, Shalimov, Kolivanov, Dobrovolski, Kiriakov, Yuran (Salenko 46).

Group 5

	P	W	D	L	F	A	Pts
Greece	8	6	2	0	10	2	14
Russia	8	5	2	1	15	4	12
Iceland	8	3	2	3	7	6	8
Hungary	8	2	1	5	6	11	5
Luxembourg	8	0	1	7	2	17	1

Russia and Greece qualified

Group 6
Helsinki, 14 May 1992, 10,000
Finland (0) 0

Bulgaria (2) 3 *(Balakov 16, Kostadinov 25, 85)*

Finland: Huttunen; Petaja, Holmgren, Heikkinen, Eriksson, Rinne (Huhtamaki 76), Litmanen, Myyry, Jarvinen, Vanhala (Tegelberg 60), Tarkkio.
Bulgaria: Mikhailov; Ivanov, Tzvetanov, Iliev, Hubchev, Sirakov, Yankov, Stoichkov (Yordanov 69), Penev, Balakov, Kostadinov.

Sofia, 9 September 1992, 45,000
Bulgaria (2) 2 *(Stoichkov 21 (pen), Balakov 29)*

France (0) 0

Bulgaria: Mikhailov; Kiriakov, Ivanov, Tzvetanov, Iliev, Yankov, Kostadinov (Yordanov 75), Stoichkov, Penev (Stoilov 76), Sirakov, Balakov.
France: Martini; Fournier, Petit, Boli, Roche, Casoni, Deschamps, Sauzee, Papin, Ginola, Vahirua (Durand 61).

Helsinki, 9 September 1992, 13,617
Finland (0) 0

Sweden (0) 1 *(Ingesson 77 (pen))*

Finland: Laukkanen; Hjelm, Tarkkio (Tauriainen 72), Ukkonen, Litmanen, Myyry (Vanhala 85), Paatelainen, Jarvinen, Holmgren, Kanerva, Remes.
Sweden: Ravelli (Eriksson L 88); Andersson P, Bjorklund, Erlingmark, Ljung, Ingesson, Limpar, Pettersson (Ekstrom 62), Schwarz, Thern, Dahlin.

Stockholm, 7 October 1992, 20,625
Sweden (0) 2 *(Dahlin 56, Pettersson 76)*

Bulgaria (0) 0

Sweden: Eriksson L; Erlingmark, Andersson P, Bjorklund, Ljung, Limpar, Thern, Schwarz, Pettersson, Ingesson, Dahlin (Andersson K 87).
Bulgaria: Mikhailov; Mladenov, Kiriakov, Ivanov, Tzvetanov, Kostadinov (Yordanov 83), Sirakov, Stoilov, Yankov, Balakov, Penev.

Paris, 14 October 1992, 39,186
France (1) 2 *(Papin 3, Cantona 77)*

Austria (0) 0

France: Martini; Sauzee, Boli, Casoni, Deschamps, Sassus, Fournier (Gnako 63), Durand, Gravelaine (Vahirua 73), Papin, Cantona.
Austria: Wohlfahrt; Feiersinger, Streiter, Zsak, Wazinger, Stoger (Pfeifenberger 84), Artner, Herzog, Baur, Schinkels (Ogris 46), Polster.

Vienna, 28 October 1992, 20,000
Austria (2) 5 *(Herzog 41, 46, Polster 49, Stoger 56, Ogris 87)*
Israel (0) 2 *(Zohar 57, 77)*

Austria: Wohlfahrt; Zsak, Streiter (Baur 71), Wazinger, Prosenik, Stoger, Artner, Herzog, Schinkels (Flogel 76), Ogris, Polster.
Israel: Ginzburg; Ben-Shimon, Yeuda, Harazi, Avi Cohen (Berkovich 52), Zohar, Klinger, Hazan, Nimny, Rosenthal, Tikva (Drieks 78).

Tel Aviv, 11 November 1992, 40,000
Israel (1) 1 *(Banin 42)*
Sweden (1) 3 *(Limpar 37, Dahlin 58, Ingesson 74)*

Israel: Ginzburg; Avi Cohen, Harazi (Berkovich 61), Hazan, Ben-Shimon, Klinger, Banin, Nimny, Revivo (Tikva 70), Zohar, Rosenthal.
Sweden: Ravelli; Nilsson R, Andersson P, Bjorklund, Ljung, Limpar, Rehn, Ingesson, Thern, Dahlin (Ekstrom 82), Brolin (Landberg 87).

Paris, 14 November 1992, 30,000
France (2) 2 *(Papin 17, Cantona 31)*
Finland (0) 1 *(Jarvinen 54)*

France: Martini; Roche, Boli, Casoni, Durand (Karembeu 71), Sauzee, Deschamps, Lizarazu, Papin, Cantona, Gravelaine (Vahirua 78).
Finland: Laukkanen; Holmgren, Kanerva, Ukkonen, Petaja (Kinnunen 85), Hjelm, Litmanen, Myyry, Jarvinen, Tarkkio, Paatelainen (Tauriainen 23).

Tel Aviv, 2 December 1992, 15,000
Israel (0) 0
Bulgaria (0) 2 *(Sirakov 55, Penev 83)*

Israel: Ginzburg; Halfon, Hilel, Shelach, Ben-Shimon, Klinger, Banin, Mizrahi (Hazan 80), Berkovich (Harazi R 84), Revivo, Rosenthal.
Bulgaria: Mikhailov; Kiriakov, Ivanov, Bezinski, Iliev, Yankov, Kostadinov, Stoichkov, Penev, Sirakov, Yordanov (Iskrenov 89).

Tel Aviv, 17 February 1993, 29,000
Israel (0) 0
France (1) 4 *(Cantona 28, Blanc 62, 84, Roche 89)*

Israel: Ginzburg; Klinger, Halfon, Hazan, Harazi A, Hilel, Atar (Drieks 56), Banin, Nimny, Harazi R, Rosenthal.
France: Lama; Boli, Roche, Blanc, Lizarazu (Loko 82), Deschamps, Sauzee, Le Guen, Ginola (Petit 63), Papin, Cantona.

Vienna, 27 March 1993, 37,500
Austria (0) 0
France (0) 1 *(Papin 58)*

Austria: Wohlfahrt; Pecl, Zsak, Artner, Feiersinger, Cerny, Kuhbauer, Schinkels (Ogris 71), Herzog, Polster, Pfeifenberger.
France: Lama; Angloma, Roche, Blanc, Petit, Lizarazu, Deschamps, Le Guen, Sauzee (Martins 87), Papin, Gravelaine (Loko 71).

Vienna, 14 April 1993, 19,500
Austria (2) 3 *(Pfeifenberger 11, Kuhbauer 25, Polster 89)*

Bulgaria (0) 1 *(Ivanov 54)*

Austria: Wohlfahrt; Streiter, Pecl, Zsak, Feiersinger, Kuhbauer (Cerny 86), Lainer, Baur, Polster, Herzog, Pfeifenberger (Ogris 68).
Bulgaria: Mikhailov; Dochev (Lechkov 73), Ivanov, Iliev, Bezinski (Iskrenov 82), Yankov, Kostadinov, Kiriakov, Balakov, Stoichkov, Penev.

Paris, 28 April 1993, 43,000
France (1) 2 *(Cantona 42 (pen), 82)*

Sweden (1) 1 *(Dahlin 14)*

France: Lama; Angloma, Petit, Boli, Blanc, Le Guen, Deschamps, Sauzee, Ginola (Vahirua 46), Martins (Lizarazu 89), Cantona.
Sweden: Ravelli; Nilsson R, Andersson P, Bjorklund, Ljung, Rehn, Thern (Kamark 27), Brolin, Schwarz, Ingesson, Dahlin (Pettersson 65).

Sofia, 28 April 1993, 35,000
Bulgaria (2) 2 *(Stoichkov 14, Yankov 43)*

Finland (0) 0

Bulgaria: Mikhailov; Kiriakov, Rakov, Markov (Besinski 89), Yankov, Lechkov, Kostadinov (Iskrenov 56), Stoichkov, Penev, Sirakov, Balakov.
Finland: Jakonen; Kinnunen, Kanerva, Heikkinen, Holmgren, Suominen, Litmanen, Lindberg, Hjelm, Paatelainen, Petaja (Rajamaki 62).

Sofia, 12 May 1993, 25,000
Bulgaria (1) 2 *(Stoichkov 35 (pen), Sirakov 60)*

Israel (0) 2 *(Harazi R 52, Rosenthal 53)*

Bulgaria: Mikhailov; Kiriakov, Ratkov, Markov, Ivanov, Lechkov (Borimirov 65), Balakov, Sirakov, Iskrenov (Yankov 37), Penev, Stoichkov.
Israel: Ginzburg; Halfon, Hilel, Hazan, Shelach, Klinger, Banin, Schwarz, Rosenthal, Harazi R (Atar 88), Ohana (Harazi A 89).

Pori, 13 May 1993, 13,682
Finland (2) 3 *(Paatelainen 17, Rajamaki 20, Hjelm 50)*

Austria (0) 1 *(Zisser 89)*

Finland: Jakonen; Heikkinen, Kanerva, Holmgren (Lindberg 60), Kinnunen, Petaja, Rajamaki, Hjelm, Suominen, Litmanen, Paatelainen (Gronholm 76).
Austria: Wohlfahrt; Streiter, Zsak (Cerny 60), Zisser, Baur, Kuhbauer, Herzog, Artner, Lainer, Ogris, Polster (Stoger 58).

Stockholm, 19 May 1993, 27,800
Sweden (0) 1 *(Eriksson J 50)*

Austria (0) 0

Sweden: Ravelli; Nilsson R, Eriksson J, Bjorklund, Ljung, Rehn, Schwarz, Brolin, Ingesson, Ekstrom (Zetterberg 80), Dahlin (Eklund 87).
Austria: Wohlfahrt; Streiter, Pecl, Lainer, Stoger, Baur, Herzog (Janeschitz 62), Artner, Feiersinger, Ogris, Pfeifenberger.

Stockholm, 2 June 1993, 22,000
Sweden (2) 5 *(Brolin 17, 41, 65, Zetterberg 55, Landberg 89)*
Israel (0) 0

Sweden: Ravelli; Nilsson R, Eriksson J, Bjorklund, Ljung, Rehn (Landberg 74), Andersson P, Zetterberg, Ingesson, Brolin, Dahlin.
Israel: Ginzburg; Halfon, Hilel, Klinger, Shelach, Bromer, Ohana (Revivo 65), Hazan, Schwarz, Harazi R, Rosenthal (Harazi A 46).

Lahti, 16 June 1993, 4620
Finland (0) 0
Israel (0) 0

Finland: Jakonen; Kinnunen (Lindberg 84), Holmgren, Kanerva, Heikkinen, Petaja, Suominen, Litmanen, Rajamaki, Paatelainen, Gronholm (Ruhanan 75).
Israel: Ginzburg; Klinger, Halfon, Bromer, Shelach, Amsalem, Hazan, Schwarz, Banin, Harazi R (Atar 89), Ohana.

Stockholm, 22 August 1993, 30,530
Sweden (0) 1 *(Dahlin 87)*
France (0) 1 *(Sauzee 76)*

Sweden: Ravelli; Nilsson R, Eriksson J, Andersson P, Ljung, Ingesson, Thern, Zetterberg (Rehn 68), Landberg (Limpar 79), Brolin, Dahlin.
France: Lama; Desailly, Blanc, Roche, Lizarazu, Deschamps, Le Guen, Sauzee, Pedros (Vahirua 79), Papin, Cantona.

Vienna, 25 August 1993, 21,000
Austria (2) 3 *(Kuhbauer 28, Pfeifenberger 41, Herzog 90 (pen))*
Finland (0) 0

Austria: Wohlfahrt; Streiter, Kogler, Pfeffer, Feiersinger (Flogel 83), Stoger, Artner, Herzog, Kuhbauer (Baur 85), Ogris, Pfeifenberger.
Finland: Jakonen; Kinnunen, Heikkinen, Kanerva, Petaja, Suominen, Litmanen (Gronholm 76), Lindberg (Ruhanen 69), Hjelm, Rajamaki, Paatelainen.

Sofia, 8 September 1993, 38,000
Bulgaria (1) 1 *(Stoichkov 21 (pen))*
Sweden (1) 1 *(Dahlin 26)*

Bulgaria: Ananiev; Kremeliev, Ivanov, Zvetanov, Rakov, Jankov, Kostadinov (Yordanov 75), Stoichkov, Alexandrov (Donkov 53), Lechkov, Balakov.
Sweden: Ravelli; Nilsson R, Andersson P, Eriksson J, Ljung, Ingesson, Thern, Limpar, Schwarz, Dahlin (Rehn 75), Brolin (Ekstrom 77).

Tampere, 8 September 1993, 10,000
Finland (0) 0
France (0) 2 *(Blanc 47, Papin 55 (pen))*

Finland: Jakonen; Kinnunen, Petaja, Kanerva, Eriksson, Suominen (Paavola 75), Hjelm, Lindberg, Litmanen, Rajamaki (Ruhanen 76), Paatelainen.
France: Lama; Desailly, Roche, Blanc, Petit, Deschamps (Guerin 87), Le Guen, Martins (Pedros 73), Sauzee, Papin, Cantona.

Sofia, 13 October 1993, 25,000
Bulgaria (2) 4 *(Penev 6, 76, Stoichkov 33 (pen), Lechkov 87)*

Austria (0) 1 *(Herzog 51)*

Bulgaria: Mikhailov; Hubchev, Ivanov, Yankov (Todorov 83), Zvetvanov, Lechkov, Balakov, Stoichkov, Kremeliev, Kostadinov (Borimirov 63), Penev.
Austria: Wohlfahrt; Baur, Streiter, Flogel, Pfeffer, Artner, Herzog, Stoger, Kogler, Polster, Ogris.

Paris, 13 October 1993, 32,741
France (2) 2 *(Sauzee 30, Ginola 40)*

Israel (1) 3 *(Harazi R 21, Berkovich 85, Atar 89)*

France: Lama; Desailly, Blanc, Roche (Lizarazu 22), Petit, Le Guen, Deschamps, Sauzee, Ginola (Djorkaeff 87), Papin, Cantona.
Israel: Ginzburg; Halfon, Hazan, Harazi A, Glam, Klinger, Levi, Nimny (Berkovich 65), Atar, Harazi R, Rosenthal.

Stockholm, 13 October 1993, 30,177
Sweden (3) 3 *(Dahlin 27, 45, Larsson H 40)*

Finland (1) 2 *(Suominen 15, Litmanen 60)*

Sweden: Ravelli; Nilsson R, Eriksson J, Ljung, Kamark, Ingesson (Landberg 8), Zetterberg, Schwarz, Dahlin, Larsson H (Martinsson 80), Limpar.
Finland: Jakonen; Kinnunen, Heikkinen, Eriksson (Jarvinen 46), Kanerva, Suominen, Lindberg, Aaltonen, Petaja, Hjelm, Litmanen.

Tel Aviv, 27 October 1993, 27,000
Israel (1) 1 *(Rosenthal 3)*

Austria (1) 1 *(Reinmayr 15)*

Israel: Ginzburg; Halfon, Hazan, Harazi A, Glam, Klinger, Levi, Berkovich (Schwartz 78), Atar (Ohan 65), Rosenthal, Harazi R.
Austria: Wohlfahrt; Kogler, Streiter, Pfeffer, Winklhofer, Feiersinger, Artner, Stoger, Reinmayr, Ogris A, Polster (Pfeifenberger 65).

Vienna, 10 November 1993, 25,000
Austria (0) 1 *(Herzog 70)*

Sweden (0) 1 *(Mild 67)*

Austria: Wohlfahrt; Winklhofer, Lainer, Kogler, Feiersinger, Stoger, Artner, Herzog, Reinmayr, Polster, Pacult (Westerhaler 71).
Sweden: Ravelli; Nilsson R, Andersson P, Kamark, Ljung, Landberg (Alexandersson 80), Zetterberg, Mild, Jansson, Schwarz, Larsson (Lilienberg 73).

Tel Aviv, 10 November 1993, 10,000
Israel (0) 1 *(Harazi R 90)*

Finland (0) 3 *(Hyrylainen 53, Paavola 72, Hjelm 84)*

Israel: Ginzburg; Harazi A, Klinger, Shelach, Glam, Hazan, Levi, Nimny, Rosenthal, Harazi R, Ohana.
Finland: Jakonen; Kinnunen, Heikkinen, Petaja, Hyrylainen, Suominen, Litmanen, Lindberg, Hjelm, Aaltonen, Paavola.

Paris, 17 November 1993, 48,402
France (1) 1 *(Cantona 33)*
Bulgaria (1) 2 *(Kostadinov 36, 90)*

France: Lama; Blanc, Desailly, Roche, Petit, Le Guen, Deschamps, Sauzee (Guerin 85), Pedros, Papin (Ginola 75), Cantona.
Bulgaria: Mikhailov; Kremenliev, Hubschev, Zvetanov (Borimirov 86), Ivanov, Yankov, Balakov, Lechkov (Alexandrov 86), Kostadinov, Penev, Stoichkov.

Group 6

	P	W	D	L	F	A	Pts
Sweden	10	6	3	1	19	8	15
Bulgaria	10	6	2	2	19	10	14
France	10	6	1	3	17	10	13
Austria	10	3	2	5	15	16	8
Finland	10	2	1	7	9	18	5
Israel	10	1	3	6	10	27	5

Sweden and Bulgaria qualified

South America
Group A
Barranquilla, 2 August 1993, 70,000
Colombia (0) 0
Paraguay (0) 0

Colombia: Cordoba; Herrera, Perea, Mendoza, Wilson Perez, Alvarez, Gomez G (Garcia A 46), Rincon, Valderrama, Asprilla, Trellez (Valenciano 67).
Paraguay: Chilavert; Duarte, Rivarola, Ayala, Suarez, Acuna, Struway, Gonzalez, Monzon (Nunes 56), Cabanas, Mendoza (Gamarra 74).

Lima, 1 August 1993, 45,000
Peru (0) 0

Argentina (1) 1 *(Batistuta 29)*

Peru: Miranda; Reynoso, Jorge Soto, Barco, Olivares, Carranza, Martinez (Muchotrigo 60), Del Solar, Palacios, Gonzalez (Maestri 60), Rivera.
Argentina: Goycochea; Basualdo F, Borelli, Ruggeri, Altamirano, Zapata, Redondo, Simeone, Leo Rodriguez (Basualdo JH 68), Batistuta, Acosta (Garcia C 79).

Lima, 8 August 1993, 18,000
Peru (0) 0

Colombia (1) 1 *(Rincon 44)*

Peru: Rivera (Charun 14), Jose Soto, Barco, Olivares, Carranza, Palacios, Del Solar, Zegarra (Saenz 65), Muchotrigo, Maestri.
Colombia: Cordoba; Herrera, Perea, Mendoza, Wilson Perez, Gomez, Lozanco, Rincon, Valderrama, Asprilla, Trellez (Aristizabal 62).

Asuncion, 8 August 1993, 25,000
Paraguay (1) 1 *(Struway 44)*

Argentina (1) 3 *(Medina Bello 15, 78, Redondo 65)*

Paraguay: Chilavert; Duarte, Rivarola, Ayala, Suarez, Struway, Acuna, Nunes (Ferreira 63), Gonzalez (Monzon 65), Cabanas, Mendoza.
Argentina: Goycochea; Basualdo F, Borelli, Ruggeri, Altamirano, Villarreal (Basualdo JH 46), Redondo, Simeone, Leo Rodriguez (Caceres 46), Medina Bello, Batistuta.

Asuncion, 15 August 1993, 20,000
Paraguay (2) 2 *(Mendoza 14, Chilavert 30 (pen))*

Peru (1) 1 *(Del Solar 44)*

Paraguay: Chilavert; Duarte, Sanabria R, Gamarra, Suarez, Cabanas, Struway, Monzon (Sanabria V 83), Gonzalez, Torres, Mendoza (Acuna 53).
Peru: Miranda; Charun (Valencia 63), Barco, Jose Soto, Olivares, Carranza, Zegarra, Del Solar, Reynoso, Baroni (Muchotrigo 60), Carty.

Barranquilla, 15 August 1993, 60,000
Colombia (1) 2 *(Valenciano 2, Valencia 52)*

Argentina (0) 1 *(Medina Bello 67)*

Colombia: Cordoba; Herrera, Perea, Mendoza, Wilson Perez, Gaviria, Lozano, Rincon, Valderrama, Valenciano (Asprilla 76), Valencia.
Argentina: Goycochea; Basualdo F, Borelli, Caceres, Altamirano, Redondo, Zapata, Basualdo JH (Zamora 46), Simeone, Medina Bello, Acosta (Leo Rodriguez 81).

Buenos Aires, 22 August 1993, 60,000
Argentina (2) 2 *(Batistuta 32, Medina Bello 37)*

Peru (0) 1 *(Palacios 66)*

Argentina: Goycochea; Craviotto, Ruggeri, Borelli, Caceres (Altamirano 27), Zapata, Redondo, Gorosito, Leo Rodriguez (Basualdo JH 70), Medina Bello, Batistuta.
Peru: Miranda; Carranza, Reynoso, Barco, Olivares, Jose Soto, Del Solar, Palacios, Zegarra, Gonzalez (Muchotrigo 65), Baroni (Maestri 86).

Asuncion, 22 August 1993, 20,000
Paraguay (0) 1 *(Rivarola 54)*

Colombia (1) 1 *(Rincon 22)*

Paraguay: Chilavert; Duarte (Barrios 46), Rivarola, Ayala, Suarez, Acuna, Struway, Cabanas, Gonzalez, Torres, Mendoza.
Colombia: Cardoba; Herrera, Perea (Gaviria 71), Mendoza, Wilson Perez, Gomez, Alvarez, Valderrama, Rincon, Valenciano (Asprilla 46), Valencia.

Barranquilla, 29 August 1993, 70,000
Colombia (2) 4 *(Valenciano 40, Rincon 45, Mendoza 66, Wilson Perez 76)*

Peru (0) 0

Colombia: Cordoba; Cabrera, Perea, Mendoza, Wilson Perez, Alvarez, Gomez, Rincon, Valderrama, Valenciano, Asprilla.
Peru: Miranda; Carranza, Reynoso, Jorge Soto, Olivares (Charun 74), Barco, Del Solar, Jose Soto, Zegarra, Gonzalez (Muchotrigo 46), Baroni.

Buenos Aires, 29 August 1993, 60,000
Argentina (0) 0

Paraguay (0) 0

Argentina: Goycochea; Basualdo F, Borelli, Ruggeri, Altamirano, Zapata, Redondo (Leo Rodriguez 63), Simeone, Gorosito (Zamora 70), Medina Bello, Batistuta.
Paraguay: Chilavert; Barrios, Rivarola, Suarez, Ayala, Struway, Gonzalez (Monzon 85), Sanabria V, Acuna, Torres, Mendoza (Ferreira 63).

Lima, 5 September 1993, 2000
Peru (1) 2 *(Muchotrigo 22, Jorge Soto 77)*
Paraguay (0) 2 *(Mendoza 61, 81)*
Peru: Miranda; Jorge Soto, Reynoso, Jose Soto, Olivares, Barco, Del Solar, Zegarra, Valencia, Muchotrigo, Baroni.
Paraguay: Chilavert; Barrios (Ferreira 81), Rivarola, Ayala, Suarez, Sanabria V (Monzon 81), Struway, Acuna, Torres, Cabanas, Mendoza.

Buenos Aires, 5 September 1993, 60,000
Argentina (0) 0
Colombia (1) 5 *(Asprilla 41, 50, 76, Rincon 74, Valencia 85)*
Argentina: Goycochea; Saldana, Ruggeri, Borelli, Altamirano, Zapata, Redondo (Garcia 54), Simeone, Leo Rodriguez (Acosta 71), Medina Bello, Batistuta.
Colombia: Cordoba; Herrera, Perea, Mendoza, Wilson Perez, Gomez, Alvarez, Rincon, Valderrama, Asprilla, Valencia.

Group A

	P	W	D	L	F	A	Pts
Colombia	6	4	2	0	13	2	10
Argentina	6	3	1	2	7	9	7
Paraguay	6	1	4	1	6	7	6
Peru	6	0	1	5	4	12	1

Colombia qualified; Argentina in play-off v Australia

Group B
Cuidad Guyana, 18 July 1993, 12,500
Venezuela (1) 1 *(Palencia 14)*
Bolivia (4) 7 *(Sanchez 27, 39, 54, Ramallo 39, 61, 68, Cristaldo 40)*
Venezuela: Gomez; Garcia C, Mathias (Rivas H 46), Echenique (Milillo 31), Morales, Hernandez, Rodriguez, Palencia, Camacho, Echenausi, Dolgetta.
Bolivia: Rojas; Rimba, Sandy, Borja, Cristaldo, Quinteros, Melgar, Baldivieso, Etcheverry (Castillo 85), Ramallo (Alvaro Pena 76), Sanchez E.

Guayaquil, 18 July 1993, 40,000
Ecuador (0) 0
Brazil (0) 0
Ecuador: Espinoza; Coronel, Tenorio B, Noriega, Capurro, Tenorio M, Carcelen, Carabali (Hurtado I 65), Aguinaga, Chala (Hurtado E 67), Munoz.
Brazil: Taffarel; Jorginho, Marcio Santos, Valber, Branco, Luis Henrique (Evair 70), Mauro Silva, Zinho, Rai, Bebeto, Careca (Dunga 70).

San Cristobal, 25 July 1993, 12,000
Venezuela (0) 0
Uruguay (0) 1 *(Herrera 59)*
Venezuela: Gomez; Echenausi, Mathias (Garcia 80), Gonzalez, Filosa, Hernandez, Palencia, Dolgetta, Rodriguez, Rivas S, Rivas H.
Uruguay: Siboldi; Herrera (De los Santos 71), Sanchez, Kanapkis, Cabrera, Moran, Ostolaza, Zalazar, Francescoli, Fonseca, Ruben Sosa (Aguilera 85).

La Paz, 25 July 1993, 45,000
Bolivia (0) 2 *(Etcheverry 88, Pena 89)*

Brazil (0) 0

Bolivia: Trucco; Borja, Rimba, Quinteros, Cristaldo, Sandy, Melgar, Baldivieso, Etcheverry, Ramallo (Alvaro Pena 73), Sanchez E (Castillo 81).
Brazil: Taffarel; Cafu, Marcio Santos, Valber, Leonardo, Luis Henrique (Jorginho 42), Mauro Silva, Zinho, Rai (Palinha 63), Bebeto, Muller.

Montevideo, 1 August 1993, 55,000
Uruguay (0) 0

Ecuador (0) 0

Uruguay: Siboldi; Herrera, Sanchez, Kanapkis, Cabrera, Moran (Da Silva J 80), Ostolaza, Zalazar, Francescoli, Fonseca (Aguilera 46), Ruben Sosa.
Ecuador: Espinoza; Noriega, Capurro, Tenorio B (Carabali 80), Carcelen, Tenorio M, Hurtado I, Coronel, Aguinaga (Chala 40), Munoz, Hurtado E.

San Cristobal, 1 August 1993, 26,000
Venezuela (0) 1 *(Garcia 84)*

Brazil (1) 5 *(Rai 34 (pen), Bebeto 70, 79, Branco 71, Palinha 88)*

Venezuela: Gomez; Filosa, Echenausi, Gonzalez, Mathias, Hernandez, Rivas H, Chacon, Rivas S (Contreras 80), Dolgetta (Garcia J 72), Rodriguez.
Brazil: Taffarel; Jorginho, Antonio Carlos, Elivelton, Valber, Marcio Santos, Branco, Mauro Silva, Dunga, Rai (Palinha 64), Bebeto, Careca (Evair 64).

La Paz, 8 August 1993, 45,000
Bolivia (0) 3 *(Sanchez 71, Etcheverry 81, Melgar 86)*

Uruguay (0) 1 *(Francescoli 89)*

Bolivia: Trucco; Borja, Quinteros, Rimba, Sandy, Cristaldo, Baldivieso, Melgar, Castillo (Etcheverry 53), Sanchez E, Ramallo (Alvaro Pena 84).
Uruguay: Siboldi; Herrera, Sanchez, Kanapkis, Cabrera, Moran, Gutierrez, Zalazar, Francescoli, Fonseca (Moas 66), Ruben Sosa (Aguilera 59).

Guayaquil, 8 August 1993, 30,000
Ecuador (2) 5 *(Munoz 23, Hurtado E 40, 50, 75, Chala 60)*

Venezuela (0) 0

Ecuador: Espinoza; Coronel (Zambrano 69), Capurro, Montanero, Hurtado I, Carcelen, Carabali, Munoz, Fernandez, Hurtado E, Chala (Aviles 69).
Venezuela: Gomez; Filosa, Gonzalez, Rivas H, Mathias, Milillo, Morales (Garcia C 54), Chacon (Contreras 88), Rivas S, Dolgetta, Garcia J.

Montevideo, 15 August 1993, 55,000
Uruguay (0) 1 *(Fonseca 79)*

Brazil (1) 1 *(Marcio Santos 28)*

Uruguay: Siboldi; Sanguinetti, Kanapkis, Sanchez, Cabrera, Ostolaza (Zalazar 71), Moran, Francescoli, Fonseca, Aguilera, Ruben Sosa (Adrian Paz 59).
Brazil: Taffarel; Jorginho, Marcio Santos, Ricardo Rocha, Branco, Dunga, Mauro Silva, Zinho, Rai, Bebeto (Antonio Carlos 71), Muller (Valdeir 84).

La Paz, 15 August 1993, 35,000
Bolivia (1) 1 *(Ramallo 18)*

Ecuador (0) 0

Bolivia: Trucco; Borja, Sandy, Quinteros, Rimba, Cristaldo, Melgar, Sanchez E, Baldivieso, Etcheverry (Villarroel 82), Ramallo (Alvaro Pena 70).
Ecuador: Espinoza; Noriega, Tenorio B, Capurro, Carabali, Hurtado I, Carcelen, Coronel, Aguinaga (Fernandez 65), Munoz (Chala 60), Hurtado E.

Sao Paulo, 22 August 1993, 77,916
Brazil (1) 2 *(Bebeto 34, Dunga 54)*

Ecuador (0) 0

Brazil: Taffarel; Jorginho, Marcio Santos, Ricardo Gomes, Branco (Cafu 75), Dunga, Mauro Silva, Zinho, Rai (Palinha 81), Bebeto, Muller.
Ecuador: Espinoza; Tenorio M, Hurtado I, Capurro, Coronel, Carcelen, Carabali, Fernandez (Gavica 77), Munoz (Aviles 65), Chala, Hurtado E.

La Paz, 22 August 1993, 35,000
Bolivia (1) 7 *(Ramallo 8, Melgar 58, 90, Sanchez 69, Sandy 75, Etcheverry 78, 82)*

Venezuela (0) 0

Bolivia: Trucco; Borja, Sandy, Quinteros, Rimba, Villarroel (Castillo 70), Cristaldo, Melgar, Etcheverry, Sanchez, Ramallo (Alvaro Pena 70).
Venezuela: Gomez; Filosa, Garcia J (Garcia C 30), Tortolero, Echenausi, Contreras, Hernandez, Rodriguez, Gonzalez, Rivas S (Morales 46), Paezpumar.

Montevideo, 29 August 1993, 60,000
Uruguay (3) 4 *(Kanapkis 7, 31, Cedres 41, Ruben Sosa 64)*

Venezuela (0) 0

Uruguay: Siboldi; Mendez, Herrera, Kanapkis, Soca (De los Santos 34), Dorta, Gutierrez, Francescoli, Aguilera (Adrian Paz 65), Cedres, Ruben Sosa.
Venezuela: Gomez; Rivas H, Gonzalez, Garcia C, Filosa, Echenausi (Contreras 78), Mathias, Paezpumar, Chacon, Rivas S, Garcia J (Rodriguez 46).

Recife, 29 August 1993, 76,636
Brazil (5) 6 *(Rai 12, Muller 18, Bebeto 22, 60, Branco 36, Ricardo Gomes 44)*

Bolivia (0) 0

Brazil: Taffarel; Jorginho, Ricardo Rocha, Ricardo Gomes, Branco, Mauro Silva, Dunga, Rai, Zinho (Palinha 55), Bebeto (Evair 71), Muller.
Bolivia: Trucco; Rimba, Borja, Sandy, Quinteros, Cristaldo, Melgar, Baldivieso, Sanchez, Etcheverry (Juan Pena 41), Ramallo (Alvaro Pena 71).

Guayaquil, 5 September 1993, 60,000
Ecuador (0) 0

Uruguay (1) 1 *(Ruben Sosa 9)*

Ecuador: Espinoza; Capurro, Tenorio B, Noriega, Hurtado I (Aviles 63), Carcelen (Chala 75), Carabali, Aguinaga, Gavica, Hurtado E, Munoz.
Uruguay: Siboldi; Canals, Mendez, Herrera, Kanapkis, Batista, Dorta, Gutierrez, Francescoli (Fonseca 66), Aguilera (Saralegui 63), Ruben Sosa.

Belo Horizonte, 5 September 1993, 64,000
Brazil (3) 4 *(Ricardo Gomes 27, 90, Palinha 29, Evair 31)*
Venezuela (0) 0

Brazil: Taffarel; Jorginho, Ricardo Rocha, Ricardo Gomes, Branco, Mauro Silva, Palinha, Rai, Zinho, Valdeir (Luis Henrique 75), Evair.
Venezuela: Gomez; Filosa, Tortolero, Rivas H, Garcia C, Rodriguez, Chacon (Hernandez 83), Echenausi, Paezpumar (Milillo 75), Garcia J, Morales.

Montevideo, 12 September 1993, 65,000
Uruguay (1) 2 *(Francescoli 3 (pen), Fonseca 51)*
Bolivia (1) 1 *(Ramallo 22)*

Uruguay: Siboldi; Mendez, Herrera, Canals, Batista, Dorta, Gutierrez (Zalazar 46), Francescoli, Aguilera, Fonseca (Saralegui 73), Cedres.
Bolivia: Trucco; Quinteros, Rimba, Rivero, Juan Pena, Cristaldo, Melgar, Borja, Baldivieso (Pinedo 80), Sanchez, Ramallo (Alvaro Pena 62).

Ciudad Guyana, 12 September 1993, 2000
Venezuela (1) 2 *(Garcia J l, Morales 47)*
Ecuador (1) 1 *(Tenorio B 5)*

Venezuela: Gomez; Filosa, Tortolero, Morales, Gonzalez, Paezpumar, Echenausi, Rivas H, Rivas S, Garcia J (Contreras 46), Camacho (Rodriguez 80).
Ecuador: Espinoza; Munoz (Aviles 58), Noriega, Capurro, Hurtado I, Carcelen, Coronel, Tenorio B, Fernandez, Hurtado E, Chala (Gavica 58).

Rio, 19 September 1993, 101,500
Brazil (0) 2 *(Romario 72, 82)*
Uruguay (0) 0

Brazil: Taffarel; Jorginho, Ricardo Rocha, Ricardo Gomes, Branco, Mauro Silva, Dunga, Rai, Zinho, Bebeto, Romario.
Uruguay: Siboldi; Herrera, Canals (Adrian Paz 68), Mendez, Kanapkis, Batista, Gutierrez, Dorta, Francescoli (Zalazar 68), Ruben Sosa, Fonseca.

Guayaquil, 19 September 1993, 5000
Ecuador (0) 1 *(Noriega 72)*
Bolivia (1) 1 *(Ramallo 45)*

Ecuador: Espinoza; Coronel, Noriega, Hurtado I, Capurro, Fernandez, Chala (Carcelen 54), Tenorio M, Aguinaga, Aviles, Munoz (Gavica 43).
Bolivia: Trucco; Soruco (Pinedo 78), Sandy, Quinteros, Cristaldo, Rivero, Borja, Melgar, Baldivieso, Sanchez, Ramallo (Etcheverry 58).

Group B

	P	W	D	L	F	A	Pts
Brazil	8	5	2	1	20	4	12
Bolivia	8	5	1	2	22	11	11
Uruguay	8	4	2	2	10	7	10
Ecuador	8	1	3	4	7	7	5
Venezuela	8	1	0	7	4	34	2

Brazil and Bolivia qualified

Concacaf
USA qualified as hosts
Pre-preliminary round
Dominican Republic 1, Puerto Rico 2
Puerto Rico 1, Dominican Republic 1
St Lucia 1, St Vincent 0
St Vincent 3, St Lucia 1

Preliminary round
Bermuda 1, Haiti 0
Haiti 2, Bermuda 1
Jamaica 2, Puerto Rico 1
Puerto Rico 0, Jamaica 1
Cuba withdrew, St Vincent w.o
Netherlands Antilles 1, Antigua 1
Antigua 3, Netherlands Antilles 0
Guyana 1, Surinam 2
Surinam 1, Guyana 1
Barbados 1, Trinidad & Tobago 2
Trinidad & Tobago 3, Barbados 0

First round
Central Region
Guatemala 0, Honduras 0
Honduras 2, Guatemala 0
Panama 1, Costa Rica 0
Costa Rica 5, Panama 1
Nicaragua 0, El Salvador 5
El Salvador 5, Nicaragua 1

Caribbean Region
Surinam 0, St Vincent 0
St Vincent 2, Surinam 1
Antigua 0, Bermuda 3
Bermuda 2, Antigua 1
Trinidad & Tobago 1, Jamaica 2
Jamaica 1, Trinidad & Tobago 1

Second round
Group A
Costa Rica 2, Honduras 3
St Vincent 0, Mexico 4
Mexico 2, Honduras 0
St Vincent 0, Costa Rica 1
Mexico 4, Costa Rica 0
St Vincent 0, Honduras 4
Honduras 4, St Vincent 0
Costa Rica 2, Mexico 0
Honduras 2, Costa Rica 1
Mexico 11, St Vincent 0
Costa Rica 5, St Vincent 0
Honduras 1, Mexico 1

Group B
Bermuda 1, El Salvador 0
Jamaica 1, Canada 1
Bermuda 1, Jamaica 1
El Salvador 1, Canada 1
Canada 1, Jamaica 0
El Salvador 4, Bermuda 1
Canada 2, El Salvador 3
Jamaica 3, Bermuda 2
Canada 4, Bermuda 2
Jamaica 0, El Salvador 2
Bermuda 0, Canada 0
El Salvador 2, Jamaica 1

Third Round
Honduras 2, Canada 1
El Salvador 2, Mexico 1
Canada 2, El Salvador 0
Mexico 3, Honduras 0
Canada 3, Honduras 1
Mexico 3, El Salvador 1
Honduras 2, El Salvador 0
Mexico 4, Canada 0
Honduras 1, Mexico 4
El Salvador 1, Canada 2
Canada 1, Mexico 2
El Salvador 2, Honduras 1

Mexico qualified

Oceania
Group 1
Solomon Islands 1, Tahiti 1
Solomon Islands 1, Australia 2
Tahiti 0, Australia 3
Australia 2, Tahiti 0
Australia 6, Solomon Islands 1
Tahiti 4, Solomon Islands 2

Group 2
New Zealand 3, Fiji 0
Vanuatu 1, New Zealand 4
New Zealand 8, Vanuatu 0
Fiji 3, Vanuatu 0
Fiji 0, New Zealand 0
Vanuatu 0, Fiji 3

Second Round
New Zealand 0, Australia 1
Australia 3, New Zealand 0

Winner Oceania v Second Concacaf
Canada 2, Australia 1
Australia 2, Canada 1
Australia won 4-1 on penalties

Winner Oceania/Concacaf v 4th South America
Sydney, 31 October 1993, 43,967
Argentina (1) 1 *(Aurelio Vidmar 42)*
Australia (1) 1 *(Balbo 37)*
Australia: Bosnich; Tony Vidmar (Mitchell 72), Tobin, Zelic, Van Bierk, Durakovic, Ivanovic, Wade, Slater, Aurelio Vidmar, Arnold.
Argentina: Goycochea; Chamot, Borelli, Vazquez, MacAlister, Perez, Redondo, Basualdo JH (Zapata 70), Maradona, Balbo (Careres 88), Batistuta.

Buenos Aires, 17 November 1993, 60,000
Argentina (0) 1 *(Batistuta 60)*
Australia (0) 0
Argentina: Goycochea; Chamot, Vazquez, Ruggeri, MacAlister, Simeone, Perez, Redondo, Maradona, Balbo (Zapata 68), Batistuta.
Australia: Zabica; Ivanovic, Tony Vidmar (Veart 63), Durakovic, Tobin, Van Bierk, Slater, Wade, Aurelio Vidmar, Arnold, Farina.

Argentina qualified

Africa
First Round
Group A
Algeria 3, Burundi 1
Burundi 1, Ghana 0
Ghana 2, Algeria 0
Burundi 0, Algeria 0
Ghana 1, Burundi 0
Algeria 2, Ghana 1
Uganda withdrew

Group B
Zaire 4, Liberia 2
Cameroon 5, Swaziland 0
Swaziland 1, Zaire 0
Zaire 1, Cameroon 2
Swaziland 0, Cameroon 0
Zaire v Swaziland not played

Cameroon 0, Zaire 0
Liberia withdrew

Group C
Zimbabwe 1, Togo 0
Egypt 1, Angola 0
Togo 1, Egypt 4
Zimbabwe 2, Egypt 1
Angola 1, Zimbabwe 1
Togo 1, Zimbabwe 2
Angola 0, Egypt 0
Egypt 3, Togo 0
Zimbabwe 2, Angola 0
Angola v Togo not played
Egypt 0, Zimbabwe 0 (after 2-1 win declared null and void after crowd trouble)
Togo 0, Angola 1

Group D
Nigeria 4, South Africa 0
South Africa 1, Congo 0
Congo 0, Nigeria 1
South Africa 0, Nigeria 0
Congo 0, South Africa 1
Nigeria 2, Congo 0
Libya withdrew

Group E
Ivory Coast 6, Botswana 0
Niger 0, Ivory Coast 0
Botswana 0, Niger 1
Botswana 0, Ivory Coast 0
Ivory Coast 1, Niger 0
Niger 2, Botswana 1
Sudan withdrew

Group F
Morocco 5, Ethiopia 0
Tunisia 5, Benin 1
Benin 0, Morocco 1
Ethiopia 0, Tunisia 1
Ethiopia 3, Benin 1
Tunisia 1, Morocco 1
Benin 0, Tunisia 5
Ethiopia 0, Morocco 1
Morocco 5, Benin 0
Tunisia 3, Ethiopia 0
Benin 1, Ethiopia 0
Morocco 0, Tunisia 0

Group G
Gabon 3, Mozambique 1
Mozambique 0, Senegal 1

238

Gabon 3, Senegal 2
Mozambique 1, Gabon 1
Senegal 6, Mozambique 1
Senegal 1, Gabon 0
Mauritania withdrew

Group H
Madagascar 3, Namibia 0
Zambia 2, Tanzania 0
Tanzania 0, Madagascar 0
Namibia 0, Zambia 4
Tanzania 2, Namibia 0
Madagascar 2, Zambia 0
Tanzania 1, Zambia 3
Namibia 0, Madagascar 1
Zambia 4, Namibia 0
Zambia 3, Madagascar 1
Tanzania withdrew

Group I
Guinea 4, Kenya 0
Kenya 2, Guinea 0
Mali and Gambia withdrew

Second round
Group A
Algeria 1, Ivory Coast 1
Ivory Coast 2, Nigeria 1
Nigeria 4, Algeria 1
Ivory Coast 1, Algeria 0
Nigeria 4, Ivory Coast 1
Algeria 1, Nigeria 1

Group B
Morocco 1, Senegal 0
Zambia 2, Morocco 1
Senegal 1, Morocco 3
Senegal 0, Zambia 1
Zambia 4, Senegal 0
Morocco 1, Zambia 0

Morocco qualified

Group C
Cameroon 3, Guinea 1
Guinea 3, Zimbabwe 0
Zimbabwe 1, Cameroon 0
Guinea 0, Cameroon 1
Zimbabwe 1, Guinea 0
Cameroon 3, Zimbabwe 1

Cameroon qualified

Asia
First round
Group A (in Jordan)
China, Iraq, Jordan, Yemen, Pakistan
Jordan 1, Yemen 1
Pakistan 0, China 5
Jordan 1, Iraq 1
Yeman 5, Pakistan 1
Iraq 6, Yemen 1
Jordan 0, China 3
Iraq 8, Pakistan 0
Yemen 1, China 0
Iraq 1, China 0
Jordan 3, Pakistan 1
(in China)
China 3, Pakistan 0
Yemen 1, Jordan 1
Iraq 4, Jordan 0
Yemen 3, Pakistan 0
China 4, Jordan 1
Iraq 3, Yemen 0
Iraq 4, Pakistan 0
China 1, Yemen 0
Pakistan 1, Jordan 0
China 2, Iraq 1

Group B (in Iran)
Iran, Syria, Oman, Taiwan, Myanmar
(withdrew)
Syria 2, Taiwan 0
Iran 0, Oman 0
Iran 6, Taiwan 0
Oman 0, Syria 0
Iran 1, Syria 1
Oman 2, Taiwan 0
(in Syria)
Oman 0, Iran 1
Syria 8, Taiwan 1
Taiwan 0, Iran 6
Syria 2, Oman 0
Taiwan 1, Oman 7
Syria 1, Iran 1

Group C (in Qatar)
Korea DPR 3, Vietnam 0
Qatar 3, Indonesia 0
Korea DPR 2, Singapore 1
Qatar 4, Vietnam 0
Korea DPR 4, Indonesia 0
Vietnam 2, Singapore 3
Qatar 4, Singapore 1
Vietnam 1, Indonesia 0
Indonesia 0, Singapore 2
Qatar 1, Korea DPR 2

239

(in Singapore)
Indonesia 1, Qatar 4
Vietnam 0, Korea DPR 1
Singapore 1, Korea DPR 3
Vietnam 0, Qatar 4
Indonesia 1, Korea DPR 2
Singapore 1, Vietnam 0
Indonesia 2, Vietnam 1
Singapore 1, Qatar 0
Korea DPR 2, Qatar 2
Singapore 2, Indonesia 1

Group D (in Lebanon)
Hong Kong 2, Bahrain 1
Lebanon 2, India 2
Bahrain 0, Korea Rep 0
Lebanon 2, Hong Kong 2
India 1, Hong Kong 2
Lebanon 0, Korea Rep 1
India 0, Korea Rep 3
Lebanon 0, Bahrain 0
Bahrain 2, India 1
Hong Kong 0, Korea Rep 3
(in Korea Rep)
Bahrain 0, Lebanon 0
Korea Rep 4, Hong Kong 1
Bahrain 3, India 0
Korea Rep 2, Lebanon 0
Korea Rep 7, India 0
Lebanon 2, Hong Kong 1
Lebanon 2, India 1
Bahrain 3, Hong Kong 0
Korea Rep 3, Bahrain 0
India 3, Hong Kong 1

Group E (in Malaysia)
Macao 0, Saudi Arabia 6
Malaysia 1, Kuwait 1
Macao 1, Kuwait 10
Malaysia 1, Saudi Arabia 1
Kuwait 0, Saudi Arabia 0
Malaysia 9, Macao 0
(in Saudi Arabia)
Kuwait 2, Malaysia 0
Saudi Arabia 8, Macao 0

Kuwait 8, Macao 0
Saudi Arabia 3, Malaysia 0
Macao 0, Malaysia 5
Saudi Arabia 2, Kuwait 0

Group F (in Japan)
Japan 1, Thailand 0
Sri Lanka 0, UAE 4
Japan 8, Bangladesh 0
Thailand 1, Sri Lanka 0
Sri Lanka 0, Bangladesh 1
UAE 1, Thailand 0
Japan 5, Sri Lanka 0
UAE 1, Bangladesh 0
Japan 2, UAE 0
Thailand 4, Bangladesh 1
(in UAE)
Thailand 0, Japan 1
UAE 3, Sri Lanka 0
Bangladesh 1, Japan 4
Thailand 1, UAE 2
Bangladesh 0, UAE 7
Sri Lanka 0, Thailand 3
Bangladesh 1, Thailand 4
Sri Lanka 0, Japan 6
Bangladesh 3, Sri Lanka 0
UAE 1, Japan 1
Second Round (in Qatar)
Korea DPR 3, Iraq 2
Saudi Arabia 0, Japan 0
Iran 0, Korea Rep 3
Korea DPR 1, Saudi Arabia 2
Japan 1, Iran 2
Iraq 2, Korea Rep 2
Korea DPR 0, Japan 3
Iran 1, Iraq 2
Korea Rep 1, Saudi Arabia 1
Iraq 1, Saudi Arabia 1
Japan 1, Korea Rep 0
Iran 2, Korea DPR 1
Korea Rep 3, Korea DPR 0
Saudi Arabia 4, Iran 3
Iraq 2, Japan 2

Saudi Arabia and Korea Rep qualified

240

WORLD CUP 1994 Final Tournament

First Round
Group A
Detroit, 18 June 1994, 77,557
USA (1) 1 *(Wynalda 45)*

Switzerland (1) 1 *(Bregy 40)*

USA: Meola; Kooiman, Balboa, Lalas, Caligiuri, Ramos, Dooley, Sorber, Wynalda (Wegerle 59), Harkes, Stewart (Cobi Jones 81).
Switzerland: Pascolo; Hottiger, Herr, Geiger, Quentin, Ohrel, Bregy, Sforza (Wyss 77), Sutter, Bickel (Subiat 73), Chapuisat.
Referee: Lamolina (Argentina).

Los Angeles, 18 June 1994, 91,856
Colombia (1) 1 *(Valencia 42)*

Romania (2) 3 *(Raducioiu 15, 87, Hagi 33)*

Colombia: Cordoba; Herrera, Perea, Escobar, Perez, Alvarez, Valderrama, Rincon, Gomez, Asprilla, Valencia.
Romania: Stelea; Belodedici, Prodan, Mihali, Petrescu, Lupescu, Popescu, Hagi, Munteanu, Dumitrescu (Selymes 63), Raducioiu (Papura 90).
Referee: Al Sharif (Syria).

Detroit, 22 June 1994, 61,428
Romania (1) 1 *(Hagi 36)*

Switzerland (1) 4 *(Sutter 16, Chapuisat 53, Knup 66, 73)*

Romania: Stelea; Belodedici, Prodan, Mihali, Petrescu, Lupescu (Panduru 85), Popescu, Munteanu, Hagi, Dumitrescu (Vladiou 71), Raducioiu.
Switzerland: Pascolo; Hottiger, Herr, Geiger, Quentin, Ohrel (Sylvestre 84), Bregy, Sforza, Sutter (Bickel 71), Knup, Chapuisat.
Referee: Jouini (Tunisia).

Los Angeles, 23 June 1994, 93,194
USA (1) 2 *(Escobar (og) 35, Stewart 53)*

Colombia (0) 1 *(Valencia 90)*

USA: Meola; Balboa, Clavijo, Lalas, Caligiuri, Ramos, Harkes, Dooley, Sorber, Stewart (Cobi Jones 76), Wynalda (Wegerle 61).
Colombia: Cordoba; Perez, Perea, Escobar, Herrera, Alvarez, Valderrama, Rincon, Gaviria, Asprilla (Valencia 46), De Avila (Valenciano 46).
Referee: Baldas (Italy).

Los Angeles, 26 June 1994, 93,869
USA (0) 0

Romania (1) 1 *(Petrescu 17)*

USA. Meola; Clavijo, Balboa, Lalas, Caligiuri, Harkes, Dooley, Ramos (Cobi Jones 64), Sorber (Wegerle 75), Stewart, Wynalda.
Romania. Prunea; Belodedici (Mihali 89), Petrescu, Selymes, Lupescu, Prodan, Hagi, Popescu, Munteanu, Dumitrescu, Raducioiu (Galca 84).
Referee: Van der Ende (Holland).

San Francisco, 26 June 1994, 83,769
Switzerland (0) 0

Colombia (1) 2 *(Gaviria 44, Lozano 90)*

Switzerland: Pascolo; Hottiger, Herr, Geiger, Quentin, Ohrel, Bregy, Sforza, Sutter (Subiat 82), Knup (Grassi 82), Chapuisat.
Colombia: Cordoba; Herrera, Mendoza, Escobar, Perez, Gaviria (Lozano 79), Alvarez, Valderrama, Rincon, Valencia (De Avila 64), Asprilla.
Referee: Mikkelsen (Denmark).

Group A

	P	W	D	L	F	A	Pts
Romania	3	2	0	1	5	5	6
Switzerland	3	1	1	1	5	4	4
USA	3	1	1	1	3	3	4
Colombia	3	1	0	2	4	5	3

Group B

Los Angeles, 20 June 1994, 83,959
Cameroon (1) 2 *(Embe 32, Omam-Biyik 47)*

Sweden (1) 2 *(Ljung 8, Dahlin 75)*

Cameroon: Bell; Song-Bahanag, MBouh, Kalla-Nkongo, Tataw, Libiih, MFede (Maboang-Kessack 87), Foe, Agbo, Omam-Biyik, Embe (Mouyeme 80).
Sweden: Ravelli; Nilsson, Patrik Andersson, Bjorklund, Ljung, Ingesson (Kennet Andersson 75), Thern, Schwarz, Blomqvist (Larsson 61), Brolin, Dahlin.
Referee: Tejada (Peru).

San Francisco, 20 June 1994, 81,061
Brazil (1) 2 *(Romario 26, Rai (pen) 53)*

Russia (0) 0

Brazil: Taffarel; Jorginho, Ricardo Rocha (Aldair 75), Marcio Santos, Leonardo, Dunga (Mazinho 84), Rai, Mauro Silva, Zinho, Bebeto, Romario.
Russia: Kharine; Nikiforov, Khlestov, Ternavski, Gorlukovich, Karpin, Kuznetsov, Piatnitski, Radchenko (Boryduk 78), Tsymbalar, Yuran (Salenko 56).
Referee: Lim Kee Chon (Mauritius).

San Francisco, 24 June 1994, 83,410
Brazil (1) 3 *(Romario 39, Marcio Santos 65, Bebeto 73)*

Cameroon (0) 0

Brazil: Taffarel; Jorginho, Aldair, Marcio Santos, Leonardo, Rai (Muller 82), Mauro Silva, Dunga, Zinho (Paulo Sergio 75), Bebeto, Romario.
Cameroon: Bell; Song-Bahanag, Kalla-Nkono, MBouh, Tataw, Libiih, MFede (Maboang-Kessack 72), Foe, Agbo, Embe (Milla 64), Omam-Biyik.
Referee: Arturo Brizio Carter (Mexico).

Detroit, 25 June 1994, 71,528
Sweden (1) 3 *(Brolin 39 (pen), Dahlin 60, 82)*

Russia (1) 1 *(Salenko (pen) 4)*

;Sweden: Ravelli; Nilsson, Patrik Andersson, Bjorklund (Erlingmark 89), Ljung, Brolin, Schwarz, Thern, Ingesson, Dahlin, Kennet Andersson (Larsson 84).
Russia: Kharine; Nikiforov, Gorlukovich, Kuznetsov, Mostovoi, Khlestov, Onopko, Borodyuk (Galjamin 51), Popov (Karpin 41), Radchenko, Salenko.
Referee: Quiniou (France).

Detroit, 28 June 1994, 77,217
Brazil (0) 1 *(Romario 47)*

Sweden (1) 1 *(Kennet Andersson 24)*

Brazil: Taffarel; Jorginho, Aldair, Marcio Santos, Leonardo, Dunga, Mauro Silva (Mazinho 46), Rai (Paulo Sergio 73), Zinho, Romario, Bebeto.
Sweden: Ravelli; Nilsson, Patrik Andersson, Kamark, Ljung, Larsson (Blomqvist 65), Schwarz (Mild 75), Thern, Ingesson, Kennet Andersson, Brolin.
Referee: Puhl (Hungary).

San Francisco, 28 June 1994, 74,914
Russia (3) 6 *(Salenko l6, 41, 44 (pen), 72, 75, Radchenko 82)*

Cameroon (0) 1 *(Milla 47)*

Russia: Cherchesov; Nikiforov, Ternavski, Khlestov, Tetradze, Onopko, Korneyev (Radchenko 66), Karpin, Lediakhov (Beschastnykh 78), Tsymbalar, Salenko.
Cameroon: Songoo; Tataw, Kalla-Nkongo, Ndip-Akem, Agbo, Libiih, Kana-Biyik, MFede (Milla 46), Foe, Omam-Biyik, Embe (Tchami 49).
Referee: Al Sharif (Syria).

Group B

	P	W	D	L	F	A	Pts
Brazil	3	2	1	0	6	1	7
Sweden	3	1	2	0	6	4	5
Russia	3	1	0	2	7	6	3
Cameroon	3	0	1	2	3	11	1

Group C
Chicago, 17 June 1994, 63,117
Germany (1) 1 *(Klinsmann 61)*

Bolivia (0) 0

Germany: Illgner; Matthaus, Kohler, Berthold, Effenberg, Hassler (Strunz 83), Sammer, Moller, Brehme, Riedle (Basler 60), Klinsmann.
Bolivia: Trucco; Quinteros, Rimba, Sandy, Borja, Soria, Erwin Sanchez, Melgar, Cristaldo, Romallo (Etcheverry 79), Baldivieso (Moreno 66).
Referee: Arturo Brizio Carter (Mexico).

Dallas, 18 June 1994, 56,247
Spain (0) 2 *(Salinas 50, Goicoechea 55)*

South Korea (0) 2 *(Hong Myung-Bo 84, Seo Jung-Won 90)*

Spain: Canizares; Nadal, Ferrer, Sergi, Fernandez, Alkorta, Goicoechea, Hierro, Guerrero (Caminero 46), Luis Enrique, Salinas (Felipe 63).
South Korea: Choi In-Young; Hong-Gi, Kim Pan-Keun, Park Jung-Bae, Lee Young-Jin, Noh Jung-Yoon (Ha Seok-Ju 72), Kim Joo-Sung (Seo Jung-Won 59), Ko Jeong-Woon, Choi Young-Il, Hong Myong-Bo, Hwang Sun-Hong.
Referee: Mikkelsen (Denmark).

Chicago, 21 June 1994, 63,113
Germany (0) 1 *(Klinsmann 48)*

Spain (1) 1 *(Goicoechea 14)*

Germany. Illgner; Matthaus, Kohler, Berthold, Strunz, Hassler, Effenberg, Sammer, Brehme, Moller (Voller 62), Klinsmann.
Spain: Zubizarreta; Ferrer, Abelardo, Alkorta, Sergi, Goicoechea (Bakero 65), Hierro, Caminero, Guardiola (Camarasa 78), Luis Enrique, Salinas.
Referee. Ernesto Filippi Cavani (Uruguay).

Boston, 24 June 1994, 53,000
South Korea (0) 0

Bolivia (0) 0

South Korea: Choi In-Young; Hong Myung-Bo, Kim Pan-Keun, Shin Hong-Gi, Noh Jung-Yoon (Choi Young-Il 71), Park Jung-Bae, Ko Jeong-Woon, Lee Young-Jin, Kim Joo-Sung, Hwang Sun-Hong, Seo Jung-Won (Ha Seok-Ju 65).
Bolivia: Trucco; Rimba, Quinteros, Sandy, Cristaldo, Borja, Melgar, Soria, Erwin Sanchez, Baldivieso, Ramallo (Pena 66).
Referee: Mottram (Scotland).

Chicago, 27 June 1994, 63,089
Bolivia (0) 1 *(Erwin Sanchez 67)*

Spain (1) 3 *(Guardiola 20 (pen), Caminero 66, 71)*

Bolivia: Trucco; Rimba, Pena, Sandy, Soruco, Borja, Erwin Sanchez, Soria (Castillo 63), Melgar, Ramallo, Ramos (Morena 46).
Spain: Zubizarreta; Ferrer, Voro, Abelardo, Sergi, Goicoechea, Guardiola, Guerrero, Caminero, Felipe (Hierro 46), Salinas.
Referee: Badilla (Costa Rica).

Dallas, 27 June 1994, 63,998
Germany (3) 3 *(Klinsmann 12, 37, Riedle 20)*

South Korea (0) 2 *(Hwang Sun-Hong 52, Hong Myung-Bo 63)*

Germany: Illgner; Matthaus (Moller 64), Kohler, Berthold, Effenberg (Helmer 75), Hassler, Buchwald, Sammer, Brehme, Riedle, Klinsmann.
South Korea: Choi In-Young (Lee Won-Jae 46); Hong Myung-Bo, Kim Pan-Keun, Choi Young-Il, Park Jung-Bae, Cho Jin-Ho (Seo Jung-Won 46), Lee Young-Jin (Chung Jong-Son 40), Kim Joo-Sung, Shin Hong-Gi, Ko Jeong-Woon, Hwang Sun-Hong.
Referee: Quiniou (France).

Group C

	P	W	D	L	F	A	Pts
Germany	3	2	1	0	5	3	7
Spain	3	1	2	0	6	4	5
South Korea	3	0	2	1	4	5	2
Bolivia	3	0	1	2	1	4	1

Group D
Boston, 21 June 1994, 53,644
Argentina (2) 4 *(Batistuta 2, 45, 90 (pen), Maradona 60)*

Greece (0) 0

Argentina: Islas; Ruggeri, Sensini, Caceres, Chamot, Simeone, Redondo, Maradona (Ortega 84), Balbo (Mancuso 81), Caniggia, Batistuta.
Greece: Minou; Manolas, Apostolakis, Kolitsidakis, Kalitzakis, Tsiantakis (Marangos 46), Tsalouchidis, Nioplias, Koifidis, Saravakos, Machlas (Mistropoulos 59).
Referee: Angeles (USA).

244

Dallas, 22 June 1994, 44,932
Bulgaria (0) 0
Nigeria (2) 3 *(Yekini 21, Amokachi 43, Amunike 54)*

Bulgaria: Mikhailov; Hubchev, Kremenliev, Ivanov, Tzvetanov, Borimirov (Yordanov 71), Lechkov (Sirakov 57), Balakov, Jankov, Kostadinov, Stoichkov.
Nigeria: Rufai; Nwanu, Eguavoen, Uche, Iroha, Siasia (Adepoju 67), Finidi (Ezeugo 76), Oliseh, Amunike, Amokachi, Yekini.
Referee: Badilla (Costa Rica).

Boston, 25 June 1994, 54,453
Argentina (2) 2 *(Caniggia 22, 29)*
Nigeria (1) 1 *(Siasia 9)*

Argentina: Islas; Sinisi (Diaz 87), Caceres, Ruggeri, Chamot, Balbo (Mancuso 71), Simeone, Maradona, Redondo, Batistuta, Caniggia.
Nigeria: Rufai; Nwanu, Eguavoen, Okechukwu, Finidi, Siasia (Adepoju 57), Emenalo, Oliseh (Okocha 87), Amokachi, Yekini, Amunike.
Referee: Karlsson (Sweden).

Chicago, 26 June 1994, 63,160
Bulgaria (1) 4 *(Stoichkov 5 (pen), 56 (pen), Lechkov 66, Borimirov 90)*
Greece (0) 0

Bulgaria: Mikhailov; Hubchev, Kremenliev, Ivanov, Tzvetanov (Kiriakov 77), Yankov, Lechkov, Balakov, Kostadinov (Borimirov 82), Sirakov, Stoichkov.
Greece: Atmatzidis; Apostolakis, Karataidis, Karagiannis, Kalitzakis, Marangos, Nioplias, Hantzidis (Mistropoulos 46), Kofidis, Machlas, Alexoudis (Dimitriadis 59).
Referee: Bujsaim (UAE).

Boston, 1 July 1994, 53,001
Greece (0) 0
Nigeria (1) 2 *(Finidi 45, Amokachi 90)*

Greece: Karkamanis; Alexiou, Hantzidis, Karagiannis, Kofidis (Dimitriadis 79), Nioplias, Kalitzakis, Tsalouchidis, Alexandris, Machlas, Mitropoulos (Tsiantakis 73).
Nigeria: Rufai; Keshi, Okechukwu, Nwanu, Siasia, Amokachi, Oliseh, Finidi (Adepoju 83), Emenalo, Yekini (Okocha 79), Amunike.
Referee: Mottram (Scotland).

Dallas, 1 July 1994, 63,998
Argentina (0) 0
Bulgaria (0) 2 *(Stoichkov 61, Sirakov 90)*

Argentina: Islas; Caceres, Ruggeri, Chamot, Diaz, Rodriguez (Medina 66), Simeone, Redondo, Balbo, Batistuta, Caniggia (Ortega 27).
Bulgaria: Mikhailov; Hubchev, Kremenliev, Ivanov, Kostadinov (Kiriakov 74), Lechkov (Borimirov 76), Yankov, Balakov, Tzvetanov, Sirakov, Stoichkov.
Referee: Jouini (Tunisia).

Group D

	P	W	D	L	F	A	Pts
Nigeria	3	2	0	1	6	2	4
Bulgaria	3	2	0	1	6	3	6
Argentina	3	2	0	1	6	3	6
Greece	3	0	0	3	0	10	0

Group E
New York, 18 June 1994, 73,511
Italy (0) 0

Republic of Ireland (1) 1 *(Houghton 12)*

Italy: Pagliuca; Tassotti, Baresi, Costacurta, Maldini, Donadoni, Dino Baggio, Albertini, Evani (Massaro 46), Roberto Baggio, Signori (Berti 84).
Republic of Ireland: Bonner; Irwin, McGrath, Babb, Phelan, Houghton (McAteer 68), Keane, Sheridan, Townsend, Staunton, Coyne (Aldridge 90).
Referee: Van der Ende (Holland).

Washington, 19 June 1994, 52,359
Norway (0) 1 *(Rekdal 85)*

Mexico (0) 0

Norway: Thorstvedt; Haaland, Bratseth, Berg, Bjornebye, Flo, Bohinen, Mykland (Rekdal 79), Leonhardsen, Jakobsen (Halle 46), Fjortoft.
Mexico: Campos; Gutierrez (Bernal 70), Suarez, Juan de Dios Ramirez, Jesus Ramirez, Ambriz, Del Olmo, Valdez (Galdino 46), Luis Garcia, Zague, Sanchez.
Referee: Puhl (Hungary).

New York, 23 June 1994, 74,624
Italy (0) 1 *(Dino Baggio 68)*

Norway (0) 0

Italy: Pagliuca; Benarrivo, Costacurta, Baresi (Apolloni 48), Maldini, Berti, Albertini, Dino Baggio, Signori, Casiraghi (Massaro 67), Roberto Baggio (Marchegiani 21).
Norway: Thorstvedt; Haaland, Berg, Bratseth, Bjornebye, Rushfeldt (Jakobsen 46), Leonhardsen, Mykland (Rekdal 80), Bohinen, Flo, Fjortoft.
Referee: Krug (Germany).

Florida, 24 June 1994, 61,219
Mexico (1) 2 *(Luis Garcia 44, 66)*

Republic of Ireland (0) 1 *(Aldridge 84)*

Mexico: Campos; Del Olmo, Suarez, Juan de Dios Ramirez, Rodriguez (Salvador 80), Bernal, Ambriz, Luis Garcia, Garcia Aspe, Hermosillo (Gutierrez 80), Zague.
Republic of Ireland: Bonner; Irwin, McGrath, Babb, Phelan, Houghton, Keane, Sheridan, Townsend, Staunton (Aldridge 69), Coyne (McAteer 66).
Referee: Rothlisberger (Switzerland).

New York, 28 June 1994, 76,332
Republic of Ireland (0) 0

Norway (0) 0

Republic of Ireland: Bonner; Kelly G, McGrath, Babb, Staunton, Keane, McAteer, Sheridan, Townsend (Whelan 74), Houghton, Aldridge (Kelly D 64).
Norway: Thorstvedt; Berg, Bratseth, Johnsen, Halle (Jakobsen 35), Flo, Mykland, Leonhardsen (Bohinen 68), Rekdal, Bjornebye, Sorloth.
Referee: Torres Cadena (Colombia).

Washington, 28 June 1994, 53,186
Italy (0) 1 *(Massaro 48)*

Mexico (0) 1 *(Bernal 58)*

Italy: Marchegiani; Benarrivo, Apolloni, Costacurta, Maldini, Berti, Albertini, Dino Baggio (Donadoni 66), Signori, Roberto Baggio, Casiraghi (Massaro 46).
Mexico: Campos; Rodriguez, Suarez, Juan de Dios Ramirez, Del Olmo, Bernal, Ambriz, Luis Garcia (Chabaz 83), Garcia Aspe, Hermosillo, Zague.
Referee: Lamolina (Argentina).

Group E

	P	W	D	L	F	A	Pts
Mexico	3	1	1	1	3	3	4
Republic of Ireland	3	1	1	1	2	2	4
Italy	3	1	1	1	2	2	4
Norway	3	1	1	1	1	1	4

Group F

Florida, 19 June 1994, 60,790
Belgium (1) 1 *(Degryse 11)*

Morocco (0) 0

Belgium: Preud'homme; De Wolf, Grun, Smidts, Staelens, Van der Elst, Scifo, Boffin (Borkelmans 85), Degryse, Weber, Nilis (Emmers 54).
Morocco: Azmi (Alaoui El Achraf 88); Naybet, Abdella, Triki, El Hadrioui, Hababi, Azzouzi, El Haddaoui (Bahja 68), Daoudi, Hadji, Chaouch (Samadi 81).
Referee: Torres Cadena (Colombia).

Washington, 21 June 1994, 52,535
Holland (0) 2 *(Jonk 50, Taument 87)*

Saudi Arabia (1) 1 *(Amin 19)*

Holland: De Goey; Koeman, Van Gobbel, Frank de Boer, Rijkaard, Jonk, Wouters, Bergkamp, Overmars (Taument 59), Ronald de Boer, Roy (Van Vossen 82).
Saudi Arabia: Al Deayea; Al Dosari, Al Khlaiwi, Madani, Al Jawad, Al Bishi, Owairan (Saleh 69), Amin, Jebreen, Al Muwallid, Majed Mohammed (Falatah 46).
Referee: Vega Diaz (Spain).

Florida, 25 June 1994, 61,219
Belgium (0) 1 *(Albert 66)*

Holland (0) 0

Belgium: Preud'homme; De Wolf, Grun, Albert, Emmers (Medved 78), Scifo, Van der Elst, Staelens, Borkelmans (Smidts 60), Weber, Degryse.
Holland: De Goey; Koeman, Valckx, Frank de Boer, Taument (Overmars 64), Rijkaard, Bergkamp, Jonk, Wouters, Roy, Ronald de Boer (Witschge 46).
Referee: Marsiglia (Brazil).

New York, 25 June 1994, 72,404
Saudi Arabia (1) 2 *(Al Jaber 8 (pen), Amin 46)*

Morocco (1) 1 *(Chaouch 28)*

Saudi Arabia: Al Deayea; Al Jawad, Al Anazi (Zebermawi 30), Madani, Al Khlaiwi, Al Bishi, Amin, Jebreen, Al Muwallid, Al Jaber (Al Ghesheyan 81), Owairan.
Morocco: Azmi; Naybet, Abdellah (El Ghrissi 57), Triki, El Hadrioui, Hababi (Hadji 74), Azzouzi, El Khalej, Daoudi, Bahja, Chaouch.
Referee: Don (England).

Orlando, 29 June 1994, 60,578
Morocco (0) 1 *(Nader 47)*

Holland (1) 2 *(Bergkamp 43, Roy 78)*

Morocco: Alaoui; El Khalej, Neqrouz, Triki, El Hadrioui, Samadi, Azzouzi (Daoudi 60), Hababi, Nader, Bahja, Bouyboud (Hadji 46).
Holland: De Goey; Koeman, Frank de Boer, Valckx, Winter, Jonk, Wouters, Witschge, Overmars (Taument 55), Bergkamp, Van Vossen (Roy 66).
Referee: Tejada (Peru).

Washington, 29 June 1994, 52,959
Belgium (0) 0

Saudi Arabia (1) 1 *(Owairan 5)*

Belgium: Preud'homme; De Wolf, Smidts, Albert, Medved, Staelens, Van der Elst, Scifo, Boffin, Degryse (Nilis 24), Wilmots (Weber 54).
Saudi Arabia: Al Deayea; Zebermawi, Madani, Al Khaiwi, Al Jawad, Al Bishi, Saleh, Owairan (Al Dosari 63), Jebreen, Mohammed (Al Muwallid 46), Falatah.
Referee: Krug (Germany).

Group F

	P	W	D	L	F	A	Pts
Holland	3	2	0	1	4	3	6
Saudi Arabia	3	2	0	1	4	3	6
Belgium	3	2	0	1	2	1	6
Morocco	3	0	0	3	2	5	0

Second Round
Chicago, 2 July 1994, 60,246
Germany (3) 3 *(Voller 6, 39, Klinsmann 11)*

Belgium (1) 2 *(Grun 8, Albert 90)*

Germany: Illgner; Matthaus (Brehme 46), Helmer, Kohler, Berthold, Hassler, Buchwald, Sammer, Wagner, Voller, Klinsmann (Kuntz 86).
Belgium: Preud'homme; De Wolf, Grun, Albert, Emmers, Van der Elst, Scifo, Staelens, Smidts (Bovin 66), Weber, Nilis (Czerniatynski 77).
Referee: Rothlisberger (Switzerland).

Washington, 2 July 1994, 53,141
Spain (1) 3 *(Hierro 15, Luis Enrique 74, Beguiristain 86 (pen))*

Switzerland (0) 0

Spain: Zubizarreta; Alkorta, Nadal, Abelardo, Ferrer, Hierro (Otero 76), Camarasa, Goicoechea (Beguiristain 62), Bakero, Sergi, Luis Enrique.
Switzerland: Pascolo; Hottiger, Herr, Geiger, Quentin (Studer 58), Ohrel (Subiat 73), Bregy, Sforza, Bickel, Knup, Chapuisat.
Referee: Van der Ende (Holland).

Dallas, 3 July 1994, 60,277
Saudi Arabia (0) 1 *(Al Ghesheyan 85)*

Sweden (1) 3 *(Dahlin 6, Kennet Andersson 51, 88)*

Saudi Arabia: Al Deayea; Madani, Zebermawi, Al Khlaiwi, Al Jawad (Al Ghesheyan 55), Al Bishi (Al Muwallid 61), Amin, Owairan, Saleh, Al Jaber, Falatah.
Sweden: Ravelli; Nilsson, Patrik Andersson, Bjorklund (Kamark 55), Ljung, Brolin, Schwarz, Thern (Mild 69), Ingesson, Kennet Andersson, Dahlin.
Referee: Marsiglia (Brazil).

Los Angeles, 3 July 1994, 90,469
Romania (2) 3 *(Dumitrescu 11, 18, Hagi 58)*
Argentina (1) 2 *(Batistuta 16 (pen), Balbo 75)*

Romania. Prunea; Belodedici, Petrescu, Prodan, Munteanu, Mihali, Hagi (Galca 86),
Lupescu, Popescu, Selymes, Dumitrescu (Papura 89).
Argentina: Islas; Sensini (Medina Bello 63), Caceres, Ruggeri, Chamot, Simeone,
Basualdo, Redondo, Ortega, Balboa, Batistuta.
Referee: Parietto (Italy).

Orlando, 4 July 1994, 61,355
Holland (2) 2 *(Bergkamp 12, Jonk 41)*
Republic of Ireland (0) 0

Holland: De Goey; Koeman, Valckx, Frank de Boer, Rijkaard, Winter, Jonk,
Witschge (Numan 79), Overmars, Bergkamp, Van Vossen (Roy 70).
Republic of Ireland: Bonner; Kelly G, McGrath, Babb, Phelan, Houghton, Keane,
Sheridan, Townsend, Staunton (McAteer 64), Coyne (Cascarino 74).
Referee: Mikkelsen (Denmark).

San Francisco, 4 July 1994, 84,147
Brazil (0) 1 *(Bebeto 74)*
USA (0) 0

Brazil: Taffarel; Jorginho, Aldair, Marcio Santos, Leonardo; Mazinho, Dunga,
Mauro Silva, Zinho (Cafu 69), Romario, Bebeto.
USA: Meola; Clavijo, Balboa, Lalas, Caligiuri, Ramos (Wynalda 46), Sorber, Dooley,
Perez (Wegerle 66), Cobi Jones, Stewart.
Referee: Quiniou (France).

Boston, 5 July 1994, 54,367
Nigeria (1) 1 *(Amunike 26)*
Italy (0) 2 *(Roberto Baggio 87, 103 (pen)) aet*

Nigeria: Rufai; Nwanu, Eguavoen, Okechukwu, Emenalo, Finidi, Okocha, Oliseh,
Amunike (Oliha 57), Amokachi (Adepoju 36), Yekini.
Italy: Marchigiani; Mussi, Costacurta, Maldini, Benarrivo, Berti (Dino Baggio 46),
Albertini, Donadoni, Signori (Zola 63), Roberto Baggio, Massaro.
Referee: Arturo Brizio Carter (Mexico).

New York, 5 July 1994, 71,030
Mexico (1) 1 *(Garcia Aspe (pen) 18)*
Bulgaria (1) 1 *(Stoichkov 7) aet*

Mexico: Campos; Rodriguez, Juan de Dios Ramirez, Suarez, Jesus Ramirez, Bernal,
Ambriz, Luis Garcia, Garcia Aspe, Zague, Galindo.
Bulgaria: Mikhailov; Hubchev, Yordanov, Kremenliev, Kiriakov, Sirakov (Guentchev
104), Borimirov, Lechkov, Balakov, Stoichkov, Kostadinov (Mitarski 120).
Bulgaria won 3-1 on penalties
Referee: Al Sharif (Syria).

Quarter-finals
Boston, 9 July 1994, 53,644
Italy (1) 2 *(Dino Baggio 26, Roberto Baggio 88)*

Spain (0) 1 *(Caminero 59)*

Italy: Pagliuca; Tassotti, Costacurta, Maldini, Benarrivo, Conte (Berti 66), Dino Baggio, Albertini (Signori 46), Donadoni, Roberto Baggio, Massaro.
Spain: Zubizarreta; Nadal, Ferrer, Abelardo, Alkorta, Otero, Goicoechea, Bakero (Hierro 65), Caminero, Sergi (Salinas 60), Luis Enrique.
Referee: Puhl (Hungary).

Dallas, 9 July 1994, 63,998
Holland (0) 2 *(Bergkamp 63, Winter 76)*

Brazil (0) 3 *(Romario 52, Bebeto 61, Branco 81)*

Holland: De Goey; Koeman, Valckx, Wouters, Winter, Rijkaard (Ronald de Boer 65), Jonk, Witschge, Overmars, Bergkamp, Van Vossen (Roy 54).
Brazil: Taffarel; Jorginho, Aldair, Marcio Santos, Branco (Cafu 90), Mazinho (Rai 81), Dunga, Mauro Silva, Zinho, Bebeto, Romario.
Referee: Badilla (Costa Rica).

New York, 10 July 1994, 72,416
Bulgaria (0) 2 *(Stoichkov 75, Lechkov 79)*

Germany (0) 1 *(Matthaus 48 (pen))*

Bulgaria: Mikhailov; Hubchev, Ivanov, Yankov, Kiriakov, Lechkov, Sirakov, Balakov, Tzvetanov, Kostadinov (Guentchev 90), Stoichkov (Yordanov 84).
Germany: Illgner; Matthaus, Kohler, Helmer, Berthold, Hassler (Brehme 83), Buchwald, Moller, Wagner (Strunz 58), Voller, Klinsmann.
Referee: Torres Cadena (Colombia).

San Francisco, 10 July 1994, 81,715
Sweden (0) 2 *(Brolin 79, Kennet Andersson 115)*

Romania (0) 2 *(Raducioiu 89, 101) aet*

Sweden. Ravelli; Nilsson, Patrik Andersson, Bjorklund (Kamark 84), Ljung, Brolin, Schwarz, Mild, Ingesson, Kennet Andersson, Dahlin (Larsson).
Romania: Prunea; Belodedici, Prodan, Popescu, Lupescu, Petrescu, Selymes, Hagi, Munteanu (Panduru 84), Dumitrescu, Raducioiu.
Referee: Don (England).
Sweden won 5-4 on penalties

Semi-finals
New York, 13 July 1994, 77,094
Italy (2) 2 *(Roberto Baggio 21, 26)*

Bulgaria (1) 1 *(Stoichkov 44 (pen))*

Italy. Pagliuca; Mussi, Costacurta, Maldini, Benarrivo, Berti, Albertini, Dino Baggio (Conte 56), Donadoni, Casiraghi, Roberto Baggio (Signori 71).
Bulgaria. Mikhailov; Kiriakov, Ivanov, Hubchev, Tzvetanov, Yankov, Lechkov, Balakov, Sirakov, Kostadinov (Yordanov 72), Stoichkov (Guentchev 79).
Referee: Quiniou (France).

Los Angeles, 13 July 1994, 84,569
Brazil (0) 1 *(Romario 80)*

Sweden (0) 0

Brazil: Taffarel; Jorginho, Aldair, Marcio Santos, Branco, Dunga, Mauro Silva, Mazinho (Rai 46), Zinho, Bebeto, Romario.
Sweden: Ravelli; Nilsson, Patrik Andersson, Bjorklund, Ljung, Mild, Brolin, Thern, Ingesson, Dahlin (Rehn), Kennet Andersson.
Referee: Torres Cadena (Colombia).

Third/Fourth place match
Los Angeles, 16 July 1994, 83,716
Sweden (4) 4 *(Brolin 8, Mild 30, Larsson 37, Kennet Andersson 39)*

Bulgaria (0) 0

Sweden: Ravelli; Nilsson, Patrik Andersson, Bjorklund, Kamark, Brolin, Schwarz, Mild, Ingesson, Kennet Andersson, Larsson (Limpar 79).
Bulgaria: Mikhailov (Nikolov 46); Kiriakov, Ivanov (Kremenliev 42), Hubchev, Tzvetanov, Yankov, Lechkov, Sirakov (Yordanov 46), Balakov, Stoichkov, Kostadinov.
Referee: Bujsaim (UAE).

Final
Los Angeles, 17 July 1994, 94,194
Brazil (0) 0

Italy (0) 0 *aet*

Brazil: Taffarel; Jorginho (Cafu 21), Marcio Santos, Aldair, Branco, Mazinho, Mauro Silva, Dunga, Zinho (Viola 109), Bebeto, Romario.
Italy: Pagliuca; Mussi (Apolloni 34), Maldini, Baresi, Benarrivo, Donadoni, Albertini, Dino Baggio (Evani 101), Berti, Roberto Baggio, Massaro.
Brazil won 3-2 on penalties
Referee: Puhl (Hungary).
Penalty sequence: Baresi (shot over); Marcio Santos (saved); Albertini (scored); Romario (scored off upright); Evani (scored); Branco (scored); Massaro (saved); Dunga (scored), Roberto Baggio (shot over).

EUROPEAN SUPER CUP

Played annually between the winners of the European Champions' Cup and the European Cup-Winners' Cup. AC Milan replaced Marseille in 1993–94.

Previous Matches
1972 Ajax beat Rangers 3-1, 3-2
1973 Ajax beat AC Milan 0-1, 6-0
1974 Not contested
1975 Dynamo Kiev beat Bayern Munich 1-0, 2-0
1976 Anderlecht beat Bayern Munich 4-1, 1-2
1977 Liverpool beat Hamburg 1-1, 6-0
1978 Anderlecht beat Liverpool 3-1, 1-2
1979 Nottingham F beat Barcelona 1-0, 1-1
1980 Valencia beat Nottingham F 1-0, 1-2
1981 Not contested
1982 Aston Villa beat Barcelona 0-1, 3-0
1983 Aberdeen beat Hamburg 0-0, 2-0
1984 Juventus beat Liverpool 2-0
1985 Juventus v Everton not contested due to UEFA ban on English clubs
1986 Steaua Bucharest beat Dynamo Kiev 1-0
1987 FC Porto beat Ajax 1-0, 1-0
1988 KV Mechelen beat PSV Eindhoven 3-0, 0-1
1989 AC Milan beat Barcelona 1-1, 1-0
1990 AC Milan beat Sampdoria 1-1, 2-0
1991 Manchester U beat Red Star Belgrade 1-0
1992 Barcelona beat Werder Bremen 1-1, 2-1

1993-94

First Leg, 12 January 1994, Parma

Parma (0) 0

AC Milan (1) 1 (*Papin 43*), 8083

Parma: Ballotta; Balleri, Benarrivo (Di Chiara 77), Minotti, Apolloni, Sensini, Brolin, Pin, Crippa, Zola, Asprilla.
AC Milan: Rossi; Tassotti, Maldini, Albertini (Massaro 70), Costacurta, Baresi, Eranio, Desailly, Papin, Savicevic (Panucci 87), Donadoni.
Referee: Diaz Vega (Spain).

Second Leg, 2 February 1994, Milan

AC Milan (0)

Parma (1) 2 (*Sensini 23, Crippa 95*) aet 24,074

AC Milan: Rossi; Panucci, Maldini, Albertini (Lentini 64), Costacurta, Baresi, Laudrup (Carbone 76), Desailly, Papin, Donadoni, Massaro
Parma: Ballotta; Benarrivo, Di Chiara, Minotti, Matrecano, Sensini, Brolin, Pin, Crippa, Zola (Zoratto 104), Asprilla.
Referee: Rothlisberger (Switzerland).

SOUTH AMERICAN CHAMPIONSHIP

(Copa America)

1916 Uruguay	1935 Uruguay	1957 Argentina
1917 Uruguay	1937 Argentina	1959 Argentina
1919 Brazil	1939 Peru	1959 Uruguay
1920 Uruguay	1941 Argentina	1963 Bolivia
1921 Argentina	1942 Uruguay	1967 Uruguay
1922 Brazil	1945 Argentina	1975 Peru
1923 Uruguay	1946 Argentina	1979 Paraguay
1924 Uruguay	1947 Argentina	1983 Uruguay
1925 Argentina	1949 Brazil	1987 Uruguay
1926 Uruguay	1953 Paraguay	1989 Brazil
1927 Argentina	1955 Argentina	1991 Argentina
1929 Argentina	1956 Uruguay	1993 Argentina

SOUTH AMERICAN CUP

(Copa Libertadores)

1960 Penarol (Uruguay)	1977 Boca Juniors (Argentina)
1961 Penarol	1978 Boca Juniors
1962 Santos (Brazil)	1979 Olimpia (Paraguay)
1963 Santos	1980 Nacional
1964 Independiente (Argentina)	1981 Flamengo (Brazil)
1965 Independiente	1982 Penarol
1966 Penarol	1983 Gremio Porto Alegre (Brazil)
1967 Racing Club (Argentina)	1984 Independiente
1968 Estudiantes (Argentina)	1985 Argentinos Juniors (Argentina)
1969 Estudiantes	1986 River Plate (Argentina)
1970 Estudiantes	1987 Penarol
1971 Nacional (Uruguay)	1988 Nacional (Uruguay)
1972 Independiente	1989 Nacional (Colombia)
1973 Independiente	1990 Olimpia
1974 Independiente	1991 Colo Colo (Chile)
1975 Independiente	1992 Sao Paulo (Brazil)
1976 Cruzeiro (Brazil)	1993 Sao Paulo

OTHER BRITISH AND IRISH
INTERNATIONAL MATCHES 1993–94

Wembley, 9 March 1994, 71,970
England (1) 1 *(Platt)*

Denmark (0) 0

England: Seaman, Parker, Adams, Pallister, Le Saux, Anderton, Platt, Ince (Batty), Gascoigne (Le Tissier), Beardsley, Shearer.
Denmark: Schmeichel; Kjeldbjerg, Olsen, Rieper, Vilfort (Hoegh), Laudrup B, Laudrup M, Larsen, Jensen, Dethlefsen, Christensen (Fredrikson).

Cardiff, 9 March 1994, 10,000
Wales (0) 1 *(Coleman)*

Norway (1) 3 *(Flo, Mykland, Jakobsen)*

Wales: Southall; Melville, Young, Coleman, Perry, Horne, Phillips, Blake (Pembridge), Rush, Speed (Saunders), Hughes M (Hughes C).
Norway: Grodas; Loken, Berg, Pedersen, Bjornebye, Flo, Mykland, Rekdal (Solbakken), Bohinen, Jakobsen, Fjortoft (Frigaard).

Windsor Park, 23 March 1994, 5500
Northern Ireland (1) 2 *(Morrow, Gray)*

Romania (0) 0

Northern Ireland: Wright; Fleming, Donaghy, Taggart, Morrow, Wilson, Lomas, Magilton, Hughes (Black), Gray, Quinn (Dowie).
Romania: Prunea (Stelea); Petrescu, Lupescu (Mihali), Belodedici, Prodan, Munteanu, Sabau, Popescu (Gilca), Hagi, Dumitrescu, Raducioiu (Panduru).

Dublin, 23 March 1994, 34,000
Republic of Ireland (0) 0

Russia (0) 0

Republic of Ireland: Bonner (Kelly A); Kelly G, Carey, Babb, McGoldrick, McAteer, O'Brien, Whelan, McLoughlin, Kelly D (Coyne), Cascarino.
Russia: Kharine; Rakhimov, Gorlukovich, Kovtoun, Tetradze, Popov, Komeev (Tchertshev), Radchenko (Kossolapov), Borodyuk, Kuznetsov, Salenko.

Hampden Park, 23 March 1994, 36,809
Scotland (0) 0

Holland (0) 1 *(Roy)*

Scotland: Goram; McKimmie, McLaren, Hendry, Levein (Boyd), Robertson (Collins), McCall, McStay (McKinlay), McAllister, Durie, Nevin (Jess).
Holland: De Goey; Van Gobbel, Blind, Frank De Boer, Witschge, Jonk, Rijkaard, Bosman (Winter), Taument (Overmars), Bergkamp (Gillhaus), Roy.

Windsor Park, 20 April 1994, 7000
Northern Ireland (3) 4 *(Quinn 2, Lomas, Dowie)*

Liechtenstein (0) 1 *(Hasler)*

Northern Ireland: Wright; Fleming, Taggart, Donaghy, Worthington, Magilton (O'Neill), Wilson, Lomas, Hughes, Quinn, Dowie (Gray).
Liechtenstein: Oehry; Stocker, Frick C, Ospelt, Moser, Quaderer, Ritter, Zech, Telser, Matt (Hasler), Frick M.
European Championship Group 6.

Vienna, 20 April 1994, 35,000
Austria (1) 1 *(Hutter)*

Scotland (1) 2 *(McGinlay, McKinlay)*

Austria: Wohlfahrt; Prosenik (Kuhbauer), Kogler, Schottel, Hochmaier, Hutter, Stoger, Herzog, Baur, Polster (Weissenberger), Cerny.
Scotland: Leighton; McKimmie, McLaren, Hendry, Irvine, Boyd (Ferguson I), McKinlay, McAllister, Collins (McCall), McGinlay (Shearer), Jess (Nevin).

Tilburg, 20 April 1994, 30,000
Holland (0) 0

Republic of Ireland (0) 1 *(Coyne)*

Holland: De Goey; Valckx, Koeman (De Wolf), Frank de Boer, Rijkaard, Jonk (Winter), Overmars, Bergkamp (Taument), Roy, Ronald de Boer.
Republic of Ireland: Bonner; Kelly G, Moran, Babb, Phelan (McLoughlin), Whelan, McGoldrick (McAteer), Sheridan, Townsend, Staunton, Coyne (O'Coyle).

Wrexham, 20 April 1994, 4694
Wales (0) 0

Sweden (0) 2 *(Larsson, Brolin)*

Wales: Southall; Horne, Melville, Neilson, Bodin, Bowen (Blackmore), Goss (Blake), Phillips, Speed, Roberts (Hughes C), Rush.
Sweden: Ravelli; Nilsson R (Nilsson M), Andersson P, Bjorklund, Ljung, Larsson, Ingesson (Rehn), Schwarz, Limpar (Blomqvist), Andersson K, Brolin.

Wembley, 17 May 1994, 23,659
England (3) 5 *(Anderton, Beardsley, Platt 2 (1 pen), Shearer)*

Greece (0) 0

England: Flowers; Jones (Pearce), Adams, Bould, Le Saux, Anderton (Le Tissier), Richardson, Merson, Beardsley (Wright), Platt, Shearer.
Greece: Karkamanis; Apostolakis, Kalitzakis, Kolitsidakis (Karataidis), Karagiannis, Tsalouchidis, Nioplias, Hantzidis (Saravakos), Kofidis (Kostis), Tsiantakis, Machlas (Mitropoulos).

Wembley, 22 May 1994, 64,327
England (0) 0

Norway (0) 0

England: Seaman; Jones, Bould, Adams, Le Saux, Anderton (Le Tissier), Ince (Wright), Wise, Platt, Beardsley, Shearer.
Norway: Thorstvedt (By Rise); Berg H, Johnsen, Bratseth, Nilsen (Haaland), Flo, Berg O (Ingebrigtsen), Rekdal, Bohinen, Jakobsen, Fjortoft (Sorloth).

Tallinn, 23 May 1994, 3500
Estonia (0) 1 *(Reim (pen))*

Wales (0) 2 *(Rush, Phillips)*

Estonia: Poom; Kallaste, Lemsalu, Prins, Kaljend, Koauan, Olumets (Pari), Linnumae, Kristal, Reim, Lindmaa.
Wales: Southall; Williams, Melville (Bodin), Neilson, Coleman, Phillips, Horne, Jones R, Hughes, Rush, Bowen J.

Dublin, 24 May 1994, 32,500
Republic of Ireland (0) 1 *(Sheridan)*

Bolivia (0) 0

Republic of Ireland: Bonner; Irwin (Kelly G), Moran (Kernaghan), Babb, Phelan, Houghton (McAteer), Keane, Townsend, Sheridan, Staunton, Coyne (Cascarino).
Bolivia: Trucco; Rimba, Quinteros, Sandy, Sporuco (Pena J), Baldivieso, Melgar, Cristaldo, Pinedo (Borja), Pena A (Castillo), Ramos (Moreno).

Utrecht, 27 May 1994, 17,500
Holland (1) 3 *(Roy, Van Vossen, Irvine (og))*

Scotland (0) 1 *(Shearer)*

Holland: De Goey; Valckx, Jonk, Frank de Boer, Winter, Wouters, Witschge, Ronald de Boer (Numan), Overmars, Gullit (Van Vossen), Roy (Taument).
Scotland: Leighton (Gunn); Clarke, Hendry, Irvine, McKimmie, McCall, McKinlay (Nevin), McAllister, Collins (Ferguson I), McGinlay (Shearer), Durie (Jess).

Hannover, 29 May 1994, 50,000
Germany (0) 0

Republic of Ireland (1) 2 *(Cascarino, Kelly G)*

Germany: Illgner; Kohler (Effenberg), Buchwald (Berthold), Strunz, Basler, Sammer, Wagner, Moller (Hassler), Klinsmann, Riedle (Voller).
Republic of Ireland: Kelly A; Irwin (Kelly G), McGrath, Babb, Phelan, Keane, McAteer (Houghton), Sheridan (Whelan), Townsend, Staunton, Cascarino (Coyne).

Boston, 4 June 1994, 21,153
Colombia (2) 2 *(Perez, Valencia)*

Northern Ireland (0) 0

Colombia: Cordoba; Escobar, Herrera, Gomez, Valderrama, Valencia (De Avila), Alvarez, Perea, Asprilla (Aristizabal), Perez, Rincon.
Northern Ireland: Wright; Fleming, Worthington, Taggart, Donaghy, Magilton (Dennison), Wilson (Lomas), Morrow, Quinn (O'Boyle), Dowie (Patterson), Hughes.

Dublin, 5 June 1994, 43,465
Republic of Ireland (1) 1 *(Townsend)*

Czech Republic (1) 3 *(Kuka 2 (1 pen), Suchoparek)*

Republic of Ireland: Bonner; Kelly G, McGrath (Babb), Kernaghan, Phelan, McGoldrick (McAteer), Sheridan, Townsend, Staunton, Aldridge (Keane), Cascarino (Coyne).
Czech Republic: Kouba; Kubik, Kotulek, Repka, Suchoparek, Nemec, Novotny, Oborsky, Smejkal (Nedved), Frydek (Samec), Kuka.

Miami, 11 June 1994, 8418
Mexico (2) 3 *(Garcia 2 (1 pen), Hermosillo)*

Northern Ireland (0) 0

Mexico: Campos; Gutierrez, Perales, Suarez, Ambriz, Ramirez, Valdes, Del Olmo, Sanchez (Hermosillo 70), Garcia (Galindo) (Espinoza), Zague.
Northern Ireland: Fettis (Wright); Fleming (Morrow), Donaghy, Taggart, Worthington, Wilson (Lennon), Lomas, Magilton (Patterson), Hughes, O'Boyle, Quinn (Dowie).

ENGLAND UNDER–21 TEAMS 1993–94

England Under–21 internationals
7 Sept
England (0) 1 *(Ehiogu)*
Poland (1) 2   5390
England: Walker; Jackson, Ehiogu, Cox, Small, Anderton (Sheron), Flitcroft, Redknapp (Ardley), McManaman, Cole, Sutton.

12 Oct
Holland (0) 1
England (0) 1 *(Flitcroft)*   3330
England: Watson D; Ardley, Minto, Sutton, Ehiogu, Awford, Flitcroft, Sheron, Cole, Clark (Redknapp), Sinclair.

17 Nov
San Marino (0) 0
England (3) 4 *(Fowler, Anderton, Sutton, Sheron)*   200
England: Watson D; Ardley, Small, Newton, Ehiogu, Cox, Anderton, Sheron, Sutton, Fowler (Shipperley), Sinclair (Watson S).

8 Mar
England (0) 1 *(Sinclair)*
Denmark (0) 0   11,553
England: Gerrard (Oakes); Watson S, Edghill, Campbell, Nethercott, Parlour, Redknapp, Barmby (Joachim), Sutton, Bart-Williams, Sinclair.

30 May
Russia (0) 0
England (1) 2 *(Sinclair, Bart-Williams (pen))*
Endgland: Gerrard; Edghill (Makin), Nethercott, Campbell, Gordon, Parlour (Selley), Redknapp, Bart-Williams, Sinclair, Fear, Dyer (Fowler).

31 May
France (1) 3
England (0) 0
England: Nicholls (Oakes); Makin, Nethercott, Campbell, Gordon (Matteo), Sinclair, Fear (Eadie), Redknapp, Bart-Williams (Selley), Dyer, Fowler.

2 June
USA (0) 0
England (1) 3 *(Dyer, Fowler, Redknapp (pen))*
England: Oakes; Makin, Nethercott, Campbell, Gordon, Sinclair, Selley, Redknapp, Eadie, Dyer, Fowler (Fear).

5 June
Belgium (0) 1
England (1) 2 (*Campbell, Dyer*)
England: Oakes; Makin, Nethercott, Campbell, Gordon, Sinclair, Parlour, Redknapp, Matteo, Bart-Williams, Dyer.

7 June
Portugal (0) 0
England (0) 2 (*Sinclair, Dyer*)
England: Oakes; Makin, Nethercott, Campbell, Gordon, Sinclair, Parlour, Redknapp, Matteo, Bart-Williams, Dyer.

POST-WAR INTERNATIONAL APPEARANCES
As at July 1994

ENGLAND

A'Court, A. (5) (Liverpool) 1957/8, 1958/9.

Adams, T.A. (31) (Arsenal) 1986/7, 1987/8, 1988/9, 1990/91, 1992/93, 1993/94.

Allen, C. (5) (QPR) 1983/4, 1986/7 (Tottenham Hotspur) 1987/8.

Allen, R. (5) (West Bromwich Albion) 1951/2, 1953/4, 1954/5.

Allen, T. (3) (Stoke City) 1959/60.

Anderson, S. (2) (Sunderland) 1961/2.

Anderson, V. (30) (Nottingham Forest) 1978/9, 1979/80, 1980/1, 1981/2, 1983/84, (Arsenal) 1984/5, 1985/6, 1986/7, (Manchester United).

Anderton, D.R. (3) (Tottenham Hotspur) 1993/94.

Angus, J. (1) (Burnley) 1960/1.

Armfield, J. (43) (Blackpool) 1958/9, 1959/60, 1960/1, 1961/2, 1962/3, 1963/4, 1965/6.

Armstrong, D. (3) (Middlesbrough) 1979/80, (Southampton) 1982/3, 1983/4.

Armstrong, K. (1) (Chelsea) 1954/5.

Astall, G. (2) (Birmingham) 1955/6.

Astle, J. (5) (West Bromwich Albion) 1968/9, 1969/70.

Aston, J. (17) (Manchester United) 1948/9, 1949/50, 1950/1.

Atyeo, J. (6) (Bristol City) 1955/6, 1956/7.

Bailey, G.R. (2) Manchester United) 1984/5.

Bailey, M. (2) (Charlton) 1963/4, 1964/5.

Baily, E. (9) (Tottenham Hotspur) 1949/50, 1950/1, 1951/2, 1952/3.

Baker, J. (8) (Hibernian) 1959/60, 1965/6, (Arsenal).

Ball, A. (72) (Blackpool) 1964/5, 1965/6, 1966/7, (Everton) 1967/8, 1968/9, 1969/70, 1970/1, 1971/2 (Arsenal) 1972/3, 1973/4, 1974/5.

Banks, G. (73) (Leicester) 1962/3, 1963/4, 1964/5, 1965/6, 1966/7, 1967/8, (Stoke) 1968/9, 1969/70, 1970/1, 1971/2.

Banks, T. (6) (Bolton Wanderers) 1957/8, 1958/9.

Bardsley, D. (2) (QPR) 1992/93.

Barham, M. (2) (Norwich City) 1982/3.

Barlow, R. (1) (West Bromwich Albion) 1954/5.

Barnes, J. (73) (Watford) 1982/3, 1983/4, 1984/5, 1985/6, 1986/7, (Liverpool) 1987/8, 1988/9, 1989/90, 1990/91, 1991/2, 1992/93.

Barnes, P. (22) (Manchester City) 1977/8, 1978/9, 1979/80 (West Bromwich Albion) 1980/1, 1981/2 (Leeds United).

Barrass, M. (3) (Bolton Wanderers) 1951/2, 1952/3.

Barrett, E.D. (3) (Oldham Athletic) 1990/91 (Aston Villa) 1992/93.

Batty, D. (15) (Leeds United) 1990/91, 1991/2, 1992/93, (Blackburn Rovers) 1993/94.

Baynham, R. (3) (Luton Town) 1955/6.

Beardsley P.A. (52) (Newcastle United) 1985/6, 1986/7 (Liverpool) 1987/8, 1988/9, 1989/90, 1990/1, (Newcastle United) 1993/94.

Beasant, D.J. (2) (Chelsea), 1989/90.

Beattie, T.K. (9) (Ipswich Town) 1974/5, 1975/6, 1976/7, 1977/8.

Bell, C. (48) (Manchester City) 1967/8, 1968/9, 1969/70, 1971/2, 1972/3, 1973/4, 1974/5, 1975/6.
Bentley, R. (12) (Chelsea) 1948/9, 1949/50, 1952/3, 1954/5.
Berry, J. (4) (Manchester United) 1952/3, 1955/6.
Birtles, G. (3) (Nottingham Forest) 1979/80, 1980/1 (Manchester United).
Blissett, L. (14) (Watford) 1982/3, 1983/4 (AC Milan).
Blockley, J. (1) (Arsenal) 1972/3.
Blunstone, F. (5) (Chelsea) 1954/5, 1956/7.
Bonetti, P. (7) (Chelsea) 1965/6, 1966/7, 1967/8, 1969/70.
Bould, S.A. (2) (Arsenal) 1993/94.
Bowles, S. (5) (QPR) 1973/4, 1976/7.
Boyer, P. (1) (Norwich City) 1975/6.
Brabrook, P. (3) (Chelsea) 1957/8, 1959/60.
Bracewell, P.W. (3) (Everton) 1984/5, 1985/6.
Bradford, G. (1) (Bristol Rovers) 1955/6.
Bradley, W. (3) (Manchester United) 1958/9.
Bridges, B. (4) (Chelsea) 1964/5, 1965/6.
Broadbent, P. (7) (Wolverhampton Wanderers) 1957/8, 1958/9, 1959/60.
Broadis, I. (14) (Manchester City) 1951/2, 1952/3 (Newcastle United) 1953/4.
Brooking, T. (47) (West Ham United) 1973/4, 1974/5, 1975/6, 1976/7, 1977/8, 1978/9, 1979/80, 1980/1, 1981/2.
Brooks, J. (3) (Tottenham Hotspur) 1956/7.
Brown, A. (1) (West Bromwich Albion) 1970/1.
Brown, K. (1) (West Ham United) 1959/60.
Bull, S.G. (13) (Wolverhampton Wanderers) 1988/9, 1989/90, 1990/1
Butcher, T. (77) (Ipswich Town) 1979/80, 1980/1, 1981/2, 1982/3, 1983/4, 1984/5, 1985/6, 1986/7 (Rangers) 1987/8, 1988/9, 1989/90.
Byrne, G. (2) (Liverpool) 1962/3, 1965/6.
Byrne, J. (11) (Crystal Palace) 1961/2, 1962/3, (West Ham United) 1963/4, 1964/5.
Byrne, R. (33) (Manchester United) 1953/4, 1954/5, 1955/6, 1956/7, 1957/8.

Callaghan, I. (4) (Liverpool) 1965/6, 1977/8.
Carter, H. (7) (Derby County) 1946/7.
Chamberlain, M. (8) (Stoke City) 1982/3, 1983/4, 1984/5.
Channon, M. (46) (Southampton) 1972/3, 1973/4, 1974/5, 1975/6, 1976/7, (Manchester City) 1977/8.
Charles, G.A. (2) (Nottingham Forest) 1990/1.
Charlton, J. (35) (Leeds United) 1964/5, 1965/6, 1966/7, 1967/8, 1968/9, 1969/70.
Charlton, R. (106) (Manchester United) 1957/8, 1958/9, 1959/60, 1960/1, 1961/2, 1962/3, 1963/4, 1964/5, 1965/6, 1966/7, 1967/8, 1968/9, 1969/70.
Charnley, R. (1) (Blackpool) 1961/2.
Cherry, T. (27) (Leeds United) 1975/6, 1976/7, 1977/8, 1978/9, 1979/80.
Chilton, A. (2) (Manchester United) 1951/2.
Chivers, M. (24) (Tottenham Hotspur) 1970/1, 1971/2, 1972/3, 1973/4.
Clamp, E. (4) (Wolverhampton Wanderers) 1957/8.
Clapton, D. (1) (Arsenal) 1958/9.
Clarke, A. (19) (Leeds United) 1969/70, 1970/1, 1972/3, 1973/4, 1974/5, 1975/6.
Clarke, H. (1) (Tottenham Hotspur) 1953/4.
Clayton, R. (35) (Blackburn Rovers) 1955/6, 1956/7, 1957/8, 1958/9, 1959/60.
Clemence, R (61) (Liverpool) 1972/3, 1973/4, 1974/5, 1975/6, 1976/7, 1977/8, 1978/9, 1979/80, 1980/1, 1981/2, (Tottenham Hotspur) 1982/3, 1983/4.
Clement, D. (5) (QPR) 1975/6, 1976/7.
Clough, B. (2) (Middlesbrough) 1959/60.
Clough, N.H. (14) (Nottingham Forest) 1988/9, 1990/91, 1991/2, 1992/93.

Coates, R. (4) (Burnley) 1969/70, 1970/1, (Tottenham Hotspur).
Cockburn, H. (13) (Manchester United) 1946/7, 1947/8, 1948/9, 1950/1, 1951/2.
Cohen, G. (37) (Fulham) 1963/4, 1964/5, 1965/6, 1966/7, 1967/8.
Compton, L. (2) (Arsenal) 1950/1.
Connelly J. (20) (Burnley) 1959/60, 1961/2, 1962/3, 1964/5 (Manchester United) 1965/6.
Cooper, T. (20) (Leeds United) 1968/9, 1969/70, 1970/1, 1971/2, 1974/5
Coppell, S. (42) (Manchester United) 1977/8, 1978/9, 1979/80, 1980/1, 1981/2, 1982/3.
Corrigan J. (9) (Manchester City) 1975/6, 1977/8, 1978/9, 1979/80, 1980/1, 1981/2
Cottee, A.R. (7) (West Ham United) 1986/7, 1987/8, (Everton) 1988/9.
Cowans, G. (10) (Aston Villa) 1982/3, 1985/6 (Bari) 1990/1 (Aston Villa).
Crawford, R. (2) (Ipswich Town) 1961/2.
Crowe, C. (1) (Wolverhampton Wanderers) 1962/3.
Cunningham, L. (6) (West Bromwich Albion) 1978/9 (Real Madrid) 1979/80, 1980/1.
Curle, K. (3) (Manchester City) 1991/2.
Currie, A. (17) (Sheffield United) 1971/2, 1972/3, 1973/4, 1975/6 (Leeds United) 1977/8, 1978/9.

Daley, A.M. (7) (Aston Villa) 1991/2.
Davenport, P. (1) (Nottingham Forest) 1984/5.
Deane, B.C. (3) (Sheffield United) 1990/91, 1992/93.
Deeley, N. (2) (Wolverhampton Wanderers) 1958/9.
Devonshire, A. (8) (West Ham United) 1979/80, 1981/2, 1982/3, 1983/4
Dickinson, J. (48) (Portsmouth) 1948/9, 1949/50, 1950/1, 1951/2, 1952/3, 1953/4, 1954/5, 1955/6, 1956/7.
Ditchburn, E. (6) (Tottenham Hotspur) 1948/9, 1952/3, 1956/7.
Dixon, K.M. (8) (Chelsea) 1984/5, 1985/6, 1986/7.
Dixon, L.M. (21) (Arsenal) 1989/90, 1990/1, 1991/2, 1992/93, 1993/94.
Dobson, M. (5) (Burnley) 1973/4, 1974/5 (Everton).
Dorigo, A.R. (15) (Chelsea) 1989/90, 1990/1, (Leeds United) 1991/2, 1992/93, 1993/94.
Douglas, B. (36) (Blackburn Rovers) 1957/8, 1958/9, 1959/60, 1960/1, 1961/2, 1962/3.
Doyle, M. (5) (Manchester City) 1975/6, 1976/7
Duxbury, M. (10) (Manchester United) 1983/4, 1984/5.

Eastham, G. (19) (Arsenal) 1962/3, 1963/4, 1964/5, 1965/6.
Eckersley, W. (17) (Blackburn Rovers) 1949/50, 1950/1, 1951/2, 1952/3, 1953/4.
Edwards, D. (18) (Manchester United) 1954/5, 1955/6, 1956/7, 1957/8.
Ellerington, W. (2) (Southampton) 1948/9.
Elliott, W. H. (5) (Burnley) 1951/2, 1952/3.

Fantham, J. (1) (Sheffield Wednesday) 1961/2.
Fashanu, J. (2) (Wimbledon) 1988/9.
Fenwick, T. (20) (QPR) 1983/4, 1984/5, 1985/6 (Tottenham Hotspur) 1987/8.
Ferdinand, L. (6) (QPR) 1992/93, 1993/94.
Finney, T. (76) (Preston) 1946/7, 1947/8, 1948/9, 1949/50, 1950/1, 1951/2, 1952/3, 1953/4, 1954/5, 1955/6, 1956/7, 1957/8, 1958/9.
Flowers R. (49) (Wolverhampton Wanderers) 1954/5, 1958/9, 1959/60, 1960/1, 1961/2, 1962/3, 1963/4, 1964/5, 1965/6.
Flowers T. (2) (Southampton) 1992/93, (Blackburn Rovers) 1993/94.
Foster, S. (3) (Brighton) 1981/2.

Foulkes, W. (1) (Manchester United) 1954/5.
Francis, G. (12) (QPR) 1974/5, 1975/6.
Francis, T. (52) (Birmingham City) 1976/7, 1977/8 (Nottingham Forest) 1978/9, 1979/80, 1980/1, 1981/2 (Manchester City) 1982/3, (Sampdoria) 1983/4, 1984/5, 1985/6.
Franklin, N. (27) (Stoke City) 1946/7, 1947/8, 1948/9, 1949/50.
Froggatt, J. (13) (Portsmouth) 1949/50, 1950/1, 1951/2, 1952/3.
Froggatt, R. (4) (Sheffield Wednesday) 1952/3.

Garrett, T. (3) (Blackpool) 1951/2, 1953/4.
Gascoigne, P.J. (29) (Tottenham Hotspur) 1988/9, 1989/90, 1990/1 (Lazio) 1992/93, 1993/94.
Gates, E. (2) (Ipswich Town) 1980/1.
George, F.C. (1) (Derby County) 1976/7.
Gidman, J. (1) (Aston Villa) 1976/7.
Gillard, I. (3) (QPR) 1974/5, 1975/6.
Goddard, P. (1) (West Ham United) 1981/2.
Grainger, C. (7) (Sheffield United) 1955/6, 1956/7 (Sunderland).
Gray, A.A. (1) (Crystal Palace) 1991/2.
Greaves, J. (57) (Chelsea) 1958/9, 1959/60, 1960/1, 1961/2 (Tottenham Hotspur) 1962/3, 1963/4, 1964/5, 1965/6, 1966/7.
Greenhoff, B. (18) (Manchester United) 1975/6, 1976/7, 1977/8, 1979/80.
Gregory, J. (6) (QPR) 1982/3, 1983/4.

Hagan, J. (1) (Sheffield United) 1948/9.
Haines, J. (1) (West Bromwich Albion) 1948/9.
Hall, J. (17) (Birmingham City) 1955/6, 1956/7
Hancocks, J. (3) (Wolverhampton Wanderers) 1948/9, 1949/50, 1950/1
Hardwick, G. (13) (Middlesbrough) 1946/7, 1947/8.
Harford, M.G. (2) (Luton Town) 1987/8, 1988/9.
Harris, G. (1) (Burnley) 1965/6.
Harris, P. (2) (Portsmouth) 1949/50, 1953/4.
Harvey, C. (1) (Everton) 1970/1.
Hassall, H. (5) (Huddersfield Town) 1950/1, 1951/2 (Bolton Wanderers) 1953/4.
Hateley, M. (32) (Portsmouth) 1983/4, 1984/5, (AC Milan) 1985/6, 1986/7, (Monaco) 1987/8, (Rangers) 1991/2.
Haynes, J. (56) (Fulham) 1954/5, 1955/6, 1956/7, 1957/8, 1958/9, 1959/60, 1960/1, 1961/2.
Hector, K. (2) (Derby County) 1973/4.
Hellawell, M. (2) (Birmingham City) 1962/3.
Henry, R. (1) (Tottenham Hotspur) 1962/3.
Hill, F. (2) (Bolton Wanderers) 1962/3.
Hill, G. (6) (Manchester United) 1975/6, 1976/7, 1977/8.
Hill, R. (3) (Luton Town) 1982/3, 1985/6.
Hinton A. (3) (Wolverhampton Wanderers) 1962/3, 1964/5 (Nottingham Forest)
Hirst, D.E. (3) (Sheffield Wednesday) 1990/91, 1991/2.
Hitchens, G. (7) (Aston Villa) 1960/1, (Inter Milan) 1961/2.
Hoddle, G. (53) (Tottenham Hotspur) 1979/80, 1980/1, 1981/2, 1982/3, 1983/4, 1984/5, 1985/6, 1986/7 (Monaco) 1987/8.
Hodge, S.B. (24) (Aston Villa) 1985/6, 1986/7, (Tottenham Hotspur), (Nottingham Forest) 1988/9, 1989/90, 1990/1.
Hodgkinson, A. (5) (Sheffield United) 1956/7, 1960/1
Holden, D. (5) (Bolton Wanderers) 1958/9.
Holliday, E. (3) (Middlesbrough) 1959/60.

Hollins, J. (1) (Chelsea) 1966/7.
Hopkinson, E. (14) (Bolton Wanderers) 1957/8, 1958/9, 1959/60.
Howe, D. (23) (West Bromwich Albion) 1957/8, 1958/9, 1959/60.
Howe, J. (3) (Derby County) 1947/8, 1948/9.
Hudson, A. (2) (Stoke City) 1974/5.
Hughes, E. (62) (Liverpool) 1969/70, 1970/1, 1971/2, 1972/3, 1973/4, 1974/5, 1976/7, 1977/8, 1978/9 (Wolverhampton Wanderers) 1979/80.
Hughes, L. (3) (Liverpool) 1949/50.
Hunt, R. (34) (Liverpool) 1961/2, 1962/3, 1963/4, 1964/5, 1965/6, 1966/7, 1967/8, 1968/9.
Hunt, S. (2) (West Bromwich Albion) 1983/4.
Hunter, N. (28) (Leeds United) 1965/6, 1966/7, 1967/8, 1968/9, 1969/70, 1970/1, 1971/2, 1972/3, 1973/4, 1974/5.
Hurst, G. (49) (West Ham United) 1965/6, 1966/7, 1967/8, 1968/9, 1969/70, 1970/1, 1971/2.

Ince, P. (14) (Manchester United) 1992/93, 1993/94.

Jezzard, B. (2) (Fulham) 1953/4, 1955/6.
Johnson, D. (8) (Ipswich Town) 1974/5, 1975/6, (Liverpool) 1979/80.
Johnston, H. (10) (Blackpool) 1946/7, 1950/1, 1952/3, 1953/4.
Jones, M. (3) (Sheffield United) 1964/5 (Leeds United) 1969/70.
Jones, R. (4) (Liverpool) 1991/2, 1993/94.
Jones, W.H. (2) (Liverpool) 1949/50.

Kay, A. (1) (Everton) 1962/3.
Keegan, K. (63) (Liverpool) 1972/3, 1973/4, 1974/5, 1975/6, 1976/7 (SV Hamburg) 1977/8, 1978/9, 1979/80 (Southampton) 1980/1, 1981/2.
Kennedy, A. (2) (Liverpool) 1983/4.
Kennedy, R. (17) (Liverpool) 1975/6, 1977/8, 1979/80.
Keown, M.R. (11) (Everton) 1991/2 (Arsenal) 1992/93.
Kevan, D. (14) (West Bromwich Albion) 1956/7, 1957/8, 1958/9, 1960/1.
Kidd, B. (2) (Manchester United) 1969/70.
Knowles, C. (4) (Tottenham Hotspur) 1967/8.

Labone, B. (26) (Everton) 1962/3, 1966/7, 1967/8, 1968/9, 1969/70.
Lampard, F. (2) (West Ham United) 1972/3, 1979/80.
Langley, J. (3) (Fulham) 1957/8.
Langton, R. (11) (Blackburn Rovers) 1946/7, 1947/8, 1948/9, (Preston North End) 1949/50, (Bolton Wanderers) 1950/1.
Latchford, R. (12) (Everton) 1977/8, 1978/9.
Lawler, C. (4) (Liverpool) 1970/1, 1971/2.
Lawton, T. (15) (Chelsea) 1946/7, 1947/8, (Notts County) 1948/9.
Lee, F. (27) (Manchester City) 1968/9, 1969/70, 1970/1, 1971/2.
Lee, J. (1) (Derby County) 1950/1.
Lee, S. (14) (Liverpool) 1982/3, 1983/4.
Le Saux, G.P. (3) (Blackburn Rovers) 1993/94.
Le Tissier, M.P. (3) (Southampton) 1993/94.
Lindsay, A. (4) (Liverpool) 1973/4.
Lineker, G. (80) (Leicester City) 1983/4, 1984/5 (Everton) 1985/6, 1986/7, (Barcelona) 1987/8, 1988/9 (Tottenham H) 1989/90, 1990/1, 1991/2.
Little, B. (1) (Aston Villa) 1974/5.
Lloyd, L. (4) (Liverpool) 1970/1, 1971/2, (Nottingham Forest) 1979/80.

Lofthouse, N. (33) (Bolton Wanderers) 1950/1, 1951/2, 1952/3, 1953/4, 1954/5, 1955/6, 1958/9

Lowe, E. (3) (Aston Villa) 1946/7.

Mabbutt, G. (16) (Tottenham Hotspur) 1982/3, 1983/4, 1986/7, 1987/8, 1991/2.

Macdonald, M. (14) (Newcastle United) 1971/2, 1972/3, 1973/4, 1974/5, (Arsenal) 1975/6.

Madeley, P. (24) (Leeds United) 1970/1, 1971/2, 1972/3, 1973/4, 1974/5, 1975/6, 1976/7.

Mannion, W. (26) (Middlesbrough) 1946/7, 1947/8, 1948/9, 1949/50, 1950/1, 1951/2.

Mariner, P. (35) (Ipswich Town) 1976/7, 1977/8, 1979/80, 1980/1, 1981/2, 1982/3, 1983/4, 1984/5 (Arsenal)

Marsh, R. (9) (QPR) 1971/2 (Manchester City) 1972/3.

Martin, A. (17) (West Ham United) 1980/1, 1981/2, 1982/3, 1983/4, 1984/5, 1985/6, 1986/7.

Marwood, B. (1) (Arsenal) 1988/9

Matthews, R. (5) (Coventry City) 1955/6, 1956/7.

Matthews, S. (37) (Stoke City) 1946/7, (Blackpool) 1947/8, 1948/9, 1949/50, 1950/1, 1953/4, 1954/5, 1955/6, 1956/7.

McDermott, T. (25) (Liverpool) 1977/8, 1978/9, 1979/80, 1980/1, 1981/2.

McDonald, C. (8) (Burnley) 1957/8, 1958/9.

McFarland, R. (28) (Derby County) 1970/1, 1971/2, 1972/3, 1973/4, 1975/6, 1976/7

McGarry, W. (4) (Huddersfield Town) 1953/4, 1955/6.

McGuinness, W. (2) (Manchester United) 1958/9

McMahon, S. (17) (Liverpool) 1987/8, 1988/9, 1989/90, 1990/1

McNab, R. (4) (Arsenal) 1968/9.

McNeil, M. (9) (Middlesbrough) 1960/1, 1961/2.

Martyn, A.N. (3) (Crystal Palace) 1991/2, 1992/93.

Meadows, J. (1) (Manchester City) 1954/5

Medley, L. (Tottenham Hotspur) 1950/1, 1951/2.

Melia, J. (2) (Liverpool) 1962/3.

Merrick, G. (23) (Birmingham City) 1951/2, 1952/3, 1953/4

Merson, P.C. (14) (Arsenal) 1991/2, 1992/93, 1993/94.

Metcalfe, V. (2) (Huddersfield Town) 1950/1

Milburn, J. (13) (Newcastle United) 1948/9, 1949/50, 1950/1, 1951/2, 1955/6

Miller, B. (1) (Burnley) 1960/1.

Mills, M. (42) (Ipswich Town) 1972/3, 1975/6, 1976/7, 1977/8, 1978/9, 1979/80, 1980/1, 1981/2.

Milne, G. (14) (Liverpool) 1962/3, 1963/4, 1964/5

Milton, C.A. (1) (Arsenal) 1951/2.

Moore, R. (108) (West Ham United) 1961/2, 1962/3, 1963/4, 1964/5, 1965/6, 1966/7, 1967/8, 1968/9, 1969/70, 1970/1, 1971/2, 1972/3, 1973/4

Morley, A. (6) (Aston Villa) 1981/2, 1982/3.

Morris, J. (3) (Derby County) 1948/9, 1949/50

Mortensen, S. (25) (Blackpool) 1946/7, 1947/8, 1948/9 1949/50, 1950/1, 1953/4

Mozley, B. (3) (Derby County) 1949/50.

Mullen, J. (12) (Wolverhampton Wanderers) 1946/7, 1948/9, 1949/50, 1953/4.

Mullery, A. (35) (Tottenham Hotspur) 1964/5, 1966/7, 1967/8, 1968/9, 1969/70, 1970/1, 1971/2.

Neal, P. (50) (Liverpool) 1975/6, 1976/7, 1977/8, 1978/9, 1979/80, 1980/1, 1981/2, 1982/3, 1983/4.

Newton, K. (27) (Blackburn Rovers) 1965/6, 1966/7, 1967/8, 1968/9, 1969/70, (Everton).

Nicholls, J. (2) (West Bromwich Albion) 1953/4.
Nicholson W. (1) (Tottenham Hotspur) 1950/1.
Nish, D. (5) (Derby County) 1972/3, 1973/4.
Norman, M. (23) (Tottenham Hotspur) 1961/2, 1962/3, 1963/4, 1964/5.

O'Grady, M. (2) (Huddersfield Town) 1962/3, 1968/9 (Leeds United).
Osgood, P. (4) (Chelsea) 1969/70, 1973/4.
Osman, R. (11) (Ipswich Town) 1979/80, 1980/1, 1981/2, 1982/3, 1983/4.
Owen, S. (3) (Luton Town) 1953/4.

Paine, T. (19) (Southampton) 1962/3, 1963/4, 1964/5, 1965/6.
Pallister, G. (13) (Middlesbrough) 1987/8, 1990/91 (Manchester United), 1991/2, 1992/93, 1993/94.
Palmer, C.L. (18) (Sheffield Wednesday) 1991/2, 1992/93, 1993/94.
Parker, P.A. (19) (QPR) 1988/9, 1989/90, 1990/1, (Manchester United) 1991/2, 1993/94.
Parkes, P. (1) (QPR) 1973/4.
Parry, R. (2) (Bolton Wanderers) 1959/60.
Peacock, A. (6) (Middlesbrough) 1961/2, 1962/3, 1965/6 (Leeds United).
Pearce, S. (56) (Nottingham Forest) 1986/7, 1987/8, 1988/9, 1989/90, 1990/1, 1991/2, 1992/93, 1993/94.
Person, Stan (8) (Manchester United) 1947/8, 1948/9, 1949/50, 1950/1, 1951/2.
Pearson, Stuart (15) (Manchester United) 1975/6, 1976/7, 1977/8.
Pegg, D. (1) (Manchester United) 1956/7.
Pejic, M. (4) (Stoke City) 1973/4.
Perry, W. (3) (Blackpool) 1955/6.
Perryman, S. (1) (Tottenham Hotspur) 1981/2.
Peters, M. (67) (West Ham United) 1965/6, 1966/7, 1967/8, 1968/9, 1969/70, (Tottenham Hotspur) 1970/1, 1971/2, 1972/3, 1973/4.
Phelan, M.C. (1) (Manchester United) 1989/90.
Phillips, L. (3) (Portsmouth) 1951/2, 1954/5.
Pickering, F. (3) (Everton) 1963/4, 1964/5.
Pickering, N. (1) (Sunderland) 1982/3.
Pilkington, B. (1) (Burnley) 1954/5.
Platt, D. (48) (Aston Villa) 1989/90, 1990/1, (Bari) 1991/2 (Juventus), 1992/93, 1993/94.
Pointer, R. (3) (Burnley) 1961/2.
Pye, J. (1) (Wolverhampton Wanderers) 1949/50.

Quixall, A. (5) (Sheffield Wednesday) 1953/4, 1954/5.

Radford, J. (2) (Arsenal) 1968/9, 1971/2.
Ramsey, A. (32) (Southampton) 1948/9, 1949/50, (Tottenham Hotspur) 1950/1, 1951/2, 1952/3, 1953/4.
Reaney, P. (3) (Leeds United) 1968/9, 1969/70, 1970/1.
Reeves, K. (2) (Norwich City) 1979/80.
Regis, C. (5) (West Bromwich Albion) 1981/2, 1982/3, (Coventry City).
Reid, P. (13) (Everton) 1984/5, 1985/6, 1986/7.
Revie, D. (6) (Manchester City) 1954/5, 1955/6, 1956/7
Richards, J. (1) (Wolverhampton Wanderers) 1972/3.
Richardson, K. (1) (Aston Villa) 1993/94.
Rickaby, S. (1) (West Bromwich Albion) 1953/4.
Rimmer, J. (1) (Arsenal) 1975/6.
Ripley, S.E. (1) (Blackburn Rovers) 1993/94.

Rix, G. (17) (Arsenal) 1980/1, 1981/2, 1982/3, 1983/4.
Robb, G. (1) (Tottenham Hotspur) 1953/4.
Roberts, G. (6) (Tottenham Hotspur) 1982/3, 1983/4.
Robson, B. (90) (West Bromwich Albion) 1979/80, 1980/1, 1981/2, (Manchester United) 1982/3, 1983/4, 1984/5, 1985/6, 1986/7, 1987/8, 1988/9, 1989/90, 1990/1, 1991/2.
Robson, R. (20) (West Bromwich Albion) 1957/8, 1959/60, 1960/1, 1961/2.
Rocastle, D. (14) (Arsenal) 1988/9, 1989/90, 1991/2.
Rowley, J. (6) (Manchester United) 1948/9, 1949/50, 1951/2.
Royle, J. (6) (Everton) 1970/1, 1972/3, (Manchester City) 1975/6, 1976/7.

Sadler, D. (4) (Manchester United) 1967/8, 1969/70, 1970/1.
Salako, J.A. (5) (Crystal Palace) 1990/91, 1991/2.
Sansom, K. (86) (Crystal Palace) 1978/9, 1979/80, 1980/1, (Arsenal) 1981/2, 1982/3, 1983/4, 1984/5, 1985/6, 1986/7, 1987/8.
Scott, L. (17) (Arsenal) 1946/7, 1947/8. 1948/9.
Seaman, D.A. (14) (QPR) 1988/9, 1989/90, 1990/1 (Arsenal), 1991/2, 1993/94.
Sewell, J. (6) (Sheffield Wednesday) 1951/2, 1952/3, 1953/4.
Shackleton, L. (5) (Sunderland) 1948/9, 1949/50, 1954/5.
Sharpe, L.S. (8) (Manchester United) 1990/1, 1992/93, 1993/94.
Shaw, G. (5) (Sheffield United) 1958/9, 1962/3.
Shearer, A. (10) (Southampton) 1991/2 (Blackburn Rovers), 1992/93, 1993/94.
Shellito, K. (1) (Chelsea) 1962/3.
Sheringham, E. (2) (Tottenham Hotspur) 1992/93.
Shilton, P. (125) (Leicester City) 1970/1, 1971/2, 1972/3, 1973/4, 1974/5, (Stoke City) 1976/7, (Nottingham Forest) 1977/8, 1978/9, 1979/80, 1980/1, 1981/2, (Southampton) 1982/3, 1983/4, 1984/5, 1985/6, 1986/7, (Derby County) 1987/8, 1988/9, 1989/90.
Shimwell, E. (1) (Blackpool) 1948/9.
Sillett, P. (3) (Chelsea) 1954/5.
Sinton, A. (12) (QPR) 1991/2, 1992/93 (Sheffield Wednesday) 1993/94.
Slater, W. (12) (Wolverhampton Wanderers) 1954/5, 1957/8, 1958/9, 1959/60.
Smith, A.M. (13) (Arsenal) 1988/9, 1990/1, 1991/2.
Smith, L. (6) (Arsenal) 1950/1, 1951/2, 1952/3.
Smith, R. (15) (Tottenham Hotspur) 1960/1, 1961/2, 1962/3, 1963/4.
Smith, Tom (1) (Liverpool) 1970/1.
Smith, Trevor (2) (Birmingham City) 1959/60.
Spink, N. (1) (Aston Villa) 1982/3.
Springett, R. (33) (Sheffield Wednesday) 1959/60, 1960/1, 1961/2, 1962/3, 1965/6.
Staniforth, R. (8) (Huddersfield Town) 1953/4, 1954/5.
Statham, D. (3) (West Bromwich Albion) 1982/3.
Stein, B. (1) (Luton Town) 1983/4.
Stepney, A. (1) (Manchester United) 1967/8.
Sterland, M. (1) (Sheffield Wednesday) 1988/9.
Steven, T.M. (36) (Everton) 1984/5, 1985/6, 1986/7, 1987/8, 1988/9 (Glasgow Rangers) 1989/90, 1990/1, (Marseille) 1991/2.
Stevens, G.A. (7) (Tottenham Hotspur) 1984/5, 1985/6.
Stevens, M.G. (46) (Everton) 1984/5, 1985/6, 1986/7, 1987/8 (Rangers) 1988/9, 1989/90, 1990/1, 1991/2.
Stewart, P.A. (3) (Tottenham Hotspur) 1991/2.
Stiles, N. (28) (Manchester United) 1964/5, 1965/6, 1966/7, 1967/8, 1968/9, 1969/70.
Storey-Moore, I. (1) (Nottingham Forest) 1969/70.
Storey, P. (19) (Arsenal) 1970/1, 1971/2, 1972/3.
Streten, B. (1) (Luton Town) 1949/50.

266

Summerbee, M. (8) (Manchester City) 1967/8, 1971/2, 1972/3.
Sunderland, A. (1) (Arsenal) 1979/80.
Swan, P. (19) (Sheffield Wednesday) 1959/60, 1960/1, 1961/2.
Swift, F. (19) (Manchester City) 1946/7, 1947/8, 1948/9.

Talbot, B. (6) (Ipswich Town) 1976/7, 1979/80.
Tambling, R. (3) (Chelsea) 1962/3, 1965/6.
Taylor, E. (1) (Blackpool) 1953/4.
Taylor, J. (2) (Fulham) 1950/1.
Taylor, P.H. (3) (Liverpool) 1947/8.
Taylor, P.J. (4) (Crystal Palace) 1975/6.
Taylor, T. (19) (Manchester United) 1952/3, 1953/4, 1955/6, 1956/7, 1958/9.
Temple, D. (1) (Everton) 1964/5.
Thomas, Danny (2) (Coventry City) 1982/3.
Thomas, Dave (8) (QPR) 1974/5, 1975/6.
Thomas, G.R. (9) (Crystal Palace) 1990/1, 1991/2.
Thomas, M.L. (2) (Arsenal) 1988/9, 1989/90.
Thompson, P. (16) (Liverpool) 1963/4, 1964/5, 1965/6, 1967/8, 1969/70.
Thompson, P.B. (42) (Liverpool) 1975/6, 1976/7, 1978/9, 1979/80, 1980/1, 1981/2, 1982/3.
Thompson, T. (2) (Aston Villa) 1951/2, (Preston North End) 1956/7.
Thomson, R. (8) (Wolverhampton Wanderers) 1963/4, 1964/5.
Todd, C. (27) (Derby County) 1971/2, 1973/4, 1974/5, 1975/6, 1976/7.
Towers, T. (3) (Sunderland) 1975/6.
Tueart, D. (6) (Manchester City) 1974/5, 1976/7.

Ufton, D. (1) (Charlton Athletic) 1953/4.

Venables, T. (2) (Chelsea) 1964/5.
Viljoen, C. (2) (Ipswich Town) 1974/5.
Viollet, D. (2) (Manchester United) 1959/60, 1961/2.

Waddle, C.R. (62) (Newcastle United) 1984/5, (Tottenham Hotspur) 1985/6, 1986/7, 1987/8, 1988/9, (Marseille) 1989/90, 1990/1, 1991/2.
Waiters, A. (5) (Blackpool) 1963/4, 1964/5.
Walker, D.S. (59) (Nottingham Forest) 1988/9, 1989/90, 1990/1, 1991/2 (Sampdoria) 1992/93, (Sheffield Wednesday) 1993/94.
Wallace, D.L. (1) (Southampton) 1985/6.
Walsh, P. (5) (Luton Town) 1982/3, 1983/4.
Walters, K.M. (1) (Rangers) 1990/91.
Ward, P. (1) (Brighton) 1979/80.
Ward, T. (2) (Derby County) 1947/8, 1948/9.
Watson, D. (12) (Norwich City) 1983/4, 1984/5, 1985/6, 1986/7 (Everton) 1987/8.
Watson D.V. (65) (Sunderland) 1973/4, 1974/5, 1975/6 (Manchester City) 1976/7, 1977/8, (Manchester City) 1978/9 (Werder Bremen), 1979/80, (Southampton) 1980/1 , 1981/2, (Stoke City).
Watson, W. (4) (Sunderland) 1949/50, 1950/1.
Webb, N. (26) (Nottingham Forest) 1987/8, 1988/9 (Manchester United) 1989/90, 1991/2.
Weller, K. (4) (Leicester City) 1973/4.
West, G. (3) (Everton) 1968/9.
Wheeler, J. (1) (Bolton Wanderers) 1954/5.
White, D. (1) (Manchester City) 1992/93.
Whitworth, S. (7) (Leicester City) 1974/5, 1975/6

Whymark, T. (1) (Ipswich Town) 1977/8.
Wignall, F. (2) (Nottingham Forest) 1964/5.
Wilkins, R. (84) (Chelsea) 1975/6, 1976/7, 1977/8, 1978/9, (Manchester United) 1979/80, 1980/1, 1981/2, 1982/3, 1983/4, 1984/5, (AC Milan) 1985/6, 1986/7
Williams, B. (24) (Wolverhampton Wanderers) 1948/9, 1949/50, 1950/1, 1951/2, 1954/5, 1955/6.
Williams, S. (6) (Southampton) 1982/3, 1983/4, 1984/5.
Willis, A. (1) (Tottenham Hotspur) 1951/2.
Wilshaw, D. (12) (Wolverhampton Wanderers) 1953/4, 1954/5, 1955/6, 1956/7
Wilson, R. (63) (Huddersfield Town) 1959/60, 1961/2, 1962/3, 1963/4, 1964/5, (Everton) 1965/6, 1966/7, 1967/8.
Winterburn, N. (2) (Arsenal) 1989/90, 1992/93.
Wise, D.F. (6) (Chelsea) 1990/91, 1993/94.
Withe, P. (11) (Aston Villa) 1980/1, 1981/2, 1982/3, 1983/4, 1984/5.
Wood, R. (3) (Manchester United) 1954/5, 1955/6.
Woodcock, A. (42) (Nottingham Forest) 1977/8, 1978/9, 1979/80 (FC Cologne) 1980/1, 1981/2, (Arsenal) 1982/3, 1983/4, 1984/5, 1985/6.
Woods, C.C.E. (43) (Norwich City) 1984/5, 1985/6, 1986/7, (Rangers) 1987/8, 1988/9, 1989/90, 1990/1, (Sheffield Wednesday) 1991/2. 1992/93.
Worthington, F. (8) (Leicester City) 1973/4, 1974/5.
Wright, I.E. (18) (Crystal Palace) 1990/1, 1991/2 (Arsenal) 1992/93, 1993/94.
Wright M. (43) (Southampton) 1983/4, 1984/5, 1985/6, 1986/7, (Derby County) 1987/8, 1988/9, 1989/90, 1990/1, (Liverpool) 1991/2, 1992/93.
Wright, T. (11) (Everton) 1967/8, 1968/9, 1969/70.
Wright, W. (105) (Wolverhampton Wanderers) 1946/7, 1947/8, 1948/9, 1949/50, 1950/1, 1951/2, 1952/3, 1953/4, 1954/5, 1955/6, 1956/7, 1957/8, 1958/9.
Young, G. (1) (Sheffield Wednesday) 1964/5.

NORTHERN IRELAND

Aherne, T. (4) (Belfast Celtic) 1946/7, 1947/8, 1948/9, 1949/50 (Luton Town).
Anderson, T. (22) (Manchester United) 1972/3, 1973/4, 1974/5, (Swindon Town) 1975/6, 1976/7, 1977/8, (Peterborough United) 1978/9.
Armstrong, G. (63) (Tottenham Hotspur) 1976/7, 1977/8, 1978/9, 1979/80, 1980/1, (Watford) 1981/2, 1982/3, (Real Mallorca) 1983/4, 1984/5, (West Bromwich Albion) 1985/6 (Chesterfield).

Barr, H. (3) (Linfield) 1961/2, 1962/3, (Coventry City).
Best, G. (37) (Manchester United) 1963/4, 1964/5, 1965/6, 1966/7, 1967/8, 1968/9, 1969/70, 1970/1 , 1971/2, 1972/3, 1973/4 (Fulham) 1976/7, 1977/8.
Bingham, W. (56) (Sunderland) 1950/1, 1951/2, 1952/3, 1953/4, 1954/5, 1955/6, 1956/7, 1957/8, 1958/9 (Luton Town) 1959/60, 1960/1 (Everton) 1961/2, 1962/3, 1963/4 (Port Vale).
Black, K. (30) (Luton Town) 1987/8, 1988/9, 1989/90, 1990/1, (Nottingham Forest) 1991/2, 1992/93, 1993/94.
Blair, R. (5) (Oldham Athletic) 1974/5, 1975/6.
Blanchflower, D. (54) (Barnsley) 1949/50, 1950/1 (Aston Villa) 1951/2, 1952/3, 1953/4, 1954/5, (Tottenham Hotspur) 1955/6, 1956/7, 1957/8, 1958/9, 1959/60, 1960/1, 1961/2, 1962/3.
Blanchflower, J. (12) (Manchester United) 1953/4, 1954/5, 1955/6, 1956/7, 1957/8.
Bowler, G. (3) (Hull City) 1949/50.
Braithwaite, R. (10) (Linfield) 1961/2, 1962/3 (Middlesbrough) 1963/4, 1964/5.
Brennan, R. (5) (Luton Town) 1948/9, 1949/50 (Birmingham City) (Fulham), 1950/1.

Briggs, R. (2) (Manchester United) 1961/2, 1964/5 (Swansea).
Brotherston, N. (27) (Blackburn Rovers) 1979/80, 1980/1, 1981/2, 1982/3, 1983/4, 1984/5.
Bruce, W. (2) (Glentoran) 1960/1, 1966/7.

Campbell, A. (2) (Crusaders) 1962/3, 1964/5.
Campbell, D.A. (10) (Nottingham Forest) 1985/6, 1986/7, 1987/8 (Charlton Athletic).
Campbell, J. (2) (Fulham) 1950/1.
Campbell, R.M. (2) (Bradford City) 1981/2.
Campbell, W. (6) (Dundee) 1967/8, 1968/9, 1969/70.
Carey, J. (7) (Manchester United) 1946/7, 1947/8, 1948/9.
Casey, T. (12) (Newcastle United) 1954/5, 1955/6, 1956/7, 1957/8, 1958/9, (Portsmouth).
Caskey, A. (7) (Derby County) 1978/9, 1979/80, 1981/2 (Tulsa Roughnecks).
Cassidy, T. (24) (Newcastle United) 1970/1, 1971/2, 1973/4, 1974/5, 1975/6, 1976/7, 1979/80 (Burnley) 1980/1, 1981/2
Caughey, M. (2) (Linfield) 1985/6.
Clarke, C.J. (38) (Bournemouth) 1985/6, 1986/7 (Southampton) 1987/8, 1988/9, 1989/90, 1990/1 (Portsmouth), 1991/2, 1992/93.
Cleary, J. (5) (Glentoran) 1981/2, 1982/3, 1983/4, 1984/5.
Clements, D. (48) (Coventry City) 1964/5, 1965/6, 1966/7, 1967/8, 1968/9, 1969/70, 1970/1, 1971/2 (Sheffield Wednesday) 1972/3 (Everton) 1973/4, 1974/5, 1975/6 (New York Cosmos).
Cochrane, D. (10) (Leeds United) 1946/7, 1947/8, 1948/9, 1949/50.
Cochrane, T. (26) (Coleraine) 1975/6, (Burnley) 1977/8, 1978/9, (Middlesbrough) 1979/80, 1980/1, 1981/2, (Gillingham) 1983/4.
Cowan, J. (1) (Newcastle United) 1969/70.
Coyle, F. (4) (Coleraine) 1955/6, 1956/7, 1957/8 (Nottingham Forest).
Coyle, L. (1) (Derry C) 1988/9.
Coyle, R. (5) (Sheffield Wednesday) 1972/3, 1973/4.
Craig, D. (25) (Newcastle United) 1966/7, 1967/8, 1968/9, 1969/70, 1970/1, 1971/2, 1972/3, 1973/4, 1974/5.
Crossan, E. (3) (Blackburn Rovers) 1949/50, 1950/1, 1954/5.
Crossan, J. (23) (Rotterdam Sparta) 1959/60, 1962/3 (Sunderland), 1963/4, 1964/5, (Manchester City) 1965/6, 1966/7, 1967/8 (Middlesbrough).
Cunningham, W. (30) (St Mirren) 1950/1, 1952/3, 1953/4, 1954/5, 1955/6, 1956/7, (Leicester City) 1957/8, 1958/9, 1959/60, 1960/1 (Dunfermline Athletic) 1961/2.
Cush, W. (26) (Glentoran) 1950/1, 1953/4, 1956/7, 1957/8 (Leeds United) 1958/9, 1959/60, 1960/1 (Portadown) 1961/2.

D'Arcy, S. (5) (Chelsea) 1951/2, 1952/3 (Brentford).
Dennison, R. (17) (Wolverhampton Wanderers) 1987/8, 1988/9, 1989/90, 1990/1, 1991/2, 1992/93, 1993/94.
Devine, J. (1) (Glentoran) 1989/90.
Dickson, D. (4) (Coleraine) 1969/70, 1972/3.
Dickson, T. (1) (Linfield) 1956/7.
Dickson, W. (12) (Chelsea) 1950/1, 1951/2, 1952/3 (Arsenal) 1953/4, 1954/5.
Doherty, L. (2) (Linfield) 1984/5, 1987/8.
Doherty P. (6) (Derby County) 1946/7, (Huddersfield Town) 1947/8, 1948/9, (Doncaster Rovers) 1950/1.
Donaghy, M. (91) (Luton Town) 1979/80, 1980/1, 1981/2, 1982/3, 1983/4, 1984/5, 1985/6, 1986/7, 1987/8, (Manchester United) 1988/9, 1989/90, 1990/1, 1991/2 (Chelsea) 1992/93, 1993/94.

Dougan D. (43) (Portsmouth) 1957/8, 1959/60, (Blackburn Rovers), 1960/1, 1962/3 (Aston Villa) 1965/6 (Leicester City), 1966/7 (Wolverhampton Wanderers) 1967/8, 1968/9, 1969/70, 1970/1, 1971/2, 1972/3.

Douglas, J.P. (1) (Belfast Celtic) 1946/7.

Dowd, H. (3) (Glentoran) 1972/3, 1974/5 (Sheffield Wednesday).

Dowie, I. (25) (Luton Town) 1989/90, 1990/1, (Southampton) 1991/2, 1992/93, 1993/94.

Dunlop, G. (4) (Linfield) 1984/5, 1986/7.

Eglington T. (6) (Everton) 1946/7, 1947/8, 1948/9.

Elder, A. (40) (Burnley) 1959/60, 1960/1, 1961/2, 1962/3, 1963/4, 1964/5, 1965/6, 1966/7, (Stoke City) 1967/8, 1968/9, 1969/70.

Farrell, P. (7) (Everton) 1946/7, 1947/8, 1948/9.

Feeney, J. (2) (Linfield) 1946/7 (Swansea City) 1949/50.

Feeney, W. (1) (Glentoran) 1975/6.

Ferguson, W. (2) (Linfield) 1965/6, 1966/7.

Ferris, R. (3) (Birmingham City) 1949/50, 1950/1, 1951/2.

Fettis, A. (4) (Hull City) 1991/2, 1992/93, 1993/94.

Finney, T. (14) (Sunderland) 1974/5, 1975/6 (Cambridge United), 1979/80.

Fleming, J.G. (28) (Nottingham Forest) 1986/7, 1987/8, 1988/9 (Manchester City) 1989/90, 1990/1 (Barnsley), 1991/2, 1992/93, 1993/94.

Forde, T. (4) (Ards) 1958/9, 1960/1.

Gallogly, C. (2) (Huddersfield Town) 1950/1.

Garton, R. (1) (Oxford United) 1968/9.

Gorman, W. (2) (Brentford) 1946/7, 1947/8.

Graham, W. (14) (Doncaster Rovers) 1950/1, 1951/2, 1952/3, 1953/4, 1954/5, 1955/6, 1958/9.

Gray, P. (9) (Luton Town) 1992/93, (Sunderland) 1993/94.

Gregg, H. (25) (Doncaster Rovers) 1953/4, 1956/7, 1957/8, (Manchester United) 1958/9, 1959/60, 1960/1, 1961/2, 1963/4.

Hamilton, B. (50) (Linfield) 1968/9, 1970/1, 1971/2 (Ipswich Town), 1972/3, 1973/4, 1974/5, 1975/6 (Everton) 1976/7, 1977/8, (Millwall), 1978/9 (Swindon Town).

Hamilton, W. (41) (QPR) 1977/8, 1979/80 (Burnley) 1980/1, 1981/2, 1982/3, 1983/4, 1984/5, (Oxford United) 1985/6.

Harkin, T. (5) (Southport) 1967/8, 1968/9 (Shrewsbury Town), 1969/70, 1970/1.

Harvey, M. (34) (Sunderland) 1960/1, 1961/2, 1962/3, 1963/4, 1964/5, 1965/6, 1966/7, 1967/8, 1968/9, 1969/70, 1970/1.

Hatton, S. (2) (Linfield) 1962/3.

Healy, F. (4) (Coleraine) 1981/2 (Glentoran) 1982/3.

Hegan, D. (7) (West Bromwich Albion) 1969/70, 1971/2 (Wolverhampton Wanderers) 1972/3.

Hill, C.F. (6) (Sheffield U) 1989/90, 1990/1, 1991/2.

Hill, J. (7) (Norwich City) 1958/9, 1959/60, 1960/1, (Everton) 1961/2, 1963/4.

Hinton, E. (7) (Fulham) 1946/7, 1947/8 (Millwall) 1950/1.

Hughes, M.E. (18) (Manchester City) 1991/2 (Strasbourg) 1992/93, 1993/94.

Hughes, P. (3) (Bury) 1986/7.

Hughes, W. (1) (Bolton Wanderers) 1950/1.

Humphries, W. (14) (Ards) 1961/2 (Coventry City) 1962/3, 1963/4, 1964/5 (Swansea Town).

Hunter, A. (53) (Blackburn Rovers) 1969/70, 1970/1, 1971/2 (Ipswich Town) 1972/3, 1973/4, 1974/5, 1975/6, 1976/7, 1977/8, 1978/9, 1979/80.

Irvine, R. (8) (Linfield) 1961/2, 1962/3 (Stoke City) 1964/5.
Irvine, W. (23) (Burnley) 1962/3, 1964/5, 1965/6, 1966/7, 1967/8, 1968/9 (Preston North End) (Brighton & Hove Albion) 1971/2.

Jackson, T. (35) (Everton) 1968/9, 1969/70, 1970/1 (Nottingham Forest) 1971/2, 1972/3, 1973/4, 1974/5 (Manchester United) 1975/6, 1976/7.
Jamison, A. (1) (Glentoran) 1975/6.
Jennings, P. (119) (Watford) 1963/4, 1964/5, (Tottenham Hotspur), 1965/6, 1966/7, 1967/8, 1968/9, 1969/70, 1970/1, 1971/2, 1972/3, 1973/4, 1974/5, 1975/6, 1976/7, (Arsenal) 1977/8, 1978/9, 1979/80, 1980/1, 1981/2, 1982/3, 1983/4, 1984/5, (Tottenham Hotspur) 1985/6.
Johnston, W. (1) (Glentoran) 1961/2, (Oldham Athletic) 1965/6.
Jones, J. (3) (Glenavon) 1955/6, 1956/7.

Keane, T. (1) (Swansea Town) 1948/9.
Kee, P.V. (7) (Oxford United), 1989/90, 1990/91.
Keith, R. (23) (Newcastle United) 1957/8, 1958/9, 1959/60, 1960/1, 1961/2.
Kelly, H. (4) (Fulham) 1949/50 (Southampton) 1950/1.
Kelly, P. (1) (Barnsley) 1949/50.

Lawther, I. (4) (Sunderland) 1959/60, 1960/1, 1961/2 (Blackburn Rovers).
Lockhart, N. (8) (Linfield) 1946/7, 1949/50, (Coventry City) 1950/1, 1951/2, 1953/4, (Aston Villa) 1954/5, 1955/6.
Lennon, N.F. (1) (Crewe Alexandra) 1993/94.
Lomas, S.M. (4) (Manchester City) 1993/94.
Lutton, B. (6) (Wolverhampton Wanderers) 1969/70, 1972/3 (West Ham United) 1973/4.

Magill, E. (26) (Arsenal) 1961/2, 1962/3, 1963/4, 1964/5, 1965/6 (Brighton & Hove Albion).
Magilton, J. (22) (Oxford United) 1990/1, 1991/2, 1992/93, (Southampton) 1993/94.
Martin, C. (6) (Glentoran) 1946/7, 1947/8 (Leeds United) 1948/9 (Aston Villa) 1949/50.
McAdams, W. (15) (Manchester City) 1953/4, 1954/5, 1956/7, 1957/8, 1960/1 (Bolton Wanderers) 1961/2 (Leeds United).
McAlinden, J. (2) (Portsmouth) 1946/7, 1948/9, (Southend United).
McBride, S. (4) (Glenavon) 1990/1, 1991/2.
McCabe, J. (6) (Leeds United) 1948/9, 1949/50, 1950/1, 1952/3, 1953/4.
McCavana, T. (3) (Coleraine) 1954/5, 1955/6.
McCleary, J.W. (1) (Cliftonville) 1954/5.
McClelland, J. (6) (Arsenal) 1960/1, 1965/6 (Fulham).
McClelland, J. (53) (Mansfield Town) 1979/80, 1980/1, 1981/2 (Rangers) 1982/3, 1983/4, 1984/5 (Watford) 1985/6, 1986/7, 1987/8, 1988/9 (Leeds U) 1989/90.
McCourt, F. (6) (Manchester City) 1951/2, 1952/3.
McCoy, R. (1) (Coleraine) 1986/7.
McCreery, D. (67) (Manchester United) 1975/6, 1976/7, 1977/8, 1978/9, 1979/80 (QPR) 1980/1 (Tulsa Roughnecks) 1981/2, 1982/3 (Newcastle United), 1983/4, 1984/5, 1985/6, 1986/7, 1987/8, 1988/9 (Hearts) 1989/90.
McCrory, S. (1) (Southend United) 1957/8.
McCullough, W. (10) (Arsenal) 1960/1, 1962/3, 1963/4, 1964/5, 1966/7, (Millwall).
McCurdy, C. (1) (Linfield) 1979/80.
McDonald, A. (43) (QPR) 1985/6, 1986/7, 1987/8, 1988/9, 1990/1, 1991/2, 1992/93, 1993/94.

McElhinney, G. (6) (Bolton Wanderers) 1983/4, 1984/5.
McFaul, I. (6) (Linfield) 1966/7, 1969/70 (Newcastle United) 1970/1, 1971/2, 1972/3, 1973/4.
McGarry, J.K. (3) (Cliftonville) 1950/1.
McGaughey, M. (1) (Linfield) 1984/5.
McGrath, R. (21) (Tottenham Hotspur) 1973/4, 1974/5, 1975/6 (Manchester United) 1976/7, 1977/8, 1978/9.
McIlroy, J. (55) (Burnley) 1951/2, 1952/3, 1953/4, 1954/5, 1955/6, 1956/7, 1957/8, 1958/9, 1959/60, 1960/1, 1961/2, 1962/3, 1965/6 (Stoke City).
McIlroy, S.B. (88) (Manchester United) 1971/2, 1973/4, 1974/5, 1975/6, 1976/7, 1977/8, 1978/9, 1979/80, 1980/1, 1981/2, (Stoke City), 1982/3, 1983/4, 1984/5 (Manchester City) 1985/6, 1986/7.
McKeag, W. (2) (Glentoran) 1967/8.
McKenna, J. (7) (Huddersfield Town) 1949/50, 1950/1, 1951/2.
McKenzie, R. (1) (Airdrieonians) 1966/7.
McKinney, W. (1) (Falkirk) 1965/6.
McKnight, A. (10) (Celtic) 1987/8, (West Ham United) 1988/9.
McLaughlin, J. (12) (Shrewsbury Town) 1961/2, 1962/3 (Swansea City), 1963/4, 1964/5, 1965/6.
McMichael, A. (39) (Newcastle United) 1949/50, 1950/1, 1951/2, 1952/3, 1953/4, 1954/5, 1955/6, 1956/7, 1957/8, 1958/9, 1959/60.
McMillan, S. (2) (Manchester United) 1962/3.
McMordie, E. (21) (Middlesbrough) 1968/9, 1969/70, 1970/1, 1971/2, 1972/3.
McMorran, E. (15) (Belfast Celtic) 1946/7 (Barnsley) 1950/1, 1951/2, 1952/3, (Doncaster Rovers) 1953/4, 1955/6, 1956/7.
McNally, B.A. (5) (Shrewsbury Town) 1985/6, 1986/7, 1987/8.
McParland, P. (34) (Aston Villa) 1953/4, 1954/5, 1955/6, 1956/7, 1957/8, 1958/9, 1959/60, 1960/1, 1961/2 (Wolverhampton Wanderers).
Montgomery, F.J. (1) (Coleraine) 1954/5.
Moore, C. (1) (Glentoran) 1948/9.
Moreland, V. (6) (Derby County) 1978/9, 1979/80.
Morgan, S. (18) (Port Vale) 1971/2, 1972/3, 1973/4 (Aston Villa), 1974/5, 1975/6 (Brighton & Hove Albion) (Sparta Rotterdam) 1978/9.
Morrow, S.J. (13) (Arsenal) 1989/90, 1990/1, 1991/2, 1992/93, 1993/94.
Mullan, G. (4) (Glentoran) 1982/3.

Napier, R. (1) (Bolton Wanderers) 1965/6.
Neill, T. (59) (Arsenal) 1960/1, 1961/2, 1962/3, 1963/4, 1964/5, 1965/6, 1966/7, 1967/8, 1968/9, 1969/70 (Hull City) 1970/1, 1971/2, 1972/3.
Nelson, S. (51) (Arsenal) 1969/70, 1970/1, 1971/2, 1972/3, 1973/4, 1974/5, 1975/6, 1976/7, 1977/8, 1978/9, 1979/80, 1980/1, 1981/2 (Brighton & Hove Albion).
Nicholl, C. (51) (Aston Villa) 1974/5, 1975/6, 1976/7 (Southampton), 1977/8, 1978/9, 1979/80, 1980/1, 1981/2, 1982/3 (Grimsby Town) 1983/4.
Nicholl, J.M. (73) (Manchester United) 1975/6, 1976/7, 1977/8, 1978/9, 1979/80, 1980/1, 1981/2 (Toronto Blizzard) 1982/3 (Sunderland) (Toronto Blizzard) (Rangers) 1983/4 (Toronto Blizzard) 1984/5 (West Bromwich Albion) 1985/6.
Nicholson, J. (41) (Manchester United) 1960/1, 1961/2, 1962/3, 1964/5, (Huddersfield Town) 1965/6, 1966/7, 1967/8, 1968/9, 1969/70, 1970/1, 1971/2.

O'Boyle, G. (2) (Dunfermline Athletic) 1993/94.
O'Doherty, A. (2) (Coleraine) 1969/70.
O'Driscoll, J. (3) (Swansea City) 1948/9
O'Kane, L. (20) (Nottingham Forest) 1969/70, 1970/1, 1971/2, 1972/3, 1973/4, 1974/5.

O'Neill, C. (3) (Motherwell) 1988/9, 1989/90, 1990/91.
O'Neill, H.M. (64) (Distillery) 1971/2 (Nottingham Forest) 1972/3, 1973/4, 1974/5, 1975/6, 1976/7, 1977/8, 1978/9, 1979/80, 1980/1 (Norwich City) 1981/2 (Manchester City) (Norwich City) 1982/3 (Notts County) 1983/4, 1984/5.
O'Neill, J. (1) (Sunderland) 1961/2.
O'Neill, J. (39) (Leicester City) 1979/80, 1980/1, 1981/2, 1982/3, 1983/4, 1984/5, 1985/6.
O'Neill, M.A. (23) (Newcastle United) 1987/8, 1988/9 (Dundee United) 1989/90, 1990/1, 1991/2, 1992/93, (Hibernian) 1993/94.

Parke, J. (13) (Linfield) 1963/4 (Hibernian), 1964/5 (Sunderland), 1965/6, 1966/7, 1967/8.
Patterson, D.J. (2) (Crystal Palace) 1993/94.
Peacock, R. (31) (Celtic) 1951/2, 1952/3, 1953/4, 1954/5, 1955/6, 1956/7, 1957/8, 1958/9, 1959/60, 1960/1 (Coleraine) 1961/2.
Penney, S. (17) (Brighton & Hove Albion) 1984/5, 1985/6, 1986/7, 1987/8, 1988/9.
Platt, J.A. (23) (Middlesbrough) 1975/6, 1977/8, 1979/80, 1980/1, 1981/2, 1982/3, (Ballymena United) 1983/4 (Coleraine) 1985/6.

Quinn, J.M. (41) (Blackburn Rovers) 1984/5, 1985/6, 1986/7, 1987/8 (Leicester) 1988/9 (Bradford City) 1989/90 (West Ham United) 1990/1, (Bournemouth) 1991/2 1992/93, 1993/94.

Rafferty, P. (1) (Linfield) 1979/80.
Ramsey, P. (14) (Leicester City) 1983/4, 1984/5, 1985/6, 1986/7, 1987/8, 1988/9.
Rice, P. (49) (Arsenal) 1968/9, 1969/70, 1970/1, 1971/2, 1972/3, 1973/4, 1974/5, 1975/6, 1976/7, 1977/8, 1978/9, 1979/80.
Rogan, A. (17) (Celtic) 1987/8, 1988/9, 1989/90, 1990/1, 1991/2.
Ross, E. (1) (Newcastle United) 1968/9.
Russell, A. (1) (Linfield) 1946/7.
Ryan, R. (1) (West Bromwich Albion) 1949/50.

Sanchez, L.P. (3) (Wimbledon) 1986/7, 1988/9.
Scott, J. (2) (Grimsby Town) 1957/8.
Scott, P. (10) (Everton) 1974/5, 1975/6, (York City) 1977/8, (Aldershot) 1978/9.
Sharkey, P. (1) (Ipswich Town) 1975/6.
Shields, J. (1) (Southampton) 1956/7.
Simpson, W. (12) (Rangers) 1950/1, 1953/4, 1954/5, 1956/7, 1957/8, 1958/9.
Sloan, D. (2) (Oxford) 1968/9, 1970/1.
Sloan, T. (3) (Manchester United) 1978/9.
Sloan, W. (1) (Arsenal) 1946/7.
Smyth, S. (9) (Wolverhampton Wanderers) 1947/8, 1948/9, 1949/50 (Stoke City) 1951/2.
Smyth, W. (4) (Distillery) 1948/9, 1953/4.
Spence, D. (29) (Bury) 1974/5, 1975/6, (Blackpool) 1976/7, 1978/9, 1979/80, (Southend United) 1980/1, 1981/2.
Stevenson, A. (3) (Everton) 1946/7, 1947/8.
Stewart, A. (7) (Glentoran) 1966/7, 1967/8 (Derby) 1968/9.
Stewart, D. (1) (Hull City) 1977/8.
Stewart, I. (31) (QPR) 1981/2, 1982/3, 1983/4, 1984/5, (Newcastle United) 1985/6, 1986/7.
Stewart, T. (1) (Linfield) 1960/1.

Taggart, G.P. (28) (Barnsley) 1989/90, 1990/1, 1991/2, 1992/93, 1993/94.

Todd, S. (11) (Burnley) 1965/6, 1966/7, 1967/8, 1968/9, 1969/70 (Sheffield Wednesday) 1970/1.
Trainor, D. (1) (Crusaders) 1966/7.
Tully, C. (10) (Celtic) 1948/9, 1949/50, 1951/2, 1952/3, 1953/4, 1955/6, 1958/9.

Uprichard, N. (18) (Swindon Town) 1951/2, 1952/3 (Portsmouth) 1954/5, 1955/6, 1957/8, 1958/9.

Vernon, J. (17) (Belfast Celtic) 1946/7 (West Bromwich Albion) 1947/8, 1948/9, 1949/50, 1950/1 , 1951/2.

Walker, J. (1) (Doncaster Rovers) 1954/5.
Walsh, D. (9) (West Bromwich Albion) 1946/7, 1947/8, 1948/9, 1949/50.
Walsh, W. (5) (Manchester City) 1947/8, 1948/9.
Watson, P. (1) (Distillery) 1970/1.
Welsh, S. (4) (Carlisle United) 1965/6, 1966/7.
Whiteside, N. (38) (Manchester United) 1981/2, 1982/3, 1983/4, 1984/5, 1985/6, 1986/7, 1987/8, (Everton) 1989/90.
Williams, P. (1) (WBA) 1990/1.
Wilson, D.J. (24) (Brighton & Hove Albion) 1986/7 (Luton) 1987/8, 1988/9, 1989/90, 1990/1, (Sheffield Wednesday) 1991/2.
Wilson, K.J. (40) (Ipswich Town) 1986/7 (Chelsea) 1987/8, 1988/9, 1989/90, 1990/1, 1991/2 (Notts County) 1992/93, 1993/94.
Wilson, S. (12) (Glenavon) 1961/2, 1963/4, (Falkirk) 1964/5 (Dundee), 1965/6, 1966/7, 1967/8.
Worthington, N. (50) (Sheffield Wednesday) 1983/4, 1984/5, 1985/6, 1986/7, 1987/8, 1988/9, 1989/90, 1990/1, 1991/2, 1992/93, 1993/94.
Wright, T.J. (22) (Newcastle United) 1988/9, 1989/90, 1991/2, 1992/93, (Nottingham Forest) 1993/94.

SCOTLAND

Aird, J. (4) (Burnley) 1953/4.
Aitken, G.G. (8) (East Fife) 1948/9, 1949/50, 1952/3 (Sunderland) 1953/4.
Aitken, R. (57) (Celtic) 1979/80, 1982/3, 1983/4, 1984/5, 1985/6, 1986/7, 1987/8, (Newcastle United) 1989/90, (St Mirren) 1991/2.
Albiston, A. (14) (Manchester United) 1981/2, 1983/4, 1984/5, 1985/6.
Allan, T. (2) (Dundee) 1973/4.
Anderson, J. (1) (Leicester City) 1953/4.
Archibald, S. (27) (Aberdeen) 1979/80 (Tottenham Hotspur) 1980/1, 1981/2, 1982/3, 1983/4, 1984/5, (Barcelona) 1985/6.
Auld, B. (3) (Celtic) 1958/9, 1959/60.

Baird, H. (1) (Airdrieonians) 1955/6.
Baird, S. (7) (Rangers) 1956/7, 1957/8.
Bannon, E. (11) (Dundee United) 1979/80, 1982/3, 1983/4, 1985/6.
Bauld, W. (3) (Heart of Midlothian) 1949/50.
Baxter, J. (34) (Rangers) 1960/1, 1961/2, 1962/3, 1963/4, 1964/5 (Sunderland) 1965/6, 1966/7, 1967/8.
Bell, W. (2) (Leeds United) 1965/6.
Bett, J. (25) (Rangers) 1981/2, 1982/3 (Lokeren) 1983/4, 1984/5 (Aberdeen) 1985/6, 1986/7, 1987/8, 1988/9, 1989/90.
Black, E. (2) (Metz) 1987/8.
Black, I. (1) (Southampton) 1947/8.

Blacklaw, A. (3) (Burnley) 1962/3, 1965/6.
Blackley, J. (7) (Hibernian) 1973/4, 1975/6, 1976/7.
Blair, J. (1) (Blackpool) 1946/7.
Blyth, J. (2) (Coventry City) 1977/8.
Bone, J. (2) (Norwich City) 1971/2, 1972/3.
Booth, S. (5) (Aberdeen) 1992/93, 1993/94.
Bowman, D. (6) (Dundee United) 1991/2, 1992/93, 1993/94.
Boyd, T. (21) (Motherwell) 1990/1 (Chelsea) 1991/2 (Celtic) 1992/93, 1993/94.
Brand, R. (8) (Rangers) 1960/1, 1961/2.
Brazil, A. (13) (Ipswich Town) 1979/80, 1981/2, 1982/3 (Tottenham Hotspur).
Bremner, D. (1) (Hibernian) 1975/6.
Bremner, W. (54) (Leeds United) 1964/5, 1965/6, 1966/7, 1967/8, 1968/9, 1969/70, 1970/1, 1971/2, 1972/3, 1973/4, 1974/5, 1975/6.
Brennan, F. (7) (Newcastle United) 1946/7, 1952/3, 1963/4.
Brogan, J. (4) (Celtic) 1970/1.
Brown, A. (14) (East Fife) 1949/50 (Blackpool) 1951/2, 1952/3, 1953/4.
Brown, H. (3) (Partick Thistle) 1946/7.
Brown, J. (1) (Sheffield United) 1974/5.
Brown, R. (3) (Rangers) 1946/7, 1948/9, 1951/2.
Brown, W. (28) (Dundee) 1957/8, 1958/9, 1959/60 (Tottenham Hotspur) 1961/2, 1962/3, 1963/4, 1964/5, 1965/6.
Brownlie, J. (7) (Hibernian) 1970/1, 1971/2, 1972/3, 1975/6.
Buchan, M. (34) (Aberdeen) 1971/2 (Manchester United), 1972/3, 1973/4, 1974/5, 1975/6, 1976/7, 1977/8, 1978/9.
Buckley, P. (3) (Aberdeen) 1953/4, 1954/5.
Burley, G. (11) (Ipswich Town) 1978/9, 1979/80, 1981/2.
Burns, F. (1) (Manchester United) 1969/70.
Burns, K. (20) (Birmingham City) 1973/4, 1974/5, 1976/7 (Nottingham Forest) 1977/8, 1978/9, 1979/80, 1980/1.
Burns, T. (8) (Celtic) 1980/1, 1981/2, 1982/3, 1987/8.

Caldow, E. (40) (Rangers) 1956/7, 1957/8, 1958/9, 1959/60, 1960/1, 1961/2, 1962/3.
Callaghan, W. (2) (Dunfermline) 1969/70.
Campbell, R. (5) (Falkirk) 1946/7 (Chelsea) 1949/50.
Campbell, W. (5) (Morton) 1946/7, 1947/8.
Carr, W. (6) (Coventry City) 1969/70, 1970/1, 1971/2, 1972/3.
Chalmers, S. (5) (Celtic) 1964/5, 1965/6, 1966/7.
Clark, J. (4) (Celtic) 1965/6, 1966/7.
Clark, R. (17) (Aberdeen) 1967/8, 1969/70, 1970/1, 1971/2, 1972/3.
Clarke, S. (6) (Chelsea) 1987/8, 1993/94.
Collins, J. (18) (Hibernian) 1987/8, 1989/90, 1990/1 (Celtic) 1991/2, 1992/93, 1993/94.
Collins, R. (31) (Celtic) 1950/1, 1954/5, 1955/6, 1956/7, 1957/8, 1958/9, (Everton) 1964/5, (Leeds United).
Colquhoun, E. (9) (Sheffield United) 1971/2, 1972/3.
Colquhoun, J. (1) (Hearts) 1987/8.
Combe, R. (3) (Hibernian) 1947/8.
Conn, A. (1) (Heart of Midlothian) 1955/6.
Conn, A. (2) (Tottenham Hotspur) 1974/5.
Connachan, E. (2) (Dunfermline Athletic) 1961/2.
Connelly, G. (2) (Celtic) 1973/4.
Connolly, J. (1) (Everton) 1972/3.
Connor, R. (4) (Dundee) 1985/6 (Aberdeen) 1987/8, 1988/9, 1990/91.
Cooke, C. (16) (Dundee) 1965/6 (Chelsea) 1967/8, 1968/9, 1969/70, 1970/1, 1974/5.

Cooper, D. (22) (Rangers) 1979/80, 1983/4, 1984/5, 1985/6, 1986/7 (Motherwell) 1989/90.
Cormack, P. (9) (Hibernian) 1965/6, 1969/70 (Nottingham Forest) 1970/1, 1971/2.
Cowan, J. (25) (Morton) 1947/8, 1948/9, 1949/50, 1950/1, 1951/2 (Motherwell).
Cowie, D. (20) (Dundee) 1952/3, 1953/4, 1954/5, 1955/6, 1956/7, 1957/8.
Cox, C. (1) (Hearts) 1947/8.
Cox, S. (24) (Rangers) 1947/8, 1948/9, 1949/50, 1950/1, 1951/2, 1952/3, 1953/4.
Craig, J. (1) (Celtic) 1976/7.
Craig, J.P. (1) (Celtic) 1967/8.
Craig, T. (1) (Newcastle United) 1975/6.
Crerand, P. (16) (Celtic) 1960/1, 1961/2, 1962/3 (Manchester United) 1963/4, 1964/5, 1965/6.
Cropley, A. (2) (Hibernian) 1971/2.
Cruickshank, J. (6) (Heart of Midlothian) 1963/4, 1969/70, 1970/1, 1975/6.
Cullen, M. (1) (Luton Town) 1955/6.
Cumming, J. (9) (Heart of Midlothian) 1954/5, 1959/60.
Cunningham, W. (8) (Preston North End) 1953/4, 1954/5.
Curran, H. (5) (Wolverhampton Wanderers) 1969/70, 1970/1.

Dalglish, K. (102) (Celtic) 1971/2, 1972/3, 1973/4, 1974/5, 1975/6, 1976/7, (Liverpool) 1977/8, 1978/9, 1979/80, 1980/1, 1981/2, 1982/3, 1983/4, 1984/5, 1985/6, 1986/7.
Davidson, J. (8) (Partick Thistle) 1953/4, 1954/5.
Dawson, A. (5) (Rangers) 1979/80, 1982/3.
Deans, D. (2) (Celtic) 1974/5.
Delaney, J. (4) (Manchester United) 1946/7, 1947/8.
Dick, J. (1) (West Ham United) 1958/9.
Dickson, W. (5) (Kilmarnock) 1969/70, 1970/1.
Docherty, T. (25) (Preston North End) 1951/2, 1952/3, 1953/4, 1954/5, 1956/7, 1957/8, 1958/9 (Arsenal).
Dodds, D. (2) (Dundee United) 1983/4.
Donachie, W. (35) (Manchester City) 1971/2, 1972/3, 1973/4, 1975/6, 1976/7, 1977/8, 1978/9.
Dougall, C. (1) (Birmingham City) 1946/7.
Dougan, R. (1) (Heart of Midlothian) 1949/50.
Doyle, J. (1) (Ayr United) 1975/6.
Duncan, A. (6) (Hibernian) 1974/5, 1975/6.
Duncan, D. (3) (East Fife) 1947/8.
Duncanson, J. (1) (Rangers) 1946/7.
Durie, G.S. (27) (Chelsea) 1987/8, 1988/9, 1989/90, 1990/1, (Tottenham Hotspur) 1991/2, 1992/93, (Rangers) 1993/94.
Durrant, I. (11) (Rangers) 1987/8, 1988/9, 1992/93, 1993/94.

Evans, A. (4) (Aston Villa) 1981/2.
Evans, R. (48) (Celtic) 1948/9, 1949/50, 1950/1, 1951/2, 1952/3, 1953/4, 1954/5, 1955/6, 1956/7, 1957/8, 1958/9, 1959/60 (Chelsea).
Ewing, T. (2) (Partick Thistle) 1957/8.

Farm, G. (10) (Blackpool) 1952/3, 1953/4, 1958/9.
Ferguson, D. (2) (Rangers) 1987/8.
Ferguson, D. (4) (Dundee United) 1991/2, 1992/93.
Ferguson, I. (8) (Rangers) 1988/9, 1992/93, 1993/94.
Ferguson, R. (7) (Kilmarnock) 1965/6, 1966/7.
Fernie, W. (12) (Celtic) 1953/4, 1954/5, 1956/7, 1957/8.
Flavell, R. (2) (Airdrieonians) 1946/7.

Fleck, R. (4) (Norwich City) 1989/90, 1990/1.
Fleming, C. (1) (East Fife) 1953/4.
Forbes, A. (14) (Sheffield United) 1946/7, 1947/8 (Arsenal) 1949/50, 1950/1, 1951/2.
Ford, D. (3) (Heart of Midlothian) 1973/4.
Forrest, J. (1) (Motherwell) 1957/8.
Forrest, J. (5) (Rangers) 1965/6 (Aberdeen) 1970/1.
Forsyth, A. (10) (Partick Thistle) 1971/2, 1972/3 (Manchester United) 1974/5, 1975/6.
Forsyth, C. (4) (Kilmarnock) 1963/4, 1964/5.
Forsyth, T. (22) (Motherwell) 1970/1 (Rangers) 1973/4, 1975/6, 1976/7, 1977/8.
Fraser, D. (2) (West Bromwich Albion) 1967/8, 1968/9.
Fraser, W. (2) (Sunderland) 1954/5.

Gabriel, J. (2) (Everton) 1960/1, 1961/2.
Gallacher, K.W. (19) (Dundee United) 1987/8, 1988/9, 1990/91 (Coventry City), 1991/2 (Blackburn Rovers) 1992/93, 1993/94.
Galloway, M. (1) (Celtic) 1991/2.
Gardiner, W. (1) (Motherwell) 1957/8.
Gemmell, T. (2) (St Mirren) 1954/5.
Gemmell, T. (18) (Celtic) 1965/6, 1966/7, 1967/8, 1968/9, 1969/70, 1970/1.
Gemmill, A. (43) (Derby County) 1970/1, 1971/2, 1975/6, 1976/7, 1977/8 (Nottingham Forest) 1978/9 (Birmingham City) 1979/80, 1980/1.
Gibson, D. (7) (Leicester City) 1962/3, 1963/4, 1964/5.
Gillespie, G.T. (13) (Liverpool) 1987/8, 1988/9, 1989/90, (Celtic) 1990/91.
Gilzean, A. (22) (Dundee) 1963/4, 1964/5 (Tottenham Hotspur) 1965/6, 1967/8, 1968/9, 1969/70, 1970/1.
Glavin, R. (1) (Celtic) 1976/7.
Glen, A. (2) (Aberdeen) 1955/6.
Goram, A.L. (29) (Oldham Athletic) 1985/6, 1986/7, (Hibernian) 1988/9, 1989/90, 1990/1, (Rangers) 1991/2, 1992/93, 1993/94.
Gough, C.R. (61) (Dundee United) 1982/3, 1983/4, 1984/5, 1985/6, 1986/7 (Tottenham Hotspur) 1987/8 (Rangers) 1988/9, 1989/90, 1990/1, 1991/2, 1992/93.
Govan, J. (6) (Hibernian) 1947/8, 1948/9.
Graham, A. (10) (Leeds United) 1977/8, 1978/9, 1979/80, 1980/1.
Graham, G. (12) (Arsenal) 1971/2, 1972/3 (Manchester United).
Grant, J. (2) (Hibernian) 1958/9.
Grant, P. (2) (Celtic) 1988/9.
Gray, A. (20) (Aston Villa) 1975/6, 1976/7, 1978/9 (Wolverhampton Wanderers) 1979/80, 1980/1, 1981/2, 1982/3, 1984/5 (Everton).
Gray, E. (12) (Leeds United) 1968/9, 1969/70, 1970/71, 1971/2, 1975/6, 1976/7.
Gray F. (32) (Leeds United) 1975/6, 1978/9, 1979/80 (Nottingham Forest) 1980/1, (Leeds United) 1981/2, 1982/3.
Green, A. (6) (Blackpool) 1970/1 (Newcastle United) 1971/2.
Greig, J. (44) (Rangers) 1963/4, 1964/5, 1965/6, 1966/7, 1967/8, 1968/9, 1969/70, 1970/1, 1975/6.
Gunn, B. (6) (Norwich C) 1989/90, 1992/93, 1993/94.

Haddock, H. (6) (Clyde) 1954/5, 1957/8.
Haffey, F. (2) (Celtic) 1959/60, 1960/1.
Hamilton, A. (24) (Dundee) 1961/2, 1962/3, 1963/4, 1964/5, 1965/6.
Hamilton, G. (5) (Aberdeen) 1946/7, 1950/1, 1953/4.
Hamilton, W. (1) (Hibernian) 1964/5.

Hansen, A. (26) (Liverpool) 1978/9, 1979/80, 1980/1, 1981/2, 1982/3, 1984/5, 1985/6, 1986/7.

Hansen J. (2) (Partick Thistle) 1971/2.

Harper, J. (4) (Aberdeen) 1972/3, 1975/6, 1978/9.

Hartford, A. (50) (West Bromwich Albion) 1971/2, 1975/6 (Manchester City) 1976/7, 1977/8, 1978/9, 1979/80 (Everton) 1980/1, 1981/2 (Manchester City).

Harvey, D. (16) (Leeds United) 1972/3, 1973/4, 1974/5, 1975/6, 1976/7.

Haughney, M. (1) (Celtic) 1953/4.

Hay, D. (27) (Celtic) 1969/70, 1970/1, 1971/2, 1972/3, 1973/4.

Hegarty, P. (8) (Dundee United) 1978/9, 1979/80, 1982/3.

Henderson, J. (7) (Portsmouth) 1952/3, 1953/4, 1955/6, 1958/9 (Arsenal).

Henderson, W. (29) (Rangers) 1962/3, 1963/4, 1964/5, 1965/6, 1966/7, 1967/8, 1968/9, 1969/70.

Hendry, E.C.J. (6) (Blackburn Rovers) 1992/93, 1993/94.

Herd, D. (5) (Arsenal) 1958/9, 1960/1.

Herd, G. (5) (Clyde) 1957/8, 1959/60, 1960/1.

Herriot, J. (8) (Birmingham City) 1968/9, 1969/70.

Hewie, J. (19) (Charlton Athletic) 1955/6, 1956/7, 1957/8, 1958/9, 1959/60.

Holt, D. (5) (Heart of Midlothian) 1962/3, 1963/4.

Holton, J. (15) (Manchester United) 1972/3, 1973/4, 1974/5.

Hope, R. (2) (West Bromwich Albion) 1967/8, 1968/9.

Houliston, W. (3) (Queen of the South) 1948/9.

Houston, S. (1) (Manchester United) 1975/6.

Howie, H. (1) (Hibernian) 1948/9.

Hughes, J. (8) (Celtic) 1964/5, 1965/6, 1967/8, 1968/9, 1969/70.

Hughes, W. (1) (Sunderland) 1974/5.

Humphries, W. (1) (Motherwell) 1951/2.

Hunter, A. (4) (Kilmarnock) 1971/2, 1972/3, (Celtic) 1973/4.

Hunter, W. (3) (Motherwell) 1959/60, 1960/1.

Husband, J. (1) (Partick Thistle) 1946/7.

Hutchison, T. (17) (Coventry City) 1973/4, 1974/5, 1975/6.

Imlach, S. (4) (Nottingham Forest) 1957/8.

Irvine, B. (9) (Aberdeen) 1990/1, 1992/93, 1993/94.

Jackson, C. (8) (Rangers) 1974/5, 1975/6.

Jardine, A. (38) (Rangers) 1970/1, 1971/2, 1972/3, 1973/4, 1974/5, 1976/7, 1977/8, 1978/9, 1979/80.

Jarvie, A. (3) (Airdrieonians) 1970/1.

Jess, E. (7) (Aberdeen) 1992/93, 1993/94.

Johnston, M. (38) (Watford) 1983/4, 1984/5 (Celtic) 1985/6, 1986/7, (Nantes) 1987/8, 1988/9 (Rangers) 1989/90, 1991/2.

Johnston, W. (22) (Rangers) 1965/6, 1967/8, 1968/9, 1969/70, 1970/1 (West Bromwich Albion) 1976/7, 1977/8.

Johnstone, D. (14) (Rangers) 1972/3, 1974/5, 1975/6, 1977/8, 1979/80.

Johnstone, J. (23) (Celtic) 1964/5, 1965/6, 1966/7, 1967/8, 1968/9, 1969/70, 1970/1, 1971/2, 1973/4, 1974/5.

Johnstone, L. (2) (Clyde) 1947/8.

Johnstone, R. (17) (Hibernian) 1950/1, 1951/2, 1952/3, 1953/4, 1954/5, (Manchester City) 1955/6.

Jordan, J. (52) (Leeds United) 1972/3, 1973/4, 1974/5, 1975/6, 1976/7, 1977/8, (Manchester United) 1978/9, 1979/80, 1980/1, 1981/2 (AC Milan).

Kelly, H. (1) (Blackpool) 1951/2.

278

Kelly, J. (2) (Barnsley) 1948/9.

Kennedy, J. (6) (Celtic) 1963/4, 1964/5.

Kennedy, S. (8) (Aberdeen) 1977/8, 1978/9, 1981/2.

Kennedy, S. (5) (Rangers) 1974/5.

Kerr, A. (2) (Partick Thistle) 1954/5.

Law, D. (55) (Huddersfield Town) 1958/9, 1959/60 (Manchester City) 1960/1, 1961/2 (Torino) 1962/3 (Manchester United) 1963/4, 1964/5, 1965/6, 1966/7, 1967/8, 1968/9, 1971/2, 1973/4 (Manchester City).

Lawrence, T. (3) (Liverpool) 1962/3, 1968/9.

Leggat, G. (18) (Aberdeen) 1955/6, 1956/7, 1957/8, 1958/9 (Fulham) 1959/60.

Leighton, J. (61) (Aberdeen) 1982/3, 1983/4, 1984/5, 1985/6, 1986/7, 1987/8, (Manchester United) 1988/9, 1989/90 (Hibernian) 1993/94.

Lennox, R. (10) (Celtic) 1966/7, 1967/8, 1968/9.

Leslie, L. (5) (Airdrieonians) 1960/1.

Levein, C. (13) (Hearts) 1989/90, 1991/2, 1992/93, 1993/94.

Liddell, W. (28) (Liverpool) 1946/7, 1947/8, 1949/50, 1950/1, 195/2, 1952/3, 1953/4, 1954/5, 1955/6.

Linwood, A. (1) (Clyde) 1949/50.

Little, A. (1) (Rangers) 1952/3.

Logie, J. (1) (Arsenal) 1952/3.

Long, H. (1) (Clyde) 1946/7.

Lorimer, P. (21) (Leeds United) 1969/70, 1970/1, 1971/2, 1972/3, 1973/4, 1974/5, 1975/6.

Macari, L. (24) (Celtic) 1971/2, 1972/3 (Manchester United) 1974/5, 1976/7, 1977/8, 1978/9.

Macaulay, A. (7) (Brentford) 1946/7 (Arsenal) 1947/8.

MacDougall, E. (7) (Norwich City) 1974/5, 1975/6.

Mackay, D. (22) (Heart of Midlothian) 1956/7, 1957/8, 1958/9 (Tottenham Hotspur) 1959/60, 1960/1, 1962/3, 1963/4, 1965/6.

Mackay, G. (4) (Heart of Midlothian) 1987/8.

Malpas, M. (55) (Dundee United) 1983/4, 1984/5, 1985/6, 1986/7, 1987/8, 1988/9, 1989/90, 1990/1, 1991/2, 1992/93.

Marshall, G. (1) (Celtic) 1991/2.

Martin, F. (6) (Aberdeen) 1953/4, 1954/5.

Martin, N. (3) (Hibernian) 1964/5, 1965/6 (Sunderland).

Martis, J. (1) (Motherwell) 1960/1.

Mason, J. (7) (Third Lanark) 1948/9, 1949/50, 1950/1.

Masson, D. (17) (QPR) 1975/6, 1976/7, 1977/8 (Derby County) 1978/9.

Mathers, D. (1) (Partick Thistle) 1953/4.

McAllister, G. (28) (Leicester City) 1989/90, 1990/1 (Leeds United), 1991/2, 1992/93, 1993/94.

McAvennie, F. (5) (West Ham United) 1985/6 (Celtic) 1987/8.

McBride, J. (2) (Celtic) 1966/7.

McCall, S.M. (27) (Everton) 1989/90, 1990/1, (Rangers) 1991/2, 1992/93, 1993/94.

McCalliog, J. (5) (Sheffield Wednesday) 1966/7, 1967/8, 1968/9, 1970/1 (Wolverhampton Wanderers).

McCann, R. (5) (Motherwell) 1958/9, 1959/60, 1960/1.

McClair, B. (30) (Celtic) 1986/7 (Manchester United) 1987/8, 1988/9, 1989/90, 1990/1, 1991/2, 1992/93.

McCloy, P. (4) (Rangers) 1972/3.

McCoist, A. (46) (Rangers) 1985/6, 1986/7, 1987/8, 1988/9, 1989/90, 1990/1, 1991/2, 1992/93.

McColl, I. (14) (Rangers) 1949/50, 1950/1, 1956/7, 1957/8.

McCreadie, E. (23) (Chelsea) 1964/5, 1965/6, 1966/7, 1967/8, 1968/9.

MacDonald, A. (1) (Rangers) 1975/6.

MacDonald, J. (2) (Sunderland) 1955/6.

McFarlane, W. (1) (Heart of Midlothian) 1946/7.

McGarr, E. (2) (Aberdeen) 1969/70.

McGarvey, F. (7) (Liverpool) 1978/9 (Celtic) 1983/4.

McGhee, M. (4) (Aberdeen) 1982/3, 1983/4.

McGinlay, J. (2) (Bolton Wanderers) 1993/94.

McGrain, D. (62) (Celtic) 1972/3, 1973/4, 1974/5, 1975/6, 1976/7, 1977/8, 1979/80, 1980/1, 1981/2.

McGrory, J. (3) (Kilmarnock) 1964/5, 1965/6.

McInally, A. (8) (Aston Villa) 1988/9 (Bayern Munich) 1989/90.

McInally, J. (10) (Dundee United) 1986/7, 1987/8, 1990/1, 1991/2, 1992/93.

McKay, D. (14) (Celtic) 1958/9, 1959/60, 1960/1, 1961/2.

McKean, R. (1) (Rangers) 1975/6.

McKinlay, W. (4) (Dundee United) 1993/94.

McKenzie, J. (9) (Partick Thistle) 1953/4, 1954/5, 1955/6.

McKimmie, S. (27) (Aberdeen) 1988/9, 1989/90, 1990/1, 1991/2, 1992/93, 1993/94.

McKinnon, R. (28) (Rangers) 1965/6, 1966/7, 1967/8, 1968/9, 1969/70, 1970/1.

McKinnon, R. (1) (Motherwell) 1993/94.

McLaren, A. (4) (Preston North End) 1946/7, 1947/8.

McLaren, A. (12) (Heart of Midlothian) 1991/2, 1992/93, 1993/94.

McLean, G. (1) (Dundee) 1967/8.

McLean, T. (6) (Kilmarnock) 1968/9, 1969/70, 1970/1.

McLeish, A. (77) (Aberdeen) 1979/80, 1980/1, 1981/2, 1982/3, 1983/4, 1984/5, 1985/6, 1986/7, 1987/8, 1988/9, 1989/90, 1990/1, 1992/93.

McLeod, J. (4) (Hibernian) 1960/1.

MacLeod, M. (20) (Celtic) 1984/5, 1986/7 (Borussia Dortmund) 1987/8, 1988/9, 1989/90, 1990/1 (Hibernian).

McLintock, F. (9) (Leicester City) 1962/3, 1964/5 (Arsenal) 1966/7, 1969/70, 1970/1.

McMillan, I. (6) (Airdrieonians) 1951/2, 1954/5, 1955/6 (Rangers) 1960/1.

McNaught, W. (5) (Raith Rovers) 1950/1, 1951/2, 1954/5.

McNeill, W. (29) (Celtic) 1960/1, 1961/2, 1962/3, 1963/4, 1964/5, 1965/6, 1966/7, 1967/8, 1968/9, 1969/70, 1971/2.

McPhail, J. (5) (Celtic) 1949/50, 1950/1, 1953/4.

McPherson, D. (27) (Hearts) 1988/9, 1989/90, 1990/1, 1991/2 (Rangers) 1992/93.

McQueen, G. (30) (Leeds United) 1973/4, 1974/5, 1975/6, 1976/7, 1977/8, (Manchester United) 1978/9, 1979/80, 1980/1.

McStay, P. (69) (Celtic) 1983/4, 1984/5, 1985/6, 1986/7, 1987/8, 1988/9, 1989/90, 1990/1, 1991/2, 1992/93, 1993/94.

Millar, J. (2) (Rangers) 1962/3.

Miller, W. (6) (Celtic) 1946/7, 1947/8.

Miller, W. (65) (Aberdeen) 1974/5, 1977/8, 1979/80, 1980/1, 1981/2, 1982/3, 1983/4, 1984/5, 1985/6, 1986/7, 1987/8, 1988/9, 1989/90.

Mitchell, R. (2) (Newcastle United) 1950/1.

Mochan, N. (3) (Celtic) 1953/4.

Moir, W. (1) (Bolton Wanderers) 1949/50.

Moncur, R. (16) (Newcastle United) 1967/8, 1969/70, 1970/1, 1971/2.

Morgan, W. (21) (Burnley) 1967/8 (Manchester United) 1971/2, 1972/3, 1973/4.

Morris, H. (1) (East Fife) 1949/50.

Mudie, J. (17) (Blackpool) 1956/7, 1957/8.
Mulhall, G. (3) (Aberdeen) 1959/60, 1962/3 (Sunderland) 1963/4.
Munro, F. (9) (Wolverhampton Wanderers) 1970/1, 1974/5.
Munro, I. (7) (St Mirren) 1978/9, 1979/80.
Murdoch, R. (12) (Celtic) 1965/6, 1966/7, 1967/8, 1968/9, 1969/70.
Murray, J. (5) (Heart of Midlothian) 1957/8.
Murray, S. (1) (Aberdeen) 1971/2.

Narey, D. (35) (Dundee United) 1976/7, 1978/9, 1979/80, 1980/1, 1981/2, 1982/3, 1985/6, 1986/7, 1988/9.
Nevin, P.K.F. (22) (Chelsea) 1985/6, 1986/7, 1987/8 (Everton) 1988/9, 1990/1, 1991/2 (Tranmere Rovers) 1992/93, 1993/94.
Nicholas, C. (20) (Celtic) 1982/3, (Arsenal) 1983/4, 1984/5, 1985/6, 1986/7, (Aberdeen) 1988/9.
Nicol, S. (27) (Liverpool) 1984/5, 1985/6, 1987/8, 1988/9, 1989/90, 1990/1, 1991/2.

O'Donnell, P. (1) (Motherwell) 1993/94.
O'Hare, J. (13) (Derby County) 1969/70, 1970/1, 1971/2.
Ormond, W. (6) (Hibernian) 1953/4, 1958/9.
Orr, T. (2) (Morton) 1951/2.

Parker, A. (15) (Falkirk) 1954/5, 1955/6, 1956/7, 1957/8.
Parlane, D. (12) (Rangers) 1972/3, 1974/5, 1975/6, 1976/7.
Paton, A. (2) (Motherwell) 1951/2.
Pearson, T. (2) (Newcastle United) 1946/7.
Penman, A. (1) (Dundee) 1965/6.
Pettigrew, W. (5) (Motherwell) 1975/6, 1976/7.
Plenderleith, J. (1) (Manchester City) 1960/1.
Provan, D. (5) (Rangers) 1963/4, 1965/6.
Provan, D. (10) (Celtic) 1979/80, 1980/1, 1981/2.

Quinn, P. (4) (Motherwell) 1960/1, 1961/2.

Redpath, W. (9) (Motherwell) 1948/9, 1950/1, 1951/2.
Reilly, L. (38) (Hibernian) 1948/9, 1949/50, 1950/1, 1951/2, 1952/3, 1953/4, 1954/5, 1955/6, 1956/7.
Ring, T. (12) (Clydebank) 1952/3, 1954/5, 1956/7, 1957/8.
Rioch, B. (24) (Derby County) 1974/5, 1975/6, 1976/7, (Everton) 1977/8, (Derby County) 1978/9.
Robb, D. (5) (Aberdeen) 1970/1.
Robertson, A. (5) (Clyde) 1954/5, 1957/8.
Robertson, D. (3) (Rangers) 1991/2, 1993/94.
Robertson, H. (1) (Dundee) 1961/2.
Robertson, J. (1) (Tottenham Hotspur) 1964/5.
Robertson, J. (11) (Heart of Midlothian) 1990/1, 1991/2, 1992/93.
Robertson, J.N. (28) (Nottingham Forest) 1977/8, 1978/9, 1979/80, 1980/1, 1981/2, 1982/3 (Derby County) 1983/4.
Robinson, B. (4) (Dundee) 1973/4, 1974/5.
Rough, A. (53) (Partick Thistle) 1975/6, 1976/7, 1977/8, 1978/9, 1979/80, 1980/1, 1981/2, (Hibernian) 1985/6.
Rougvie, D. (1) (Aberdeen) 1983/4.
Rutherford, E. (1) (Rangers) 1947/8.

281

St John, I. (21) (Motherwell) 1958/9, 1959/60, 1960/1, 1961/2 (Liverpool) 1962/3, 1963/4, 1964/5.
Schaedler, E. (1) (Hibernian) 1973/4.
Scott, A. (16) (Rangers) 1956/7, 1957/8, 1958/9, 1961/2 (Everton) 1963/4, 1964/5, 1965/6.
Scott, J. (1) (Hibernian) 1965/6.
Scott, J. (2) (Dundee) 1970/1.
Scoular, J. (9) (Portsmouth) 1950/1, 1951/2, 1952/3.
Sharp, G.M. (12) (Everton) 1984/5, 1985/6, 1986/7, 1987/8.
Shaw, D. (8) (Hibernian) 1946/7, 1947/8, 1948/9.
Shaw, J. (4) (Rangers) 1946/7, 1947/8.
Shearer, D. (2) (Aberdeen) 1993/94.
Shearer, R. (4) (Rangers) 1960/1.
Simpson, N. (4) (Aberdeen) 1982/3, 1983/4, 1986/7, 1987/8.
Simpson, R. (5) (Celtic) 1966/7, 1967/8, 1968/9.
Sinclair, J. (1) (Leicester City) 1965/6.
Smith, D. (2) (Aberdeen) 1965/6, 1967/8 (Rangers).
Smith, E. (2) (Celtic) 1958/9.
Smith, G. (18) (Hibernian) 1946/7, 1947/8, 1951/2, 1954/5, 1955/6, 1956/7.
Smith, H.G. (3) (Heart of Midlothian) 1987/8, 1991/2.
Smith, J. (4) (Aberdeen) 1967/8, 1973/4 (Newcastle United).
Souness, G. (54) (Middlesbrough) 1974/5 (Liverpool) 1977/8, 1978/9, 1979/80, 1980/1, 1981/2, 1982/3, 1983/4, (Sampdoria)K1984/5, 1985/6.
Speedie, D.R. (10) (Chelsea) 1984/5, 1985/6, (Coventry City) 1988/9.
Stanton, P. (16) (Hibernian) 1965/6, 1968/9, 1969/70, 1970/1, 1971/2, 1972/3, 1973/4.
Steel, W. (30) (Morton) 1946/7, 1947/8 (Derby County) 1948/9, 1949/50, (Dundee) 1950/1, 1951/2, 1952/3.
Stein, C. (21) (Rangers) 1968/9, 1969/70, 1970/1, 1971/2 (Coventry City).
Stephen, J. (2) (Bradford City) 1946/7, 1947/8.
Stewart, D. (1) (Leeds United) 1977/8.
Stewart, J. (2) (Kilmarnock) 1976/7 (Middlesbrough) 1978/9.
Stewart, R. (10) (West Ham United) 1980/1, 1981/2, 1983/4, 1986/7.
Strachan, G. (50) (Aberdeen) 1979/80, 1980/1, 1981/2, 1982/3, 1983/4 (Manchester United) 1984/5, 1985/6, 1986/7, 1987/8, 1988/9 (Leeds United) 1989/90, 1990/1, 1991/2.
Sturrock, P. (20) (Dundee United) 1980/1, 1981/2, 1982/3, 1983/4, 1984/5, 1985/6, 1986/7.

Telfer, W. (1) (St Mirren) 1953/4.
Thomson, W. (7) (St Mirren) 1979/80, 1980/1, 1981/2, 1982/3, 1983/4.
Thornton, W. (7) (Rangers) 1946/7, 1947/8, 1948/9, 1951/2.
Toner, W. (2) (Kilmarnock) 1958/9.
Turnbull, E. (8) (Hibernian) 1947/8, 1950/1, 1957/8.

Ure, I. (11) (Dundee) 1961/2, 1962/3 (Arsenal) 1963/4, 1967/8.

Waddell, W. (17) (Rangers) 1946/7, 1948/9, 1949/50, 1950/1, 1951/2, 1953/4, 1954/5.
Walker, A. (1) (Celtic) 1987/8.
Walker, N. (1) (Heart of Midlothian) 1992/93.
Wallace, L.A. (3) (Coventry City) 1977/8, 1978/9.
Wallace, W.S.B. (7) (Heart of Midlothian) 1964/5, 1965/6, 1966/7 (Celtic) 1967/8, 1968/9.
Wardhaugh, J. (2) (Heart of Midlothian) 1954/5, 1956/7.

Wark, J. (29) (Ipswich Town) 1978/9, 1979/80, 1980/1, 1981/2, 1982/3, 1983/4 (Liverpool) 1984/5.
Watson, J. (2) (Motherwell) 1947/8 (Huddersfield Town) 1953/4.
Watson, R. (1) (Motherwell) 1970/1.
Weir, A. (6) (Motherwell) 1958/9, 1959/60.
Weir, P. (6) (St Mirren) 1979/80, 1982/3, (Aberdeen) 1983/4.
White, J. (22) (Falkirk) 1958/9, 1959/60 (Tottenham Hotspur) 1960/1, 1961/2, 1962/3, 1963/4.
Whyte,   D. (6) (Celtic) 1987/8, 1988/9, 1991/2 (Middlesbrough) 1992/93.
Wilson, A. (1) (Portsmouth) 1953/4.
Wilson, D. (22) (Rangers) 1960/1, 1961/2, 1962/3, 1963/4, 1964/5.
Wilson, I.A. (5) (Leicester City) 1986/7, (Everton) 1987/8.
Wilson, P. (1) (Celtic) 1974/5.
Wilson, R. (2) (Arsenal) 1971/2.
Wood, G. (4) (Everton) 1978/9, 1981/2 (Arsenal).
Woodburn, W. (24) (Rangers) 1946/7, 1947/8, 1948/9, 1949/50, 1950/1, 1951/2.
Wright, K. (1) (Hibernian) 1991/2.
Wright, S. (2) (Aberdeen) 1992/93.
Wright, T. (3) (Sunderland) 1952/3.

Yeats, R. (2) (Liverpool) 1964/5, 1965/6.
Yorston, H. (1) (Aberdeen) 1954/5.
Young, A. (9) (Heart of Midlothian) 1959/60. 1960/1 (Everton) 1965/6.
Young, G. (53) (Rangers) 1946/7, 1947/8, 1948/9, 1949/50, 1950/1, 1951/2, 1952/3, 1953/4, 1954/5, 1955/6, 1956/7.
Younger, T. (24) (Hibernian) 1954/5, 1955/6, 1956/7 (Liverpool) 1957/8.

WALES

Aizlewood, M. (38) (Charlton Athletic) 1985/6, 1986/7 (Leeds United) 1987/8, 1988/9 (Bradford City) 1989/90, 1990/1 (Bristol City), 1991/2, 1992/93, 1993/94.
Allchurch, I. (68) (Swansea Town) 1950/1, 1951/2, 1952/3, 1953/4, 1954/5, 1955/6, 1956/7, 1957/8, 1958/9 (Newcastle United) 1959/60, 1960/1, 1961/2, 1962/3 (Cardiff City) 1963/4, 1964/5, 1965/6 (Swansea Town).
Allchurch L. (11) (Swansea Town) 1954/5, 1955/6, 1957/8, 1958/9, 1961/2, (Sheffield United) 1963/4.
Allen, B. (2) (Coventry City) 1950/1.
Allen, M. (14) (Watford) 1985/6, (Norwich City) 1988/9 (Millwall) 1989/90, 1990/1, 1991/2, 1992/93 (Newcastle United) 1993/94.

Baker, C. (7) (Cardiff City) 1957/8, 1959/60. 1960/1, 1961/2.
Baker, W. (1) (Cardiff City) 1947/8.
Barnes, W. (22) (Arsenal) 1947/8, 1948/9, 1949/50, 1950/1, 1951/2, 1953/4, 1954/5.
Berry, G. (5) (Wolverhampton Wanderers) 1978/9, 1979/80, 1982/3 (Stoke City).
Blackmore, C.G. (38) (Manchester United) 1984/5, 1985/6, 1986/7, 1987/8, 1988/9, 1989/90, 1990/1, 1991/2, 1992/93, 1993/94.
Blake, N. (2) (Sheffield United) 1993/94.
Bowen, D. (19) (Arsenal) 1954/5, 1956/7, 1957/8, 1958/9.
Bowen, M.R. (27) (Tottenham Hotspur) 1985/6 (Norwich City) 1987/8, 1988/9, 1989/90, 1991/2, 1992/93, 1993/94.
Bodin, P.J. (22) (Swindon Town) 1989/90, 1990/1 (Crystal Palace), 1991/2 (Swindon Town) 1992/93, 1993/94.
Boyle, T. (2) (Crystal Palace) 1980/1.

Burgess, R. (32) (Tottenham Hotspur) 1946/7, 1947/8, 1948/9, 1949/50, 1950/1, 1951/2, 1952/3, 1953/4.
Burton, O. (9) (Norwich City) 1962/3 (Newcastle United) 1963/4, 1968/9, 1971/2.

Cartwright, L. (7) (Coventry City) 1973/4, 1975/6, 1976/7 (Wrexham) 1977/8, 1978/9.
Charles, J. (38) (Leeds United) 1949/50, 1950/1, 1952/3, 1953/4, 1954/5, 1955/6, 1956/7 (Juventus) 1957/8, 1959/60, 1961/2, 1962/3, (Leeds United) (Cardiff City) 1963/4, 1964/5.
Charles, J.M. (19) (Swansea Town) 1980/1, 1981/2, 1982/3, 1983/4 (QPR), (Oxford United) 1984/5, 1985/6, 1986/7.
Charles, M. (31) (Swansea Town) 1954/5, 1955/6, 1956/7, 1957/8, 1958/9 (Arsenal) 1960/1, 1961/2 (Cardiff City) 1962/3.
Clarke, R. (22) (Manchester City) 1948/9, 1949/50, 1950/1, 1951/2, 952/3, 1953/4, 1954/5, 1955/6.
Coleman, C. (4) (Crystal Palace) 1991/2, 1992/93, 1993/94.
Crowe, V. (16) (Aston Villa) 1958/9, 1959/60, 1960/1, 1961/2, 1962/3.
Curtis, A. (35) (Swansea City) 1975/6, 1976/7, 1977/8, 1978/9, 1979/80, 1981/2, 1982/3, 1983/4 (Southampton) 1984/5, 1985/6, 1986/7 (Cardiff City).

Daniel, R. (21) (Arsenal) 1950/1, 1951/2, 1952/3, 1953/4 (Sunderland) 1954/5, 1956/7.
Davies, A. (13) (Manchester United) 1982/3, 1983/4, 1984/5, (Newcastle United) 1985/6 (Swansea City) 1987/8, 1988/9 (Bradford City) 1989/90.
Davies, D. (52) (Everton) 1974/5, 1975/6, 1976/7, 1977/8, (Wrexham) 1978/9, 1979/80, 1980/1 (Swansea City) 1981/2, 1982/3.
Davies, G. (16) (Fulham) 1979/80, 1981/2, 1982/3, 1983/4, 1984/5 (Chelsea), (Manchester City) 1985/6.
Davies, R. Wyn (34) (Bolton Wanderers) 1963/4, 1964/5, 1965/6, 1966/7 (Newcastle United) 1967/8, 1968/9, 1969/70, 1970/1, 1971/2 (Manchester City), (Blackpool) 1972/3 (Manchester United) 1973/4.
Davies, Reg (6) (Newcastle United) 1952/3, 1953/4, 1957/8.
Davies, Ron (29) (Norwich City) 1963/4, 1964/5, 1965/6, 1966/7, (Southampton) 1967/8, 1968/9, 1969/70, 1970/1, 1971/2, 1973/4 (Portsmouth).
Davis, C. (1) (Charlton Athletic) 1971/2.
Davis, G. (4) (Wrexham) 1977/8.
Deacy, N. (11) (PSV Eindhoven) 1976/7, 1977/8 (Beringen) 1978/9.
Derrett, S. (4) (Cardiff City) 1968/9, 1969/70, 1970/1.
Dibble, A. (3) (Luton Town) 1985/6, (Manchester City) 1988/9.
Durban, A. (27) (Derby County) 1965/6, 1966/7, 1967/8, 1968/9, 1969/70, 1970/1, 1971/2.
Dwyer, P. (10) (Cardiff City) 1977/8, 1978/9, 1979/80.

Edwards, I. (4) (Chester) 1977/8, 1978/9, 1979/80.
Edwards, G. (12) (Birmingham City) 1946/7, 1947/8 (Cardiff City) 1948/9, 1949/50.
Edwards, T. (2) (Charlton Athletic) 1956/7.
Emanuel, J. (2) (Bristol City) 1972/3.
England, M. (44) (Blackburn Rovers) 1961/2, 1962/3, 1963/4, 1964/5, 1965/6, 1966/7 (Tottenham Hotspur) 1967/8, 1968/9, 1969/70, 1970/1, 1971/2, 1972/3, 1973/4, 1974/5.
Evans, B. (7) (Swansea City) 1971/2, 1972/3 (Hereford United) 1973/4.
Evans, I. (13) (Crystal Palace) 1975/6, 1976/7, 1977/8.
Evans, R. (1) (Swansea Town) 1963/4.

Felgate, D. (1) (Lincoln City) 1983/4.
Flynn, B. (66) (Burnley) 1974/5, 1975/6, 1976/7, 1977/8 (Leeds United) 1978/9, 1979/80, 1980/1, 1981/2, 1982/3 (Burnley) 1983/4.
Ford, T. (38) (Swansea City) 1946/7 (Aston Villa) 1947/8, 1948/9, 1949/50, 1950/1 (Sunderland) 1951/2, 1952/3 (Cardiff City) 1953/4, 1954/5, 1955/6, 1956/7.
Foulkes, W. (11) (Newcastle United) 1951/2, 1952/3, 1953/4.

Giggs, R.J. (11) (Manchester United) 1991/2, 1992/93, 1993/94.
Giles, D. (12) (Swansea City) 1979/80, 1980/1, 1981/2 (Crystal Palace) 1982/3.
Godfrey, B. (3) (Preston North End) 1963/4, 1964/5.
Goss, J. (6) (Norwich City) 1990/1, 1991/2, 1993/94.
Green, C. (15) (Birmingham City) 1964/5, 1965/6, 1966/7, 1967/8, 1968/9.
Griffiths, A. (17) (Wrexham) 1970/1, 1974/5, 1975/6, 1976/7.
Griffiths, H. (1) (Swansea Town) 1952/3.
Griffiths, M. (11) (Leicester City) 1946/7, 1948/9, 1949/50, 1950/1, 1953/4.

Hall, G.D. (9) (Chelsea) 1987/8, 1988/9, 1990/91, 1991/2.
Harrington, A. (11) (Cardiff City) 1955/6, 1956/7, 1957/8, 1960/1, 1961/2.
Harris, C. (24) (Leeds United) 1975/6, 1977/8, 1978/9, 1979/80, 1980/1, 1981/2.
Harris, W. (6) (Middlesbrough) 1953/4, 1956/7, 1957/8.
Hennessey, T. (39) (Birmingham City) 1961/2, 1962/3, 1963/4, 1964/5, 1965/6, (Nottingham Forest) 1966/7, 1967/8, 1968/9, 1969/70 (Derby County) 1971/2, 1972/3.
Hewitt, R. (5) (Cardiff City) 1957/8.
Hill, M. (2) (Ipswich Town) 1971/2.
Hockey, T. (9) (Sheffield United) 1971/2, 1972/3 (Norwich City) 1973/4, (Aston Villa).
Hodges, G. (16) (Wimbledon) 1983/4, 1986/7 (Newcastle United) 1987/8, (Watford) 1989/90, (Sheffield United) 1991/2.
Holden, A. (1) (Chester City) 1983/4.
Hole, B. (30) (Cardiff City) 1962/3, 1963/4, 1964/5, 1965/6, 1966/7, (Blackburn Rovers) 1967/8, 1968/9 (Aston Villa) 1969/70 (Swansea Town) 1970/71.
Hollins, D. (11) (Newcastle United) 1961/2, 1962/3, 1963/4, 1964/5, 1965/6.
Hopkins, J. (16) (Fulham) 1982/3, 1983/4, 1984/5 (Crystal P) 1989/90.
Hopkins, M. (34) (Tottenham Hotspur) 1955/6, 1956/7, 1957/8, 1958/9, 1959/60, 1960/1, 1961/2, 1962/3.
Horne, B. (44) (Portsmouth) 1987/8, (Southampton) 1988/9, 1989/90, 1990/1, 1991/2 (Everton) 1992/93, 1993/94.
Howells, R. (2) (Cardiff City) 1953/4.
Hughes, C.M. (4) (Luton Town) 1991/2, 1993/94.
Hughes, I. (4) (Luton Town) 1950/1.
Hughes, L.M. (53) (Manchester United) 1983/4, 1984/5, 1985/6, 1986/7 (Barcelona) 1987/8, 1988/9 (Manchester United) 1989/90, 1990/1, 1991/2, 1992/93, 1993/94.
Hughes, W. (3) (Birmingham City) 1946/7.
Hughes, W.A. (5) (Blackburn Rovers) 1948/9.
Humphreys, J. (1) (Everton) 1946/7.

Jackett, K. (31) (Watford) 1982/3, 1983/4, 1984/5, 1985/6, 1986/7, 1987/8.
James, G. (9) (Blackpool) 1965/6, 1966/7, 1967/8, 1970/1.
James, L. (54) (Burnley) 1971/2, 1972/3, 1973/4, 1974/5, 1975/6 (Derby County) 1976/7, 1977/8 (QPR) (Burnley) 1978/9, 1979/80 (Swansea City) 1980/1, 1981/2 (Sunderland) 1982/3.

James, R.M. (47) (Swansea City) 1978/9, 1979/80, 1981/2, 1982/3 (Stoke City) 1983/4, 1984/5 (QPR) 1985/6, 1986/7 (Leicester City) 1987/8 (Swansea City).

Jarvis, A. (3) (Hull City) 1966/7.

Johnson, M. (1) (Swansea City) 1963/4.

Jones, A. (6) (Port Vale) 1986/7, 1987/8 (Charlton Athletic) 1989/90.

Jones, Barrie (15) (Swansea Town) 1962/3, 1963/4, 1964/5 (Plymouth Argyle) 1968/9 (Cardiff City).

Jones, Bryn. (4) (Arsenal) 1946/7, 1947/8, 1948/9.

Jones, C. (59) (Swansea Town) 1953/4, 1955/6, 1956/7, 1957/8 (Tottenham Hotspur) 1958/9, 1959/60, 1960/1, 1961/2, 1962/3, 1963/4, 1964/5, 1966/7, 1967/8, 1968/9 (Fulham) 1969/70.

Jones, D. (8) (Norwich City) 1975/6, 1977/8, 1979/80.

Jones, E. (4) (Swansea Town) 1947/8 (Tottenham Hotspur) 1948/9.

Jones, J. (72) (Liverpool) 1975/6, 1976/7, 1977/8 (Wrexham) 1978/9, 1979/80, 1980/1, 1981/2, 1982/3 (Chelsea) 1983/4, 1984/5 (Huddersfield Town) 1985/6.

Jones, K. (1) (Aston Villa) 1949/50.

Jones, R. (1) (Sheffield Wednesday) 1993/94.

Jones, T.G. (13) (Everton) 1946/7, 1947/8, 1948/9, 1949/50.

Jones W. (1) (Bristol City) 1970/1.

Kelsey, J. (41) (Arsenal) 1953/4, 1954/5, 1955/6, 1956/7, 1957/8, 1958/9, 1959/60, 1960/1, 1961/2.

King, J. (1) (Swansea Town) 1954/5.

Kinsey, N. (7) (Norwich City) 1950/1, 1951/2, 1953/4 (Birmingham City) 1955/6.

Knill, A.R. (1) (Swansea City) 1988/9.

Krzywicki, R. (West Bromwich Albion) 1969/70 (Huddersfield Town) 1970/1, 1971/2.

Lambert, R. (5) (Liverpool) 1946/7, 1947/8, 1948/9.

Law, B.J. (1) (QPR), 1989/90.

Lea, C. (2) (Ipswich Town) 1964/5.

Leek, K. (13) (Leicester City) 1960/1, 1961/2 (Newcastle United) (Birmingham City) 1962/3, 1964/5.

Lever, A. (1) (Leicester City) 1952/3.

Lewis, D. (1) (Swansea City) 1982/3.

Lloyd, B. (3) (Wrexham) 1975/6.

Lovell, S. (6) (Crystal Palace) 1981/2 (Millwall) 1984/5, 1985/6.

Lowndes, S. (10) (Newport County) 1982/3 (Millwall) 1984/5, 1985/6, 1986/7, (Barnsley) 1987/8.

Lowrie, G. (4) (Coventry City) 1947/8, 1948/9 (Newcastle United).

Lucas, M. (4) (Leyton Orient) 1961/2, 1962/3.

Lucas, W. (7) (Swansea Town) 1948/9, 1949/50, 1950/1.

Maguire, G.T. (7) (Portsmouth) 1989/90, 1991/2.

Mahoney, J. (51) (Stoke City) 1967/8, 1968/9, 1970/1, 1972/3, 1973/4, 1974/5, 1975/6, 1976/7 (Middlesbrough) 1977/8, 1978/9 (Swansea City) 1979/80, 1981/2, 1982/3.

Marustik, C. (6) (Swansea City) 1981/2, 1982/3.

Medwin, T. (30) (Swansea Town) 1952/3, 1956/7 (Tottenham Hotspur) 1957/8, 1958/9, 1959/60, 1960/1, 1962/3.

Melville, A.K. (20) (Swansea C), 1989/90, 1990/1 (Oxford United), 1991/2, 1992/93 (Sunderland) 1993/94.

Mielczarek, R. (1) (Rotherham United) 1970/1.

Millington, A. (21) (West Bromwich Albion) 1962/3, 1964/5 (Crystal Palace) 1965/6 (Peterborough United) 1966/7, 1967/8, 1968/9, 1969/70 (Swansea City) 1970/1, 1971/2.
Moore, G. (21) (Cardiff City) 1959/60, 1960/1, 1961/2 (Chelsea) 1962/3, (Manchester United) 1963/4 (Northampton Town) 1965/6, 1968/9 (Charlton Athletic) 1969/70, 1970/1.
Morris, W. (5) (Burnley) 1946/7, 1948/9, 1951/2.

Nardiello, D. (2) (Coventry City) 1977/8.
Neilson, A.B. (3) (Newcastle United) 1991/2, 1993/94.
Nicholas, P. (73) (Crystal Palace) 1978/9, 1979/80, 1980/1 (Arsenal) 1981/2, 1982/3, 1983/4 (Crystal Palace) 1984/5 (Luton Town) 1985/6, 1986/7, 1987/8 (Aberdeen), (Chelsea) 1988/9, 1989/90, 1990/1 (Watford), 1991/2.
Niedzwiecki, E.A. (2) (Chelsea) 1984/5, 1987/8.
Nogan, L.M. (1) (Watford) 1991/2.
Nurse, E.A. (2) (Chelsea) 1984/5, 1987/8.
Norman, A.J. (5) (Hull City) 1985/6, 1987/8.
Nurse, M. (12) (Swansea Town) 1959/60, 1960/1, 1962/3 (Middlesbrough) 1963/4.

O'Sullivan, P. (3) (Brighton & Hove Albion) 1972/3, 1975/6, 1978/9.

Page, M. (28) (Birmingham City) 1970/1, 1971/2, 1972/3, 1973/4, 1974/5, 1975/6, 1976/7, 1977/8, 1978/9.
Palmer, D. (3) (Swansea Town) 1956/7, 1957/8.
Parry, J. (1) (Swansea Town) 1950/1.
Pascoe, C. (10) (Swansea Town) 1983/4, (Sunderland) 1988/9, 1989/90 1990/91, 1991/2.
Paul, R. (33) (Swansea Town) 1948/9, 1949/50 (Manchester City) 1950/1, 1951/2, 1952/3, 1953/4, 1954/5, 1955/6.
Pembridge, M.A. (8) (Luton Town) 1991/2 (Derby County) 1992/93, 1993/94.
Perry, J. (1) (Cardiff City) 1993/94.
Phillips, D. (52) (Plymouth Argyle) 1983/4 (Manchester City) 1984/5, 1985/6, 1986/7 (Coventry City) 1987/8, 1988/9 (Norwich City) 1989/90, 1990/1, 1991/2, 1992/93 (Nottingham Forest) 1993/94.
Phillips, J. (4) (Chelsea) 1972/3, 1973/4, 1974/5, 1977/8.
Phillips, L. (58) (Cardff City) 1970/1, 1971/2, 1972/3, 1973/4,H1974/5, (Aston Villa) 1975/6, 1976/7, 1977/8, 1978/9 (Swansea City) 1979/80, 1980/1, 1981/2 (Charlton Athletic).
Pontin, K. (2) (Cardiff City) 1979/80.
Powell, A. (8) (Leeds United) 1946/7, 1947/8, 1948/9 (Everton) 1949/50, 1950/1 (Birmingham City).
Powell, D. (11) (Wrexham) 1967/8, 1968/9 (Sheffield United) 1969/70, 1970/1.
Powell, I. (8) (QPR) 1946/7, 1947/8, 1948/9 (Aston Villa) 1949/50, 1950/1.
Price, P. (25) (Luton Town) 1979/80, 1980/1, 1981/2 (Tottenham Hotspur) 1982/3, 1983/4.
Pring, K. (3) (Rotherham United) 1965/6, 1966/7.
Pritchard, H.K. (1) (Bristol City) 1984/5.

Rankmore, F. (l) (Peterborough United) 1965/6.
Ratcliffe, K. (59) (Everton) 1980/1, 1981/2, 1982/3, 1983/4, 1984/5, 1985/6, 1986/7, 1987/8, 1988/9, 1989/90, 1990/1, 1991/2 (Cardiff City) 1992/93.
Reece, G. (29) (Sheffield United) 1965/6, 1966/7, 1969/70, 1970/1, 1971/2, (Cardiff City) 1972/3, 1973/4, 1974/5.
Reed, W. (2) (Ipswich Town) 1954/5.

287

Rees, A. (1) (Birmingham City) 1983/4.
Rees, J.M. (1) (Luton Town) 1991/2.
Rees, R. (39) (Coventry City) 1964/5, 1965/6, 1966/7, 1967/8 (West Bromwich Albion) 1968/9 (Nottingham Forest) 1969/70, 1970/1, 1971/2.
Rees, W. (4) (Cardiff City) 1948/9 (Tottenham Hotspur) 1949/50.
Richards, S. (1) (Cardiff City) 1946/7.
Roberts, A. M. (1) (QPR) 1992/93.
Roberts, D. (17) (Oxford United) 1972/3, 1973/4, 1974/5 (Hull City) 1975/6, 1976/7, 1977/8.
Roberts, I.W. (5) (Watford) 1989/90, (Huddersfield Town) 1991/2, (Leicester City) 1993/94.
Roberts, J.G. (22) (Arsenal) 1970/1, 1971/2, 1972/3, (Birmingham City) 1973/4, 1974/5, 1975/6..
Roberts, J.H. (1) (Bolton Wanderers) 1948/9.
Roberts, P. (4) (Portsmouth) 1973/4, 1974/5.
Rodrigues, P. (40) (Cardiff City) 1964/5, 1965/6 (Leicester City) 1966/7, 1967/8, 1968/9, 1969/70 (Sheffield Wednesday) 1970/1, 1971/2, 1972/3, 1973/4.
Rouse, V. (1) (Crystal Palace) 1958/9.
Rowley, T. (1) (Tranmere Rovers) 1958/9.
Rush, I. (66) (Liverpool) 1979/80, 1980/1, 1981/2, 1982/3, 1983/4, 1984/5, 1985/6, 1986/7 (Juventus) 1987/8, (Liverpool) 1988/9, 1989/90, 1990/1, 1991/2, 1992/93, 1993/94.

Saunders, D. (44) (Brighton & Hove Albion) 1985/6, 1986/7 (Oxford United) 1987/8, (Derby County) 1988/9, 1989/90, 1990/91, (Liverpool) 1991/2 (Aston Villa) 1992/93, 1993/94.
Sayer, P. (7) (Cardiff City) 1976/7, 1977/8.
Scrine, F. (2) (Swansea Town) 1949/50.
Sear, C. (1) (Manchester City) 1962/3.
Sherwood, A. (41) (Cardiff City) 1946/7, 1947/8, 1948/9, 1949/50, 1950/1, 1951/2, 1952/3, 1953/4, 1954/5, 1955/6, 1956/7 (Newport County).
Shortt, W. (12) (Plymouth Argyle) 1946/7, 1949/50, 1951/2, 1952/3.
Showers, D. (2) (Cardiff City) 1974/5.
Sidlow, C. (7) (Liverpool) 1946/7, 1947/8, 1948/9, 1949/50.
Slatter, N. (22) (Bristol Rovers) 1982/3, 1983/4, 1984/5 (Oxford United) 1985/6, 1986/7, 1987/8, 1988/9.
Smallman, D. (7 (Wrexham) 1973/4 (Everton) 1974/5, 1975/6.
Southall, N. (74) (Everton) 1981/2, 1982/3, 1983/4, 1984/5, 1985/6, 1986/7, 1987/8, 1988/9, 1989/90, 1990/1, 1991/2, 1992/93, 1993/94.
Speed, G.A. (25) (Leeds U) 1989/90, 1990/91, 1991/2, 1992/93, 1993/94.
Sprake, G. (37) (Leeds United) 1963/4, 1964/5, 1965/6, 1966/7, 1967/8, 1968/9, 1969/70, 1970/1, 1971/2, 1972/3, 1973/4 (Birmingham City) 1974/5.
Stansfield, F. (1) (Cardiff City) 1948/9.
Stevenson, B. (15) (Leeds United) 1977/8, 1978/9, 1979/80, 1981/2 (Birmingham City).
Stevenson, N. (4) (Swansea City) 1981/2, 1982/3.
Stitfall, R. (2) (Cardiff City) 1952/3, 1956/7.
Sullivan, D. (17) (Cardiff City) 1952/3, 1953/4, 1954/5, 1956/7, 1957/8, 1958/9, 1959/60.
Symons, C.J. (13) (Portsmouth) 1991/2, 1992/93, 1993/94.

Tapscott, D. (14) (Arsenal) 1953/4, 1954/5, 1955/6, 1956/7, 1958/9 (Cardiff City).
Thomas, D. (2) (Swansea Town) 1956/7, 1957/8.

Thomas, M. (51) (Wrexham) 1976/7, 1977/8, 1978/9 (Manchester United) 1979/80, 1980/1, 1981/2 (Everton) (Brighton) 1982/3 (Stoke City) 1983/4, (Chelsea) 1984/5, 1985/6 (West Bromwich Albion).
Thomas, M.R. (1) (Newcastle United) 1986/7
Thomas, R. (50) (Swindon Town) 1966/7, 1967/8, 1968/9, 1969/70, 1970/1, 1971/2, 1972/3, 1973/4 (Derby County) 1974/5, 1975/6, 1976/7, 1977/8 (Cardiff City).
Thomas, S. (4) (Fulham) 1947/8, 1948/9
Toshack, J. (40) (Cardiff City) 1968/9, 1969/70 (Liverpool) 1970/1, 1971/2, 1972/3, 1974/5, 1975/6, 1976/7, 1977/8 (Swansea City) 1978/9, 1979/80.

Van Den Hauwe, P.W.R. (13) (Everton) 1984/5, 1985/6, 1986/7, 1987/8, 1988/9
Vaughan, N. (10) (Newport County) 1982/3, 1983/4 (Cardiff City) 1984/5.
Vearncombe, G. (2) (Cardiff City) 1957/8, 1960/1.
Vernon, R. (32) (Blackburn Rovers) 1956/7, 1957/8, 1958/9, 1959/60 (Everton) 1960/1, 1961/2, 1962/3, 1963/4, 1964/5 (Stoke City) 1965/6, 1966/7, 1967/8.
Villars, A. (3) (Cardiff City) 1973/4.

Walley, T. (1) (Watford) 1970/1
Walsh, I. (18) (Crystal Palace) 1979/80, 1980/1, 1981/2 (Swansea City).
Ward, D. (2) (Bristol Rovers) 1958/9, 1961/2 (Cardiff City).
Webster, C. (4) (Manchester United) 1956/7, 1957/8.
Williams, A. (1) (Reading) 1993/94.
Williams, D.G. (12) 1987/8 (Derby County) 1988/9, 1989/90 (Ipswich Town) 1992/93.
Williams, D.M. (5) (Norwich City) 1985/6, 1986/7
Williams, G. (1) (Cardiff City) 1950/1
Williams, G.E. (26) (West Bromwich Albion) 1959/60, 1960/1, 1962/3, 1963/4, 1964/5, 1965/6, 1966/7, 1967/8, 1968/9.
Williams, G.G. (5) (Swansea Town) 1960/1, 1961/2.
Williams, H. (4) (Newport County) 1948/9 (Leeds United) 1949/50, 1950/1
Williams, Herbert (3) (Swansea Town) 1964/5, 1970/1
Williams, S. (43) (West Bromwich Albion) 1953/4, 1954/5, 1955/6, 1957/8, 1958/9, 1959/60, 1960/1, 1961/2, 1962/3 (Southampton) 1963/4, 1964/5, 1965/6.
Witcomb, D. (3) (West Bromwich Albion) 1946/7 (Sheffield Wednesday).
Woosnam, P. (17) (Leyton Orient) 1958/9 (West Ham United) 1959/60, 1960/1, 1961/2, 1962/3 (Aston Villa).

Yorath, T. (59) (Leeds United) 1969/70, 1970/1, 1971/2, 1972/3, 1973/4, 1974/5, 1975/6 (Coventry City) 1976/7, 1977/8, 1978/9 (Tottenham Hotspur) 1979/80, 1980/1
Young, E. (20) (Wimbledon) 1989/90, 1990/1 (Crystal Palace), 1991/2, 1992/93, 1993/94.

EIRE

Aherne, T. (16) (Belfast Celtic) 1945/6 (Luton Town) 1949/50, 1950/1, 1951/2, 1952/3, 1953/4.
Aldridge, J.W. (60) (Oxford United) 1985/6, 1986/7 (Liverpool) 1987/8, 1988/9 (Real Sociedad) 1989/90, 1990/1, (Tranmere Rovers) 1991/2, 1992/93, 1993/94
Ambrose, P. (5) (Shamrock Rovers) 1954/5, 1963/4
Anderson, J. (16) (Preston North End) 1979/80, 1981/2 (Newcastle United) 1983/4, 1985/6, 1986/7, 1987/8, 1988/9.

Babb, P. (9) (Coventry City) 1993/94
Bailham, E. (1) (Shamrock Rovers) 1963/4

289

Barber, E. (2) (Shelbourne) 1965/6 (Birmingham City) 1965/6.
Beglin, J. (15) (Liverpool) 1983/4, 1984/5, 1985/6, 1986/7.
Bonner, P. (77) (Celtic) 1980/1, 1981/2, 1983/4, 1984/5, 1985/6, 1986/7, 1987/8, 1988/9, 1989/90, 1990/1, 1991/2, 1992/93, 1993/94.
Braddish, S. (1) (Dundalk) 1977/8.
Brady T.R. (6) (QPR) 1963/4.
Brady, W. L. (72) (Arsenal) 1974/5, 1975/6, 1976/7, 1977/8, 1978/9, 1979/80 (Juventus) 1980/1, 1981/2 (Sampdoria) 1982/3, 1983/4 (Internazionale) 1984/5, 1985/6 (Ascoli) 1986/7 (West Ham United) 1987/8, 1988/9, 1989/90.
Breen, T. (3) (Shamrock Rovers) 1946/7.
Brennan, F. (1) (Drumcondra) 1964/5.
Brennan, S.A. (19) (Manchester United) 1964/5, 1965/6, 1966/7, 1968/9, 1969/70 (Waterford) 1970/1.
Browne, W. (3) (Bohemians) 1963/4.
Buckley, L. (2) (Shamrock Rovers) 1983/4 (Waregem) 1984/5.
Burke, F. (1) (Cork Athletic) 1951/2.
Byrne, A.B (14) (Southampton) 1969/70, 1970/1, 1972/3, 1973/4.
Byrne, J. (23) (QPR) 1984/5, 1986/7, 1987/8 (Le Havre) 1989/90, 1990/1 (Brighton & Hove Albion), 1991/2 (Sunderland) 1992/93 (Millwall).
Byrne, P. (8) (Shamrock Rovers) 1983/4, 1984/5, 1985/6.

Campbell, A. (3) (Santander) 1984/5.
Campbell, N. (11) (St Patrick's Athletic) 1970/1 (Fortuna Cologne) 1971/2, 1972/3, 1974/5, 1975/6.
Cantwell, N. (36) (West Ham United) 1953/4, 1955/6, 1956/7, 1957/8, 1958/9, 1959/60, 1960/1 (Manchester United) 1960/1,K1961/2, 1962/3, 1963/4, 1964/5, 1965/6, 1966/7.
Carey, B.P. (3) (Manchester United) 1991/2, 1992/93 (Leicester City) 1993/94.
Carey, J.J. (21) (Manchester United) 1945/6, 1946/7, 1947/8, 1948/9, 1949/50, 1950/1, 1952/3.
Carolan, J. (2) (Manchester United) 1959/60.
Carroll, B. (2) (Shelbourne) 1948/9, 1949/50.
Carroll, T.R. (17) (Ipswich Town) 1967/8, 1968/9, 1969/70, 1970/1 (Birmingham City) 1971/2, 1972/3.
Cascarino, A.G. (51) (Gillingham) 1985/6 (Millwall) 1987/8, 1988/9, 1989/90 (Aston Villa), 1990/9 (Celtic) 1991/2 (Chelsea) 1992/93, 1993/94.
Chandler, J. (2) (Leeds United) 1979/80.
Clarke, J. (1) (Drogheda United) 1977/8.
Clarke, K. (2) (Drumcondra) 1947/8.
Clarke, M. (1) (Shamrock Rovers) 1949/50.
Clinton, T.J. (3) (Everton) 1950/1, 1953/4.
Coad, P. (11) (Shamrock Rovers) 1946/7, 1947/8, 1948/9, 1950/1, 1951/2.
Coffey, T. (1) (Drumcondra) 1949/50.
Colfer, M.D. (2) (Shelbourne) 1949/50, 1950/1.
Conmy, O.M. (5) (Peterborough United) 1964/5, 1966/7, 1967/8, 1969/70.
Conroy, G.A. (27) (Stoke City) 1969/70, 1970/1, 1972/3, 1973/4, 1974/5, 1975/6, 1976/7.
Conway, J.P. (20) (Fulham) 1966/7, 1967/8, 1968/9, 1969/70, 1970/1, 1973/4, 1974/5, 1975/6 (Manchester City) 1976/7.
Corr, P.J. (4) (Everton) 1948/9.
Courtney, E. (1) (Cork United) 1945/6.
Coyle, O. (1) (Bolton Wanderers) 1993/94.
Coyne, T. (16) (Celtic) 1991/2, (Tranmere Rovers) 1992/93, (Motherwell) 1993/94.

290

Cummins, G.P. (19) (Luton Town) 1953/4, 1954/5, 1955/6, 1957/8, 1958/9, 1959/60, 1960/1.

Cuneen, T. (1) (Limerick) 1950/1.

Curtis, D.P. (17) (Shelbourne) 1956/7 (Bristol City) 1956/7, 1957/8, (Ipswich Town) 1958/9, 1959/60, 1960/1, 1961/2, 1962/3 (Exeter City) 1963/4.

Cusack, S. (1) (Limerick) 1952/3.

Daish, L.S. (1) (Cambridge United) 1991/2.

Daly, G.A. (48) (Manchester United) 1972/3, 1973/4, 1974/5, 1976/7 (Derby County) 1977/8, 1978/9, 1979/80 (Coventry City) 1980/1, 1981/2, 1982/3, 1983/4 (Birmingham City) 1984/5, 1985/6 (Shrewsbury Town) 1986/7.

Daly, M. (2) (Wolverhampton Wanderers) 1977/8.

Daly, P. (1) (Shamrock Rovers) 1949/50.

De Mange, K.J.P.P. (2) (Liverpool) 1986/7, (Hull City) 1988/9.

Deacy, E. (4) (Aston Villa) 1981/2.

Dempsey, J.T. (19) (Fulham) 1966/7, 1967/8, 1968/9 (Chelsea) 1968/9, 1969/70, 1970/1, 1971/2.

Dennehy, J. (11) (Cork Hibernian) 1971/2 (Nottingham Forest) 1972/3, 1973/4, 1974/5 (Walsall) 1975/6, 1976/7.

Desmond, P. (4) (Middlesbrough) 1949/50.

Devine, J. (12) (Arsenal) 1979/80, 1980/1, 1981/2, 1982/3 (Norwich City) 1983/4, 1984/5.

Donovan, D.C. (5) (Everton) 1954/5, 1956/7.

Donovan, T. (1) (Aston Villa) 1979/80.

Doyle, C. (1) (Shelbourne) 1958/9.

Duffy, B. (1) (Shamrock Rovers) 1949/50.

Dunne, A.P. (33) (Manchester United) 1961/2, 1962/3, 1963/4, 1964/5, 1965/6, 1966/7, 1968/9, 1969/70, 1970/1 (Bolton Wanderers) 1973/4, 1974/5, 1975/6.

Dunne, J.C. (1) (Fulham) 1970/1.

Dunne, P.A.J. (5) (Manchester United) 1964/5, 1965/6, 1966/7

Dunne, S. (15) (Luton Town) 1952/3, 1953/4, 1955/6, 1956/7, 1957/8, 1958/9, 1959/60.

Dunne, T. (3) (St Patrick's Athletic) 1955/6, 1956/7.

Dunning, P. (2) (Shelbourne) 1970/1.

Dunphy, E.M. (23) (York City) 1965/6 (Millwall) 1965/6, 1966/7, 1967/8, 1968/9, 1969/70, 1970/1.

Dwyer, N.M. (14) (West Ham United) 1959/60 (Swansea Town) 1960/1, 1961/2, 1963/4, 1964/5.

Eccles, P. (1) (Shamrock Rovers) 1985/6.

Eglington, T.J. (24) (Shamrock Rovers) 1945/6 (Everton) 1946/7, 1947/8, 1948/9, 1950/1, 1951/2, 1952/3, 1953/4, 1954/5, 1955/6.

Fagan, E. (1) (Shamrock Rovers) 1972/3

Fagan, F. (8) (Manchester City) 1954/5, 1959/60 (Derby County) 1959/60, 1960/1

Fairclough, M. (2) (Dundalk) 1981/2.

Fallon, S. (8) (Celtic) 1950/1, 1951/2, 1952/3, 1954/5.

Farrell, P.D. (28) (Shamrock Rovers) 1945/6 (Everton) 1946/7, 1947/8, 1948/9, 1949/50, 1950/1, 1951/2, 1952/3, 1953/4, 1954/5, 1955/6, 1956/7

Finucane, A. (11) (Limerick) 1966/7, 1968/9, 1969/70, 1970/1, 1971/2.

Fitzgerald, F.J. (2) (Waterford) 1954/5, 1955/6.

Fitzgerald, P.J. (5) (Leeds United) 1960/1 (Chester) 1961/2.

Fitzpatrick, K. (1) (Limerick) 1969/70.

Fitzsimons, A.G. (26) (Middlesbrough) 1949/50, 1951/2, 1952/3, 1953/4, 1954/5, 1955/6, 1956/7, 1957/8, 1958/9 (Lincoln City) 1958/9.

Fogarty, A. (11) (Sunderland) 1959/60, 1960/1, 1961/2, 1962/3, 1963/4, (Hartlepool United) 1963/4.

Foley, T.C. (9) (Northampton Town) 1963/4, 1964/5, 1965/6, 1966/7

Fullam, J. (Preston North End) 1960/1 (Shamrock Rovers) 1963/4, 1965/6, 1967/8, 1968/9, 1969/70.

Gallagher, C. (2) (Celtic) 1966/7.

Gallagher, M. (1) (Hibernian) 1953/4.

Galvin, A. (29) (Tottenham Hotspur) 1982/3, 1983/4, 1984/5, 1985/6, 1986/7 (Sheffield Wednesday) 1987/8, 1988/9, 1989/90.

Gannon, E. (14) (Notts County) 1948/9 (Sheffield Wednesday) 1948/9, 1949/50, 1950/1, 1951/2, 1953/4, 1954/5 (ShelbourneK1954/5.

Gannon, M. (1) (Shelbourne) 1971/2.

Gavin, J.T. (7) (Norwich City) 1949/50, 1952/3, 1953/4 (Tottenham Hotspur) 1954/5 (Norwich City) 1956/7.

Gibbons, A. (4) (St Patrick's Athletic) 1951/2, 1953/4, 1955/6.

Gilbert, R. (1) (Shamrock Rovers) 1965/6.

Giles, C. (1) (Doncaster Rovers) 1950/1.

Giles, M.J. (59) (Manchester United) 1959/60, 1960/1, 1961/2, 1962/3 (Leeds United) 1963/4, 1964/5, 1965/6, 1966/7, 1968/9, 1969/70, 1970/1, 1972/3, 1973/4, 1974/5 (West Bromwich Albion) 1975/6, 1976/7 (Shamrock Rovers) 1977/8, 1978/9.

Givens, D.J. (56) (Manchester United) 1968/9, 1969/70 (Luton Town) 1969/70, 1970/1, 1971/2 (QPR) 1972/3, 1973/4, 1974/5, 1975/6, 1976/7, 1977/8 (Birmingham City) 1978/9, 1979/80, 1980/1 (Neuchatel Xamax) 1981/2.

Glynn, D. (2) (Drumcondra) 1951/2, 1954/5.

Godwin, T.F. (13) (Shamrock Rovers) 1948/9, 1949/50 (Leicester City) 1949/50, 1950/1 (Bournemouth) 1955/6, 1956/7, 1957/8.

Gorman, W.C. (2) (Brentford) 1946/7.

Grealish, A. (44) (Orient) 1975/6, 1978/9 (Luton Town) 1979/80, 1980/1, (Brighton & Hove Albion) 1981/2, 1982/3, 1983/4 (West Bromwich Albion) 1984/5, 1985/6.

Gregg, E. (8) (Bohemians) 1977/8, 1978/9, 1979/80.

Grimes, A.A. (17) (Manchester United) 1977/8, 1979/80, 1980/1, 1981/2, 1982/3 (Coventry City) 1983/4 (Luton Town) 1987/8.

Hale, A. (13) (Aston Villa) 1961/2 (Doncaster Rovers) 1962/3, 1963/4, (Waterford) 1966/7, 1967/8, 1968/9, 1969/70, 1970/1, 1971/2.

Hamilton, T. (2) (Shamrock Rovers) 1958/9.

Hand, E.K. (20) (Portsmouth) 1968/9, 1969/70, 1970/1, 1972/3, 1973/4, 1974/5, 1975/6.

Hartnett, J.B. (2) (Middlesbrough) 1948/9, 1953/4.

Haverty, J. (32) (Arsenal) 1955/6, 1956/7, 1957/8, 1958/9, 1959/60, 1960/1, (Blackburn Rovers) 1961/2 (Millwall) 1962/3, 1963/4 (Celtic) 1964/5, (Bristol Rovers) 1964/5 (Shelbourne) 1965/6, 1966/7.

Hayes, A.W.P. (1) (Southampton) 1978/9.

Hayes, W.E. (2) (Huddersfield Town) 1946/7.

Hayes, W.J. (1) (Limerick) 1948/9.

Healey, R. (2) (Cardiff City) 1976/7, 1979/80.

Heighway, S.D. (34) (Liverpool) 1970/1, 1972/3, 1974/5, 1975/6, 1976/7, 1977/8, 1978/9, 1979/80, 1980/1 (Minnesota Kicks) 1981/2.

Henderson, B. (2) (Drumcondra) 1947/8.

Hennessy, J. (5) (Shelbourne) 1955/6, 1965/6 (St Patrick's Athletic) 1968/9.

Herrick, J. (3) (Cork Hibernians) 1971/2 (Shamrock Rovers) 1972/3.

Higgins, J. (1) (Birmingham City) 1950/1.
Holmes, J. (Coventry City) 1970/1, 1972/3, 1973/4, 1974/5, 1975/6, 1976/7 (Tottenham Hotspur) 1977/8, 1978/9, 1980/1 (Vancouver Whitecaps) 1980/1.
Houghton, R.J. (62) (Oxford United) 1985/6, 1986/7, 1987/8 (Liverpool) 1987/8, 1988/9, 1989/90, 1990/1, 1991/2 (Aston Villa) 1992/93, 1993/94.
Howlett, G. (1) (Brighton & Hove Albion) 1983/4.
Hughton, C. (53) (Tottenham Hotspur) 1979/80, 1980/1, 1981/2, 1982/3, 1983/4, 1984/5, 1985/6, 1986/7, 1987/8, 1988/9, 1989/90, 1990/1 (West Ham United), 1991/2.
Hurley, C.J. (40) (Millwall) 1956/7, 1957/8 (Sunderland) 1958/9, 1959/60, 1960/1, 1961/2, 1962/3, 1963/4, 1964/5, 1965/6, 1966/7, 1967/8 (Bolton Wanderers) 1968/9.

Irwin, D.J. (28) (Manchester United) 1990/1, 1991/2, 1992/93, 1993/94.

Keane, R.M. (26) (Nottingham Forest) 1990/1, 1991/2, 1992/93, 1993/94.
Keane, T.R. (4) (Swansea Town) 1948/9.
Kearin, M. (1) (Shamrock Rovers) 1971/2.
Kearns, F.T. (1) (West Ham United) 1953/4.
Kearns, M. (18) (Oxford United) 1969/70 (Walsall) 1973/4, 1975/6, 1976/7, 1977/8, 1978/9 (Wolverhampton Wanderers) 1979/80.
Kelly, A.T. (3) (Sheffield United) 1992/93, 1993/94.
Kelly, D.T. (17) (Walsall) 1987/8 (West Ham) 1988/9 (Leicester City) 1989/90, 1990/1 (Newcastle United) 1991/2, 1992/93 (Wolverhampton Wanderers) 1993/94.
Kelly, G. (7) (Leeds United) 1993/94.
Kelly, J.A. (48) (Drumcondra) 1956/7 (Preston North End) 1961/2, 1962/3, 1963/4, 1964/5, 1965/6, 1966/7, 1967/8, 1969/70, 1970/1, 1971/2, 1972/3.
Kelly, J.P.V. (5) (Wolverhampton Wanderers) 1960/1, 1961/2.
Kelly, M.J. (4) (Portsmouth) 1987/8, 1988/9, 1990/1.
Kelly, N. (1) (Nottingham Forest) 1953/4.
Kennedy, M.F. (2) (Portsmouth) 1985/6.
Keogh, J. (1) (Shamrock Rovers) 1965/6.
Keogh, S. (1) (Shamrock Rovers) 1958/9.
Kernaghan, A.N. (11) (Middlesbrough) 1992/93 (Manchester City) 1993/94.
Kiernan, F.W. (5) (Shamrock Rovers) 1950/1 (Southampton) 1951/2.
Kinnear, J.P. (26) (Tottenham Hotspur) 1966/7, 1967/8, 1968/9, 1969/70, 1970/1, 1971/2, 1972/3, 1973/4, 1974/5 (Brighton & Hove Albion) 1975/6.

Langan, D. (25) (Derby County) 1977/8, 1979/80 (Birmingham City) 1980/1, 1981/2 (Oxford United) 1984/5, 1985/6, 1986/7, 1987/8.
Lawler, J.F. (8) (Fulham) 1952/3, 1953/4, 1954/5, 1955/6.
Lawlor, J.C. (3) (Drumcondra) 1948/9 (Doncaster Rovers) 1950/1.
Lawlor, M. (5) (Shamrock Rovers) 1970/1, 1972/3.
Lawrenson, M. (38) (Preston North End) 1976/7 (Brighton & Hove Albion) 1977/8, 1978/9, 1979/80, 1980/1 (Liverpool) 1981/2, 1982/3, 1983/4, 1984/5, 1985/6, 1986/7, 1987/8.
Leech, M. (8) (Shamrock Rovers) 1968/9, 1971/2, 1972/3.
Lowry, D. (1) (St Patrick's Athletic) 1961/2.

McAlinden, J. (2) (Portsmouth) 1945/6.
McAteer, J.W. (9) (Bolton Wanderers) 1993/94.
McCann, J. (1) (Shamrock Rovers) 1956/7.
McCarthy, M. (57) (Manchester City) 1983/4, 1984/5, 1985/6, 1986/7 (Celtic) 1987/8, 1988/9 (Lyon) 1989/90, 1990/1 (Millwall) 1991/2.

McConville, T. (6) (Dundalk) 1971/2 (Waterford) 1972/3.
McDonagh, J. (24) (Everton) 1980/1 (Bolton Wanderers) 1981/2, 1982/3, (Notts County) 1983/4, 1984/5, 1985/6.
McDonagh, Joe (3) (Shamrock Rovers) 1983/4, 1984/5.
McEvoy, M.A. (17) (Blackburn Rovers) 1960/1, 1962/3, 1963/4, 1964/5, 1965/6, 1966/7.
McGee, P. (15) (QPR) 1977/8, 1978/9, 1979/80 (Preston North End) 1980/1.
McGoldrick, E.J. (12) (Crystal Palace) 1991/2, 1992/93, (Arsenal) 1993/94.
McGowan, D. (3) (West Ham United) 1948/9.
McGowan, J. (1) (Cork United) 1946/7.
McGrath, M. (22) (Blackburn Rovers) 1957/8, 1958/9, 1959/60, 1960/1, 1961/2, 1962/3, 1963/4, 1964/5, 1965/6 (Bradford Park Avenue) 1965/6, 1966/7.
McGrath, P. (69) (Manchester United) 1984/5, 1985/6, 1986/7, 1987/8, 1988/9 (Aston Villa) 1989/90, 1990/1, 1991/2, 1992/93, 1993/94.
Macken, A. (1) (Derby County) 1976/7.
Mackey, G. (3) (Shamrock Rovers) 1956/7.
McLoughlin, A.F. (16) (Swindon T) 1989/90, 1990/1 (Southampton) 1991/2 (Portsmouth) 1992/93, 1993/94.
McMillan, W. (2) (Belfast Celtic) 1945/6. McNally, J.B. (3) (Luton Town) 1958/9, 1960/1, 1962/3.
Malone, G. (1) (Shelbourne) 1948/9.
Mancini, T.J. (5) (QPR) 1973/4 (Arsenal) 1974/5.
Martin, C.J. (30) (Glentoran) 1945/6, 1946/7 (Leeds United) 1946/7, 1947/8, (Aston Villa) 1948/9, 1949/50 1950/1, 1951/2,K1953/4, 1954/5, 1955/6.
Martin, M.P. (51) (Bohemians) 1971/2, 1972/3 (Manchester United) 1972/3, 1973/4, 1974/5 (West Bromwich Albion) 1975/6, 1976/7 (Newcastle United) 1978/9, 1979/80, 1981/2, 1982/3.
Meagan, M.K. (17) (Everton) 1960/1, 1961/2, 1962/3, 1963/4 (Huddersfield Town) 1964/5, 1965/6, 1966/7, 1967/8 (Drogheda) 1969/70.
Milligan, M.J. (1) (Oldham Athletic) 1991/2.
Mooney, J. (2) (Shamrock Rovers) 1964/5.
Moran, K. (70) (Manchester United) 1979/80, 1980/1, 1981/2, 1982/3, 1983/4, 1984/5, 1985/6, 1986/7, 1987/8 (Sporting Gijon) 1988/9 (Blackburn Rovers) 1989/90, 1990/1, 1991/2, 1992/93, 1993/94.
Moroney, T. (12) (West Ham United) 1947/8, 1948/9, 1949/50, 1950/1, 1951/2, 1953/4.
Morris, C.B. (35) (Celtic) 1987/8, 1988/9, 1989/90, 1990/1, 1991/2 (Middlesbrough) 1992/93.
Moulson, G.B. (3) (Lincoln City) 1947/8, 1948/9.
Mucklan, C. (1) (Drogheda) 1977/8.
Mulligan, P.M. (50) (Shamrock Rovers) 1968/9, 1969/70 (Chelsea) 1969/70, 1970/1, 1971/2 (Crystal Palace) 1972/3, 1973/4, 1974/5 (West Bromwich Albion) 1975/6, 1976/7, 1977/8, 1978/9 (Shamrock Rovers) 1979/80.
Munroe, L. (1) (Shamrock Rovers) 1953/4.
Murphy, A. (1) (Clyde) 1955/6.
Murphy, B. (1) (Bohemians) 1985/6.
Murphy, J. (1) (Crystal Palace) 1979/80.
Murray, T. (1) (Dundalk) 1949/50.

Newman, W. (1) (Shelbourne) 1968/9.
Nolan, R. (10) (Shamrock Rovers) 1956/7, 1957/8, 1959/60, 1961/2, 1962/3.

O'Brien, F. (4) (Philadelphia Fury) 1979/80.

O'Brien, L. (11) (Shamrock Rovers) 1985/6 (Manchester United) 1986/7, 1987/8 (Newcastle United) 1988/9, 1991/2, 1992/93 (Tranmere Rovers) 1993/94.
O'Brien R. (4) (Notts County) 1975/6, 1976/7.
O'Byrne, L.B. (1) (Shamrock Rovers) 1948/9.
O'Callaghan, B.R. (6) (Stoke City) 1978/9, 1979/80, 1980/1, 1981/2.
O'Callaghan, K. (20) (Ipswich Town) 1980/1, 1981/2, 1982/3, 1983/4, 1984/5, (Portsmouth) 1985/6, 1986/7.
O'Connnell, A. (2) (Dundalk) 1966/7 (Bohemians) 1970/1.
O'Connor, T. (4) (Shamrock Rovers) 1949/50.
O'Connor, T. (7) (Fulham) 1967/8 (Dundalk) 1971/2 (Bohemians) 1972/3.
O'Driscoll, J.F. (3) (Swansea Town) 1948/9.
O'Driscoll, S. (3) (Fulham) 1981/2.
O'Farrell, F. (9) (West Ham United) 1951/2, 1952/3, 1953/4, 1954/5, 1955/6 (Preston North End) 1957/8, 1958/9.
O'Flanagan, K.P. (3) (Arsenal) 1946/7.
O'Flanagan, M. (1) (Bohemians) 1946/7.
O'Hanlon, K.G. (1) (Rotherham United) 1987/8.
O'Keefe, E. (5) (Everton) 1980/1 (Port Vale) 1983/4.
O'Leary, D. (67) (Arsenal) 1976/7, 1977/8, 1978/9, 1979/80, 1980/1, 1981/2, 1982/3, 1983/4, 1984/5, 1985/6, 1988/9, 1989/90, 1990/1, 1991/2, 1992/93.
O'Leary, P. (7) (Shamrock Rovers) 1979/80, 1980/1.
O'Neill, F.S. (20) (Shamrock Rovers) 1961/2, 1964/5, 1965/6, 1966/7, 1968/9, 1971/2.
O'Neill, J. (17) (Everton) 1951/2, 1952/3, 1953/4, 1954/5, 1955/6, 1956/7, 1957/8, 1958/9.
O'Neill, J. (1) (Preston North End) 1960/1.
O'Regan, K. (4) (Brighton & Hove Albion) 1983/4, 1984/5.
O'Reilly, J. (2) (Cork United) 1945/6.

Peyton, G. (33) (Fulham) 1976/7, 1977/8, 1978/9, 1979/80, 1980/1, 1981/2, 1984/5, 1985/6 (Bournemouth) 1987/8, 1988/9, 1989/90, 1990/1 (Everton) 1991/2.
Peyton, N. (6) (Shamrock Rovers) 1956/7 (Leeds United) 1959/60, 1960/1, 1962/3.
Phelan, T. (25) (Wimbledon) 1991/2 (Manchester City) 1992/93, 1993/94.

Quinn, N.J. (42) (Arsenal) 1985/6, 1986/7, 1987/8, 1988/9 (Manchester City) 1989/90, 1990/1, 1991/2, 1992/93, 1993/94.

Richardson, D.J. (3) (Shamrock Rovers) 1971/2 (Gillingham) 1972/3, 1979/80.
Ringstead, A. (20) (Sheffield United) 1950/1, 1951/2, 1952/3, 1953/4, 1954/5, 1955/6, 1956/7, 1957/8, 1958/9.
Robinson, M. (23) (Brighton & Hove Albion) 1980/1, 1981/2, 1982/3, (Liverpool) 1983/4, 1984/5 (QPR) 1985/6.
Roche, P.J. (8) (Shelbourne) 1971/2 (Manchester United) 1974/5, 1975/6.
Rogers, E. (19) (Blackburn Rovers) 1967/8, 1968/9, 1969/70, 1970/1, (Charlton Athletic) 1971/2, 1972/3.
Ryan, G. (16) (Derby County) 1977/8 (Brighton & Hove Albion) 1978/9, 1979/80, 1980/1, 1982/3, 1983/4, 1984/5.
Ryan, R.A. (16) (West Bromwich Albion) 1949/50, 1950/1, 1951/2, 1952/3, 1953/4, 1954/5 (Derby County) 1955/6.

Saward, P. (18) (Millwall) 1953/4 (Aston Villa) 1956/7, 1957/8, 1958/9, 1959/60, 1960/1 (Huddersfield Town) 1960/1, 1961/2, 1962/3.
Scannell, T. (1) (Southend United) 1953/4.
Scully, P.J. (1) (Arsenal) 1988/9.

Sheedy, K. (45) (Everton) 1983/4, 1984/5, 1985/6, 1986/7, 1987/8, 1988/9, 1989/90, 1990/1 (Newcastle United) 1991/2, 1992/93.

Sheridan, J.J. (24) (Leeds United) 1987/8, 1988/9 (Sheffield Wed) 1989/90, 1990/1, 1991/2, 1992/93, 1993/94.

Slaven, B. (7) (Middlesbrough) 1989/90, 1990/91, 1992/93.

Sloan, J.W. (2) (Arsenal) 1945/6.

Smyth, M. (1) (Shamrock Rovers) 1968/9.

Stapleton, F. (70) (Arsenal) 1976/7, 1977/8, 1978/9, 1979/80, 1980/1 (Manchester United) 1981/2, 1982/3, 1983/4, 1984/5, 1985/6, 1986/7 (Ajax) 1987/8 (Derby County) 1987/8 (Le Havre) 1988/9 (Blackburn Rovers) 1989/90.

Staunton, S. (51) (Liverpool) 1988/9, 1989/90, 1990/1 (Aston Villa) 1991/2, 1992/93, 1993/94.

Stevenson, A.E. (6) (Everton) 1946/7, 1947/8, 1948/9.

Strahan, F. (5) (Shelbourne) 1963/4, 1964/5, 1965/6.

Swan, M.M.G. (1) (Drumcondra) 1959/60.

Synott, N. (3) (Shamrock Rovers) 1977/8, 1978/9.

Thomas, P. (2) (Waterford) 1973/4.

Townsend, A.D. (49) (Norwich City) 1988/9, 1989/90, 1990/1 (Chelsea) 1991/2, 1992/93 (Aston Villa) 1993/94.

Traynor, T.J. (8) (Southampton) 1953/4, 1961/2, 1962/3, 1963/4.

Treacy, R.C.P. (42) (West Bromwich Albion) 1965/6, 1966/7, 1967/8 (Charlton Athletic) 1967/8, 1968/9, 1969/70, 1970/1 (Swindon Town) 1971/2, 1972/3, 1973/4 (Preston North End)K1973/4, 1974/5, 1975/6 (West Bromwich Albion) 1976/7, 1977/8 (Shamrock Rovers) 1979/80.

Tuohy, L. (8) (Shamrock Rovers) 1955/6, 1958/9 (Newcastle United) 1961/2, 1962/3 (Shamrock Rovers) 1963/4, 1964/5.

Turner, A. (2) (Celtic) 1962/3, 1963/4.

Vernon, J. (2) (Belfast Celtic) 1945/6.

Waddock, G. (20) (QPR) 1979/80, 1980/1, 1981/2, 1982/3, 1983/4, 1984/5, 1985/6 (Millwall) 1989/90.

Walsh, D.J. (20) (West Bromwich Albion) 1945/6, 1946/7, 1947/8, 1948/9, 1949/50, 1950/1 (Aston Villa) 1951/2, 1952/3, 1953/4.

Walsh, J. (1) (Limerick) 1981/2.

Walsh, M. (21) (Blackpool) 1975/6, 1976/7 (Everton) 1978/9 (QPR) 1978/9 (Porto) 1980/1, 1981/2, 1982/3, 1983/4, 1984/5.

Walsh, M. (4) (Everton) 1981/2, 1982/3 (Norwich City) 1982/3.

Walsh, W. (9) (Manchester City) 1946/7, 1947/8, 1948/9, 1949/50.

Waters, J. (2) (Grimsby Town) 1976/7, 1979/80.

Whelan, R. (2) (St Patrick's Athletic) 1963/4.

Whelan, R. (51) (Liverpool) 1980/1, 1981/2, 1982/3, 1983/4, 1984/5, 1985/6, 1986/7, 1987/8, 1988/9, 1989/90, 1990/1, 1991/2, 1992/93, 1993/94.

Whelan, W. (4) (Manchester United) 1955/6, 1956/7.

Whittaker, R. (1) (Chelsea) 1958/9.

BRITISH ISLES INTERNATIONAL GOALSCORERS SINCE 1946

ENGLAND

A'Court, A.	1
Adams, T.A.	4
Allen, R.	2
Anderson, V.	2
Anderton, D.R.	1
Astall, G.	1
Atyeo, P.J.W.	5
Baily, E.F.	5
Baker, J.H.	3
Ball, A.J.	8
Barnes, J.	11
Barnes, P.S.	4
Beardsley, P.A.	9
Beattie, I.K.	1
Bell, C.	9
Bentley, R.T.F.	9
Blissett, L.	3
Bowles, S.	1
Bradford, G.R.W.	1
Bradley, W.	2
Bridges, B.J.	1
Broadbent, P.F.	2
Broadis, I.A.	8
Brooking, T.D.	5
Brooks, J.	2
Bull, S.G.	4
Butcher, T.	3
Byrne, J.J.	8
Carter, H.S.	7
(inc. 2 scored pre-war)	
Chamberlain, M.	1
Channon, M.R.	21
Charlton, J.	6
Charlton, R.	49
Chivers, M.	13
Clarke, A.J.	10
Connelly, J.M.	7
Coppell, S.J.	7
Cowans, G.	2
Crawford, R.	1
Currie, A.W.	3
Dixon, L.M.	1
Dixon, K.M.	4
Douglas, B.	11

Eastham, G.	2
Edwards, D.	5
Elliott, W.H.	3
Ferdinand, L.	3
Finney, T.	30
Flowers, R.	10
Francis, G.C.J.	3
Francis, J.	12
Froggatt, J.	2
Froggatt, R.	2
Gascoigne, P.J.	6
Goddard, P.	1
Grainger, C.	3
Greaves, J.	44
Haines, J.T.W.	2
Hancocks, J.	2
Hassall, H.W.	4
Hateley, M.	9
Haynes, J.N.	18
Hirst, D.E.	1
Hitchens, G.A.	5
Hoddle, G.	8
Hughes, E.W.	1
Hunt, R.	18
Hunter, N.	2
Hurst, G.C.	24
Johnson, D.E.	6
Kay, A.H.	1
Keegan, J.K.	21
Kennedy, R.	3
Keown, M.R.	1
Kevan, D.T.	8
Kidd, B.	1
Langton, R.	1
Latchford, R.D.	5
Lawler, C.	1
Lawton, T.	22
(inc.6 scored pre-war)	
Lee, F.	10
Lee, J.	1
Lee, S.	2
Lineker, G.	48
Lofthouse, N.	30

Mabbutt, G.	1
McDermott, T.	3
Macdonald, M.	6
Mannion, W.J.	11
Mariner, P.	13
Marsh, R.W.	1
Matthews, S.	11
(inc. 8 scored pre-war)	
Medley, L.D.	1
Melia, J.	1
Merson, P.C.	1
Milburn, J.E.T.	10
Moore, R.F.	2
Morris, J.	3
Mortensen, S.H.	23
Mullen, J.	6
Mullery, A.P.	1
Neal, P.G.	5
Nicholls, J.	1
Nicholson, W.E.	1
O'Grady, M.	3
Own goals	23
Paine, T.L.	7
Palmer, C.L.	1
Parry, R.A.	1
Peacock, A.	3
Pearce, S.	4
Pearson, J.S.	5
Pearson, S.C.	5
Perry, W.	2
Peters, M.	20
Pickering, F.	5
Platt, D.	23
Pointer, R.	2
Ramsay, A.E.	3
Revie, D.G.	4
Robson, B.	26
Robson, R.	4
Rowley, J.F.	6
Royle, J.	2
Sansom, K.	1
Sewell, J.	3
Shackleton, L.F.	1
Shearer, A.	3

Smith, A.M.	2	Collins, J.	4	Johnston, M.	14
Smith, R.	13	Collins, R.V.	10	Johnstone, D.	2
Steven, T.M.	4	Combe, J.R.	1	Johnstone, J.	4
Stiles, N.P.	13	Conn, A.	1	Johnstone, R.	9
Summerbee, M.G.	1	Cooper, D.	6	Jordan, J.	11
		Craig, J.	1		
Tambling, R.V.	1	Curran, H.P.	1	Law, D.	30
Taylor, P.J.	2			Leggat, G.	8
Taylor, T.	16	Dalglish, K.	30	Lennox, R.	3
Thompson, P.B.	1	Davidson, J.A.	1	Liddell, W.	6
Tueart, D.	2	Docherty, T.H.	1	Linwood, A.B.	1
		Dodds, D.	1	Lorimer, P.	4
Viollet, D.S.	1	Duncan, D.M.	1		
		Durie, G.S.	4	Macari, L.	5
Waddle, C.R.	6			McAllister, G.	4
Wallace, D.L.	1	Fernie, W.	1	MacDougall, E.J.	3
Walsh, P.	1	Flavell, R.	2	MacKay, D.C.	4
Watson, D.V.	4	Fleming, C.	2	Mackay, G.	1
Webb, N.	4			MacKenzie, J.A.	1
Weller, K.	1	Gallacher, K.W.	2	MacLeod, M.	1
Wignall, F.	2	Gemmell, T.K		McAvennie, F.	1
Wilkins, R.G.	3	*(St Mirren)*	1	McCall, S.M.	1
Wilshaw, D.J.	10	Gemmell, T.K		McCalliog, J.	1
Wise, D.F.	1	*(Celtic)*	1	McClair, B.	2
Withe, P.	1	Gemmill, A.	8	McCoist, A.	15
Woodcock, T.	16	Gibson, D.W.	3	McGhee, M.	2
Worthington, F.S.	2	Gilzean, A.J.	12	McGinlay, J.	1
Wright, I.E.	5	Gough, C.R.	6	McInally, A.	3
Wright, M.	1	Graham, A.	2	McKimmie, S.I.	1
Wright, W.A.	3	Graham, G.	3	McKinlay, W.	2
		Gray, A.	7	McKinnon, R.	1
SCOTLAND		Gray, E.	3	McLaren, A.	4
		Gray, F.	1	McLean, T.	1
Aitken, R.	1	Greig, J.	3	McLintock, F.	1
Archibald, S.	4			McMillan, I.L.	2
		Hamilton, G.	4	McNeill, W.	3
Baird, S.	2	Harper, J.M.	2	McPhail, J.	3
Bannon, E.	1	Hartford, R.A.	4	McQueen, G.	5
Bauld, W.	2	Henderson, J.G.	1	McStay, P.	9
Baxter, J.C.	3	Henderson, W.	5	Mason, J.	4
Bett, J.	1	Hendry, E.C.J.	1	Masson, D.S.	5
Bone, J.	1	Herd, D.G.	4	Miller, W.	1
Booth, S.	1	Hewie, J.D.	2	Mitchell, R.C.	1
Brand, R.	8	Holton, J.A.	1	Morgan, W.	1
Brazil, A.	1	Houliston, W.	2	Morris, H.	3
Bremner, W.J.	3	Howie, H.	1	Mudie, J.K.	9
Brown, A.D.	6	Hughes, J.	1	Mulhall, G.	1
Buckley, P.	1	Hunter, W.	1	Murdoch, R.	5
Burns, K.	1	Hutchison, T.	1	Murray, J.	1
Caldow, E.	4	Jackson, C.	1	Narey, D.	1
Campbell, R.	1	Jardine, A.	1	Nevin, P.K.F.	4
Chalmers, S.	3	Johnston, L.H.	1	Nicholas, C.	5

O'Hare, J. 5
Ormond, W.E. 1
Orr, T. 1
Own goals 7

Parlane, D. 1
Pettigrew, W. 2
Provan, D. 1

Quinn, J. 7
Quinn, P. 1

Reilly, L. 22
Ring, T. 2
Rioch, B.D. 6
Robertson, A. 2
Robertson, J. 2
Robertson, J.N. 8

St John, I. 9
Scott, A.S. 5
Sharp, G. 1
Shearer, D. 1
Smith, G. 4
Souness, G.J. 3
Steel, W. 12
Stein, C. 10
Stewart, R. 1
Strachan, G. 5
Sturrock, P. 3

Thornton, W. 1

Waddell, W. 6
Wallace, I.A. 1
Wark, J. 7
Weir, A. 1
White, J.A. 3
Wilson, D. 9

Young, A. 2

WALES
Allchurch, I.J. 23
Allen, M. 3

Barnes, W. 1
Blackmore, C.G. 1
Bodin, P.J. 3
Bowen, D.I. 3
Bowen, M. 2

Boyle, T. 1
Burgess, W.A.R. 1

Charles, J. 1
Charles, M. 6
Charles, W.J. 15
Clarke, R.J. 5
Coleman, C. 2
Curtis, A. 6

Davies, G. 2
Davies, R.T. 8
Davies, R.W. 7
Deacy, N. 4
Durban, A. 2
Dwyer, P. 2

Edwards, G. 2
Edwards, R.I. 4
England, H.M. 3
Evans, I. 1

Flynn, B. 7
Ford, T. 23
Foulkes, W.J. 1

Giggs, R.J. 2
Giles, D. 2
Godfrey, B.C. 2
Griffiths, A.T. 6
Griffiths, M.W. 2

Harris, C.S. 1
Hewitt, R. 1
Hockey, T. 1
Hodges, G. 2
Horne, B. 2
Hughes, L.M. 12

James, L. 10
James, R. 8
Jones, A. 1
Jones, B.S. 2
Jones, Cliff 15
Jones, D.E. 1
Jones, J.P. 1

Kryzwicki, R.I. 1

Leek, K. 5
Lovell, S. 1
Lowrie, G. 2

Mahoney, J.F. 1
Medwin, T.C. 6
Moore, G. 1

Nicholas, P. 2

O'Sullivan, P.A. 1
Own goals 5

Palmer, D. 1
Paul, R. 1
Pembridge, M.A. 1
Phillips, D. 2
Powell, A. 1
Powell, D. 1
Price, P. 1

Reece, G.I. 2
Rees, R.R. 3
Roberts, P.S. 1
Rush, I. 28

Saunders, D. 14
Slatter, N. 2
Smallman, D.P. 1

Tapscott, D.R. 4
Thomas, M. 4
Toshack, J.B. 13

Vernon, T.R. 8
Walsh, I. 7
Williams, G.E. 1
Williams, G.G. 1
Woosnam, A.P. 4

Yorath, T.C. 2
Young, E. 1

NORTHERN IRELAND
Anderson, T. 4
Armstrong, G. 12

Barr, H.H. 1
Best, G. 9
Bingham, W.L. 10
Black, K. 1
Blanchflower, D. 2
Blanchflower, J. 1

Brennan, R.A. 1	McGarry, J.K. 1	Bradshaw, P. 4
Brotherston, N. 3	McGrath, R.C. 4	Brady, L. 9
	McIlroy, J. 10	Brown, D. 1
Campbell, W.G. 1	McIlroy, S.B. 5	Byrne, J. (Bray) 1
Casey, T. 2	McLaughlin, J.C. 6	Byrne, J. (QPR) 4
Caskey, W. 1	McMordie, A.S. 3	
Cassidy, T. 1	McMorran, E.J. 4	Cantwell, J. 14
Clarke, C.J. 13	McParland, P.J. 10	Carey, J. 3
Clements, D. 2	Moreland, V. 1	Carroll, T. 1
Cochrane, T. 1	Morgan, S. 3	Cascarino, A. 12
Crossan, E. 1	Morrow, S.J. 1	Coad, P. 3
Crossan, J.A. 10		Conroy, T. 2
Cush, W.W. 5	Neill, W.J.T. 2	Conway, J. 3
	Nelson, S. 1	Coyne, T. 4
D'Arcy, S.D. 1	Nicholl, C.J. 3	Cummings, G. 5
Doherty, I. 1	Nicholl, J.M. 2	Curtis, D. 8
Doherty, P.D. 3	Nicholson, J.J. 6	
(inc. 1 scored pre-war)		Daly, G. 13
Dougan, A.D. 8	O'Kane, W.J. 1	Davis, T. 4
Dowie, I. 2	O'Neill, J. 1	Dempsey, J. 1
	O'Neill, M. 1	Dennehy, M. 2
Elder, A.R. 1	O'Neill, M.H. 8	Donnelly, J. 3
	Own goals 4	Donnelly, T. 1
Ferguson, W. 1		Duffy, B. 1
Ferris, R.O. 1	Peacock, R. 2	Duggan, H. 1
Finney, T. 2	Penney, S. 2	Dunne, J. 12
		Dunne, L. 1
Gray, P. 2	Quinn, J.M. 10	
		Eglinton, T. 2
Hamilton, B. 4	Simpson, W.J. 5	Ellis, P. 1
Hamilton, S. 5	Smyth, S. 5	
Harkin, J.T. 2	Spence, D.W. 3	Fagan, F. 5
Harvey, M. 3	Stewart, I. 2	Fallon, S. 2
Hill, C.F. 1		Fallon, W. 2
Humphries, W. 1	Taggart, G.P. 5	Farrell, P. 3
Hughes, M.E. 1	Tully, C.P. 3	Fitzgerald, J. 1
Hunter, A. 1		Fitzgerald, P. 2
	Walker, J. 1	Fitzsimons, A 7
Irvine, W.J. 8	Walsh, D.J. 5	Flood, J.J. 4
	Welsh, E. 1	Fogarty, A. 3
Johnston, W.C. 1	Whiteside, N 9	Fullam, J. 1
Jones, J. 1	Wilson, D.J. 1	Fullam, R. 1
	Wilson, K.J 6	
Lockhart, N. 3	Wilson, S.J 7	Galvin, A. 1
Lomas, S.M. 1		Gavin, J. 2
		Geoghegan, M 2
Magilton, J. 4	**EIRE**	Giles, J. 5
McAdams, W.J 7	Aldridge, J. 14	Givens, D. 19
McClelland, J. 1	Ambrose, P. 1	Glynn, D. 1
McCrory, S. 1	Anderson, J. 1	Grealish, T. 8
McCurdy, C. 1		Grimes, A.A 1
McDonald, A. 3	Bermingham, P 1	Hale, A. 2

9th UEFA UNDER-21 CHAMPIONSHIP 1992–94

Finals in France
Semi-finals
Portugal 2, Spain 0
France 0, Italy 0
Italy won 5-3 on penalties.

Third place
Spain 2, France 1

Final
Italy 1, Portugal 0
In sudden death extra time.

10th UEFA UNDER-17 CHAMPIONSHIP 1993–94

Semi-finals
Ghana 3, Chile 0
Nigeria 2, Poland 1
Third place
Chile 1, Poland 1
Chile won 4-2 on penalties.

Final
Ghana 1, Nigeria 2

OTHER AWARDS 1993–94

FA Carling Premiership Manager of the Year
Alex Ferguson (Manchester United)
Endsleigh Insurance Managers of the Year
Division 1 - Alan Smith (Crystal Palace); Division 2   Mark McGhee (Reading);
Division 3   Fred Davies (Shrewsbury Town).

The PFA awards 1994
Player of the Year: Eric Cantona (Manchester United).

Football Writers Player of the Year
Alan Shearer (Blackburn Rovers).

European Footballer of the Year 1993
Roberto Baggio (Juventus and Italy).

Scottish PFA Awards 1993
Mark Hateley (Rangers).

Scottish Football Writers Player of the Year 1993
Mark Hateley (Rangers).

GM VAUXHALL CONFERENCE 1993-94

GM VAUXHALL CONFERENCE TABLE 1993-94

		Home			Goals		Away			Home		
	Pl	W	D	L	F	A	W	D	L	F	A	Pts
Kidderminster Harriers	42	13	5	3	31	12	9	4	8	32	23	75
Kettering Town	42	9	7	5	23	14	10	8	3	23	10	72
Woking	42	12	5	4	35	25	6	8	7	23	33	67
Southport	42	10	7	4	26	21	8	5	8	31	30	66
Runcorn	42	12	6	3	41	26	2	13	6	22	31	61
Dagenham & Redbridge	42	12	5	4	41	23	3	9	9	21	31	59
Macclesfield Town	42	7	8	6	24	18	9	3	9	24	31	59
Dover Athletic	42	9	3	9	28	24	8	4	9	20	25	58
Stafford Rangers	42	10	7	4	39	22	4	8	9	17	30	57
Altrincham	42	8	5	8	23	22	8	4	9	18	20	57
Gateshead	42	10	6	5	23	18	5	6	10	22	35	57
Bath City	42	6	8	7	28	21	7	9	5	19	17	56
Halifax Town	42	7	9	5	28	18	6	7	8	27	31	55
Stalybridge Celtic	42	6	6	9	27	30	8	6	7	27	25	54
Northwich Victoria	42	9	5	9	26	19	4	10	7	18	26	52
Welling United	42	7	7	7	25	23	6	5	10	22	26	51
Telford United	42	8	7	6	24	22	5	5	11	17	27	51
Bromsgrove Rovers	42	5	8	8	26	32	7	7	7	28	34	51
Yeovil Town	42	7	4	10	23	26	7	5	9	26	36	51
Merthyr Tydfil	42	8	7	6	34	26	4	8	9	26	35	49
Slough Town	42	8	8	5	30	24	3	6	12	14	34	47
Witton Albion	42	4	8	9	18	30	3	5	13	19	33	34

VAUXHALL CONFERENCE LEADING GOALSCORERS 1993-94

Conf.			FAC	FAT	DC
25	Paul Dobson (Gateshead)	+	3	4	2
23	Karl Thomas (Runcorn)	+	—	5	2
17	Paul Adcock (Bath City)	+	4	1	-
	Terry Robbins (Welling United)	+	-	2	2
16	Mickey Spencer (Yeovil Town)	+	-	1	1
	Clive Walker (Woking)	+	-	3	-
15	David Gamble (Southport)	+	2	2	-
	David Leworthy (Dover Athletic)	+	1	1	3
14	Carl Alford (Macclesfield Town)	+	3	2	6
	Paul Davies (Kidderminster Harriers)	+	1	-	3
	Morrys Scott (Slough Town)	+	2	1	-
13	Recky Carter (Bromsgrove Rovers)	+	3	2	-
	Jamie Paterson (Halifax Town)	+	-	2	1
	Delwyn Humphreys (Kidderminster H.)	+	3	-	1

FAC; FA Cup. FAT; FA Trophy. DC; Drinkwise Cup.

GM VAUXHALL CONFERENCE RESULTS GRID 1993-94

	Altrincham	Bath City	Bromsgrove Rovers	Dagenham & Redbridge	Dover Athletic	Gateshead	Halifax Town	Kettering Town	Kidderminster Harriers	Macclesfield Town	Merthyr Tydfil	Northwich Victoria	Runcorn	Slough Town	Southport	Stafford Rangers	Stalybridge Celtic	Telford United	Welling United	Witton Albion	Woking	Yeovil Town
Altrincham	—	0-1	3-0	3-0	2-1	1-0	1-0	1-0	1-0	2-0	2-0	2-2	2-1	2-0	1-2	0-0	0-0	0-1	2-0	1-3	0-2	1-0
Bath City	0-2	—	0-1	0-0	0-0	3-0	0-0	0-4	0-0	1-1	0-3	0-0	0-0	3-0	1-2	2-3	1-1	2-0	2-0	1-1	1-1	3-0
Bromsgrove Rovers	2-3	0-1	—	4-2	4-3	0-0	0-1	0-1	4-3	3-0	0-0	1-1	0-0	0-0	2-2	3-3	0-1	0-5	1-1	3-3	0-0	1-2
Dagenham & Redbridge	1-2	0-0	1-0	—	1-2	3-1	2-1	0-2	3-0	0-2	2-2	3-0	1-1	1-0	5-0	2-0	1-2	4-1	5-0	2-1	1-8	2-1
Dover Athletic	2-0	0-0	2-1	1-2	—	1-1	0-0	3-2	0-2	0-1	0-1	1-1	2-3	1-0	3-1	0-0	0-1	0-1	0-1	2-1	3-0	1-3
Gateshead	0-3	2-3	1-1	3-1	3-1	—	0-1	1-1	0-1	6-1	3-0	0-0	1-1	2-1	3-1	3-1	1-1	2-3	1-1	3-0	2-1	1-1
Halifax Town	0-0	1-0	3-0	2-0	2-1	2-1	—	0-1	0-1	3-0	0-2	2-0	5-0	1-1	1-1	1-1	3-2	0-1	3-2	2-2	2-6	0-0
Kettering Town	1-1	0-3	0-4	2-0	2-1	0-0	1-0	—	0-2	1-1	1-1	0-0	0-2	1-5	1-0	1-1	2-3	0-5	2-0	0-1	1-0	1-0
Kidderminster Harriers	1-0	0-0	0-1	3-0	1-0	0-0	1-1	2-0	—	1-0	1-2	2-0	1-1	2-0	2-0	3-2	3-0	1-2	2-2	2-0	1-1	1-1
Macclesfield Town	1-0	0-0	4-3	3-0	0-2	1-0	0-1	0-0	0-0	—	1-2	0-0	3-0	2-2	2-0	1-3	1-3	0-3	1-0	0-1	3-1	2-3
Merthyr Tydfil	1-0	0-4	1-0	0-1	0-0	0-0	2-0	1-1	0-0	1-2	—	5-0	1-1	5-1	0-1	1-2	2-3	3-2	3-1	2-0	2-3	1-1
Northwich Victoria	2-0	3-1	2-2	2-2	0-1	0-0	0-1	0-2	0-0	1-0	1-2	—	1-1	3-2	2-1	0-2	0-2	1-1	2-4	4-3	1-1	1-1
Runcorn	2-1	0-0	4-1	1-0	2-3	1-1	1-1	0-2	1-4	2-2	3-0	0-0	—	3-0	1-1	2-2	2-0	2-1	1-1	1-1	1-1	4-0
Slough Town	0-2	0-0	1-2	1-0	1-0	0-2	1-0	1-0	1-0	1-0	0-0	2-2	3-0	—	1-0	3-0	2-0	5-1	1-0	1-0	0-0	5-2
Southport	3-1	1-0	0-0	2-0	0-0	1-1	2-1	1-0	2-3	2-1	1-0	2-2	3-0	1-1	—	2-2	1-2	0-2	1-3	1-3	3-0	1-1
Stafford Rangers	0-2	1-0	1-2	5-0	3-2	3-1	1-1	0-2	2-3	2-0	0-2	3-0	1-1	0-2	1-2	—	1-2	3-3	3-0	2-1	2-0	4-2
Stalybridge Celtic	1-3	1-3	0-0	2-0	0-1	1-1	2-2	0-3	2-0	1-2	2-2	3-1	1-1	2-1	1-3	0-2	—	0-1	2-3	0-3	2-2	1-1
Telford United	0-2	0-0	0-0	0-1	0-1	1-2	0-3	2-0	0-3	1-3	2-1	2-1	1-1	4-1	6-2	2-1	1-2	—	2-0	2-1	0-0	2-1
Welling United	2-1	1-1	0-0	1-2	1-0	2-2	2-2	0-1	0-0	2-0	0-0	0-0	1-1	0-2	0-2	1-1	1-2	0-0	—	3-1	0-2	1-0
Witton Albion	1-1	0-3	4-1	1-1	0-1	2-2	2-2	2-0	2-0	3-0	0-0	0-3	0-0	1-0	1-0	1-1	1-3	0-0	0-5	—	3-1	4-1
Woking	1-1	4-1	0-0	1-8	3-0	2-6	2-6	1-0	1-1	3-1	3-0	0-3	0-0	2-1	1-0	4-0	3-0	0-0	0-2	3-1	—	0-1
Yeovil Town	0-0	1-2	2-3	2-1	1-3	1-1	0-0	1-0	1-1	2-3	1-1	0-3	4-2	0-2	3-2	0-1	1-1	1-0	0-1	2-0	1-2	—

BEAZER HOMES LEAGUE 1993–94

Premier Division

	P	W	D	L	F	A	Pts
Farnborough Town	42	25	7	10	74	44	82
Cheltenham Town	42	21	12	9	67	38	75
Halesowen Town	42	21	11	10	69	46	74
Atherstone United	42	22	7	13	57	43	73
Crawley Town	42	21	10	11	56	42	73
Chelmsford City	42	21	7	14	74	59	70
Trowbridge Town	42	16	17	9	52	41	65
Sittingbourne	42	17	13	12	65	48	64
Corby Town	42	17	8	17	52	56	59
Gloucester City	42	17	6	19	55	60	57
Burton Albion	42	15	11	16	57	49	56
Hastings Town	42	16	7	19	51	60	55
Hednesford Town	41	15	9	18	67	66	54
Gresley Rovers	41	14	11	17	61	72	53
Worcester City	42	14	9	19	61	70	51
Solihull Borough	42	13	11	18	52	57	50
Cambridge City	42	13	11	18	50	60	50
Dorchester Town	42	12	11	19	38	51	47
Moor Green	42	11	10	21	49	66	43
Waterlooville	42	11	10	21	47	69	43
Bashley	42	11	10	21	47	80	43
Nuneaton Borough	42	11	8	23	42	66	41

LEADING GOALSCORERS

Premier Division

L. Ryan (Cambridge City)	28
T. Senior (Farnborough Town)	26
C. Boothe (Farnborough Town)	24
P. Joinson (Halesowen Town)	22
L. McRobert (Sittingbourne)	21
S. Restarick (Chelmsford City)	21

BEAZER HOMES SOUTHERN LEAGUE PREMIER DIVISION RESULTS 1993–94

	Atherstone United	Bashley	Burton Albion	Cambridge City	Chelmsford City	Cheltenham Town	Corby Town	Crawley Town	Dorchester Town	Farnborough Town	Gloucester City	Gresley Rovers	Halesowen Town	Hastings Town	Hednesford Town	Moor Green	Nuneaton Borough	Sittingbourne	Solihull Borough	Trowbridge Town	Waterlooville	Worcester City
Atherstone United	—	4-0	1-0	0-1	3-0	3-2	2-0	2-0	1-0	1-0	1-1	3-0	1-2	1-2	0-2	0-1	1-0	0-1	4-1	0-1	1-0	2-1
Bashley	1-2	—	2-1	0-2	1-5	2-1	2-1	1-1	1-1	1-0	1-1	2-0	3-0	1-5	1-2	2-0	1-0	0-3	2-3	1-1	1-1	2-1
Burton Albion	0-0	1-0	—	1-1	1-3	1-1	1-0	1-1	0-6	2-1	0-1	1-0	2-1	3-0	3-0	1-3	6-1	2-0	0-0	1-0	1-0	1-0
Cambridge City	0-0	4-0	3-1	—	5-0	1-1	1-1	1-2	3-0	1-2	0-0	1-1	3-2	1-0	4-1	1-0	1-1	1-2	0-2	2-0	3-0	4-3
Chelmsford City	5-1	1-0	2-1	1-3	—	0-1	1-3	1-2	3-0	3-0	0-1	1-1	3-1	1-0	3-0	4-3	2-2	0-2	3-2	2-0	1-0	2-0
Cheltenham Town	1-0	1-2	2-1	0-1	0-0	—	4-1	1-1	0-6	0-1	1-2	0-1	0-1	3-0	3-0	1-3	0-1	1-3	1-0	1-0	1-1	1-0
Corby Town	1-0	6-2	2-1	4-1	7-6	1-1	—	1-1	0-0	1-0	5-0	0-1	0-1	3-0	4-1	1-0	1-1	3-3	1-0	1-1	2-1	0-3
Crawley Town	2-2	1-3	2-1	5-1	2-5	0-1	1-0	—	0-1	0-0	0-6	5-0	3-0	3-1	3-0	3-3	2-2	1-2	1-1	3-1	1-2	1-2
Dorchester Town	2-2	1-1	2-3	0-0	2-1	0-1	1-0	1-2	—	0-1	0-1	1-1	3-0	1-0	1-4	1-0	2-2	1-3	1-0	1-0	1-0	3-1
Farnborough Town	3-0	1-0	2-1	0-6	3-0	1-3	1-0	0-0	0-1	—	2-3	1-1	3-1	0-2	1-0	2-1	4-1	2-0	1-0	1-1	2-1	1-2
Gloucester City	1-1	1-1	4-2	1-2	3-1	1-3	2-4	1-2	2-3	1-2	—	2-1	3-0	1-4	1-0	5-2	3-3	2-1	1-1	1-1	2-1	3-4
Gresley Rovers	0-0	0-4	1-1	2-1	1-2	1-3	3-0	0-1	2-3	4-0	1-0	—	0-1	1-2	0-2	2-2	3-1	3-2	3-1	1-3	1-1	2-1
Halesowen Town	1-2	1-0	2-2	3-2	2-0	2-0	2-2	3-0	2-4	1-1	1-0	1-1	—	1-1	1-2	2-2	5-3	0-1	0-1	1-0	4-0	3-2
Hastings Town	1-2	3-2	1-0	1-2	2-1	1-2	3-1	2-2	1-0	2-3	2-4	3-1	1-1	—	2-1	0-0	1-2	2-1	1-3	2-2	3-2	4-2
Hednesford Town	0-1	6-0	2-0	3-0	2-4	2-0	0-4	0-1	0-0	2-4	2-2	2-4	0-3	0-2	—	0-3	2-2	2-1	2-1	1-1	3-0	0-2
Moor Green	2-0	1-1	2-0	1-3	2-0	1-2	1-2	3-1	2-3	0-1	2-4	0-0	3-2	2-2	0-0	—	2-2	2-3	2-1	1-3	3-0	4-0
Nuneaton Borough	2-0	2-0	1-2	6-1	2-2	1-3	1-0	2-0	1-0	2-3	4-2	4-0	1-4	2-2	3-0	2-1	—	1-0	0-3	2-1	1-1	1-1
Sittingbourne	4-1	2-0	0-0	1-2	2-0	0-3	1-2	0-1	2-3	2-3	1-3	1-2	2-2	4-1	3-0	2-2	1-0	—	1-0	0-3	2-1	0-1
Solihull Borough	0-3	3-2	3-2	2-0	0-1	1-0	1-0	1-0	0-2	1-0	2-4	1-3	1-4	2-0	2-0	2-2	0-3	1-0	—	1-1	1-0	2-2
Trowbridge Town	3-0	1-0	1-0	2-0	1-1	2-0	2-0	1-0	0-0	0-2	1-1	2-0	2-0	3-1	2-0	0-0	2-1	0-3	2-2	—	0-0	2-2
Waterlooville	0-3	1-1	3-1	3-0	1-3	0-2	2-1	2-0	2-4	0-2	2-2	2-2	0-2	3-2	2-0	3-3	1-1	2-1	0-4	0-0	—	3-2
Worcester City	3-0	2-0	2-0	1-2	0-3	3-2	2-1	2-0	3-1	1-2	2-2	2-2	3-2	4-2	0-1	4-0	1-1	0-1	2-2	2-1	1-2	—

NORTHERN PREMIER FOOTBALL LEAGUE
PREMIER DIVISION

	P	W	D	L	F	A	Pts
Marine	42	27	9	6	106	62	90
Leek Town	42	27	8	7	79	50	89
Boston United	42	23	9	10	90	43	78
Bishop Auckland	42	23	9	10	73	58	78
Frickley Athletic	42	21	12	9	90	51	75
Colwyn Bay	42	18	14	10	74	51	68
Morecambe	42	20	7	15	90	56	67
Barrow	42	18	10	14	59	51	64
Hyde United	42	17	10	15	80	71	61
Chorley	42	17	10	15	70	67	61
Whitley Bay	42	17	9	16	61	72	60
Gainsborough Trini	42	15	11	16	64	66	56
Emley	42	12	16	14	63	71	52
Matlock Town	42	13	23	17	71	76	51
Buxton	42	13	10	19	67	73	49
Accrington Stanley	42	14	7	21	63	85	49
Droylsden	42	11	14	17	57	82	47
Knowsley United	42	11	11	20	52	66	44
Winsford United	42	9	11	22	50	74	38
Horwich RMI (1)	42	8	12	22	50	75	35
Bridlington Tn (3)	42	7	10	25	41	91	28
Fleetwood Town	42	7	7	28	55	114	28

Leading goalscorers

Lge	Cup	Tot.	
24	16	40	Darren Twigg (Leek Town)
26	8	34	Andy Hayward (Frickley Athletic)
21	13	34	Steve Jones (Colwyn Bay)
31	2	33	Tony McDonald (Chorley)
26	6	32	Chris Camden (Marine)
21	11	32	Jim McCluskie (Morecambe)
26	3	29	Brian Ross (Marine)
25	4	29	Neil Grayson (Boston United)

NORTHERN PREMIER LEAGUE—PREMIER DIVISION RESULTS 1993–94

	Accrington Stanley	Barrow	Bishop Auckland	Boston United	Bridlington Town	Buxton	Chorley	Colwyn Bay	Droylsden	Emley	Fleetwood Town	Frickley Ath	Gainsborough Trinity	Horwich RMI	Hyde United	Knowsley United	Leek Town	Marine	Matlock Town	Morecambe	Whitley Bay	Winsford United
Accrington Stanley	—	1-0	0-2	1-3	2-1	3-1	1-1	5-5	2-0	1-2	3-1	2-4	2-4	1-0	4-1	2-1	0-3	0-2	0-2	3-2	0-1	4-2
Barrow	0-5	—	0-2	0-2	4-0	4-0	3-1	0-2	2-2	2-1	3-1	1-3	1-1	0-2	1-4	2-0	2-3	1-2	0-2	1-2	1-0	1-1
Bishop Auckland	0-2	2-1	—	1-1	5-0	1-2	1-1	3-1	2-2	4-0	3-2	1-3	1-0	0-2	2-1	0-3	3-3	1-4	2-0	2-1	1-0	4-2
Boston United	0-1	0-1	1-1	—	3-1	2-2	2-0	6-1	4-0	2-0	4-1	1-1	6-1	0-2	2-1	2-1	0-1	0-0	2-4	0-3	1-1	1-1
Bridlington Town	3-0	5-0	3-1	2-2	—	1-1	2-0	6-1	1-1	4-0	3-2	0-3	2-5	0-2	4-0	3-0	3-3	0-2	2-2	0-4	1-1	3-2
Buxton	3-0	3-0	0-2	3-1	3-1	—	2-3	2-3	0-1	2-2	5-2	0-3	2-5	4-4	3-0	1-1	1-2	0-4	4-1	0-2	5-4	1-0
Chorley	2-2	3-1	1-1	2-0	4-0	2-0	—	1-1	4-0	1-0	5-2	2-2	2-5	1-0	2-1	2-0	0-0	1-4	2-2	3-2	1-1	0-0
Colwyn Bay	2-3	0-2	4-0	2-0	6-1	2-0	0-2	—	3-3	3-3	3-2	1-1	2-3	1-1	1-2	1-5	1-0	1-4	3-0	2-3	6-0	0-0
Droylsden	4-2	2-3	4-2	0-2	1-0	3-1	0-3	4-0	—	3-3	3-2	0-1	1-1	2-3	2-1	2-1	2-1	1-1	3-2	1-0	3-1	1-2
Emley	2-0	2-3	0-0	1-1	3-1	1-4	2-1	2-1	0-3	—	3-2	3-3	2-0	2-0	0-0	1-1	4-1	0-2	2-0	0-2	3-1	1-3
Fleetwood Town	2-0	3-1	3-2	3-2	4-1	3-2	5-2	2-2	3-2	3-2	—	2-2	5-1	4-0	3-0	6-1	4-0	4-0	3-0	4-3	1-4	3-1
Frickley Ath	2-4	1-3	1-3	0-3	2-0	0-3	2-2	6-1	4-0	2-2	2-2	—	1-0	1-1	2-3	4-1	1-5	2-2	0-0	0-2	2-2	0-2
Gainsborough Trinity	2-0	1-1	6-1	2-5	1-0	1-2	2-3	2-3	0-2	1-0	4-0	1-2	—	5-2	3-0	5-2	3-0	1-0	2-2	3-1	0-1	1-0
Horwich RMI	1-4	0-2	0-2	0-2	4-4	1-0	1-0	2-3	5-2	2-0	4-0	0-1	1-2	—	1-0	1-1	2-3	0-1	1-1	3-1	1-3	3-1
Hyde United	4-0	3-0	2-1	1-0	3-0	2-1	1-2	2-1	1-0	2-1	4-0	2-1	4-0	4-1	—	3-0	1-1	2-0	5-1	2-3	3-0	3-1
Knowsley United	1-4	2-0	0-3	2-1	3-0	4-0	0-1	1-5	2-1	3-1	3-0	0-2	0-1	3-0	1-1	—	0-3	1-4	3-2	5-0	1-3	2-2
Leek Town	2-1	2-3	3-3	0-1	3-3	1-2	0-0	1-0	2-1	4-1	4-0	1-5	3-0	2-3	1-1	0-3	—	1-4	0-0	1-3	2-0	1-0
Marine	2-1	1-2	1-4	0-0	0-2	0-4	1-4	1-4	1-1	0-2	4-0	2-2	1-0	0-1	2-0	1-4	1-4	—	4-2	1-4	3-1	2-0
Matlock Town	3-3	2-2	2-0	2-4	2-2	4-1	2-2	3-0	3-2	2-0	3-0	0-0	2-2	1-1	5-1	3-2	0-0	4-2	—	0-0	1-3	1-0
Morecambe	5-0	1-2	2-1	3-0	0-4	0-2	3-2	2-3	1-0	0-2	4-3	0-2	3-1	3-1	2-3	5-0	1-3	1-4	0-0	—	4-2	2-1
Whitley Bay	4-1	1-0	1-0	1-1	1-1	5-4	1-1	6-0	3-1	3-1	1-4	2-2	0-1	1-3	3-0	1-3	2-0	3-1	1-3	4-2	—	2-0
Winsford United	3-1	1-2	4-2	2-1	3-2	1-0	0-0	0-0	1-2	1-3	3-1	0-2	1-0	3-1	3-1	2-2	1-0	4-1	1-0	2-1	2-0	—

DIADORA FOOTBALL LEAGUE 1993–94

Premier Division

		Home			Away			Totals			Goals		
	P	W	D	L	W	D	L	W	D	L	F	A	Pts
Stevenage Borough	42	15	2	4	16	2	3	31	4	7	88	39	97
Enfield	42	14	4	3	14	4	3	28	8	6	80	28	92
Marlow	42	14	3	4	11	4	6	25	7	10	90	67	82
Chesham United	42	13	1	7	11	7	3	24	8	10	73	45	80
Sutton United	42	13	5	3	10	5	6	23	10	9	77	31	79
Carshalton Athletic	42	12	2	7	10	5	6	22	7	13	81	53	73
St. Albans City	42	12	5	4	9	5	7	21	10	11	81	54	73
Hitchin Town	42	11	2	8	10	5	6	21	7	14	81	56	70
Harrow Borough	42	9	8	4	9	3	9	18	11	13	54	56	65
Kingstonian	42	9	3	9	9	6	6	18	9	15	101	64	63
Hendon	42	8	4	9	10	5	6	18	9	15	61	51	63
Aylesbury United	42	8	3	10	9	4	8	17	7	18	64	67	58
Hayes	42	7	6	8	8	2	11	15	8	19	63	72	53
Grays Athletic	42	8	1	12	7	4	10	15	5	22	56	69	50
Bromley	42	7	5	9	7	2	12	14	7	21	56	69	49
Dulwich Hamlet	42	4	6	11	9	2	10	13	8	21	52	74	47
Yeading	42	7	5	9	4	8	9	11	13	18	58	66	46
Molesey	42	5	8	8	6	3	12	11	11	20	44	62	44
Wokingham Town	42	6	3	12	5	3	13	11	6	25	38	67	39
Dorking	42	6	1	14	3	3	15	9	4	29	58	104	31
Basingstoke Town	42	7	2	12	3	5	13	5	12	25	38	86	27
Wivenhoe Town	42	2	3	16	3	0	18	5	3	34	38	152	18

LEADING GOALSCORERS

Premier Division

		Lge	Lge Cup	Carlsberg
35	Jimmy Bolton (Carshalton Athletic)	29	5	1
27	Martin Gittings (Stevenage Borough)	27		
	David Lay (Marlow)	21	6	

DIADORA LEAGUE PREMIER DIVISION

	Aylesbury Utd	Basingstoke	Bromley	Carshalton Ath	Chesham Utd	Dorking	Dulwich Hamlet	Enfield	Grays Athletic	Harrow Borough	Hayes	Hendon	Hitchin Town	Kingstonian	Marlow	Molesey	St. Albans	Stevenage Boro	Sutton Utd	Wivenhoe Town	Wokingham	Yeading
Aylesbury Utd	—	4-4	2-1	3-0	0-2	2-0	1-3	1-0	0-1	0-4	1-0	2-3	1-1	3-6	1-5	2-1	1-2	0-1	1-2	3-0	3-0	1-1
Basingstoke	2-3	—	1-3	0-2	3-3	0-0	1-2	2-0	2-0	4-1	6-0	1-0	3-4	1-0	3-0	0-0	0-2	1-2	1-0	6-2	6-2	1-1
Bromley	0-0	3-0	—	2-1	1-1	3-1	3-2	0-1	0-2	3-1	2-1	3-3	1-0	2-2	2-3	0-1	2-0	1-2	1-4	6-0	1-0	2-0
Carshalton Ath	1-3	0-2	2-1	—	1-1	3-0	3-2	1-4	0-2	0-3	0-1	3-3	0-3	2-2	0-1	2-0	3-3	1-2	1-4	6-3	1-2	2-0
Chesham Utd	1-4	3-0	5-0	1-4	—	3-0	0-1	2-2	2-3	1-1	4-1	3-0	1-3	1-4	2-3	2-1	1-2	1-5	1-0	4-3	3-0	2-0
Dorking	1-2	2-0	2-1	3-0	3-0	—	0-1	1-4	3-0	3-0	2-0	3-0	0-3	1-6	2-0	0-3	1-3	1-2	1-0	4-1	3-0	4-3
Dulwich Hamlet	4-0	1-1	1-2	2-1	3-4	1-0	—	2-2	1-3	1-2	3-2	1-2	0-0	1-7	2-3	1-0	1-0	2-5	1-3	8-0	2-1	4-3
Enfield	4-0	1-2	3-0	1-1	0-1	6-0	3-0	—	1-4	1-1	2-0	1-2	0-2	0-3	4-7	1-0	0-1	3-0	1-0	3-0	0-3	0-0
Grays Athletic	0-1	2-0	2-0	3-0	0-4	3-2	2-1	0-1	—	1-1	3-3	0-3	2-4	2-4	2-0	1-2	0-1	1-3	1-0	0-1	2-1	2-1
Harrow Borough	0-1	2-0	4-0	3-0	0-4	3-2	1-2	1-4	1-1	—	0-1	1-1	2-2	0-3	2-0	3-0	1-3	3-5	1-8	3-0	0-3	1-0
Hayes	2-2	4-0	3-1	1-1	1-1	3-1	2-1	2-0	1-1	1-1	—	0-2	1-2	0-3	2-0	2-0	1-3	0-3	0-4	0-2	2-1	5-2
Hendon	5-1	4-0	0-3	3-3	1-2	3-0	2-1	0-1	1-3	2-3	0-2	—	2-2	0-3	2-0	3-0	1-3	1-3	1-8	3-1	1-0	4-2
Hitchin Town	1-0	6-0	1-0	0-3	1-0	0-3	3-0	2-0	1-0	2-2	4-3	1-3	—	2-4	4-7	3-1	0-3	3-5	0-2	8-1	5-0	0-0
Kingstonian	1-0	5-1	1-0	0-2	2-0	1-2	4-2	1-0	3-1	7-0	3-2	1-3	3-3	—	3-3	0-0	4-2	0-0	0-2	0-2	3-0	4-2
Marlow	1-0	1-0	3-4	0-6	3-4	2-3	3-0	1-1	3-1	2-1	4-3	0-4	1-0	1-1	—	2-1	4-1	0-0	0-6	4-0	2-0	1-1
Molesey	1-1	0-0	2-3	0-1	0-1	0-1	4-2	3-0	3-2	2-3	3-2	0-0	3-5	1-4	1-1	—	2-1	0-3	0-2	2-0	3-2	3-0
St. Albans	6-1	2-0	3-1	2-2	0-0	4-3	2-3	3-0	5-3	3-0	3-0	2-3	1-2	1-4	4-2	4-1	—	1-3	1-0	4-2	1-0	1-0
Stevenage Borov	4-0	2-2	2-1	4-0	3-1	0-0	0-1	0-1	3-0	0-6	2-1	0-4	1-2	0-7	4-2	3-4	4-1	—	0-0	0-0	1-1	4-1
Sutton Utd	3-1	3-1	1-0	2-1	1-0	3-1	0-3	1-2	1-0	3-1	0-6	0-2	0-1	1-1	2-3	3-4	0-3	4-1	—	1-3	3-2	2-4
Wivenhoe Town	0-4	0-0	0-0	0-4	1-0	1-0	3-4	2-3	0-4	2-3	0-6	0-4	0-7	2-3	0-6	0-3	1-3	0-3	1-0	—	1-0	4-1
Wokingham	0-3	3-1	2-1	0-4	2-0	3-1	0-0	1-1	1-1	0-1	2-3	0-2	2-1	1-1	0-6	0-0	0-1	0-1	0-0	3-2	—	1-3
Yeading	1-2	3-1	2-3	2-1	0-2	1-2	0-0	1-2	2-1	2-0	2-3	1-1	2-1	2-1	1-2	3-0	1-1	0-2	0-0	4-1	2-4	—

THE PONTIN'S LEAGUE

Division One

	P	W	D	L	F	A	Pts
Manchester United	34	22	7	5	77	38	73
Aston Villa	34	18	9	7	61	29	63
Bolton Wanderers	34	15	10	9	88	65	55
Wolverhampton Wanderers	34	15	9	10	45	38	54
Derby County	34	14	8	12	55	51	50
Nottm. Forest	34	14	8	12	55	51	50
Sunderland	34	12	13	9	47	53	49
Blackburn Rovers	34	14	7	13	40	47	49
Leeds United	34	13	8	13	42	48	47
Coventry City	34	13	7	14	42	41	46
Sheffield United	34	12	9	13	57	60	45
Notts. County	34	12	8	14	43	50	44
Everton	34	12	7	15	54	50	43
Liverpool	34	10	11	13	42	51	41
Newcastle United	34	10	8	16	46	53	38
Sheffield Wednesday	34	7	12	15	46	63	33
Leicester City	34	8	7	19	37	58	31
York City	34	6	10	18	36	67	28

Division Two

	P	W	D	L	F	A	Pts
Tranmere Rovers	34	25	4	5	77	36	79
West Bromwich Albion	34	20	7	7	64	38	67
Stoke City	34	21	3	10	54	41	66
Rotherham United	34	18	8	8	61	35	62
Manchester City	34	18	8	8	57	31	62
Oldham Athletic	34	17	5	12	61	46	56
Burnley	34	16	4	14	55	49	52
Huddersfield Town	34	15	6	13	69	56	51
Port Vale	34	11	14	9	43	40	47
Preston North End	34	14	5	15	54	54	47
Bradford City	34	12	7	15	47	52	43
Grimsby Town	34	11	7	16	48	61	40
Barnsley	34	11	7	16	38	54	40
Middlesbrough	34	8	11	15	39	55	35
Hull City	34	10	4	20	36	62	34
Blackpool	34	7	7	20	33	61	28
Mansfield Town	34	6	7	21	33	60	25
Scunthorpe United	34	7	4	23	41	79	25

THE NEVILLE OVENDEN FOOTBALL COMBINATION

Division One

	P	W	D	L	F	A	Pts
Chelsea	38	24	8	6	79	41	80
Ipswich Town	38	19	8	11	71	52	65
Tottenham	38	19	6	13	69	47	63
Crystal Palace	38	17	11	10	63	40	62
Norwich City	38	18	7	13	68	54	61
Wimbledon	38	16	13	9	53	48	61
Q.P.R.	38	17	8	13	58	49	59
West Ham	38	16	10	12	59	45	58
Swindon Town	38	18	4	16	54	53	58
Bristol Rovers	38	15	12	11	50	52	57
Southampton	38	15	10	13	62	66	55
Millwall	38	12	11	15	57	67	47
Charlton Athletic	38	13	7	18	61	62	46
Luton Town	38	12	9	17	64	70	45
Arsenal	38	13	6	19	67	76	45
Oxford Utd	38	11	10	17	53	66	43
Portsmouth	38	10	11	17	43	60	41
Brighton & Hove Albion	38	9	10	19	38	58	37
Watford	38	9	8	21	49	75	35
Bristol City	38	8	9	21	47	84	33

Division Two

	P	W	D	L	F	A	Pts
Birmingham City	18	13	1	4	53	17	40
Plymouth Argyle	18	12	2	4	63	18	38
Swansea City	18	11	4	3	47	26	37
Torquay Utd	18	11	2	5	33	18	35
A.F.C. Bournemouth	18	9	3	6	36	38	30
Exeter City	18	7	2	9	40	41	23
Hereford Utd	18	6	1	11	36	52	19
Cardiff City	18	4	4	10	28	44	16
Yeovil Town	18	4	2	12	21	47	14
Cheltenham Town	18	2	1	15	16	72	7

League Cup Table
Group "A"

	P	W	D	L	F	A	Pts
Torquay Utd	8	5	2	1	17	9	17
A.F.C. Bournemouth	8	4	1	3	10	11	13
Exeter City	8	3	2	3	15	17	11
Plymouth Argyle	8	3	1	4	15	14	10
Yeovil Town	8	2	1	6	11	18	6

Group "B"

	P	W	D	L	F	A	Pts
Birmingham City	8	6	2	0	22	10	20
Cardiff City	8	4	1	3	8	10	13
Swansea City	8	3	3	2	20	9	12
Cheltenham Town	8	1	2	5	9	18	5
Hereford Utd	8	1	2	5	15	27	5

SOUTH EAST COUNTIES LEAGUE

Division One

	P	W	D	L	F	A	Pts
Queens Park Rangers	30	24	2	4	121	49	50
Tottenham Hotspur	30	20	4	6	85	40	44
West Ham United	30	19	5	6	78	44	43
Chelsea	30	19	3	8	67	39	41
Millwall	30	18	4	8	86	59	40
Fulham	30	19	2	9	59	46	40
Arsenal	30	15	7	8	66	42	37
Ipswich Town	30	11	8	11	50	49	30
Watford	30	11	5	14	52	63	27
Norwich City	30	11	2	17	42	60	24
Cambridge United	30	6	9	15	40	69	21
Portsmouth	30	7	5	18	44	76	19
Southend United	30	8	3	19	40	78	19
Leyton Orient	30	6	6	18	32	65	18
Charlton Athletic	30	6	3	21	46	87	15
Gillingham	30	4	4	22	30	72	12

Division Two

	P	W	D	L	F	A	Pts
Crystal Palace	26	15	5	6	56	32	35
Swindon Town	26	14	6	6	49	26	34
Wimbledon	26	15	1	10	61	44	31
Reading	26	10	9	7	39	36	29
Oxford United	26	11	6	9	46	38	28
Brentford	26	10	8	8	40	34	28
Luton Town	26	11	4	11	40	47	26
Brighton & Hove Albion	26	10	6	10	37	44	26
Southampton	26	8	7	11	29	30	23
Bristol Rovers	26	9	5	12	40	48	23
Bristol City	26	8	6	12	35	44	22
AFC Bournemouth	26	9	2	15	40	53	20
Tottenham Hotspur	26	8	4	14	35	49	20
Colchester United	26	6	7	13	33	55	19

REPUBLIC OF IRELAND

Qualifying Table 1993–94

	P	W	D	L	F	A	Pts
Shamrock Rovers	22	15	3	4	43	16	48
Cork City	22	12	5	5	43	24	41
Shelbourne	22	10	6	6	33	27	36
Galway U	22	9	7	6	30	26	34
Bohemians	22	8	7	7	23	17	31
Derry City	22	8	7	7	21	21	31
Dundalk	22	7	8	7	25	20	29
St Patrick's Ath	22	6	9	7	24	24	27
Monaghan U	22	9	3	10	27	27	30
Cobh Ramblers	22	5	4	13	20	34	19
Limerick City	22	3	8	11	15	40	17
Drogheda U	22	4	5	13	16	44	17

Final Round

	P	W	D	L	F	A	Pts
Shamrock Rovers	32	21	3	8	62	30	66
Cork City	32	17	8	7	60	36	59
Galway U	32	14	8	10	47	42	50
Derry City	32	12	10	10	37	35	46
Shelbourne	32	11	10	11	42	42	43
Bohemians	32	11	8	12	34	35	41

HIGHLAND LEAGUE

	P	W	D	L	F	A	Pts
Huntly	34	27	4	3	95	21	85
Caledonian	34	20	7	7	80	44	67
Ross County	34	21	4	9	80	51	67
Cove Rangers	34	20	4	10	89	46	64
Lossiemouth	34	19	6	9	74	45	63
Elgin City	34	19	6	9	60	33	63
Keith	34	16	6	12	57	40	54
Buckie Thistle	34	16	6	12	54	48	54
Fraserburgh	34	15	8	11	52	36	53
Brora Rangers	34	13	9	12	60	61	48
Peterhead	34	12	8	14	55	56	44
Clachnacuddin	34	11	7	16	49	60	40
Forres Mechanics	34	11	4	17	56	67	39
Deveronvale	34	7	8	19	46	84	29
Inverness Thistle	34	6	9	19	38	62	27
Fort William	34	8	3	23	26	78	27
Nairn County	34	6	3	25	30	114	21
Rothes	34	4	6	24	42	97	18

First Qualifying Round

Bridlington Town v Ferryhill Athletic	4-0
Peterlee Newton v Workington	0-2
Ashton United v Chester-Le-Street Town	1-2
Dunston Federation Brewery v Easington Colliery	3-0
Fleetwood Town v Great Harwood Town	0-6
Durham City v Tow Law Town	0-1
Whitley Bay v Chorley	1-1, 1-3
Shildon v Harrogate Town	1-1, 2-4
Consett v Hebburn	2-2, 2-1
Brandon United v Seaham Red Star	0-2
Matlock Town v Knowsley United	0-0, 1-1, 3-0
Tamworth v Worksop Town	3-2
Buxton v Curzon Ashton	0-0, 4-2
Dudley Town v Mossley	3-2
Grantham Town v Bedworth United	5-2
Burton Albion v Caernarfon Town	3-0
Horwich RMI v Congleton Town	0-2
Gainsborough Trinity v Eastwood Town	5-3
Gresley Rovers v Goole Town	1-2
Sutton Coldfield Town v Colwyn Bay	1-1, 0-4
Atherstone United v Redditch United	1-1, 0-2
Leicester United v Moor Green	0-2
Droylsden v Solihull Borough	2-0
Barking v Billericay Town	0-1
Bishop's Stortford v Braintree Town	1-0
Hitchin Town v Boreham Wood	0-2
Hendon v Marlow	1-2
Ruislip Manor v Chelmsford City	1-4
Sudbury Town v Purfleet	3-3, 0-3
Leyton v Chalfont St Peter	6-4
Berkhamsted Town v Yeading	1-1, 0-2
Uxbridge v Harrow Borough	1-2
Ashford Town v Windsor & Eton	3-1
Bromley v Molesey	0-2
Gravesend & Northfleet v Bognor Regis Town	3-0
Tooting & Mitcham United v Whyteleafe	3-1
Dorking v Sittingbourne	1-5
Margate v Worthing	0-2
Fisher 93 v Walton & Hersham	1-0
Croydon v Canterbury City	3-0
Dulwich Hamlet v Hastings Town	2-1
Wokingham Town v Maidenhead United	1-0
Fareham Town v Weston-Super-Mare	1-2
Salisbury City v Poole Town	1-3
Newport AFC v Havant Town	1-0
Basingstoke Town v Abingdon Town	0-2
Weymouth v Witney Town	0-2

Second Qualifying Round

Guiseley v Tow Law Town	4-3
Dunston Federation Brewery v Newcastle Blue Star	2-1
Harrogate Town v Chorley	3-1
Stockton v Great Harwood Town	2-1
Workington v Bridlington Town	0-2
Seaham Red Star v West Auckland Town	3-1
Consett v Chester-Le-Street Town	3-0
Gainsborough Trinity v Matlock Town	1-2
Goole Town v Dudley Town	3-1
Alfreton Town v Congleton Town	2-0
Redditch United v Moor Green	2-1
Stourbridge v Halesowen Town	0-1
Grantham Town v Droylsden	3-2
Buxton v Colwyn Bay	1-6
Rushden & Diamonds v Burton Albion	0-1
Tamworth v Emley	2-2, 0-4
Baldock Town v Purfleet	2-3
Marlow v Hayes	1-1, 3-2
Yeading v Leyton	1-1, 3-1
Cambridge City v Chelmsford City	1-1, 2-3
Bishop's Stortford v Billericay Town	1-2
Wembley v Staines Town	1-1, 0-1
Harrow Borough v Boreham Wood	0-0, 2-1
Tooting & Mitcham United v Erith & Belvedere	1-2
Molesey v Sittingbourne	0-4
Ashford Town v Gravesend & Northfleet	1-1, 0-2
Croydon v Worthing	1-7
Fisher 93 v Dulwich Hamlet	0-2

Witney Town v Dorchester
Town   0-1
Weston-Super-Mare v Newport
AFC   2-0
Abingdon Town v Wokingham
Town   1-1, 1-2
Poole Town v Waterlooville   1-1, 0-2
Third Qualifying Round
Harrogate Town v Guiseley   3-4
Consett v Billingham Synthonia   1-3
Bishop Auckland v Murton   2-2, 4-1
Stockton v Spennymoor United   0-3
Seaham Red Star v Gretna   0-3
Alfreton Town v Bridlington
Town   4-1
Goole Town v Northallerton
Town   1-1, 0-1
Colwyn Bay v Guisborough
Town   2-2, 3-2
Hyde United v Accrington
Stanley   2-0
Matlock Town v Blyth Spartans   1-3
Dunston Federation Brewery v
Frickley Athletic   1-5
Barrow v Emley   2-2, 1-2
Enfield v Corby Town   2-1
Billericay Town v Yeading   2-0
Purfleet v Heybridge Swifts   3-2
VS Rugby v Chelmsford City   0-3
Staines Town v St Albans City   0-3
Nuneaton Borough v Aylesbury
United   2-2, 2-1
Wivenhoe Town v Grantham
Town   1-2
Burton Albion v Halesowen
Town   1-2
Redditch United v Hednesford
Town   1-1, 0-1
Leek Town v Stevenage
Borough   0-2
Wealdstone v Harrow Borough 2-2, 0-3
Erith & Belvedere v
Weston-Super-Mare   1-4
Dulwich Hamlet v Gloucester
City   2-1
Dorchester Town v Bashley   0-0, 0-3
Sittingbourne v Kingstonian   1-2
Worcester City v Crawley Town 1-1, 2-1
Waterlooville v Wokingham
Town   3-0
Trowbridge Town v Cheltenham
Town   1-1, 0-1
Worthing v Carshalton Athletic   3-0
Gravesend & Northfleet v
Marlow   1-4
First Round
Alfreton Town v Runcorn   0-5
Gretna v Warrington Town   1-1, 3-2

Halifax Town v Emley   2-1
Halesowen Town v Gateshead   0-2
Stalybridge Celtic v Colwyn
Bay   1-1, 2-2, 1-2
Winsford United v Guiseley   0-1
Grantham Town v Witton
Albion   3-2
Billingham Synthonia v
Frickley Athletic   2-1
Spennymoor United v Hyde
United   2-1
Blyth Spartans v Bishop
Auckland   1-3
Hednesford Town v Whitby
Town   1-0
Boston United v Macclesfield
Town   1-1, 0-1
Morecambe v Northwich
Victoria   2-1
Telford United v Northallerton
Town   2-1
Marine v Southport   0-0, 1-3
Altrincham v Stafford Rangers   0-2
Cheltenham Town v Nuneaton
Borough   1-0
Dulwich Hamlet v Kingstonian   1-2
Welling United v Chelmsford
City   6-1
Kettering Town v Stevenage
Borough   2-1
St Albans City v Merthyr Tydfil   4-5
Billericay Town v Slough Town   0-2
Kidderminster Harriers v
Dagenham & Redbridge   0-2
Waterlooville v Bromsgrove
Rovers   1-1, 1-2
Farnborough Town v Grays
Athletic   1-1, 0-2
Bashley v Woking   2-4
Weston-Super-Mare v Dover
Athletic   0-2
Yeovil Town v Bath City   3-3, 0-4
Sutton United v Chesham
United   2-0
Enfield v Purfleet   2-0
Harrow Borough v Worcester
City   3-3, 3-5
Worthing v Marlow   3-0
Second Round
Runcorn v Telford United   2-1
Grantham Town v Bishop
Auckland   1-2
Colwyn Bay v Southport   0-3
Dagenham & Redbridge v
Woking   1-2
Worcester City v Macclesfield
Town   0-0, 2-3
Worthing v Enfield   1-1, 0-2

Spennymoor United v Halifax Town 1-2
Kettering Town v Billingham Synthonia 2-2, 1-3
Guiseley v Stafford Rangers 3-2
Kingstonian v Merthyr Tydfil 0-2
Sutton United v Bath City 6-1
Grays Athletic v Bromsgrove Rovers 1-2
Welling United v Dover Athletic 1-3
Gateshead v Gretna 0-0, 1-0
Cheltenham Town v Hednesford Town 1-0
Morecambe v Slough Town 1-0

Third Round
Macclesfield Town v Billingham Synthonia 0-1

Cheltenham Town v Guiseley 0-0, 0-1
Gateshead v Merthyr Tydfil 3-2
Sutton United v Dover Athletic 0-0, 3-2
Runcorn v Halifax Town 1-1, 2-0
Bishop Auckland v Enfield 2-2, 1-2
Woking v Bromsgrove Rovers 3-2
Morecambe v Southport 2-1

Fourth Round
Gateshead v Runcorn 0-3
Sutton United v Enfield 1-1, 0-1
Woking v Billingham Synthonia 1-1, 2-1
Guiseley v Morecambe 3-2

Semi-finals (two legs)
Woking v Enfield
1-1, 0-0, 3-0 (at Wycombe)
Runcorn v Guiseley 1-1 (at Chester), 1-0

Trophy Final at Wembley

21 May

Woking (2) 2 *(Brown D, Hay)*

Runcorn (0) 1 (Shaw (pen)) 15,818

Woking: Batty; Berry, Brown K, Tucker, Wye, Clement, Brown D (Rattray), Steele, Fielder, Hay (Puckett), Walker.
Runcorn: Williams; Bates, Lee, Brabin, Robertson, Shaw, Anderson, Connor, McKenna, McInerney (Hill), Thomas.
Referee: P. Durkin (Portland).

FA CHALLENGE VASE 1993–94

Third Round

Thackley v Lincoln United	2-1
Cammell Laird v Glossop North End	2-3
Oadby Town v Ponteland United	2-0
Nantwich Town v Bacup Borough	2-0
Belper Town v Brigg Town	2-1
Radcliffe Borough v Yorkshire Amateur	2-0
Penrith v Atherton LR	0-1
Whickham v Bamber Bridge	1-0
Dunkirk v Maltby MW	2-1
Wisbech Town v Collier Row	1-2
Great Wakering Rovers v Hinckley Athletic	3-3, 1-2
Northampton Spencer v Cogenhoe United	1-2
Boston v Bedfont	6-1
Ford United v Diss Town	1-2
Saffron Walden Town v Raunds Town	1-4
Bridgnorth Town v Cheshunt	3-1
Soham Town Rangers v Brimsdown Rovers	3-0
Buckingham Town v Kings Lynn	1-2
Pelsall Villa v Halstead Town (abandoned at 0-0 after 57 minutes; waterlogged pitch),	2-4
Eastwood Hanley v Arlesey Town	1-2
Canvey Island v Corinthian-Casuals	2-1
Taunton Town v Barnstaple Town	2-0
Elmore v Thame United	1-2
Croydon Athletic v Paulton Rovers	0-2
Tonbridge v Tiverton Town	0-1
Aldershot Town v Malden Vale	1-0
Tunbridge Wells v Torpoint Athletic	2-6
Clevedon Town v Wimborne Town	3-4
Bracknell Town v Newbury Town	1-2
Banstead Athletic v Peacehaven & Telscombe	1-0
Falmouth Town v Andover	3-1
Whitehawk v Metropolitan Police	3-2

Fourth Round

Radcliffe Borough v Boston	3-3, 1-2
Atherton LR v Thackley	0-0, 3-2
Raunds Town v Belper Town	1-2
Whickham v Dunkirk	0-0, 0-1
Kings Lynn v Nantwich Town	1-0
Bridgnorth Town v Glossop North End	3-2
Oadby Town v Cogenhoe United	5-1
Halstead Town v Wimborne Town	1-5
Canvey Island v Newbury Town	1-2
Taunton Town v Banstead Athletic	1-1, 2-0
Whitehawk v Thame United	3-2
Torpoint Athletic v Diss Town	0-3
Aldershot Town v Soham Town Rangers	5-0
Tiverton Town v Paulton Rovers	5-0
Hinckley Athletic v Collier Row	4-2
Arlesey Town v Falmouth Town	5-3

Fifth Round

Hinckley Athletic v Newbury Town	0-3
Atherton LR v Bridgnorth Town	1-0
Oadby Town v Arlesey Town	1-2
Dunkirk v Tiverton Town	0-2
Diss Town v Kings Lynn	2-0
Whitehawk v Boston	2-3
Aldershot Town v Wimborne Town	1-0
Belper Town v Taunton Town	1-3

Sixth Round

Aldershot Town v Atherton LR	0-0, 0-0, 0-2
Arlesey Town v Boston	2-3
Diss Town v Tiverton Town	1-0
Taunton Town v Newbury Town	2-0

Semi-finals (two legs)

Taunton Town v Boston	1-0, 1-0
Diss Town v Atherton LR	3-1, 0-2, 2-1 (at Rugby)

Vase Final at Wembley

7 May

Diss Town (0) 2 *(Gibbs (pen), Mendham)*

Taunton Town (1) 1 (Fowler) aet 13,450

Diss Town: Woodcock; Carter, Hartle, Smith, Wolsey (Musgrave), Casey (Bugg), Mendham, Barth, Warne, Miles, Gibbs.

Taunton Town: Maloy; Morris, Graddon, Palfrey, Walsh, Ewens, West (Hendy), Perett (Ward), Fowler, Durham, Jarvis.

Referee: K. Morton (Bury St Edmunds).

FA YOUTH CHALLENGE CUP 1993–94

Second Round

Middlesbrough v Oldham Athletic	2-0
Burnley v Leeds United	3-0
Bradford City v Manchester United	2-0
Crewe Alexandra v Huddersfield Town	4-2
York City v Blackburn Rovers	0-0, 1-1, 1-2
Doncaster Rovers v Manchester City	1-4
Everton v Grimsby Town	0-2
Rotherham United v Sunderland	2-4
Sheffield United v Liverpool	1-2
Coventry City v Leicester City	2-1
Ipswich Town v Queens Park Rangers	3-1
Tottenham Hotspur v Stoke City	1-2
West Bromwich Albion v Leighton Town	2-1
West Ham United v Leyton Orient	6-0
Watford v Aston Villa	1-3
Birmingham City v Peterborough United	1-1
(penalty kicks taken aet contrary to rules of competition),	1-2
Port Vale v Southend United	1-3
Chelsea v Norwich City	1-1, 0-1
Nottingham Forest v Nuneaton Borough	3-1
Notts County v Derby County	0-3
Colchester United v Arsenal	2-3
Southampton v Wimbledon	2-6
Torquay United v Enfield	3-1
Croydon Athletic v Wycombe Wanderers	2-3
Reading v Bristol City	0-1
Gillingham v Swindon Town	1-2
Dulwich Hamlet v Crystal Palace	0-5
Cardiff City v Harefield United	2-0
Welling United v Portsmouth	4-6
Brighton & Hove Albion v Wokingham Town	1-0
Brentford v Exeter City	5-1
Plymouth Argyle v Millwall	3-3, 1-2

Second Round

Middlesbrough v Oldham Athletic	2-0
Burnley v Leeds United	3-0
Bradford City v Manchester United	2-0
Crewe Alexandra v Huddersfield Town	4-2
York City v Blackburn Rovers	0-0, 1-1, 1-2
Doncaster Rovers v Manchester City	1-4
Everton v Grimsby Town	0-2
Rotherham United v Sunderland	2-4
Sheffield United v Liverpool	1-2
Coventry City v Leicester City	2-1
Ipswich Town v Queens Park Rangers	3-1
Tottenham Hotspur v Stoke City	1-2
West Bromwich Albion v Leighton Town	2-1
West Ham United v Leyton Orient	6-0
Watford v Aston Villa	1-3
Birmingham City v Peterborough United	1-1
(penalty kicks taken aet contrary to rules of competition),	1-2
Port Vale v Southend United	1-3
Chelsea v Norwich City	1-1, 0-1
Nottingham Forest v Nuneaton Borough	3-1
Notts County v Derby County	0-3
Colchester United v Arsenal	2-3
Southampton v Wimbledon	2-6
Torquay United v Enfield	3-1
Croydon Athletic v Wycombe Wanderers	2-3
Reading v Bristol City	0-1
Gillingham v Swindon Town	1-2
Dulwich Hamlet v Crystal Palace	0-5
Cardiff City v Harefield United	2-0
Welling United v Portsmouth	4-6
Brighton & Hove Albion v Wokingham Town	1-0
Brentford v Exeter City	5-1
Plymouth Argyle v Millwall	3-3, 1-2

Third Round

Manchester City v Norwich City	0-2
Bristol City v Aston Villa	1-4
Middlesbrough v Nottingham Forest	2-2, 3-3, 2-1
Blackburn Rovers v Bradford City	1-1, 1-1, 0-4
Wimbledon v Burnley	3-4

Ipswich Town v Peterborough
United 1-1, 0-0, 1-0
Grimsby Town v Torquay
United 3-1
West Bromwich Albion v Crewe
Alexandra 2-1
Liverpool v West Ham United 2-2, 2-3
Brentford v Arsenal 1-1, 1-3
Swindon Town v Brighton &
Hove Albion 0-1
Sunderland v Derby County 0-1
Cardiff City v Coventry City 1-2
Millwall v Wycombe Wanderers
2-2, 5-0
Southend United v Stoke City 0-4
Portsmouth v Crystal Palace 2-0

Fourth Round
Coventry City v Norwich City 0-2

Brighton & Hove Albion v
Millwall 3-4
Middlesbrough v West
Bromwich Albion 2-0
Ipswich Town v Portsmouth 2-4
Grimsby Town v Bradford City 0-0,
1-1, 0-2
Aston Villa v West Ham United 1-2
Stoke City v Derby County 3-1
Burnley v Arsenal 0-1
Fifth Round
Arsenal v Stoke City 3-1
West Ham United v Bradford
City 0-1
Middlesbrough v Portsmouth 5-0
Millwall v Norwich City 2-0
Semi-finals (two legs)
Middlesbrough v Millwall 2-2, 1-3
Bradford City v Arsenal 0-1, 0-1

FA Youth Cup Final, first leg

6 May

Millwall (1) 3 *(Gordon, Kennedy, own goal)*

Arsenal (0) 2 *(Rawlins, McGowan)* 6098

Millwall: Cronin; Irving, Luckett, Mulraney, Thatcher, Francis, Pitcher (O'Neil),
Gordon, Kennedy, Williams, Wright.
Arsenal: Imber; Griggs, Taylor, Howell, Hall, McDonald, Black, Rose, Rawlins,
McGowan, Hughes.

FA Youth Cup Final, second leg

12 May

Arsenal (1) 3 *(Clarke, Rawlins, Hughes)*

Millwall (0) 0 4750

Arsenal: Imber; Griggs, Taylor, Clarke, McDonald, Hall, Black, Rose (Howell),
Rawlins (Drake), McGowan, Hughes.
Millwall: Cronin; Irving, Luckett, Mulraney, Thatcher, Francis, Pitcher, Gordon,
Kennedy, Williams, Wright.

BRITISH FOOTBALL RECORDS

Records during 1993–94

HIGHEST SCORES
FA Premier League
Newcastle U 7, Swindon T 1 12.3.1994.

MOST GOALS IN A SEASON
FA Premier League
82 in 42 games, Newcastle U. 1993–94.

MOST GOALS IN A SEASON
Scottish League
93 in 44 games, Dunfermline Ath. New Division 1 1993–94.

FEWEST GOALS IN A SEASON
FA Premier League
35 in 42 games, Ipswich T 1993–94.

Scottish League
30 in 44 games, Brechin C Division 1, 1993–94.

MOST GOALS AGAINST IN A SEASON
FA Premier League
100 in 42 games, Swindon T 1993–94.

FEWEST GOALS AGAINST IN A SEASON
FA Premier League
28 in 42 games, Arsenal, 1993–94.
Scottish League
32 in 44 games, Falkirk, New Division 1, 1993–94.

MOST POINTS IN A SEASON
FA Premier League
92 in 42 games, Manchester U, 1993–94.
Scottish League
66 in 44 games, Falkirk, New Division 1, 1993–94.

FEWEST POINTS IN A SEASON
FA Premier League
30 in 42 games, Swindon T, 1993–94.

MOST WINS IN A SEASON
FA Premier League
27 in 42 games, Manchester U. 1993–94.

FEWEST WINS IN A SEASON
FA Premier League
5 in 42 games, Swindon T, 1993–94.

MOST DEFEATS IN A SEASON
23 in 42 games, Southampton, 1993–94.

FEWEST DEFEATS IN A SEASON
FA Premier League
4 in 42 games, Manchester U. 1993–94.
Scottish League
4 in 44 games, Falkirk, New Division 1, 1993–94.

MOST DRAWS IN A SEASON
FA Premier League
18 in 42 games, Manchester C. 1993–94.
18 in 42 games, Sheffield U. 1993–94.
Scottish League
21 in 44 games, Aberdeen. Premier Division, 1993–94.

MOST GOALS IN A GAME
FA Premier League
4, Efan Ekoku for Norwich C v Everton, 25.9.93.

322

USEFUL ADDRESSES

The Football Association: R. H. G. Kelly, F.C.I.S., 16 Lancaster Gate, London W2 3LW
Scotland: J. Farry, 6 Park Gardens, Glasgow G3 7YE. *041-332 6372*
Northern Ireland (Irish FA): D. I. Bowen, 20 Windsor Avenue, Belfast BT9 6EG. *0232-669458*
Wales: A. Evans, 3 Westgate Street, Cardiff, South Glamorgan CF1 1JF. *0222-372325*
Republic of Ireland (FA of Ireland): S. Connolly, 80 Merrion Square South, Dublin 2. *0001-766864*
International Federation (FIFA): S. Blatter, FIFA House, Hitzigweg 11, CH-8032 Zurich, Switzerland. *1-384-9595. Fax: 1-384-9696*
Union of European Football Associations: G. Aigner, Jupiter Strasse 33, PO Box 16, CH-3000 Berne 15, Switzerland. *031-321735. Fax: 031-321838.*
The Football League: J. D. Dent, F.C.I.S., The Football League, Lytham St Annes, Lancs FY8 1JG. *0253-729421. Telex 67675*
The Scottish League: P. Donald, 188 West Regent Street, Glasgow G2 4RY. *041-248 384415*
The Irish League: H. Wallace, 87 University Street, Belfast BT7 1HP. *0232-242888*
Football League of Ireland: E. Morris, 80 Merrion Square South, Dublin 2. *0001-765120*
GM Vauxhall Conference: P. D. Hunter, 24 Barnehurst Road, Bexleyheath, Kent DA7 6EZ. *0322-521116*
Northern Premier: R. D. Bayley, 22 Woburn Drive, Hale, Altrincham, Cheshire. *061-980 7007*
English Schools FA: M. R. Berry, 4a Eastgate Street, Stafford ST16 2NN. *0785-51142*
National Federation of Football Supporters' Clubs: Chairman: Tony Kershaw, 87 Brookfield Avenue, Loughborough, Leicestershire LE11 3LN. *01509 267643 (and fax)*. Hon Secretary: Mark Agate, "The Stadium", 14 Coombe Close, Lordswood, Chatham, Kent ME5 8NU. *01634 863520 (and fax)*
Professional Footballers' Association: G. Taylor, 2 Oxford Court, Bishopsgate, Off Lower Mosley Street, Manchester M2 3W2. *061-236 0575*
Referees' Association: W. J. Taylor, Cross Offices, Summerhill, Kingswinford, West Midlands DY6 9JE. *0384-288386*
Women's Football Alliance: Miss H. Jeavons, 9 Wyllyotts Place, Potters Bar, Herts EN6 2JB. *0707 651840*
The Association of Football Statisticians: R. J. Spiller, 22 Bretons, Basildon, Essex SS15 5BY. *0268-416020*
The Football Programme Directory: David Stacey, 'The Beeches', 66 Southend Road, Wickford, Essex SS11 8EN.
England Football Supporters Association: Publicity Officer, David Stacey, 66 Southend Road, Wickford, Essex SS11 8EN.
The Football League Executive Staffs Association: PO Box 52, Leamington Spa, Warwickshire.
The Football Trust: Second Floor, Walkden House, 10 Melton Street, London NW1 2EJ. *071-388 4504*
The Football Supporters Association: PO Box 11, Liverpool L26 1XP. *051-709-2594.*

VAUXHALL CONFERENCE FIXTURES 1994–95

	Altrincham	Bath City	Bromsgrove Rovers	D'ham & Redbridge	Dover Athletic	Farnborough Town	Gateshead	Halifax Town	Kettering Town
Altrincham	—	1.4	17.4	5.11	10.12	18.2	6.9	31.12	18.3
Bath City	29.10	—	25.2	12.9	20.12	14.11	10.12	18.2	4.2
Bromsgrove Rovers	24.9	23.8	—	11.3	15.4	8.10	29.10	22.4	6.5
D'ham & Redbridge	4.2	22.4	15.10	—	5.9	22.8	17.9	1.10	31.12
Dover Athletic	22.4	26.11	17.9	27.9	—	31.12	8.4	3.9	14.1
Farnborough Town	3.9	11.3	19.11	11.2	25.10	—	14.1	29.10	12.11
Gateshead	30.11	20.8	7.1	29.4	19.11	5.11	—	26.12	29.8
Halifax Town	8.10	15.10	27.8	15.4	7.1	10.9	2.1	—	26.11
Kettering Town	17.12	4.3	1.10	1.4	3.12	28.1	15.4	11.3	—
Kidderminster H.	19.11	22.10	26.12	25.3	1.10	7.1	1.5	17.9	8.4
Macclesfield Town	25.2	5.11	29.8	14.1	25.3	1.10	26.11	24.9	10.9
Merthyr Tydfil	17.9	26.12	6.9	17.4	27.8	8.4	6.5	25.2	29.10
Northwich Victoria	2.1	17.12	4.2	3.9	18.3	15.4	27.9	4.4	25.2
Runcorn	8.4	1.10	18.3	26.11	4.2	10.12	31.12	6.5	20.8
Southport	29.8	14.1	5.11	17.12	29.10	17.9	23.8	11.10	25.3
Stafford Rangers	3.12	3.9	8.4	29.8	29.4	6.5	18.3	14.1	13.9
Stalybridge Celtic	11.3	6.5	25.3	20.8	11.2	15.10	20.12	29.8	3.9
Stevenage Borough	25.3	31.12	3.12	10.10	22.8	4.3	27.8	12.11	2.1
Telford United	31.1	17.9	29.4	18.2	12.11	27.8	11.2	17.4	10.12
Welling United	6.5	28.1	11.10	4.3	26.12	6.9	4.2	10.12	22.4
Woking	7.1	27.9	17.12	26.12	28.1	3.12	25.3	20.8	8.10
Yeovil Town	20.9	6.9	28.1	7.1	4.3	26.12	25.2	19.11	24.9

Kidderminster H.	Macclesfield Town	Merthyr Tydfil	Northwich Victoria	Runcorn	Southport	Stafford Rangers	Stalybridge Celtic	Stevenage Borough	Telford United	Welling United	Woking	Yeovil Town
10.9	11.10	29.4	26.12	28.1	4.3	23.8	27.9	15.10	26.11	1.10	27.8	14.1
24.9	29.4	2.1	27.8	29.8	10.9	7.1	8.10	19.11	18.3	3.12	8.4	17.4
2.1	1.4	4.3	10.12	18.2	20.8	26.11	10.9	3.9	31.12	13.9	14.1	27.9
29.10	19.11	18.3	8.4	27.8	25.2	10.12	28.1	14.11	6.5	19.12	2.1	3.12
6.5	18.2	5.11	1.5	15.10	1.4	11.3	17.12	13.9	20.8	2.1	25.2	29.8
20.8	17.12	13.9	25.3	24.9	29.4	4.2	25.2	29.8	1.4	26.11	22.4	2.1
11.3	28.1	18.2	12.10	14.9	3.12	15.10	4.3	22.4	17.12	1.4	1.10	3.9
11.2	4.3	17.12	23.8	3.12	6.9	5.11	8.4	1.5	28.1	18.3	4.2	25.3
23.8	21.3	27.9	17.9	5.11	27.8	6.9	7.1	26.12	15.10	18.2	19.11	29.4
—	17.4	15.10	5.9	17.12	28.1	22.4	27.8	25.2	3.12	29.8	18.3	4.2
13.9	—	3.9	11.3	15.4	20.9	31.12	26.12	6.5	4.2	20.8	10.12	15.10
1.4	3.12	—	28.1	19.11	10.12	1.10	4.2	7.1	11.3	12.11	31.12	23.8
20.12	29.10	20.8	—	4.3	31.12	15.11	3.12	14.1	29.8	29.4	1.4	26.11
8.10	23.8	14.1	22.4	—	2.1	25.2	6.9	29.10	27.9	3.9	17.9	11.3
3.9	7.1	26.11	18.2	26.12	—	29.11	1.10	17.4	1.5	11.3	6.5	8.4
18.2	8.10	11.2	17.4	4.10	12.11	—	19.11	20.8	2.1	17.12	29.10	17.9
31.12	2.1	22.4	5.11	1.4	15.4	24.9	—	10.12	13.9	14.1	26.11	18.2
26.11	17.9	15.4	1.10	29.4	4.2	28.1	18.3	—	5.11	24.10	5.9	17.12
14.1	6.9	20.12	7.1	25.3	19.11	26.12	23.8	8.4	—	29.10	4.3	1.10
15.4	8.4	25.3	19.11	7.1	15.10	27.8	17.9	27.10	25.2	—	23.8	5.11
5.11	11.2	29.8	15.10	22.10	24.9	10.9	29.4	11.3	3.9	17.4	—	13.9
10.12	27.8	25.10	6.5	10.9	8.10	1.4	29.10	11.2	22.4	31.12	11.10	—

CARLING PREMIERSHIP FIXTURES 1993–94

	Arsenal	Aston Villa	Blackburn R	Chelsea	Coventry C	Crystal Palace	Everton	Ipswich T	Leeds U	Leicester C
Arsenal		26.12	31.8	15.10	22.10	1.10	14.1	15.4	17.12	11.2
Aston Villa	17.4	—	4.3	23.12	8.3	27.8	10.12	10.9	2.1	22.2
Blackburn R	7.3	24.9	—	18.3	27.8	8.4	10.9	24.1	28.12	23.8
Chelsea	13.5	15.4	18.9	—	5.11	4.3	26.11	22.10	11.3	8.10
Coventry C	21.1	29.8	11.3	4.2	—	2.11	13.5	8.10	17.9	25.2
Crystal Palace	25.2	11.3	31.12	24.9	11.2	—	22.10	5.11	30.8	14.1
Everton	29.10	20.8	1.4	18.2	15.10	21.1	—	31.12	5.12	24.9
Ipswich T	28.2	1.4	19.11	21.1	6.5	4.2	8.4	—	1.11	2.1
Leeds U	28.8	29.4	15.4	27.8	18.3	7.3	21.2	11.2	—	22.10
Leicester C	23.11	3.12	17.12	6.5	(3.10)	29.10	4.3	29.4	21.1	—
Liverpool	28.8	8.10	13.5	9.11	22.2	10.12	24.1	14.1	8.4	17.4
Manchester C	10.12	31.12	26.12	8.3	14.1	10.9	27.8	22.2	25.2	25.1
Manchester U	18.2	4.2	21.1	17.4	3.1	19.11	1.10	4.3	1.4	28.12
Newcastle U	18.3	25.2	9.10	10.9	24.8	13.5	21.12	26.11	17.4	10.12
Norwich C	10.9	13.5	1.10	10.12	25.1	24.8	5.11	18.3	8.10	26.11
Nottingham F	3.12	21.1	29.10	19.11	17.4	2.1	8.3	10.12	18.2	27.8
QPR	8.4	29.10	18.2	3.1	10.9	17.4	18.3	27.8	19.11	8.3
Sheffield W	4.2	18.2	2.11	29.10	28.12	3.12	17.4	13.5	26.9	8.4
Southampton	19.11	17.12	20.8	3.12	4.3	8.2	8.10	1.10	29.10	13.5
Tottenham H	2.1	19.11	4.2	28.11	8.4	27.12	24.8	8.3	13.5	18.3
West Ham U	25.9	17.9	29.4	25.2	26.11	10.10	11.2	26.12	20.8	5.11
Wimbledon	8.10	2.11	3.12	8.4	10.12	18.3	2.1	23.8	4.2	10.9

Liverpool	Manchester C	Manchester U	Newcastle U	Norwich C	Nottingham F	QPR	Sheffield W	Southampton	Tottenham H	West Ham U	Wimbledon
11.3	20.8	26.11	18.9	1.4	21.2	31.12	6.11	24.1	29.4	5.3	6.5
6.5	8.4	6.11	1.10	15.10	22.10	14.1	26.11	24.8	25.1	18.3	11.2
15.10	17.4	23.10	6.5	25.2	14.1	26.11	11.2	10.12	5.11	2.1	21.2
17.12	31.8	26.12	1.4	20.8	25.1	29.4	14.1	22.2	11.2	2.10	31.12
3.12	29.10	29.4	17.12	19.11	26.12	1.4	15.4	24.9	31.12	18.2	20.8
20.8	1.4	24.1	15.10	17.12	29.4	26.12	21.2	26.11	15.4	6.5	17.9
21.11	11.3	25.2	15.4	4.2	30.8	17.9	26.12	6.5	17.12	1.11	29.4
29.10	3.12	24.9	18.2	19.9	20.8	11.3	16.10	25.2	30.8	17.4	16.12
31.12	1.10	11.9	26.12	6.5	26.11	24.1	4.3	14.1	15.10	10.12	5.11
26.12	20.11	15.4	21.8	18.2	11.3	31.8	31.12	15.10	17.9	4.2	1.4
—	28.12	18.3	4.3	2.1	5.11	11.2	1.10	8.3	26.11	10.9	22.10
15.4	—	11.2	29.4	24.9	8.10	13.5	18.3	5.11	22.10	24.8	26.11
17.9	10.11	—	29.10	3.12	17.12	20.8	6.5	8.4	11.3	15.10	31.8
24.9	2.1	14.1	—	8.4	11.2	5.11	22.10	27.8	22.2	8.3	25.1
29.4	4.3	22.2	31.12	—	15.4	22.10	8.3	11.2	26.12	27.8	14.1
4.2	6.5	22.8	2.11	27.12	—	2.10	10.9	18.3	4.3	8.4	17.10
31.10	15.10	10.12	4.2	21.1	25.2	—	24.8	28.12	6.5	3.12	24.9
25.2	17.9	8.10	21.1	31.8	1.4	17.12	—	2.1	20.8	19.11	11.3
31.8	4.2	31.12	11.3	2.11	17.9	15.4	29.4	—	1.4	21.1	26.12
18.2	21.1	27.8	3.12	17.4	24.9	8.10	12.12	12.9	—	29.10	25.2
1.4	17.12	13.5	31.8	11.3	31.12	22.2	25.1	22.10	14.1	—	15.4
21.1	18.2	7.3	19.11	30.10	13.5	4.3	27.8	17.4	1.10	28.12	—

ENDSLEIGH INSURANCE FIXTURES 1993–94

DIVISION ONE

	Barnsley	Bolton W	Bristol C	Burnley	Charlton Ath	Derby Co	Grimsby T	Luton T	Middlesbrough	Millwall	Notts Co
Barnsley	—	26.11	12.11	7.3	10.12	13.8	26.12	14.1	22.4	21.2	13.9
Bolton W	18.2	—	20.8	6.5	21.1	1.10	17.12	1.4	11.3	30.8	19.11
Bristol C	4.2	10.12	—	18.3	7.3	13.9	3.12	25.2	24.9	8.10	10.9
Burnley	3.9	8.10	30.8	—	3.12	15.4	18.2	21.3	17.12	1.4	29.10
Charlton Ath	20.8	5.11	3.9	22.10	—	14.1	21.3	22.4	26.11	31.12	4.3
Derby Co	17.12	25.2	1.4	27.12	29.10	—	3.9	20.8	31.8	11.3	3.12
Grimsby T	17.4	13.8	22.10	26.11	10.9	7.3	—	11.2	5.11	12.11	2.1
Luton T	29.10	13.9	1.10	10.9	2.1	10.12	1.11	—	15.10	4.3	8.4
Middlesbrough	2.1	27.8	4.3	13.8	18.2	18.3	21.1	29.4	—	1.10	28.12
Millwall	19.11	18.3	6.5	14.9	8.4	27.8	4.2	24.9	25.2	—	19.4
Notts Co	1.4	21.2	21.3	14.1	24.9	22.10	22.4	31.12	15.4	26.12	—
Oldham Ath	24.9	29.4	26.11	27.8	13.8	25.3	15.4	12.11	11.2	22.4	18.3
Port Vale	30.8	22.10	11.3	17.4	15.10	21.2	2.1	4.39	17.9	26.11	6.5
Portsmouth	27.12	25.3	14.1	2.1	27.8	5.11	25.2	22.2	22.10	11.2	13.8
Reading	11.3	22.4	15.10	5.11	6.5	11.2	31.12	26.12	12.11	3.9	1.10
Sheffield U	15.10	10.9	5.11	21.2	18.3	12.11	6.5	22.10	26.12	14.1	27.8
Southend U	6.5	24.9	17.9	8.4	18.4	15.10	29.10	11.3	20.8	17.12	1.11
Stoke C	21.1	8.3	15.4	10.12	14.9	4.3	19.11	8.10	31.12	29.4	25.3
Sunderland	17.9	26.12	17.12	15.10	1.11	31.12	30.8	15.4	21.3	20.8	21.1
Swindon T	25.2	11.2	22.2	23.11	25.3	10.9	24.9	26.11	14.1	5.11	8.3
Tranmere R	1.11	15.4	31.12	25.2	19.11	26.12	11.3	30.8	6.5	17.9	4.2
Watford	21.3	14.1	22.4	11.2	2.5	6.5	20.8	17.9	3.9	15.4	15.10
WBA	3.12	31.12	26.12	24.9	4.2	22.4	17.9	18.12	1.4	22.3	18.2
Wolverhampton	8.4	12.11	11.2	25.3	28.12	26.11	15.10	5.11	21.2	22.10	10.2

Oldham Ath	Port Vale	Portsmouth	Reading	Sheffield U	Southend U	Stoke C	Sunderland	Swindon T	Tranmere R	Watford	WBA	Wolverhampton
4.3	18.3	15.4	27.8	29.4	8.10	5.11	25.3	1.10	11.2	10.9	22.10	31.12
15.10	3.12	17.9	2.1	21.3	4.3	3.9	17.4	1.11	27.12	29.10	8.4	4.2
18.2	27.8	29.10	29.4	21.1	25.3	27.12	13.8	19.11	8.4	2.1	17.4	1.11
11.3	26.12	22.4	21.1	19.11	31.12	20.8	29.4	4.2	1.10	1.11	4.3	17.9
17.12	29.4	11.3	8.10	30.8	26.12	1.4	11.2	17.9	21.2	1.10	12.11	15.4
17.9	19.11	21.1	2.11	4.2	29.4	24.9	8.4	22.3	17.4	8.10	2.1	18.2
27.12	13.9	1.10	8.4.	8.10	14.1	21.2	18.3	4.3	27.8	10.12	25.3	29.4
4.2	7.3	19.11	17.4	3.12	27.8	6.5	27.12	18.2	18.3	25.3	13.8	21.1
1.11	25.3	3.12	4.2	17.4	10.12	8.4	10.9	29.10	8.10	7.3	13.9	19.11
2.1	18.2	2.11	8.3	29.10	13.8	15.10	10.12	21.1	25.3	27.12	10.9	3.12
30.8	8.10	17.12	25.2	11.3	11.2	17.9	5.11	3.9	12.11	29.4	26.11	21.8
—	10.12	8.10	10.9	25.2	7.3	22.10	14.1	31.12	5.11	13.9	21.2	26.12
20.8	—	21.3	27.12	24.9	5.11	2.1	29.11	17.12	14.1	8.4	11.2	25.2
6.5	10.9	—	10.12	8.4	18.3	12.11	26.11	15.10	14.9	17.4	8.3	24.9
21.3	15.4	20.8	—	17.9	21.2	30.8	22.10	1.4	26.11	4.3	14.1	17.12
1.10	4.3	31.12	25.3	—	26.11	11.2	13.9	15.4	7.3	13.8	10.12	22.4
3.9	21.1	30.8	19.11	18.2	—	21.3	25.2	3.12	2.1	4.2	27.12	1.4
3.12	22.4	4.2	18.3	2.11	10.9	—	27.8	26.12	13.8	18.2	1.10	29.10
29.10	4.2	18.2	3.12	1.4	1.10	11.3	—	22.4	4.3	19.11	6.5	3.9
8.4	14.8	29.4	14.9	27.12	22.10	17.4	2.1	—	10.12	27.8	18.3	8.10
21.1	29.10	1.4	18.2	3.9	22.4	17.12	24.9	20.8	—	3.12	15.10	21.3
1.4	31.12	26.12	24.9	17.12	12.11	26.11	21.2	11.3	22.10	—	5.11	30.8
9.11	2.11	3.9	29.10	20.8	15.4	25.2	8.10	31.8	29.4	21.1	—	11.3
17.4	1.10	4.3	13.8	2.1	13.9	14.1	7.3	6.5	10.9	18.3	28.8	—

	Birmingham C	Blackpool	Bournemouth	Bradford C	Brentford	Brighton & HA	Bristol R	Cambridge U	Cardiff C	Chester C	Crewe Alex
Birmingham C	—	31.12	19.11	22.4	7.1	29.4	29.10	26.12	15.4	20.8	1.11
Blackpool	4.4	—	10.12	15.10	25.3	13.9	18.3	14.1	10.9	21.2	7.3
Bournemouth	21.2	20.8	—	22.10	15.10	11.2	18.4	5.11	24.9	17.9	27.12
Bradford C	2.1	29.4	7.1	—	1.11	8.10	21.1	25.2	29.10	17.12	19.11
Brentford	22.10	17.9	29.4	11.2	—	26.11	8.10	28.1	22.4	15.4	4.3
Brighton & HA	15.10	1.4	2.11	6.5	4.2	—	7.1	24.9	21.1	22.3	18.2
Bristol R	28.1	31.8	26.12	5.11	6.5	22.10	—	11.2	15.10	31.12	1.10
Cambridge U	17.4	18.2	21.1	1.10	29.10	4.3	1.11	—	7.1	30.8	4.2
Cardiff C	28.12	21.3	4.3	28.1	2.1	5.11	29.4	22.10	—	1.4	8.10
Chester C	10.12	19.11	25.3	13.8	27.12	10.9	8.4	18.3	13.9	—	17.4
Crewe Alex	11.2	3.9	15.4	21.2	24.9	14.1	25.2	26.11	6.5	26.12	—
Huddersfield T	6.5	17.12	29.10	4.3	19.11	1.10	4.2	15.10	18.2	11.3	7.1
Hull C	4.3	8.10	1.10	15.4	21.1	31.12	19.11	22.4	4.2	3.9	29.10
Leyton O	13.8	21.1	13.9	10.12	17.4	7.3	2.1	10.9	1.11	15.10	8.4
Oxford U	10.9	1.11	4.2	18.3	8.4	25.3	18.2	27.8	10.12	25.2	13.9
Peterborough U	25.3	22.4	18.3	14.1	10.12	21.2	13.8	31.12	25.2	5.11	27.8
Plymouth Arg	7.3	29.10	18.2	27.8	13.8	10.12	27.12	13.9	25.3	24.9	2.1
Rotherham U	13.9	1.10	27.8	26.12	18.3	28.1	10.9	7.3	31.12	26.11	10.12
Shrewsbury T	5.11	11.3	8.10	26.11	25.2	15.4	24.9	21.2	26.12	14.1	29.4
Stockport Co	26.11	15.4	10.9	31.12	27.8	22.4	7.3	10.12	13.8	11.2	18.3
Swansea C	27.8	7.1	22.4	10.9	17.2	13.8	13.9	25.3	7.3	6.5	21.1
Wrexham	1.10	4.3	13.8	13.9	7.3	27.8	25.3	6.5	18.3	28.1	10.9
Wycombe W	18.3	4.2	31.12	7.3	10.9	26.12	27.8	13.8	19.11	22.4	25.3
York City	14.1	26.12	7.3	25.3	13.9	18.3	10.12	15.4	27.8	22.10	13.8

Huddersfield T	Hull C	Leyton O	Oxford U	Peterborough U	Plymouth Arg	Rotherham U	Shrewsbury T	Stockport Co	Swansea C	Wrexham	Wycombe W	York City
8.10	24.9	17.12	21.3	17.9	3.9	1.4	21.1	4.2	11.3	25.2	30.8	18.2
13.8	6.5	5.11	11.2	2.1	28.1	25.2	27.8	27.12	22.10	24.9	26.11	18.4
28.1	25.2	1.4	26.11	30.8	14.1	11.3	6.5	21.3	2.1	16.12	8.4	3.9
24.9	28.12	20.8	30.8	18.2	11.3	17.4	4.2	8.4	21.3	1.4	3.9	17.9
21.2	5.11	26.12	31.12	20.8	17.12	30.8	1.10	11.3	14.1	3.9	21.3	1.4
25.2	8.4	3.9	17.9	19.11	20.8	29.10	27.12	2.1	17.12	11.3	19.4	31.8
26.11	22.2	22.4	14.1	17.12	15.4	22.3	4.3	3.9	1.4	17.9	11.3	20.8
29.4	2.1	21.3	11.3	8.4	1.4	3.9	19.11	20.8	17.9	8.10	16.12	28.12
14.1	25.11	11.2	20.8	1.10	17.9	8.4	17.4	17.12	3.9	30.8	21.2	11.3
27.8	7.3	29.4	1.10	21.1	4.3	4.2	18.2	2.11	8.10	10.30	2.1	7.1
22.10	28.1	31.12	1.4	11.3	22.4	20.8	15.10	30.8	5.11	21.3	17.9	16.12
—	17.4	30.8	3.9	1.4	21.3	27.12	2.1	17.9	8.4	1.11	20.8	21.1
26.12	—	11.3	17.12	21.3	30.8	17.9	7.1	18.2	20.8	29.4	1.4	1.11
18.3	27.8	—	4.3	4.2	1.10	7.1	25.3	29.10	27.12	18.2	6.5	19.11
7.3	13.8	24.9	—	17.4	8.10	19.11	29.10	21.1	29.4	7.1	27.12	2.1
13.9	10.9	26.11	26.12	—	11.2	24.9	7.3	15.10	28.1	15.4	22.10	6.5
10.9	18.3	25.2	6.5	1.11	—	21.1	8.4	7.1	17.4	19.11	15.10	4.2
15.4	25.3	22.10	21.2	4.3	5.11	—	13.8	6.5	11.2	22.4	14.1	15.10
22.4	22.10	17.9	28.1	3.9	31.12	17.12	—	1.4	30.8	20.8	11.2	21.3
25.3	14.1	28.1	5.11	29.4	22.10	8.10	13.9	—	21.2	26.12	24.9	25.2
31.12	10.12	15.4	15.10	29.10	26.12	1.11	17.3	19.11	—	4.2	25.2	24.9
11.2	15.10	14.1	22.10	27.12	21.2	2.1	10.12	17.4	26.11	—	5.11	8.4
10.12	13.9	8.10	15.4	7.1	29.4	18.2	1.11	4.3	1.10	21.1	—	29.10
5.11	11.2	21.2	22.4	8.10	26.11	29.4	10.9	1.10	4.3	31.12	28.1	—

DIVISION THREE

	Barnet	Bury	Carlisle U	Chesterfield	Colchester U	Darlington	Doncaster R	Exeter C	Fulham	Gillingham
Barnet	—	19.11	7.1	29.10	18.2	4.2	10.9	2.1	1.10	27.12
Bury	11.2	—	15.4	24.9	25.2	6.5	13.9	10.12	26.11	22.10
Carlisle U	22.10	27.12	—	2.1	15.10	1.10	26.11	10.9	28.1	8.4
Chesterfield	28.1	4.3	22.4	—	6.5	15.10	26.12	13.9	22.10	11.2
Colchester U	14.1	1.10	29.4	8.10	—	4.3	27.8	18.3	15.4	5.11
Darlington	26.11	8.10	25.2	29.4	24.9	—	25.3	27.8	14.1	28.1
Doncaster R	11.3	1.4	4.2	17.4	16.12	3.9	—	21.1	30.8	2.1
Exeter C	22.4	20.8	11.3	1.4	30.8	17.12	5.11	—	29.4	3.9
Fulham	25.2	4.2	29.10	7.1	27.12	18.2	18.3	15.10	—	17.4
Gillingham	15.4	7.1	31.12	19.11	21.1	29.10	22.4	25.3	26.12	—
Hartlepool U	30.8	17.12	26.12	3.9	11.3	20.8	11.2	25.2	31.12	17.9
Hereford U	6.5	18.2	19.11	21.1	8.4	7.1	13.8	27.12	4.3	15.10
Lincoln C	5.11	29.4	8.10	8.4	2.1	27.12	14.1	13.8	11.2	26.11
Mansfield T	31.12	3.9	1.4	18.12	20.8	30.8	22.10	24.9	22.4	25.2
Northampton T	15.10	2.1	24.9	27.12	17.4	8.4	10.12	6.5	5.11	14.1
Preston N.E.	17.12	18.3	18.2	4.2	7.1	17.9	4.3	29.10	11.3	1.4
Rochdale	1.4	17.9	21.1	20.8	19.11	2.1	1.10	18.2	8.10	17.12
Scarborough	20.8	21.1	17.12	17.9	3.9	18.4	15.10	4.2	1.4	11.3
Scunthorpe U	17.9	11.3	3.9	18.2	4.2	1.4	15.4	7.1	20.8	30.8
Torquay U	24.9	8.4	20.8	25.2	17.9	11.3	28.1	18.4	3.9	6.5
Walsall	26.12	29.10	30.8	11.3	1.4	21.1	31.12	19.11	17.9	24.9
Wigan Ath	3.9	18.4	17.9	30.8	29.10	19.11	6.5	8.5	17.12	20.8

Paul Alcock (S. Merstham, Surrey)
David Allison (Lancaster)
Gerald Ashby, (Worcester)
Mike Bailey, (Impington, Cambridge)
Keren Barratt, (Coventry)
Neil Barry, (Scunthorpe)
Ray Bigger, (Croydon)
Martin Bodenham, (Looe, Cornwall)
Jim Borrett, (Harleston, Norfolk)
John Brandwood, (Lichfield, Staffs.)
Kevin Breen (Liverpool)
Keith Burge, (Tonypandy)
Billy Burns, (Scarborough)
George Cain, (Bootle)
Vic Callow, (Solihull)
Brian Coddington, (Sheffield)
Keith Cooper, (Pontypridd)
Keith Cooper, (Swindon)
Ian Cruikshanks, (Hartlepool)
Paul Danson, (Leicester)
Alan Dawson, (Jarrowe)
Roger Dilkes, (Mossley, Lancs.)
Phil Don, (Hanworth Park, Middlesex)
Steve Dunn, (Bristol)
Paul Durkin, (Portland, Dorset)
David Elleray, (Harrow)
Alan Flood, (Stockport)
Peter Foakes, (Clacton-on-Sea)
David Frampton, (Poole, Dorset)
Dermot Gallagher, (Banbury, Oxon.)
Rodger Gifford, (Llanbradach, Mid. Glam.)
Ron Groves, (Weston-Super-Mare)
Allan Gunn, (South Chailey, Sussex)
Keith Hackett, (Sheffield)
Paul Harrison, (Oldham)
Robert Hart, (Darlington)
Terry Heilbron, (Newton Aycliffe)
Ian Hemley, (Ampthill, Beds.)
Brian Hill, (Kettering)

John Holbrook (Ludlow)
Terry Holbrook, (Walsall)
Peter Jones, (Loughborough)
John Key, (Sheffield)
Howard King, (Merthyr Tydfil)
John Kirkby, (Sheffield)
Ken Leach, (Wolverhampton)
John Lloyd, (Wrexham)
Stephen Lodge, (Barnsley)
Eddie Lomas (Manchester)
Terry Lunt, (Ashton-in-Makerfield, Lancs)
Ken Lupton, (Stockton-on-Tees)
Kevin Lynch, (Lincoln)
Roger Milford, (Bristol)
Kelvin Morton, (Bury St. Edmunds)
David Orr (Iver)
Jim Parker, (Preston)
Mike Peck, (Kendal)
Micky Pierce, (Portsmouth)
Graham Poll, (Berkhamsted)
Graham Pooley, (Bishops Stortford)
Richard Poulain, (Huddersfield)
Mike Reed, (Birmingham)
Jim Rushton, (Stoke-on-Trent)
Ray Shepherd, (Leeds)
Gurnam Singh, (Wolverhampton)
Arthur Smith, (Rubery, Birmingham)
Paul Vanes, (Warley, West Midlands)
John Watson, (Whitley Bay)
Trevor West, (Hull)
Clive Wilkes, (Gloucester)
Alan Wilkie, (Chester-le-Street)
Gary Willard, (Worthing, W. Sussex)
Jeff Winter, (Middlesbrough)
Roger Wiseman (Borehamwood, Herts.)
Eddie Wolstenholme, (Blackburn)
Joe Worrall, (Warrington)
Philip Wright, (Northwich)

Hartlepool U	Hereford U	Lincoln C	Mansfield T	Northampton T	Preston N.E.	Rochdale	Scarborough	Scunthorpe U	Torquay U	Walsall	Wigan Ath
18.3	8.10	21.1	8.4	29.4	27.8	13.9	10.12	13.8	4.3	17.4	25.3
27.8	14.1	15.10	25.3	22.4	30.8	13.8	5.11	10.9	31.12	28.1	26.12
17.4	11.2	6.5	13.9	4.3	14.1	5.11	27.8	25.3	10.12	18.3	13.8
25.3	5.11	31.12	21.8	15.4	26.11	10.12	13.8	14.1	1.10	10.9	18.3
10.9	31.12	22.4	10.12	26.12	22.10	11.2	25.3	26.11	13.8	13.9	28.1
10.12	22.10	15.4	18.3	31.12	13.8	22.4	26.12	13.9	10.9	5.11	11.2
19.11	16.9	18.2	7.1	20.8	24.9	25.2	29.4	27.12	29.10	8.4	8.10
1.10	15.4	17.9	4.3	8.10	28.1	14.1	26.11	22.10	26.12	11.2	31.12
8.4	24.9	19.11	2.1	21.1	10.9	6.5	13.9	10.12	25.3	13.8	27.8
13.8	29.4	4.2	1.10	18.2	13.9	27.8	10.9	18.3	8.10	4.3	10.12
—	22.4	24.9	6.5	1.4	15.10	26.11	14.1	28.1	15.4	22.10	5.11
2.1	—	29.10	17.4	4.2	20.8	25.3	18.3	1.10	13.9	27.8	10.9
4.3	28.1	—	10.9	1.10	25.3	18.3	22.10	17.4	27.8	10.12	13.9
8.10	26.12	11.3	—	17.9	5.11	28.1	15.4	11.2	29.4	26.11	14.1
13.9	26.11	25.2	11.10	—	11.2	10.9	28.1	16.12	18.3	25.3	22.10
29.4	10.12	3.9	21.1	19.11	—	26.12	31.12	8.10	22.4	1.10	15.4
4.2	3.9	30.8	29.10	11.3	17.4	—	4.3	8.4	7.1	27.12	29.4
18.2	30.8	7.1	27.12	29.10	8.4	24.9	—	2.1	19.11	6.5	25.2
29.10	25.2	26.12	19.11	27.8	6.5	31.12	22.4	—	21.1	15.10	24.9
27.12	1.4	17.12	15.10	30.8	2.1	22.10	11.2	5.11	—	14.1	26.11
7.1	17.12	20.8	4.2	3.9	25.2	15.4	8.10	29.4	18.2	—	22.4
21.1	11.3	1.4	18.2	7.1	28.12	15.10	1.10	4.3	4.2	2.1	—

OTHER FIXTURES—SEASON 1994-95

July
16 Sat   Pre Season Commences

August
10 Wed   Euro Comps Prel - 1st Leg
13 Sat   Football League Season Commences
14 Sun   FA Charity Shield
20 Sat   FA Premier League Season Commences
24 Wed   Euro Comps Prel - 2nd Leg
27 Sat   FA Challenge Cup Preliminary Rd
29 Mon   Bank Holiday

September
3 Sat   FA Vase Extra Preliminary Rd
  FA Youth Challenge Cup Extra Preliminary Rd*
7 Wed   International Date
10 Sat   FA Challenge Cup 1st Rd Qualifying
  FA Youth Challenge Cup Preliminary Rd*
14 Wed   Euro Comps 1st Rd - 1st Leg
17 Sat   FA Challenge Trophy 1st Rd Qualifying
18 Sun   FA Women's Rd (prov)
24 Sat   FA Challenge Cup 2nd Rd Qualifying
25 Sun   FA Sunday Cup Preliminary Rd (if required)
28 Wed   Euro Comps 1st Rd - 2nd Leg

October
1 Sat   FA Challenge Vase Preliminary Rd
  FA Youth Challenge Cup 1st Rd Qualifying*
8 Sat   FA Challenge Cup 3rd Rd Qualifying
12 Wed   International Date
15 Sat   FA Challenge Trophy 2nd Rd Qualifying
  FA Youth Challenge Cup 2nd Rd Qualifying*
  FA County Youth Challenge Cup 1st Rd*
16 Sun   FA Women's Cup 2nd Rd (prov)
19 Wed   Euro Comps 2nd Rd - 1st Leg

November
2 Wed   Euro Comps 2nd Rd - 2nd Leg
12 Sat   FA Challenge Cup 1st Rd Proper
  FA Youth Challenge Cup 1st Rd Proper*
13 Sun   FA Women's Cup 3rd Rd (prov)
16 Wed   International Date
19 Sat   FA Challenge Vase 2nd Rd
20 Sun   FA Sunday Cup 2nd Rd
23 Wed   Euro Comps 3rd Rd - 1st Leg
26 Sat   FA Challenge Trophy 3rd Rd Qualifying
  FA County Youth Challenge Cup 2nd Rd*

December
3 Sat   FA Challenge 2nd Rd Proper
4 Sun   FA Women's Cup 4th Rd (prov)
7 Wed   Euro Comps 3rd Rd - 2nd Leg
10 Sat   FA Challenge Vase 3rd Rd
  FA Youth Challenge Cup 2nd Rd Proper*
11 Sun   FA Sunday Cup 3rd Rd
14 Wed   International Date
25 Sun   Christmas Day
26 Mon   Boxing Day
27 Tue   Bank Holiday

January
1 Sun   New Years Day
2 Mon   Bank Holiday
7 Sat   FA Challenge Cup 3rd Rd Proper
14 Sat   FA Challenge Vase 4th Rd
  FA Youth Challenge Cup 3rd Rd Proper*
  FA County Youth Challenge Cup 3rd Rd*
15 Sun   FA Women's Cup 5th Rd (prov)
21 Sat   FA Challenge Trophy 1st Rd Proper
22 Sun   FA Sunday Cup 4th Rd
22 Sat   FA Challenge Cup 4th Rd Qualifying
29 Sat   FA Challenge Vase 1st Rd
30 Sun   FA Sunday Cup 1st Rd

28 Sat   FA Challenge Cup 4th Rd Proper

February
4 Sat   FA Challenge Vase 5th Rd
  FA Youth Challenge Cup 4th Rd Proper*
11 Sat   FA Challenge Trophy 2nd Rd Proper
12 Sun   FA Women's Cup 6th Rd (prov)
18 Sat   FA Challenge Cup 5th Rd Proper
  FA County Youth Challenge Cup 4th Rd*
19 Sun   FA Sunday Cup 5th Rd
25 Sat   FA Challenge Vase 6th Rd

March
1 Wed   Euro Comps Quarter Finals - 1st leg
4 Sat   FA Challenge Trophy 3rd Rd Proper
  FA Youth Challenge Cup 5th Rd Proper*
11 Sat   FA Challenge Cup 6th Rd Proper
15 Wed   Euro Comps Quarter Finals - 2nd Leg
18 Sat   FA Challenge Vase Semi-Final 1st Leg
  FA County Youth Challenge Cup Semi-Final*
19 Sun   FA Women's Cup Semi-Final (prov)
25 Sat   FA Challenge Trophy 4th Rd Proper
  FA Challenge Vase Semi-Final 2nd Leg
29 Wed   International Date

April
1 Sat   FA Youth Challenge Cup Semi-Finals*
2 Sun   FA Sunday Cup Semi-Final
5 Wed   Euro Comps Semi Finals - 1st Leg
8 Sat   FA Challenge Trophy Semi-Finals - 1st Leg
9 Sun   FA Challenge Cup Semi-Finals
14 Fri   Good Friday
15 Sat   FA Challenge Trophy Semi-Finals - 2nd Leg
17 Mon   Easter Monday
19 Wed   Euro Comps Semi Finals - 2nd Leg
26 Wed   International Date
29 Sat   FA County Youth Final (fixed date)
30 Sun   FA Women's Cup Final (prov)

May
1 Mon   Bank Holiday
3 Wed   European Final
6 Sat   FA Youth Challenge Cup Final*
7 Sun   FA Sunday Cup Final
10 Wed   European Final
13 Sat   FA Challenge Vase Final - Wembley Stadium
14 Sun   FA Challenge Trophy Final - Wembley Stadium
17 Wed   European Final
20 Sat   FA Challenge Cup Final - Wembley Stadium
24 Wed   European Final
25 Thu   FA Challenge Cup Final Possible Replay - Wembley Stadium
29 Mon   Bank Holiday

* = closing date of round.